Cultural Economics & the Creative Economy

This series aims to provide original and societally relevant perspectives on the modern creative economy from the perspective of cultural economics broadly understood. In the past decades it is increasingly realized that value in the economy is realized in the creative industries and the more traditional cultural sectors. This series will aim to shed light on how value is created and realized and how the creative economy shapes the broader economy. We believe that trends in the creative economy are often a sign of things to come in the broader economy, this is true for the way in which work is organized, how innovation happens, how entrepreneurs act and the relevance of cities in the modern economy.

The series will provide a collection of works of leading cultural economists on theoretical and empirical topics. It will cover the field in its most broad sense and focus on the current open problems and topics in cultural economics, covering micro, macro end methodological aspects.

Anne-Sophie V. Radermecker
Editor

Low-End Markets for Art and Cultural Goods

Understanding the Economic, Cultural and Social Dynamics of Low-Value Goods

palgrave
macmillan

Editor
Anne-Sophie V. Radermecker
Brussels, Belgium

ISSN 2662-4478 ISSN 2662-4486 (electronic)
Cultural Economics & the Creative Economy
ISBN 978-3-032-27565-3 ISBN 978-3-032-27566-0 (eBook)
https://doi.org/10.1007/978-3-032-27566-0

This Palgrave Macmillan imprint is published by the registered company Springer Nature Switzerland AG.
The registered company address is: Gewerbestrasse 11, 6330 Cham, Switzerland

Preface

This book project stems from years of dedicated research into art market segments that have long been overlooked by both the media and academic scholarship. My scholarly work began with a focus on Old Master paintings of uncertain or anonymous authorship, namely works that stand apart from a market largely driven by artist-name recognition. Over time, this focus has broadened into a wider investigation of undervalued markets, particularly those in which culturally significant yet unfashionable and economically depreciated objects circulate.

This intellectual journey has since crystallized in a research project, *MOOVA—Making Old Objects Valuable Again. The Cultural, Economic Challenges and Sustainability Opportunities of Antiques in the Twenty-first Century*, funded by the European Research Council (ERC StG—#101075828). MOOVA explores the mechanisms of value creation and price formation in the market for ordinary antiques. Engaging with such objects has compelled me to delve into the very bottom of the art and cultural goods market and to confront a core methodological challenge: this segment is far more complex and elusive than one might assume, with current knowledge in cultural economics, art history, anthropology, and art market literature remaining insufficient to fully grasp its specificities. Despite the growing field of art market studies—which has yielded significant insights into investment behavior, price formation, emergence mechanisms, and the roles and networks of intermediaries (auction houses, galleries, dealers, fairs, experts), across historical periods—much of the attention has focused, quite understandably, on the high end of the market. Though continued research in these areas is undoubtedly necessary, several mechanisms, practices, and profiles are now well documented and understood within the scholarly community. However, can the mechanisms and logics observed at the top of the art market hierarchy be meaningfully applied to its lower tiers? This is the central question this volume seeks to explore, by taking a transversal look at the so-called *low-end* of the art market—where objects of lower market value circulate.

To this end, a call for chapters was launched in June 2024, culminating in a virtual workshop held in December of the same year at the Université libre de Bruxelles, and a session at the conference of the Association for Cultural Economics International (ACEI 2025, Erasmus University Rotterdam). During these events, contributors presented their research approaches to the low-end markets. As reflected in the present volume, submissions came from a wide range of disciplinary backgrounds, showcasing the diversity of perspectives on this topic and confirming the ongoing nature of scholarly engagement with these market segments. Notably, the willingness of art market professionals to contribute also underscores the relevance of this topic at a moment when the forces shaping the art market are undergoing significant transformation.

Through various contributions, this volume aims to reframe our understanding of market segmentation and product differentiation, while challenging assumptions about what constitutes artistic, cultural and economic value. A clear and nuanced understanding of this market segment is indeed essential not only for academic purposes but also for informing policy within cultural and creative industries. One of the great strengths of this project lies in its interdisciplinarity, with all the intellectual opportunities and challenges it entails. Learning from other disciplines and from practitioners has enriched the analysis and brought new perspectives to this vibrant and multifaceted segment of the art market.

In a recent book (Radermecker 2024), I argued that some aspects of the low-end art markets have the potential to address critical issues related to accessibility, diversity, inclusivity, and sustainability. In a context where these values may be increasingly challenged, acknowledging their importance has become critical, and this book reveals some of these positive externalities of the art markets. It goes without saying that this edited volume cannot claim to exhaust such a rich topic. Its primary goal is to acknowledge the importance of the low-end within today's art market ecosystem and to draw the attention of researchers—especially cultural economists—to its singularities, which merit further investigation. I therefore invite readers to view this volume not as a definitive account, but as a point of departure for deeper and more sustained exploration of the "low-end" of the art market—a marketplace rich in complexity, contradiction, and potential.

Anne-Sophie V. Radermecker

Acknowledgments The publication of this volume would not have been possible without the support of the European Research Council and the dedication of an outstanding team of researchers hired for this project at the Université libre de Bruxelles (Cultural Management): Federica Aramu, Alessia Crotta, Marine Lagasse, Roberta Raccomandato, and Jin Wang. I am also profoundly grateful for the opportunity to work closely with a distinguished scientific committee—Ellen Loots (Erasmus University Rotterdam), Kim Oosterlinck (Royal Museums of Fine Arts of Belgium—Université Libre de Bruxelles), Claartje Rasterhoff (University of Maastricht), and Christophe Spaenjers (University of Colorado, Boulder)—whose combined expertise was instrumental in addressing the heterogeneity of this market and the interdisciplinarity of the contributions. This volume also benefited from a thorough review process, supported by the insights of internationally recognized scholars including Diana Berzina (University of Maastricht), Marie-Sophie de Clippele (UCLouvain–Saint-Louis Bruxelles), Anna de Jonge (University of Maastricht), Claire Dupin de Beyssat (Université de Tours), Catherine Janssen (Université libre de Bruxelles), Nicolette Makovicky (University of Oxford), Anne Malmendier (ULB), Nathalie Moureau (Université Paul Valéry Montpellier), Naomi Oosterman (Erasmus University Rotterdam), Adriana Turpin (IESA), and Filip Vermeylen (Erasmus University Rotterdam). Inspiring discussions with my colleagues Nathalie Nyst, Eric Van Essche, and Alexandre Pintiaux from the Master's program in Cultural Management have been equally pivotal. I would also like to thank Ellie Duncan, Commissioning Editor at Palgrave Macmillan, for her belief in and support of this project, as well as its editors Erwin Dekker, Andrej Srakar and Michael Rushton. Finally, my deepest appreciation goes to the art market studies community (TIAMSA, BAMLab, ENCATC Working Group on Art Markets and Cultural Goods Integrity, RAM-T) and to all the contributors of this book—academics and practitioners alike—whose active participation and thoughtful, original perspectives greatly enriched the discussion.

Contents

Notes on Contributors

Kaylee P. Alexander is a Research Data Librarian at the University of Utah's J. Willard Marriott Library. She holds a PhD in Art History & Visual Culture from Duke University and is the author of *A Data-Driven Analysis of Cemeteries and Social Reform in Paris, 1804–1924* (Routledge 2024).

Francesco Angelini PhD, is Adjunct Professor at the University of Bologna. His main topics of research revolve around cultural markets, tourism markets, and digital markets, with a particular focus on price formation and quality evaluation. He published his papers in Journal of Cultural Economics, Cultural Trends, and Kyklos, among others.

Federica Aramu holds Master's degrees in Arts and Heritage (Maastricht University, 2021) and Contemporary Arts (Ca' Foscari University, 2019), with prior experience as a museum assistant curator in Italy. Her research interests include the art market, collecting, sustainability, and cultural policy. Since October 2023, she is a PhD candidate in Cultural Management at the Université libre de Bruxelles, within the ERC-StG project *MOOVA*.

María Isabel Baldasarre holds a Ph.D. in Art History and a Bachelor's degree in Arts from the University of Buenos Aires. She is currently a Full Professor in the Master's Program in Art History at the Interdisciplinary School of Higher Social Studies (IDAES), National University of San Martín. She also serves as a Researcher at the National Scientific and Technical Research Council (CONICET) in Argentina.

Isabel Causadias Domingo is Associate Professor at the Faculty of Fine Arts, University of Barcelona, where she teaches cultural policy and artistic practice. Her research focuses on the primary art market, the professionalization of artists, and the impact of AI on artistic production and education. She combines qualitative and quantitative methods to explore how value and trust are constructed within contemporary art ecosystems.

Bronwyn Coate is an Associate Professor in Economics within the School of Economics, Finance & Marketing at RMIT University in Melbourne, Australia. Her research within the field of cultural economics includes topics related to art markets, cultural entrepreneurship and the role of gender in shaping preferences for art.

Laura D'hoore is a researcher at the Competence Centre Culture Management and Culture Policy, University of Antwerp.

Matilde Ferrero PhD, is currently working as a postdoctoral researcher at the Université Libre de Bruxelles (and the IHECS-*Institut des Hautes Études des Communications*) on a research evaluating the economic impact of events in the Brussels-Capital Region. She also conducts independent research on independent artist-run spaces.

Tim R. L. Fry After 35 years in Australia, Tim Fry has returned to England where he is a Fellow in the Nottingham Business School at Nottingham Trent University. He has published in a wide range of international journals and disciplines and specializes in applied micro econometrics. His recent work has been the field of cultural economics with papers concerning Australian Indigenous art at auction and with papers concerning street performers.

Douglas J. Hodgson is a Professor of Economics at UQAM-*Université du Québec à Montréal* in Montreal, Canada. He received his Ph.D. in Economics from Yale University and has published in numerous economics journals, in subfields including theoretical and applied econometrics, financial economics, international finance, and economics of the arts.

Michael Hutter is Professor Emeritus at Berlin Social Science Center (WZB). Before 2015, he was research director at WZB and research professor at Technische Universität Berlin. Before 2008, he was professor for economic theory at Universität Witten/Herdecke. He had studied mathematics and economics in Munich, Portland (Oregon) and Seattle.

Wiktor Komorowski received his PhD from the Courtauld Institute of Art in London in 2023 where he worked on the periodic exhibitions of prints in East-Central Europe. He currently works for one of the major European auction houses as a specialist on post-war prints and multiples.

Vincent Lamouraux is a *conservateur du patrimoine*. Since 2021, he has served as Collections Inspector at the Mobilier national, where he is responsible for antique furniture. Specializing mainly in furniture from the Consulate and Empire periods, he is also involved in the refurnishing of several *châteaux* in France.

Jiahui Liao is a PhD candidate in the Department of Culture, Media and Creative Industries at King's College London. She explores how art business strategies mediate cultural and economic values in transnational contexts, particularly in the visual arts and traditional crafts sectors.

Krystyna Matyjaszkiewicz an independent art historian and curator with a BA in History of Art and a Postgraduate Diploma in Art Gallery and Museum Studies (University of Manchester), has been researching and curating exhibitions for 40 years. Her interest in Victorian art dealers arose from her work on the nineteenth-century artists David Roberts and James Tissot.

Camille Mestdagh Formerly a specialist in European furniture and works of art at Bonhams Auctioneers, Camille Mestdagh has served as Collections Inspector at the Mobilier national since 2025, where she is responsible for metalwork. Prior to this role, she led the research project OBJECTive (ANR ACCESS ERC/Université Lyon-2, LARHRA), which investigated the markets for decorative arts through Parisian auctions in the nineteenth century. Her PhD, *The Beurdeleys (1818–1895): A History of Trade and Furniture Making in 19th-Century Paris*, was awarded the INHA/CTHS Prize in 2021.

Jean Minguet is Head of the Department of Econometrics at Artprice.

Emily Peacock is a doctoral researcher in the Faculty of Law at Maastricht University, exploring the trade and trafficking of cultural heritage through an interdisciplinary lens. With a background in Roman archaeology and heritage studies, she is part of the Trafficking Transformations project and recently published on illicit antiquities and fossil commodification.

Anne-Sophie V. Radermecker is an Associate Professor at the Université libre de Bruxelles, where she holds the Chair in Cultural Economics (Department of History, Arts and Archaeology). Her main research interests focus on price formation mechanisms, value construction, and rebranding strategies in the market for indeterminate art and cultural goods.

Sanne Rossel is an independent provenance researcher specializing in collecting networks and the collecting of ephemera, archaeological and ethnographic objects. Her work focuses on the online licit and illicit trade of cultural heritage, using interdisciplinary methods to examine how online platforms transform the circulation, visibility, and perceived value of cultural objects.

Annick Schramme is a Professor and Academic Director of the Master of Cultural Management and the Competence Centre Cultural Management and Cultural Policy, University of Antwerp. Since 2024, she has held the UNESCO Chair in Cultural Entrepreneurship and Policy.

Yuqing Song is a PhD candidate in Economics and Management Sciences at the Université libre de Bruxelles. Her doctoral research focuses on issues of authenticity in the Chinese art market. Her broader research interests include cultural heritage, museum studies, and art markets.

Darius A. Spieth is an art historian and San Diego Alumni Association Chapter Alumni Professor at Louisiana State University. His major books include *Revolutionary Paris and the Market for Netherlandish Art* (Brill, 2018), *Napoleon's Sorcerers: The Sophisians* (University of Delaware Press, 2007), and a forthcoming dictionary on *Art Markets, Law and Economics* (OUP).

Peter K. Tompa Esq., Executive Director of the International Association of Professional Numismatists (IAPN), is a Washington, D.C.-based attorney practicing cultural property law. He advocates for collectors and small businesses, with decades of experience in litigation, policy, and numismatics.

Cameron Weber is an independent scholar living in Brooklyn. He produces *Hardfire TV* about current events and helped to create the field of cultural economics at the New School for Social Research as part of his PhD studies in 2015. *Markets and Artists in Music* (2024) is his latest book.

Julia Marie Wendl (MA) became Germany's youngest auctioneer before studying History of Art and Art Business in London, where she freelanced for auction platforms and started guest-lecturing. She is director of Kunst-Auktionshaus WENDL, contributing to national committees, conferences and publications – most recently co-teaching a practice-based module she conceived for Friedrich-Schiller-Universität Jena.

Donna Yates is Associate Professor of Criminal Law and Criminology at Maastricht University and a leading expert on the illicit trade in cultural objects and art crime. With dual PhDs in Archaeology and Criminology, she leads major research projects including the ERC-funded *TRANSFORM*. She advises governments and international bodies on cultural heritage crime, money laundering, and art market regulation, and regularly appears in major international media.

List of Figures

Selling Eclecticism: Trickle-Round Signaling and Modular Design in French Cemeteries After 1804

A Piece of Art in Every Household: The Nationwide Subscription of Graphic Art and Its Implications on the Market for Prints in Poland

Price, Value and Originality in the Oleograph Market in Buenos Aires (1870–1920)

Sector Insights: The Valuable Low End of the Auction Art Market

Trash or Treasure? Interviews with a Dealer from the Chinese Folk Antiques Market

Sector Insights: Stay Local, Sell Global: Regional Auctioneers, Platforms and Questions of Locality in the Digital Age

From Physical to Virtual: The Shifting Landscape of a Collectors' Community of Advertising and Packaging Paraphernalia in Northwestern Europe

Outsiders or Forgotten? Independent Artists Creating Alternative Career Paths in the Low-end Market

Sector Insights: The Low-end in the *Mobilier National*'s Collections: From Splat Back Chairs to Bouillotte Lamps

Sector Insights: Coins as Cultural Goods: Promoting Conservation Over State Control

List of Tables

Recontextualizing and Modeling the "Low-end" Markets for Art and Cultural Goods

Anne-Sophie V. Radermecker and Nathalie Moureau

In recent years, the art market has undergone a notable shift in both trends and discourse. Popular television programs such as *Flog it!* Or *Affaire conclue* and the rise of online platforms for affordable art and antiques have broadened access, enabling a wider audience to engage in buying and selling. Even conceptual artist and Instagram influencer Jerry Gogosian (1985-2026) has remarked on the increasing presence of decorative paintings marketed as "artworks" by mainstream furniture retailers. This evolution is also reflected in recent market analyses. Whereas earlier editions of leading reports—such as *The Art Basel & UBS Art Market Report* and the *Artprice Report*—focused predominantly on the high-end segment, their 2025 editions emphasize the stagnation of this premium tier and the concurrent expansion of the so-called "low-end" market. As the *Artprice Report* (2025, p. 6) notes: "when striving to achieve faster sales at higher prices and breaking records is no longer viable, and when high-end market activity stagnates, sales continue to flourish at the opposite end of the

A.-S. V. Radermecker (✉)
Université libre de Bruxelles, Brussels, Belgium
e-mail: Anne-Sophie.Radermecker@ulb.be

N. Moureau
Université Paul-Valéry-Montpellier, Montpellier, France
e-mail: nathalie.moureau@univ-montp3.fr

A.-S. V. Radermecker (ed.), *Low-End Markets for Art and Cultural Goods*, Cultural Economics & the Creative Economy,
https://doi.org/10.1007/978-3-032-27566-0_1

spectrum." The same report highlights the remarkable growth in the market for prints priced under $1,000, which has surged by over 79% since 2020—reaching 193,000 transactions compared to just 72,000 a decade earlier. This broader trend culminates in *The Art Newspaper* article "End of Investment Art? Why the Bottom of the Market is Flourishing" (Reyburn, 2025), which underscores the growing relevance of lower-priced segments within the art market.

The characterization of the art market as structurally polarized—where transaction volume is concentrated in lower price segments while transaction value is heavily skewed toward the higher end—is well established. This segmentation has been consistently documented in art market analyses, particularly through price-based product differentiation and the distribution of market share across defined price tiers. For example, McAndrew (2024, p. 160) divides the fine art market into four primary segments: the low-end (prices up to $50,000), the middle market (prices between $50,000–250,000 and $250,000–1 million), the high-end (prices exceeding $1 million), and an additional ultra-high-end category (prices above $10 million). Data from 2024 illustrate this structure clearly. Works priced above $1 million and $10 million comprised only 0.3% and 0.02% of total transactions, respectively, yet accounted for 31% and 18% of total market value. In contrast, works sold for under $5,000 represented approximately 76% of all transactions, yet only 4% of total sales value—demonstrating a distribution pattern that closely follows the Pareto principle (McAndrew, 2025, p. 179). While annual variations exist, this core segmentation remains a defining and stable feature of the art market.

What is more recent is the increasing attention paid by the art market itself to a segment that has historically received limited recognition. This lack of attention can be partly attributed to the language used in market discourse. The term "low-end" inherently carries hierarchical and value-laden connotations, positioning these goods as lesser in comparison to the "high-end," and associating them with lower prices, unknown artists, and diminished cultural significance. In a market governed by superstar dynamics, unbranded or anonymous artworks do not align with the dominant narratives that define art market success—namely, scarcity, prestige, opacity and financial returns. The recognition of cultural markets as "star markets" (Adler, 1985; Rosen, 1981) has further concentrated attention on the top end of the market, inadvertently contributing to the neglect of lower-priced segments. However, over the past decade, the institutionalization and expansion of art market studies as an academic field have fostered more diverse research agendas. As scholarly interest in the art market grows, there is a corresponding shift toward more comprehensive analytical frameworks—ones that incorporate social, cultural, and heritage dimensions—moving beyond traditional economic models focused solely on art's profitability (e.g., Baumol, 1986; Mei & Moses, 2002; Worthington & Higgs, 2004).

Interestingly, an interdisciplinary review of the scholarly literature on the art market shows that the lower ends of the market have not been entirely overlooked. Across disciplines, several studies have addressed this segment—either directly or indirectly—by examining the careers of lesser-known artists, the practices of local dealers, or the circulation of lower-value objects such as decorative arts, prints, photographs, and antiques. These contributions often arise from discipline-specific research agendas, reinforcing the fragmentation that characterizes the broader field of art market studies (Radermecker and Alvarez de Toledo 2022). Such fragmentation has hindered the development of a comprehensive economic understanding of low-end markets. While this introduction does not attempt to provide an exhaustive review of interdisciplinary work on this segment, it seeks to demonstrate the existence of scholarly interest—particularly within sociology, art history, and economics.

Sociology, one of the foundational disciplines in art market research, has made significant contributions to understanding hierarchical distinctions in cultural production and consumption. Raymonde Moulin's pioneering work offered a systematic analysis of art market segmentation and differentiation, highlighting lower-value artistic outputs such as *chromos*—i.e., artworks of limited artistic recognition often produced by amateurs (Moulin 1967, pp. 409–416). Building on this, Couture (1981) critically examined the dichotomy between *l'art savant* (canonical art) and *l'art commercial* (commercial or popular art), arguing that the *chromos* industry merits recognition as a legitimate cultural industry due to its popularity among lower-income groups and its broader economic significance. The argument has recently been taken up and further developed by Pernoud (2025), who offers new scholarly insights into what has long been regarded—and often disparaged by scholars—as the *tableau du pauvre* ("poor man's painting"). In the context of antiques, Nelsen (1970) contributed substantially by showing how the antiques market—spanning both high and low ends—serves diverse social strata. As later emphasized by Bourdieu (1984), Nelsen showed that purchasing behavior in this domain is motivated by factors ranging from leisure to social distinction. Similarly, Palmer and Forsyth

(2002) analyzed antique malls as sites of low-end market activity, identifying diverse buyer profiles such as occasional shoppers, regular customers, professional dealers, and informed collectors. Socio-economic studies have also examined the necessary conditions for the emergence of local art markets, particularly outside global centers such as New York, London, and Paris. These studies often focus on structural and contextual enablers—such as clusters of players, the entry of major market actors, cultural policy developments, and institutional support—which allow decentralized areas to emerge as market spaces, regardless of whether they aim to compete with global art capitals (e.g., De Vrièse et al., 2011; Velthuis and Baia Curioni 2015; Robertson et al. 2025). Other research has investigated artist careers without focusing on superstar profiles (Duester, 2024; Moureau, 2023). Although underrepresented in art market studies, anthropology offers complementary perspectives on lower-end segments. Stuart Plattner's *High Art Down Home* (1996), an ethnographic study of the local art market in St. Louis, Missouri, revealed how economic transactions intersect with social and symbolic practices, showing parallels between local and high-end markets. Anthropologists have also studied alternative social spaces such as flea markets, providing valuable insights into the informal dynamics and interactions shaping the lower tiers of the art economy. For instance, in his study of French regional ceramic production, Bonnot (2002) examined the shift in status from ordinary consumer goods to cultural objects, directly addressing the role of everyday collecting and the ways in which the antiques market contributes to the production of heritage value. In her recently published book, Torregrossa (2026) conducted an ethnographic investigation showing that local art and collectible auctions operate as a social world in which sellers, buyers, and intermediaries transform the value of objects through narratives, emotions, personal trajectories, and processes of appropriation and separation.

In art history and economic history, the seminal work of John Michael Montias (1982) advanced our understanding of lesser-known artworks in early modern society. Through the analysis of Dutch probate inventories, Montias uncovered patterns of ownership and consumption among non-elite populations. Building on this approach, De Marchi and Van Miegroet (2006; 2007) have explored the contributions of anonymous or under-documented artists, especially in Mechelen, on the periphery of Antwerp. Their work on *petits maîtres*—artists who produced "phantom copies"—showed their critical role in the emergence of a commercially oriented art market in sixteenth-century Antwerp (Van Miegroet, 2008; Vermeylen, 2003). Art historian Sophie Raux has expanded the scope of art market historiography by foregrounding provincial markets, often overlooked in dominant narratives. Her methodological innovation lies in utilizing alternative archival sources—such as newspaper advertisements—to compensate for the survival bias that typically affects lower-end objects (Raux, 2018). Similarly, Saint-Raymond (2021; 2023) has examined marginal market segments, including the trade in decorative arts in nineteenth-century Paris and regional areas such as Toulouse. Her work highlights the significance of neglected marketplaces and artistic productions. For the contemporary period, Wong (2013)'s study of Dafen Village—a Chinese community known for mass-producing replicas of Western masterpieces—is also notable. Rather than dismissing this output as forgery or kitsch, Wong highlights how labor, value, and authorship intersect in non-Western contexts, challenging the romanticized notion of the singular artist-genius and pushing for a broader understanding of authenticity and legitimacy in today's art world.

In economics and consumer research, Belk (2013) has offered important insights into collecting behavior, following in the tradition of Stoller's (1984) foundational work on the "singular economy" of collectibles. Moureau et al. (2015), in a study commissioned by the French Ministry of Culture, also paid attention to "ordinary" collectors—those who are not ultra-wealthy. Traditionally, economic research has also treated art primarily as an asset class, concentrating on high-value works transacted through major auction houses; a focus largely driven by the availability of reliable data. However, growing awareness of the art market's stratification has prompted scholars to investigate performance differences across various market segments. For example, Pesando (1993) and Renneboog and Spaenjers (2013) used quantile-based hedonic regressions to show that the high-end market is more volatile than the low-end. Alternative assets such as violins and stamps have also been studied (Graddy & Margolis, 2011; Oosterlinck, 2017). Fry (2020) applied finite mixture modeling to segment Indigenous art markets, while Blazy and Blum (2022) examined vertical (quality) and horizontal (taste) differentiation in the comic art market. Radermecker (2021) explored valuation in markets for anonymous paintings, offering insights into pricing in the absence of name recognition. Angelini et al. (2022) developed a Nash bargaining model of price formation in the art market, showing that in information-scarce segments—especially the low tier—overconfidence and imperfect signals can inflate prices beyond underlying quality, alter the likelihood of trade, and disadvantage more sophisticated buyers. Recently, Abbing (2022) has also criticized the high/low art divide, interrogating how institutional and historical boundaries affect pricing, access, and cultural legitimacy.

This rapid overview highlights a clear divergence between the emphasis of grey literature and media—typically centered on the high-end of the market—and the broader scope of academic research, which increasingly explores lesser-known segments. Despite this growing interest, such research remains fragmented and lacks integration. Two main factors contribute to this fragmentation. First is a methodological divide: each discipline tends to narrow its analytical focus to ensure academic rigor. Economists, for example, often isolate variables within homogeneous segments to facilitate controlled modeling, while art historians, limited by the nature of archival sources, frequently concentrate on specific object categories or production periods. Second, longstanding disciplinary boundaries have shaped the organization of academic inquiry. However, gaining a comprehensive understanding of art market dynamics—particularly across different price tiers—demands interdisciplinary approaches. This is especially important in the cultural sector, where economic analysis must be enriched by historical, sociological, and aesthetic insights.

1 The Low-End Art Markets: Current Challenges

While addressing all the complexities of low-end art markets lies beyond the scope of this volume, the aim of this introductory essay is to recontextualize the notion of the "low-end" market from an academic perspective —that is, to move beyond a purely price-based classification. The objective is to highlight key challenges related to this market segment and to propose a general framework through which coherent logics driving behaviors across different segments can be identified. Readers are encouraged to keep these considerations in mind when approaching the chapters compiled in this volume that illustrate various aspects of low-end art markets.

1.1 Limitations of Price-Based Market Segmentation

The price thresholds commonly used by art market stakeholders to delineate market segments, though offering certain advantages, come with significant limitations. First, it is important to note that this segmentation only began to take shape in the 2010s, particularly through the market reports published by Artprice and Clare McAndrew for TEFAF (and later for Art Basel). It emerged in a context marked by soaring prices, largely driven by the influx of new high-net-worth individuals into the global art market. The classification helped illustrate how a small number of high-value transactions could disproportionately influence overall market value. However, beyond this descriptive function, such segmentation lacks robust analytical and theoretical foundations. It is not grounded in a coherent economic framework capable of fully explaining market dynamics. As a result, this approach risks reinforcing Alfred Marshall's early observation that works of art cannot be objectively valued due to their lack of comparables, making their pricing "a simple matter of accident" (Marshall, 1890, p. 13). Second, while price-based segmentation facilitates statistical analyses and offers a starting point for market interpretation, the thresholds themselves vary widely and inconsistently—from a few thousand to several million euros or dollars—with no standardized criteria. Cutoffs such as \$50,000, \$10,000, \$5,000, or \$1,000 are applied unevenly across sources. Although these benchmarks may serve regulatory or policy purposes (e.g., the €10,000 Anti-Money Laundering threshold or the €18,000 minimum valuation for EU import declarations), inflation, evolving regulations, and market volatility make longitudinal price comparisons challenging unless properly normalized. More importantly, price does not necessarily reflect an object's intrinsic quality, especially in contexts where key information is missing or asymmetric (Akerlof, 1970; Spence, 1973; Tirole, 1988). Third—and most critically—price alone cannot account for the full spectrum of value relevant in cultural markets. Cultural goods embody not only economic but also aesthetic, historical, social, symbolic, spiritual, emotional and functional value (Karpik, 2010; Throsby, 2001). This is particularly true for low-end artworks, where clear quality signals and expert authentication may be absent. In such cases, other value dimensions—depending on the buyer's personal needs or background—often take precedence over strict rational calculations. For example, a €20 vintage toy cannot meaningfully be equated with a nineteenth-century antique mirror priced at €2,500, given their vastly different histories, production contexts, and consumer appeals. Likewise, a Murano vase (e.g., model *Chambord*) might fetch only €20 at a local auction in Belgium, despite its artisanal quality and cultural significance—underscoring the inadequacy of price-based categorization.

To date, few alternative frameworks have been developed to conceptualize segmentation and differentiation within the art market beyond simple pricing brackets. Some scholars have sought to classify intermediaries according to their operating scale. For example, Robertson (2005) proposed a four-tier model for auction houses: Alpha (major global firms like

Christie's and Sotheby's), Beta (international firms with cross-border operations), Gamma (national-level firms), and Delta (local or regionally focused entities). This intermediary-based segmentation introduces a spatial dimension to market analysis, emphasizing geographic scope over price level. However, with the digitization of art transactions—accelerated by the rise of online platforms—even small, locally based firms can now reach global audiences, blurring the lines between traditional intermediary categories.

While intermediaries certainly shape buyer behavior, we contend that any robust analysis of market differentiation must begin with the artworks themselves rather than with transactional metrics alone. Defining the low-end solely in terms of price risks obscuring the diverse logics that shape value creation and exchange. Building on its twenty-four contributions, the book introduces from the outset a triadic model for examining traded goods through three core attributes: functionality (practical versus symbolic), scarcity, and brand strength as a proxy for quality. As shown in the box accompanying this introduction, we argue that the combination of low symbolic functionality, limited scarcity, and weak brand strenght delineates the boundaries of the low-end segments.

1.2 *Dealing with High Heterogeneity*

The difficulty of conceptualizing low-end art markets beyond price lies in the high degree of heterogeneity among the sub-segments and goods they encompass. In the upper-end segment, fine art and other culturally significant goods are at least unified by a recognized degree of scarcity and quality, such as prestigious signatures, provenance, exhibition history, or scholarly publications. In low-end markets, situated at the intersection of various cultural industries, the degree of heterogeneity is considerably higher. While one may argue that the high- and middle-end markets are also heterogeneous—encompassing fine art, decorative arts, and luxury items—there is reason to believe that this diversity, both within and across categories, reaches its peak in the low ends. This is partly due to their porous boundaries, where distinctions blur between art, craft, cultural goods, and even conventional consumer products. The intrinsic and extrinsic characteristics of these items vary greatly, as does the availability of information, complicating attempts to classify or evaluate them through conventional frameworks.

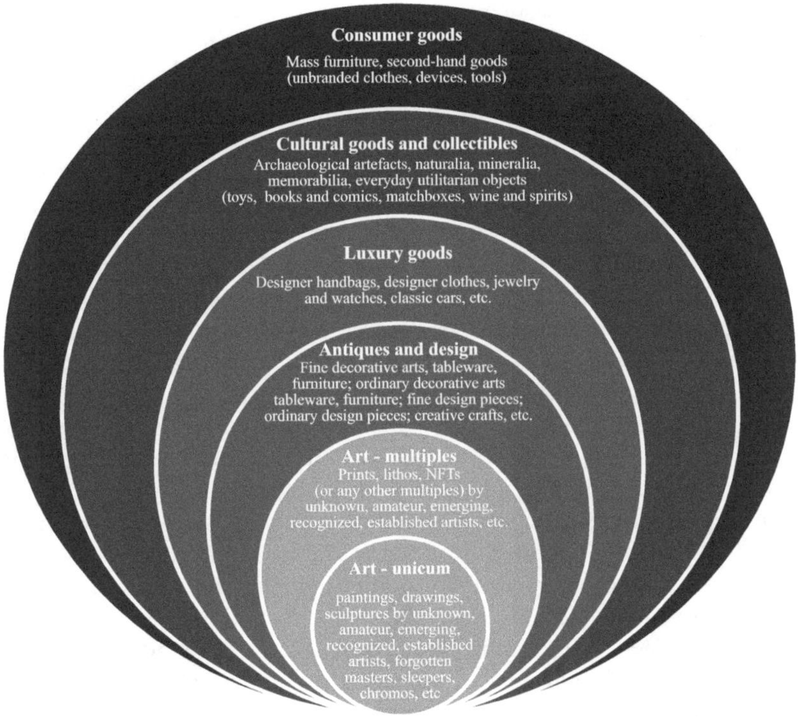

Fig. 1 Concentric diagram of the low-end art market

Drawing on Throsby's model of cultural and creative industries, which is structured around the concept of proximity to the "core arts," the concentric circle diagram presented in Fig. 1 organizes these objects based on their distance from core movable artistic goods. The diverse range of items encountered in low-end art markets—including those sold through small antique shops, local galleries, online platforms, flea markets, garage sales, and *vide-greniers*—reflects varying degrees of utility and scarcity, topics that will be further discussed in this book. Although similar types of artistic and cultural goods may occasionally appear in higher-end segments—particularly in the case of exceptional or rare specimens—the majority of the items considered here predominantly belong to low-end markets. Additionally, it is important to note that across all market segments, the presence of copies and forgeries remains a possible issue.

At the core of this diagram are fine arts—i.e., paintings, drawings, and sculptures—that are, in principle, unique works created by the hand of an artist, regardless of their level of recognition. This category includes works by unknown or amateur artists (both identified and anonymous), emerging artists whose market value is still developing, regionally or nationally recognized artists who remain outside the global "superstar" circuit, and internationally established artists. It also encompasses unattributed or misattributed works, as well as "sleepers" whose prestigious authorship remains undiscovered (Bandle, 2016). A distinct subcategory includes chromos and low-cost commercial artworks, often characterized by vivid colors and kitsch aesthetics, appealing to broader consumer segments. These are closely aligned with mass-produced art—sometimes pejoratively called "supermarket art"—which may or may not involve artist collaboration and is typically sold through furniture retailers.

The second concentric level consists of multiples—including serial prints, engravings, lithographs, chromolithographs, statuettes, etc. These items, signed or unsigned, often include reproductions or works produced in the style of Old Masters or modern and contemporary artists. Such works generally carry lower price points than unique pieces, as market value is strongly affected by medium and technique (Renneboog & Spaenjers, 2013). For example, an engraving by a renowned Old Master might be valued at only a few thousand euros, allowing buyers to acquire works by canonical names. Contemporary artists such as Jeff Koons and Damien Hirst have adopted product differentiation strategies by producing limited editions and prints to reach multiple market tiers. When editions are limited, reproducible works can also reach high prices—such as Gursky's photograph *Rhein II* (1999), number 1 in a series of six, which sold for $4.3 million at Christie's New York in 2011. It is important to note that such editions often coexist with unauthorized reproductions, further complicating market segmentation. In the case of Banksy, for instance, the artist established the company Pest Control to authenticate his works, particularly for auctions, due to the widespread circulation of counterfeits. At the lowest tier of this level are posters, especially those derived from museum collections.

The third level comprises antiques and design objects, which embody aesthetic, functional, and historical value. Antiques typically include decorative arts (e.g., clocks, mirrors, bronzes, carpets, tapestries), furniture, and tableware (e.g., porcelain plates, crystalware, silverware), and are traditionally defined as being over 100 years old (Rosenstein, 2009).

This differentiates them from vintage items, which generally date from 20 to 100 years. Design pieces from the twentieth century are also included. This category is highly heterogeneous and varies widely in quality, often prompting a distinction between "fine" and "ordinary" antiques. Fine antiques are original pieces from historical periods, while ordinary antiques are often "style of" reproductions designed for less-elite—yet bourgeois—consumers. Each category is considered high- or low-end depending on market differentiation logic. Though reproductions are produced with more economical materials and quicker techniques, they often retain significant artisanal value. For instance, late nineteenth- and early twentieth-century regional furniture—now undervalued—was once regarded as skilled craftsmanship. The value of design objects is shaped by designer reputation, production quantity, and shifting market preferences.

Traditional luxury goods—such as handbags, watches, rare sneakers, and classic cars—are also increasingly integrated into the art market. Although empirical research remains limited, such items have long appeared in the lower-end sector (below €50,000). Branded luxury items (e.g., Chanel, Louis Vuitton bags) are regularly found at local auctions, alongside vintage garments and estate-sale jewelry. While collectible cars are rarer due to higher baseline values, some lower-tier models do appear in these contexts.

Another relevant category is that of collectibles and cultural goods, which includes utilitarian or decorative archaeological artifacts, *mineralia*, *naturalia*, *memorabilia*, and vernacular objects more broadly. Virtually any object can become collectible if it evokes a nostalgic connection to the past (Belk, 2013). Examples include advertising materials, toys, comic books, and domestic items. Wine and spirits may also fall into this category, as their segmentation and differentiation resemble those of the art market.

Finally, standard consumer items without creative intent are also routinely encountered in venues like flea markets, garage sales, and *vide-greniers*. These hybrid marketplaces often serve as the entry point to the art market, where "creative" and "non-creative" goods coexist. As theorized by Thompson (1979), such venues illustrate the cyclical nature of value: formerly prized objects may lose or regain worth depending on market dynamics.

The concentric diagram presented here acknowledges the existence of distinct, porous submarkets within the broader low-end art markets—thereby justifying the use of the plural in this introductory essay—and highlights their richness and diversity from both object-based and consumer perspectives. It underscores the wide range of artistic, cultural, creative, and consumer goods that comprise these segments, while also challenging the frequent exclusion of utilitarian or decorative objects from art market analysis. In doing so, it promotes a more inclusive framework that reflects the complexity and stratification of the market beyond the canonical domains of fine and high-value art. Importantly, recognizing this heterogeneity is not meant to undermine institutional definitions of art or to equate all artistic, cultural, and creative goods. Rather, it aims to foster a productive interdisciplinary dialogue—particularly among economists, art historians, sociologists and anthropologists—on evolving conceptions of art, heritage, visual and material culture. Such engagement is crucial for broadening our understanding of value systems beyond conventional hierarchies and standard measures of price and quality, which are often insufficient to capture the nuances of these segments.

1.3 Words Matter: "High" Versus "Low"

The terminology used to distinguish "high-end" from "low-end" goods is particularly suited to commodity markets, where product differentiation is based on observable, measurable, and standardized quality attributes (Dickson & Ginter, 1987). In such contexts, price segmentation generally aligns with quality distinctions, as is the case in certain cultural and creative industries. For example, in the sparkling wine industry—comprising search and experience goods—products like Champagne are positioned as high-end relative to lower-cost alternatives such as sparkling wine made using non-traditional methods, with prices often reflecting variations in inputs, production, and brand equity. Similar principles apply in industries like fashion, where luxury clothes or accessories are typically segmented from mass-market or counterfeit alternatives based on material quality, craftsmanship, and brand reputation. Yet, in both examples, the availability of more affordable goods allows broader socio-economic groups to adopt similar consumption behaviors (e.g., celebrating a special occasion with sparkling wine or wearing a look-alike luxury accessory), without incurring the cost of premium products (Bourdieu, 1984).

Traditional product differentiation frameworks, however, are less suited to markets involving (meta)credence goods such as art (Ekelund et al., 2020), where applying conventional economic theory proves challenging. Quality in such markets is rarely observable ex ante, and information asymmetry is a fundamental characteristic. Moreover, quality is often shaped by subjective and contextual factors. This is especially true in the low-end segment, where information failures may be more acute than in the high-end, and where price alone fails to reflect the full spectrum of relevant values—historical, aesthetic, authentic, symbolic, social, spiritual, emotional or functional—due to weak demand or low visibility. While some low-priced items (e.g., mass-produced reproductions) clearly serve as lower-quality analogues of higher-end works, not all low-priced goods are necessarily inferior. Many high-quality artworks by skilled but lesser-known artists—recognized within local or national networks—remain undervalued due to shifting tastes, limited market demand, or reduced institutional support. Consider the case of decorative arts: a sixteenth-century Brussels tapestry valued at €20,000 or a fine eighteenth-century ormolu mantel clock sold for a few thousand euros may be classified as "low-end" under prevailing price-based typologies. Such classification obscures their historical and artistic significance, wrongly equating limited demand with inferior quality. Consequently, a major work may be labeled "low-end" despite representing one of the finest examples within its category. This mislabeling risks negatively impacting the perception, reception, and valuation of such works.

These observations align with longstanding art historical and sociological discourses that oppose highbrow and lowbrow culture, or major and minor arts—distinctions with enduring consequences for how value is attributed (Bourdieu, 1984; Gans, 1985). It is also essential to recognize that value is inherently relative. Drawing on a constructivist perspective (Heinich, 2017), both perceived and market value are contingent upon context and shaped by the subjectivity of those engaging with the object. What one individual may deem "low-end," another—depending on their socio-economic status or purchasing power—may regard as "high-end." Thus, both price and quality remain highly variable and relational concepts.

In other words, the pejorative connotations associated with the term "low-end" in reference to the arts call for a more nuanced conceptual framework—namely, one that avoids conflating low price with low quality or limited cultural significance. Terminology in this context is not merely descriptive but also performative as imprecise or inappropriate labels can obscure important distinctions and distort decision-making processes within the market. Since Kahneman and Tversky's seminal work (1979), extensive research (e.g., Levin et al., 1998) has shown that human behavior is highly influenced by framing effects. When presented with the same choices, individuals respond differently depending on whether the context is framed positively (potential gains) or negatively (potential losses). One may therefore argue that the neglect or even negative perception of this segment of the art market partly results from the somewhat inappropriate terminology applied to cultural and creative goods. In the concluding section of this volume, we advocate the use of an alternative term, namely "entry-level markets."

2 Structure of the Book

In addition to providing a conceptual foundation, the primary aim of this volume is to assemble scholarly and professional contributions that explicitly engage with the low-end segments of the art market, with each chapter offering a distinct disciplinary perspective. These contributions have played a critical role in shaping the reflection presented in this introduction and the proposed triadic model. The collection comprises academic essays, empirical studies, and practitioner-oriented texts referred to as *Sector Insights.* Although the inclusion of practitioner voices may depart from conventional academic norms, this editorial choice is intentional, aimed to foster constructive dialogue with stakeholders who are directly involved in the operational realities of the low-end art markets. It is important to emphasize, however, that *Sector Insights* reflect the individual perspectives and professional experiences of their authors.

Moreover, rather than following a conventional structure based on disciplinary and chronological segmentation, or the tripartite division of supply, intermediaries, and demand, this volume is organized around a series of transversal themes that emerged organically from the received contributions. These thematic clusters—though not exhaustive and shaped by the nature of the chapters—seek to highlight key characteristics and mechanisms specific to low-end art markets. In doing so, this volume offers an alternative to prior edited collections in the field, which have typically been organized around established frameworks such as legal and financial issues (Lazzaro et al., 2025) or globalization and transnational dynamics (Robertson et al., 2025).

Part 1 of the volume revisits established cultural economic theories through the lens of low-end art markets, engaging with concepts such as long-tail theory, the (in)formal economy, and art as an investment. Michael Hutter's contribution underscores that most cultural goods markets follow a power-law pattern, with value flowing upward as select low-end goods gain prestige and downward as once-elite items disperse into lower-value markets. Francesco Angelini examines the role of informal economies within Western art markets and highlights research gaps that challenge existing knowledge, which largely applies to formal, regulated art markets. Anne-Sophie Radermecker extends the discussion of investment to "everyday luxury goods" such as Val Saint Lambert crystalware, demonstrating that the tools used to construct price indices can also be applied to low-end art goods. She further shows that such goods can be understood as investments in their original context, despite their lower value and high sensitivity to changing tastes and lifestyles.

Part 2 shifts focus to the diverse range of goods that shape low-end art markets and the porous boundaries between categories of cultural and economic value, spanning art, craft, luxury, consumer goods, and even junk. Darius Spieth's chapter traces the evolution of the St. Ouen flea markets—born in late nineteenth-century Paris during Haussmannization—from recycling hubs to romanticized cultural landmarks, now facing gentrification pressures as branding pivots toward luxury and tourism. Kaylee Alexander reexamines the role of nineteenth-century *marbriers*, challenging their portrayal as subordinate to architects by demonstrating that they were the primary makers of funerary monuments for middle- and working-class clients, whose vernacular tomb designs engaged in a "trickle-round" exchange with elite architectural styles. Wiktor Komorowski's paper explores the history of Poland's Nationwide Subscription of Graphic Art, revealing how its legacy—rooted in the country's state-socialist past—continues to shape a growing, globally integrated market for affordable prints and multiples, fueled by the expanding middle class.

In Part 3, the contributions examine how actors in low-end segments seek to harness the prestige of high art to enhance the appeal of lower-end artistic and creative goods. María Isabel Baldassarre, a specialist in nineteenth-century art, analyzes how these reproductions—crafted to replicate the iconography and surface qualities of fine paintings—straddle the line between artistic reproduction and commercial commodity. Krystyna Matyjaszkiewicz investigates the diversification strategies of Victorian wholesalers Silber & Fleming, who broadened their clientele through the mass distribution of affordable artworks and copies. Bringing a contemporary angle, Jiahui Liao explores how museums indirectly stimulate art consumption by developing creative products linked to intellectual property licensing.

Part 4 explores the fluidity of boundaries within the art market, where the classification of objects as low- or high-end can shift according to context, timing, and interpretive lens. Drawing on data from Australian art auctions between 1970 and 2017, Douglas J. Hodgson, Cameron M. Weber, and Bronwyn Coate show that works by lower-consecration artists—those missing from major art historical references—have seen slower price growth, reduced sales volumes, and declining collector interest, suggesting that artists without lasting recognition gradually vanish from the market. Donna Yates examines the trade in megalodon teeth to illustrate how an object's market value fluctuates depending on the sales channel, from online platforms to elite auction houses, invoking the concept of the "desirescape" to explain these shifts. Jean Minguet, head of econometrics at Artprice, disputes the idea that the low-end market is marginal, arguing that it provides the structural foundation that sustains the high-end art market.

Part 5 examines how trust and value are constructed in market segments where conventional markers—such as authorship, provenance, or originality—may be absent. Tim R. L. Fry and Bronwyn Coate analyze the Australian Indigenous art auction market (1991–2020), demonstrating that pre-sale estimates can be an effective tool for segmenting the market and that, for low-end works, auction houses tend to set estimates closer to realized prices, likely to shape buyer perceptions. Isabel Causadias explores how trust—built through interpersonal networks, informal reputations, and flexible transaction norms—sustains Barcelona's low-end primary art market in the absence of institutional validation, revealing its invisible yet resilient role within the broader art ecosystem. In an interview-based study, Yuqing Song delves into the Chinese antiques market to show that "sleepers" are more common than often assumed, and that their discovery (*jianlou*) depends on culturally embedded practices such as gut feelings (*yanli*), exploiting regional price differences (*diqu cha*), and understanding buyer variation (*xiajia cha*). Finally, German auctioneer Julia Marie Wendl offers a valuable insider's perspective on how digitization has transformed regional art and antiques auctioneers, revealing how online platforms and live bidding have reshaped the sale of affordable cultural goods—illustrated with exclusive sales data rarely available to researchers.

Part 6 of the volume turns to motivations and consumption behaviors in the low-end art market that diverge from traditional value drivers such as the quest for authorship, authenticity, and originality. Drawing on interviews from the specialized press, Federica Aramu compares the purchasing motivations behind fine antiques, ordinary antiques, and collectibles. She finds that while fine antiques and collectibles are primarily acquired as items for building a collection, ordinary antiques are more often consumed as second-hand goods, reflecting a different logic of value attribution. Through online ethnographic research, Emily Peacock examines social media communities of low-end antiquities buyers, revealing that for many participants, the appeal of the "ancient" can outweigh conventional standards of authenticity and provenance. Likewise, Sanne Rossel explores the niche world of advertising and packaging collectors, showing how digital tools have reshaped both the scale and character of collecting practices in this domain. Finally, Matilde Ferrero investigates independent art spaces as marginal yet meaningful arenas for low-end art transactions, operating outside established institutional frameworks while offering alternative pathways for artistic exchange and value recognition.

Finally, Part 7 brings together contributions that address the heritage dimension of low-end cultural goods, highlighting their cultural significance regardless of their low perceived value. In line with the broader definition of heritage advanced by the 2005 Faro Convention, these goods are shown to play a vital role in shaping local and national identities, while also fulfilling important social and economic functions within communities. Annick Schramme and Laura D'hoore examine how public museums and private collectors in Flanders (Belgium)—drawing on comparative policy models from the Netherlands, France, and the UK—can collaborate to safeguard culturally significant yet under-recognized artworks. They argue for policy frameworks that promote complementarity rather than competition between sectors, encourage long-term investment, and provide early-stage support for local artistic practices. Vincent Lamouraux and Camille Mestdagh, collections inspectors at the Mobilier National in Paris, discuss the institution's strategies for preserving serial furniture pieces that are currently experiencing a decline in both perceived and functional value. Finally, Peter Tompa, Executive Director of the International Association of Professional Numismatists, argues that historical coins are best preserved through private collecting and a vibrant numismatic trade. He advocates for collaborative models such as the UK's Portable Antiquities Scheme over restrictive government controls, which, he contends, hinder legitimate collecting and scholarship while offering limited benefits to heritage preservation.

By documenting low-end art markets in a systematic manner for the first time, this book brings together the relevant interdisciplinary literature, helps prevent the survival bias of tomorrow, opens new research pathways, and invites scholars to reconsider the power of terminology and branding in shaping social, cultural, and economic realities. For policymakers—particularly at national and supranational levels—the book is an invitation to move beyond lingering stereotypes and to recognize the complexity, significance, and potential of the lower ends of art markets, along with their positive externalities. While goods circulating in these segments may not be recognized as objects of universal value like masterpieces, they arguably convey the value of everyday life and aesthetics—a form of cultural expression that, by resonating with a broader public, may achieve a different kind of universality.

Triadic Model

Building on the introduction to this volume and its contributions, we propose a triadic model that serves as a more effective analytical tool for understanding price formation and buyer behavior. Rather than prescribing normative pricing benchmarks, the model highlights general trends by returning to the fundamentals of the market: the traded goods themselves. The model is structured around the goods' three core attributes: (i) functionality, (ii) scarcity, and (iii) brand strength. These variables are not arbitrarily selected; they derive from Lancaster's consumer theory (1966) and interact to shape both pricing strategies and the perceived or symbolic value of objects in low-end segments. Each axis is described below, and the framework allows us to identify four sub-segments, which are introduced in turn.

Axis 1. Functionality

Functionality constitutes a key point of departure from traditional fine art models. While artworks and collectibles often serve symbolic or experiential purposes—such as aesthetic enjoyment, leisure through collecting, investment, or social signaling (Mandel, 2009)—many low-end items retain direct utilitarian functions. Decorative arts, furniture, design pieces, and handmade everyday objects were originally created to meet practical needs (e.g., storage, lighting, dining), and their direct utility as secondhand goods distinguishes them from canonical artworks.[1] More specifically, this axis spans a spectrum from low direct functionality—whether because the object's practical use has become obsolete or because its utility is primarily symbolic (i.e., collected for its decorative, social, or investment value)—to high direct functionality, when the object continues to serve its original utilitarian purpose.

Axis 2. Scarcity

Scarcity describes a situation in which supply is limited relative to demand, whereas rarity refers to how unique, uncommon or unusual an object is. In the art market, a work may be rare because few comparable examples exist, which is often the case at the high end of the market, but it becomes scarce when demand exceeds what is actually available. For the purposes of this model, we adopt the latter notion, as it appears more appropriate for a market segment characterized by a large supply of relatively substitutable goods and unequal demand for those goods. Moreover, this notion is a well-established determinant of value, particularly for collectibles (Hughes, 2022; Koford & Tschoegl, 1998). It increases desirability and, in turn, buyers' willingness to pay. However, the reasons for limited supply may vary: for antiques, age and survival are key; for editioned works, scarcity stems from limited print runs; and in fine art, it may be linked either to high demand or to low production output, thereby reconnecting with the notion of rarity. This axis spans a range from mass-produced or widely available items to objects that have become scarcer because of some of their attributes and broader consumption trends. Scarcity is also context-dependent and temporally situated: an object may be scarce in a given cultural or geographic setting but commonplace in another. It must therefore be assessed in relation to the specific market segment and time period in which the object circulates.

[1] That said, although they are often overlooked, some high-end goods also serve utilitarian purposes. Famously, after purchasing a Ming-era bowl for $36.05 million at Sotheby's in 2014, Chinese collector Liu Yiqian posted a photo of himself drinking tea from it on social media, stating, "I just want to express my excitement about this moment. The cup has such a long history, so when I got it, I just poured tea into it, and without even wiping it, I drank the tea." The bowl later entered his museum.

Axis 3. Brand Strength

Brand strength functions as a signal of quality, authenticity, and prestige. It is shaped by commercial performance, institutional validation, historical legacy, and cultural resonance (Moureau & Sagot-Duvauroux, 2016). In the art market, branding may come from an artist's name recognition (Hernando & Campo, 2017), the reputation of a manufacturer, or geographic indicators of origin (e.g., Murano glass or Sèvres porcelain), especially in the case of decorative arts and antiques (Kotler & Gertner, 2002). This axis includes a spectrum from unbranded to highly branded goods, also encompassing semi-branded objects and those with popular cultural significance (e.g., LU biscuit tins). Within low-end art markets, all these variations coexist and affect perceived value differently, depending on context. Like scarcity, brand strength is dynamic and must be evaluated against evolving market structures and symbolic meanings.

To define the market segment under study, we consider several possible combinations of these three attributes, classifying each as either "low to moderate" or "moderate to high" (e.g., low scarcity, high direct functionality, low brand strength). Although the analytical logic differs, this typology can be related to price-based segmentation: as the relative importance of these three characteristics increases, prices tend to rise and the market becomes progressively more exclusive, and vice versa. At the very top is the market for seven-figure artworks, characterized by high symbolic functionality (i.e., low direct functionality), high scarcity, and a strong brand (or signature). The buying motivation in this segment is straightforward, with all attributes converging to provide the highest possible level of distinction. The absence of direct functionality lends the work an aura of intellectual or spiritual superiority, elevating it above material concerns. The item's scarcity reinforces its exclusive nature—echoing Leibenstein's snob effect—while the renown of the artist, acting as a brand, confirms the desirability and secured nature of the piece. Paying a high price enhances this distinction even further. This is the trophy market, accessible only to high-net worth individuals. In other words, although our focus here is on low-end segments, this framework is more broadly applicable to other segments as well, and to both the primary and secondary art markets.

Beyond the high-end art market, situations in which attributes vary and combine in different ways are far more common. In such cases, consumers' willingness to pay tends to decrease, and the object is positioned in less exclusive market segments, such as mid- or low-end markets. The nature of the object and the buyer's motivation also shift accordingly. For example, a price of €10,000 might apply either to an object with high direct functionality and moderate scarcity and brand strength (such as a Louis XV-era silver household set bearing a coat of arms) or to an object with low direct functionality and low scarcity but high brand strength (such as a lithograph by Niki de Saint Phalle). Put differently, we argue that when symbolic functionality, scarcity, and brand strength are limited, their combination defines the boundaries of the low-end market segment. More specifically, we explore different configurations in which scarcity—ranging from low to moderate—is combined with the other two variables, since scarcity remains the primary economic driver of price levels. When scarcity is low, prices tend to remain low despite high symbolic functionality (i.e., low direct functionality) or strong brand legitimacy, due to competitive market pressure. Similarly, even a reputable brand paired with low functionality cannot command higher prices in the absence of scarcity. Building on these three axes, four sub-segments can be distinguished.

Sub-Segment 1: Moderate to High Direct Functionality (Low to Moderate Symbolic Functionality), Low to Moderate Scarcity, Low to Moderate Brand Strength

In its simplest form, where all attributes are low, this segment encompasses mass-produced furniture and decorative or functional objects—such as designed chairs, tables, and vases—that are widely available in domestic settings. These items are primarily valued for their utilitarian purpose, while exhibiting limited scarcity and weak brand strength. Typically associated with mainstream or affordable design brands (e.g., entry-level lines from Roche Bobois), such products may over time transition into collectible status, as evidenced by the emerging secondary market for vintage IKEA pieces.

In its more sophisticated form, where the attributes are moderate, this segment includes objects that do not display strong branding or exceptional scarcity but retain both practical and aesthetic utility. These items are not necessarily acquired for collecting, but rather for incorporation into everyday domestic environments, primarily as decorative elements. Examples include handcrafted vases from local artisan markets. Some items may also combine moderate brand strength, moderate scarcity, and high direct functionality. This includes functional furnishings—such as commercially designed pieces with moderate brand recognition, like recent editions of the Pipistrello lamp by Gae Aulenti for Martinelli Luce—or ordinary antiques such as silverware, mirrors, or chandeliers, often produced in historic revival styles (e.g., French Empire-style clocks). These objects are valued both for their utility—lighting, seating, or storage—and for their aesthetic contribution to interior spaces. They are often unique or semi-unique owing to manual production, limited distribution, or age, yet they remain relatively accessible.

Market Type: Primarily utilitarian and home decor markets, with players active in both primary market channels (e.g., craft fairs, mid-range design retailers, and decoration stores) and secondary market channels (e.g., auction houses, vintage shops, and flea markets).

Behavioral Hypothesis: Purchase motivations are predominantly functional and aesthetic. Consumption is mostly driven by immediate use rather than symbolic or investment considerations.

Indicative Price Range: Generally between a few euros (e.g., a crafted vase) and several hundred to a few thousand euros (e.g., furniture), depending on design, quality, condition, and evolving consumer trends. Higher-end exceptions may reach into the low-thousands, particularly where scarcity and brand recognition intersect.

Sub-Segment 2: Low to Moderate Direct Functionality (Moderate to High Symbolic Functionality), Low to Moderate Scarcity, Low to Moderate Brand Strength

This segment encompasses a wide variety of goods that, while all characterized by lower direct functionality, fall into distinct subcategories depending on the source of that limited utility. Demand for these items varies considerably depending on whether they are primarily intended for decorative purposes or for collecting. When low functionality is associated with the collection of mass-produced utilitarian objects or souvenirs, the result is a category of "everyday collectibles." These items generally have minimal intrinsic brand value and, when acquired on the secondary market, offer little to no direct practical use, as their original function may have become obsolete. Valued primarily as collectibles, they are typically preserved or displayed rather than used in everyday life. Although such objects may appear trivial or devoid of value to non-collectors, they can acquire speculative or symbolic significance within specific enthusiast or niche communities. This perceived value is often tied to contextual factors such as brand associations, scarcity within a subculture, or nostalgic appeal—criteria that differ substantially from those prevailing in traditional fine art or luxury markets. Representative examples include vintage postcards, matchboxes, collectible game cards (e.g., Pokémon) or absinthe spoons.

In other instances, low direct functionality is inherent to the object's purpose, particularly in the case of artworks created primarily for aesthetic appreciation rather than direct use. This applies to so-called "modest" or "amateur" art and chromos, namely paintings by amateur artists and mechanical reproductions, where the works may be treated as interchangeable and lack specific significance within a broader oeuvre. Unlike works by renowned artists, these pieces rarely possess substantial standalone value. This segment also includes prints, photographs, and other multiples produced by unknown artists. Such items are not necessarily collected for investment or prestige, but are instead incorporated into domestic settings for their decorative appeal.

Market Type: Primarily collectibles markets. Players are active in both primary market channels (e.g., local galleries, street markets, pop-up stores) and secondary market channels (e.g., auctions, vintage shops, flea markets, digital platforms).

Behavioral Hypothesis: Acquisition is typically driven by collecting as a leisure activity—motivated by personal interest, nostalgia, aesthetic appeal, or cultural affiliation. For artworks, the primary motivation is decorative, but one may not exclude that some buyers seek social distinction by acquiring such affordable objects.

Indicative Price Range: Generally between a few euros and several hundred euros, with higher values (thousands) corresponding to stronger scarcity and/or brand recognition.

Sub-Segment 3—Moderate to High Direct Functionality (Low to Moderate Symbolic Functionality), Low to Moderate Scarcity, Moderate to High Brand Strength

This category is relatively specific and includes aesthetically functional objects and furnishings associated with established luxury brands or historically significant artisanal production. These objects possess both high symbolic value and practical utility. Examples include period furniture and decorative arts (such as authenticated Sèvres porcelain services), luxury handbags (e.g., Hermès), designer sneakers (e.g., Air Jordan collaborations), and classic automobiles. While typically produced in limited quantities, their scarcity is often only moderate. Although these items remain usable in everyday contexts, they are frequently acquired for their symbolic value and may transition into higher-end market segments (e.g., museum collections or prestigious private holdings). For instance, in July 2025, the exceptional scarcity and provenance of a Hermès Birkin bag formerly owned by Jane Birkin contributed to its record-breaking sale at Sotheby's for €8.582 million. In such cases, the object's scarcity reaches its peak, and its functional utility becomes largely residual. In more typical scenarios, however, lower market valuations may result from the object's non–fine art status, prevailing market demand, or broader availability.

Market type: Luxury home furniture and accessories, operating at the intersection of symbolic consumption, functional utility, and investment potential. Players are active in both primary market channels (e.g., luxury stores, artisan workshops) and secondary market channels (e.g., antique stores, auction houses, digital platforms).

Behavioral hypothesis: Acquisition is driven by a combination of functional needs and snob effect/conspicuous consumption, often signaling taste, status, or investment intent.

Indicative price range: Typically from several thousand to several tens of thousands of euros, depending on the brand's capital, the object's scarcity (low to moderate), and perceived potential for long-term value retention.

Sub-Segment 4—Low to Moderate Direct Functionality (Moderate to High Symbolic Functionality), Low to Moderate Scarcity, Moderate to High Brand Strength

This sub-segment brings together works by artists from diverse artistic contexts and traditions. It includes paintings and other artworks by regionally emerging and recognized artists whose brand recognition is moderate and whose reputations are established primarily through local gallery representation, regional museums, or art-historical scholarship rooted in specific geographic or cultural contexts. Artists such as Maurice Musin (Liège, Belgium, 1939) or Jean-Pierre Ransonnet (Lierneux, Belgium, 1944), for instance, may not command international demand but nonetheless hold significant symbolic value within their local cultural ecosystems. Also situated in this sub-segment are anonymous or unbranded works linked to historically significant schools or stylistic traditions (e.g., Antwerp School, circa 1530), where association with a particular movement or place of origin functions as a proxy for brand equity. In such cases, although demand may be limited and scarcity low, cultural and symbolic value remain substantial.

This sub-segment also encompasses derivative or editioned works by modern and contemporary blue-chip artists—such as Jeff Koons, Damien Hirst, or Pablo Picasso—whose names serve as powerful brand indicators. Examples include limited-edition prints (e.g., Hirst), small-scale sculptures (e.g., Balloon Dog editions by Koons), and ceramics (e.g., Picasso's Madoura series). These pieces are often acquired by consumers seeking symbolic affiliation with high-status artists but who may lack the financial means to access the middle- or high-end art markets. Consumption in this context is primarily driven by aspirational motivations and symbolic signaling, consistent with

Bourdieu's theory. While significantly less expensive than unique works by the same artists, such editions may serve as entry points into art collecting or investment. Despite the diversity of object types, a common feature of this segment lies in their ability to satisfy the buyer's desire for distinction. Through moderate to high brand recognition and aesthetic appeal, these items provide symbolic capital while remaining financially accessible due to their limited scarcity.

Market type: This segment represents the lower tier of the fine art market, involving traditional players from both primary market channels (e.g., gallerists) and secondary market channels (e.g., antiques dealers and auction houses).

Behavioral hypothesis: Consumption is motivated by the pursuit of cultural distinction and symbolic capital, particularly within localized or regional cultural fields. Collecting and investment perspectives should not be excluded.

Indicative price range: Typically between several hundred and several thousand euros, depending on factors such as artist notoriety, provenance, edition size, and historical relevance.

The proposed triadic model thus suggests that consumer behavior within low-end art markets occurs at the intersection of several markets: the *home decor market* (sub-segment 1), the *collectibles market* (sub-segment 2), the *luxury goods market* (sub-segment 3), and the *fine art market* (sub-segment 4), each with porous boundaries that allow for a degree of inter-segment mobility. The upper stratum of the low-end segment—characterized by relatively higher symbolic functionality, scarcity and levels of branding—also occupies this intersection. It is, however, important to note that participants in this segment typically consume in ways aligned with their disposable income. By contrast, high-net-worth individuals may operate simultaneously across the low-, middle-, and high-end markets, depending on their collecting strategies and preferences. This contributes to the relative inclusivity and accessibility of low-end art markets, which encompass a broad spectrum of buyer profiles and motivations.

Limitations of the Triadic Model

While the model is intentionally built around three core attributes—functionality, scarcity, and brand strength—we acknowledge that other subjective parameters, particularly those related to historical, social, and spiritual value (e.g., emotional premiums, personal histories), may increase willingness to pay for certain low-end items, especially in marketplaces where objects from material culture and past generations circulate abundantly. Similarly, issues related to conditions (from new to reused), trust, bargaining and entry barriers—such as codes of conduct, access constraints, and alternative forms of exclusivity—are likely to influence how perceptions and prices are shaped in this market segment. Future research must examine how to incorporate these—often subjective—parameters more systematically in order to deepen our understanding of low-end markets.

Another crucial point is that the proposed triadic model is constructed under the simplifying assumption of perfect information. In practice, this condition is rarely met in the art market, owing to persistent and often structural information asymmetries. While traditional intermediaries such as auction houses and dealers are expected to reduce these asymmetries by providing expertise and valuation services, the structure of low-end markets—characterized by a diverse array of sales channels, including peer-to-peer platforms and informal marketplaces—frequently undermines this role. Disparities in knowledge among market participants further amplify these asymmetries. This is particularly evident in the pricing inconsistencies observed across platforms. For example, a Val Saint Lambert crystal candlestick might be listed for €15–20 on eBay, while the same item may command €50–60 on a curated platform such as 1stDibs, where brand recognition and expert curation justify a premium. In less mediated contexts, sellers may significantly underprice or overprice items depending on their level of expertise or access to information. Auction results also illustrate these dynamics: anonymous artworks estimated at a few thousand euros may occasionally sell for hundreds of thousands if bidders suspect possible reattribution to a recognized artist, thus blurring the line between the low-end and middle-end market segments. This mobility across segments reflects processes of cultural reclassification consistent with Thompson's *Rubbish Theory* (1979). More broadly, these examples underscore the complexity and volatility of price formation in low-end art markets, as well as the challenges inherent in applying standard segmentation frameworks.

As such, the triadic model is intended primarily as a heuristic tool—one that helps explain apparent price equivalences between fundamentally different objects, such as a small Jeff Koons *Balloon Dog*, a painting by a regionally established artist, an anonymous Old Master drawing, or a decorative object.

References

Abbing, H. (2022). *The economies of serious and popular art: How they diverged and reunited*. Palgrave Macmillan.

Adler, M. (1985). Stardom and talent. *The American Economic Review, 75*(1), 208–212.

Akerlof, G. A. (1970). The market for "lemons": Quality uncertainty and the market mechanism. *Quarterly Journal of Economics, 84*(3), 488–500.

Angelini, F., Castellani, M., & Zirulia, L. (2022). Overconfidence in the art market: a bargaining pricing model with asymmetric disinformation. *Economia Politica, 39*(3), 961–988.

Bandle, A.-L. (2016). *The sales of misattributed works at auction*. Edward Elgar Publishing.

Baumol, W. J. (1986). Unnatural value: Or art investment as floating crap game. *The American Economic Review, 76*(2), 10–14.

Belk, R. W. (2013). *Collecting in a consumer society*. Routledge.

Blazy, R., & Blum, M. (2022). Horizontal and vertical differentiation in comic art auctions. *Economic Inquiry, 60*(3), 1382–1415.

Bonnot, T. (2002). *La vie des objets: D'ustensiles banals à objets de collection*. Éditions de la Maison des sciences de l'homme.

Bourdieu, P. (1984). *Distinction: A social critique of the judgement of taste*. Harvard University Press.

Couture, F. (1981). Le marché des chromos: Une industrie culturelle? *Intervention, 12*, 6–8.

De Marchi, N., & Van Miegroet, H. J. (Eds.). (2006). *Mapping markets for paintings in Europe, 1450–1750*. Brepols.

De Vrièse, M., Martin, B., Melin, C., Moureau, N., & Sagot-Duvauroux, D. (2011). *Disseminating and promoting contemporary art regionally: A study of the Le Havre, Lyon, Montpellier, Nantes and Rouen areas* (CE-2011-1). French Ministry of Culture, Department of Prospective Studies and Statistics.

Dickson, P. R., & Ginter, J. L. (1987). Market segmentation, product differentiation, and marketing strategy. *Journal of Marketing, 51*(2), 1–10.

Duester, E. (2024). Precarious careers: A longitudinal study with contemporary visual artists from emerging to established career stages. *Journal of Creative Industries and Cultural Studies, 10*, 46–66.

Ekelund Jr, R. B., Higgins, R., & Jackson, J. D. (2020). ART as meta-credence: Authentication and the role of experts. *Journal of Cultural Economics, 44*(1), 155–171.

Fry, T. R. (2020). Heterogeneity in auction price distributions for Australian Indigenous artists. *Economic Record, 96*(313), 177–186.

Gans, H. J. (1985). American popular culture and high culture in a changing class structure. *Prospects, 10*, 17–37.

Graddy, K., & Margolis, P. E. (2011). Fiddling with value: Violins as an investment? *Economic Inquiry, 49*(4), 1083–1097.

Heinich, N. (2017). *Des valeurs: Une approche sociologique*. Gallimard.

Hernando, E., & Campo, S. (2017). Does the artist's name influence the perceived value of an artwork? *International Journal of Arts Management, 19*(2), 46–58.

Hughes, J. E. (2022). Demand for rarity: Evidence from a collectible good. *The Journal of Industrial Economics, 70*(1), 147–167.

Kahneman, D., & Tversky, A. (1979). Prospect theory: An analysis of decision under risk. *Econometrica, 47*(2), 263–291.

Karpik, L. (2010). *Valuing the unique: The economics of singularities*. Princeton University Press.

Koford, K., & Tschoegl, A. E. (1998). The market value of rarity. *Journal of Economic Behavior & Organization, 34*(3), 445–457.

Kotler, P., & Gertner, D. (2002). Country as brand, product, and beyond: A place marketing and brand management perspective. *Journal of Brand Management, 9*(4–5), 249–261.

Lancaster, K. J. (1966). A new approach to consumer theory. *Journal of Political Economy, 74*(2), 132–157.

Lazzaro, E., Moureau, N., & Turpin, A. (Eds.). (2025). *Law and finance in international art markets: Tools for the future*. Taylor & Francis.

Levin, I. P., Schneider, S. L., & Gaeth, G. J. (1998). All frames are not created equal: A typology and critical analysis of framing effects. *Organizational Behavior and Human Decision Processes, 76*(2), 149–188.

McAndrew, C. (2024). *The Art Basel and UBS art market report 2024*. Basel.

McAndrew, C. (2025). *The Art Basel and UBS art market report 2025*. Basel.

Mandel, B. R. (2009). Art as an investment and conspicuous consumption good. *American Economic Review, 99*(4), 1653–1663.

Marshall, A. (1890). *Principles of economics*. Macmillan and Co.

Mei, J., & Moses, M. (2002). Art as an investment and the underperformance of masterpieces. *American Economic Review, 92*(5), 1656–1668.

Montias, J. M. (1982). *Artists and artisans in Delft: A socio-economic study of the seventeenth century*. Princeton University Press.

Moureau, N., Sagot-Duvauroux, D., & Vidal, M. (2015). Collectionneurs d'art contemporain: Des acteurs méconnus de la vie artistique. *Culture Études*, *1*(1), 1–20.

Moulin, R. (1967). *Le marché de la peinture en France*. Les Éditions de Minuit.

Moureau, N., & Sagot-Duvauroux, D. (2016). *The contemporary art market* (4th ed.). La Découverte.

Moureau, N. 2023. Le boom de Paris. La scène française en profite-t-elle? *Le Quotidien de l'art*. November 28. *Hors Série The Art Market Day*.

Nelsen, H. M. (1970). The democratization of the Antique: meanings of antiques and dealers' perceptions of customers. *The Sociological Review*, *18*(3), 407–419.

Oosterlinck, K. (2017). Art as a wartime investment: Conspicuous consumption and discretion. *The Economic Journal*, *127*(607), 2665–2701.

Palmer, E. C., & Forsyth, C. (2002). Dealers and dealing in antique malls. *Sociological Spectrum*, *22*(2), 171–190.

Pernoud, E. (2025). *Chromo de bazar: Le tableau du pauvre*. Hazan.

Pesando, J. E. (1993). Art as an investment: The market for modern prints. *American Economic Review*, *83*(5), 1075–1089.

Plattner, S. (1996). *High art down home: An economic ethnography of a local art market*. University of Chicago Press.

Radermecker, A. S. V. (2021). *Anonymous art at auction: The reception of early Flemish paintings in the Western art market (1946–2015)* (Vol. 11). Brill.

Radermecker, A. S., & Alvarez de Toledo, F. (2022). The history of art markets: methodological considerations from art history and cultural economics. *InternationalJournal of Digital Art History*, *5*.

Raux, S. (2018). *Lotteries, art markets, and visual culture in the Low Countries, 15th–seventeenth centuries* (Vol. 4). Brill.

Renneboog, L., & Spaenjers, C. (2013). Buying beauty: On prices and returns in the art market. *Management Science*, *59*(1), 36–53.

Reyburn, S. (2025, April 30). *End of investment art? Why the bottom of the market is flourishing. The Art Newspaper*

Robertson, I. (Ed.). (2005). *Understanding international art markets and management*. Routledge.

Robertson, I., Chong, D., & Afonso, L. U. (Eds.). (2025). *Global art markets: History and current trends*. Taylor & Francis.

Rosen, S. (1981). The economics of superstars. *The American Economic Review*, *71*(5), 845–858.

Rosenstein, L. (2009). *Antiques: The history of an idea*. Cornell University Press.

Saint-Raymond, L. (2021). *À la conquête du marché de l'art. Le Pari(s) des enchères (1830–1939)*. Garnier.

Saint-Raymond, L. (2023). The Toulouse salons: A regional counterweight to the Parisian art scene? (1861–1939). *European Review of Economic History*, *27*(3), 362–379.

Spence, M. (1973). Job market signaling. *Quarterly Journal of Economics*, *87*(3), 355–374.

Stoller, M. A. (1984). The economics of collectible goods. *Journal of Cultural Economics*, *8*(1), 91–104.

Thompson, M. (1979). *Rubbish theory: The creation and destruction of value*. Oxford University Press.

Throsby, C. D. (2001). *Economics and culture*. Cambridge University Press.

Tirole, J. (1988). *The theory of industrial organization*. MIT Press.

Torregrossa, P. (2026). *Vivre les enchères: Raison et passion pour l'art et les objets de collection*. Éditions de la Maison des sciences de l'homme.

Van Miegroet, H. J., & De Marchi, N. (2007). The Antwerp-Mechelen production and export complex. In M. Misozuki (Ed.), *Album Amicorum J. Michael Montias* (133–147). University of Amsterdam Press.

Van Miegroet, H. J. (2008). Copies fantômes: La culture imitative au début de l'époque moderne en Europe. In S. Raux (Ed.), *L'estampe, un art multiple à la portée de tous* (47–64). Presses Universitaires de Lille.

Velthuis, O., & Curioni, S. B. (Eds.). (2015). *Cosmopolitan canvases: The globalization of markets for contemporary art*. Oxford University Press.

Vermeylen, F. (2003). *Painting for the market: Commercialisation of art in Antwerp's Golden Age*. Brepols.

Wong, W. W. Y. (2013). *Van Gogh on demand: China and the readymade*. University of Chicago Press.

Worthington, A. C., & Higgs, H. (2004). Art as an investment: Risk, return and portfolio diversification in major painting markets. *Accounting & Finance*, *44*(2), 257–271.

PART I

Revisiting Art Market Theories

The Low End of High-Tailed "Toys." Sequences of Markets for Cultural Goods

Michael Hutter

1 Power-Law Distributions of Success: From High End to Low End

Skewed probabilities in physical, biological and social phenomena have been observed since the late nineteenth century. Vilfredo Pareto was first to observe that the observed entity—in his case, annual monetary income per family in various European countries over the course of centuries—was not distributed normally throughout the population, but that the "upper tail" showed a distortion, roughly expressed by the rule that 20% of the population receive 80% of the total income.[1] Similar asymmetric distributions were found for the distribution of words in languages and in literary texts,[2] in the size of urban agglomerations and in organisms.[3] Robert Merton, eminent sociologist, coined the name "Matthew effect" for the "cumulative advantage" of successful scientists, with success measured by

[1] The first version is found in his *Manuel d'économie politique* from 1909, reprinted in Pareto (2014, p. 194).

[2] See Zipf (1949) and Yule (1925).

[3] See Fox Keller (2005).

M. Hutter (✉)
Berlin Social Science Center (WZB), Berlin, Germany
e-mail: michael.hutter@wzb.eu

A.-S. V. Radermecker (ed.), *Low-End Markets for Art and Cultural Goods*, Cultural Economics & the Creative Economy,
https://doi.org/10.1007/978-3-032-27566-0_2

their "symbolic and material rewards" (Merton, 1988).[4] The parametric mathematical form of all these distributions is a function that increases in value with the "power" of its exponent:

$$f(y) = a \cdot y^{-\alpha}$$

The data in the studies cited follow such a "power-law"- or "Pareto"-function,[5] at least in their upper part, where most of the value, economic or otherwise, is concentrated. The values measured for the exponent cluster around 2, indicating the slope of a linear function in logarithmic form.[6] More than a hundred distributions that follow a power law function have been identified, in sciences ranging from astronomy to neural networks.[7] The network structure of the diverse phenomena seems to be the unifying characteristic.

In the sphere of economic activities, power law distributions have been mostly observed in financial markets. Hudson and Mandelbrot (2004) found large variations of price changes that fit a power-law pattern.[8] They explain the operation of these markets as a series of incessant booms and busts. The turbulences follow a power-law pattern, with peaks on the local as well as on a national level. Ijiri and Simon (1977) showed that the pattern holds also for the sizes of firms in

[4] The source for the name is a line in Matthew 25.29: "For to everyone who has will more be given". The meaning of the phrase shifts when the previous sentence is considered. "You ought to have invested my money with the bankers, and at my coming I should have received what was my own with interest," chides the returned master the servant who has not invested his "talents"—historical monetary units, later generalized to any kind of human capability. Matthew's divine author encourages capital accumulation, he does not express a natural law of exponential growth.

[5] The relationship has been given many names. "Pareto function", an honorary attribution to the pioneer, is the one most frequently used. The Pareto function is the most commonly used parametric format out of a larger set of exponential functions. See Mitzenmacher (2003).

[6] For a series of visualizations of power law distributions in popular media, see https://github.com/taubergm/Powerlaw, with sources for the visualizations in Tauberg (2018). Because revenues are distributed across a wide range, from 1 to several million units, log-log-formats are frequently chosen by researchers. See Mitzenmacher (2003).

[7] See the Wikipedia entry for "Power law".

[8] The markets investigated include IBM shares, railroad stocks, currencies and commodity exchange markets, like the cotton market.

industries.[9] In markets for cultural goods, Pareto distributions came into play because of the "superstar phenomenon" in sports, music and fiction literature (Rosen, 1981; Adler, 1985). Since "bestsellers" and "blockbusters" were the focus of these studies, they concentrated on the skewed high end of the respective markets.

The prominence of the phenomenon in financial and in cultural markets is due to the nature of their products: in both of them, information is generated and travels in communication networks. In financial markets, new information shapes expectations for future prices of assets. Cultural goods are purchased because they contain messages that entertain their recipients. Videogames, sports events, music festivals or indigenous craftworks do not enter or manipulate their users physically.[10] They enter them mentally, as they are registered through one or more of the five senses. Information has properties that distinguish such goods from physical commodities, and which inhibit the formation of commodity markets: messages are inherently abundant, they can be accessed by many, and they are singular yet interconnected by meanings and narratives (Hutter, 2020). Their singularity is due to their temporal nature: they must be, in some sense, "new", thus uncertain and potentially surprising (Shackle, 1953; Hutter, 2011). New messages in cultural goods are addressed to the members of their audiences, which include all those who can decode and enjoy their qualities. All the members, spectators as well as actors, participate in a specific, highly institutionalized game of appreciation. The cultural goods serve as "toys," as *Spielzeug* (stuff to play with) in the cultural games that make up the so-called "creative industries"—as opposed to the "tools" that constitute the world of conventional economics.

Since cultural goods are produced, distributed and used in networks (Potts et al., 2008), the preferential attachment rule applies (Barabási & Albert, 1999): cultural networks generate at any given time a few "popular" nodes[11] with a high number of links (hubs), while many nodes with

[9] The phenomenon of proportional firm size growth is also known as "Gibrat' law", which spawned empirical studies after its original publication in 1931. See also Gabaix et al. (2003) on fluctuations in financial markets.

[10] Gastronomy is an interesting exception, woefully underresearched.

[11] There is no need to assume a similarly skewed distribution of talent in a population. Salganik et al. (2006) tested the proposition successfully in an artificial cultural goods market. Easley and Kleinberg (2010) suggest "popularity" as a term fitting for any kind of social attachment.

few links make up the bulk of the network. In this ever-evolving structure, patterns of temporary price peaks and long price valleys are continuously played out.[12]

Over the past two decades, revenue distributions that follow a power-law function in their upper tail have been identified in a wide range of cultural goods markets, for immaterial as well as material products. Since digitization has reached and transformed cultural goods markets, some scholarly attention has been addressed to the low end.

The present synoptic study reviews scholarly works focused on segments of the distribution function for evidence of power law structure, particularly at the low end of the distribution. Section 2 presents evidence from markets that provide access to immaterial goods: music, books, films and visual content. Section 3 reports on markets for events, and for material cultural goods: paintings, antiques and collectibles. Section 4 concludes with the major finding of a dynamic upward and downward value traffic, organized in sequences of interlocking markets.

2 Value Distribution in Markets for Immaterial Cultural Goods

Immaterial cultural goods consist only of messages. The messages are auditory, visual or, via some common vocabulary, literary.[13] They are complemented by material forms, like musical instruments and printed books. The products sold in a market are copies of some original recorded message, the "master copy." In these markets, the number of copies sold, multiplied by the price per copy, indicates the economic value of a single album, novel or film.

2.1 *Markets for Copies of Musical Recordings*

In 1981, Rosen investigated markets where the distribution of rewards follows a power-law function, epitomized by "superstars." The examples were markets for the services of comedians, for recordings of classical musicians and for textbooks. His explanation attributes the

[12] The term "preferential" invites ambiguities in an economics context. Here, it indicates a utility-maximizing choice rather than a preference, be it innate or acquired.

[13] An exception are culinary products and perfumes. See Linford (2019).

"multiplicatory effect on reward" to "superior talent and ability" (Rosen, 1981, p. 852). Four years later, Moshe Adler shifted the explanation to consumers' knowledge. His example is the appreciation of music, where listening and discussing it with other persons is "the key to the phenomenon of stars" (Adler, 1985, p. 208). The distribution is efficient, because "efficiency calls for very few artists with public recognition" (Adler, 1985, p. 211). Chung and Cox (1994) refer to Adler when they show that the distribution of gold records among performers between 1958 and 1989 follows a "Yule-Simon" function,[14] due to the "probabilistic" behavior of consumers, irrespective of the performers' talent.

The focus on the skewed distribution at the high end left little attention for the low end of these markets. Circumstances changed when digital technology and a rapidly spreading digital communication network made it possible to produce music more cheaply, to search for new music more effectively and to distribute copies via the Internet at zero marginal cost. Now, the immaterial property of music began to determine market structure.

When Anderson (2006) published his hypothesis on the long tail, his empirical argument was based on data from *Rhapsody*, an early music streaming platform that had registered the number of downloads per title during December 2005, for a million titles. Anderson notes the skewed distribution at the high end, which he calls the "head" of the distribution, but he emphasizes the endlessly long extension on the low end, which he called its "tail."

Three arguments support his claim that the economic value generated has shifted towards the low end in digital music and video markets: (i) the expansion of inventory, (ii) the lowered cost of digital production, search and distribution, and (iii) the increased accessibility of niche products through algorithmic filters. His claim was countered by Anita Elberse with results that showed a stronger increase on the high end, presumably because digital communication enforces the multiplier network effect.[15] The controversy continued over the following years, Napoli (2016) counted more than 600 studies of the long-tail phenomenon. Based on

[14] The function, which Herbert Simon identified and named after its first discoverer, is the equivalent of a power law function, expressed as a probability distribution of events along a rank-size-plot.

[15] See Elberse (2008). Her results were based on data from video sales (Elberse & Oberholzer-Gee, 2007).

evidence from music and video markets, he concludes that the advantage of the one-stop megastore with its long tail of products is outweighed by the effect of digitally boosted attachment to the megahits, leading to "an increasing gap as the long tail both retracts and fragments" (Napoli, 2016, p. 352).

Haampland tested the "cumulative advantage" theory of success with data from *Billboard 100*. He plots the share of weekly total market value against the chart positions in randomly selected weeks, and tests for path dependencies over a series of weeks. His results confirm the "Yule process of proportional growth," and he finds the same pattern on a weekly basis. "This might also provide a notion of the fractal nature of the power phenomenon" (Haampland, 2017, pp. 370–371). Coelho and Mendes presented an overview of studies on the pop-rock music market. They provide evidence for persistence of the superstar effect. They see it even strengthened by the increased share of the revenue stream coming from concert tickets, and by the recommendation algorithms of streaming platforms. The tail end of this market is remarkably long: 94% of the tracks purchased on iTunes in 2013 were downloaded less than a hundred times (Coelho and Mendes, 2019).

Gustar (2020) computed thirty power law distributions in classical and in pop music sub-markets, from "BBC Proms composers" to "UK Million-selling singles" and ordered them along their estimated power-law exponents. He claims that the distribution of success is generated by a combination of network communication, promotion, appreciation and listening habits. The process can be influenced by "inherent quality," but only to the extent that such items stay, if they are successful, somewhat longer at the top.[16] Prinz draws his explanation for power-law distributions in music from game theory. His data come from an annual voting procedure that selects the *Dutch Top 2000* songs. The distribution of song success in this non-commercial ranking "seems to follow a power law tail, combined with an exponential tempering" (Prinz, 2017, p. 392).[17] In terms of market organization, superstars—which can even rise to the status of incontestability, as the Dutch voting poll shows—are focal points in large coordination games: "they coordinate the social preferences of people" (ibid., p. 397).

[16] Gustar makes no reference to network theory and preferential attachment. Rather, he interprets power-law distributions as solutions to a maximum entropy problem.

[17] Prinz's "tail" is the high end of the market.

2.2 *Markets for Books and News*

Studies on Pareto distributions in markets for books, fiction and non-fiction, process much larger data sets. Brynsolffson, Hu and Smith used data on Amazon sale ranks of books for several weeks and came to the conclusion "that the Long Tail has grown longer over time, with niche books accounting for a larger share of total sales. Our analyses suggest that by 2008, niche books account for 36.7% of Amazon's sales and the consumer surplus generated by niche books has increased at least five-fold from 2000 to 2008" (Brynjolfsson et al., 2010, n.p.). Benghozi and Benhamou (2010) computed their Pareto distribution of sales in the French book market with survey data for 20 weeks in 2005. They detect in their time series oscillations of the Pareto curve, with the high tail getting stronger in the weeks before Christmas. Overall, they credit digitization with a strengthening of both tails. Electronic media boost popularity on one end, and they enable trade in small product numbers at the other end, due to low-cost distribution in specific market niches. Peltier, Benhamou and Touré (2016) used similar data, encompassing 170,000 positions between 2004 and 2010.[18] The French book market is dominated by a duopoly. Around these two companies, they identify a first fringe of medium-sized and a second fringe of small publishers. They distinguish online and offline distribution, and they show "that the market share lost by dominant firms is captured by small publishers online and by medium-sized publishers in conventional stores" (ibid., p. 394). Liebowitz and Zentner (2024) use Nielsen sales data on more than 250,000 U.S. book editions between 2004 and 2016 to demonstrate that the use of rankings to approximate sales data is inaccurate for the very long tail of the market where sales of less than 10 copies are common, which is misrepresented by equidistant rank numbers.

Huang and Wang (2014) studied the digital online news market. They sent questionnaires to 720 news sites: "The results of our research reveal that online news institutions have responded to the changing market trend of segmentation and niches by deploying a long tail economy in terms of content, service, and participation variety (...) online news institutions are still encountering the difficulty of turning web traffic into real profit and revenue,..." (Huang & Wang, 2014, p. 173). The market situation is complicated by the

[18] See also Peltier and Moreau (2012) on long tail effects of the Internet.

fact that news formats, be they in print or in pixels, are attractive surfaces for commercial messages. Revenue is therefore frequently a combination of advertising income and income from sales of copies or subscriptions.

2.3 *Markets for Movies and Videos*

The performance for which viewers of movies and videos pay consists in a sequence of immaterial moving images and sounds. Nevertheless, movies are the outcomes of a heavily material process. Arthur De Vany has spent a lifetime of research on the probability distribution of success and loss in the movie industry. In a handbook article, he synthesized his findings. To him, movies are "prospects, probability distributions as ephemeral as the images on the screen. It has to be that way because movies are creative products—they are pure information..." (De Vany, 2016, p. 661). Distributions with heavy Paretian tails fit the movie industry "like a glove." They "capture the winner-take-all nature of the movie business as well as the dominant influence of extreme events" (ibid., p. 538). Since he has data on the budgets of unsuccessful movies, the graph of the distribution function extends beyond zero profit to loss and shows a symmetrical tail of extreme events on the negative side.

Among De Vany's "laws of the box office," three stand out: (i) extreme events dominate: "As time expands, the size of changes grows. Thus, the largest event so far observed will, eventually, be exceeded. In fact, the variance will grow as the sample grows" (ibid., p. 646); (ii) non-linearity of momentum: "At about the fourth or fifth week of the run ... hit movies rapidly diverge from the bombs and the mapping bifurcates..." (ibid., p. 643); (iii) Biased decisions under uncertainty: "An executive must always make some assessment of the odds in choosing movies. This is harder to do when the movie or the actors are unknown entities" (ibid., p. 660).

Shapiro (2023) interprets results from visual as well as musical media markets, based on data from movie box office sales, Netflix series rankings and Spotify streaming. In such networked environments he observes that lowered search and distribution cost have fattened the high ends of media markets as well as their low ends: "The good news is that hits still matter and likely always will. The bad news is just about everything else: the lucrative middle is being hollowed out; risk is climbing; the tail is become more competitive for hits; bargaining power is shifting to the top talent; content producers are increasingly at the mercy of curators' algorithms; and paid media is being devalued" (ibid., n.p.).

3 Value Distribution in Markets for Events, and for Material Cultural Goods

Markets for immaterial cultural goods are a rather young phenomenon in the history of the sector. In contrast, markets for material cultural goods are centuries old. Physical objects, made out of substances that deteriorate over time, are bound to a physical location, and they convey messages about their own, singular historical "period." They can take the form of buildings, sculptures and *paintings*, of small editions of hand-crafted *antiques*, usually intended for domestic representation, and of objects, even industrial, that are sufficiently similar, scarce and meaningful to generate a market for that kind of *collectible*. *Events* take place in both dimensions: their subjective experiences are fleeting as immaterial cultural goods, yet their production is highly material, and therefore costly.

Pricing in markets for material cultural goods is strongly determined by their material dimensions. Therefore, it is questionable whether the power law distribution and the dynamics of frequent changes in popularity observed in markets without these constraints still hold. My presentation of available evidence concentrates on the four varieties highlighted above.

3.1 Events: Festivals, Concerts, Tourism

Events are a major means of selling experiences that carry value for those who participate in a particular culture game. Consumers buy access to an event that "is consumed jointly and in public in the same place at the same time" (De Serpa & Faith, 1996, p. 77). Events need a physical venue for unique, unrepeatable performances. Even if their format is copied, every copy is costly as well. There is great variety amongst markets for cultural events: traditional performances in concert halls, clusters of stages with concerts in the format of an annual festival at the same location, visits to sites of high cultural prestige, organized in commercial or private tours, and sittings at restaurants that provide Michelin-rated culinary experiences illustrate the disparity. Studies on revenue distribution in any of the submarkets are rare.

Connolly and Krueger (2016) did research on the rock concert business, following De Vany's methodology. They estimate that revenue is distributed along a power law function, with an exponent α of 0.45 for artists' and 0.55 for promoters' revenues. Two studies use data from tourism markets. Ulubaşoğlu and Hazari (2004) charted international tourist arrivals in 89 countries in a volume-rank plot and find that the data follow a power law function, with a very long low end.[19] Provenzano (2014) estimated power law distributions of lodging capacities—as a proxy for tourism volume—in Italy and in Germany.[20] He finds "that the size distribution of tourism industry is heavy- tailed and consistent with a power-law behavior in its upper tail" (ibid., p. 1055).

3.2 *Paintings*

Artworks use three-dimensional (sculpture) or two-dimensional (painting, drawing, photograph) visual forms. Their markets are midway between immaterial and material conditions because they are created for immaterial cultural experiences, yet they need a material medium to inscribe their messages. Paintings—framed canvases treated conventionally with oil or acrylic paint—have become the standard format of European artworks. Their sales volumes and prices are best documented in auctions. In consequence, the data for empirical studies are mostly drawn from auction sales. However, the restriction to sales in the secondary market cuts off information about sales of all the artworks transacted outside of auction salerooms, which leaves not only the low end, but also the entire dealer market unobserved.[21] The scholarly interest in auction prices for paintings has generated a few studies that focus on revenue distributions, while the markets for other auction departments have not yet been explored.[22] Over

[19] Based on the average numbers from 1986 to 1990, France is at first rank, hundred times more popular than # 52, Pakistan.

[20] The data are from 2004 to 2009, the value of exponent α is around 2.5. It is not clear whether the data also include business-related travel.

[21] Hutter et al. (2007) compare auction and dealer prices, find the same distribution pattern and explain the higher prices in gallery sales with the complementary membership in an exclusive collectors' club.

[22] Ashenfelter and Graddy (2016, p. 936) report 1996 average sale rates for 37 auction departments at Christie's, from Impressionist (£ 122.000) via furniture (£ 11.000, at 9th rank) to wine (£ 690). Revenue distributions in all these submarkets are highly skewed. In an

a series of publications, Etro and Stepanova have assembled unique data sets for sales of paintings during four historical periods with extraordinary artistic activity. They use their data sets to test for power law distributions (Etro & Stepanova, 2018). They succeed in all four periods, reporting exponent values between 2.07 (Renaissance Art, 1255–1510, 56 artists) and 3.77 (Dutch & Flemish Golden Age, 1597–1700, 277 artists). An added test with data from recent auctions of works by 575 artists yields an α-value of 3.3. These slopes, however, are only valid for the skewed upper tails, most works in the sample were sold at similar low prices. The authors seem to take it for granted that the reason for unequal success is a correspondingly unequal distribution of talent, defined as the ability to innovate successfully. They demonstrate convincingly that large teacher-student networks were formed especially during the Dutch period and attribute the skewed sizes of successful workshops to preferential attachment of new students. They do not transfer this argument to the buyers of paintings by popular artists.

Fry (2020) worked with a data set for the 100 best-selling indigenous Australian artists, thus isolating one particular submarket among the many that reach the level of auction attention. He takes a power law distribution of prices within that market for granted, his interest is with the accuracy of pre-sale estimates. He finds that the overall price distribution "is overestimated at the top of the overall distribution, and underestimated at the bottom of the distribution... In the low-price segment, where buyer preferences and (private) valuations may be important, the experts underestimate the hammer price" (ibid., p. 184). A paper with Erica Coslor (Coslor & Fry, 2024) on the price effects of accusations against an artist finds evidence for "stigma," which leads to losses in realized hammer prices. The authors suggest that similar reputation losses may be caused by rumors about the authenticity of works, or about a change in interest by key collectors.

Aloys Prinz investigated the reputation value of intermediaries in the market for contemporary art. Based on the annual "Power 100"-ranking of *ArtReview*, he finds "that the ranking of power members over time is [...] characterized by an extreme value distribution function" (Prinz, 2022, p. 19).[23] He distinguishes two market stages: an "upstream market"

unpublished dissertation, Simpson (2020) compared power law distributions for celebrities in visual art, sports and music. He finds the steepest tail in the market for artworks.

[23] The list includes mostly collectors, gallerists and directors of renowned museums.

where experts determine artistic value through judgments of quality. They "reduce the quality uncertainty for art collectors and art buyers in the downstream market by disseminating relevant information about art based on their art knowledge" (ibid., p. 26). These judgements influence the "downstream market ... [where] works are sold and bought against payment." A second study investigates the reputation distribution among 2000 German art galleries. Prinz takes the sum of "glory points"[24] attributed to the top 100 artists by a professional scoring algorithm, adds up the points of all those artists that are represented by a given gallery, and uses the resulting figure as an indicator of the gallery's capacity to succeed. The result is a power law distribution of gallery "power" with an exponent α around 2. Prinz and his co-authors attribute the success of the "few leading galleries" at the high end of the tail to their capacity for innovation, "supported by information cascades in such a way that their success advantage cannot be eroded by competition" (Prinz et al., 2015, p. 170). This incontestability resonates with the findings of his study on the most valued pop songs in the Netherlands (Prinz, 2017).

All the studies cited concentrate on the high tail of the revenue distribution in markets for artistic paintings of a particular category. There is some mention of a "mid-section" and an "upstream market," but the low end is outside of the scope of interest.[25] However, studies on artistic labor markets show that the tail is much longer than in other markets. There is "excess supply," as U.S. artists are willing to earn roughly a third of their income through non-art occupations (Alper & Wassall, 2016, p. 851).[26] The production process is impossible to industrialize, even if successful artists are able to employ a team of assistants to scale their output. Moreover, art project rooms and artist-run galleries are means to pool production, display, promotion and transaction in a common organizational unit. It is in this kind of milieu, usually strongly concentrated in

[24] The term "glory points" was coined by Willi Bongard, initiator of *Kunstkompass*, a success index that continues to be computed. Valuation points from exhibitions, reviews and other forms of recognition are juxtaposed to the artists' estimated gallery prices.

[25] Hodgson et al., (2026) (in this volume) separate their sample of Australian indigenous paintings in three hierarchical value sections. They are not interested in revenue distribution, but they provide rare evidence of movements up and down the value slide. They suggest that "artists whose status is declining tend to "fall" through the hierarchy of auction houses as demand for their works declines."

[26] See also the section on excess supply in Menger (2016).

a few metropolitan centers per continent, where aspiring artists gain their first opportunities to present their work to a trained audience that is willing to pay for it. At the low end, residency grants and invitations to funded exhibitions provide opportunities for income, in cash and in kind. The extent of this production line and its reputation for creativity have led to claims of a "schism" between conventional gallery art and experimental, yet professionally curated "Biennials" art.[27]

3.3 *Useful Cultural Goods: Antiques and Collectibles*

Immaterial cultural goods are attempted messages, with the faint prospect of becoming valuable as part of a community's or society's archive of tunes, stories and images. Instead, most material cultural goods begin their historical journey as useful commodities. Even paintings were considered part of private decoration or of religious representation until the fifteenth century. Most other man-made objects are valued as efficient solutions to a material problem: maximal effect at minimal cost. However, such objects also find communicative and thus cultural purposes: they can display the owner's taste, as is the case with furniture or glassware, or they stimulate games of collecting objects with narrowly specified forms, like shells, stamps, medals or vintage cars. Such goods are "tools" as well as "toys."

The conditions of production and consumption distort the power law curve of material cultural goods to a degree that makes it unrecognizable. The goods are not sold as copies, but as singular physical objects. Revenue is gained from a few singular items that have become very valuable. They may be manufactured in series of identical pieces, but the extent of such series is limited if the pieces are handmade. Over time, the number of specimens diminishes, and differing degrees of physical deterioration affect each item's particular market value. The high value of excellent specimens makes them attractive as stores of financial value. This secondary use as assets increases demand for objects at the high end of the distribution.

The literature on revenue distribution in markets for material cultural goods is sparse. I focus on the submarket for antique furniture, where some empirical results, quantitative and qualitative, are available. In this volume, Radermecker investigates antiques: decorative art

[27] See Baden (2018).

objects over 100 years old and produced at the intersection of craftsmanship and (semi-) industrial manufacture.[28] The study is motivated by the observation of a generational change in lifestyle, and an epochal drop in prices for antiques since the establishment of online marketplaces. Lowered search cost for sellers as well as for buyers have led to a large increase in the quantity of pieces offered, with a subsequent drop in the price level. However, uncertainty about quality and fakes limits the scope of such marketplaces to the low end, where platforms are the digital equivalent of flea markets. Radermecker uses data from Drouot.com (Paris), which excludes pieces that are sold at top-tier auctions. She finds that high-end antiques are more vulnerable to changing market trends, tastes, and lifestyles (ibid.).

Insights into the fine calibrations of this "ecosystem" can be gained from posts by the antique furniture dealer Ed Welch, published in the *Journal of Antiques and Collectibles* between 2002 and 2007. After several decades of professional experience, Welch has come to the conclusion that there are ten levels in markets for antiques. He divides them into three segments. At levels 10 and 9, items at the skewed high end of the distribution are sold. The volume of trade is shared between high-end auction houses and dealers that are specialized at these levels. Levels 8 to 3 constitute the mid-tier. At 8 and 7, reputation and specialization guarantee quality; at 6 to 4, less knowledge is required, the field is full of semi-professionals; dealers at level 3 need knowledge for picking unrecognized valuable pieces out of undocumented estates, and they need knowledge about price differentials at market locations. At levels 2 and 1, dealers sell at flea markets, and through websites targeted to specific collectibles. In 2007 prices, deals at level 1 are below $50, at level 4 below $800 and at level 8 below $8,000. At the high end, limits are there to be broken.[29] According to Welch's observation, the attempt to sell an item below or above one's level either fails or results in

[28] Radermecker cites studies on markets for fine violins, British postage stamps, silverware, glassware, diamonds and Premier Crus wines. These studies focus on average rates of return on investment at the high end, not on the spread of prices within each submarket.

[29] At a recent auction for pop culture collectibles, the ruby shoes from *The Wizard of Oz* were sold for $ 32.5 million, "becoming the most valuable movie memorabilia ever sold at auction. That sale alone accounted for the bulk of the auction's $ 38.6 million total." https://journalofantiques.com/digital-publications/january-2025-1925-2025/ p. 60. Accessed on March 25, 2025.

major price reduction.[30] At the high end, the skill lies in selling; dealers build a network of suppliers and clients, they spend time and resources on keeping in touch, and they expose their business only for a few days at prestigious fairs. At the low end, the skill lies in buying, finding items that are favored and collected by largely anonymous buyers.

The three segments apply to all markets for material cultural goods. The kind of stores, the range of journals, the type of auction house—they all differ relative to the range of potential buyers. The phenomenon is observed in markets for period furniture as well as those for postage stamps.[31] The three segments add up to a distribution of revenues that follows—adjusted to local conditions—a power law function. Not only is the pattern observable in each of the hundreds of submarkets operative in the U.S., it appears also within each market at each level, because prices for antiques are extremely sensitive to the physical condition of a specific item. The price differential from "best" to "good" is generally more than half, and items that have defects are sold at discount prices. Finally, the "eco-system"—now identified with the mid-tier of all active antiques markets—is stabilized by institutions and information channels. Dealers have firm business connections with partners at higher and lower levels, they all follow the same code of conduct. For collectors of vintage and antique objects, the major fairs are venues for interaction, often organized by associations that provide information services for their audience.

Welch refers to the low end of the antiques markets in three ways: he is a dealer who sells items year-round through websites that cater only to their specific clientele, he mentions *eBay* as "the bargain basement" of the markets, and draws attention to "pickers" who acquire wholesale lots, usually from household clearances, recognize valuable items and sell them at flea markets or on platforms like *eBay*.[32] However, not all of

[30] "The knowledge required is different, operating expenses are different and selling and buying methods are different." See https://journalofantiques.com/?s=welch+pickers. Accessed on March 25, 2025.

[31] Quote from the section of stamp collecting in the January 2025 edition of the *Journal for Antiques and Collectibles*: "While the value of the hobby is mostly in the fun of completing stamp books and meeting fellow hobbyists, some "holy grail" stamps keep all collectors on their toes. In the world of U.S. stamp collecting, the Blue Boy is akin to the *Mona Lisa*." (p. 36).

[32] Welch also suggest a distinction between rule-based and face-to-face items. The first are easy to qualify precisely according to their standardized features, while the latter are less regular and need explanation—which, again, occurs on all three tiers.

those who buy at flea market prices intend to simply keep the items in their collection. A practice specific to the music market is crate-digging, "that age-old practice of rummaging through record shop discount bins in the hopes of discovering snippets of sonic gold for sampling."[33] In a much more general approach, Thompson hypothesized that commodities go through a transient stage during which their commercial value sinks until it reaches the stage of rubbish, "which is a cultural category of a special type," distinct from "residual" (Thompson 1979, p. 101). Some of the commodities are transformed, due to their cultural connotations, and reach a state of "durable" value.[34]

The evidence from markets for material cultural goods suggests a dynamic relationship between the three market tiers, sequences of valorization and de-valorization, organized as traffic upward and downward the revenue scale.[35] Dealers move the traffic. They are experts, historians, restorers, networkers and communicators, with the mixture of skills needed to bring a fraction of items from a lower to a higher price bracket, or skills that sort items with remaining value from those that slide into negative value—rubbish.[36]

4 Conclusion: Traffic, Upward and Downward the Power Law Slide

Cultural goods are goods with low to high "symbolic functionality." The available studies confirm that revenue in markets of such goods is roughly distributed along a power law function. Moreover, they suggest that some of the items in each submarket move through

[33] From https://www.perfectcircuit.com/signal/vinyl-sampling-workflows?srsltid=AfmBOood75-AaBTzLUwdtuRJUp8GAwqX06pBh6t6tcIJjpsIkXu1Bax5. Accessed March 25, 2025.

[34] An equivalent category is proposed by Boltanski and Esquerre (2017). They distinguish between a "standard form", with declining price, and a "collecting form" of commodities, with increasing price. See also Kopytoff (1986).

[35] I use the spatial terms upward/downward to avoid confusion with the temporal upstream/downstream distinction.

[36] Beyond the scope of this review are markets for "judgment devices", e.g. guidebooks, rankings and assessments, and other forms of "knowledge" that promise to reduce uncertainty for buyers. An encompassing study of this field, based on a theory of markets for nonhomogeneous goods, is Karpik (2010).

a sequence of markets along the power law slide, as they gain or lose in "brand strength."[37]

The Low End is the beginning and the end of such value careers. It is the beginning for unknown young painters, or DJs combining music samples found at a flea market, as gallerists or music producers select those among new works that show potential for success. Most of the works do not gain reputation and remain at the low end, their creators support themselves through other financial sources. The works of artists selected by dealers and producers gain brand strength as they are traded on increasing price levels. Works that reach level 10 tend to remain there, unless they are taken off the market by public collections. Success and failure of works in contemporary music genres takes place more quickly and runs through fewer market levels, but brand strength—observed as "popularity"—is again heavily skewed. The major share of revenue goes to the small number of companies that are able to promote successful artists consistently.[38] The downward journey towards the "low end" sets in as brand strength weakens. Physical quality deteriorates, tastes change, and reputations are forgotten. At the low end of markets for goods with direct and symbolic functionality, like furniture or porcelain, dealers gain profit by identifying objects with sufficient brand value to be collectible, and marketing them through a variety of distribution channels.

Research on sequences of market levels in submarkets for cultural goods is hampered on practical as well as on theoretical grounds. It is easier to measure the distribution of success in markets for immaterial cultural goods where it can be proxied by the number of copies sold. Data on sales are often proprietary, and differ in quality depending on their sources. Readily available auction data bias research toward the high end of their markets. Moreover, the revenue differences along the sequence of markets are obscured if the underlying theory ignores the sequence and assumes homogeneous goods, single prices and constant expectations. Median values are meaningless in exponential distributions, and high average revenue figures in winner-take-most markets overestimate the chances for success of market entrants. Better information on the low end of these markets might be gained by applying qualitative methods, particularly structured interviews with primary market participants.

[37] See the introduction by Moureau and Radermecker on the notions of "symbolic functionality" and "brand strength".

[38] For examples, see Elberse (2013).

References

Adler, M. (1985). Stardom and talent. *American Economic Review, 75*, 208–212.

Alper, N., & Wassall, G. (2016). Artists' careers and their labor markets. In V. A. Ginsburgh & D. Throsby (Eds.), *Handbook of the economics of art and culture* (pp. 814–864). North-Holland.

Anderson, C. (2006). *The long tail: Why the future of business is selling less of more.* Hyperion.

Ashenfelter, O., & Graddy, K. (2016). Art auctions. In V. A. Ginsburgh & D. Throsby (Eds.), *Handbook of the economics of art and culture* (pp. 909–946). North-Holland.

Baden, S. (2018). Sebastian Baden in discussion with the *Journal for Art Market Studies* on institutionalized criticism of "art fair art" and the "aesthetic schism" in art history. *Journal for Art Market Studies, 1*, 1–5.

Barabási, A. -L., & Albert, R. (1999). Emergence of scaling in random networks. *Science, 286*, 509–512.

Benghozi, P. -J., & Benhamou, F. (2010). The long tail: Myth or reality? *International Journal of Arts Management, 12*(3), 43–53.

Boltanski, L., & Esquerre, A. (2017). Enrichment, profit, critique: A rejoinder to Nancy Fraser. *New Left Review, 106*, 67–76.

Brynjolfsson, E., Hu, Y., & Smith, M. D. (2010). The longer tail: The changing shape of Amazon's sales distribution curve. *SSRN Electronic Journal.*

Chung, K. H., & Cox, R. (1994). A stochastic model of superstardom: An application of the Yule distribution. *The Review of Economics and Statistics, 76*, 771–775.

Coelho, M. P., & Mendes, J. Z. (2019). Digital music and the "death of the long tail". *Journal of Business Research, 101*, 454–460.

Connolly, M., & Krueger, A. (2016). Rockonomics: The economics of popular music. In V. A. Ginsburgh & D. Throsby (Eds.), *Handbook of the economics of art and culture* (pp. 667–720). North-Holland.

Coslor, E., & Fry, T. R. L. (2024). Misattribution stigma and contagion: How did the art auction market react to Australian "Black art scandals"? *Journal of Cultural Economics.*

De Serpa, A. C., & Faith, R. L. (1996). "Bru-uu-uce": The simple economics of mob goods. *Public Choice, 89*(1), 77–91.

De Vany, A. (2016). The movies. In V. A. Ginsburgh & D. Throsby (Eds.), *Handbook of the economics of art and culture* (pp. 615–666). North-Holland.

Easley, D., & Kleinberg, J. (2010). *Networks, crowds, and markets: Reasoning about a highly connected world.* Cambridge University Press.

Elberse, A. & Oberholzer-Gee, F. (2007). *Superstars and underdogs:an Examination of the long-tail phenomenon in video sales.* MSI Report, (4), 7–120.

Elberse, A. (2008, July 2). The long tail debate: A response to Chris Anderson. *Harvard Business Blog*. https://web.archive.org/web/20080705190446/http://conversationstarter.hbsp.com/2008/07/the_long_tail_debate_a_respons.html

Elberse, A. (2013). *Blockbusters: Hit-making, risk-taking, and the big business of entertainment*. Henry Holt and Company.

Etro, F., & Stepanova, E. (2018). Power laws in art: From Renaissance to contemporary art. *LEM Working Paper Series, Laboratory of Economics and Management, Pisa, 32*, 1–13.

Fox Keller, E. (2005). Revisiting "scale-free" networks. *BioEssays, 27*(10), 1060–1068.

Fry, T. R. L. (2020). Heterogeneity in auction price distributions for Australian Indigenous artists. *Economic Record, 96*(313), 177–186.

Gabaix, X., Gopikrishnan, P., Plerou, V., & Stanley, E. (2003). A theory of power-law distributions in financial market fluctuations. *Nature, 423*, 267–270.

Gustar, A. (2020). Fame, obscurity and power laws in music history. *Empirical Musicology Review, 14*(3–4), 186–215.

Haampland, O. (2017). Power laws and market shares: Cumulative advantage and the Billboard Hot 100. *Journal of New Music Research, 46*(4), 356–380.

Hodgson, D., Weber, C., & Coate, B. (2026). Stratification and price in art auctions: How the presence of unconsecrated and lowly consecrated painters impacts the Australian art auction market (From this book).

Huang, J. S., & Wang, W. -C. (2014). Application of the long tail economy to the online news market: Examining predictors of market performance. *Journal of Media Economics, 27*(3), 158–176.

Hudson, R., & Mandelbrot, B. (2004). *The (mis)behavior of markets: A fractal view of risk, ruin and reward*. Basic Books.

Hutter, M. (2011). Infinite surprises: On the stabilization of value in the creative industries. In J. Beckert & P. Aspers (Eds.), *The worth of goods: Valuation and pricing in the economy* (pp. 201–222). Oxford University Press.

Hutter, M. (2020). Information goods. In R. Towse & T. Navarrete (Eds.), *Handbook of cultural economics* (3rd ed., pp. 287–293). Edward Elgar Publishing.

Hutter, M., Knebel, C., Pietzner, G., & Schäfer, M. (2007). Two games in town: A comparison of dealer and auction prices in contemporary visual arts markets. *Journal of Cultural Economics, 31*(4), 247–261. https://doi.org/10.1007/s10824-007-9045-0

Ijiri, Y., & Simon, H. A. (1977). *Skew distributions and the sizes of business firms*. North-Holland Publishing Company.

Karpik, L. (2010). *Valuing the unique: The economics of singularities*. Princeton University Press.

Kopytoff, I. (1986). The cultural biography of things: Commoditization as a process. In A. Appadurai (Ed.), *The social life of things: Commodities in cultural perspective* (pp. 64–91). Cambridge University Press.

Liebowitz, S., & Zentner, A. (2024). The challenges of using ranks to estimate sales. *Journal of Economics & Management Strategy*, *33*, 3–24. https://doi.org/10.1111/jems.12514

Linford, J. (2019). *The missing ingredient: The curious role of time in food and flavor*. Particular Books.

Menger, P. -M. (2016). Artistic labor markets: Contingent work, excess supply and occupational risk management. In V. A. Ginsburgh & D. Throsby (Eds.), *Handbook of the economics of art and culture* (pp. 766–811). North-Holland.

Merton, R. K. (1988). The Matthew effect in science, II: Cumulative advantage and the symbolism of intellectual property. *Isis*, *79*(4), 606–623. https://doi.org/10.1086/354848

Mitzenmacher, M. (2003). A brief history of generative models for power law and lognormal distributions. *Internet Mathematics*, *1*, 226–251. https://doi.org/10.1080/15427951.2004.10129088

Napoli, P. (2016). Requiem for the long tail: Towards a political economy of content aggregation and fragmentation. *International Journal of Media & Cultural Politics*, *12*(3), 341–356. https://doi.org/10.1386/macp.12.3.341_1

Pareto, V. (2014). *Manual of political economy: A critical and variorum edition*. OUP Oxford, Original work published 1909.

Peltier, S., Benhamou, F., & Touré, M. (2016). Does the long tail really favor small publishers? *Journal of Cultural Economics*, *40*, 393–412. https://doi.org/10.1007/s10824-015-9245-7

Peltier, S., & Moreau, F. (2012). Internet and the "long tail versus superstar effect" debate: Evidence from the French book market. *Applied Economics Letters*, *19*(8), 711–715.

Potts, J., Cunningham, S., Hartley, J., & Ormerod, P. (2008). Social network markets: A new definition of the creative industries. *Journal of Cultural Economics*, *32*(3), 167–185.

Prinz, A. (2017). Rankings as coordination games: The Dutch Top 2000 pop song ranking. *Journal of Cultural Economics*, *41*, 379–401.

Prinz, A. (2022). The concentration of power in the market for contemporary art: An empirical analysis of ArtReview's "Power 100". *Springer Nature Business & Economics*, *2*(11).

Prinz, A., Piening, J., & Ehrmann, T. (2015). The success of art galleries: A dynamic model with competition and information effects. *Journal of Cultural Economics*, *39*(2), 153–176.

Provenzano, D. (2014). Power laws and the market structure of the tourism industry. *Empirical Economics*, *47*, 1055–1066.

Rosen, S. (1981). The economics of superstars. *American Economic Review, 71* (1), 167–183.
Salganik, M., Dodds, P., & Watts, D. (2006). Experimental study of inequality and unpredictability in an artificial cultural market. *Science, 311*(5762), 854–856. https://doi.org/10.1126/science.1121066
Shackle, G. L. S. (1953). The logic of surprise. *Economica, 20*(78), 112–117. https://doi.org/10.2307/2550836
Shapiro, D. (2023, March 16). Power laws in culture: Why hits will persist in an infinite content world. *Medium*. https://dougshapiro.medium.com/power-laws-in-culture-27ab6461c693
Simpson, T. (2020). *Art, ability and pricing* (Unpublished doctoral thesis). University of Western Australia.
Tauberg, M. (2018, June 29). Power law in popular media. *Medium*. https://michaeltauberg.medium.com/power-law-in-popular-media-7d7efef3fb7c
Thompson, M. (1979). *Rubbish theory: The creation and destruction of value*. Oxford University Press.
Ulubaşoğlu, M. A., & Hazari, B. R. (2004). Zipf's law strikes again: The case of tourism. *Journal of Economic Geography, 4*(4), 459–472. https://doi.org/10.1093/jnlecg/lbh029
Yule, G. D. (1925). A mathematical theory of evolution, based on the conclusions of Dr. *J. C. Willis. Philosophical Transactions of the Royal Society of London, 213*, 21–87. https://doi.org/10.1098/rstb.1925.0002
Zipf, G. (1949). *Human behavior and the principle of least effort*. Addison-Wesley.

Information, Bargaining, and Relationships: Cultural Goods and Art in the Bazaar Economy in Western Markets

Francesco Angelini

1 Introduction

Cultural goods, particularly artworks, are exchanged through a diverse array of channels that vary significantly in terms of the agents involved, the quality of goods circulated, and the level of market institutionalization. These channels range from highly structured and formalized markets to more fluid and less regulated settings. Most economic research in the cultural field has focused on the high-end, formal market segment, where transactions are documented, contracts are enforceable, legal accountability is clearly defined, and authenticity and provenance are systematically verified.

By contrast, the lower tiers of the market remain significantly underexplored. Some of these less formalized arenas rely on self-regulation, social norms, or reputational mechanisms to govern exchanges. They include a variety of contexts often grouped under the umbrella of "informal markets," which can be negatively defined as settings where codified exchange rules and institutional enforcement are missing or only weakly

F. Angelini (✉)
University of Bologna, Rimini, Italy
e-mail: francesco.angelini7@unibo.it

A.-S. V. Radermecker (ed.), *Low-End Markets for Art and Cultural Goods*,
Cultural Economics & the Creative Economy,
https://doi.org/10.1007/978-3-032-27566-0_3

applied.[1] Examples include peer-to-peer transactions, digital gray or black markets, and segments of the underground economy.

In this chapter, I focus on a specific subset of these informal markets: what I refer to as the "bazaar economy." This subset is characterized by face-to-face negotiation, flexible pricing, and a strong reliance on personal networks, trust, and non-standardized cues of quality and authenticity.[2] It encompasses a variety of settings, such as traditional bazaars, flea markets, some open-air or street markets (List, 2009), and hybrid cases such as the so-called "cul de camion" or "back-of-the-truck sale".[3] While typically offline, some contemporary informal exchanges begin on digital platforms (e.g., Facebook groups or messaging apps) and culminate in in-person negotiations, preserving the above-mentioned core dynamics of the bazaar economy. These markets host a broad array of cultural goods, including crafts (e.g., handmade ceramics, textiles, wooden sculptures), vintage or second-hand items (e.g., vinyl records, old books, posters), folk and devotional objects, unsigned artworks, and ordinary antiques. While typically associated with low-visibility or uncertified goods, these markets occasionally feature items of significant cultural or economic value (so-called "sleepers," see below) that may be overlooked or misattributed at the time of exchange.

The modelling of the entry-level segments of the art market proposed in this volume suggests that low-end cultural markets should not be defined solely in terms of price, but also through dimensions such as functionality, scarcity, and quality. Such an approach presupposes contexts in which these attributes can be reasonably observed and compared. Bazaar-type markets, however, operate under conditions of significant informational asymmetry, in which functionality, scarcity, and quality are often uncertain, difficult to verify, or socially constructed through interaction. For this reason, the present chapter does not attempt to

[1] While these distinctions between formal and informal markets are not always clear-cut, they provide a useful analytical framework.

[2] Although the focus here is on fully informal contexts, informal markets often lie along a spectrum of regulation, ranging from entirely unregulated exchanges to semi-informal settings, such as licensed flea markets in France or Italy. It is also worth noting that, while the bazaar economy may partially overlap with the underground economy (particularly when transactions are undocumented or untaxed), it is not reducible to it: not all informal exchanges are illicit, and not all illicit exchanges follow a "bazaar economy logic."

[3] This term refers to an informal practice where itinerant merchants display and sell their goods at the very beginning of a fair or market, often before the official opening.

operationalize these dimensions directly, but instead focuses on the informational and relational mechanisms through which value emerges in such settings. Nonetheless, even under conditions of informational asymmetry, some of these dimensions, particularly quality and scarcity, remain conceptually relevant, especially in shaping value within these markets.

Following Geertz (1978), I will first identify the main characteristics of these markets and report the relevant literature that covered them, related to cultural goods as well as other product categories. There is no universally accepted formal definition of "bazaar economy" in the economics literature; to my knowledge, Geertz's analytical framework, centered on personalized bargaining, information asymmetries, and social embeddedness, remains the most coherent and influential reference point. This contribution builds on and extends that approach by considering additional aspects such as value uncertainty, network effects, and transitions to formal markets, proposing a research agenda outlining how future studies might develop.

This chapter contributes to the growing focus on an overlooked segment of the cultural goods market, particularly within the economic literature, where these exchanges remain underexplored. Gaining insights into the dynamics of these markets is crucial for understanding broader market phenomena. As the chapter is framed within an economic perspective, the reviewed sources are primarily drawn from economics and related disciplines. Examining these informal settings can also shed light on how certain issues that affect the higher tiers of the market, such as the emergence of "sleepers" (e.g., Marrone & Beltrametti, 2020), the circulation of fakes (e.g., Bocart & Oosterlinck, 2011), and the origin of criminal exchange of cultural goods (e.g., Oosterman & Angelini, 2021), come into play. The goal of the chapter is then to highlight existing gaps in the literature and suggest avenues for future research that could offer a more complete understanding of bazaar economy markets. This will also contribute to a deeper comprehension of how both economic and cultural value are formed and sustained in cultural markets more broadly (Angelini & Castellani, 2019).

As a caveat, since most of the reviewed literature comes from Western sources, this chapter does not aim to provide a comprehensive account of the global functioning of bazaar economies. This reflects a broader Western research bias that still characterizes much of the cultural economics field. Moreover, I have taken care to avoid transposing Western market concepts onto informal contexts, whose dynamics may follow different economic and cultural logics. Nevertheless, some of the discussed issues may also apply to non-Western settings.[4]

2 Previous Research on Informal Markets and the Bazaar Economy

While some recent papers begun to explore low-end cultural markets from an economic perspective (e.g., Radermecker, 2022; Angelini et al., 2022), the characteristics of informal markets and of the bazaar economy regarding cultural goods have not yet been studied in a systematic way. I will discuss below how information, relationships, and mechanisms are identifying features of the bazaar economy. Among these characteristics, the role of information in economic transactions has been a central theme in economic discourse for at least six decades, as demonstrated by foundational works by Stigler (1961), Nelson (1970), Akerlof (1970), and Darby and Karni (1973). Similarly, the analysis of relationships and networks (e.g., Jackson et al., 2012; Choi & Storr, 2020), as well as trade mechanisms (e.g., Binmore et al., 1986; Wolinsky, 1987), have also received significant attention in the economic literature. Despite the relevance of these characteristics to broader economic theory, there has been limited economic inquiry into how informal markets function, particularly for cultural goods.

Focusing on the bazaar economy, one of the seminal works, at the intersection of economics and anthropology, was the short paper by Geertz (1978) in the *American Economic Review*, which outlined and emphasized the main characteristics of the bazaar economy, namely the importance of interpersonal relationships between agents, the specific mechanisms of exchange employed, and the crucial role that information plays in these transactions. His observations come from the bazaar economy of a Moroccan city, Sefrou, in the 1960s, but these insights

[4] While this chapter primarily focuses on Western literature, several recent works have contributed to the analysis of cultural and art markets beyond the West. See, for example, Duarte and Pérez-Ibáñez (2023) and Shaban et al. (2022). The former includes contributions by Vermeylen and Bhat (2023), who discuss both traditional and informal art markets in India since the 2000s, as well as Hutter (2023), who examines informal economies and the role of "art games" in African contexts. The volume edited by Shaban, Vermeylen, and Handke also explores the role of informality across various sectors of the Indian creative economy.

appear applicable to many contemporary digital and physical market settings. In this economy, information is "poor, scarce, maldistributed, inefficiently communicated, and intensely valued" (ibid., p. 29), generating important transaction costs, in particular search costs. These costs, especially for non-standardized goods, tend to refer to the intensive rather than the extensive margin of search, namely trying to gain more information about the good from the same seller, instead of trying to obtain information from different sellers and then make a choice, as also confirmed by List (2009). The absence of any type of advertising, together with frictions in how information is shared in other ways, makes the evaluation of quality and, hence, prices a difficult task. This makes information even more important, for both those who lack it and those who own it. In that, wider discrepancies in information availability with respect to formal markets and the scarcity of signals that could help in the evaluation of the cultural goods (Angelini et al., 2022) make other characteristics more relevant, such as the skills in interacting with the agents operating in these markets and in the exchange itself, the luck in finding more valuable goods, and the privileged access in interactions with counterparts. Geertz also suggested search procedures aligned with the availability of these characteristics and information, namely bargaining, concerning price formation, and clientelization, regarding the potential reduction of information discrepancies. Both mechanisms are less commonly observed in other segments of the market.

A more recent and notable exception to the general lack of research on these topics is List (2009), who experimentally studied incentives to cheat within collusive agreements between sellers in open air markets, finding aligned results in the laboratory and in the field experiments conducted. In particular, the US-based open-air markets considered by the author were characterized by agreements between 2 and 4 sellers on the selling prices, which were infringed more frequently in certain cases: when the number of sellers was higher, when the days were more hectic, and when the sellers had fewer collusive agreements across the various markets they operate in. List also reported a series of facts observed in the open-air markets, which are in line with (and/or derive from) those discussed above: these markets are characterized by the opportunity for the seller to gain from price discrimination on an individual basis more easily than in other markets where prices are posted. In addition to that, there is a general level of suspicion that nothing is what it appears to be, with respect to non-standardized goods such as cultural goods.

A final couple of papers worth mentioning in this brief review are van Ours (1991) and McCrohan and Sugrue (1998), where the authors investigated the socioeconomic status of households referring to informal suppliers to purchase goods and services, with mixed results. The former explored the status of buyers in the Netherlands, finding that those who turned to informal markets (for certain products and services) have a lower family income, while the latter found for the US that informal markets consumers had higher family incomes. These papers did not focus on cultural goods.

Given the scarcity of the current investigations into the bazaar economy for cultural goods, two paths should be pursued in future research on these issues: there is a need to analyze the role of the characteristics already identified, with particular attention to cultural goods; on the other hand, further characteristics can be identified and then investigated. The next section discusses a research agenda to advance both lines of inquiry.

3 A Research Agenda for Future Investigations into the Bazaar Economy for Cultural Goods

Characterizing a market is not an easy task, as it requires considering different features separately, despite their strong interdependence. Characterizing the bazaar economy is no exception. However, examining each aspect in detail is useful for planning future research developments, whether addressing individual features or exploring their interconnections.

3.1 Examining the Previously Identified Characteristics in Greater Depth

Information

Regarding information, the first matter concerns the sources available in the bazaar economy markets, particularly the signals and both intrinsic and extrinsic cues that help determine the value of cultural goods (Angelini et al., 2023b). These signals and cues are generally more prevalent and reliable in formal markets; examples are the artist's brand, the artistic movement, and the origin and the provenance of the goods. In bazaar economy markets, however, these sources of information might be less accessible or entirely absent, leading to a more uncertain environment for buyers and sellers. For instance, the presence of authenticity certificates or provenance records can significantly influence market outcomes. In bazaar economy contexts, one or more of these sources may be totally missing, thereby creating specific market scenarios. It becomes key, then, to identify which information is generally available for each typology of cultural good exchanged in the bazaar economy, in order to assess whether this information affects price and salability. Two further research paths stem from this observation: whether broader internet access can reduce these asymmetries, and whether digital information has any impact in contexts where both sellers and buyers share limited knowledge.

A major concern (relevant to formal markets as well, though to a lesser extent) is the reliability of the available information. Uncertainty about the trustworthiness of a source can alter how people assign value to an object, whether in economic, cultural, or other terms. In these markets, information search costs are particularly shaped by two factors: the accessibility of information and the credibility of its source. Analyzing these aspects can provide insights into the functioning of these markets and the role of trust in the absence of formal certification mechanisms and institutions. For instance, a vintage print found at a flea market may lack any provenance record, label, or artist signature, forcing the buyer to rely entirely on the seller's narrative or visual cues (such as paper quality or printing techniques) to assess its authenticity and value.

Relationships

Given the previously identified characteristics of relationships in the bazaar economy—such as trust, privilege, contract repetition, and seller collusion—it remains unclear whether these features are present and function in the same way across different countries and time periods. The evidence discussed above is drawn from three countries (Morocco, Netherlands, and the USA) and pertains to distinct historical moments. This limitation is partly due to the dominant methodological approach in studies of the bazaar economy, which often relies on anthropological methods. While these provide rich, in-depth insights into local dynamics, their generalizability remains uncertain.[5] The extent to which these characteristics operate in other geographic and temporal contexts has remained systematically underexplored. Expanding research across different regions and time

[5] For a discussion on case-study research, see the interesting analysis by Flyvbjerg (2006).

periods, where possible, would not only improve our understanding of the persistence and adaptability of these mechanisms but also clarify whether they are structural features of the bazaar economy or contingent upon specific socio-economic conditions. Moreover, any attempt to broaden this analysis geographically must address key challenges such as the limited availability of reliable data, the difficulty of translating analytical categories across cultural contexts, and potential ethical or political sensitivities, especially in settings involving illicit trade.

Reputation, too, plays a key role in trust-building, though through different mechanisms than in formal markets. Rather than institutional signals, credibility here stems from repeated interactions, word-of-mouth, and local familiarity. These informal cues shape expectations and behaviors and warrant further investigation to better understand how trust operates across diverse bazaar economy settings.

Exchange Mechanisms

Bargaining, as practiced in the bazaar economy, can be analyzed using a game-theoretical approach. Previous studies have used this framework in cultural markets (e.g., Angelini & Castellani, 2018; Angelini et al., 2022), considering the role of information asymmetries in both bilateral monopoly settings (a single seller and a single buyer) and decentralized markets with multiple agents. However, empirical analyses of these value formation mechanisms remain absent in the cultural economics literature. Outside this field, such studies are primarily based on experimental findings (e.g., Nydegger & Owen, 1974; Fischer et al., 2006).

Cultural goods are often complex and symbolically charged. Their quality and value are not fully observable before, during, or even after the transaction, as they depend heavily on indirect signals, contextual interpretation, and social validation over time. Rather than functioning as experience goods, they resemble what Ekelund et al. (2020) call "meta-credence goods"—goods whose evaluation relies on sustained belief systems and external cues, and whose economic and cultural value may remain uncertain or contested even post-purchase. While this applies to both formal and informal cultural markets, the institutional arrangements, contractual norms, and types of agents involved in the bazaar economy differ substantially from those in formal settings. In such contexts, even quality (already partly inferred in formal markets) becomes more explicitly an object of negotiation and interpretation, given the absence of standardized certification and enforcement mechanisms. These differences crucially shape how value is constructed and negotiated. This aspect has, to my knowledge, not yet been addressed in cultural economics. A comparative analysis of how individuals negotiate the exchange of goods with recognized quality and value (e.g., from the high-end market) versus goods with uncertain quality, limited information, or less reliable sources (e.g., from the bazaar economy) is still missing from literature.

3.2 Exploring New Paths

Legal Frameworks (and Policy)
The legal landscape of the bazaar economy is highly fragmented, with significant differences across countries (reflecting the cultural heterogeneity previously discussed, including within Western countries). Some markets operate in regulated environments (such as licensed flea markets or second-hand vendor registries), while others function in "legal gray areas" where enforcement is weaker. Despite these variations, it is useful to investigate whether common principles apply across different contexts.

One key issue is liability: who is responsible when disputes arise or when counterfeit or illicit goods are sold? In formal markets, liability typically falls on sellers or intermediaries, but in informal settings, accountability is harder to define. Individual vendors may operate without legal recognition, and enforcement agencies often struggle to regulate transactions effectively. For example: should liability also be extended to buyers, penalizing the purchase of counterfeit goods?

Another relevant aspect is due diligence requirements. In regulated sectors (e.g., cultural goods, precious stones, high-value art), buyers and sellers must verify provenance to prevent illicit trade. In the bazaar economy, such mechanisms are rarely enforced, raising questions about whether and how responsibility for verification should be assigned. Similarly, laws against counterfeit goods vary widely: while some countries impose strict bans, others tolerate trade due to economic or enforcement constraints.

These aspects should be examined in greater depth to determine whether common regulations or customs exist in general, facilitating a comprehensive study of the bazaar economy, or whether distinct peculiarities emerge at the national or regional level. Understanding how different regulatory frameworks influence the functioning of the bazaar economy could also provide insights into the balance between oversight and informality.

Illicit Objects Passing Through and Hidden Opportunities
Policymakers are increasingly concerned about the illicit trade of cultural goods, although research on this issue remains limited (e.g., the RAND report by Sargent et al., 2020). While some of these goods are created specifically for the market (as in the case of well-known forgers like John Myatt), in all other cases they "enter" the market somehow. A key research question, therefore, is whether forged or stolen artworks and antiquities infiltrate the traditional market via low-end informal exchanges. Tracking how problematic goods emerge and circulate within the bazaar economy could reveal critical intervention points.

Furthermore, understanding the buyer profile is essential. Less-informed individuals, who lack expertise in recognizing forgeries or stolen items, are likely to be more vulnerable to fraud.[6] This suggests that illicit objects may first pass through buyers unaware of their true nature before resurfacing in higher-tier markets, sometimes aided by retroactive documentation or by passing through intermediaries who "sanitize" the provenance of the object. In this sense, the informal market can act as a staging ground for the eventual legitimization of problematic objects.

However, not all such goods are fraudulent. Some undervalued items, known as "sleepers" (Marrone & Beltrametti, 2020), may be misidentified or overlooked within informal markets before being recognized as valuable. These may be acquired by informed intermediaries (dealers, collectors, or curators) who then channel them into the formal market, often after authentication or contextual reframing. Other items may gain cultural legitimacy post-sale through institutional recognition or inclusion in curated exhibitions. Studying how these objects transition from informal to formal settings could provide insights into both illicit trade mechanisms and overlooked opportunities within the art market.

Agents
Agents operating within a market play a fundamental role in shaping its dynamics. Their characteristics, such as wealth, expertise, and their ability to process information, are critical in determining market outcomes (van Ours, 1991; McCrohan & Sugrue, 1998; Evers & Seale, 2015a). Additionally, the frequency with which these agents participate in informal markets (whether as sellers, buyers, or both) can further influence their

[6] This has been proved in other markets, finding also a role of age and income in the probability of incurring in frauds (Lee and Soberon-Ferrer, 1997).

behavior and the overall market environment. The experience level of agents, coupled with their familiarity with the market, often determines their negotiating power and overall success in these settings. Understanding who the agents are in the bazaar economy helps clarify how relationships take shape in this context. While sellers are often more familiar with the market than buyers, this is not always the case, and different configurations of knowledge and experience may emerge. In fact, experts, traders, and owners of higher-tier cultural goods shops engage in this type of market either to acquire goods at lower prices for resale or to expand their collections cost-effectively. This market failure is not only linked with information availability, but also with how information is processed and influenced by behavioral biases.

Furthermore, different trading venues serve different strategic needs for both buyers and sellers. Some agents prefer informal markets because they rely on reputation and discretion rather than formal regulation, especially when transaction values are low, verification costs are high, or when certain goods would not be accepted in more institutionalized channels. In other cases, repeated interactions and relational proximity substitute for legal guarantees. These patterns suggest that participation in the bazaar economy is not only driven by necessity, but can reflect deliberate preferences. Understanding which agents are drawn to these settings, and why, is an open question that deserves further empirical investigation. Finally, an exploration of the type of agents available in each market (depending also on the goods exchanged, e.g., old books vs. antiques vs. craftsmanship) would also inform possible policies and regulations of these trades.

Behavioral Specificities

Agents form relationships that help them reduce issues related to information availability. However, the existence of behavioral biases increases the complexity of this process. In fact, these biases significantly impact pricing and the likelihood of transactions, both in general and within the specific context of bazaar economy markets. As highlighted by Angelini et al. (2022), the high level of uncertainty in the lower end of the market increases the likelihood of overconfidence (which may manifest as overoptimism or overspecification) among sellers, buyers, or both. This overconfidence, in turn, affects final selling prices and the probability of a transaction occurring, as demonstrated in the above-mentioned paper by using a bargaining exchange mechanism, aligning with real-world market dynamics. How strong these effects are in the bazaar economy remains an open question. In particular, the intensity of these biases and distortions, if they exist, may vary depending on the type of goods exchanged and the characteristics of the agents involved.[7]

Another important aspect related to these distortions concerns the nature of relationships between agents, which can be characterized by strong or weak ties, in the sense of Granovetter (1983). These ties further influence the interactions by introducing varying levels of trust (potentially explaining what has been mentioned by Geertz). Trust, or the lack thereof, in fact plays a pivotal role in shaping market outcomes, especially in environments where formal verification and guarantees are scarce. Bazaar economy markets can then be an important study field, given their characteristics and the potentially varying strength of the agents' relationship, which may depend on the cultural background of the place hosting the market, as well as on the cultural features of the agents operating within it.

Value Formation Mechanisms

An interesting avenue for further research concerns the formation of value in the bazaar economy markets. The uniqueness of a good, particularly in these markets, can profoundly impact how agents interact and negotiate the final price, as also discussed by Geertz (1978) and List (2009). However, uniqueness is harder to characterize in the bazaar economy, due to the limited availability of information, not only about the goods themselves but also about their presence across different informal markets. A seemingly rare item may indeed be rare or, alternatively, may be widely available yet dispersed among various resellers, making it difficult for buyers to assess its true scarcity. Consequently, economic value is largely shaped by the perceived rarity of goods. In this respect, scarcity plays a central role, although it operates here as a matter of perception and inference rather than objective verification. Exchange mechanisms suggested by Geertz are clearly at work in forming the economic value of those goods, though, as discussed in the previous section, bargaining may sometimes be based on distorted valuations.

It remains unclear how cultural value is assessed in these markets: this type of evaluation is surely made harder by information scarcity and asymmetry and can be critical to recognizing whether such value exists

[7] This may be due, for example, to their different experience (e.g., List, 2003).

at all. As in the high tier, this value is related to the economic one (Angelini & Castellani, 2019). It is conceivable that a form of bargaining may also occur in the construction of cultural value. During negotiation, the two parties may exchange information about the good's characteristics, revealing aspects that were initially known only to one side. Through this process, the less-informed party gains insights from the reactions of the better-informed party, not only regarding economic value (as reflected in price) but also concerning cultural value. For instance, a buyer engaged in negotiation with a seller might learn about a piece's historical significance, authenticity, or artistic merit, thereby refining their perception of its cultural value. Whether and how this process operates within the bazaar economy remains an open question that warrants further investigation, as well as whether and how this possible value formation mechanism is reflected in the economic value formation.

Typical and General Risks

A final but no less important issue concerns the risks inherent in the bazaar economy. All the characteristics we discussed above generate risks for the buyer, the seller, or both, to varying degrees. Identifying and analyzing these risks is essential to understanding their actual relevance and impact. Notably, some of these risks are also present in formal and high-end markets. However, in the latter, they tend to occur less frequently due to stricter regulations and stronger enforcement mechanisms. That said, assessing their relative importance remains crucial, as a single fraudulent artwork in the high-end market represents the economic equivalent of numerous counterfeits circulating in bazaar economy markets.

The first major risk concerns authenticity. Determining the authenticity of goods is particularly challenging in the bazaar economy, where verification mechanisms are often weak or absent. Interestingly, the significance attributed to authenticity varies across market segments. Counterfeit goods are more prevalent in the bazaar economy, but they differ in nature. Hepworth (2015) distinguishes between "fake-fakes", inferior imitations with entirely fabricated brand identities, and "true-fakes", high-quality replicas made from the same materials as the original (see also Oosterman & Angelini, 2021). This issue (as well as the one that will follow below) is also strictly linked with the illicit market for cultural goods, which tend to circulate more easily in lower segments, as previously noted.

A second, related risk involves the provenance of cultural goods. Stolen items find their way into these markets with relative ease, as provenance verification is often nonexistent, and certificates of authenticity are typically absent. The perceived risk of purchasing stolen artworks or other cultural objects influences buyers' valuations, as highlighted by Posner and Landes (1996) and Landes and Levine (2006). However, it remains unclear whether this holds true for bazaar economy markets as well. Intuitively, the attention paid to the provenance is likely to be proportional to the monetary and cultural value one attaches to the exchange made or about to be made, in the absence of regulations fostering or requiring due diligence. A similar concern applies to traded goods that do not originate from thefts or forgery but are of illicit provenance (such as international illicitly traded goods).[8]

A third risk is due to the potential misalignment of the traded good and its assessed value, not necessarily due to its illicit origin. This would be the case of an overvaluation of goods made by the buyer, or an undervaluation of goods made by the seller. The likelihood of such discrepancies increases as information asymmetry grows. An agent's ability to accurately assess the nature and worth of a good plays a critical role in the value formation process within bazaar economy markets.

A final remark on risk in the bazaar economy concerns its connection with liquidity—defined here as the ease of exchanging a cultural good—and how this is shaped by both the perceived risks of trade and the presence (or absence) of enforcement mechanisms. A general principle is that *ceteris paribus* the higher the risk linked to a certain good, the lower its liquidity should be. A high-risk good typically requires a risk premium to be exchanged, effectively a discount compensating the buyer for potential losses.[9] For example, a buyer may be willing to buy a stolen artwork, knowing that this is risky; to do so, the buyer asks for a discount to cover the potential loss (e.g., being discovered after the purchase). This discount increases the ease with which the good can be sold. However, in the absence of a regulatory framework, as is often the case in bazaar economy

[8] See the discussion on this theme by Fisman and Wei (2009) on art smuggling. Some scholars also investigated the role of regulations, such as artworks' export veto and their impact on prices, which can lead to export through illicit ways, and which could lead artworks to be exchanged in less transparent markets (e.g., Onofri, 2009; Angelini et al., 2023a).

[9] Along these lines, see the analysis by d'Este (2020) on pawnshops and stolen goods.

markets, these risks are perceived as less severe and thus may have limited impact on a good's liquidity. At the same time, in certain contexts, these risks may extend beyond the transactional level, exposing buyers or sellers to legal consequences or, in rare cases, to reprisals, especially where informal markets intersect with criminal networks or operate in regulatory gray zones. A particularly interesting avenue for further research concerns the liquidity of the various segments of the market for cultural goods, considering varying degrees of risk and regulation. These regulations take the form of formal legal frameworks or informal systems of trust, shaped by the strength of relationships between market participants.

4 Conclusions and Challenges

The matters mentioned in this chapter are clearly interrelated and understanding their respective roles within this segment of the market, particularly in relation to the type of good being exchanged, can pave the way for new lines of research. Such research would not only reveal previously overlooked issues related to the ones discussed above but also suggest targeted interventions to address them. Given the distinctive characteristics of these informal markets, new analytical tools and approaches may be necessary to effectively tackle emerging issues.

In fact, the divergence in arrangements and practices between bazaar economy and high-end markets suggests that conventional solutions may fall short, requiring alternative strategies tailored to these unique conditions. The peculiarities of informal markets also underscore the need for diverse information sources and analytical methods to analyze them effectively. Traditional economic data tend to be sparse or entirely unavailable due to the organization and nature of these markets, making it necessary to rely on methods commonly used in anthropology and ethnography (Evers & Seale, 2015b), or to use experimental approaches (List, 2009) or interviews (Radermecker, 2022) to gather insights. Addressing these challenges calls for a more explicitly interdisciplinary approach, integrating economic theory with insights from anthropology, legal studies, and behavioral research to capture the full complexity of bazaar economy markets and guide future empirical and policy-oriented research.

References

Akerlof, G. A. (1970). The market for "Lemons": Quality uncertainty and the market mechanism. *The Quarterly Journal of Economics, 84*(3), 488–500.

Angelini, F., & Castellani, M. (2018). Private pricing in the art market. *Economics Bulletin, 38*(4), 2371–2378.

Angelini, F., & Castellani, M. (2019). Cultural and economic value: A critical review. *Journal of Cultural Economics, 43*, 173–188.

Angelini, F., Castellani, M., & Pattitoni, P. (2023a). You can't export that! Export ban for modern and contemporary Italian art. *European Journal of Law and Economics, 56*, 533–557.

Angelini, F., Castellani, M., & Ventrucci, M. (2023b). Cumulative information on quality and willingness to pay: A study on wine evaluation. *Journal of Foodservice Business Research, 28*(2), 295–333.

Angelini, F., Castellani, M., & Zirulia, L. (2022). Overconfidence in the art market: A bargaining pricing model with asymmetric disinformation. *Economia Politica, 39*(3), 961–988.

Binmore, K., Rubinstein, A., & Wolinsky, A. (1986). The Nash bargaining solution in economic modelling. *The RAND Journal of Economics, 17*(2), 176–188.

Bocart, F., & Oosterlinck, K. (2011). Discoveries of fakes: Their impact on the art market. *Economics Letters, 113*(2), 124–126.

Choi, G. S., & Storr, V. H. (2020). Market interactions, trust and reciprocity. *PLoS One, 15*(5), e0232704.

d'Este, R. (2020). The effects of stolen-goods markets on crime: Pawnshops, property theft, and the gold rush of the 2000s. *The Journal of Law & Economics, 63*(3), 449–472.

Darby, M. R., & Karni, E. (1973). Free competition and the optimal amount of fraud. *The Journal of Law & Economics, 16*(1), 67–88.

Duarte, A., & Pérez-Ibañez, M. (Eds.). (2023). *The art market and the Global South*. Brill.

Ekelund, R. B., Higgins, R., & Jackson, J. D. (2020). Art as meta-credence: Authentication and the role of experts. *Journal of Cultural Economics, 44*(1), 155–171.

Evers, C., & Seale, K. (2015a). Informal urban street markets: International perspectives. In C. Evers & K. Seale (Eds.), *Informal urban street markets: International perspectives* (1–14). Routledge.

Evers, C., & Seale, K. (Eds.). (2015b). *Informal urban street markets: International perspectives*. Routledge.

Fischer, S., Güth, W., Müller, W., & Stiehler, A. (2006). From ultimatum to Nash bargaining: Theory and experimental evidence. *Experimental Economics, 9*, 17–33.

Fisman, R., & Wei, S.-J. (2009). The smuggling of art, and the art of smuggling: Uncovering the illicit trade in cultural property and antiques. *American Economic Journal: Applied Economics*, *1*, 82–96.

Flyvbjerg, B. (2006). Five misunderstandings about case-study research. *Qualitative Inquiry*, *12*(2), 219–245.

Geertz, C. (1978). The bazaar economy: Information and search in peasant marketing. *The American Economic Review*, *68*(2), 28–32.

Granovetter, M. (1983). The strength of weak ties: A network theory revisited. *Sociological Theory*, *1*, 201–233.

Hepworth, K. (2015). Geographies of unauthorized street trade in the "Fight Again Counterfeiting" in Milan. In C. Evers & K. Seale (Eds.), *Informal urban street markets: International perspectives* (pp. 167–175). Routledge.

Hutter, M. (2023). Toward global transmodernity: Contemporary visual art games in twelve African cities. In A. Duarte & M. Pérez-Ibañez (Eds.), *The art market in the Global South* (pp. 127–153). Brill.

Jackson, M. O., Rodriguez-Barraquer, T., & Tan, X. (2012). Social capital and social quilts: Network patterns of favor exchange. *American Economic Review*, *102*(5), 1857–1897.

Landes, W., & Levine, D. B. (2006). The economic analysis of art law In V. A. Ginsburgh & D. Throsby (Eds.), *Handbook of the economics of art and culture* (Vol. 1, pp. 211–225). Elsevier.

Lee, J., & Soberon-Ferrer, H. (1997). Consumer vulnerability to fraud: Influencing factors. *Journal of Consumer Affairs*, *31*, 70–89.

List, J. A. (2003). Does market experience eliminate market anomalies? *The Quarterly Journal of Economics*, *118*(1), 41–71.

List, J. A. (2009). *The economics of open air markets*. NBER Working Paper n. 15420. Retrieved January 29, 2025, from https://www.nber.org/papers/w15420

Marrone, J., & Beltrametti, S. (2020). "Sleeper" antiquities: Misattributions in sales of ancient art. *International Journal of Cultural Property*, *27*(1), 3–51.

McCrohan, K. F., & Sugrue, T. F. (1998). An empirical analysis of informal markets participation. *Social Science Quarterly*, *79*(1), 211–226.

Nelson, P. (1970). Information and consumer behavior. *Journal of Political Economy*, *78*(2), 311–329.

Nydegger, R. V., & Owen, G. (1974). Two-person bargaining: An experimental test of the Nash axioms. *International Journal of Game Theory*, *3*, 239–249.

Onofri, L. (2009). Old master paintings, export veto and price formation: An empirical study. *European Journal of Law and Economics*, *28*, 149–161.

Oosterman, N., & Angelini, F. (2021). One flew over the cuckoo's clock: Selling exclusivity through conspicuous goods on Evolution. In N. Oosterman & D. Yates (Eds.), *Crime and Art* (pp. 267–284). Springer.

Posner, R. A., & Landes, W. (1996). The economics of legal disputes over the ownership of works of art and other collectibles. In V. A. Ginsburgh & P.-M. Menger (Eds.), *Economics of the arts: Selected essays* (pp. 177–219).

Radermecker, A.-S. (2022). Selling low-brow art and cultural goods in times of pandemic: The case of a provincial art market. *International Journal of Cultural Property*, *29*(3), 283–310.

Sargent, M., Marrone, J. V., Evans, A. T., Lilly, B., Nemeth, E., & Dalzell, S. (2020). *Tracking and disrupting the illicit antiquities trade with open source data*. Homeland Security Operational Analysis Center operated by the RAND Corporation. Retrieved October 10, 2025 from https://www.rand.org/pubs/research_reports/RR2706.html.

Shaban, A., Vermeylen, F., & Handke, C. (Eds.). (2022). *Creative industries in India*. Routledge.

Stigler, G. J. (1961). The economics of information. *Journal of Political Economy*, *69*(3), 213–225.

van Ours, J. (1991). Self-service activities and formal or informal market services. *Applied Economics*, *23*(3), 505–516.

Vermeylen, F., & Bhat, S. (2023). New markets for Indian Art: The growth of an ecosystem in the new millennium. In A. Duarte & M. Pérez-Ibañez (Eds.), *The art market in the Global South* (19–38). Brill.

Wolinsky, A. (1987). Matching, search, and bargaining. *Journal of Economic Theory*, *42*(2), 311–333.

"Semi-luxury Goods" as an Investment. The Case of Val Saint Lambert Crystalware

Anne-Sophie V. Radermecker

1 Introduction

Since Baumol's seminal paper (1986), the notion of art as an investment has predominantly been examined through the lens of high-end artworks and blue-chip artists (Oosterlinck, 2025). While this focus is understandable when conceptualizing art as an asset class, it tends to obscure the multifaceted nature of investment, which does not necessarily require substantial expenditure on the finest art pieces but can be relative to buyers' purchasing power and extended to other categories of more affordable cultural goods. At its core, investment refers to the allocation of resources—such as capital, time, or effort—into an asset or activity with the expectation of future returns. Economists broadly define investment as a commitment of money intended to yield greater returns over time, typically in the form of capital gains, income streams, or both (Gerlis, 2014). This distinguishes investment from consumption or intermediate spending, as it implies the potential to generate long-term value.

With fine art, the core investment principles remain similar, i.e., the allocation of capital into assets expected to yield returns, particularly through profitable resale. Investing in art entails the application of fundamental economic concepts such as capital allocation, risk–return

A.-S. V. Radermecker (✉)
Université libre de Bruxelles, Brussels, Belgium
e-mail: Anne-Sophie.Radermecker@ulb.be

A.-S. V. Radermecker (ed.), *Low-End Markets for Art and Cultural Goods*, Cultural Economics & the Creative Economy,
https://doi.org/10.1007/978-3-032-27566-0_4

optimization, and strategic holding periods to assets that, as (meta) credence goods, diverge from standard financial instruments (Mei & Mose, 2005). However, much like conventional investments, art investment decisions are shaped by the availability of information and the influence of expert signaling. Art's dual character—simultaneously hedonic and financial—requires a combination of qualitative expertise (e.g., authenticity, artist reputation) and quantitative metrics (e.g., price indices, rankings) to legitimize its role as an investment category.

Although fine art is widely recognized for its potential to yield financial returns, support portfolio diversification, and provide an emotional premium to its owner (e.g., Goetzmann, 1993; Mandel, 2009; Renneboog & Spaenjers, 2013; Li et al., 2024), other categories of cultural goods, such as everyday collectibles and luxury items, can also be considered investment-worthy when approached strategically. Consider the example of an informed collector or *chineur* who acquires undervalued items and resells them in more favorable markets or to specific buyers, thereby realizing a considerable premium. Alternatively, through minor restoration and compelling marketing, an antique chair can be repositioned to command a significantly higher resale price, potentially generating noteworthy profits (Shoop, 2004; 2011). Historically, various generations have regarded such goods as investments, particularly in social contexts where households allocated resources not only to real estate but also to valuable domestic furnishings and decorative objects—such as porcelain sets, silverware, or period-specific furniture (Nelsen, 1970; Graeser, 1993). These items were often intended to be passed down to future generations. While not always viewed as collectibles in the strict sense (e.g., like stamps or violins) nor high-end luxury items, they were nevertheless considered durable, high-quality domestic assets. The underlying logic was that objects crafted from noble materials or bearing the marks of reputable manufacturers—unlike ordinary consumer goods—would retain or even appreciate in value over time. These antique "everyday luxury goods" can be regarded as precursors to what Silverstein and Fiske describe as "masstige" products—a contraction of "mass" and "prestige"—defined as goods that "occupy a sweet spot between mass and class." Such products command a premium over conventional items while remaining priced well below super-premium offerings, and are closely tied to generational lifestyle preferences (Silverstein & Fiske, 2003, pp. 48–49; Kumar et al., 2020).

Due to the relatively lower monetary value of these goods compared to fine art or high-end luxury items—and the limited availability of accessible data—economists have largely overlooked these segments of the cultural goods markets. However, the expansion of online sales platforms has led to the frequent appearance of such domestic assets in digital marketplaces, often accompanied by basic descriptions and pricing information. This development enables empirical analysis using methods traditionally applied to fine art markets. Applying analytical tools to these data offers a valuable opportunity to assess whether these goods have retained their value and can be considered viable investment assets.

This paper fills this gap by focusing on a specific creative industry and object category: crystal manufacturing and Val Saint Lambert crystalware. Established in Seraing (Belgium) in 1826, the Val Saint Lambert manufactory became a hallmark of the Industrial Revolution in the Mosan basin, rivalling prestigious firms such as Baccarat and Saint-Louis (Philippe, 1974; Chevalier et al., 1999). Throughout the nineteenth and early twentieth centuries, the company exported a wide range of high-quality crystal products—including glasses, vases, plates, decorative and gift objects—significantly contributing to the international recognition of local craftsmanship in glassmaking and glassblowing. After decades of prosperity, however, the company experienced repeated financial setbacks, eventually entering a period of drastically reduced production. Today, the legacy of its historical success is evidenced by the widespread presence of Val Saint Lambert pieces in private homes and the secondary antiques market. In line with the triadic model proposed in the introduction, Val Saint Lambert crystalware arguably fits within the home decor market (i.e., sub-segment 1). Beyond their creative dimension as designed objects, these pieces retain a strong functional value, display low scarcity, and benefit from a recognized, though relative, brand name. The fact that they were mostly sold directly by the manufacture or through specialized decoration stores, for which the sales catalogs were produced according to a B2B model, further supports their affiliation with this category.

Using an adjusted Hedonic Pricing Model, this paper reveals the dramatic decline in the market value of what was once a highly esteemed production, associated with a lack of specialized expertise—a trend that mirrors the broader downturn in the antiques sector (Javerlhiac, 2021). Among the key objects' characteristics associated with stronger market performance, the analysis shows that maintaining a relevant functionality, demonstrating a higher degree of technical sophistication, and being linked to a recognized designer or stylistic tradition enable certain pieces to outperform others. These items remain "safe bets" within this production category, even amid overall market contraction.

The remainder of this paper is structured as follows. Section 2 presents a review of the key literature addressing collectibles as investment assets and Val Saint Lambert crystalware. Section 3 outlines the methodology, while Section 4 reports the empirical findings—first analyzing recent market trends in terms of volume and value, then identifying the main price determinants. Section 5 concludes.

2 Literature Review

2.1 *Fine Art and Collectibles as Assets*

While the majority of financial studies on art as an investment focus on fine art—such as painting, drawing, and sculpture (see Oosterlinck, 2025, for a review)—some scholars have extended this analysis to collectibles, which offer both financial returns and non-pecuniary benefits, including aesthetic enjoyment and enhanced social status (Dimson & Spaenjers, 2014). For example, Graeser (1993) analyzed sales data for fine American furniture from 1967 to 1986, revealing modest long-term returns, with declines of 8.24% in the first decade and 5.71% in the second. Graddy and Margolis (2011), using a combination of repeat-sales regression and hedonic pricing models, found that fine violins yielded an annualized return of 3.5% between 1850 and 2008, while exhibiting minimal correlation with traditional financial assets such as stocks and bonds. Dimson and Spaenjers (2011) estimated real annual returns of 2.9% (7% nominal) for British collectible postage stamps from 1900 to 2008, outperforming bonds but underperforming equities. Renneboog and Spaenjers (2012) reported annualized returns of 6.4% for white diamonds and 2.9% for colored diamonds (1999–2010), noting a strong correlation with stock market performance. Wu (2014) constructed both short-term hedonic and long-term repeat-sales price indices for vintage furniture, analyzing 4,485 auction records from twentieth-century design sales (1966–2013), and reported an average return of 3.23%. Bordeaux wines generated average annual returns of 4.1% between 1900 and 2012, with superior performance observed for young, high-quality vintages (Dimson et al., 2015). Ursprung (2021) extended this research to rare books, identifying a 2.8% return from 1975 to 2019. More recently, Radermecker and Brosens

(2023) employed adjusted hedonic regression to examine price determinants in the antique tapestry market, focusing on value drivers rather than investment returns.

With the exception of Graeser (1993), most of these studies highlight the investment potential of cultural goods akin to fine art, yet focus predominantly on objects that have lost their original function and are now primarily appreciated for their scarcity, craftsmanship, or historical significance—traits that categorize them as "fine" collectibles. In contrast, more accessible yet still valuable forms of antique *masstige* goods—such as domestic decorative or functional objects strongly associated with lifestyle—remain largely underexplored in the financial literature. The following section introduces a specific example of this type of production: crystalware and the Val Saint Lambert manufactory.

2.2 *Val Saint Lambert Crystalware*

Crystal, renowned for its clarity, brilliance, and elegance, has a long and rich history that spans centuries. The origins of crystal glassmaking can be traced to ancient civilizations such as Egypt, Mesopotamia, and Rome, where artisans first developed techniques to produce glass with exceptional transparency and luster (Cummings, 2002). Specifically, it was during the Renaissance in Europe that crystal glassmaking truly flourished, particularly in northeastern France, Bohemia and the Venetian region. Venice, long celebrated for its glassmaking tradition, played a pivotal role in the development of high-quality crystal. Venetian glassmakers perfected the production of *cristallo*, a clear, high-purity glass that quickly became a symbol of luxury and refinement, widely imitated around the world (Page, 2004). The introduction of lead oxide into glass formulations—giving rise to lead crystal—was a major innovation that achieved industrial scale with the English businessman George Ravenscroft (1632–1683). This technique dramatically enhanced the refractive properties of glass, producing a distinctive sparkle that revolutionized the industry. Over time, innovations in crystal glassmaking have continued to advance. Improvements in furnace technology, glass chemistry, and cutting machinery have enabled the production of increasingly intricate and refined designs (Toso, 2006). Beyond its technical evolution, crystal glassware also holds deep cultural and symbolic significance. It is often associated with luxury, prestige, and celebration, making it a staple in formal dining, ceremonial events, and high-society rituals. Its presence in such contexts underscores its role as a marker of wealth and social status. Moreover, crystal has served as a source of inspiration for artists, designers, and collectors worldwide (Thiry, 1987, 1990; Chevalier et al., 1999). The aesthetic appeal of crystal vessels, chandeliers, and sculptures has been celebrated in both artistic literature and major decorative arts exhibitions. In the contemporary era, however, the crystal glassmaking industry has faced multiple challenges. Increasing competition from mass-produced, low-cost glassware—often made from synthetic substitutes—has threatened the market share of traditional producers, urging them to find new models and creative solutions (Communian & England, 2019). Shifting consumer preferences toward minimalist or more sustainable alternatives further complicate the landscape. In response to growing environmental concerns and regulatory pressures, some manufacturers have begun to explore eco-friendlier formulations and production processes in an effort to reduce the environmental footprint of crystal production (Giusti & Polo, 2002).

Val Saint Lambert, founded in 1826 in Seraing (Belgium), rapidly evolved from a regional glasswork into a globally recognized producer of high-end crystal glassware. Benefiting from its strategic location—rich in natural resources and skilled labor—the company transitioned from basic glass production to refined crystal manufacturing during the nineteenth century (Philippe, 1974; Chevalier et al., 1999; Kremer & Pluymaekers, 2007). Emphasizing artisanal precision and technical innovation, Val Saint Lambert introduced its signature technique, which involved layering colored glass to create complex and vibrant designs (Chevalier et al., 1999; Fontaine-Hodiamont, 2010). These innovations, combined with sustained investment in manufacturing quality, earned the brand numerous international accolades, including honors at the *Exposition Universelle* in Paris (1867), thereby reinforcing its prestige and global market presence. By the early twentieth century, Val Saint Lambert had established itself as a symbol of European luxury, with showrooms in Paris, London, and New York. Its clientele included royalty, diplomats, and members of high society, and its pieces became synonymous with opulence and refined taste (Philippe, 1974). The company's product diversification—from chandeliers to decorative tableware and everyday glassware—broadened its appeal among the bourgeoisie, encompassing both functional and collectible markets (Kremer & Pluymaekers, 2007; Philippe, 1974). This is particularly evident in the Luxval line—more affordable yet still refined—as well as in several collaborations with contemporary designers aimed at modernizing its product aesthetics (de Pessemier, 1998). Nevertheless, post-war shifts in consumer preferences, increased competition, and globalization gradually eroded Val Saint Lambert's market dominance. Despite its efforts, Val Saint Lambert faced recurrent financial crises, resulting in bankruptcies in 1980, 2008, and 2013. The high cost of artisanal production, vulnerability to economic downturns, and waning demand for traditional crystalware posed structural challenges in a market increasingly dominated by mass-produced alternatives (Heyvaert, 1978). Today, the company operates on a much smaller scale, producing bespoke and limited-edition pieces aimed at collectors and amateurs.

This rapid historical overview helps contextualize the investment potential of Val Saint Lambert crystalware. Unlike generic, everyday glassware, the appeal of high-end crystal as an asset lies in the interplay between artisanal craftsmanship, brand heritage, and material-specific attributes—such as brilliance, refraction, and the complexity of cut—which contribute to both its symbolic and economic value as *masstige* goods. Many crystal pieces are handcrafted and produced in limited quantities, resulting in supply constraints that help sustain their value over time (Philippe, 1974; Kremer & Pluymaekers, 2007). Drawing on Nelsen's (1970) analysis on the democratization of antiques across socio-economic strata and Bourdieu's (1984) theory of distinction, one may argue that the materiality and dual function of crystalware as both decorative and utilitarian enhance its appeal to individuals seeking to accumulate cultural capital and convey social status. This duality, coupled with the enduring market recognition of legacy brands, renders crystalware particularly responsive to investment potential.

To support this claim, archival research conducted into the company's price catalogs provides evidence of a Val Saint Lambert premium compared to regular glassware. For instance, in 1972, a small engraved double-layered crystal candy dish was priced at 3,000 BEF (Catalog 1972, p. 29), while regular crystal glasses ranged between 200 and 300 BEF. Adjusted for inflation, the candy dish would be valued at approximately €560 in 2023. Insights gathered from semi-structured interviews with antiques dealers based in the Liège region further support this investment-oriented interpretation (Radermecker, 2022). When specifically asked about Val Saint Lambert today, several responses explicitly highlight the investment potential of these items, both past and present (e.g., "Certain Val Saint Lambert pieces could make very good investments in the past;" "With Val Saint Lambert it's always good to invest. Even a small amount of money. You never know what will happen in 10 or 20 years;" "The good thing with Val Saint Lambert and other antiques, like all these 'Louis XV, XVI style' or 'Empire style' objects is that they have material value—crystal, mahogany, marble—that is always worth something;" "Val Saint Lambert items are not always very expensive, but these objects last in time, and that's an advantage"). Nevertheless, these conversations also underscored the currently low market value of objects that were once regarded as investment goods. The following section further examines their recent market performance and identifies the primary price formation mechanisms, in order to assess whether these domestic assets have retained their value and to determine which factors currently influence their valuation.

3 Data and Methodology

To construct a reliable price index and identify the factors that continue to influence prices in this segment of the art market, I employed a Hedonic Pricing Model (Ginsburgh et al., 2006). Previous research has thoroughly evaluated the strengths and limitations of the three primary techniques for constructing art price indices: average-based price indices (e.g., Stein, 1977), repeat-sales regression (e.g., Goetzmann, 1993), and hedonic pricing models (e.g., Renneboog & Spaenjers, 2013). Drawing on Lancaster's (1966) theory of goods as bundles of characteristics, the hedonic model treats prices as functions of observable attributes such as authenticity (e.g., artist's name, signature), quality (e.g., provenance, exhibition history), aesthetics (e.g., technique, style), and the sale context (e.g., auction house, year). Given the limitations associated with average-based indices and the data requirements of repeat-sales regressions, the hedonic approach has proven most appropriate for analyzing the recent performance of antiques markets. Prior studies (e.g., Bauwens & Ginsburgh, 2000; Draper et al., 2013) have demonstrated its adaptability to three-dimensional decorative objects, provided suitable methodological adjustments are applied.

The dataset, composed of Val Saint Lambert crystalware sales sourced from Drouot.com and manually compiled, spans from 2010 to 2023. It includes 9,869 entries, of which 5,776 contain price data. All prices are adjusted for inflation and expressed in 2023 euros. A close examination of the auction lot descriptions enabled the extraction of a comprehensive set of variables hypothesized to influence the market value of these items. These variables differ in several respects from those typically used in fine art analysis, introducing a necessary degree of complexity to adequately capture the nuances of price formation in this market segment. As outlined in Appendix 1, the variables fall into several broad categories: the object's functionality (direct utility and decorative value); crystal's characteristics and technical attributes; material integrity; indicators of authenticity and quality; and, finally, contextual information related to the sale. Unlike fine art, decorative arts frequently serve utilitarian purposes and were historically used in domestic settings. To address the heterogeneity of this product category—which includes a broad array of functionally distinct items—I used a typology of object types that strikes a balance between generalizability (allowing replication for other brands of decorative arts) and sufficient specificity (to reflect the diversity of objects involved). The decorative value of such items often lies in their formal, stylistic, and aesthetic dimensions. Accordingly, I coded variables such as styles, shapes, colors, models, and decorative motifs. By combining these detailed item-specific variables with standard hedonic controls, the equation can be read as:

$$\begin{aligned} \mathrm{Ln}_{(p)} = \beta_0 + \beta_1 \text{functionality (direct\_utility} \\ \beta_2 \text{crystal\_characteristics} + \beta_3 \text{crystal\_techniques} + \\ \beta_4 \text{material\_integrity} + \beta_5 \text{authenticity} + \beta_6 \text{quality} + \beta_7 \text{salecontext} + \\ \beta_8 \text{years} + \varepsilon. \end{aligned} \quad (1)$$

Where:

- $\mathrm{Ln}_{(p)}$ denotes the natural logarithm of the hammer price, used to normalize the distribution of price data and interpret coefficients in percentage terms;
- β_0 is the intercept term;
- Functionality (β_1) captures both the direct utility (i.e., practical use such as glassware, bowls) and decorative value (i.e., colors, shapes, models) of the item;
- Crystal characteristics (β_2) includes variables such as transparency and thickness;
- Crystal techniques (β_3) reflects the use of specific manufacturing processes (e.g., engraving, casing, cutting);

- Material integrity (β_4) accounts for the item's condition, presence of damage, or restoration;
- Authenticity (β_5) incorporates brand marks, signatures, or verifiable attributions;
- Quality (β_6) includes proxies such as provenance, inclusion of qualitative adjectives, etc.;
- Sale context (β_7) captures potential regional price differentials and indirectly local auction houses' reputation;
- Years (β_8) is a set of annual dummies accounting for time effects and enabling the construction of the price index;
- ε is the error term.

Despite not controlling for transaction costs, this model allows for isolating the marginal contribution of each attribute to the observed price, thereby revealing which characteristics are most strongly associated with value retention or appreciation in the secondary market for Val Saint Lambert crystalware. Using the antilog of the yearly coefficients, the price index is modeled as follows, with the baseline year 2010 set to 0:

$$\prod_t \equiv \exp(\hat{Y}_t) \times 100, \tag{2}$$

The estimated return for year t is[1]:

$$r_t \equiv \frac{\prod_t - 1}{\prod_{t-1}} \tag{3}$$

4 Empirical Analysis and Findings

4.1 Recent Trends (Volume and Value) in the Market for Val Saint Lambert Crystalware

Figure 1 illustrates the evolution of lots offered for sale, both online and offline, with a first notable increase in 2014 and a second significant rise in 2020. The latter coincides with the COVID-19 pandemic and the

[1] With the subsequent application of the price index correction as required by Triplett (2004).

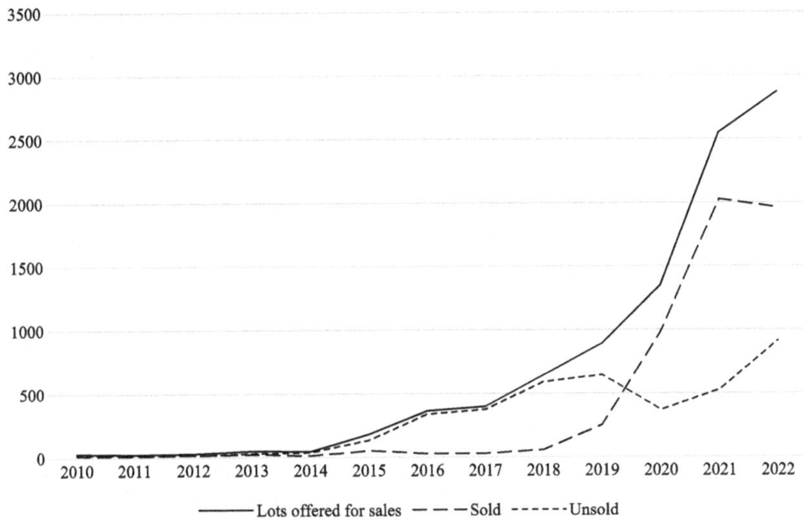

Fig. 1 Val Saint Lambert Crystalware—Total number of lots offered for sale (Sold and Unsold). *Source* Author

subsequent surge in online sales, as clearly reflected in the graph. While the pre-2014 period should not be interpreted as a time with minimal online listings, the increase in volume is largely attributable to the growing popularity and operational efficiency of Drouot.com. A noteworthy trend also emerges when distinguishing between lots sold and those bought-in. Until 2017, the proportion of bought-in lots closely mirrored the total supply, indicating limited demand. However, a marked reversal occurred in 2019–2020, with a decline in bought-in rates and a corresponding increase in successful sales. This shift suggests improved market liquidity for Val Saint Lambert crystalware in online channels, likely driven by the enhanced international visibility afforded by digital platforms

The analysis of hammer prices and their corresponding estimates (in 2023 EUR) reveals several noteworthy patterns. The average hammer price is €365.15, with a median of €165. The lowest recorded hammer price is €3.89, while the highest reaches €17,631. A standard deviation of €714.18 indicates substantial variability in realized prices. Regarding low estimates, the average stands at €280, with a median of €136, ranging from €0 to €21,480, and a standard deviation of €535. High estimates are slightly higher, with an average of €379, a median of €200, a minimum of €0, and a maximum of €28,640, accompanied by a standard deviation of €684. These figures highlight the significant heterogeneity of the low-end market, with large discrepancies between minimum and maximum values across all variables. The high standard deviations underscore the variability in both estimated and actual prices, reflecting the diverse characteristics and perceived value of the items sold. Notably, the descriptive statistics show that—despite current market volatility—Val Saint Lambert crystalware retains a relatively elevated position in the glassware market, with both average and median prices situated in the three-figure range. However, in the case of drinking glasses, these prices typically refer to sets of four to six items, rather than individual pieces.

Before constructing the price index, I also examined whether the increased prevalence of online sales correlated with improved information provision by auction houses, distinguishing between "general" and "specialized" expertise (as proxied by the length of lot descriptions).[2] As in other segments of the art market, the availability of information is critical for buyers. Figure 2 clearly shows that, despite the rise in sales volume, general expertise continues to dominate over specialized expertise. Contrary to expectations, the entry of new auction houses into the online market has not resulted in more detailed or better-documented lot notes. In fact, the relative share of lots accompanied by specialized descriptions tends to decline over time: 2011 = 25%, 2012 = 38.8%, 2013 = 12.5%, 2014 = 18.9%, 2015 = 21.6%, 2016 = 29%, 2017 = 31%, 2018 = 47%, 2019 = 25.6%, 2020 = 15.3%, 2021 = 14.3%, 2022 = 13%. This is surprising, as one might have expected auction houses operating in an increasingly competitive online environment to enhance the quality of their offerings by providing more detailed information and stronger quality signals about the lots for sale.

Furthermore, the descriptive statistics do not indicate a significantly different average price between sales in Belgium and those conducted abroad (Belgium: €362 vs. abroad: €380, with median prices of €170 and €106, respectively). Notably, the four main Liège-based auction

[2] This variable was created by successively accumulating all technical information provided in each lot description, ranging from 1 (limited expertise) to 10 (high level of expertise). This continuous variable was then divided into two categories: *GENERAL_EXPERTISE*, aggregating information from 1 to 5, and *SPECIALIZED_EXPERTISE*, from 6 to 10.

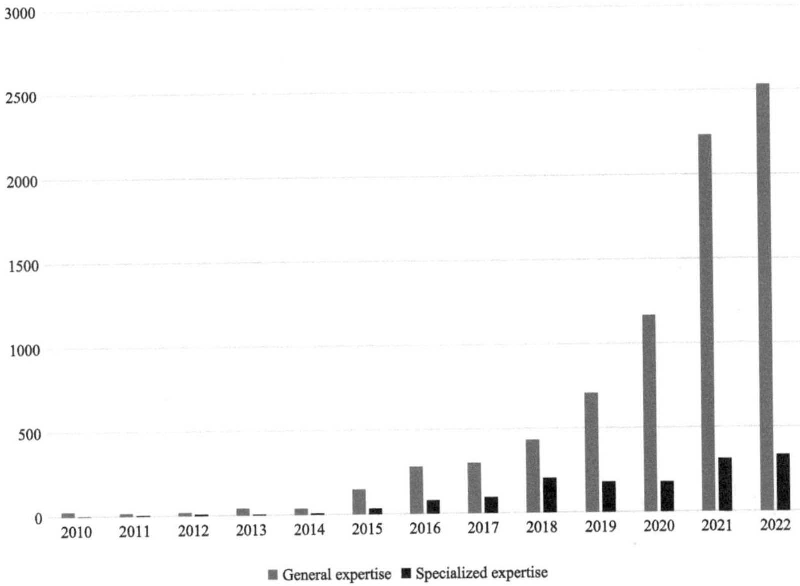

Fig. 2 General versus specialized expertise in Val Saint Lambert auction listings over time. *Source* Author

houses—located just a few kilometers from the original manufactory—predominantly provide only general expertise on these items. The exception is the Hôtel des Ventes Mosan, a historic auction house that offers specialized expertise for approximately 45% of its listings. In Wallonia (the French-speaking area of Belgium), specialized expertise is provided for only around 10% of the lots. This proportion is even lower in Flanders, with the notable exception of Bernaerts Auction House in Antwerp—ranked among the top ten by value—which offers specialized expertise for nearly 40% of its listings. In Brussels, Belgium's main art market hub, the situation is more mixed: several auction houses offer more detailed cataloguing for approximately 20% of their lots.

Figure 3 and Table 1 retrace the market performance of Val Saint Lambert crystalware over the past thirteen years.

As anticipated in interviews with antique dealers, the price index confirms a significant downward trend in the market for Val Saint Lambert crystalware in recent years, with an average annual return of −2.7%.

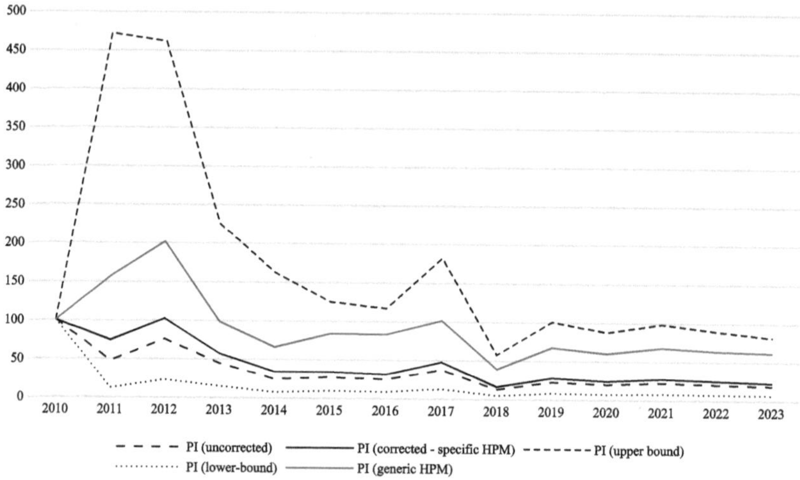

Fig. 3 Val Saint Lambert—Price Index (2010–2023). *Source* Author

Table 1 Val Saint Lambert—Price index value and annual returns. (All years are statistically significant from 2014 onward, except for 2017)

Year-end	*PI (Uncorrected)*	*PI (Corrected—specific HPM)*	*PI (Upper bound)*	*PI (Lower-bound)*	*Return (Corrected PI)*
2010	100.0	100.0	100.0	100.0	–
2011	47.2	73.8	471.4	11.6	−26.2%
2012	75.4	101.5	460.9	22.4	37.5%
2013	44.4	56.7	224.6	14.3	−44.1%
2014	24.2	33.5	161.8	6.9	−41.0%
2015	26.8	33.5	124.6	9.0	0.1%
2016	24.5	30.8	116.2	8.2	−8.0%
2017	37.3	47.2	181.9	12.3	53.2%
2018	12.3	15.4	57.1	4.1	−67.4%
2019	22.2	27.6	100.1	7.6	79.1%
2020	19.4	24.1	87.1	6.7	−12.7%
2021	21.9	27.2	98.1	7.5	12.8%
2022	19.8	24.6	89.1	6.8	−9.2%
2023	18.1	22.5	81.2	6.2	−8.8%

Source Author

Although certain years show positive returns, these gains are insufficient to counterbalance the overall decline. While Val Saint Lambert items remain proportionally more valuable than mass-produced glassware, the growing influx of pieces offered through online sales has likely led to oversupply and market saturation, exerting downward pressure on prices. This trend raises questions about the benefits of increased online visibility from the perspective of owners, for whom value preservation typically outweighs sales volume—unlike dealers, who may prioritize turnover. This situation is particularly concerning for a type of production whose quality is no longer adequately reflected in market prices.

It is, however, important to recall that while auctions of Val Saint Lambert items generally reflect the lower end of the market due to modest price points, there exists considerable differentiation in object quality and value even within this segment. As in the fine art market—where returns vary significantly across high-, mid-, and low-end tiers—further segmentation may help identify the mechanisms underpinning market decline and clarify whether all price levels are equally affected. Following the methodological recommendations of Pesando (1993), Renneboog and Spaenjers (2013), and Vosilov (2015) regarding segmentation by price range, I divided the dataset into quartiles and quantiles. The 90th and 75th percentiles (Q90 and Q75) represent the upper market segments, while the 10th and 25th percentiles (Q10 and Q25) reflect the lower ends. Middle-range values are captured by Q25–50 and Q20–80. Since none of the annual coefficients for the low-end segment were statistically significant, I focus on reporting price indices for the "high-end" and "middle-end" segments of Val Saint Lambert crystalware. Figure 4 illustrates the trends across these sub-segments.

An analysis of the "high-end" and "middle-end" segments of the Val Saint Lambert market reveals some unexpected trends. Contrary to the assumption that finer pieces would outperform average-quality items—particularly in the context of oversupply resulting from the online antiques boom—the data suggests otherwise. Since 2014, the Q90 percentile, representing higher-quality items, has shown a consistently low and flat trajectory, while the middle-end segment has—*ceteris paribus*—exhibited a stronger performance since 2015. Several factors may account for this trend. First, oversupply has likely pushed the finest pieces, such as Art Nouveau and Art Deco, towards high-end auction houses like Sotheby's and Christie's or to specialized dealers. This exclusion introduces a selection bias that may render our "high-end" segment unrepresentative of the actual upper tier of the low-end market. Additionally, concerns over generic attributions, counterfeits, or

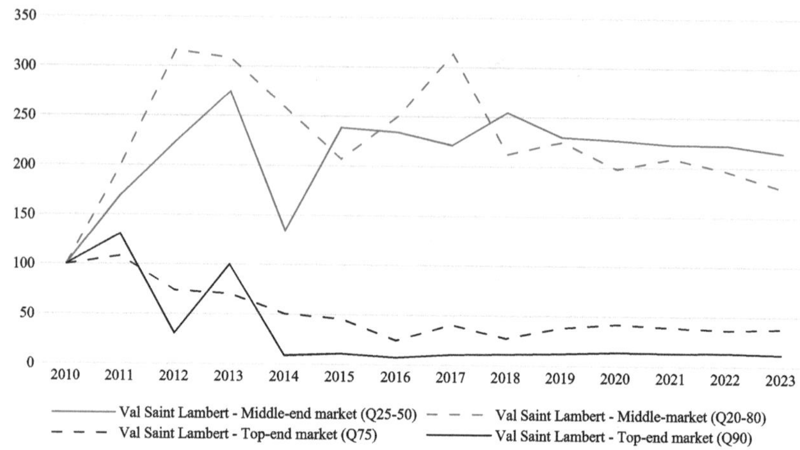

Fig. 4 Val Saint Lambert—Price index (High-end and Middle-end Markets). (All years are statistically significant for Q20-80, from 2012 for Q90 and Q25-50, and from 2016 for Q75). *Source* Author

misidentified crystalware disproportionately affect demand for high-end pieces, while having less impact on average-quality items. Moreover, high-end pieces often require greater care and maintenance to preserve their value, whereas average pieces are less condition-sensitive, making them more appealing to casual buyers. These more affordable and accessible decorative items tend to attract a broader buyer base, particularly among online consumers. This wider demand supports more consistent price growth and presents lower perceived risk, thereby encouraging market participation. Furthermore, high-end antiques are generally more vulnerable to shifting tastes, changing trends, and macroeconomic fluctuations. In contrast, average-quality items—typically purchased for functional purposes—may benefit from more stable demand. This relative stability supports modest but consistent growth, ultimately making average pieces more resilient over time within the auction market, owing to their broader appeal, lower volatility, and dependable demand, as recently observed in the fine art market (Artprice, 2025).

More broadly, this contrasted trend and devaluation—relative to Val Saint Lambert's former status as semi-luxury goods—can be attributed to several interrelated factors. The investment potential of Val Saint Lambert crystalware, long regarded as a hallmark of European craftsmanship, is increasingly challenged by evolving market dynamics that mirror broader shifts in the luxury and decorative arts sectors. One of the most pressing issues is the intensification of competition within the luxury glassware market. The resurgence of legacy brands such as Saint Louis (in collaboration with Dior), alongside the emergence of new market entrants, has eroded Val Saint Lambert's share in both the primary and secondary markets, placing pressure on its pricing power and brand distinctiveness. Globalization further exacerbates this situation. In addition to the surge in online sales, consumers now have access to cheaper glassware produced in lower-cost manufacturing hubs, often replicating the aesthetic qualities of premium crystal without the associated price tag. This trend undermines the comparative advantage once held by artisanal European producers. Shifting consumer tastes present another structural challenge. Whereas previous generations valued ornate, hand-cut crystal as a marker of prestige, contemporary preferences lean toward minimalist and modern designs that diverge sharply from Val Saint Lambert's traditional aesthetic. This transformation in consumer values affects not only primary market sales but also the collectability of vintage and historical items in the secondary market. Modern buyers may no longer assign the same cultural or emotional capital to collectible glassware, resulting in diminished demand and lower resale values (Javerlhiac, 2021). Indeed, auction and resale data reflect this waning enthusiasm, particularly in cases where market saturation has driven prices downward. Macroeconomic factors have further constrained demand for luxury crystal. Economic downturns and inflationary pressures reduce discretionary spending, as consumers increasingly prioritize essential expenditures over non-necessities such as high-end decorative goods—although the pandemic did briefly generate a surge in antiques sales (Radermecker, 2022). Rising living costs particularly affect middle- and upper-middle-class buyers—once key demographics for crystalware—curbing their appetite for such purchases. In this context, brand perception becomes critical. If a heritage brand such as Val Saint Lambert is perceived as static or disconnected from the tastes and values of newer generations, it risks losing its aspirational appeal. A failure to renew product lines, adopt contemporary marketing strategies, or engage effectively with digital platforms can render even the most storied brands obsolete. Finally, and as suggested earlier, the secondary market plays a pivotal role in shaping the investment profile of crystalware. The increasing visibility of price declines in auction houses, antique fairs, and online marketplaces signals a broader devaluation trend. As supply on these platforms grows—whether through estate liquidations or the divestment of aging collectors—oversaturation further depresses value, eroding the perception of crystalware as a stable investment category. These multiple factors thus suggest that while Val Saint Lambert crystalware retains its historical and aesthetic significance, its status as an investment good is being redefined by market forces that privilege adaptability, contemporary relevance, and sustained consumer engagement.

Nevertheless, despite the decline in value, demand for such goods persists and is driven by the search for specific characteristics inherent to crystal glassware. The Hedonic Pricing Model allows for a better understanding of price formation mechanisms and helps identify which attributes contribute to stronger market performance nowadays.

4.2 *Main Determinants of Val Saint Lambert's Market Value*

Table 2 presents the main results of the hedonic regression, with several traditional variables showing expected levels of significance, in line with previous research (for example, positive effects for provenance, rarity, and quality signals (qualitative adjectives), and negative effects for poor condition (e.g., Renneboog & Spaenjers, 2013; Radermecker, 2021; Li et al., 2024)). Within the wide array of crystal items produced by the Val Saint Lambert manufactory, three characteristics emerge as particularly critical in relation to the original investment potential of crystalware and its capacity to retain value over time.

Functionality

As expected, the typology of objects—each associated with a specific function—shows distinct price differentials when using the generic category "other objects" as the baseline. Carafes with glassware sets and bowls achieve significantly higher prices, while items such as candy dishes, ashtrays, lighting fixtures, paperweights, and miscellaneous objects do not. Notably, the former group consists of the most common and stereotypical items, whereas the latter includes objects that are less representative of Val Saint Lambert's core production. Although both groups possess direct utilitarian value, the second category is also more eclectic and less aligned with contemporary usage (e.g., drinking versus smoking, storing paper, or serving candy). The loss of original function likely contributes to the market devaluation of these items, even though, historically, owning such objects of high sophistication was a clear marker of refined lifestyle.

Table 2 Results of the hedonic regression (Preferred model)

Variable (Dependent variable = log real price 2023)	*Coefficient*	*Standard error*
FUNCTIONAlITY		
Direct utility—Object type		
Bonbonnière (candy dish)	−0.304**	0.118
Carafe	−0.0719	0.0537
Carafe with glasses	0.519***	0.0674
Ashtray	−0.892***	0.119
Bowl	0.300***	0.0435
Lamp	−0.294**	0.134
Centerpiece	0.0425	0.202
Paperweight	−0.280***	0.0897
Vase	0.0164	0.0375
Glasses	0.337***	0.0440
Mixed objects	−0.158***	0.0527
Other objects	Baseline	Baseline
Decorative value		
Style		
Art nouveau	0.376***	0.109
Art déco	0.0727*	0.0418
Modernist	0.216	0.415
Style not mentioned	Baseline	Baseline
Type		
Ball-shaped	0.0167	0.137
Soliflore	−0.195**	0.0932
On-foot	0.152**	0.0688
Type not mentioned	Baseline	Baseline
Shape		
Circular/conical/cylindrical/ovoid	0.258**	0.126
Hexagonal	0.0832	0.112
Octogonal	0.178	0.132
Other shapes	0.00625	0.314
Shape not mentioned	Baseline	Baseline
Spiral	−0.107	0.132
Triangular	−0.463*	0.270
Tulip	−0.0456	0.0948
Model		
Jupiter	0.886***	0.0790
Nestor	0.372***	0.0850
Poitiers	0.424	0.277
Yale	0.513***	0.0797

(continued)

Table 2 (continued)

Variable (Dependent variable = log real price 2023)	*Coefficient*	*Standard error*
Model mentioned	0.276***	0.0393
Model not mentioned	Baseline	Baseline
Decoration		
Frieze	0.343***	0.107
Patterns	0.182**	0.0802
Decoration mentioned	0.380***	0.0448
Decoration not mentioned	Baseline	Baseline
Cristal color		
Blue (and derivatives)	0.0527	0.0395
Brown	0.166	0.156
Yellow (and derivatives)	−0.0886	0.186
Multicolored	0.264***	0.0503
Black	−0.0935	0.204
Orange	−0.0624	0.161
Pink (and derivatives)	−0.169*	0.0931
Red (and derivatives)	−0.106***	0.0383
Green (and derivatives)	0.0735*	0.0382
Purple (and derivatives)	−0.00904	0.0686
Color not mentioned in the lot note	Baseline	Baseline
CRYSTAL'S CHARACTERISTICS		
Cristal explicit mention		
Cristal specified in the lot note	0.0345	0.0307
Cristal type		
White crystal	0.0633	0.110
Clear crystal	−0.214***	0.0601
Transparent/translucent/colorless	−0.0318	0.0508
Cristal type not mentioned	Baseline	Baseline
Cristal texture		
Thick crystal	0.346	0.230
Cristal weight		
0 to 1,000 g	−0.0788	0.259
1000 to 5,000 g	0.338	0.250
Over 5,000 g	0.693**	0.285
Weight not mentioned	Baseline	Baseline
Mix glassware		
Baccarat	−0.0114	0.297
Bohème	−0.240	0.304
Daum	−0.268	0.275
Lalique	0.142	0.373

(continued)

Table 2 (continued)

Variable (Dependent variable = log real price 2023)	*Coefficient*	*Standard error*
Murano	−0.439*	0.261
On y joint	−0.297	0.222
Saint Louis	–	–
Val Saint Lambert (alone)	Baseline	Baseline
TECHNIQUE		
Technique A		
Engraved	0.0663	0.0817
Cut/Hand cut	0.192***	0.0346
Engraved/Cut and double-layered	0.0892**	0.0389
Double layered/multilayer	0.113**	0.0445
Technique A not mentioned	Baseline	Baseline
Technique Abis (more specific)		
Point cutting	−0.0238	0.0779
Rich cutting	0.156	0.117
American-style cutting	−0.149	0.198
Wheel cutting	0.316*	0.187
Technique Abis not mentioned	Baseline	Baseline
Technique B		
Cast crystal	−0.357**	0.182
Molded crystal	−0.262***	0.0953
Pressed crystal	−0.286	0.203
Mouth-blown crystal	0.0249	0.121
Hand-pulled crystal	−0.232	0.522
Hot-stretched crystal	−0.340***	0.0735
Technique B not mentioned	Baseline	Baseline
Technique C		
Frosted/iridescent/matter crystal	0.344***	0.111
Tinted crystal	−0.141	0.0911
Gold or silver inclusion	−0.0583	0.0919
Technique C not mentioned	Baseline	Baseline
Specific tools		
Acid-etched	0.556***	0.0877
Fluogravure	1.641***	0.242
Galvanoplasty	−0.0970	0.101
Sandblasting	0.945***	0.267
Specific tools not mentioned	Baseline	Baseline

(continued)

Table 2 (continued)

Variable (Dependent variable = log real price 2023)	*Coefficient*	*Standard error*
MATERIAL INTEGRITY		
Condition scale	−0.0358**	0.0176
Chips/cracks/missing elements	−0.113***	0.0395
AUTHENTICITY		
Origins		
Belgium	−0.0928	0.118
Seraing	0.0833	0.134
Origins not mentioned	Baseline	Baseline
Designer's name		
Alfred Collard	0.245	0.262
C. Genard	−0.875***	0.221
R. Carrera	0.662**	0.301
Charles Graffart	−0.0347	0.0759
Hubert Lega	−0.0289	0.194
L. Jacobs	–	–
Joseph Simon	0.755***	0.0695
Louis Leloup	0.628***	0.120
René Delvenne	−0.816**	0.338
René Julien	−0.556***	0.138
Camille Renard	0.0614	0.234
Hubert Fouarge	0.256	0.161
Léon Ledru	0.218*	0.120
Samuel Herman	0.117	0.0916
Other designers	−0.824	0.626
No designers	Baseline	Baseline
Attribution qualifiers		
Attribution qualifier	−0.115	0.0814
Intrinsic marks of authenticity		
VSL/monogram/mark	0.0280	0.140
Stamp	0.165	0.280
Signature	−0.0815	0.118
No intrinsic marks of authenticity	Baseline	Baseline
Serial number mention	0.401***	0.102
Extrinsic marks of authenticity		
Sticker/label	0.135**	0.064
Original box	0.295	0.214
No extrinsinc marks of authenticity	baseline	baseline

(continued)

Table 2 (continued)

Variable (Dependent variable = log real price 2023)	*Coefficient*	*Standard error*
Date		
Year	0.203***	0.034
Century	0.0151	0.097
No date	Baseline	Baseline
QUALITY		
Provenance		
Provenance mentioned	0.351**	0.143
Adjective		
Beautiful	0.223**	0.0925
Important	0.976***	0.121
Magnificient/superb/Exceptional	1.088***	0.219
Unique piece (UP)	0.199	0.133
Of quality	0.0752	0.203
Rare/very rare	0.634***	0.114
No adjective	Baseline	Baseline
CONTEXT OF THE SALE		
Type of auction		
Online	−0.514***	0.0510
Bilingual lot notes		
Multiple languages	0.0754	0.0724
Location		
Belgium	−0.914	1.088
Auction houses		
Anténor (Brussels)	1.803*	1.070
Art Auction (Brussels)	0.449	1.047
Asté (Liège)	0.180	1.046
Bernaerts (Antwerpen)	1.574	1.071
Béguinages (Brussels)	0.864	1.069
Campo and Campo (Antwerpen)	0.676	1.056
Carlo Bonte (Bruges)	1.689	1.050
Cnock (Knokke)	0.866	1.052
Coronari Auctions (Gent)	1.329	1.070
De Ruiter (Klaaswaal, Neth)	−0.432	0.377
Debaveye (Harelbeke)	1.116	1.051
Dewit Auction (Oostend)	0.0684	1.046
Elysée (Liège)	0.957	1.045
FW Auction (Namur)	−0.292	1.051
Flanders Auctions (Wingene)	1.002	1.046
Galerie Athena (Brussels)	1.140	1.047

(continued)

Table 2 (continued)

Variable (Dependent variable = log real price 2023)	*Coefficient*	*Standard error*
Galerie Moderne (Brussels)	0.942	1.046
Germany-based auction houses	−0.411	0.348
Goldfield (Luxemburg)	−0.490	0.365
Haynault (Brussels)	1.100	1.052
Horta (Brussels)	2.425**	1.046
Hôtel Drouot (Paris)	−0.329	0.331
Italy-based auction houses	0.338	0.368
Kanerz Art (Luxemburg)	−1.029***	0.324
La Régence (Namur)	0.138	1.047
Legros (Verviers)	0.796	1.046
Lhomme (Liège)	0.955	1.071
Lux-Auction (Luxemburg)	−0.513	0.352
Légia (Hannut)	0.552	1.046
MJV Soudant (Gerpinnes)	1.387	1.046
Maison Jules (Gent)	1.068	1.045
Millon (Brussels)	0.501	1.055
MonsAntic (Mons)	0.196	1.048
Mont de Piété (Brussels)	0.391	1.047
Mosan (Liège)	1.025	1.052
Paris-based auction houses	−0.642*	0.332
Phoenix Auction (Wavre)	0.400	1.051
Pierre Bergé and Associés (Brussels)	2.649**	1.088
Regional french auction houses	−0.802**	0.313
Rops (Namur)	1.638	1.051
Salle de ventes ABC (Brussels)	0.759	1.048
Spain-based auction houses	0.100	0.460
Stanley (Diegem)	0.569	1.108
Uccle St Job (Brussels)	−0.316	0.325
Vanderkindere (Brussels)	1.572	1.046
Other auction houses	Baseline	Baseline
Year of the sale		
2010	Baseline	Baseline
2011	−0.751	0.946
2012	−0.283	0.772
2013	−0.813	0.702
2014	−1.418*	0.804
2015	−1.318**	0.670
2016	−1.406**	0.677
2017	−0.987	0.688
2018	−2.095***	0.669

(continued)

Table 2 (continued)

Variable (Dependent variable = log real price 2023)	*Coefficient*	*Standard error*
2019	−1.505**	0.658
2020	−1.639**	0.656
2021	−1.518**	0.655
2022	−1.615**	0.655
2023 (January-April)	−1.707***	0.655
Constant	6.456***	0.724
Observations	5.757	
R-squared	0.513	
Adj—R-squared	0.497	

Robust standard errors in column 2
*** $p < 0.01$, ** $p < 0.05$, * $p < 0.1$
Source Author

Scarcity Through Technical Sophistication
Several techniques associated with crystal glassmaking appear to be significant determinants of value. Findings related to TECH_A suggest that the more elaborate the engraving and cutting processes, the higher the resulting prices—an effect already observed in historical Val Saint Lambert catalogs. These combined techniques reflect a degree of craftsmanship and sophistication that remains particularly appreciated by buyers. However, the provision of more granular information, such as the precise type of engraving, generally does not result in substantial price differentials, with the exception of wheel-cut crystal, which commands a premium. This may indicate that the technical terminology used to describe such processes does not consistently resonate with buyers and is instead interpreted through more immediately visible features. TECH_B encompasses a range of glassworking methods. Interestingly, although mouth-blown crystal implies significant artisanal labor, it does not emerge as a statistically significant price determinant. By contrast, more industrial production techniques—such as cast or molded crystal—are associated with lower valuations, likely reflecting perceptions of mass production and diminished artisanal value. TECH_C indicates that decorative surface treatments—such as iridescent and frosted finishes—are particularly appreciated by buyers. Similarly, TECH_D, which includes distinctive methods such as fluogravure, acid etching, and sandblasting, also positively

influences price, likely due to their association with iconic Val Saint Lambert production styles and recognizable aesthetic signatures. Overall, these findings suggest that items featuring a higher degree of technical sophistication—reflecting more intensive production efforts—continue to convey added value compared to those lacking such attributes. Likewise, the inclusion of technique-related descriptors in auction lot notes can significantly affect valuation. These details not only signal greater expertise on the part of the auction house but also help differentiate individual pieces within an increasingly saturated market.

Brand Strength Through Authenticity

Just as brand names significantly influence value in the fine art market (Schroeder, 2005), they also play a crucial role in the decorative arts, where manufactory brand recognition can be a key determinant of price, especially when reinforced by other brands such as a designer's name. Val Saint Lambert, as a manufactory brand, enjoys a certain degree of recognition and competes directly with other renowned crystal producers. However, within its broad production, several characteristics serve to reinforce—or in some cases, dilute—the strength of this original brand identity.

Although the explicit mention of national origin does not significantly affect pricing (likely due to the strong association of Val Saint Lambert with Belgium), the inclusion of the designer's name proves to be an important value driver. Historically, the manufactory collaborated with numerous artists and designers who contributed to the Seraing-based production center, and many of these contributors are identifiable by name. Designers such as Louis Leloup (1929–2025) and Joseph Simon (1874–1960) appear particularly influential, with their works commanding premium prices. In contrast, some other names are associated with negative price effects—possibly reflecting styles that are no longer in vogue or widely available items that lack exclusivity. Interestingly, attribution qualifiers which typically affect price significantly in the fine arts by casting doubt on authorship, do not appear to have a statistically significant impact in this context (Renneboog & Spaenjers, 2013; Radermecker, 2021). While some uncertainty remains around the attribution of certain pieces (especially due to visual similarities with works from other decorative arts centers), this appears to have a limited effect on price. This may be due to the relatively lower overall value of these goods, which entails less perceived risk from a buyer's perspective. The ability of auction houses to temporally situate objects also contributes positively to valuation, particularly when an approximate date of production is provided, rather than vague references to a general era or century. As demonstrated by Radermecker (2019), precision in information supply is particularly valuable in markets dealing with indeterminate goods. Two categories of authenticity criteria can also be distinguished: intrinsic and extrinsic. Intrinsic indicators—such as signatures, marks, and monograms—do not appear to be statistically significant price determinants, although their effect may be subsumed under the designer variable (as signatures are often used to confirm attribution). The common Val Saint Lambert monogram (VSL) is so frequently encountered that it adds little additional value. However, limited edition production with serial numbering does appear to enhance desirability, suggesting that scarcity remains a relevant driver of price—echoing findings in the market for prints and multiples (Lazzaro, 2006). Extrinsic indicators of authenticity, such as a manufacturer's sticker affixed to the object or the presence of the original box, present mixed effects. The presence of a sticker appears to be a positive value indicator, while the original box does not significantly influence price—unlike in other market segments such as antique toys, where packaging is often a decisive factor.

From a stylistic perspective, older designs such as Art Nouveau and Art Deco command higher average prices. These highly recognizable styles are linked to emblematic visual features that contributed to the success of the manufactory (Kremer & Pluymaekers, 2007). Objects characterized by round, organic shapes—less angular and rigid than typical crystal—tend to fetch higher prices, as do footed items, which often carry connotations of elegance and prestige. Model identification also enhances valuation, as it reflects a deeper level of expertise. Certain iconic designs—such as the *Jupiter* vase or the *Nestor* series of glassware—are particularly valued for their clear stylistic identity and exemplary craftsmanship, marking them as standout pieces within Val Saint Lambert's production (Philippe, 1974).

5 Conclusion

In the vein of prior research examining the investment potential of fine art and collectibles (e.g., Graeser, 1993; Graddy & Margolis, 2011; Dimson & Spaenjers, 2014), this chapter has explored the notion of investment in the low-end art market by investigating the recent market reception of "semi-luxury" goods traditionally regarded as domestic assets. Using Val Saint Lambert crystalware as a case study, the analysis has demonstrated that the hedonic pricing model can be methodologically applied to this segment—provided appropriate adjustments in model specification—and has evidenced the significant decline in value experienced by these once highly esteemed goods. Among the contributing factors, this decline can be attributed to evolving market dynamics, including increased competition from multinational companies specializing in home furnishings and accessories, online market saturation, and shifting tastes and lifestyles among younger generations (Javerlhiac, 2021). In addition to conventional price determinants such as quality and scarcity (Renneboog & Spaenjers, 2013; Li et al., 2024), items that continue to perform better on average are those that retain functional utility, demonstrate technical craftsmanship in crystal-making, and are associated with notable designers or established art movements (e.g., Art Nouveau, Art Deco). While the extent of this decline requires further investigation across other categories of antique semi-luxury goods—such as "brown" furniture, Limoges or Sèvres porcelain, and silverware sets—the findings already raise important questions from an investment perspective. Many of these objects now command low market value or suffer from illiquidity, rendering them difficult to sell, despite the significant expenditures once made by previous upper-middle-class generations. The reluctance of younger generations to retain such inherited items—or to resell for price levels that fail to properly reflect their quality—has led to a structural mismatch between supply and demand, ultimately diminishing the long-term value of these family assets.

In other words, the investment dimension cannot be ignored when analyzing the low ends of the art market, which include the home decor market (sub-segment 1), regardless of the modest monetary value of the goods at time *t*. Similar behavioral mechanisms may operate even in lower price contexts. Future research should explore these dynamics more deeply, both quantitatively and qualitatively, leveraging the growing availability of sales data and investigating purchasing behaviors through an investment lens—one that includes not only financial returns but also human and cultural capital. This chapter also encourages further empirical inquiry into these markets by ideally including historical archival sources to provide more longitudinal perspectives on patterns of appreciation or depreciation in value. Although not examined in detail here, it is worth noting that Val Saint Lambert's historical sales catalogs—dating back to the nineteenth century—display a structure that remarkably resembles the logic of hedonic pricing frameworks. These catalogs assign progressively increasing prices to similar items based on specific characteristics (e.g., a crystal vase without color/with color/with mechanical engraving/with manual engraving). Such documents represent a rich yet underexplored resource for cultural economists and economic historians interested in price formation mechanisms and export strategies among manufacturers operating at the intersection of commodity, art, and craft. Finally, because semi-luxury goods were mass-produced and now encompass hundreds or even thousands of distinct models traded across numerous online sales platforms, issues related to the reliability and granularity of information also become increasingly important. The use of machine learning and AI-generated information to improve data classification and interpretation presents a promising avenue for enhancing existing models and better predicting the long-term evolution of these market segments.

Funding This research is part of the project *MOOVA—Making Old Objects Valuable Again. The Cultural, Economic Challenges and Sustainability Opportunities of Antiques in the Twenty-first Century*, funded by the European Research Council (ERC). ERC Starting Grant 2022 (Horizon Europe—HORIZON). Reference number: 101075828.

Appendix Section

Appendix 1. HPM Specification

Variables Related to Functionality (Direct Utility and Decorative Value)

- *DIRECT UTILITY—OBJECT TYPE* (categorical variables): candy dish (*bonbonnière*), carafe, carafe and glasses (*carafe* and *verres*), ashtray (*cendrier*), bowl (*coupe*), lighting (*lampe*), center piece (*milieu de table*), paper weight (*presse-papier*), vase, glasses (*verres*), mix of objects, other objects (base line).

Decorative Value

- *STYLE* (categorical variables): art nouveau, art déco, moderniste, style not mentioned (base line);

- *SHAPEa* (categorical variables): ball (*boule*), single-flower shape (*soliflore*), on-foot (*sur pied*), shapea not mentioned (base line);
- *SHAPEb* (categorical variables): Circular/conical/cylindrical/ovoid, hexagonal, octogonal, twisted, tulipe-shaped, triangular, other shapesb, shapeb not mentioned;
- *MODEL* (categorical variables): Jupiter, Nestor, Poitiers, Yale, model mentioned, model not mentioned (baseline);
- *COLORS* (categorical variables): blue (and derivatives), brown, yellow (and derivatives), multicolors, black, orange, pink (and derivatives), red (and derivatives), green (and derivatives), purple (and derivatives), colors not mentioned in the lot note (baseline);
- *DECORATION* (categorical variables): frieze, patterns (*motifs*), decoration mentioned, decoration not mentioned (baseline).

Variables Related to Crystal Characteristics

- *CRYSTAL* (1 if specifically mentioned in the description of the lot, 0 otherwise);
- *HEIGHT* (categorical variables): not mentioned (baseline), upto100 mm between 100 and 200 mm, between 200_500 mm, above 500 mm);[3]
- *WEIGHT* (categorical variables): 0_to_1000 g, 1000_5000 g, more_than_5000 g, weight not mentioned (baseline);
- *CRYSTAL FEATURES* (categorical variables): (lead cristal (*cristal clair*), white crystal, translucid/transparent/colorless crystal), crystal feature not mentioned (baseline);
- *CRYSTAL TEXTURE* (1 if mentioned as thick crystal (*cristal épais*), 0 otherwise);
- *MIX GLASSWARE* (categorical variables): Baccarat, Bohème, Daum, Lalique, Murano, Saint Louis, *on y joint*, Val saint Lambert alone (baseline).

[3] Due to the complexity of measuring all lot items, certain lot descriptions do not provide the dimension or weight of the items. To avoid the loss of data, I created categorical variables instead of a continuous variable.

Variables Related to Techniques

- *TECH_A* (categorical variables): engraved (*gravé*), cut/hand cut (*taillé/taillé main*), engraved/cut and overlaid (*gravé/taillé et double*), overlaid/multilayered (*doublé/multicouche*), technique A not mentioned (baseline);
- *TECH_Ab* is (categorical variables): point cutting (*taille à la pointe*), rich cutting (*taille riche*), american cutting (*taille à l'américaine*), wheel cutting (*taille à la roue*), technique Ab not mentioned (baseline);
- *TECH_B* (categorical variables): cast crystal (*cristal coulé*), molded crystal (*cristal moulé*), pressed crystal (*cristal pressé*), mouth-blown crystal (*cristal soufflé à la bouche*), pincered crystal (*cristal travaillé à la pince*), hot-streched crystal (*cristal étiré à chaud*), Technique B not mentioned (baseline);
- *TECH_C* (categorical variables): frosted/iridescent crystal (*cristal dépoli, givré*), irisé, tinted crystal (*cristal teinté*), gold or silver inclusion (*inclusion d'or or d'argent*), technique C not mentioned (baseline);
- *TECH_D* (categorical variables): acid etched (*dégagé à l'acide*), fluogravure, electroplating (*galvanoplastie*), *sandblasting* (jet de sable), technique D not mentioned (baseline).

Variables Related to Material Integrity

- *CONDITION* (ordinal variable, using a scale of damages, running from minor to major damages);
- *ACCIDENTS/CHIPS/NICKS* (*accident, éclats, égrenures*) (1 if those specific damages are mentioned, 0 otherwise).

Variables related to authenticity

- *ORIGINS* (1 if the Belgian or Seraing origins are explicitly mentioned, 0 otherwise);
- *DESIGNERS* (categorical variables): Charles Graffart, Alfred Genard, Joseph Simon, René Julien, Louis Leloup, Léon Ledru, René Delvenne, Samuel Herman, Camille Renard, Hubert Fouarge, Hubert Lega, designer not mentioned (baseline);

- *AUTHENTICITY_INTRINSIC* (categorical variables): signed, monogram, mark, number, no intrinsic authenticity indicator mentioned (baseline);
- *AUTHENTICITY_EXTRINSIC* (categorical variables): stickers, box, no extrinsic authenticity indicator mentioned (baseline);
- *DATE* (categorical variables): years, epoch, date not mentioned (baseline)
- *ATTRIBUTIONS* (categorical variables): attributed to, studio/workshop of, style of, Val Saint Lambert (baseline), probably/possibly.

Variables Related to Quality

- *PROVENANCE* (1 if provenance information is provided, 0 otherwise);
- *ADJECTIVE* (categorical variables): beautiful (*beau, belle*), important, gorgeous/superb/exceptional, unique piece (*PU-pièce unique*), rare/very rare, quality, no adjective (baseline).

Variables Related to the Context of the Sale

These variables are common to those traditionally used to analyze the market for fine arts.

- *SALE_TYPE* (1 if online, 0 if live). We suspect online auction to be the place where items of lower value are traded;
- *BILINGUAL_NOTES* (1 if the description is in multiple language, 0 otherwise);
- *BELGIUM* (1 if sold in Belgium, 0 otherwise). This variable aims to control for a possible home biais (Velthuis & Baia Curioni, 2015);
- *AUCTION HOUSES* (categorical variables): Anténor (Brussels); Art Auction (Brussels); Asté (Liège); Bernaerts (Antwerpen); Bonhams-Cornette de Saint Cyr (Brussels); Béguinages (Brussels); Campo and Campo (Antwerpen); Carlo Bonte (Bruges); Cnock (Knokke); Coronari Auctions (Gent); De Ruiter (Klaaswaal, Neth); De Ruiter (Klaaswaal, Neth); Debaveye (Harelbeke); Dewit Auction (Oostend); Elysée (Liège); FW Auction (Namur); FW Auction (Namur); Flanders

Auctions (Wingene); Galerie Athena (Brussels); Galerie Moderne (Brussels); Germany-based auction houses; Goldfield (Luxemburg); Haynault (Brussels); Horta (Brussels); Hôtel Drouot (Paris); Italy-based auction houses; Kanerz Art (Luxemburg); La Régence (Namur); Legros (Verviers); Lhomme (Liège); Lux-Auction (Luxemburg); Légia (Hannut); MJV Soudant (Gerpinnes); Maison Jules (Gent); Millon (Brussels); MonsAntic (Mons); Mont de Piété (Brussels); Mosan (Liège); Paris-based auction houses; Phoenix Auction (Wavre); Pierre Bergé and Associés (Brussels); Regional french auction houses; Rob Michiels (Bruges); Rops (Namur); Salle de ventes ABC (Brussels); Spain-based auction houses; Stanley (Diegem); Uccle St Job (Brussels); Vanderkindere (Brussels); Venduehuis Dickaut (Maastricht, Neth), other auction houses (baseline).

- *YEARS* (categorical variables from 2010 to 2023 (January-March).

References

Artprice (2025). *The global art market report in 2024.* Lyon.

Baumol, W. J. (1986). Unnatural value: Or art investment as floating-crap game. *The American Economic Review, 76*(2), 10–14.

Bauwens, L., & Ginsburgh, V. (2000). Art experts and auction: Are pre-sale estimates unbiased and fully informative? *Recherches Économiques de Louvain/ Louvain Economic Review, 66*(2), 131–144.

Bourdieu, P. (1984). *A social critique of the judgement of taste.* Cambridge, MA.

Catalog (1972). *Price list 1972.* Seraing: Cristalleries Val Saint Lambert.

Chevalier, A., Delande, J.-P., Laurent, I., Toussaint, J., & Wallonie-Bruxelles, C. (1999). *L'aventure du cristal et du verre en Wallonie.* Renaissance du Livre.

Communian, R., & England, L. (2019). Creative clusters and the evolution of knowledge and skills: From industrial to creative glassmaking. *Geoforum, 99*, 238–247.

Cummings, K. (2002). *A history of glassforming.* A & C Black.

De Pessemier, C. (1998). Les cristalleries du Val-Saint-Lambert: Étude de la série "Luxval" (Mémoire de licence, Département d'art et archéologie. Université libre de Bruxelles).

Dimson, E., Rousseau, P. L., & Spaenjers, C. (2015). The price of wine. *Journal of Financial Economics, 118*(2), 431–449.

Dimson, E., & Spaenjers, C. (2011). Ex post: The investment performance of collectible stamps. *Journal of Financial Economics, 100*(2), 443–458.

Dimson, E., & Spaenjers, C. (2014). Investing in emotional assets. *Financial Analysts Journal, 70*(2), 20–25.
Draper, P., Thornton, R., & Vickers, D. (2013). Auctions, market efficiency, and the trade in second-hand and antique silver. *Economics Letters, 162*, 45–48.
Fontaine-Hodiamont, C. (Ed.). (2010). *D'Ennion au Val Saint Lambert: Le verre soufflé-moulé* (Vol. 5, Scientia Artis). Institut Royal du Patrimoine Artistique.
Gerlis, M. M. (2014). *Art as an investment?: A survey of comparative assets.* Ashgate Publishing, Ltd.
Ginsburgh, V., Mei, J., & Moses, M. (2006). The computation of price indices In V. Ginsburgh & D. Throsby (Eds.), *Handbook of the economics of art and culture* (Vol. 1, pp. 947–979). Elsevier.
Giusti, L., & Polo, M. C. (2002). A review of the glass-making industry of Murano (Venice, Italy) under an environmental perspective. *Environmental Management and Health, 13*(1), 40–54. https://doi.org/10.1108/09566160210417813
Goetzmann, W. N. (1993). Accounting for taste: Art and the financial markets over three centuries. *American Economic Review, 83*(5), 1370–1376.
Graddy, K., & Margolis, P. E. (2011). Fiddling with value: Violins as an investment? *Economic Inquiry, 49*(4), 1083–1097.
Graeser, P. (1993). Rate of return to investment in American antique furniture. *Southern Economic Journal*, 817–821.
Heyvaert, H. (1978). Le cas des Cristalleries du Val Saint Lambert. In A. -M. Kumps, P. Grand-Jean, & R. Wtterwulghe (Eds.), *Entreprises en difficulté et initiative publique* (pp. 159–164). Presses universitaires Saint-Louis.
Javerlhiac, S. (2021). *Être antiquaire.* Presses de l'Université Laval.
Kremer, C., & Pluymaekers, A. (2007). *Val Saint Lambert: 180 ans de savoir-faire et de création.* La Renaissance du Livre/Versant Sud.
Kumar, A., Paul, J., & Unnithan, A. B. (2020). 'Masstige'marketing: A review, synthesis and research agenda. *Journal of Business Research, 113*, 384–398.
Lancaster, K. (1966). A new approach to consumer theory. *Journal of Political Economy, 74*(2), 132–157.
Lazzaro, E. (2006). Assessing quality in cultural goods: The hedonic value of originality in Rembrandt's prints. *Journal of Cultural Economics, 30*, 15–40.
Li, Y., Ma, X., & Renneboog, L. (2024). In art we trust. *Management Science, 70*(1), 98–127.
Mandel, B. R. (2009). Art as an investment and conspicuous consumption good. *American Economic Review, 99*(4), 1653–1663.
Mei, J., & Moses, M. (2005). Vested interest and biased price estimates: Evidence from an auction market. *The Journal of Finance, 60*(5), 2409–2435.
Nelsen, P. (1970). The democratization of the antique: Meanings of antiques and dealers' perceptions of customers. *The Sociological Review, 18*(3), 407–419.

Oosterlinck, K. (2025). Art as an asset class and as a component of a financial portfolio. In I. Robertson, D. Chong, & L. U. Afonso (Eds.), *Global art markets: History and current trends* (pp. 295–306). Taylor & Francis.

Page, J. -A. (2004). *Beyond venice: Glass in venetian style, 1500–1750*. Hudson Hills Press.

Pesando, J. E. (1993). Art as an investment: The market for modern prints. *American Economic Review*, 1075–1089.

Philippe, J. (1974). *Le Val Saint Lambert: Ses cristalleries et l'art du verre en Belgique* (2nd ed.). Librairie Halbart.

Radermecker, A. S. (2021). *Anonymous art at auction: The reception of early Flemish paintings in the Western art market (1946–2015)*, Vol. 11.

Radermecker, A. S. (2022). Selling lowbrow art and cultural goods in times of pandemic: The case of a provincial art market. *International Journal of Cultural Property, 29*(3), 283–310.

Radermecker, A. S. V. (2019). Artworks without names: An insight into the market for anonymous paintings. *Journal of Cultural Economics, 43*(3), 443–483.

Radermecker, A. S. V., & Brosens, K. (2023). Valuing European tapestry: From riches to rags. *Journal of Cultural Economics, 47*(3), 359–406.

Renneboog, L., & Spaenjers, C. (2012). Hard assets: The returns on rare diamonds and gems. *Finance Research Letters, 9*(4), 220–230.

Renneboog, L., & Spaenjers, C. (2013). Buying beauty: On prices and returns in the art market. *Management Science, 59*(1), 36–53.

Schroeder, J. E. (2005). The artist and the brand. *European Journal of Marketing, 39*(11/12), 1291–1305. https://doi.org/10.1108/03090560510623325

Shoop, F. (2004). *Buying and selling antiques: Insider knowledge and trade tips to help you make money from your hobby* (2nd ed.). Little, Brown Book Group.

Shoop, F. (2011). *How to deal in antiques* (5th ed.). Robinson Non-Fiction.

Silverstein, M. J., & Fiske, N. (2003). Luxury for the masses. *Harvard Business Review, 81*(4), 48–59.

Stein, J. P. (1977). The monetary appreciation of paintings. *Journal of Political Economy, 85*(5).

Thiry, M. (1987). *De l'art déco aux années cinquante: Le verre et le cristal belges dans le monde*. Rotary Club de Charleroi-Ouest.

Thiry, M. (1990). *Val Saint-Lambert: Art & design 1880–1990*. Remo Zandoná.

Toso, G. (2006). *Murano: A history of glass* (First ed.). Arsenale Editrice.

Triplett, J. (2004). *Handbook on hedonic indexes and quality adjustments in price indexes*. OECD Publishing.

Ursprung, H. W. (2021). Financial returns to collecting rare political economy books. *European Journal of Political Economy, 70*, 102139.

Velthuis, O., & Curioni, S. B. (Eds.). (2015). *Cosmopolitan canvases: The globalization of markets for contemporary art*. Oxford University Press.

Vosilov, R. (2015). Sculpture as an alternative investment: An analysis of price dynamics between sculpture and equity and bond markets. *The Journal of Alternative Investments*, 20–46.

Wu, L. T. (2014). *Financial returns and price determinants in the twentieth-century design market: Evidence from Sotheby's New York, 2007–2013 & 1966–2013*. Sotheby's Institute of Art.

PART II

Between Art, Craft, Luxury, Consumer Goods, and Junk

Flea Markets From a Historical Perspective and Their Contemporary Challenges: The Example of St. Ouen

Darius A. Spieth

1 Introduction

"One person regrets their career choice, or the wealth they did not gain; another one thinks of failed loves or travels not undertaken; still others of all of the above. Every human—even those with lives so filled with events as Molière or Lenin—keeps in their past some empty spot where precious memories could have found their place, and, in this way, I have my regrets, too. One of which, a modest one but one that is still no less burning, is to not have spent more time at Saint Ouen, in this land of enchantment which is called the *marché aux puces* (Clair, 1951)".

As paradigmatic low-end exchanges for art and antiques, flea markets have a way of lingering in the shadows of other, seemingly more important things. The second half of the twentieth century was their "golden age"; the twenty-first century, due to changes in mentalities and the pressures of digitization, that of their decline. The proliferation of flea markets in advanced consumer economies during the last quarter of the twentieth century should not obscure the fact that, by this time, they had already existed for about a century. The history of flea markets, especially from

D. A. Spieth (✉)
Louisiana State University, Baton Rouge, USA
e-mail: dspieth@lsu.edu

A.-S. V. Radermecker (ed.), *Low-End Markets for Art and Cultural Goods*,
Cultural Economics & the Creative Economy,
https://doi.org/10.1007/978-3-032-27566-0_5

a macro-economic and trans-national perspective, remains largely to be written, but even more topical studies on the subject are apt to reveal baffling attitudinal shifts to material culture.

The very first flea markets seem to have come into existence in the 1870s and 1880s in Paris and Brussels, respectively. The one in Brussels, on the Place du Jeu de Balle, is documented as early as 1873 (Mardaga, 1995), but it remains a much smaller and less consequential venue than that at St. Ouen, situated just beyond the city limits of Paris, which would eventually occupy permanently several city blocks. Both markets, however, have their origins in the nineteenth-century recycling business. The case of St. Ouen is particularly intriguing because its evolution is tied up with the urban renewal of Paris since the 1850s, which is also known as Haussmannization.

Georges-Eugène Haussmann became Prefect of the Seine (i.e., governor of Paris) in 1853. He was appointed by Emperor Napoleon III, who famously tasked him with building "modern" Paris. Large parts of "old" Paris, the city of winding, medieval streets without sewers or running water, were demolished in the process, as were those areas of the city inhabited by the poor: the slums, shantytowns, and tenement settlements, which existed even in the city's center (Poisson, 1995; Pinon, 2002; Blanc-Chaléard, 2006). They were replaced by wide, open boulevards, lined with bourgeois limestone apartment buildings and their hallmark wrought-iron balconies. The straight boulevards facilitated inner-city traffic and commerce; Haussmanization at large was designed to improve the hygienic situation, as the last Cholera epidemic took place as recently as 1831. The boulevards were furthermore instruments of riot control in a city that had seen three revolutions since the end of the eighteenth century. Haussmann also set out to beautify Paris with parks, street furniture, and public fountains. In the process, the city limits were expanded from the eighteenth-century walls of the *fermiers-généraux* (tax farmers), where the city toll used to be collected during the Old Regime, to the current location of the Boulevard Périphérique encircling the city.

In the 1840s, the Prime Minister of King Louis-Philippe, Auguste Thiers was tasked with building a defensive system around the city of Paris. Beyond the new fortification walls, where today the notoriously congested Boulevard Péripherique runs, a "zone *non aedificandi*" was established. It comprised the area beyond the fortifications themselves, up to 250 m after the glacis; in total, 777 ha surrounding Paris. The "zone" was formally put under military administration, and, for strategic reasons, any construction was prohibited on this strip of land. In the northeast, the "zone" lay adjacent to the town of St. Ouen in the St. Denis département.

2 The Beginnings of the Recycling Business at St. Ouen

The Franco-Prussian War of 1870–1871 proved the utter uselessness of Thiers' defensive system of Paris, and the military increasingly abandoned its installations. Vincent van Gogh still painted the intact ramparts and the adjacent glacis in 1887 (Manchester, Whitworth Art Gallery, University of Manchester); it was only in the 1920s that Thiers' walls were finally demolished. Intermittently, the glacis had attracted a small tribe of squatters, the poorest of the poor, who were displaced by the progressive gentrification at the center of Paris. The working classes, which Karl Marx began calling proletariat at that time, had mostly found a home in the newly erected tenement houses of the "petite banlieue," between the walls of the *fermiers-généraux* and the "zone." But rag and old iron pickers, beggars, gypsies, and anybody who did not hold a regular job often could not even afford the "petite banlieue." They found a refuge in the "zone," where squatters, whose presence was technically illegal but was practically tolerated, did not have to pay any rent and could go about their business without being bothered too much by officialdom. Many of these individuals built small huts or enclosures where they lived and worked; others held out in caravans. By 1913, the "zone" counted some 30,000 inhabitants. They were called "zoniers" or "zonards," while the word "zone" became increasingly synonymous with slums.

The fringes between Paris and St. Ouen especially attracted self-employed individuals in the recycling business for rags and old iron. The supply of these materials, of course, came from the refuse of the city of Paris, which these *chiffoniers*, *fripiers*, or *biffins* combed through during their nightly raids (Bedel, 2003). As their pursuits were the most picturesque, the rag pickers attracted most of the attention. They inspired both Edouard Manet's portrait from 1869 of one such individual (Pasadena, Norton Simon Museum) as well as the Marxist term *Lumpenproletariat* described in *Der achtzehnte Brumaire des Louis Bonaparte*:

> Rejects, trash, dropouts of all classes [. . .] lust-for-lifers of dubious means and dubious origins who face hard times; rotten and adventurous outcasts of

> the bourgeoisie, vagabonds, discharged soldiers, released prisoners, galley slaves on the run, crooks, showmen, bums, thieves, magicians, gamblers, pimps, brothel operators, porters, writers, organ grinders, rag pickers, knife grinders, tinkers, beggars; in short, all these ill-defined, dispersed, and tossed-around masses, which the French call *la bohème* (Marx & Engels, 1960).

Rags were key to this identity. Rags were always in high demand because they were needed for the manufacture of paper. But not all rags ended up in the paper mills, and not all iron was melted down in the forges. What could still be used, or what could be fixed, was resold "as is." But since old clothing was often infested with vermin, like fleas and lice, the term *marché aux puces*—flea markets—was born. Its original humorous and ironic undertones have long since been lost on us.

The best evidence for the expansion and eventual legalization of the flea markets north of Paris comes from the city ordinances of St. Ouen (Bedel, 2003). On February 4, 1884 the major of St. Ouen sent a petition to the local police prefect, asking for a night watch on the fortifications because of the danger from "bohemians." There followed an ordinance from April 17, 1883, which prohibited the littering of trash, including "cadavers of dead animals, broken glass, etc.," in response to which a "commission on cleanliness is established." The wording suggests problems with the remains from the sales activities of the earliest *puciers.* A year later, in Spring 1884, the hours of operation of markets in the municipality were standardized; in this context a "market of old iron" along the Avenue Michelet, which still marks the eastern boundary of the market district currently, is mentioned. Similar wording can be found in an official urban study of the Prefecture of the Seine (i.e. the city of Paris) from 1902, which mentions a "market of varied objects, known as the Market of Old Iron, frequented by 130 merchants every Sunday."

In 1885, finally, one finds the first official mention of the flea markets at St. Ouen in the context of "parking fees" (*droits de stationnement*), imposed by the municipality after the paving of the Rue des Rosiers and the Avenue Michelet. By 1891, a fee of "10 centimes per square meter" was established, which was soon raised to 20 centimes. The increase triggered a revolt of the *puciers*, who then moved to the glacis of the fortifications, where they did not have to pay any fee at all. This idyll lasted until the first Sunday of October 1925. By then, the city of Paris had bought the fortifications from the French government and proceeded immediately to expel the *puciers* from the "zone." The Communist mayor of the nearby commune of St. Denis intervened and offered an "asylum" to the syndicate of *chiffoniers* and *puciers* on the Plaine St. Denis, but his rivalry with the socialist mayor of St. Ouen led to a counteroffer and most members stayed in St. Ouen. They were accommodated at their new, old venue along the Avenue Michelet.

Another important contributor to the growth of flea markets in the area was the 1896 opening of an innovative trash disposal plant—the prototype of other such treatment facilities which began dotting the suburbs of Paris around the turn of the century—the *usine de broyage d'ordures* à *Saint-Ouen* (Mazerolle, 1914). Located on the Rue Ardoin, to the northwest of the flea markets, its location abuts the Seine. The site continues to house even today one of the largest and most powerful trash incinerators in France.

The establishment of the "trash mill of Saint-Ouen" came in the wake of the 1885 mandatory introduction, in Paris, of standardized trash cans—the first generalized use of such receptacles in human civilization—fittingly named after the Prefect of the Seine who imposed them in the name of improved hygiene, Eugène Poubelle. The introduction of the *poubelles* created an immediate uproar amongst the suburban *chiffoniers* and other recycling professionals—men, women, and children—and especially so at Saint-Ouen (Anonymous, 1901). In 1901, their number was estimated at 40,000 individuals. To appease the revolt, the city of Paris conceded the continuation of an informal arrangement for the multi-tiered, hierarchical access to the picking of refuse. Early in the morning, the *placiers* took the *poubelles* from the interiors of the buildings to the street, where the *coureurs* picked through the contents; the cans were then emptied onto trucks by the *tombereautiers*; and, upon arrival at Saint Ouen, before the refuse was sent to the mill, the *secondeurs* feeding the machine glanced the contents over one last time. Each turn, of course, afforded the workers an opportunity to secure for themselves items of larger or smaller value: for recycling, reuse, and resale. Although the establishment of the *usine de broyage d'ordures* was deeply resented by locals, it provided many pickers with a livelihood and made the local flea markets flourish. Despite the self-evident hazards and despised social rank of their occupation, some of the trash workers assembled smaller and larger private fortunes. Thus, "rags to riches" stories were sometimes cut out of the cloth of the *Lumpenproletariat.*

3 The Establishments of Formal Markets at St. Ouen

Although St. Ouen would attain eventually a population density even higher than that of Paris, it was still mostly a rural place at the turn of the twentieth century. A large portion of the land was taken up by the vineyards and vegetable gardens which provisioned the nearby city (Bedel, 2003). But by about 1900, a Phylloxera outbreak killed all the remaining vineyards at St. Ouen. To prevent the further spread of the bugs, the growing of vines was prohibited. Since the vines from St. Ouen and the northern *arrondissements* of Paris were never of great quality anyhow, the loss was not widely lamented. By the 1920s, upon the relocation of the *puciers* from the ramparts to the municipality of St. Ouen, a regularization and legalization process commenced. It manifested itself in the form of a network of named, privately owned markets with permanent or semi-permanent structures for the merchants. Many of these new markets were founded on land where the vegetable gardens and vineyards had once blossomed.

The first such formal flea market was the Marché Vernaison, which was founded by the entrepreneur Romain Vernaison as the "baraques Villegrain" in 1920. Vernaison had earned his fortune as a subcontractor of the Halles Baltard, the produce market in the heart of Paris, and with a rental business for chairs in the Parisian public parks. He parceled out some 9,000 square meters wedged between the Avenue Michelet, the Rue des rosiers, and the Rue Voltaire, on which he built prefabricated wooden booths for his renters, the *puciers.*

At about the same time, the Marché Malik, facing today the Boulevard Périphérique, came into existence. In its current form, it is a market specializing in new textiles, which has little to do with the antique trade for which St. Ouen is best known; historically, it was a market for rags, old uniforms, helmets, and technical equipment (photography, phonographs, radios, etc.). The market is named after an Albanian World War I veteran and coffee house owner, Malik Hajrulac, who in 1919 acquired the café-brasserie "A. Picolo." The business came with a plot of empty land across the street on which the owner established his namesake market.

The heart of the antique trade at St. Ouen, along the Rue des Rosiers, is circumscribed by the Markets Biron, Paul Bert, Jules Vallès, and Serpette. Of the four, the Marché Biron is the oldest. It was founded by a syndicate of *puciers* looking for a new home after their eviction from the ramparts in 1925. The dealers approached the owner of a piece of land occupied by vegetable farmers close to the Marché Vernaison. The landlord, a silversmith, agreed to parcel out the plot and to rent the parcels to members of the syndicate. Seeking to distinguish themselves and their merchandise from their lowly origins and competitors, they branded their market as a "brocante," suggesting higher-value antiques and art instead of recycled wares.

The history of the Marché Paul Bert, further down the Rue des Rosiers, follows similar lines. Before World War II, grazing cows and vineyards defined the appearance of the plot of land owned by the Poré family. By the 1940s, the concrete Poré garages were built, while other parts of the Poré land that were still sitting empty were populated by the first *puciers* from 1946 onwards. In 1949, a syndicate of dealers secured permission to build permanent structures for their businesses on this L-shaped land. Nearby, the much smaller Marché Jules Vallès had already been in operation since 1938. Founded and developed by a Venetian immigrant named Amadeo Cesana, this simple, two-aisled structure has a surface of only 1900 sq m. For a long time, the Marché Jules Vallès retained, as a reminder of its rural origins, a floor of beaten earth. Today, most visitors would not much likely notice the transition between the Paul Bert and the Serpette markets, if it were not for the fact that the Serpette market is completely sheltered. In fact, it is of much more recent date and is nestled in the old Poré garages. The Serpette market came into existence only in 1977, when a young dealer specializing in historical armor, Alain Serpette, converted the still operable garages on 110 Rue des Rosiers into a covered market for the more upper end of the antique trade.

The story of the converted garages of St. Ouen deserves a quick digression. St. Ouen, like other communities defined by the light industries rimming Paris, was quite rich in garages and automobile maintenance businesses during the early and mid-twentieth century. There are still traces of them, such as old signage, visible in some parts of the municipality today. Of course, there were a lot fewer garages, if any, in the "beaux quartiers" of Louis Aragon. However, garages were important places of sociability, business, and the making of quick fortunes from the mid-1920s until about 1970, as any astute reader of Octave Mirbeau and Patrick Modiano's novels will know. At mid-century, the transient demimonde of the garages was in some sense a perfect fit with that of the *marché aux puces*.

The Marché Serpette signaled an important shift in the social self-reinvention of the flea markets at St. Ouen, away from working-class recycling businesses and closer to the luxury industries of the late twentieth and early twenty-first centuries—a place that could compete, albeit in its own terms and aided by some make-believe, with Louis Vuitton, Moët, Yves Saint-Laurent, Sotheby's, or the Ritz. The last two markets added to the infrastructure of St. Ouen, that of Malassis and Dauphine, opened in 1989 and 1991, respectively, bear out this rebranding trend. The Marché Malassis is perhaps the only custom-built flea market structure in the world. With its architectural details hovering somewhere between a neo-Art Nouveau and neo-Art Deco style, it lays unambiguous claim to the luxury segment of the art, design, and antique trade. Much of the merchandise consists of designer furniture, lighting fixtures, Oriental carpets, and Asian art. Because it emerged from a remodeled warehouse, the two-storey Marché Dauphine has a more modest appearance. It is composed of several distinct sections that deal in such items as vintage clothing, fashion accessories, vinyl discs, historical entertainment appliances, comics, postcards, toys, books, maps, and other collectibles. Since 2013, the focal point of the Marché Dauphine became a permanently installed, fiberglass-molded and brightly orange "UFO" saucer of giant proportions, whose neo-1970s design was the brainchild of Finnish architect Matti Suuronen. The Marché Dauphine stands out as the most specialized market at St. Ouen and the one best attuned to twenty-first-century collector taste among younger audiences.

4 The Flea Markets at St. Ouen in Art and Literature

Despite the many untoward episodes of their history, the markets at St. Ouen lent themselves to romanticization from a very early date. In writings, art, and representation, they were portrayed as a haunt for artists, writers, bohemians, non-conformists, and dreamers. The first manifestation of this romanticization came in the form of a large variety of black-and-white postcards from the early twentieth century. Dozens of photographic motifs of the *marché aux puces* at St. Ouen were released before World War I and the fact that so many of them have survived shows that they found a market of eager buyers. Postcards generally do not feature outright poverty, but, if they do, it is framed as picturesque. Falling into this latter category, cheap photographic images of the markets at St. Ouen—snapshots from the ramparts of the fortifications, or of the unauthorized huts and caravans for business and living, as well as the "headquarters" of the rag pickers—were made for popular souvenirs. One such postcard, extant in multiple copies all mailed around 1908 (series of "Saint-Ouen illustré," P. Sudan, éd., St.-Ouen), even foregrounds a dealer specializing in old paintings who tends to his impromptu, open-air exhibition. The title of the image labels it an impression from the "section de peinture" of the flea market, an ironic pun aimed at institutions at the pinnacle of cultural sophistication and prestige: the departments of the Louvre Museum, or the official Salon, which, by this time, was housed in the Grand Palais.

In 1910, the satirical weekly *L'Assiette au beurre* dedicated a special issue filled with some twenty color lithographs by Paul Bour and Francisque Poulbot to *Le Marché aux puces* (Bour & Poulbot, 1910). Many of the scenes still capture the vastness of the plains on the glacis with their scattered sellers lost across the pasture, while others focus on the narrow streets of St. Ouen, where sellers spread out their wares against palisade backdrops. Distant silhouettes of the smoking chimneys of nearby factories round up the setting's special character. Nevertheless, the tone is humorous: a teenage *pucier* admonishes an elderly client interested in a pair of pincers "to watch out for his nose," while a matronly female seller chases away a client who mistook her sleeping child for a pile of rags for sale. The gruff and sketch-like style of the lithographs is perfectly attuned to the working-class ambiance, and although *L'Assiette au beurre* had no openly avowed political leanings, its sympathies were often anarchist. As a typical product of its time, the special 1910 issue of *L'Assiette au beurre* stands symptomatically for the increasing interest by artists and writers in the markets at St. Ouen even before the outbreak of World War I.

Luigi Loir, who became the first painter to repeatedly engage with the picturesque aspects of the flea markets at St. Ouen, is another case in point (Willer, 2004). Loir is an artist who surprises. His choice of subject matter and his handling of the paint qualify him as a follower of post-Impressionism. One can discern in his canvases Monet's daubed-on touches of paint and the love for atmospheric effects. Although he was born in Austria in 1845, only five years after the founder of the Impressionist group, and studied art in Parma, Loir comes across at hindsight primarily as a chronicler of the technological transformations of early twentieth-century Paris. His perhaps best work, the canvases from the final years of his life, are humming with the noise of engines and the boisterousness of popular quarters. Loir was often attracted to the seedier side of the city, especially mass transportation. He captured the steamboats going up and down the Seine, the Haussmannian boulevards torn open to build the métro, and the glittering lights of the Merry Go Rounds (*manèges*) in Luna Park, opened in 1907. And he was attracted to St. Ouen, where he captured, probably sometime around 1910, the hunkered down store fronts and the hustle-bustle of the *puciers* lining the Avenue Michelet just as Claude Monet had rendered the Boulevard des Capucines and Camille Pissarro the Boulevard Montmartre.

The literary world discovered the markets at St. Ouen during the Second World War and the immediate post-war years. Lucien Aressy and Antoine Parménie's *La Cité des épaves: Le Marché aux Puces* was published in 1943, during the German occupation of Paris (Aressy et al., 1943). However, the manuscript must have been completed by 1939, since the text ends with the outbreak of World War II. Aressy and Parménie were best known for their portraits of the Parisian literary bohème at the turn of the century, such as Baudelaire and Verlaine. *La Cité des épaves* presents itself as a literary walk across the different corners of the flea markets, flavored with character studies of the people who live and make a living at St. Ouen, the bistros, bars, and cafés they frequent, as well as picturesque descriptions of the merchandise on offer. The appeal of the book was enhanced by about two dozen wood engravings of objects, booths, streets, and people by André Deslignères, who specialized in prints depicting "romantic misery." Deslignères was not the first printmaker to commemorate *les puces*. Around 1910, the etcher August Brouet had already completed a series of plates with similar subjects, stylistically and iconographically closely inspired by Rembrandt's genre scenes, which were marketed by the Chalcography (in today's terms, the gift store) of the Louvre. André Deslignères, by contrast, used much larger and thicker lines, which align more closely with the aesthetics of twentieth-century German Expressionist woodcuts.

There were deeper intellectual concerns underlying Lucien Aressy and Antoine Parménie's investigation, as they sought to explore the psychology of the people they encountered and interviewed, which resulted in a mosaic of micro-biographies. Their view of the flea market was a romantic rough-and-tumble place that did not exclude transgressions of any kind, or even violence for that matter. The authors repeatedly show how St. Ouen became a refuge of last resort for individuals who had failed at other pursuits in life and who found a second chance behind the broken chairs, rusty bicycles, torn paintings, and worn cloths. The emphasis on self-reliance made St. Ouen a haven for individuals who had problems with formal hierarchies, as it was a place that offered freedom from fixed working hours and bosses. Another disenfranchised group of importance was foreigners marginalized by French mainstream society, from a Tunisian fortune teller and a Romanian orphan to Russian émigrés who fled the Bolshevik revolution of 1917. In the end, *La Cité des épaves* was perhaps a much more political book than it seemed, a eulogy for cosmopolitanism and individualism, for anarchism *and* capitalism at the same time.

Jean-Marc Campagne and René Clair's *Les Week-end de Saint-Ouen* from 1951 was evidently indebted to the "impressions-from-a-random-walk" approach of *La Cité des épaves*, but takes on a much more jovial and hedonistic tone (Campagne, 1951). It was marketed as an oversized, limited-edition art book, illustrated with pastel-colored vignettes and full-page illustrations of the flea markets by Emilio Grau Sala, a Spanish artist active in Paris, who was noted for his flowery, post-Impressionist paintings and book illustrations, often featuring young women. The volume was prefaced by an autobiographical and sentimental appreciation of the markets at St. Ouen by the film director and soon-to–be member of French Academy, René Clair, whose cinematographic work was widely regarded as old-fashioned after World War II.

As a writer, Jean-Marc Campagne was also outmoded when the book appeared. Before the war he had worked as a journalist, art critic, fashion specialist, and exhibition curator, who regularly contributed to *Marianne*, *Aujourd'hui*, *L'Intransigeant*, and *Le Figaro*. His scattered post-war publication, however, dabbled in things like the occult, the fantastic, and magic in art, but without any apparent links to Surrealism; by this time, he preferred to publish on eccentric French outsider artists, such as Clovis Trouille and Alfred Courmes. Clearly, Grau Sala's many color lithographs—and not the writings of the two authors—constitute the main attraction of the volume. Overall, *Les Week-end de Saint-Ouen* remained conceptually a product more at home in the inter-war than the post-war years. It was a continuation and the end point of the short-lived genre which had begun with the *L'Assiette au beurre* and *La Cité des épaves*.

5 Tourism, Alignment with Luxury Industries, and the Twilight of Gentrification

The *trente glorieuses* (1945–1975) did not show much sympathy for the recycling business or its romanticization. Louis Malle's *Zazie dans le métro* from 1960 was the exception to the Zeitgeist because it contained some sequences filmed at the markets at St. Ouen. Otherwise, movie buffs would have to wait until 2011, when Woody Allen released *Midnight in Paris*, to see the *puces* return to the big screen. By this point, St. Ouen had metamorphosed into an outpost of the luxury industry. The interiors for the central restaurant of the Marché Serpette, "Ma Cocotte aux Puces," for example, were created in 2012 by the star designer Philippe Starck. The transformation was also apparent in the publication of the French-English periodical, *Le Village des Puces: Le Journal du Grenier du Monde*, whose ten complementary issues were distributed to visitors between 2015 and 2019 (Village des Puces, 2015–2019). Its elegant contents moved effortlessly from sales promotion to philosophy, lifestyle, and art history. Most importantly, the *Le Village des Puces* highlighted the fluid transition between the market for antiquities and the market for (recent or upcycled) design objects. A further indicator for these shifts was the appointment, in 2019, of Surrealist interior designer Vincent Darré, a former assistant of fashion czar Karl Lagerfeld, to the position of "ambassador" of the flea markets, in which function he created the "Puces, mon trésor" marketing campaign (Hemonet, 2019). Finally, in August 2024, the review of Kate van den Boogert's newly released coffee table book, *The Paris Flea Market* (van den Boogert & Glanville, 2024), with its many photographs and short dealer biographies, even attained a place among the opening articles on the website of the *New York Times* (Meltzer, 2024).

Today, the market infrastructure at St. Ouen consists of about eleven distinct markets, each with their own name and identity, spread out over seven hectares. They are populated by an estimated total of more than 1,100 dealers and create some 10,000 jobs (Bedel, 2003; Puces de Saint-Ouen, 2025). Another one thousand or more individuals work in related service industries, such as art/furniture restoration and repair, art materials supply, shipping, catering, etc. On a good weekend, the markets attract between 150,000 and 200,000 visitors; an estimated five million or more individuals flock to St. Ouen per year. The annual turnover runs in the hundreds of millions of euros; by some optimistic estimates, it may be as high as €400 million. If accurate, this would put it at 45% of France's entire yearly auction turnover, which stood in 2023 at roughly €875 million. All of these figures need to be contextualized by the global importance of the French tourism industry. In 2024, France was the most visited country in the world, hosting an estimated 80–100 million international visitors. The flea markets at St. Ouen, in turn, are cited in some statistics as the fourth or fifth most visited tourist site in France.

Despite their success story, the flea markets at St. Ouen remain very fragile places. A cautionary tale is the fate of the ephemeral "Habitat 1964—Espace vintage," a micro-market that existed between 2016 and 2019 on the site of the former Wonder batteries factory, wedged between the Rue des Rosiers and the Rue Marie-Curie (Louison, 2016; Bourdon, 2017; Haus, 2017). Opened in 1918, the Wonder factory was bought in 1984 by France's foremost corporate raider of the 1980s, Bernard Tapie, who closed the plant in 1986 and fired its 600 employees. In the early 1990s, Tapie sold the empty factory to the "the Prince of the Antique Dealers," Bernard Steinitz, who transformed it into a storage space for his business, the "Espace Steinitz." When Steinitz died in 2012, the structure and the land on which it sits was bought by SNC Paris-Périph, which belongs to the holding company Foncière Volta, whose CEO, Hervé Giaoui, also owns the Groupe Habitat. Four years later, the site was opened to the public with the inauguration of "Habitat 1964—Espace vintage." Admittedly, "Habitat 1964" was planned from the beginning as an "ephemeral" market, bound to disappear as plans for future development evolved. The dealers clustered around the open courtyard of "Habitat 1964" specialized frequently in upcycled industrial equipment from the early twentieth century or vintage furniture from the 1960s and 1970s, such as plastic-molded chairs in bright colors. But their selection also included designer furniture of the 1990s and early 2000s from the upper end of the market, such as interiors by Sido & François Thévenin. The "ephemeral bar" Sonnenkönig, best known for the Parisian-brewed beer that it served, attracted large crowds each weekend to the "Habitat 1964."

In July 2017, a demolition permit for the "Espace Steinitz" was issued, together with a municipal building permit for the luxury "Le village des rosiers" complex (Fig. 1) that has subsequently replaced it. Upon its completion in 2025, this neo-Art Deco, eight-floor compound, constructed at a cost of €110 million, houses 520 apartments and 745 parking units. As a consequence, *Le Figaro Immobilier* reported in November 2019 that the price per square meter of real estate at St. Ouen surpassed the 10,000 euro threshold for the first time (Errard, 2019). The "Village des rosiers"

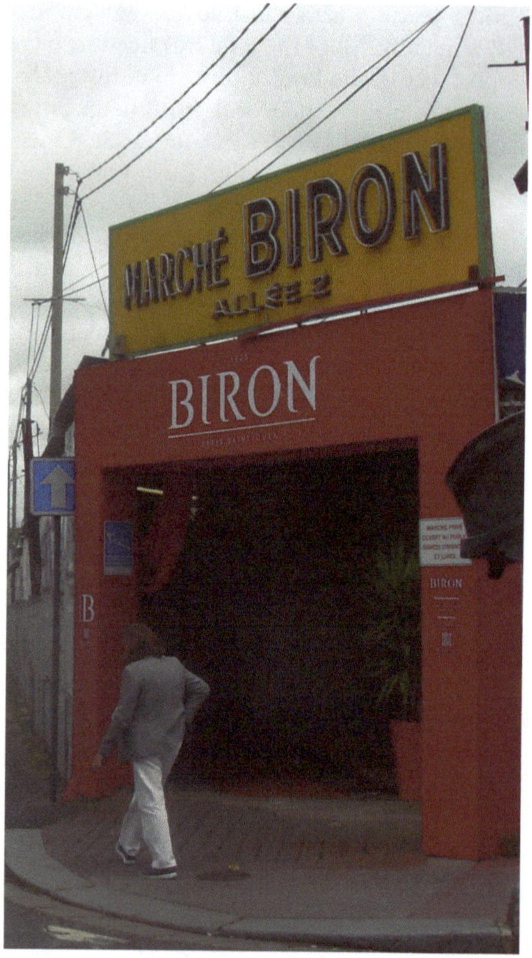

Fig. 1 Construction site of the "Le village des rosiers" at Saint Ouen, with the entry to the Marché Biron in the Background. *Source* Author, June 2024

currently overshadows the nearby Marché Biron, crouching and shabby by comparison, but the protests of the *puciers*, worried about increased traffic volume, environmental problems, and fears of eventually being driven out, went largely unheard.

The "Village des rosiers" is a foreshadowing of more such developments to come. If one looks around the neighborhood of the flea markets, one cannot fail to observe that the few remaining, abandoned industrial sites and the crumbling, ramshackle working-class houses of St. Ouen, usually only one or two floors high and built any time between 1880 and 1950, are quickly disappearing. They are replaced by "sustainable" boutique hotels, more upscale apartment buildings, and student housing. All of the shifts noted make St. Ouen a case study for the role which the art and antique trade plays in gentrification. Ironically, the buyers and renters of the newly built or renovated apartments at St. Ouen are mostly quite affluent "refugees" from Paris, who can no longer afford to reside inside the city, where so much space for domestic living has been converted in recent years to Airbnb rentals for foreign visitors (Hehli, 2024).

The oversized role of tourism—and here in particular American buyers —in the "rags to riches" story of St. Ouen always becomes painfully apparent in moments of crisis, such as the economic downturn of 2008 (Robert, 2009) or the COVID travel restrictions of the early 2020s. For many sellers, and the location overall, such events can quickly turn into an existential crisis. While St. Ouen can rightly claim to hold the veritable founding charter of twentieth-century flea markets across the world, it also represents a great anomaly. As we saw, it is much older than almost all other markets and evolved in very idiosyncratic ways. In the current conditions of the twenty-first century, when so many flea market venues globally have disappeared or are struggling, that of St. Ouen, for now, is prospering despite its fragility—to the extent that it has even become a victim of its own success due to the synergies of the tourism and luxury industries on which it depends.

References

Anonymous (1901, October 18). Les Chiffonniers protestent. *L'écho de Paris, 18* (6350), 2.

Aressy, L., Parménie, A., & Deslignères, A. (1943). *La Cité des épaves: Le Marché aux puces.* Éditions littéraires et artistiques.

Bedel, J. (2003). *Les Puces sautent les siècles: Du Chiffonier à l'antiquaire.*

Blanc-Chaléard, M.-C. (2006, November-December). Les Immigrés et le logement en France depuis le XIXe siècle. *Hommes et migrations, 1264,* 20–34.

Bour, P., & Poulbot, F. (1910, March 12). Le Marché aux puces. *L'Assiette au beurre, 467,* 1653–1688.

Bourdon, G. (2017, September 26). Saint-Ouen: Inquiétudes autour du Projet immobilier des Puces. *Le Parisien.* https://www.leparisien.fr/seine-saint-denis-93/saint-ouen-93400/saint-ouen-inquietudes-autour-du-projet-immobilier-des-puces-25-09-2017-7285569.php. Accessed Jan 11, 2025.

Campagne, J.-M. (1951). *Les Week-End à Saint-Ouen*. Groupe d'amateurs.
Clair, R. (1951). Préface. In J.- M. Campagne, (Ed.), *Les week-end à Saint-Ouen* (pp. 9–13). Groupe d'amateurs.
de Saint-ouen, P. (2025) *Histoire des Puces*. https://www.pucesdeparissaintouen.com/les-puces/. Accessed Jan 11, 2025.
Errard, G. (2019, November 13, updated, November 14, 2019). Aux puces de Saint-Ouen, le mètre carré peut dépasser 10.000 euros. *Le Figaro immobilier*. https://immobilier.lefigaro.fr/article/aux-puces-de-saint-ouen-le-metre-carre-peut-depasser-10-000-euros_eb3a6678-0226-11ea-8e9d-d047f0a34a0c/. Accessed Jan 11, 2025.
Haus, H. (2017, May 6). Saint-Ouen: Le Projet immobilier des Puces inquiète. *Le Parisien*. https://www.leparisien.fr/seine-saint-denis-93/saint-ouen-le-projet-immobilier-des-puces-inquiete-06-05-2017-6923112.php. Accessed Jan 11, 2025.
Hehli, S. (2024, April 12). Airbnb statt Familienwohnungen: Darum leben immer weniger Menschen in Paris. *Neue Züricher Zeitung*. https://www.nzz.ch/international/pariser-ziehen-weg-paris-hat-wegen-airbnb-weniger-einwohner-ld.1825701. Accessed Jan 11, 2025.
Hemonat, M. (2019, September 17). Vincent Darré, ambassadeur des Puces Mon Trésor. *AD Magazine*. https://www.admagazine.fr/art/marche-art/diaporama/vincent-darre-ambassadeur-des-puces-mon-tresor/58625. Accessed Jan 11, 2025.
Louison, F. (2016, June 14). Saint-Ouen: Au cœur des Puces, l'ex-usine Wonder va disparaître. *Le Parisien*. https://www.leparisien.fr/seine-saint-denis-93/saint-ouen-93400/saint-ouen-au-coeur-des-puces-l-ex-usine-wonder-va-disparaitre-14-06-2016-5884005.php. Accessed Jan 11, 2025.
Mardaga, P. (ed.) (1995). *Le Patrimoine monumental de la Belgique* (vol. 1/B, 256–257).
Marx, K., & Engels, F. (1960). Der achtzehnte Brumaire des Louis Bonaparte. In *Werke*, vol. 8, ch. V, 160–161.
Mazerolle, L. (1914, April 1). Le Traitement de ordures ménagères à Paris. *La Science Et la Vie*, *5*(13), 45–55.
Meltzer, M. (2024, August 27, updated, 2024, November 11). One Woman's Quest to Map the Paris Flea Market. *The New York Times*. https://www.nytimes.com/2024/08/27/style/paris-puces-flea-market.html
Pinon, P. (2002). *Le 'dépeuplement' du centre*. In *Atlas du Paris haussmannien* (pp. 92–94). Parigramme.
Poisson, G. (1995, September-October). Haussmann transforme Paris. *Historia spécial: Napoléon III et le Second Empire 37*.
Robert, M. (2009, November 6). Les Puces de Saint-Ouen, un monument en péril. *Les Echos*. https://www.lesechos.fr/2009/11/les-puces-de-saint-ouen-un-monument-en-peril-467626. Accessed Jan. 11, 2025.

Van den Boogert, K., & Glanville, T. (2024). *The Paris flea market.* Prestel.
Village des Puces: Le Journal du Grenier du Monde (2015, Sept.-2019, Nov.). vols. 1–8, 2 special issues.
Willer, N. (2004). *Luigi Loir, 1845–1916: Peintre de la Belle Époque à la publicité. Catalogue raisonné.* Noë Willer.

Selling Eclecticism: Trickle-Round Signaling and Modular Design in French Cemeteries After 1804

Kaylee P. Alexander

1 Introduction

The 1804 Imperial Decree on Burials was issued in response to ongoing concerns about public health and municipal cemeteries, which, by the end of the eighteenth century, had become severely overcrowded. Regulating where future cemeteries could be established and stipulating the ideal conditions for public burial grounds, the decree also introduced a highly regulated concession system that guaranteed individual plots to all regardless of financial means (see, e.g., Ariès, 1981; Etlin, 1984; Kselman, 1993; Legacey, 2019). In radically modernizing burial practices, these regulations transformed the practice of marking a loved-one's grave from a privilege of the elite few to a popular (and expected) custom. Most impactfully, the market for funerary monuments expanded greatly as an independent, specialized industry developed out of preexisting, generalist networks for stonework (Alexander, 2020). As such, the market for funerary monuments became itself a fully-fledged cultural industry in which tomb markers functioned as cultural goods. In other words, as funerary monuments became more widely accessible, they became imbued with a multidimensional set of values—aesthetic, symbolic, spiritual, social, etc.—that comprised what Throsby and Zednik describe as cultural value: "a distinct form of value … related

K. P. Alexander (✉)
University of Utah, Salt Lake City, Utah, USA
e-mail: kaylee.alexander@utah.edu

A.-S. V. Radermecker (ed.), *Low-End Markets for Art and Cultural Goods*,
Cultural Economics & the Creative Economy,
https://doi.org/10.1007/978-3-032-27566-0_6

to, but not synonymous with, the goods' economic value" (Throsby & Zednik, 2013, p. 81).

Guaranteeing individual plots for all, however, did not establish a fully democratic system of burial. Initially limited to only those of significant means, Reglementary Order of 15 Ventôse year XIII (March 6, 1805) established two options for concessions: "long-term" and "perpetual." The long-term burial, which would eventually be known as the temporary concession, provided a more affordable option for burials lasting beyond five years (Kselman, 1993).[1] The price difference between temporary and perpetual burials, however, was substantial, with the price of temporary concessions set throughout most of the nineteenth century at 50 francs per five-year increment (up to a maximum of 150 francs) and perpetual concessions starting at 250 francs but achieving rates well into the thousands (Bureau des Cimetières, 1889; Alexander, 2024, pp. 88–89). Only a fraction of Paris's population was able to afford a permanent resting place. Thus, most burials—free or paid—and their attendant monuments were temporary from conception (Alexander, 2024, pp. 23–54).

What art historians typically consider cemetery *architecture* and *sculpture* was only constitutive of the uppermost end of the market and therefore a much rarer occurrence than surviving nineteenth-century texts, modern guidebooks, scholarship, and present-day cemetery views suggest. These works have simply outlived other monuments by having been initially erected over perpetual concessions and having now achieved the status of cultural heritage, a loophole that protects them from twentieth-century legal reinterpretations of, and restrictions on, perpetual burial.[2]

[1] Among other provisions for burial conditions at Père-Lachaise, Frochot's Reglementary Order of 15 Ventôse year XIII divided the cemetery into public and private terrain. While public territory referred to free five-year plots, private territory referred to concessions, or lands that could be conceded either as "long-term" (i.e., longer than the five years limited to free, public plots) or "in perpetuity." In defining these three burial options, Frochot set the precedent for the three categories of burial—free (i.e., *fosse commune* or, later, *tranchée gratuite*), temporary concession, and perpetual concession—that would later be offered in all new and reformed cemeteries of Paris until 1843.

[2] The Law of January 3, 1924, granted French townships the authority to recuperate any perpetual or perennial concession that is deemed to be in a state of abandonment, which is defined as unmaintained by a direct descendent of the initial concession holder for thirty or more years. This further complicated the meaning of *perpetuity*, essentially rendering all burials as potentially temporary regardless of their initial status. Such abandoned plots are subject to state recuperation if, within three years of being declared abandoned, no direct relatives are identified and/or willing to maintain the concession. This law is upheld today by

At its core, the survival of these monuments over others is a matter of material culture; however, as will be discussed, the durability of materials used to construct funerary monuments was rarely linked to the duration of their presence in the cemetery.

Therefore, the immediate goal of this research was to reevaluate the visual culture of French cemeteries through the lens of the nonelite majority that one no longer encounters. In analyzing the "low end" of the funerary monuments market and situating vernacular, temporary structures as key drivers of taste in the nineteenth century, we can begin to uncover a more nuanced view of how modern styles—including those still in high demand today—developed out of changing attitudes toward death and opportunities for commemoration at the turn of the nineteenth century.

2 Literature Review and Context

Although much has been written about French funerary monuments and the development of the first Modern cemeteries, art historical research has tended to focus on monuments by or to notable individuals, extant or otherwise well-documented (see, e.g., Le Normand-Romain, 1995; Pantano, 1997). Such approaches have lessened or completely ignored the influence of *marbriers* (stonecutters) and average consumers on this body of visual material. Often seen secondary to architects, *marbriers*, already in the nineteenth century, were denigrated as manual laborers who lacked any design ability to match those of architects. Although it is true that *marbriers* did undertake the manual labor involved in executing architectural designs, my research demonstrates that *marbriers* also produced original and highly customizable objects at nearly any price point. Yet studies of such objects and the contemporary texts written about them would have you believe that the architects played a much more significant visual role in the nineteenth century than was the case.

The bias against non-architectural work for the cemetery already began in the first half of the nineteenth century (Alexander, 2020). Criticized both by the public and the architects alongside whom they often worked, *marbriers* were referred to as subpar copyists who would prove detrimental to the legacy of French civilization. The architect Jean Boussard, for

Article L.2223–17 of the *Code général des collectivités territoriales* (CGCT), and Article L361–17 of the "Code des communes" stipulates the procedures for such acts of recuperation.

example, made this especially clear when he wrote in 1870 that monuments in French cemeteries were "in great majority only numbers 1, 2, 3 from the *marbrier*'s album, resembling one another too often and generally being devoid of the special character of architectural works" (Boussard, 1870, n.p.).[3]

An examination of extant *marbriers*' model books and catalogues reveals that their products were significantly more customizable than they have traditionally been understood. Most importantly, we see evidence quite early on for a nascent form of modular design resulting from clients and *marbriers* working together to create custom monuments suiting the client's budgetary constraints while satisfying individual tastes. Though not fully bespoke in nature, the production of funerary monuments could be seen as a commission process in which creators and patrons collaborated toward a final output. Contrary to conventional views of low-end markets as sites in which ready-made goods tend to be traded over custom ones, this system is evidence of yet another way tomb markers constituted cultural goods with more than just an economic value. Satirical works also gestured toward pricing structures based on clients' picking-and-choosing, providing further evidence for modular design strategies (Alexander, 2020; 2024, pp. 65–70).

3 Data and Methodology

Despite lacking a robust body of extant monuments to study directly, several archival sources provide abundant data yielding insights into the scale of the funerary monuments market, popular forms and features, and "low end" market mechanisms that likely influenced stylistic trends. Chief among these are the *Registres journaliers d'inhumation* (Daily Registers of Inhumation), which document all burials taking place in Paris from 1804 to 1969, albeit with some gaps.[4] From 1819 onward, these records consistently account for

[3] "ne sont en grande majorité que les numéros 1, 2, 3 de l'album des marbriers, qu'ils se ressemblent trop souvent et sont généralement dépourvus du caractère spécial aux œuvres d'architecture."

[4] Reporting for several cemeteries is incomplete, particularly for those that did not come under Parisian jurisdiction until 1860. The records for the three public cemeteries in Paris prior to 1860—Père-Lachaise, Montparnasse, and Montmartre—are the most complete, although free burials for Père-Lachaise were excluded until July 20, 1818, and the earliest records for Père-Lachaise show evidence of material loss that affect data accuracy.

plot types—free, temporary, or perpetual—and are therefore instrumental in gauging potential market output (Alexander, 2023a).

As all plots were entitled to a monument, accounting for the number of burials annually evidences the potential demand for monuments annually by providing the maximum number of monuments that could have been erected. Additionally, while we cannot account for the percentage of monuments produced by *marbriers* over architects, the high number of active *marbriers* in Paris during this period makes it reasonable to assume *marbriers* were responsible for most monument sales (Alexander, 2020).[5] These records can also not tell us anything about what monuments looked like or cost. Coupled with the present-day absence of these objects, it is nearly impossible to discern broad stylistic trends directly. There are, however, a handful of proxy bodies of evidence. The most comprehensive of these sources is Roger and Roger's *Le champ du repos* (1816), which provides illustrations and transcribed epitaphs for over two thousand monuments present in Père-Lachaise by the end of 1815. This source—which self-describes as a comprehensive account of all the monuments then present in the cemetery and includes no information about the makers of the monuments it documents—is the most comprehensive extant documentation for structures in situ during this period (see also, Alexander, 2025). Though imperfect, as many historical data sources are, *Le champ du repos* provided the second dataset for this study. Having transcribed and organized the text into a structured dataset for an earlier iteration of this research (Alexander, 2018), I supplemented existing data with additional variables accounting for monument forms, ornaments, and iconographic features based on a visual observation (Alexander, 2023b).

4 Empirical Analysis and Findings

As shown in Table 1, approximately 96% of burials between 1819 and 1835 would have expired, at most, after fifteen years; in reality, most were likely never intended to last beyond five. Yet their temporary status did not preclude the construction of highly personalized and, at times, quite elaborate and presumably expensive markers. Although it is impossible

[5] The number of marbriers active in Paris rose from just 38 in 1801 to 393 by 1876 before gradually dropping off to around 300 by the end of the nineteenth century. When compared to population, marbriers peaked in 1856 at 2.37 marbriers per 10,000 people, compared to 0.69 per 10,000 in 1801 (Alexander, 2020, pp. 5–8).

Table 1 Share of total burials taking place annually in free, temporary, and perpetual plots, aggregated for the cemeteries of Père-Lachaise, Montparnasse, and Montmartre from 1818 to 1835 (n = 14,459)

Year	*Free (%)*	*Temporary (%)*	*Perpetual (%)*
1818	69.03	25.54	5.43
1819	79.74	16.35	3.91
1820	77.12	18.12	4.76
1821	77.91	16.71	5.39
1822	75.98	18.07	5.95
1823	75.73	18.84	5.43
1824	79.61	16.92	3.47
1825	78.46	18.89	2.65
1826	77.43	19.19	3.38
1827	76.80	19.51	3.69
1828	75.65	20.54	3.81
1829	75.39	20.53	4.08
1830	75.23	21.30	3.47
1831	76.73	20.15	3.12
1832	74.50	21.88	3.62
1833	76.31	19.20	4.49
1834	74.88	20.88	4.24
1835	73.64	21.80	4.56
Average	76.12	19.69	4.19

Source Registres journaliers d'inhumation (Alexander, 2023a)

to link all burial records for Paris to visual evidence of design, it is possible to get a sense of which types of markers would have accompanied certain types of plots by comparing burial records to the illustrations and epitaphs included in *Le champ du repos*. In examining the markers recorded in *Le champ du repos* and joining them to the burial records, I was able to make one-to-one matches and analyze the appearance of monuments for each free, temporary, and perpetual burial included in the volume (concession status was information excluded from *Le champ du repos* but present in the state records). Though not accounted for in official documentation, free burials were included in *Le champ du repos*, and, contrary to what has been previously assumed, plots in the *fosse commune* (free burial section) did have individual monuments.

Though typically modest in nature, the monuments over free plots ranged from wooden crosses to stonework markers comparable to those found in paid areas of the cemetery. In fact, 35% of the markers over free plots recorded in *Le champ du repos* can confidently be assumed to have been made of stone and approximately 25% had iron grillwork around their perimeter (Fig. 1). The fosse commune's monumental impact

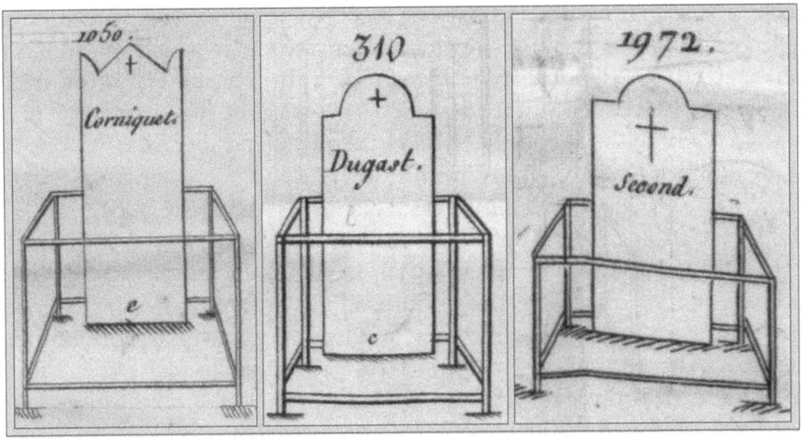

Fig. 1 Examples of simple stone monuments with iron grillwork. From left to right: Plot nos. 1050 (perpetual), 310 (temporary), and 1972 (free) from *Le champ du repos*. BnF/Gallica. *Source* Image in the public domain

should therefore not be disregarded, despite its status as the lowest end of the "low-end." Additionally, the three-tiered segmentation of burial plots into free, temporary, and perpetual as indicative of a parallel market for monuments and, by proxy, an intuitive indicator of a decedent's socioeconomic status emerges as reductive and misleading. As Moureau and Radermecker astutely point out in their introduction to the present volume, purely price-driven classifications of low and high ends of the market are insufficient and assume quality distinctions that are inherently context dependent and, more importantly, highly subjective. Given the complex, consumer preference–driven reality of this cultural industry, much nuance is needed when attempting to examine social stratification in the cemetery.

Additionally, we find a diverse range of iconographic references and formal characteristics. Markers seemingly came in all shapes and sizes with more than eight variations on steles having been identified as well as columns, chapels, sarcophagi-style structures, and pedestal tombs with both Christian and Greco-Roman motifs: winged hourglasses, laurel wreaths, urns, decorative crosses, inverted torches, and acanthus leaves. Other than crosses, which were included on 68% of all tombs with some form of decoration, no single motif emerged as significantly prominent. The result of this was a somewhat eclectic space in which monuments reflected the individual taste preferences of consumers more than a unified style that could be identified as "typical of the period."

Based on this evidence, it is also useful to consider the market for funerary monuments, even in this early phase, according to Kelvin Lancaster's theory of consumer demand (Lancaster, 1966, 1971). Taking a hedonic pricing approach to consumer goods, Lancaster's theory argues that consumers derive utility from the characteristics that a good provides rather than from the good itself. Therefore, Lancaster's theory positions consumption as a process of selecting goods that offer optimal bundles of desired characteristics, thereby accounting for consumer choice in markets with diverse offerings. Within this model, a consumer selects the best option for them, considering all available options and their willingness—and ability—to pay.

Comparing monument features (shape, iconography, ironwork, etc.) to burial duration proved my hypothesis that it was not only the most modest of markers that were temporary. In fact, the markers for temporary concessions and even free plots were often elaborately decorated, and presumably quite costly, stone monuments. Counter-intuitively—albeit in line with Lancaster—this suggests that when budgets were too tight to allow for the ideal bundle of burial characteristics (i.e., a long duration burial and an elaborate monument), families were more likely to opt for the more costly marker and substitute in the shorter duration burial. In short, looking permanent was more important that truly being permanent. Below, I elaborate on the effect of these economic factors on monument designs as the century progressed.

4.1 *Eclecticism and the Popular Market for Funerary Monuments*

Véron's (1877) short story *Regrets éternels* provides the most vivid, albeit satirical, description of how grave markers were commissioned in the nineteenth century. Here, a young widow visits a *marbrier*'s shop to purchase a marker for her recently deceased husband's grave. She is shown a catalogue with the newest designs, and, as she peruses the catalogue, the *marbrier* starts asking her about her late husband (Véron, 1877, pp. 126–127). Learning that her husband had been a medical doctor, the *marbrier* proposes an elaborate—and expensive—chapel-style tomb adorned with a portrait of the deceased as his namesake saint (a feature the *marbrier* pitches as very *à la mode* in the faubourg Saint-Germain). Finding the chapel horribly overpriced, the widow settles on a simple broken column design. Then, they advance to the inscription. The *marbrier* presents several options, quoting a price to which the widow retorts that her husband was never one for pomp. "Besides," she continues with a feigned earnestness, "the real inscription is engraved into our hearts." And with that, she opts to inscribe only the deceased's name (Véron, 1877, p. 132).[6]

This fictionalized encounter illustrates what was likely the very real experience of purchasing a monument, which itself mirrored the process of arranging a funeral service (see Trompette, 2008, 2012; Alexander, 2024, pp. 63–65). It would not have been simply a matter of walking into a shop, selecting a standard model, and purchasing it, as Boussard suggested in his 1870 treatise. Instead, there would have been a process of negotiating the client's preferences and budget against many options the *marbrier* could offer. Although one could begin with a catalogue model, there would have always been room for customization—from the addition of various sculptural and decorative elements to the length and style of the inscription—to suit the patron's needs.

One of the earliest surviving examples of such a catalogue is a small, undated model book authored by Pierre Lachave. Though little is known about Lachave himself, evidence suggests that this volume would have been produced in the late 1820s or 1830s. An example in the collection the of Historical Library of the City of Paris is particularly interesting because we know it belonged to a specific *marbrier*, identified only as Dumont, who inscribed his name in the book and made marginal notes working out the price of monuments according to a set of specific characteristics (Fig. 2). Here, it is apparent that the idea was not to use this book as a series of designs to be copied exactly, but rather to provide some ideas for possibilities that could be customized according to a specific client's needs. At the top left of one page, for instance, Dumont has indicated the type of stone (*marbre blanc* [white marble]) to be used and the estimated cost (15 francs) per one hundred letters in the inscription; at the bottom of the page, he records additional information such as the price of the marble face (300 francs) and stone socle (200 francs).

[6] "D'ailleurs la vraie inscription est gravée dans nos cœurs."

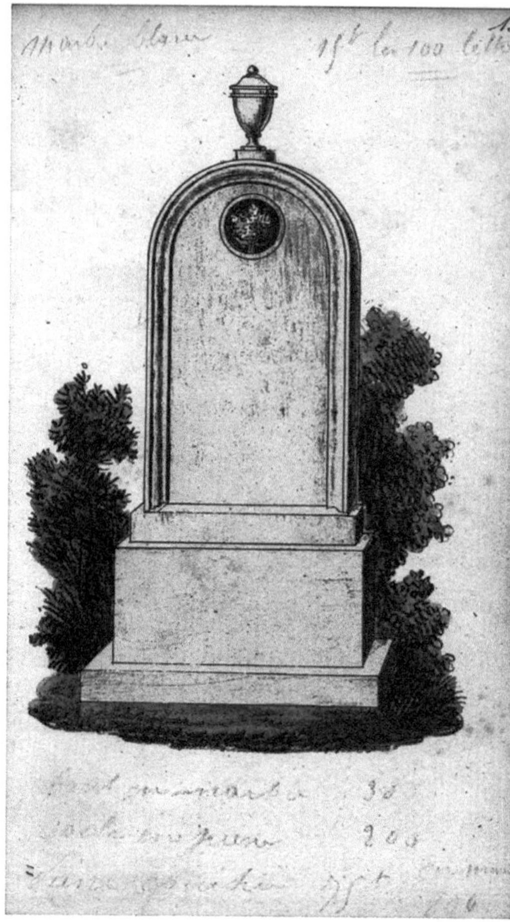

Fig. 2 Example of a die and base headstone with *Marbrier's* marginalia, plate 13 from L. Lachave, *Recueil de monuments funèbres*, ca. 1830s. Ville de Paris/ Bibliothèque historique, Paris. *Source* Image in the public domain

Lachave's book contains a wide range of monument types from small, simple designs to more elaborate family chapels, demonstrating how *marbriers* worked within a highly segmented market. Examples such as this demonstrate the different types of stone, fonts, ironwork, and other decorative elements available, suggesting that, while one might have started with a basic design, it would have been expected that one would pick and choose different elements to create something unique to the client and decedent.

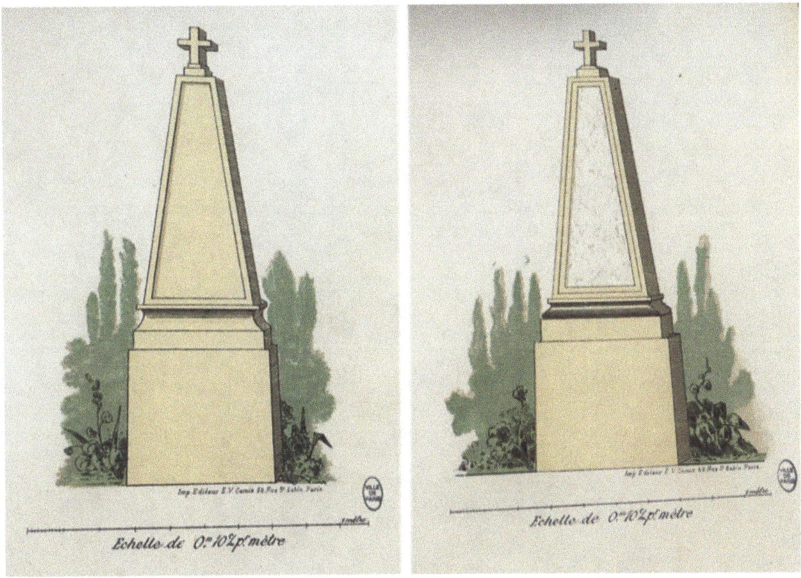

Fig. 3 Variations on a monument design, plates 6 and 7 from E. V. Camis, *Sépultures nouvelles*, 1885. Ville de Paris/Bibliothèque historique, Paris. *Source* Image in the public domain

Confirmation of these modular design strategies is demonstrated in several model books within which alternate options for modifying a given design appear on adjacent pages. In Fig. 3, for example, we see how one could have upgraded a granite monument by adding a white marble plaque to its face. Even more conspicuous evidence, however, appears in an 1895 catalogue for the Gourdon-Docq company, in which price structures are defined according to whether one chose to follow the design exactly or alter dimensions, ornaments, or materials. In Fig. 4, for example, we can see how changing out the classical-style urn for a Latin cross would have not only altered the look but increased the price by 180 francs.

Another important characteristic of these catalogues is the seemingly deliberate fusion of architectural traditions that, at least by the 1870s, had become known as the *style moderne* (modern style). In an 1871 model book by the *marbrier* Leblanc, *style moderne* (Fig. 5) is the most

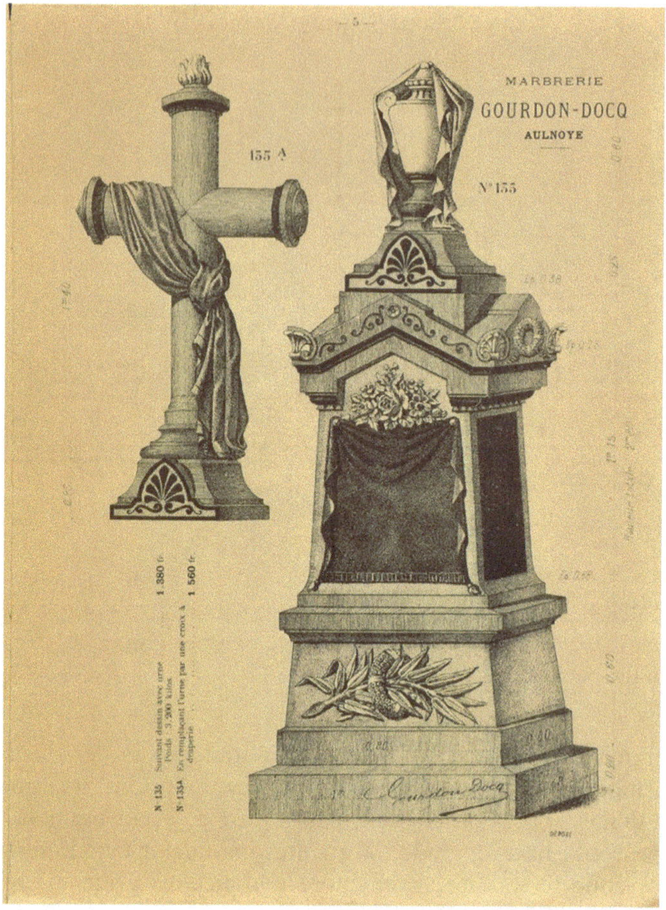

Fig. 4 Funerary monument model nos. 135 from Gourdon-Docq sales catalogue, July 10, 1895. Ville de Paris/Bibliothèque Forney, Paris. *Source* Image in the public domain

common design designation. The volume also contains several overt examples of revivalist designs that draw on classical, gothic, and neoclassical forms. Most monuments, however, exhibit a commingling of various architectural and iconographic influences that is decidedly not revivalist. Rather, I argue, these designs—juxtaposed against those

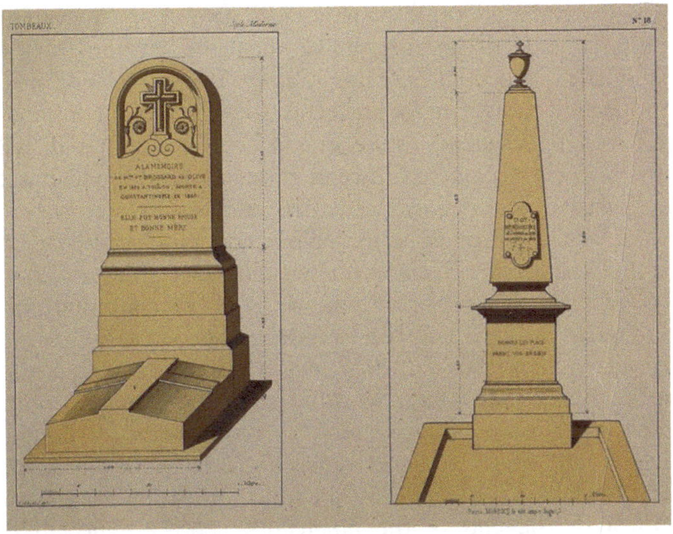

Fig. 5 Examples of *style moderne* monuments from E. Leblanc, *Recueil de monuments funèbres d'après tous les styles*, 1871. New York Public Library, New York. *Source* Image in the public domain, retrieved from HathiTrust

labeled Greek, Roman, Ogival, or Louis XVI—were intended to stand in stark contrast to revivalist designs as something uniquely modern: a composite of historical influences presented in a uniquely modern format for modern consumers.

Of the seventy-four examples included in Leblanc's catalogue, 41% constitute a composite or eclectic style (Alexander, 2024, p. 136).[7] Whereas the Gothic-style tombs in LeBlanc's volume are defined by elements such as pinnacles, trefoils, and pointed arches, classical designs possess features such as ionic columns, rounded arches, pediments, urns, and laurel wreaths. None of the Gothic-style designs possess typically classical design elements, but nearly all Classical-style models included some Christian iconography (e.g., crosses, hourglasses) or elements

[7] *Style moderne* is the most common term used in Leblanc, but other terms—e.g., *style contemporaine* (contemporary style), *sépultures nouvelles* (new tombs), *style composé* (composite style—are also used to refer to this composite design trend in Leblanc as well as other model books (Alexander, 2024, pp. 132–136).

recalling a particularly Gothic element, such as trefoils. Such tombs suggest a modest eclecticism not unlike the early monuments at Père-Lachaise, where—as documented in *Le champ du repos*—mixing and matching Antique and Christian forms seems to have been common. What Leblanc's volume designates as the *style moderne* is, I argue, directly connected to eclecticism, a nineteenth-century design trend generally addressed through the lens of academic, Beaux-Arts architecture. Promoted by the architect César Daly through his journalistic endeavors—such as the *Revue générale de l'architecture et des Travaux publics*, which he had founded in 1839—eclecticism played a significant role in Daly's conception of a new, uniquely French architectural style (see Daly, 1863).

What Leblanc describes as the *style moderne* in his catalogue—as well as those monuments that appear in other surviving funerary monuments catalogues of this period as new or contemporary designs—are, I suggest, directly related to the eclecticism that has generally been understood as a key feature of Beaux-Arts architecture, dating roughly from the 1830s through the end of the nineteenth century. Though drawing inspiration from the past, eclecticism is not to be confused with revivalism, which sought to recover and reproduce historical forms. Instead, eclecticism drew together a variety of architectural influences, amassed from diverse cultural and historical sources, into a single design (see, e.g., Van Zanten, 1994; Schoonjans, 2008). Eclecticism has also been acknowledged as a key characteristic of architectural designs for nineteenth-century French cemeteries (Bertrand & Groud, 2016, pp. 200–203). Although widely understood as an academic architectural style, my research demonstrates how eclecticism was also characteristic of monuments commissioned from *marbriers*. In fact, one can already see traces of this eclecticism in Roger and Roger, where the synthesis of Antique and Christian elements—both formal and iconographic—consistently occurred. This early tendency towards funerary eclecticism was further stimulated and perhaps informed by the *marbriers'* modular strategies, a finding that unseats architects from their position as the originators of eclectic architecture and repositions "low-end" trends as key influences on "high-end" taste.

4.2 *Funerary Eclecticism and the "Trickle Round" Effect*

Despite limited past scholarship on vernacular funerary monuments in France, the assumption seems to be that monuments produced by *marbriers* either represented work that directly fulfilled architectural designs or that, using cheaper materials or executed with reduced decoration or precision, represent attempts to emulate elite styles for middle-class consumers. The former constitute what we traditionally understand as luxury goods, while the latter are what we might call semi-luxury goods: objects made for lower market segments that imitate luxuries. Semi-luxury goods act as markers of distinction between the middle and lower classes as true luxury goods signal differences between the elite and middle classes. Consequently, the tendency in monument studies has been to understand style as a function of the trickling down of elite, luxury taste preferences into the more popular market; hence also the tendency to view eclecticism—as defined through Daly's work and exemplified through architectural endeavors associated with the Beaux-Arts movement—as having trickled down into vernacular funerary monument designs.

Part of this assumption that middle- and lower-class monuments were styled after high architecture comes directly from the architects themselves; they are known to have decried the work of the *marbriers* as tasteless imitations (Boussard, 1870) or exaggeratedly endorsed the ability of academically trained architects (Daly, 1871). With limited surviving direct evidence to the contrary, it stands to reason that one would assume architectural designs for funerary monuments were objects to be emulated by the lower classes in a trickle-down fashion. However, when one considers the regulatory context within which grave markers became accessible to a broader public; the picking-and-choosing process of purchasing lower segment monuments; and the rise of eclecticism in funerary architecture after the 1830s without the bias of the architect (who had a vested interest in promoting funerary architecture over *marbrerie* [stonework]), then it is more precise to consider other mechanisms of influence and status signaling than the trickle-down theories associated with traditional theories of consumption.

Several consumer studies over the past decade have explored trickle-up mechanisms, particularly in relation to popular fashion. Trickle-up refers to bottom-up rather than top-down processes of influence wherein utilitarian trends among working classes come to influence high-end, luxury fashions. The quintessential example is denim, which originated among the working classes as a durable, practical material that eventually trickled up the social hierarchy until luxury brands, too, began producing denim clothing, often without the functional quality that they once had (see, e.g., Ordabayeva &

Chandon, 2011; Atik & Firat, 2013; Bellezza et al. 2017). But it would be incorrect to suggest that eclecticism in architecture broadly was, like denim in the twentieth century, the result of a purely trickle-up effect. It is unlikely that eclectic tendencies resulting from picking-and-choosing purchasing strategies from the low-end funerary monuments market is the direct predecessor of eclecticism in architecture. However, given the specific regulatory factors surrounding the development of the popular funerary monuments market, it is my contention that we must consider the rise of eclecticism, at least in funerary architecture, as resulting from a "trickle-round" model of taste change and status signaling.

Bellezza and Berger (2020) describe how the presence of a wealthier middle class since the Industrial Revolution has resulted in an increased demand for luxuries that mass production has met with the production of larger supplies of these goods. They argue that, consequently, the signal value of luxury goods has decreased, eventually ceasing to function as reliable indicators of elite status. Thus, for high-status individuals to distinguish themselves from the middle class, they either (i) turn away from wealth signals that have been appropriated by the middle class in a Bourdieusian urge toward distinction and adopt new products to further distance themselves from the middle or (ii) turn toward low-status items as new sources of cultural distinction. The appropriation of these "tasteless" trends among elites becomes acceptable because, Bellezza and Berger write:

> only some individuals, equipped with the right knowledge or cultural capital, can decode these newer, more sophisticated signals. Thus, rather than accruing distinction from luxury goods and pecuniary rarity, high-status individuals consume objects that are ideationally difficult and can be appreciated only by the few who have acquired the ability to do so. (p. 120)

This process is known as the trickle-round effect (see also Nelsen, 1970; Trigg, 2001). Like the Industrial Revolution for Bellezza and Berger's analysis of luxury goods, the 1804 burial reforms is an exogenous shock that precipitated a massive increase in demand for funerary monuments, the production of which was met by an increasingly specialized funerary monuments industry. Like other luxury goods, funerary monuments were once status signals only available to the highest tiers of society. Once middle- and working-class individuals gained the right to erect monuments and the ability to purchase them, having a grave marker for a loved one ceased to be a luxury and became a semi-luxury available to a larger, more socioeconomically diverse audience.

Following Bellezza and Berger's trickle-round formula, we can begin to see how this mechanism might have latently been at play in the rise of eclecticism in architecture. *Le champ du repos* revealed that, for early monuments in Père-Lachaise, stylistic choices were drawn both from Christian and Antique traditions, with neither emerging as particularly dominant (Alexander, 2024, pp. 117–121). In fact, already in this early period one can discern a tendency toward a fusion of stylistic forms, with elements from both traditions often combined on a single monument. While there is no concrete evidence that this "eclectic" tendency constituted a recognized style of funerary monuments in this early phase, the deliberate fusion of architectural traditions is what I contend became known as the *style moderne* by the second half of the century.[8]

As a larger population gained the minimally regulated ability to mark the graves of their loved ones, a popular market for funerary monuments burgeoned throughout Paris (Alexander, 2020). With the resulting increased supply, elites needed a new manner of distinguishing themselves. This manifested in the form of the chapel-style tomb, an option that was only permitted for perpetual concessions and therefore only accessible to the wealthiest individuals and families. The chapel tomb, however, was not the only stylistic development resulting from widened access to funerary monuments.

Allowing the consumer to maximize utility by selecting the ornaments, materials, inscriptions, and more that best suited individual taste preferences and budgets, this mode of piecing together a monument almost certainly resulted in an inadvertent eclecticism that emerged concurrent to, or perhaps even predated, the academic eclecticism that art and architectural historians discuss in relation to architectural theory and practice. Intentionally or not, then, the eclecticism of Beaux-Arts architects such as Daly (1871) and Boussard (1870) appears to be embedded in a "low-end" model of buying monuments. In this conception of funerary architectural designs, eclecticism works in much the same way as kitsch in the mid-

[8] While Leblanc's 1871 *Recueil de monuments funèbres d'après tous les styles*, unambiguously labels monument designs as *moderne* or *contemporaine* (contemporary), other volumes do not explicitly label styles. The designs do, however, adhere to the same stylistic conventions.

twentieth century. It then follows that this "tasteless" eclecticism of the masses becomes high architecture through the presumed interpretive skills and artistic prowess of architects, in other words, through their cultural capital. Indeed Daly himself claimed it was the architect's responsibility to translate emotions into architectural forms:

> In literature, comedy laughs, tragedy weeps; and if architecture has its operas, its circuses and its columns, celebratory and triumphant structures, it also has its tears, its monuments of pain and mourning: its tombs. Thus a need for the architect to learn how to express, through combinations of line and color—especially line—the two great essential characteristics of human sensibility.[9] (Daly, 1871, p. 3)

As arbiters of taste, the academically trained architects of the École des Beaux-Arts were, in theory, uniquely equipped with the cultural capital required to translate the sophisticated signals of low-end eclecticism for an elite audience who would commission their designs as a means of distinguishing themselves from the economically inferior. Hence, a trickling round of eclectic funerary monument trends.

This effect is further compounded by the fact that the producers of architect-designed and *marbrier*-designed monuments were one in the same: the *marbriers*. Just as *praticiens* were regularly employed by sculptors to execute the designs of sculptors, including those like Auguste Rodin who have now become household names, architects employed *marbriers*—many of whom, according to their own descriptions of their ateliers in commercial almanacs, operated independently—to realize their commissions. Ostensibly, this reduces the architect to nothing more than a brand: an intangible marker of quality that cannot be measured materially and effectively negates the idea that the presumed lower price of works not designed by architects denotes an innately—i.e., materially—inferior quality.

[9] "En littérature, la comédie rit, la tragédie pleure; et si l'architecture a ses opéras, ses cirques et ses colonnes, édifices de fête et de triomphe, elle a aussi ses sanglots, ses monuments de douleur ou de deuil: ses tombeaux. De là une nécessité pour l'architecte d'apprendre à exprimer par des combinaisons de lignes et de couleurs—de lignes surtout—les deux grands caractères essentiels de la sensibilité humaine."

5 Conclusion

Beginning with Roger and Roger's *Le champ du repos*, I demonstrated how a database-driven approach to somewhat nebulous material evidence might allow us to identify otherwise undetectable trends and thus ask new questions about topics we think we already know well. In undertaking this examination monuments known to have been in Père-Lachaise in 1815, I identified popular modes of grave marking during this early period, which, when examined alongside models for monuments produced later in the century, permitted an analysis of how styles developed over time. Most critically, in taking this approach, I have proposed a revised, and more nuanced, view of eclecticism's emergence in post-1830s Paris. Rather than privileging "high art" as the model to be emulated in popular fashions, I have demonstrated the necessity of examining circular flows of influence, such as the trickle-round theory of taste change and status signaling, to more precisely understand how styles were formulated and dispersed among socioeconomically diverse consumers. Stimulated by an emergent and then a developing ability to individualize death on a large scale, the underlying incentive of funerary commemoration was both a matter of distinction and permanence signaling. Except for the chapel tombs that remained exclusive to perpetual burials and could thus only function as signals of elite status, relatively few visual differences could be discerned among free, temporary, and perpetual monuments. From the use of materials like stone and iron to the eclectic *style moderne* that would come to define an emerging French aesthetic rooted in historical visual cues, socioeconomically diverse consumers responded to burial reforms by embracing a visual culture of permanence. In doing so, low- and high-end monuments alike projected an enduring appearance, regardless of whether they were intended to stand for five years or an eternity.

Regardless of the plausibility of the trickle-round effect I have proposed here, however, it has become the architect's brand of eclecticism that has stood the test of time in the cemeteries of Paris. But in re-examining stylistic developments of funerary monuments over the course of the nineteenth century through proxy evidence for tomb markers that have not survived to the present, this research repositions this legacy as one rooted in a "low-end," largely ephemeral tradition of grave marking. In terms of this volume's proposed triadic model of market segmentation, what emerges are two competing sub-segments, each at opposing ends of the spectrum. Here, the *marbriers*' production, which undoubtedly dominated historically in terms of sheer volume, constitutes sub-segment 1, while the architect's output, which has won out in terms of survival and thus scholarly and popular attention, constitutes sub-segment 2. Importantly, however, we must understand these sub-segment categorizations as context dependent. While the brand strength—low to moderate among *marbriers* and moderate to high among architects—remains relatively stable over time (even if some names are more recognizable now than they were then or vice versa) because the designation *architect* itself evokes a level quality—then as now—that is, in many ways, timeless albeit highly subjective and effectively immeasurable. Functionality and rarity, on the other hand, are transmutable across time because of the regulatory environment within which these objects were created and removed. Those objects that were once rare have become what one commonly associates with these spaces while those that were once abundant are now a relative scarcity. Likewise, function is highly dependent on context and subject to wide interpretation, especially with such historical distance from the the time in which the monuments were created. While one could argue for high direct functionality in both cases because of the monuments' purpose of grave marking, both categories of monuments also possess a high level of symbolic functionality in terms of their design and their very presence in the cemetery as markers of individuals who, prior to 1804, would have been relegated to anonymous mass graves and charnel houses.

Data Availability Statement

The data informing this chapters are publicly available under CC–BY–NC licenses:

Alexander, K. P. (2023a). *Dataset for: After 23 prairial.* The Hive: University of Utah Research Data Repository. https://doi.org/10.7278/S50d-d18q-yfzt

Alexander, K. P. (2023b). *Dataset for: A data-driven analysis of cemeteries and social reform in Paris, 1804–1924.* The Hive: University of Utah Research Data Repository. https://doi.org/10.7278/S50d-4cbs-yrv1

References

Alexander, K. P. (2018). Père-Lachaise in 1815: A new method in the study of ephemeral funerary monuments. In E. Doss & C. Snay (Eds.), *Monumental troubles: Rethinking what monuments mean today* (pp. 16–28). Midwest Art History Society and the Snite Museum of Art. https://doi.org/10.7274/r0-30e5-2840

Alexander, K. P. (2020). *Marbriers de Paris*: The popular market for funerary monuments in nineteenth-century Paris. *Early Popular Visual Culture*, *18*(2), 127–148. https://doi.org/10.1080/17460654.2020.1804964

Alexander, K. P. (2023a). *Dataset for: After 23 prairial*. The Hive: University of Utah Research Data Repository. https://doi.org/10.7278/S50d-d18q-yfzt

Alexander, K. P. (2023b). *Dataset for: A data-driven analysis of cemeteries and social reform in Paris, 1804–1924*. The Hive: University of Utah Research Data Repository. https://doi.org/10.7278/S50d-4cbs-yrv1

Alexander, K. P. (2024). *A data-driven analysis of cemeteries and social reform in Paris, 1804–1924*. Routledge.

Alexander, K. P. (2025). Le champ du repos: A tidy approach to early epitaphs in Père-Lachaise Cemetery. In V. Brandis, J. L. de Jong, & R. Seidel (Eds.), *Funerary inscriptions in early modern Europe. Shaping identities to remember* (pp. 431–451). Brill. https://doi.org/10.1163/9789004711709_018

Ariès, P. (1981). *The hour of our death: The classic history of Western attitudes toward death over the last one thousand years* (H. Weaver, Trans.). Knopf.

Atik, D., & Firat, A. F. (2013). Fashion creation and diffusion: The institution of marketing. *Journal of Marketing Management*, *29*(7–8), 836–860. https://doi.org/10.1080/0267257X.2012.729073

Bellezza, S., & Berger, J. (2020). Trickle-round signals: When low status is mixed with high. *Journal of Consumer Research*, *47*(1), 100–127. https://doi.org/10.1093/jcr/ucz049

Bellezza, S., Paharia, N., & Keinan, A. (2017). Conspicuous consumption of time: When busyness and lack of leisure time become a status symbol. *Journal of Consumer Research*, *44*(1), 118–138. https://doi.org/10.1093/jcr/ucw076

Bertrand, R., & Groud, G. (2016). *Patrimoine funéraire français: Cimetières et tombeaux*. Centre des monuments nationaux.

Boussard, J. (1870). *Recueil des tombeaux les plus remarquables exécutés de nos jours et représentés en perspective*. Librairie Polytechnique de J. Baudry.

Bureau des Cimetières. (1889). *Notes sur les cimetières de la Ville de Paris*. A. Maulde.

Daly, C. (1863). *Nos doctrines: Réponse à deux objections adressées à la direction de la Revue de l'Architecture*. J. Claye.

Daly, C. (1871). *Architecture funéraire contemporaine*. Ducher et Cie.

Etlin, R. (1984). *The architecture of death: The transformation of the cemetery in eighteenth-century Paris*. The MIT Press.
Kselman, T. A. (1993). *Death and the afterlife in modern France*. Princeton University Press.
Lancaster, K. J. (1966). A new approach to consumer theory. *Journal of Political Economy, 74*(2), 132–157.
Lancaster, K. J. (1971). *Consumer demand: A new approach*. Columbia University Press.
Le Normand-Romain, A. (1995). *Mémoire de marbre: La sculpture funéraire en France, 1804–1914*. Bibliothèque historique de la Ville de Paris.
Legacey, E.-M. (2019). *Making space for the dead: Catacombs, cemeteries, and the reimagining of Paris, 1780–1830*. Cornell University Press.
Nelsen, H. M. (1970). The democratization of the antique: Meanings of antiques and dealers' perceptions of customers. *The Sociological Review, 18*(3), 407–419. https://doi.org/10.1111/j.1467-954X.1970.tb00474.x
Ordabayeva, N., & Chandon, P. (2011). Getting ahead of the Joneses: When equality increases conspicuous consumption among bottom-tier consumers. *Journal of Consumer Research, 38*(1), 27–41. https://doi.org/10.1086/658165
Pantano, N. A. (1997). Liberal politics and the Parisian cemetery: David d'Angers and Léon Vaudoyer's monument to General Foy, 1825–1831. *Oxford Art Journal, 20*(1), 23–34. https://doi.org/10.1093/oxartj/20.1.23
Roger,, & Roger,. (1816). *Le champ du repos, ou le cimetière Mont-Louis dit du Père Delachaise* (Vol. 2). Lebégue.
Schoonjans, Y. (2008). Regional architecture as an element of cosmopolitanism in César Daly's vision of eclecticism. In L. van Santvoort, J. de Maeyer, & T. Verschaffel (Eds.), *Sources of regionalism in the nineteenth century: Architecture, art and literature* (33–47). Leuven University Press.
Throsby, D., & Zednik, A. (2013). The economic and cultural value of paintings: Some empirical evidence In V. A. Ginsburgh & D. Throsby (Eds.), *Handbook of the economics of art and culture* (Vol. 2, pp. 81–99). North Holland.
Trigg, A. B. (2001). Veblen, Bourdieu, and conspicuous consumption. *Journal of Economic Issues, 35*(1), 99–115.
Trompette, P. (2008). *Le marché des défunts*. Sciences Po.
Trompette, P. (2012). Pompes funèbres and the overflowing of ostentatious funerals. In B. Czarniawsja & O. Löfgren (Eds.), *Managing overflow in affluent societies* (pp. 19–42). Routledge.
Van Zanten, D. (1994). *Building Paris: Architectural institutions and the transformation of the French capital, 1830–1870*. Cambridge University Press.
Véron, P. (1877). Regrets éternels. In *Le nouvel art d'aimer* (pp. 125–135). E. Dentu.

A Piece of Art in Every Household: The Nationwide Subscription of Graphic Art and Its Implications on the Market for Prints in Poland

Wiktor Komorowski

1 Introduction

This paper examines the history of the Nationwide Subscription of Graphic Art (*Ogólnopolska Subskrypcja Grafiki*), founded in 1965 in the Polish People's Republic, and its impact on the modern-day market for prints and multiples in Poland. It argues that the Nationwide Subscription of Graphic Art was one of the most tangible manifestations of a state-controlled art trade (Walczak, 1965, p. 7) and can be considered a major factor behind the significant modern-day oversupply of prints and their low prices. The paper compares current characteristics of the Polish market for prints with the historical characteristics of the state-controlled art market to outline the reasons for the recent surge of interest in prints, which have traditionally occupied the "low end" of the market. It draws on quantitative evidence from historical overviews prepared by Wiesław Walczak, Secretary General of the Committee for the Cooperation of Societies of Friends of Fine Arts (*Sekretarz Generalny Komisji Porozumienia Towarzystw Przyjaciół Sztuk Pięknych*), as published in the

W. Komorowski (✉)
Independent researcher, London, UK
e-mail: wiktorkomorowski1@gmail.com

A.-S. V. Radermecker (ed.), *Low-End Markets for Art and Cultural Goods*, Cultural Economics & the Creative Economy,
https://doi.org/10.1007/978-3-032-27566-0_7

catalogues of successive iterations of the Nationwide Subscription of Graphic Art, and compares these with statistical data from the Central Statistical Office (*Główny Urząd Statystyczny*) on recent changes in the Polish art market.[1]

This study highlights the impact of the centrally planned art trade on the modern-day art market in Poland. The Polish modern-day art market has its roots in an era when the art trade was fully regulated by the state. During the Polish People's Republic (1952–1989), the state held a monopoly over the country's art trade. After the market transformation in the 1980s, with its symbolic landmark in 1989 (Kołodko, 2010, p. 362), the Polish art market shifted to a free economy. In the 1990s, the market developed slowly and was dominated by attempts to privatize previously state-controlled art outlets, mainly the former art galleries of the state-led Auction House and Gallery DESA "Works of Art and Antiques." Following the economic downturn of the 1990s, the standard of living steadily increased, resulting in greater demand for luxury goods and art (Kompa & Witkowska, 2014).

A major stimulus for the development of the Polish art market was Poland's accession to the European Union in 2004, but an even more substantial breakthrough came in 2022, coinciding with the peak of the COVID-19 pandemic. In that year, the Polish art market reached a record turnover of 650.7 million Polish złoty (PLN) (approx. $167.9 million). The rapid growth around 2022 was driven by the popularization of digital bidding platforms, shifts in customers' investment strategies, and auction houses' market strategies. In 2021, Desa Group, the owner of Desa Unicum—Poland's largest auction house in

[1] Central Statistical Office (*Główny Urząd Statystyczny*) is the Polish government's chief executive agency responsible for collecting and publishing statistics related to the economy in Poland. The data regarded the Polish art market provided by Central Statistical Office is based on the financial statements of companies which are submitted by the auction houses, art galleries and art dealers, and which are shared by the National Court Register (*Krajowy Rejestr Sądowy*). The financial statements of companies only present the official absolute sale numbers. This makes it difficult to provide precise estimates on the percentage split between each medium on the market. This data does not include the "grey zone" of the market where artwork moves between collectors without registering the sale. The size of the "grey zone" on the Polish art market is difficult to estimate. The Committee for the Cooperation of Societies of Friends of Fine Arts was the main body responsible for organising the Nationwide Subscription of Graphic Art.

2022 with a 51% market share—announced plans to enter the Polish stock market. From around 2020, Desa Unicum began stimulating the market to increase the potential valuation of the company's shares. The impact of this campaign on the structure of the art market in Poland remains to be investigated. According to the Central Statistical Office (2022), auction houses were the primary distribution channel, accounting for more than 60% of the market. The Internet has become a significant trade platform, reaching 10% of the total market in 2021. Although the Polish economy has experienced rapid growth in recent years, with increasing GDP per capita, this trend has not translated into widespread interest in art investment. Among Poland's middle class, the frequency of art purchases remains lower than in Western Europe, reflected in lower price levels (Lucińska, 2021). In contrast to societies with a long history of free-market economies, post-communist societies do not tend to view art as a sustainable, long-term investment (Białowąs et al., 2018, p. 609). Many purchases seem to be driven more by emotion than by careful investment analysis. A clear manifestation of this trend is the growing interest in the "low end" of the art market, particularly among buyers seeking works with starting prices around PLN 1,000 (approx. $280). Such collectors often view buying art as a leisure activity or as a way to decorate newly purchased apartments. Since 2008, the Polish art market has seen the growth of auctions dedicated to so-called "young artists," most often offering works by less-established creators born after 1975. Each year, more than 55 such auctions take place in Poland, with starting prices of PLN 1,000 for an oil-on-canvas painting. The average sale price reaches PLN 1,200 (approx. $330) (Białowąs et al., 2018, p. 596). A similar trend can be observed in the field of prints, often considered the "minor arts." This common disregard is reflected in the relatively low prices prints and works on paper fetch on the global art market compared with higher-valued paintings or sculptures. The position of prints in the Polish art market reflects this trend; however, as this paper demonstrates, it is also marked by significant growth in absolute sales volume, an oversupply of prints produced since 1945, and a rising number of emotion-driven purchases. This paper focuses on the history of the Nationwide Subscription of Graphic Art (*Ogólnopolska Subskrypcja Grafiki*), founded in 1965 in the Polish People's Republic, and its impact on the modern-day market for prints and multiples in Poland.

2 "A Piece of Art in Every Household"

One of the traits of the contemporary Polish market for prints is the significant supply of high-quality works produced since the 1950s; a result of the strong interest in printed media that emerged in the Polish People's Republic in the early 1960s. Print, as the so-called "people's medium," came to the attention of the communist authorities as early as the 1950s, but the true surge in its popularity began after 1960. Prints can be easily multiplied and circulated in large numbers. They can be packed in tubes and sent to distant places by post. Their production is often a collective process, requiring input from an artist, a master printmaker, and paper producers—characteristics that aligned with the slogans of collective socialist work. These characteristics made prints the medium of choice for the communist authorities.

The printmaking boom originated in a number of state-funded initiatives devoted, often exclusively, to this specific segment. In the 1960s, about 50 printmakers graduated each year from the academies of fine arts in Warsaw and Kraków. In addition, two large-scale international exhibitions of prints and posters were funded by the state. The International Graphic Art Biennale (*Międzynarodowe Biennale Grafiki*), founded in Kraków in 1966 (Weichardt, 2006, pp. 21–29), and the International Poster Biennale (*Międzynarodowe Biennale Plakatu*), founded in Warsaw in the same year (Matul, 2015, p. 22), created a specific internal competition between these cities and their academies of fine arts. Since 1959, printmakers in Kraków have organized the cyclical Competition for the Best Graphics of the Month (*Konkurs na Najlepszą Grafikę Miesiąca*) (Waltoś, 1975). This competition was a strong emancipatory stimulus and was immediately embraced by the younger generation of artists, who were granted the opportunity to exhibit their works and, in a rare occurrence, to compete for monetary prizes. The prize-winning prints were presented at the exhibitions of the International Press and Books Club (*Klub Międzynarodowej Prasy i Książki, KMPiK*).

Prints occupied a special place in the wider social consciousness of Polish citizens from around the mid-1960s, and their popularization was promoted under the slogan "A Piece of Art in Every Household." Interestingly, prints were not only associated with cheap state propaganda, nor were they regarded merely as craft or anonymously produced folk art; rather, they were recognized as an independent medium in their own right. Additionally, prints offered a breath of freedom, as they could be considered early beacons of a free market. From 1965, members of the Association of Polish Artists and Designers (*Związek Polskich Artystów Plastyków*), along with members of the Society of Friends of Fine Arts in Warsaw (*Towarzystwo Przyjaciół Sztuk Pięknych w Warszawie*), carried out yearly subscriptions of graphic art. The subscription was an annual traveling exhibition of around 50 prints submitted by invited printmakers. Works at the Nationwide Subscription of Graphic Art were exhibited with prices and could be purchased directly from the organizers—a rare possibility given the various restrictions on the art trade in the country. Before reaching the nationwide level, the Subscription of Graphic Art was organized on a smaller, local scale.[2] The Warsaw Society of Friends of Fine Arts undertook its first subscription campaign in December 1959. In total, 47 graphic artists took part in this subscription, and 7,000 people visited the exhibitions (Walczak, 1978, 3). The prints were sold for a total amount of PLN 72,850.[3] This was a major success, and the organizers quickly decided to hold another edition of the show. It took place between 1961 and 1962 and was titled *Artistic Creativity in the 15th Anniversary of the Polish People's Republic* (*Twórczość plastyczna w XV-lecie Polskiej Republiki Ludowej*). The second, smaller edition brought in only PLN 8,750 in revenue; however, over 29 exhibitions were organized in workplaces. These encouraging results led the Warsaw Society of Friends of Fine Arts to announce the 1st Nationwide Subscription of Graphic Art in 1965. The initiative to organize the Nationwide

[2] The National Artistic Graphics Subscription is the successor of a similar prewar initiative. In 1912, the Society of Friends of Graphic Arts was founded. Graphic art was gaining on popularity. In 1922, the Circulating Graphic Art Exhibition was organised, which was displayed in almost all major cities in Poland. At that time, Warsaw began to increasingly take over the role of the center of graphic art, especially after the woodcut artist Władysław Skoczylas (1883–1934) moved from Zakopane to Warsaw in 1923 to take over the Print Department at the School of Fine Arts in Krakow. In addition to the General Association of Polish Graphic Artists in Warsaw, which had existed since 1919, in 1925 the Association of Polish Artists "Ryt" was founded, gathering mainly Skoczylas' students. In 1935, "Czerń i Biel" group was established, bringing together the youngest graphic artists who, like their master Władysław Skoczylas, preferred the woodcut technique. The "Ryt" association, in addition to exhibition and popularisation activities, ran a graphic art subscription. The first subscription was announced in 1935 together with the "ABC" daily newspaper. The subscription turned out to be a great success and by 1938, seven nationwide subscriptions had been organised, thanks to which about 8000 graphics had been sold.

[3] According to Central Statistical Office (*Główny Urząd Statystyczny*) (2025), in 1965, the average monthly salary in Poland reached 1 867 PLN.

Subscription of Graphic Art was undertaken by the Coordinating Committee of the Society of Friends of Fine Arts in Warsaw and can be seen as a bottom-up initiative on the part of the printmakers. The Central Council of Trade Unions and the Main Board of the Association of Polish Artists and Designers assumed patronage over the subscription activities, while the Ministry of Culture and Art provided financial support. In the 1970s, this support came through the specially established Fund for the Development of Fine Arts (*Fundusz Rozwoju Twórczości Plastycznej*), which operated under the auspices of the Department of Fine Arts of the Ministry of Culture (Walczak, 1978, p. 3). The official program stated that the Nationwide Subscription would seek to enhance the role of visual arts and create conditions conducive to the development and popularization of graphic art by bringing the creative community closer to broader circles of society. The organizer's manifesto, printed in the opening pages of the first catalogue of the Nationwide Subscription, stated: "We aim to create conditions in which the popularization of contemporary works of graphic artists does not involve diminishing their significance or lowering their value" (Walczak, 1965, p. 7). This appeal reflected the neglected position of graphic arts within the creative sector and pointed to the high hopes of the organizers, who sought to make the event a powerful educational platform. The Nationwide Subscription was intended to become a widely accessible review of different trends in contemporary graphic arts. Its educational dimension was meant to change the prevailing social belief that prints were mainly craft or folk art and not associated with higher artistic value. Additionally, the event was designed to encourage "noble collecting of unique graphic prints" and to promote the creation of galleries at state-funded companies. Already in the first edition, the organizers decided to clearly define the main group of potential customers in order to avoid any accusations of undermining the centrally planned economy by introducing elements of a free market. This precaution was expressed in the foreword to the first catalogue, which stated:

> (...) it is considered right that works of art purchased at exhibitions from union, administration and company funds should be designated for the gradual setting up of art galleries in workplaces (cultural centres), for the interior decoration of cultural and educational institutions, workers' hotels and schools, as well as for awards for champions of socialist work and rationalisers and outstanding social activists. (Walczak, 1965, p. 7)

The Nationwide Subscription was directed primarily at associations, workplaces, cultural centers, clubs, community centers, and libraries, and to a lesser extent at individual collectors (Walczak, 1978, p. 3). This was a compromise between enabling the unobstructed circulation of artworks and economically supporting artists, especially printmakers, who often struggled financially.

In order to obtain a wide range of works, the Board of the Graphics Section of the Association of Polish Artists and Designers asked all regional boards of the Association to designate printmakers who might take part in the event. As a result, the Main Board invited 50 graphic artists and secured a high variety of entries. The event followed an invitation-only pattern, which arguably might have led to nepotism or other forms of malpractice; however, every edition included a group of new artists. The selection committee consisted of members of the Board of the Graphics Section of the Association of Polish Artists and Designers, as well as members of the Board of the Society of Friends of Fine Arts in Warsaw. The subscription also included works by artists whose prints had received recognition in the Competition of the Central Council of Trade Unions and the Main Board of the Association of Polish Artists and Designers (Walczak, 1978, p. 3). Artists selected to participate in the Nationwide Subscription could submit only one design, although they could take part in several editions. Each print had to be hand-signed and numbered, and the size of the edition was to be specified according to UNESCO standards. The majority of prints included in the subscription were issued in editions of 50. Artists were also required to submit a short biographical note along with an address for correspondence, which was included in the catalogue. Publishing the artist's address often led to direct contact from potential buyers—a deliberately planned loophole in the centrally planned system, intended to further support printmakers economically.

Usually, four full sets of numbered and signed prints were purchased with funds granted by the Ministry of Culture and Art, and one full set of all prints selected for the Subscription was donated to the collection of the Warsaw Society of Friends of Fine Arts. The sets of subscription prints were then assembled into traveling exhibitions and displayed throughout the country at regional museums, cultural centers located at state-funded companies, and the regional branches of the Society of Friends of Fine Arts. Catalogues were printed for every edition of the show and made available in the exhibition rooms. The catalogues featured all the details about each artwork, including its price (Walczak, 1965, p. 7).

Prints could be ordered by filling out a special form, which was then sent to the headquarters of the Society of Friends of Fine Arts in Warsaw. The prints were sent by post to customers. The initial intention of the organizers was to donate entire sets to various institutions, which could then use them as traveling exhibitions. Every new edition would provide additional prints for the collections, which were intended to meet the urgent need for establishing cultural centers and galleries. These print collections would then be scattered across the country and displayed in various locations, providing a strong propagandistic message. In 1965, Poland was introducing a policy of decentralization, and the Nationwide Subscriptions served as an optimal example of its successful implementation.

As for the results of the campaign, data exists only for the first two editions combined, 1965 and 1966. Together, they generated purchases worth a total of PLN 534,000. A total of 166 exhibitions were organized, which were visited by over 200,000 people. In addition, 109 lectures and thematic meetings were held. In 1969–1970, the third edition of the event took place, resulting in 80 exhibitions and a record purchase total of PLN 408,000. Subscription exhibitions were viewed by over 100,000 visitors. The fourth edition took place between 1971 and 1972 as part of the Trade Unions Culture Festival. It also achieved strong results, with 52 exhibitions organized nationwide, attracting over 100,000 visitors, and generating a total turnover of PLN 313,200 (Walczak, 1978, p. 3).

3 Towards the New Face of Graphic Art

During the subscription exhibitions, feedback books were displayed on the tables, which turned out to be substantial sources for legitimizing the decisions taken by the organizational committee. The feedback books often contained a recurring postulate emphasizing the need to organize accompanying events for the opening of the subscription exhibition—for example, meetings with artists and critics, lectures, or even seminars at which issues of contemporary graphic art could be discussed and explained by competent speakers (Walczak, 1978, p. 3). Without these accompanying events, graphic art was often considered too complex for newcomers to understand. This perceived complexity was also strongly reflected in an introductory essay by Polish art history professor Karol Estreicher, included in the first catalogue of the Nationwide Subscription. Estreicher (1965, pp. 9–10) noted:

> Currently, the main assumptions behind graphic art have changed. It is not the purity of the technique, nor the accentuation of the texture by means of technology, but the painterly effects which are the most valued by graphic artists. That is why a multitude of techniques are being used nowadays. They are mixed; mechanical techniques are even combined with hand-drawn techniques or with a free-hand staining which is obtained from flat surface of the printing plate, what is more, often unintentionally. The boundary between a painted picture, a coloured engraving and a monotype cannot always be determined. If we add to this abstract art, or breaking of forms, searches and experiments, then the divisions will turn out to be illusory. Everything can be actually considered painting that is not sculpture nor architecture. Today, modern prints are more related to everyday life then they were before. They occupy the walls of small modern flats and are way more popular for decorative use.

The feedback also suggested that the duration of the subscription campaign should be extended to at least two years (Walczak, 1978, p. 3). This would allow recipients who encountered it for the first time to get involved in the process and gather funds for acquiring artworks. A longer duration of the event would also help engage more local institutions. The feedback received from the participants of the 4th edition mentioned that the subscription campaigns were by all means desirable, because of the egalitarian access to culture they provided, and also because of their educational opportunities (Walczak, 1978, p. 5).

The aim of the Nationwide Subscription was to provide Poles not only with firsthand contact with this neglected field of art, but also to grant them an opportunity to purchase prints by printmakers who were often underrepresented on the Polish art scene. For lesser-known, young printmakers, this was a significant opportunity to leave the shadows and sell their first artwork. At the same time, the Nationwide Subscription addressed the demand expressed by the members of the Association of Polish Artists and Designers, who advocated for more opportunities to exhibit and sell their work. For the printmakers' community, the Nationwide Subscription was an opportunity to protect the value of their craft and stop the influx of chromolithographs and other cheap printed reproductions that, in the 1960s, were flooding the apartments of Polish citizens. The popularization of reproductive media spoiled the understanding of the correlation between the monetary value and the quality of prints and could result in the monetary depreciation of their work. Polish printmaker Halina Chrostowska (1929–1990), in an article published in the catalogue of the 1st Nationwide Subscription of Graphic Art, argued that graphic art had to maintain its distinctiveness and could not be confused with reproductive media (Chrostowska, 1965, p. 11).

From the perspective of the cultural authorities, the Nationwide Subscription could be perceived as an important tool for incorporating artists—especially printmakers whose work was less in demand—into the country's economic system. The authorities envisioned the Nationwide Subscription as a significant opportunity to execute the so-called "social patronage" (*mecenat społeczny*) and to smuggle various propaganda slogans. For example, the 1st subscription included a group of printmakers who were awarded in the competition titled *Human Being and Work in the People's Poland* (*Człowiek i Praca w Polsce Ludowej*).

Prices for one print at the Nationwide Subscription started from around PLN 500 for a sheet measuring circa 30 cm by 40 cm. This was a substantial price relative to the average monthly salary in the country, which in 1965 did not exceed PLN 1,900; however, it was not beyond the reach of an ordinary Polish citizen. The sale of prints was often advertised in newspapers such as *Express Wieczorny* (*The Evening Express*), and many Poles could afford an original piece of art. After a few weeks, the print arrived at the local post office for them to collect. The prints were sold in large quantities; however, even greater numbers were produced. This was due to the fact that many artists wanted to take part in the subscription, while the Association of Polish Artists and Designers insisted on introducing some aspects of free-market economy for the artists, who, in turn, supplied large numbers of prints in the hope of more substantial profits.

Over time, and partially thanks to the Nationwide Subscription, Poles developed a specific taste for prints, which resulted in an increase in the technical and programmatic quality of graphic media. For example, at the first edition of the Nationwide Subscription, potential customers encountered prints that combined superior technical skills with compelling programs. Some of the prints might have appeared to uninformed visitors as simplistic developments of folk motifs; however, many printmakers used folk tradition or pre-war woodcut in a self-reflexive manner in order to comment on it and expand its notion beyond mere craft.

Among these artists, Jerzy Panek (1918–2001) held a special place; his works were regarded as exemplifying a profound mastery of the woodcut technique. Making compelling woodcut prints requires a lot of practice, supported by a thorough study of the material and its properties. In the process of cutting a woodcut, the artist must apply pressure on the woodblock in a way not to chip the growth rings. The best woodcuts are executed with respect for the natural layout of the growth rings. For the first edition of the show, Panek prepared a woodcut titled *Bleating Goat* (*Becząca koza*) (Fig. 1) (Burkamp 1995, p. 143).

The print was designed in a minimalist way that could be seen almost as a combination of folk art with an abstract, Picasso-inspired design. It depicted a schematically outlined goat, sketched with only a few thin, black lines. The rest of the composition was left white, which, for the woodcut, meant that the printmaker had to remove all the wooden material on the matrix apart from the spots that constituted the black lines. Arguably, Panek's simplistic woodcut must have been difficult for

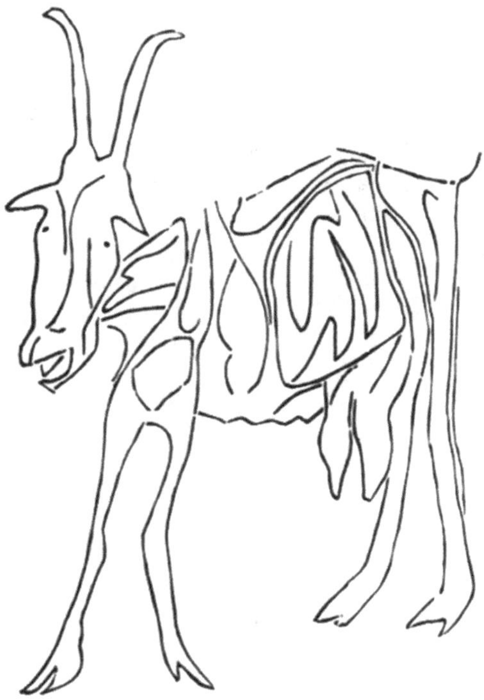

Fig. 1 Jerzy Panek, Bleating Goat (*Becząca koza*), 1964, Woodcut, 52 × 38 cm, Edition Size 50. *Source* Warszawskie Towarzystwo Przyjaciół Sztuk Pięknych w Warszawie (Ed.), *Ogólnopolska Subskrypcja Grafiki Artystycznej*, Warszawskie Towarzystwo Przyjaciół Sztuk Pięknych w Warszawie, 1965, p. 69

a wider audience to comprehend and might have appeared accidental or almost childish; however, the selection committee decided to distinguish this print among 50 others selected for the first subscription. Selecting Panek's print was very telling and highlighted the organizers' programmatic assumptions for the Nationwide Subscription. The event was meant to present a strong educational character, not only in regard to the propaganda stipulated by the state, but also in terms of developing a general understanding and appreciation of art.

Another manifestation of a compelling, though hidden under the guise of naïve art, program were the linocuts by Teresa Jakubowska (1930–2025), who used a children's illustration-inspired artistic language. Her designs were usually full of bitter irony, as in the case of her linocut titled *Smallpox* (*Ospa*) (Prymlewicz, 2021, pp. 11–12) (Fig. 2).

In her linocut, Jakubowska depicted a comic strip-like cross-section through a hospital building. Her work can be read as an allusion to the smallpox epidemic that broke out in 1963 in Wrocław. The patient zero was Bonifacy Jedynak, an officer of the Security Services of the Polish

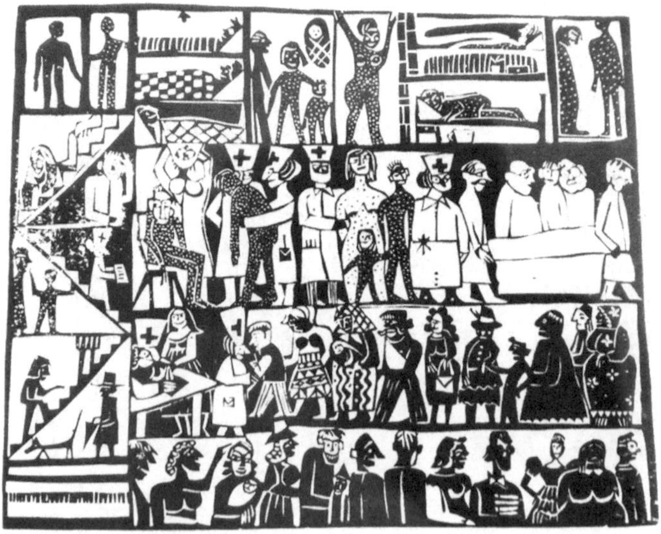

Fig. 2 Teresa Jakubowska, Smallpox (*Ospa*), 1964, Linocut, 66 × 55 cm, Edition Size 50. *Source* The Archive of Teresa Jakubowska

People's Republic (*Służba Bezpieczeństwa*), who most likely became infected during his travels to Myanmar and India and brought the disease to Poland. Jakubowska's print was a witty commentary on everyday life in the country, yet also presented a tongue-in-cheek narration about the effectiveness of the communist public services.

These prints, which today populate auctions in large numbers, competed with each other at the national exhibitions. The best ones were also sent abroad for international competitions, often to Western countries. Newspapers covered these major shows of graphic art, and artists whose work was sent abroad could count on social recognition and also significant monetary profit paid in foreign currency. Today, these prints can still be found in houses around Poland, hanging on the walls or stored in cardboard folders. Their prices on the market vary from around PLN 1,000 ($250) to PLN 10,000 ($2,500) for the scarcest prints by artists such as Józef Gielniak (1932–1972), Jerzy Panek (1918–2001), Teresa Jakubowska (1930–2025), or Stanisław Fijałkowski (1922–2022). In many cases, the prints bought via the subscription of graphic art return to the art market after 60 years, having hung on the wall since their first purchase.

4 From State Monopoly to Free Market

Despite the extensive campaign to popularize graphic art, for many years only a small number of Poles were able to acquire original prints and display them in their homes. Prior to the mid-1960s, artworks were difficult to obtain for a regular Polish citizen, and this situation was caused mostly by the monopolization of the art trade by the state. In the centrally planned economy, the art trade was severely restricted and was fully supervised and controlled by the state. The state monopoly on the art trade was exercised by the DESA Auction House and Gallery, "Works of Art and Antiques" (Bołdok, 2004, pp. 203–218). This state-supervised entity was created in 1950 by the Ministry of Culture and Art, which profited mostly from selling artworks that were created before 1945 (Białowąs et al., 2018, p. 593). The main customers were the state-owned museums and tourists who often paid in foreign currency. Another group constituted some privileged citizens, who could afford expensive goods. Prices often fluctuated and could change dramatically, even overnight (Banasiak, 2020, p. 135). Moreover, they were rarely disclosed to the public and the auction and sale results were not publicly available. For these reasons, a large portion of the market in the socialist economy constituted the informal sector, where the transaction currency was the US dollar. Modern art was not commonly offered by DESA; however, the Foreign Trade Office within DESA bought and sold modern art starting from the beginning of the 1960s. Prices were sometimes deliberately kept low so that the state-owned museums could exercise their preemption right (Białowąs et al., 2018, p. 593).

An exchange of goods in US currency was particularly lucrative. In the 1970s, DESA, operating under the name of Foreign Trade Enterprise Desa (*Przedsiębiorstwo Handlu Zagranicznego Desa*), participated in Art Basel, where it offered works by Henryk Stażewski (1894–1988) and Edward Krasiński (1925–2004). The absolute monopolization of the market by the state lasted until 1974, when the total ban on private art dealing was relaxed, which resulted in several grassroots initiatives aimed at establishing the first private art galleries in the country (Dz.U. 1974 nr 27 poz. 158). In the 1960s and 1970s, small galleries called "author" or "independent" galleries (*galerie autorskie*) sporadically emerged in larger cities; however, given their aura of elitism, they remained detached from the mainstream cultural events in the country. Their audience could view and engage with modern art but could not acquire the pieces on display, at least not through the official channels. Among these galleries, Piotr Nowicki's Gallery (*Galeria Piotra Nowickiego*), which opened in 1977 in Warsaw, was among the most prominent (Banasiak, 2020, p. 140). The small degree of market freedom did not lead to any further opening of the market, and the state maintained a monopoly over the art trade until 1989. Interestingly, in 1984, one year after martial law was lifted in the Polish People's Republic, the state attempted to introduce a simulation of a free market and organized in Poznań the first Art Fair of Socialist Countries Interart (*Targi Sztuki Krajów Socjalistycznych Interart*). This cyclical event heralded the opening of the art market that was about to happen after the collapse of the Soviet Union (Banasiak, 2020, p. 135).

As Poland's centrally planned economy transitioned to a free-market system, the country's art market took several years to emerge and stabilize. The Polish art market was particularly affected by the stagnation of the communist era due to the lack of previous institutional foundations. Apart from DESA, there were no other auction houses that could legitimize the trade through their operations. Secondly, all the previous art market operations were centrally planned, and after the introduction of a free market economy, it was difficult to judge its basic parameters such as supply and demand. Early attempts to research the demand structure of Polish households were made in the early 1970s and were out of date. Moreover, they did not include non-consumer goods such as artworks (Markowski, 1972). Finally, the lack of proper legitimization and unstable currency resulted in an incomparably higher level of risk connected with investing in the Polish art market, which slowed down the implementation of the art market for more than ten years (Białowąs et al., 2018, pp. 593–594). The period of stagnation lasted until the late 2000s. During that time, the market was dominated by pre-war artworks, and graphic art occupied a margin, which resulted in a large accumulation of prints kept in the hands of the artists themselves, customers who bought samples of graphic art mostly thanks to various subscriptions, and a very narrow group of collectors.

Interest in postwar Polish printmaking revived around the middle of 2010, following the growth of other sectors of the art market and a major popularization of the products of Soviet culture in mass media. This growing interest in prints is reflected in the statistics on the Polish art market. According to the Central Statistical Office (2023), prints and works on paper constituted 3.3% of the total sale value of the Polish market for art and antiques. This amounts to PLN 18.7 million (approx. $4.8 million, 1 PLN = $0.26 [31.08.2024]) (Central Statistical Office, 2024). According to the Central Statistical Office (2024), in 2023 the total sale value of art and antiques in Poland reached PLN 567.7 million ($146.2 million), representing a decrease of 12.8% compared to 2022. Paintings constituted the largest part of the total sale value of works of art and antiques, amounting to PLN 471.9 million ($121.5 million, 83.1% of the total sale value). Post-1945 paintings brought in PLN 242.1 million ($62.5 million, 42.6% of the total sale value), and pre-1945 paintings amounted to PLN 229.8 million ($59.3 million, 40.5% of the total sale value).[4] Compared with 2022, the value of painting sales decreased by 16.2 percent, with the sales of post-1945 paintings increasing by 9.9% and pre-1945 paintings decreasing by 33.0%.

In 2022, which is considered the peak performance year for the Polish art market since the economic reforms of 1990, the total sales value of prints and works on paper constituted 4.1% of the total sales value of art and antiques (Central Statistical Office, 2023). This equals

[4] The Polish art market is traditionally divided into pre-1945 and post-1945 fields.

PLN 26.7 million (approx. $6.9 million) (Central Statistical Office, 2023). That year, the total sale value of art and antiques in Poland reached PLN 650.7 million (approx. $167.9 million) and increased by 10.1% compared to 2021. As in previous years, painting constituted the largest part of the total sale value of works of art and antiques, reaching PLN 563.0 million ($145.3 million, 86.5% of the total sale value). Post-1945 paintings brought 220.2 million PLN ($56.8 million, 33.8% of the total sale value), and pre-1945 paintings brought 342.8 million PLN ($88.5 million, 52.7% of the total sale value). Compared with 2021, sales of paintings increased by 20.2%, with sales of post-1945 paintings decreasing by 3.6% and sales of pre-1945 paintings increasing by 42.8%. These figures demonstrate that interest in works on paper in Poland, including prints, has remained stable in recent years, consistent with the global market share of approximately 4%.

However, when the total sale value of prints and works on paper is considered in absolute terms, the Polish art market more than doubled its size in less than five years. This means that the Polish art market attracted not only the wealthiest collectors but also a proportionally large group of collectors interested in the low-end segment of the art market. Since 2017, the total sale value of prints and works on paper in Poland grew from PLN 11.6 million ($2.9 million, 8.4% of the total sale value) to PLN 26.7 million ($6.9 million, 4.1% of the total sale value) in 2022. In comparison, the global market for prints in absolute terms doubled its revenue between 2011 and 2021, reaching a record high of $529 million in 2021 (Bertrand, 2023).

Finally, it is worth pointing out that the print market performed particularly well in Poland during the pandemic. Interest in graphic art was likely stimulated by the growth of online auctions, which favored low-end and mid-range works. This trend coincided with the emergence of new sales formats for prints, particularly short-duration online auctions, as well as a revival of interest in cultural goods produced under state socialism. Together, these developments made the Polish print market one of the country's fastest-growing art-market sectors in recent years, alongside the market for works by emerging artists.

5 Conclusion

The steady rise in revenue generated by prints and works on paper corresponds with the growth of the Polish economy in recent years, as well as with increasing interest among the country's expanding middle class in the lower end of the art market. The Polish print market follows global trends and in many respects resembles its foreign counterparts. However, because of Poland's state-socialist past, it also has several distinctive characteristics, including substantial growth in overall sales, an oversupply of prints produced since 1945, and a rising number of emotionally driven purchases. The mechanism behind the dynamic growth of the print market in Poland can also be explained through the triadic model based on functionality, scarcity, and brand strength to describe both price formation and buyer behavior. The significant interest in this segment of the art market has been shaped by the "rediscovery" of the original functionality of prints. Originally purchased as a form of home decoration, prints produced during state socialism have recently regained their original purpose. The revival of prints as accessible and popular home décor has coincided with a broader revival of interest in cultural goods produced during state socialism, which has itself become a distinct and self-standing cultural phenomenon. Nostalgia for the material culture of this bygone era has recently developed into a recognizable market brand whose characteristics and leading figures are now familiar to collectors. In addition, growing interest in this segment of the art market has been fueled by greater awareness and appreciation of the quality of its craftsmanship, as well as by the scarcity of certain prints, some of which may be the only surviving impressions from their original editions.

References

Banasiak, J. (2020). *Proteuszowe czasy: Rozpad państwowego systemu sztuki 1982–1993: Stan wojenny, druga odwilż, transformacja ustrojowa.* Akademia Sztuk Pięknych w Warszawie, Muzeum Sztuki Nowoczesnej w Warszawie.

Bertrand, L. (2023). TIAMSA Blog: Overview of the print market. https://www.artmarketstudies.org/tiamsa-blog-overview-of-the-print-market/. Accessed August 31, 2024.

Białowąs, S., Potocki, T., & Rogozińska, A. (2018). Financial returns and cultural price determinants on the polish art market, 1991–2012. *Acta Oeconomica*, *68*(4), 591–615.

Bołdok, S. (2004). Historia kolekcjonerstwa polskiego i zasady obyczaju aukcyjnego. In J. Rapicka (Ed.), *Malarze Polscy XIX i XX Wieku. Mała Encyklopedia Rynku Sztuki* (pp. 203–218). Antiquarius Sp. Z o.o.

Burkamp, D. (Ed.). (1995). *Jerzy Panek: Werkverzeichnis der graphischen Arbeiten 1939–1993*. Kerber.

Central Statistical Office. (2022). *Culture and national heritage in 2021*. https://stat.gov.pl/obszary-tematyczne/kultura-turystyka-sport/kultura. Accessed June 29, 2025.

Central Statistical Office. (2023). *Rynek dzieł sztuki i antyków w 2022*. https://stat.gov.pl/obszary-tematyczne/kultura-turystyka-sport/kultura/rynek-dziel-sztuki-i-antykow-w-2022-roku,17,7.html. Accessed August 31, 2024.

Central Statistical Office. (2024). *Rynek dzieł sztuki i antyków w 2023*. https://stat.gov.pl/obszary-tematyczne/kultura-turystyka-sport/kultura/rynek-dziel-sztuki-i-antykow-w-2023-roku,17,8.html. Accessed August 31, 2024.

Central Statistical Office. (2025). *Przeciętne miesięczne wynagrodzenie w gospodarce narodowej w latach 1950–2024*. https://stat.gov.pl/obszary-tematyczne/rynek-pracy/pracujacy-zatrudnieni-wynagrodzenia-koszty-pracy/przeciętne-miesieczne-wynagrodzenie-w-gospodarce-narodowej-w-latach-1950-2024,2,1.html. Accessed June 29, 2025.

Chrostowska, H. (1965). [Untitled]. In Warszawskie Towarzystwo Przyjaciół Sztuk Pięknych w Warszawie (Ed.), *Ogólnopolska Subskrypcja Grafiki Artystycznej* (pp. 11–12). Warszawskie Towarzystwo Przyjaciół Sztuk Pięknych w Warszawie.

Estreicher, K. (1965). [Untitled]. In Warszawskie Towarzystwo Przyjaciół Sztuk Pięknych w Warszawie (Ed.), *Ogólnopolska Subskrypcja Grafiki Artystycznej* (pp. 9–10). Warszawskie Towarzystwo Przyjaciół Sztuk Pięknych w Warszawie.

Kołodko, G. W. (2010). Two decades of great postsocialist transformation—And what next? *Acta Oeconomica*, *60*(4), 361–373.

Kompa, K., & Witkowska, D. (2014). Prices of paintings on polish art market in years 2007–2010: Hedonic price index application. *Acta Oeconomia*, *13*(3), 127–141.

Lucińska, A. (2021). *Obrazy na rynku finansowym. Analiza efektywności inwestowania*. Difin.

Markowski, S. (1972). *Spożycie w Polsce Ludowej*. Instytut Wydawniczy CRZZ.

Matul, K. (2015). *Międzynarodowego Biennale Plakatu w Warszawie*. Towarzystwo Autorów i Wydawców Prac Naukowych Universitas.

Prymlewicz, K. (2021). Z życia wycięte... In K. Prymlewicz (Ed.), *Teresa Jakubowska: Z życia wycięte*. Muzeum Karykatury im. Eryka Lipińskiego.

Ustawa z dnia 18 lipca 1974 r. o wykonywaniu handlu oraz niektórych innych rodzajów działalności przez jednostki gospodarki nie uspołecznionej, Dz.U. 1974 nr 27 poz. 158.

Walczak, W. (1965). [Untitled]. In Warszawskie Towarzystwo Przyjaciół Sztuk Pięknych w Warszawie (Ed.), *Ogólnopolska Subskrypcja Grafiki Artystycznej* (pp. 7–8). Warszawskie Towarzystwo Przyjaciół Sztuk Pięknych w Warszawie.

Walczak, W. (1978) [Untitled]. In Towarzystwo Przyjaciół Sztuk Pięknych (Ed.), *V Ogólnopolska Subskrypcja Grafiki Artystycznej 1978–1980* (pp. 3–5). Instytut Wydawniczy Centralnej Rady Związków Zawodowy.

Waltoś, J. (1975) *NGM: Najlepsza Grafika Miesiąca: XV lat konkursu* (np.). Związek Polskich Artystów Plastyków w Krakowie.

Weichardt, J. (2006). Krakowskie biennale do przełomu 1989 roku. In D. Wróblewska, W. Wierzchowska, & J. Mansfeld (Eds.), *Grafika i pamięć: Rok 1966 największa przygoda polskiej grafiki* (pp. 21–29). Stowarzyszenie Międzynarodowe Triennale Grafiki.

PART III

Capitalizing on High-End Art

Price, Value and Originality in the Oleograph Market in Buenos Aires (1870–1920)

María Isabel Baldasarre

1 Introduction

The nineteenth century was a time of great exploration in terms of image reproduction. The possibility of replicating images in color thanks to chromolithography allowed for the wide circulation of visually striking prints with strong commercial appeal. This involved both the reproduction of famous paintings and the creation of images conceived ad hoc, such as posters, almanacs, or prints, designed to circulate and be consumed, to be treasured in albums, collected, or used to decorate the walls of various types of homes. Buenos Aires, like many other metropolitan centers, participated in the so-called chromo-mania, which lasted from the middle of the century until the First World War (Slautterback, 2012).

This proliferation of lower-value images, compared to original works, allowed broader sectors of the population—surpassing the wealthy elite who could afford to acquire original paintings and sculptures—to access the consumption of images and collecting practices. However, they can clearly be considered an example of pieces that, both in their materiality and iconography, belong to the vast and diverse segment of the "low-end" market. That is, their very status as reproductions with a commercial

M. I. Baldasarre (✉)
Universidad Nacional de San Martín, Buenos Aires, Argentina;
CONICET, Buenos Aires, Argentina
e-mail: mbaldasarre@unsam.edu.ar

A.-S. V. Radermecker (ed.), *Low-End Markets for Art and Cultural Goods*,
Cultural Economics & the Creative Economy,
https://doi.org/10.1007/978-3-032-27566-0_8

purpose and their fragile materiality—mostly ink on paper—has determined their fate in terms of preservation and scholarly study. In general, archives and repositories hold very few of these pieces, while museums and institutions have disregarded them in favor of so-called masterpieces.

Additionally, canonical narratives and genealogies built within art history, focused on ideas of originality and unique authorship, have largely ignored them. However, in recent years, scholarship more interested in exploring the complexity and scale of nineteenth-century visual culture has begun to pay attention to these ephemeral objects. This shift has led to the formation of public collections dedicated to them, as well as solid analyses centered on graphic culture, reproduction techniques, and circulation mechanisms. Some of these studies will be revisited in the next section.

Specifically, this article focuses on chromolithographs and, more particularly, on a subset known as oleographs, which gained popularity in the second half of the nineteenth century. The oleograph technique was a form of mechanical reproduction that allowed for the large-scale replication of well-known images. The finished print was heavily varnished and then passed through patterned rollers, creating a texture that mimicked canvas. Many such reproductions were referred to as oleographs not necessarily because the original was an oil painting, but because the final print, varnished and often enhanced with a canvas-like texture or simulated impasto brushstrokes, gave the illusion of one, especially to the untrained eye. It was precisely this appearance that conferred an "artistic" quality upon them, making them desirable decorative objects for the urban middle classes and other aspirational social groups. To put it in marketing terms, we can consider oleographs 'copycat products'—imitation goods that emulate both the formal qualities and the semantic meaning of a leading brand and its market reputation (Van Horen & Pieters, 2012); in this case, the established prestige rooted in the materiality of pictorial technique and its iconographic repertoire. Viewers with limited expertise often mistook oleographs for original paintings—a confusion similarly observed between copycat products and their source models, due to the varying degrees of imitation.

Oleographs may be situated within Sub-segment 2 of the low-end art market through the triadic model proposed in this volume, which articulates functionality, scarcity, and brand strength. With regard to the first dimension, oleographs fulfilled a symbolic function, operating primarily as decorative goods. In this respect, they shared a dimension with unique artworks; however, their value derived from imitation and visual resemblance, rather than from authorship or originality. Their scarcity is structurally low, given their industrial mode of production and wide circulation. Unlike multiples issued in limited and numbered editions, the degree of scarcity of chromolithographs could not be guaranteed at the time of acquisition. On the contrary, their very nature was mass circulation. At present, their historical valuation is often linked to the fact that their ephemeral status resulted in low rates of preservation, making surviving examples privileged testimonies to the circulation and consumption of images in the past. Finally, oleographs display a weak and unstable form of brand strength: while they often relied on the reputational capital of canonical artists, prestigious European schools, or national iconographies, this legitimacy remained indirect and mediated, detached from individual authorship. Certain examples nevertheless achieved higher valuation, depending on the capacity of technical reproduction to imitate the visual and material qualities of the originals, as well as to the degree of detail and color achieved by the chromolithographs.

Focusing on how these three dimensions intersected in Buenos Aires between 1870 and 1920, this paper analyzes the circulation and commercialization of oleographs in the Argentine capital and their role in shaping the consumption of cultural goods. Using qualitative methodology and case studies, I examine how these prints were advertised, sold, and valued in comparison to oil paintings. More broadly, the Buenos Aires case contributes to a deeper understanding of the international art market and the circulation of cultural goods, which expanded on an unprecedented scale in the late nineteenth century in search of new business opportunities. What happened in the Argentine capital is relevant to understanding the dynamics and internationalization of an art market that, since the last quarter of the nineteenth century, required active and steady purchasers, even if this meant exporting artifacts to a distant capital.

Within this context, this chapter shows that oleographs occupied a distinctive position in the low-end art market—one that neither simply competed with original paintings nor functioned as their degraded substitute, but rather expanded access to art consumption and reshaped local dynamics of valuation and cultural exchange.

2 Literature Review

In 1883, painter and art critic Eduardo Schiaffino (1858–1935) bemoaned the Buenos Aires public's fondness for oleographs. They were, he claimed, "aberrations" acquired by undiscerning individuals at prices not unlike those paid for "original sketches" of "indisputably superior quality." For the future founder of the local National Museum of Fine Arts, if taste followed its "natural evolution" then those "imitations and forgeries" would "miserably" end in fire. In Schiaffino's opinion, oleographs displayed the originality of a laborer rather than that of an artist (Schiaffino, 1883, p. 1).[1]

Schiaffino's words testify to the tension that defined the nineteenth century between the prevailing conception of art and the expanding possibilities of reproductive technologies. According to Robert Verhooght: "on the one hand, art reproduction burgeoned on an unprecedented scale; on the other, the period was permeated as never before by concepts of originality and authenticity" (Verhooght, 2007, p. 18). Despite this, there was a true craze for the consumption of reproductions, part of what several historians of graphic culture have referred to as chromo-mania, a phenomenon driven by the new possibilities for the technical reproduction of artistic works made available by the chromolithography market. By 1870, this very technique enabled the mass production of prints—cheaply and with relative speed—flooding markets such as the United States with a wide range of products, from art reproductions to advertisements, business cards, sheet music covers, city views and book illustrations. Those known as "hanging prints" were specifically intended to be framed and used as decoration in middle-class interiors (Slautterback, 2012) and even categorized according to the room of the house in which they were to be placed (Fig. 1).

[1] *El público de Buenos Aires es desconfiado en materia artística, como todos los que no son conocedores [. . .], teme si compra un cuadro o un bosquejo, que el vendedor lo engañe. Por esto es que se ven tantas aberraciones. Prefiere una oleografía y suele pagarla a 500 pesos, aun cuando solo valga 10 francos, pero se dice a sí mismo que sabe lo que compra y que nadie lo engaña. No compraría seguramente un bosquejo original por la misma cantidad, de una composición naturalmente más sencilla, pero de mérito indiscutiblemente superior [. . .] cuelgan en sus casas imitaciones y falsificaciones de las que sus herederos no sabrán qué hacerse—si el gusto en Buenos Aires siguiendo la evolución natural, acaba por implantarse–, y que irán a concluir miserablemente en una fogata* (In this and the following quotes, the Spanish has been adapted to contemporary spelling for better understanding).

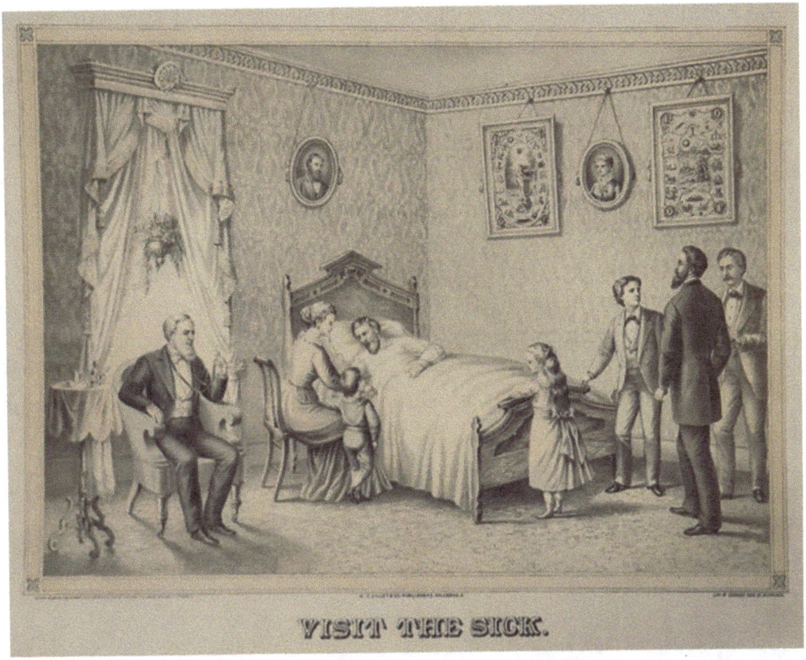

Fig. 1 M. C. Lilley & Co. (1877). *Visit the sick*, color lithograph, 60.4 × 47.7 cm, Chapin Library, Williams College. *Photo* Author

As in Argentina, this new technology also had its detractors, who regarded it as a mechanical contrivance with no artistic value, appealing only to an ignorant audience. Their advocates, on the other hand, considered the medium a way to extend artistic taste and to elevate the aesthetic standards of broader audiences. In fact, artistic lithographs that reproduced original paintings were considered a "democratic art" available to everyone (Marzio, 1979). Besides, as expressed by Laura Anne Kalba "full color reproductions of artworks added an allure of prestige to chromolithography not afforded by other types of prints" (Kalba, 2017, p. 156).

One of the most comprehensive studies of this process is Twyman's work, which provides a detailed account of the development, techniques, and impact of chromolithography, focusing on its role in mass visual culture. Specifically, he explains that in the 1870s the word "oleograph" began to be used to describe chromolithographed reproductions that, using between 15 and 20 colors, looked like oil paintings (Twyman, 2013, p. 216). As stated by English book dealer R. A. Peddie in the early twentieth century: "The 'oleograph,' a rather *distressing* form of the chromo-lithograph, was of German origin. The finished print was thickly coated with varnish and then passed between patterned rollers giving the impression of canvas" (Peddie, 1915, p. 158). Many such reproductions were named oleographs, not necessarily because the original was an oil painting, but because the final print, varnished and often provided with a texture of canvas or simulated impasto brush strokes, made it look like one (Twyman, 2013, p. 216). However, as Peddie's quote conveyed, there was something deceptive or fraudulent in the status of oleography, as it allowed for the existence of artifacts that sought to pass for what they were not. It was precisely that appearance which made them "artistic," and as such worthy of decorating the homes of the rising bourgeoisie (Fig. 2).

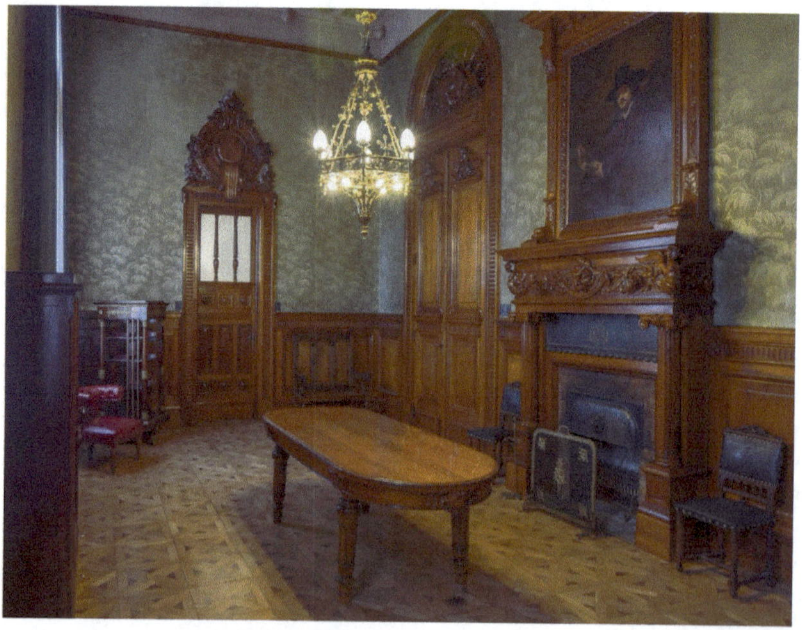

Fig. 2 Interior of the Borges room at the National Library with the oleograph after a follower of Rembrandt, *Portrait of a Man*, undated, Buenos Aires. *Photo* Estudio Giménez Duhau

The preference for oleographs extended even to rural and remote areas. In 1899, the son of a widely reproduced nineteenth-century artist, the Pre-Raphaelite John Everett Millais, was astonished to find oleographs of his father's most popular scenes in unexpected places such as huts in Samoa and South Africa (quoted in Verhoogt, 2007, pp. 221–222). Half a century later, a witness from the English countryside recorded: "Fifty years ago, this process of picture reproduction was so popular that no cottage interior was complete without one or two specimens." Yet, he also observed that "today not only has the oleograph disappeared; it has disappeared almost without a trace." As a possible explanation for this phenomenon, he argued that it was precisely its status as a non-original that led to its downfall: "It was, in fact, a fake: and its disappearance is probably due to nothing but this—not to improvements in color printing, for the modern products of the color screen would lend themselves to similar treatment, but because it pretended to be what it was not" (Johnson, 1950, p. 683).

The first oleographs that circulated in Argentina were imported and came from major production centers such as Paris, London, and Milan. However, by the second quarter of the nineteenth century, the first workshops producing black-and-white lithographs, began to emerge in the city, and some of them would achieve a high level of specialization by the end of the century, focusing on its more artistic variations (Szir, 2018). For example, the establishments of German immigrants Guillermo Kraft and Jacobo Peuser became printing emporiums. In addition to illustrated books, they published maps, albums, almanacs, and various types of chromolithographs, aiming to compete with imported publications. According to María Eugenia Costa, Kraft pioneered steam-powered lithography, in 1906, proudly claimed to have produced the country's first fourteen-color chromolithograph (Costa, 2018, p. 188). Peuser, in turn, published portfolios with reproductions of engravings or paintings, mainly European, advertised as works of "indisputable artistic merit" (Costa, 2018, p. 203). Regarding technical innovations and the conditions that enabled printed materials, Sandra Szir makes a fundamental contribution to understanding how print culture became professionalized and expanded on a massive scale in Argentina. In the case of chromolithography, she argues that it became a privileged medium for both commercial and artistic initiatives. She also notes that the status of these objects—generally ephemeral and of low value—makes it difficult to reconstruct narratives about their consumption circuits (Szir, 2023, p. 16).

Regarding the art market in a broader sense, between 1870 and 1920, Buenos Aires became a major hub for contemporary art brought from Europe. Numerous dealers and intermediaries either traveled to this distant capital in the Southern Hemisphere or established alliances with local merchants to supply a thriving demand for artworks. This topic has been the focus of my doctoral research, which is synthesized in articles addressing the development of the art trade, collecting, and the circulation of foreign artworks in Buenos Aires (Baldasarre, 2017), as well as the international art market and dealers' strategies at the turn of the twentieth century (Baldasarre, 2024).

Oleographs became an essential part of visual culture, mimicking oil paintings through varnishing and texturization. Marketed as artistic objects, they were broadly distributed in cities worldwide, including Buenos Aires. Despite their widespread presence, no studies to date have focused on the commerce of chromolithographs, the specific characteristics of oleographs, or comparisons between their value and circulation mechanisms and those of original artworks. This paper aims to reflect on how the supply, circulation and trade of oleographs in Buenos Aires took place in parallel with the consumption of other forms of artistic production such as original paintings, copies of old and new masters, forgeries and engravings. The coexistence of these objects is key to understanding the distinctive dynamics of the aesthetic market that unfolded in Buenos Aires between 1870 and 1920, as well as the diversity of cultural goods that shaped visual culture during this period.

3 Methodology

In this contribution, I propose to reconstruct and analyze the material circulation of oleographs using a qualitative methodology. By examining specific case studies, I will identify the emergence of this technique within the promising market for cultural goods that was taking shape in Buenos Aires.

Based on a survey of newspapers, periodicals, gallery and auction catalogues, and commercial guides, this study traces the moment when oleographs emerged as a marketable product in Buenos Aires and identifies their points of sale. Additionally, textual analysis sheds light on the advertising strategies used to promote them, as well as on the critiques from those who deemed them inadequate for fostering artistic refinement.

Moreover, the visual and physical examination of prints and paintings allows for a comparison of their distinct material qualities and an assessment of how these differences played a role in determining both their economic and symbolic value. The analysis focuses on how oleographs were advertised, where they were sold, and the prices paid for them, while also comparing their costs and resulting symbolic value to those of more prestigious and canonical artifacts, such as oil paintings.

By examining the prices paid for different goods—including lithographs, prints, and original paintings—it is possible to contextualize their relative value within a specific historical framework. However, we must note that the price comparisons between different types of goods are based on limited available data, mainly drawn from information found in the printed press and exhibition or sales catalogues. In other words, these comparisons should not be understood as representative average estimates, but rather as indicative of relative value based on the evidence at hand. Considering these variables, lithographs and oleographs help elucidate the dynamics of the low end of the market, while also taking into account that, in the case of Buenos Aires, the high end was still in formation and largely dependent on the flow of leftover works from European markets.

On the basis of simultaneous study of both the oil painting and the oleograph market, I question whether the latter actually diminished sales of original works. My hypothesis is that while oleographs, with a material and economic status more precarious than oil paintings, were not valorized by connoisseurs or later art history, they did expand access to the practice of art consumption as part of the growing visual culture of the late nineteenth and early twentieth-century Argentina.

4 Analysis and Findings

Chromolithographs emerged in Argentina at a time when its art system, based in its capital city, was still going through the process of institutionalization. Before 1895, there was no museum specifically dedicated to the Fine Arts in the country, nor was there a university or academy where art history could be studied (Baldasarre, 2018). The first professional galleries importing foreign art and marketing local pieces were not established until the early twentieth century, following the pattern of the prominent Witcomb Gallery, opened in 1897. The main art school was a private entity created in 1876, the *Sociedad Estímulo de Bellas Artes*, which was not nationalized as an academy until 1905.

In a context of great economic expansion due to the incorporation of Argentina into the world market as supplier of agricultural raw materials, many members of the bourgeoisie devoted themselves to the acquisition of luxury goods to decorate their homes. Some of them focused systematically on building up artistic collections, generally of European origin. As said earlier between the last quarter of the nineteenth century and the beginning of the First World War, Buenos Aires was flooded with artworks and sumptuary objects coming from Europe. They were mostly oils on canvas, but also bronzes, marbles, terracottas, tapestries, drawings, engravings and medals, which quickly found a place in the Buenos Aires market. In September 1888, a chronicle recorded that Buenos Aires was "a great city with an astonishing art scene" and that so far that year "there has been an offer [. . .] of more than five thousand canvases, some very good, others good, others bad and shameful eyesores" resulting from "daring speculation which relies on ignorance as its capital and success in the business" (La Nación, 1888, September 9).[2]

In the face of that literal invasion of pieces from Europe, those who purchased works of art did not necessarily have the relevant knowledge or seek advice from specialists to avoid deceptions or unreliable attributions. Thus, engravings and oleographs of well-known works served as mechanisms for engaging with reputed artworks. Their status as reproductions made them more affordable and therefore accessible to an audience willing to acquire cultural goods but lacking the means to purchase high art.

This democratization of images was significant, as the fervor for the acquisition and collecting was not an exclusive practice of the wealthy. A photograph of the interior of an immigrant ranch, taken by the Witcomb photographic studio, bears witness to the so-called chromomania in a local context (Fig. 3). The humble adobe walls of the ranch were covered with satirical lithographs, fashion plates, portraits, and

[2] *Buenos Aires es una gran ciudad con un movimiento artístico asombroso [. . .]. El año presente, hasta la semana anterior, arrojaba una oferta al público [. . .] de más de cinco telas, muy buenas algunas, buenas otras, malas las siguientes y vergonzosos mamarrachos las más, sea dicho esto en honor [. . .] de la verdad y en defensa del público al que hemos advertido siempre de la especulación atrevida que se lanza contando con la ignorancia como capital y éxito en el negocio.*

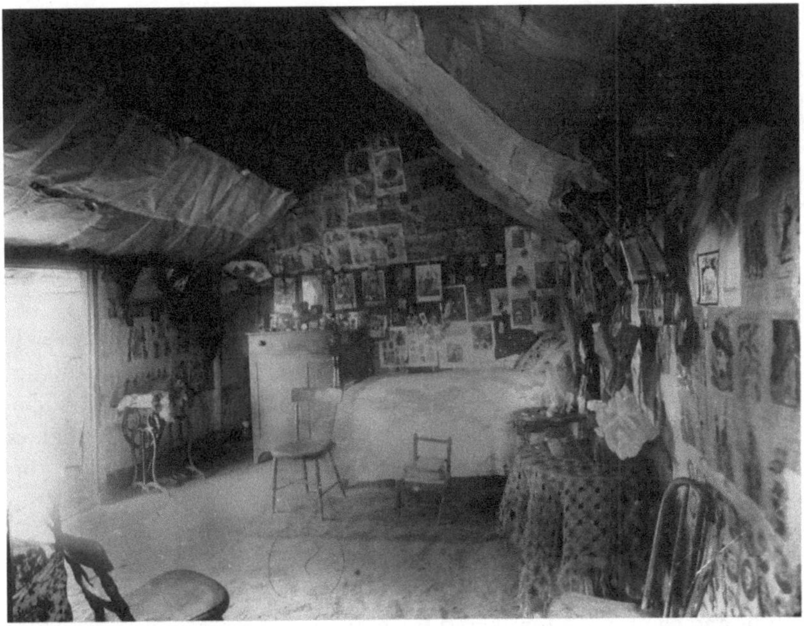

Fig. 3 Estudio Witcomb. (ca. 1880). *Interior of an Immigrant Ranch. Source* Buenos Aires, Archivo General de la Nación, Argentina, Department of Photographic Documents, inv. 543. Public Domain

religious iconography. Taken from magazines and almanacs, and some even framed as standalone pieces, their proliferation demonstrates that it was not only the bourgeois sectors that sought to surround themselves with images in their daily lives. If in the less privileged sectors of society, this passion for products from the low end of the market could be tolerated and even encouraged, among the consumption habits of more affluent sectors, a greater expertise was expected—one that would lead to discernment and refinement.

A very important Buenos Aires almanac proclaimed in 1900 that many wealthy, educated men exhibited "a deplorable hodgepodge of forgeries, copies and discarded materials from workshops" in their residences and told naive visitors that they were "authentic works by Murillo, Velázquez, Goya, Zurbarán, Ribera, Rafael, Alonso Cano—all the gods of painting"

(Un espectador, 1900, pp. 67–76).[3] Price was a central element in this favoritism, leading those who appreciated the good to be scared off and end up covering their walls with the medium-quality and the cheap. Beyond the ambitious attributions, the money investment was an almost unequivocal indication of the authenticity of what was acquired. For example, in 1892, at the auction of Gabriel Larsen del Castaño's collection, the works supposedly painted by old masters such as Titian, Brueghel or Bronzino were sold for trifling sums, similar or even lower than those paid for some modern artists such as Spanish painters Salvador Sánchez Barbudo and José Casado del Alisal (Uno che c'era, 1893, p. 171).

Thus, along with the formalization of a market for original works by contemporary artists, Buenos Aires also witnessed an extensive circulation of copies and reproductions. By including iconic names and reproducing works celebrated by the canon of art history, these images represented less daring investments for less experienced buyers. At the same time, they allowed "the art of painting, until now reserved for the wealthy classes, to be affordable for the poor and to decorate the most modest rooms" (El Correo Español, 1899, p. 2).[4]

Around 1870, before the emergence of professional art galleries, oleographs and paintings often shared the same spaces for sale and circulation. In other words, there was not yet a "commercial specialization indicating the existence of an autonomous market with its own rules and agents" (Amigo, 2008, p. 3). Bazaars, bookstores, photography studios, and art supply stores frequently displayed both original works and reproductions. Later, with the establishment of the first professional galleries in the final years of the nineteenth century, original paintings and sculptures became largely confined to these venues. However, overlaps persisted, and the system remained more porous than it might appear at first glance. Many galleries continued to alternate exhibitions of renowned masters with certified copies well into the twentieth century.

[3] *No pueden seguir los poseedores de galerías particulares creyendo, o queriendo hacer creer a los inteligentes mismos, que son dueños de colecciones valiosas cuando en realidad no cuelgan de los muros de sus palacios sino una deplorable mezcolanza de falsificaciones y copias y de desechos de los talleres [. . .] No se puede asegurar a los visitantes de esas galerías, a menos que se cuente con su ignorancia [. . .] que son obras auténticas de Murillo, Velázquez, Goya, Zurbarán, Ribera, Rafael, Alonso Cano, de todos los dioses de la pintura, las que forman esa colección.*

[4] [. . .] *el arte de la pintura, privativo hasta hoy de las clases acomodadas, sea asequible al bolsillo de los pobres y pueda adornar las más modestas habitaciones.*

The first records of oleograph sales in Buenos Aires date back to 1858, just a few years after the technique emerged in Europe. An article published in *La Tribuna* acknowledged the novelty of the process and introduced it as capable of "reproducing oil paintings, preserving not only their tonality and vigor, but even imitating them in their most minute details, such as the roughness of the surface, the weave of the canvas, the brushstrokes, the transparency of the glazes—everything with such perfection and meticulousness that even the most experienced are mistaken and believe they are looking at an actual oil painting" (Elio, 1858).[5]

As was the case with many of the technological advances associated with consumption, the propagation of oleographs was almost immediate in the Western world. In Buenos Aires, the trade in oleographs boomed in the 1870s. They were sold by general stores, dealers in imported goods, and bookstores, and sometimes even by businesses specializing in antiques and oil paintings, such as Pascual Quesnel e Hijos, E. Galli y Cía., Pinturerías de Montserrat, Cooperativa Artística Limitada, and Repetto y Cía. (Demissolz, 1879; Junior & Stein, 1876; Kuntz, 1886). Known as *casas introductoras*—stores primarily dedicated to importing European products—most of these establishments were located in the southwest sector of the civic center, the city's main commercial hub. Later on, some would relocate to the more elegant Florida Street, where professional art galleries would also be established, following the northward movement of the upper classes

In the last quarter of the century, these shops offered a wide but undifferentiated range of goods, including art supplies, mirrors, porcelain, and furniture. Their selection of artistic images—oleographs, lithographs, watercolors, and paintings—was similarly varied and non-specialized, reflecting a clientele that made little distinction among media when decorating their homes. Other outlets were printing shops such as that of Professione, Costa y Cia., which, besides offering books and educational supplies, imported engravings and "facsimiles" of famous European paintings (La Mujer, 1899). Mostly run by foreign owners, these individuals cannot properly be considered art dealers, but rather more or less specialized merchants engaged in various trades—either oriented towards home decoration or focused on supplying artists and

[5] [...] *reproducir los cuadros al óleo, conservándoles no solo su entonación y su vigor, pero hasta imitándolos en sus más minuciosos detalles, como son la aspereza de la superficie, el tejido del lienzo, los golpes de pincel, la transparencia de las veladuras y todo con una perfección y una prolijidad que hasta los más experimentados se equivocan y creen tener adelante de sí una pintura al óleo.*

photographers with the necessary materials. Even though these businesses were not formal artistic venues, they were undoubtedly frequented by those who practiced art at the time or were interested in its consumption.

It is important to note that the oleograph market, criticized by those who saw it as an obstacle for the trade of original works, in fact preceded and laid the foundations for the influx of oil paintings into Buenos Aires towards the end of the following decade, which would not be formalized with the installation of professional galleries until twenty years later. In other words, the marketing of chromolithographs and different kinds of reproductions installed the practice of conceiving daily life in coexistence with images, becoming an essential milestone, rather than a harmful instance, for the development of the art market.

For example, in 1880, Espasa y Cia editors of Barcelona introduced the two volumes of *Los Dioses de Grecia y Roma o Mitología greco-romana*, by Spanish writer Víctor Gebhardt, which contained a "rich collection of reproductions of works of art by the best ancient and modern authors [. . .] with works to be found in the public museums of Madrid, Paris, Rome and Florence", oleographs that in and of themselves constituted "artistic work" (La Nación, 1880, November 16).[6] That is to say, the publishing enterprise allowed those who could not afford original paintings to hang images by Bouguereau, Boucher, Gérôme, Girardon, Guido Reni, Murillo, Rafael, Rubens, Tiepolo, Titian, Velázquez or Veronese on the walls of their homes (Fig. 4).

By the beginning of the twentieth century, oleographs were already being produced in Buenos Aires, and their iconography expanded to include allegories of Argentina and its national heroes. In 1900, *La Mujer* magazine advertised an immense oleograph of the Argentine Republic, measuring 210 by 110 cm, made by the publication's director, Eduardo Sojo—a Galician cartoonist active in Buenos Aires—and printed in Mr. Volante's printing house (Fig. 5). The piece had taken Sojo a year's work and was categorized as "the greatest effort in graphic art made so far in the country."[7] It was offered for sale at $20 m/n–$22 m/n if mounted on canvas—and increased by half its price if the frame was also included (La Mujer, 1900, November 9).

[6] *Las oleografías que lo adornan constituyen por sí solas una obra artística. Orladas en oro, y de una ejecución perfecta, forman una rica colección de reproducciones de obras de arte de los mejores autores antiguos y modernos, algunas inéditas y otras que se hallan en los museos públicos y particularmente en Madrid, París, Roma, Florencia.*

[7] *Es esta obra de mérito positivo y uno de los mayores esfuerzos de arte gráfico en el país.*

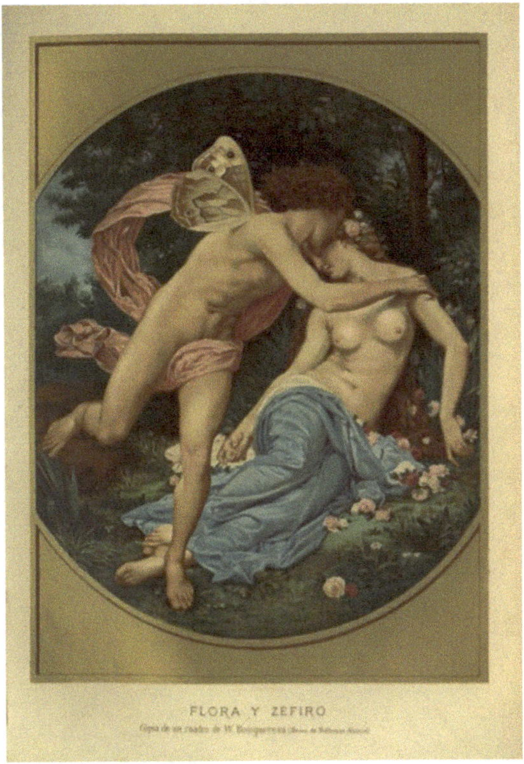

Fig. 4 Espasa y Comp. Ed. (1880–1881). Flora and Zéphyr, copy of a painting by W. Bouguereau. Gebhardt y Coll, V. *Los Dioses de Grecia y Roma ó Mitología greco-romana*. Biblioteca Ilustrada de Espasa y Compañía. *Photo* Author

These figures are relevant as they help us understand the relative prices of these objects and put Schiaffino's complaints into perspective. The value of the oleograph of the Argentine Republic was significantly lower than that of an oil painting by a contemporary artist, placing it in another price range and therefore oriented to another type of consumer. For instance, in 1900, *Sin pan y sin trabajo*, a social painting by Argentine artist Ernesto de la Cárcova—highly praised at its 1894 exhibition and considered one of his masterpieces—was acquired by the National Museum of Fine Arts for $1000 m/n. This was fifty times the price of Sojo's oleograph. That same year, the Museum also purchased the landscape *Silencio*, by Catalan painter Eliseo Meifrén, for $1500 m/n (Schiaffino, 1897). However, the prices of oleographs were closer to those of drawings, small panels, or sketches which also circulated in

Fig. 5 The Argentine Republic by Demócrito (1900). *La Mujer* (41), 20. *Photo* Author

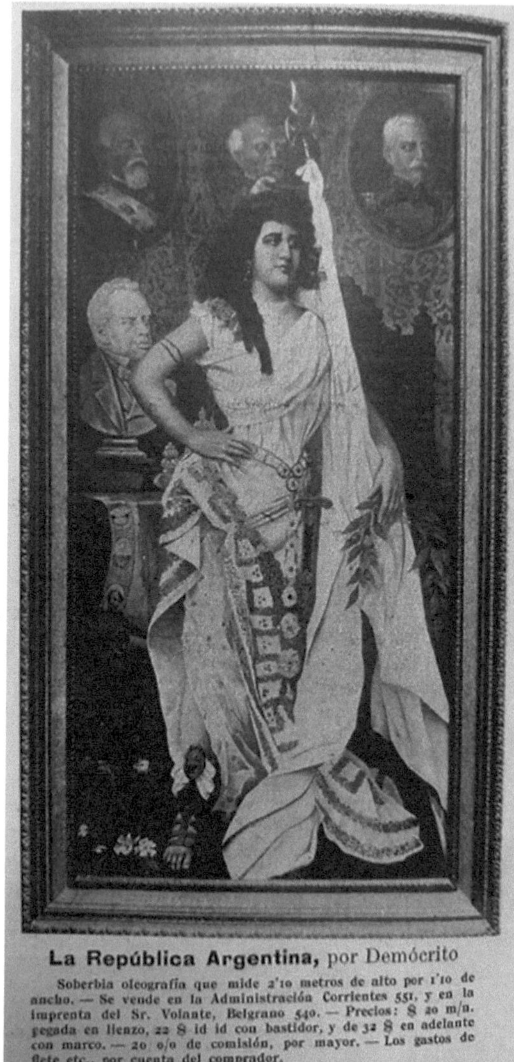

Buenos Aires at that time and rarely exceeded one hundred pesos. For example, a small landscape by French painter Eugène Ciceri was acquired at auction for $75 m/n, while *Parisienne*, a lithograph by the refined Antonio de La Gándara, sold for $32 m/n.

As we can see, oleographs were priced similarly to artist-signed prints. However, a clear difference in status positioned them at the lowest end of the market. While engravings still carried an authorial mark—a direct link to the creator of the original image—this connection was lost in the oleograph, which was generally unsigned and explicitly intended as an imitation of something else: an oil painting held in a museum collection and thus beyond the reach of private ownership. In the case of Sojo, for instance, the oleograph was assimilated to a poster or an illustration—an object intended to contribute to civic memory.

A revealing example of the circulation of originals, engravings and oleographs was the collection of politician and lawyer Rufino Varela (1838–1911), offered at auction by Bravo y Cia. in July 1896. In addition to furniture, bronzes, paintings with ambitious attributions (such as Zurbarán or Rembrandt) and contemporary pictures by realist, naturalist and academic artists, the collection contained more than 5,000 engravings, copies and reproductions of famous works from the fifteenth to the nineteenth centuries. These included titles such as Rembrandt's *The Anatomy Lesson*, a portrait by Van Dyck, landscapes by J. M. W. Turner and *Saint Geneviève in Prayer* by Puvis de Chavannes (Fig. 6).

This graphic section was not included in the auction but offered in 1898 to the National Museum of Fine Arts for $180,000 m/n to form the basis of a national cabinet of prints. However, it was Schiaffino himself who rejected it, noting that "its artistic value was very little" since it comprised mostly anonymous drawings "attributed without much reason to various masters", while other pieces, considered to be originals, were nothing more than "vulgar facsimiles, such as a chromo reproduction of a 'Landscape of Italy' by Turner, a chromolithographic portrait of Marat attributed to Gericault, and so on and so forth" (Schiaffino, 1900).[8] In Schiaffino's conception of the museum, the canon of art history should be

[8] *Hecha la tasación y el inventario de la colección Rufino Varela, de dibujos y grabados, resultó que su valor artístico era muy escaso; la casi totalidad de los dibujos eran anónimos, atribuidos sin mayor razón a diversos maestros […] había facsímiles vulgares, como un cromo reproducción de un "Paisaje de Italia" de Turner, un retrato cromolitográfico de Marat atribuido a Gericault, etc. etc.* (underlined in the original).

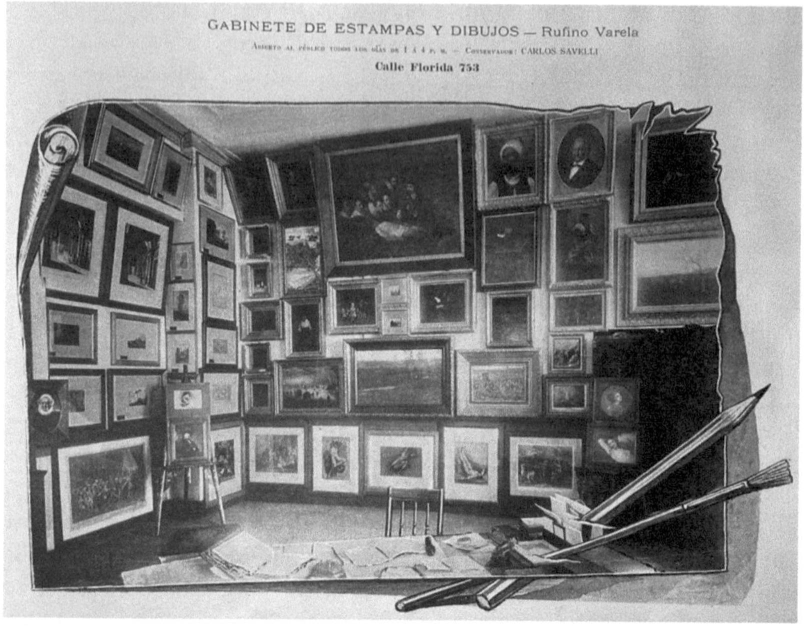

Fig. 6 Rufino Varela's Print and Drawing Cabinet (1900). Savelli, C. *La Argentina Monumental en la Exposición de París 1900*. Buenos Aires. *Photo* Author

formed mainly by originals. Although he gave some space to plaster casts of Greek and Roman antiquity and the Renaissance, that was only because sculpture allowed an "almost perfect mechanical reproduction" superior to the "mental copy of the works of art" (quoted in Gallipoli, 2021, p. 10). In later decades, casts would also be removed from the institution's display, which, in concordance with contemporary museums, favored a narrative based on originality.

Nevertheless, the evolution of the art market and its gradual specialization have many more nuances than those desired by the authorities in the art sphere. In fact, the establishment of a much more professionalized art system and the appearance of salons dedicated to living painters and sculptors in the early twentieth century did not prevent oleographs from being promoted as a sort of insurance against works of "dubious artistic taste." In 1912, in the main newspaper published in the city, an advertisement by the *Sociedad Internacional* asked why one should buy works by "unknown painters" at "exorbitant prices" instead of "exact reproductions" of "masters of universal fame" from the Louvre, Dresden, London and Saint Petersburg museums.[9] The advertisement aimed at educational and artistic dissemination: besides providing an illustrative booklet on the personalities of the masters, it offered payment plans with affordable monthly installments (La Nación, February 4, 1912, p. 5). In the same vein, a few years later, in 1918, renowned galleries such as Witcomb offered "reproductions of famous paintings" from the Prado Museum for $250 (Witcomb, 1918).

In a context of increasing professionalization within the Argentine art system, that sum was far from what a painting by a recognized artist would have cost at the time. It amounted to only 10% to 25% of the prices paid for *El chico de los gallos* by Jorge Bermúdez ($1,000) or *Sendero florido* by Fernando Fader ($3,000), two Argentine artists who received the highest awards in the local artistic sphere, as determined by the Salón Nacional de Bellas Artes in 1913 and 1914, respectively. However, if the goal had been to invest in national art, $250 would have been sufficient to acquire a couple of watercolors or etchings by young talents such as Rodolfo Franco, who was then exhibiting in the salons of the National Commission of Fine Arts (Augusta, March 1919). By that time, the circuits of validation and valuation in the art world were already well established. The context had shifted significantly from 1870 to fifty years later, when the term oleograph had come to be equated with low-quality art, and uninspired paintings were dismissed as "cheap oleographs" (La Nación, June 10, 1920).

5 Conclusion

Rather than threatening the trade of original works, as Eduardo Schiaffino feared, oleographs widened access to the artistic experience as part of the expanded visual culture of the late nineteenth century. That is to say, we should not think of two antithetical systems but rather of the coexistence of mediums and the possibility of diversified consumption. Different materialities—some closer to graphic or

[9] *¿Por qué adquiere Ud. cuadros de dudoso gusto artístico ejecutados por pintores desconocidos en el mundo del arte, pagando por ellos precios exorbitantes cuando por poco dinero puede Ud. obtener una reproducción exacta en todo sentido de los originales existentes en los Museos de Louvre, Dresde, Londres, San Petersburgo, etc?.*

decorative arts—proved beneficial to the global circulation of the imaginary of European art at a time of oversaturation in traditional markets and the need to create new consumers. Indeed, the persistence of oleographs and their widespread popularity as a form of commercial art in the nineteenth century even led to the term *chromo* being applied to all inexpensive paintings with sentimental themes. These works continued to be mass-produced—generally unsigned—into the twentieth century and were aimed at a middle-class audience (Couture, 1981).

The consumption and circulation of oleographs allow us to reconstruct precisely these porous spaces of the art market, often overlooked by art history in its effort to consolidate a narrative centered on singular authorship, originality, and great names. It was the circulation of these works—of lesser material and economic status compared to oil paintings and even artist-signed prints—that enabled artistic images to reach most Buenos Aires homes at the time. Focusing on this low end of the market from a thriving yet distant city from the centers of artistic production highlights the diversity of cultural consumption. At the same time, it brings us closer to understanding what a transatlantic art market meant in a period before the so-called globalization. Far from being mere reproductions, oleographs played a key role in shaping visual culture. They broadened access to artistic imagery and redefined—in a less elitist way—how art was experienced and valued more than a hundred years ago.

References

Primary sources

Augusta. (1919, March-April). Plática de Augusta. Ventas de arte. *Augusta*, *2*(10–11).

Colección Rufino Varela: Obras de arte y muebles en la casa-habitación calle Maipú 466. (1896). *Román Bravo y Cía.*

Demissolz, A. (1879). *Guía Comercial e Industrial.* Buenos Aires.

Elio. (1858, September 1). Olografía. *La Tribuna 2.*

El Correo Español. (1899, June 12–13). Un colmo artístico. *El Correo Español 2.*

Johnson, R. F. (1950, September 1). The disappearance of the oleograph. *Country Life*, *CVIII*(2798), 683.

Junior, C., & Stein, E. (eds.). (1876). *Almanaque comercial y guía de forasteros para 1877.* Imp. y Lit. del Courrier de la Plata.

Kuntz, H. (ed.). (1886). *Gran Guía de la Ciudad de Buenos Aires.* Lit. Italo Platense.

La Mujer. (1899). Casa Professione, Costa y Cia. *La Mujer, 137*.

La Mujer. (1900, November 9). La República Argentina por Demócrito, *La Mujer* (*41*), 20.

La Nación. (1880, November 16). *La Nación*, 1.

La Nación. (1888, September 9). Crónica de arte. Cosas de Pero Grullo-6000 cuadros-Arte, comercio, fin y causas ... *La Nación*, 1.

La Nación. (1912, February 4). ¿Por qué? *La Nación 5*.

La Nación. (1920, June 6). Pintores austríacos. *La Nación 4*.

Peddie, R. A. (1915, January 15). The history and practice of the art of printing. Lecture IV. *Journal of the Royal Society of Arts*, *63*(3243), 158–162.

Savelli, C. (1900). *La Argentina Monumental en la Exposición de París 1900*.

Schiaffino, E. (1883, September 21). Apuntes sobre el arte en Buenos Aires. IV. *El Diario, 1*.

Schiaffino, E. (1897–1910). *M.N.B.A. 2º Catálogo. Notas y apuntes personales*. Archivo Schiaffino (AS)-MNBA. Manuscript.

Schiaffino, E. (1900, May). *Manuscript*. Legajo 1–3325, Archivo Schiaffino, Archivo General de la Nación.

Un espectador (1900). Arte moderno. Escuela Española. 3° Exposición. *Almanaque Peuser 1900*, 67–76.

Uno che c'era. (1893). L'arte in remate. La collezione artistica del Dr. D. Gabriel Larsen del Castaño. *El Mundo Del Arte*, *3*, 171.

Witcomb, S. (1918). *Exposición de copias del Museo del Padre. Velázquez, Murillo, Goya, Rubens*.

Secondary sources

Amigo, R. (2008). El resplandor de la cultura del bazar. Arte y política. Mercados y violencia. *Razón Y Revolución*, *4*. Electronic reissue.

Baldasarre, M. I. (2017). Buenos Aires: An art metropolis in the late nineteenth century. *19th-Century Art Worldwide: A Journal of 19th-Century Visual Culture*, *16*(2). https://doi.org/10.29411/ncaw.2017.16.1.5

Baldasarre, M. I. (2018). From universalist to national art: Argentina's Museo Nacional de Bellas Artes, Buenos Aires. In M. Greet & G. M. Tarver (Eds.), *Art museums of Latin America: Structuring representation* (pp. 17–30). Routledge.

Baldasarre, M. I. (2024). The expansion of an international art market: Buenos Aires at the beginning of the twentieth century. In G. Feigenbaum, S. van Ginhoven, & E. Sterrett (Eds.), *Money in the Air: Art Dealers and the Making of a Transatlantic Market, 1880–1930* (pp. 182–197). Getty Research Institute.

Costa, M. E. (2018). Los talleres multigráficos de Guillermo Kraft y Jacobo Peuser en los inicios de la industria editorial argentina. In F. Ares (Ed.), *En torno a la Imprenta de Buenos Aires* (pp. 179–226). Dirección General de Patrimonio, Museos y Casco Histórico.

Couture, F. (1981). Le marché des chromos: Une industrie culturelle? *Intervention*, (*12*), 6–8.https://id.erudit.org/iderudit/1231ac

Gallipoli, M. (2021). *La victoria de las copias. Dinámicas de circulación y exhibición de calcos escultóricos en la consolidación de un canon estético occidental entre el Louvre y América (1863–1945)* [Unpublished doctoral dissertation]. Universidad de San Martín.

Kalba, L. A. (2017). *Color in the age of impressionism: Commerce, technology, and art*. The Pennsylvania State University Press.

Marzio, P. C. (1979). *The democratic art: An exhibition on the history of chromolithography in America, 1840–1900*. Amon Carter Museum of Western Art.

Slautterback, C. (2012). *Chromo-mania!: The art of chromolithography in Boston, 1840–1910*. Boston Athenæum.

Szir, S. (2018). El fabricante de imágenes César Hipólito Bacle y el establecimiento de la litografía en Buenos Aires (1828–1838). In F. Ares (Ed.), *En torno a la Imprenta de Buenos Aires* (pp. 105–134). Dirección General de Patrimonio, Museos y Casco Histórico.

Szir, S. (2023). *Las conquistas de lo efímero: Gráfica e industria en tiempos de Caras y Caretas*. Ministerio de Cultura de la Nación.

Twyman, M. (2013). *A history of chromolithography*. The British Library.

Van Horen, F., & Pieters, R. (2012). Consumer evaluation of copycat brands: The effect of imitation type. *International Journal of Research in Marketing*, *29*(3), 246–255. https://doi.org/10.1016/j.ijresmar.2012.04.001

Verhoogt, R. (2007). *Art in reproduction: 19th-century prints after Lawrence Alma-tadema, Jozef Israëls and Ary Scheffer*. Amsterdam University Press.

Cheap Art by the Crate-Load: Victorian Wholesalers of "Fine Art" Silber & Fleming

Krystyna Matyjaszkiewicz

1 Introduction

Economic expansion during the nineteenth century spurred the development of enterprises such as Silber & Fleming (S&F), selling goods or services to others. Founders Albert Marcius Silber and Noble Hutchinson Fleming, both recent immigrants to England, had different business networks, Silber in Europe and Hutchinson among the Irish/Scottish diaspora. Beginning their partnership as "Warehousemen," they developed a stock of "Foreign and fancy goods," including "Fine art," and by 1885 were "Complete house furnishers," like John Lewis or IKEA today—dealing in high volume of low value goods—but selling to other wholesalers or retailers, not directly to the public.

Their "Fine art" offer—in terms of Moureau and Radermecker's triadic model—spanned items of moderate-to-high symbolic functionality with low-to-moderate scarcity and moderate-to-high brand strength. It comprised oil paintings, chromolithographs, oleographs, photographs, engravings and other prints, from mass-market "German" lithographs to high-quality framed "artist's proofs" that London-based, Belgian-born art dealer Ernest Gambart marketed as luxury goods to higher-end collectors (Maas, 1975). Advertising themselves from 1880 as "Picture Dealers & Importers" alongside Gambart's business heirs and competitors, S&F

K. Matyjaszkiewicz (✉)
Independent researcher, Canterbury, UK

A.-S. V. Radermecker (ed.), *Low-End Markets for Art and Cultural Goods*, Cultural Economics & the Creative Economy,
https://doi.org/10.1007/978-3-032-27566-0_9

specialized in bulk-selling inexpensive artworks, unframed or framed-and-glazed. They had vast showrooms and warehousing in London's "City" business heartland, as well as branches in Birmingham and Paris, and traded worldwide via mail order and agents.

Expanding their trade over forty years, S&F were clearly a successful business, but detailed aspects remain unclear. What precisely did S&F's "Fine art" offer comprise, and where was it sourced? What customers were S&F aiming at, where did S&F position themselves in the art market, and what were their unique selling propositions? To answer these questions, a set of S&F trade catalogues has been analyzed and set in context, drawing on the author's research concerning art dealers in Victorian London (Matyjaszkiewicz, 2025) and on published studies of the nineteenth-century art market (including Fletcher & Israel, 2007; Fletcher & Helmreich, 2011), as well as analysis of nineteenth-century trade catalogues and newspaper advertisements.

S&F developed their business when photographs and reproductive prints were being produced "for the Million" (Dyson, 1984), with commensurate growth in sellers across the British Isles and Empire to whom S&F could tailor their offer. Through contacts in Europe, S&F accessed low-end lithographs and oil paintings. They also had financial backing that enabled them to negotiate discounts for cash payments when purchasing stock, allowing them to sell cheaply. By giving their clients the option of framed-and-glazed works ready for retail, S&F saved them time and effort, as did their bulk-crated "selections." S&F's expanding stock provided a one-stop shop for wholesale art, from low-end landscape or celebrity photographs to high-end engravings sourced from all available publishers, and items such as frame moldings, picture-glass, and mirrors that were sold by provincial retailers who styled themselves "picture-framers and art dealers." Fully illustrated catalogues enabled S&F to trade worldwide through agents with little or no knowledge of art.

This chapter begins with background detail about Silber and Fleming, introducing their contacts and networks in the British Isles and Europe. Their "Fine art" offer is summarized in Table 1, with different media in descending order of value. Stock is surveyed and sourcing evidence explored, with analysis of S&F's art-market positioning, stock quality, pricing, and unique selling propositions, in the context of other picture dealers as well as nineteenth-century earnings and cost of living.

2 Literature Review

S&F were discussed by the author among Jewish art dealers in Victorian London (Matyjaszkiewicz, 2025), but their "Fine art" stock was not analyzed in detail, nor has much been published about their backgrounds, business networks, and backers. Victorian trade in low-end artworks like S&F has received much less scholarly attention than high-to-mid-range art, about which Fletcher and Helmreich (2011) have written in the context of art dealers and the modern art market in nineteenth-century London, and Macleod (1996) on Victorian middle-class art-collecting. The production and marketing of high-quality reproductive engravings after popular Victorian paintings was detailed by Maas (1975) in his major study of Gambart, who came to London as Goupil & Co.'s representative and pioneered the subscription sale of such prints to high-end art collectors alongside newly-wealthy middle classes. Goupil's reproductive prints and photographs business, explored in Gérôme and Goupil (2000) and Renié (2005), ranged across lower-end art, from "artist's proof" engravings (i.e., high symbolic functionality, moderate-to-high scarcity, and high brand strength) to widely affordable "carte-de-visite" photographs (i.e., high symbolic functionality, low scarcity, moderate-to-high brand strength). S&F extended their stock beyond this, with cheap, mass-market lithographs that even working classes could afford, but these have been little studied.

Regarding print multiples, Dyson (1984) focused on pre-Victorian popular engravings rather than on those from the 1850s–1890s. Marzio (1979) explored the "democratic art" of chromolithographs in America, while Ward (2020) wrote about collecting in America and Australasia of Arundel Society chromolithographs after European Old Masters. Inglis (1988) looked at a broader range of reproductive prints collected in mid-nineteenth-century Australia, including those distributed to Art Union subscribers, and King (1985) made a detailed study of the Art Union of London's prints and subscribers. Engraved reproductions of nineteenth-century paintings have been explored by Rix (1983), Bann (2001), Tedeschi (2005), Verhooght (2007), and others, but print wholesalers like S&F were not discussed. Oil-painted reproductions have been referred to in the context of fakes and forgeries, notably by Briefel (2006), and the development of collections in Australia by Galbally and Inglis (1992). However, wholesalers like S&F and their prices have not been discussed in published research except by Zalesch (1996) in the case of American 1880s trade in cheap oil paintings. Similar or earlier non-American trade has been little examined.

3 Data and Methodology

For this chapter ten S&F trade catalogues in London's National Art Library, Victoria & Albert Museum—the most comprehensive set traced—were examined closely to analyze what S&F stocked in their Fine Art Department and how that changed over the period 1876–1889/1890 covered by the catalogues. None have publication dates but the earliest (S&F, 1876) can be dated from internal evidence ("just published" a picture titled *Look Mamma* for which S&F registered Copyright [April] 1876). Subsequent catalogues date from around 1877/1878 to mid/late 1882 (before S&F's premises fire in December 1882), 1885 (with new premises), and 1889/1890 (after Silber's death). Catalogue prices are summarized in Table 1. Some stock items were identified through digitized museum-collection catalogues and nineteenth-century newspapers. Information about Silber, Fleming and their business draws on genealogical records, trade directories and newspapers. Comparisons are made with nineteenth-century prices published by the Printsellers' Association and in newspapers, as well as with oil painting sales recorded in the ledgers of the art dealer Thomas Agnew & Sons (Agnew's).

4 Silber & Fleming's Foundation and History

Co-founder Albert Marcius Silber (1834–1887), born to a Friedrichstadt (Frederiksstad) merchant in Denmark, left after the city's severe bombardment under Prussian siege in 1850. By October 1856, when he applied for Naturalization as a British subject, Silber was a "General and Commission Agent" based in London (Naturalization Papers, 1856). In 1858 he married Amelia Isaacs, daughter of British-born "Commercial Traveler" Ralph Isaacs, who supported Silber's Naturalization. Two other supporters, also of Jewish heritage, were involved in textile trades connected with Silber's future partner. Noble Hutchinson Fleming (1826–1915), born in Cork, Ireland, was a merchant of shirts and collars in Limerick (1850), a major port on Ireland's west coast. He may have worked for, with, or in competition to Scottish-born Limerick shirt-manufacturer Peter Tait.

Table 1 Summary of selected Silber & Fleming "Fine art" prices. (£ = Pounds Sterling, s = Shillings, d = Pence. 12d = 1s, 20s = £1, £1 1s = 1 Guinea. Unit-prices rounded up to nearest fraction. Prices are nominal values, not adjusted for gradual deflation over this period that reduced the value of £100 in 1876 to £89 in 1889 (Allen, 2012))

Year	*Description*	*Framed*	*Unframed*	*Unit price*	*Discount offers*
Oil Paintings					
1876	Oil paintings on canvas	14s 6d–52s 6d each		14s 6d–52s 6d	2.5% discount for cash
1877/1878	French oval paintings	7s 6d–63s each	["In stock", no price]	7s 6d–63s	
1877/1878	Oil-painted copies on metal	57s–114s per dozen		4s 9d–9s 6d	
1877/1878	Ditto on glass	39s per dozen		3s 3d	
1877/1878	Ditto on canvas	32s–39s per dozen		2s 8d–3s 3d	
1877/1878	Ditto on millboard	12s 6d–105s per dozen		1s ½d–8s 9d	
1879/1880	Original oil paintings	2–100 guineas per pair		1–50 guineas	
1879/1880	Oil paintings on canvas [copies]	10s–45s each		10s–45s	9s each not 10s for 12 including crate
1882	Works by the best English Artists	1–100 guineas		1–100 guineas	
1882	Oil-painted copies, very fine	300s per 8		37s 6d	
1882	Oil-painted copies	135s per 50		2s 8½d	
1889/1890	Ditto on panel	12s 6d–45s each		12s 6d–45s	
1889/1890	Ditto on canvas	8s 9d–31s 6d each		8s 9d–31s 6d	
1889/1890	Ditto on metal	69s–105s per dozen		3s 9d–8s 9d	

(continued)

Table 1 (continued)

Year	*Description*	*Framed*	*Unframed*	*Unit price*	*Discount offers*
Water Colors					
1882	Watercolor drawings	17s 6d–45s each		17s 6d–45s	
1882		69s–105s per dozen		3s 9d–8s 9d	
1885	Watercolor drawings, superior	£15 per dozen		25s	
1885	Watercolor drawings	£9 per dozen		15s	
1889/1890	Watercolors	17s 6d–37s 6d each		17s 6d–37s 6d	
1889/1890		57s–150s per dozen		4s 9d–12s 6d	
Engravings & Etchings					
1876	Engravings		7s 6d–£10 10s each	7s 6d–£10 10s	2.5% discount for cash
1882			1s–98s each	1s–98s	
1889/1890			1s–70s each	1s–70s	
1882	Etchings		14s–56s each	14s–56s	
1889/1890			14s each	14s	
Oleographs & Chromolithographs					
1876	Oleographs	13s 6d–35s each		13s 6d–35s	2.5% discount for cash
1877/1878		14s 6d–35s each		14s 6d–35s	
1877/1878			9s 6d–84s each	9s 6d–84s	33⅓% discount
1879/1880			9s–24s or more per dozen	9d–2s or more	Ditto
1882		10 guineas for 20		10s 6d	

(continued)

Table 1 (continued)

Year	*Description*	*Framed*	*Unframed*	*Unit price*	*Discount offers*
1882	Oleographs strained on canvas	34s–96s per dozen		2s 10d–7s 10d	
1882	Oleographs	2s 6d–22s 7d each		2s 6d–22s 7d	
1882		12s–54s per dozen		1s–4s 6d	
1889/1890	Oleographs strained on canvas	13s 6d each		13s 6d	
1889/1890	Oleographs	9s–93s per dozen		9d–7s 9d	
1882	Peinture-Bogaerts		9d–50s each	9d–50s	
1876	Chromolithographs	16s 6d–54s per dozen		1s 4½d–4s 6d	2.5% discount for cash
1877/1878			3s 4d–63s each	3s 4d–63s	33⅓% discount
1877/1878		57s per 144		4¾d	
1882		12s 9d–144s per dozen		1s ¾d–12s	
1882			33s 3d–67s per 100	4d–8d	
1889/1890		8s 6d–81s per dozen		8½d–6s 9d	
1879/1880	Chromo mottoes		8s per dozen	8d	
1889/1890		5s 6d–18s per dozen		5½d–1s 6d	
Photographs & Photomechanical Prints					
1876	Photographs of statuary	8s 6d–31s 6d each		8s 6d–31s 6d	2.5% discount for cash
1876		5s 9d–84s per dozen		5¾d–4s 4d	Ditto

(continued)

Table 1 (continued)

Year	*Description*	*Framed*	*Unframed*	*Unit price*	*Discount offers*
1876	Photographs, hand-colored		7s 6d–42s each	7s 6d–42s	Ditto
1876	Photographs of paintings, hand-colored	21s–31s each		21s–31s	Ditto
1876	Photograph[ic] views	7s 6d each		7s 6d	Ditto
1876			20s per dozen	1s 8d	Ditto
1877/1878	Photographs of paintings, hand-colored		25s–63s each	25s–63s	33⅓% discount
1877/1878	Ditto plain		5s–42s each	5s–42s	Ditto
1877/1878	Photographs	57s per 144		4¾d	
1879/1880	Photographs of paintings, plain		8s–18s per dozen	8d–1s 6d	
1882	Colored photographs of landscapes & from drawings	24s–35s each		24s–35s	
1882		16s 6d–28s per dozen		1s 6½d–2s 4d	
1882	Photographs of paintings, hand-colored		48s per dozen	4s	
1882	Ditto plain		18s per dozen	1s 6d	
1882	Fine art medallions [photographs]	8s 6d–42s per dozen		8½d–3s 6d	
1889/1890	Photogravures		14s each	14s	
German Prints					
1876	Colored	10s 6d–64s per dozen		10½d–5s 4d	2.5% discount for cash
1876			13s 6d per dozen	1s 1½d	Ditto

(continued)

Table 1 (continued)

Year	*Description*	*Framed*	*Unframed*	*Unit price*	*Discount offers*
1876			21s per 100	2½d	Ditto
1876	Plain	37s–57s per dozen		3s 1d–4s 9d	Ditto
1876			6s per dozen	6d	Ditto
1877/1878	Colored		22s 6d per 100	2¾d	33⅓% discount
1877/1878	Plain		8s per dozen	8d	Ditto
1882	Colored	10s–64s per dozen		10d–5s 4d	
1882			16s 6d–74s per 100	2d–8¾d	
1882	Plain	30s–50s per dozen		2s 6d–4s 2d	
1882			40s per 100	4¾d	
1889/1890	Colored	12s per dozen		1s	

Source Author

By 1858 Fleming was London-based, renting a warehouse in Wood Street at the heart of the old "City" district, in an area dominated by textile businesses. Silber gave Wood Street as his address in 1859.

London's 1860 Post Office (PO) Directory lists "Silber & Fleming, warehousemen" at 56½ Wood Street (PO London, 1860). Warehousemen were wholesale merchants, trading especially in textiles. Silber had a brother in France[1] and, in December 1861, S&F established a Paris branch to conduct "the agency and commissioning for purchase and sale of English, French and other merchandise." The business registration mentions a sleeping partner, whose £20,000 Sterling share extended to the Paris branch (*Sociétés*, 1861). He was almost certainly Gloucestershire-born entrepreneur George Cannock, a textile trader who in 1858 sold his Limerick business to Peter Tait and in 1869 "sold his share in the business of Silber and Fleming for £44,000" (Assize, 1871). Ready access to money enabled S&F to negotiate discounts for cash payment and invest in their own manufacturing.

4.1 Trading c. 1860–1875

S&F likely began trading with shirts and collars (still stocked in 1876–1889/1890) and their associated accessories—shirt-studs and cufflinks—which are among "English and Foreign Gold, Silver and Imitation Jewelry" in their earliest catalogues. In 1867, S&F were listed as "importers & dealers in foreign stones" (gemstones) in Birmingham, a center of jewelry-making (PO Directory, 1867), and, in 1863, as "importers of fancy goods" in Manchester (Slaters, 1863). "Fancy goods" were anything ornamental and low-end, from jewelry to purses, photo-frames to prints. Having been "Warehousemen" until 1870, S&F listed themselves under "Foreign & Fancy Goods Importers," "Bronzists," "Clockmakers," "Jewelers" and "Leather Goods Manufacturers, Fancy" in 1875 (PO London, 1875).

From 1862 onwards, Silber patented various inventions and in 1873 set up the Silber Light Company (Limited), becoming managing director. In January 1876, his partnership with Fleming was "dissolved by mutual consent" (Notice, 1876). At that time S&F had premises in London and Birmingham as well as their Paris branch.

[1] He died in Paris in 1887 shortly before Silber (Obituary, 1887).

4.2 *Trading 1876–1898*

Under Silber's direction, and with specialist departmental buyers, S&F expanded their household-related stock, manufacturing capacities and trademarking. By 1880 their "Fine Art" department was so extensive that S&F listed themselves under "Picture Dealers & Importers" (PO London, 1880). After a disastrous fire destroyed S&F's London premises in December 1882, a vast showroom-warehouse was built and opened in September 1884. S&F then advertised themselves as "Complete House Furnishers," with stock detailed and illustrated in two hefty volumes. Advertisements for "Agents or Travelers" to represent the company were placed in scores of newspapers, resulting in a network of agents worldwide. Versions of S&F's catalogues were printed without prices or company name alongside a separate price list, so agents could quote their own prices including mark-up.

In June 1886, S&F registered as a private limited company with six shareholders, "all old assistants," and Silber as "sole proprietor" (Money, 1886). After his sudden death in May 1887, the company continued, with his son Martin Albert Silber (1862–1941) as one of the directors, but trading difficulties led to S&F liquidation in June 1898.

5 Silber & Fleming's "Fine Art" Stock: Sourcing, Pricing and Art-Market Positioning

From the mid-nineteenth century onward, art had become a subject of interest to a wide range of British society, stimulated by mass-attendance of international exhibitions, visits to public museums and galleries, reading, debate, and illustrations in press, periodicals and annuals. Growing demand for images to display at home led to increasing numbers of picture-dealers, framers and other sellers in Britain and abroad, including stationers and bookshops that stocked a range of prints. London-based "Picture Dealers" increased from 78 in PO trade directories of 1850 to 97 in 1860–1870 and 117 in 1880 (Matyjaszkiewicz, 2025). There were also picture and print-sellers in all cities and most towns. While high-profile art-dealers like Gambart bought work direct from living artists, most picture-dealers sourced their stock from auctions, wholesalers and one another, including picture-importers like S&F. Many traders were opportunists with limited knowledge of art.

As summarized by Burnett (1969) in a cost-of-living history, prices for goods in Britain rose after 1850 but wages rose more rapidly. Wage advancement continued during 1873–1896 while prices fell, in what was termed the "Great Depression". On a scale where 1850 = 100, average retail prices fell to 83 in 1896; real wages increased to 176. In 1889, people could buy for £89 what had cost £100 in 1876 (Allen, 2012). Cost-of-living calculations for wage-earners in 1881 found that 56.9% of wages were spent on food and drink, 16.8% on clothes, 13.9% on housing (rent, furniture, fuel and water), 5.4% on tax and the remaining 7% on "recreation and education", which could include any low-end art. The average price of a standard 4lb loaf of bread—staple food—was 7d in 1875, 6d in 1887, 5d in 1895 (Burnett, 1969). Working-class wages at that time were 12–35s per week, depending on skills.

During the 1860s an "upper middle-class ... professional man or tradesman" earned an average £500 a year, could rent a house at £50 a year and keep three servants. "Small mercantile income" averaged £300 a year; "lower middle-class" clerks earned £99 a year. The latter would have struggled to afford the one-guinea annual subscription to prints from the Arundel Society or Art Union of London (see 5.1), which targeted higher middle-classes, who like Mrs Meyrick in George Eliot's *Daniel Deronda* (1876) filled their houses with "black and white" reproductions of paintings.[2] Numbers of people employed in certain "middle-class" occupations increased 1851–1881: clerks, accountants and bankers from 0.5% of the occupied population to 1.9%; retail and wholesale traders from 6.5% to 7.8%. Law, medicine and religion remained fairly constant, but numbers involved in education increased from 1% to 1.6% (Best, 1979).

The wealthiest people in Britain were peers of the realm, with annual incomes of £3000–£50,000 or more, £10,000 per year being "probably the minimum for maintaining a country seat and a London season." Local landed "gentry" had annual incomes of £1,000–£10,000; the least that could support the leisured life of a "gentleman" was £1,000. Numerous merchants, industrialists, bankers and shop-owners became "as wealthy as many of the landed aristocracy" (Best, 1979). It was from these echelons that the wealthier art collectors came who patronized luxury-purveyors Gambart and the longer-established Agnew's, often paying spectacular prices for works by living artists (Macleod, 1996). S&F instead catered

[2] Eliot (1876), p. 201.

for retailers to the burgeoning middle-classes and to working-class people above the "poverty line" of nutritional requirement who could spare money for cheap prints or photographs of symbolic functionality.

Although no details have been found of S&F's "Fine art" stock before 1876, by then, the department was sufficiently well established to have been in existence for several years. Photographs, frames and prints were standard "fancy goods," which S&F had imported from at least 1862. Their 1876 catalogue boasts "the Artistic world ... fully represented" in "choice collections" of oil paintings, chromolithographs, oleographs, "German Prints," photographs, "First-Class Engravings," frames and mirrors. Table 1 summarizes "Fine art" detailed in S&F trade catalogues dated 1876–1889/1890. Groups of media are arranged in descending order of value, from highest-priced oil paintings to lowest-priced "German prints," with chronological pricing in each group.

5.1 *Silber & Fleming's Oil Painting Stock*

Oil paintings headed S&F's "Fine art" stock. The highest-priced were "Original oil paintings" by English artists—"original" implying moderate-to-high scarcity—at 2–100 guineas a pair (1–50 guineas each) in 1879/1880, 1–100 guineas each in 1882. One guinea was the annual subscription price to the Arundel Society, which published chromolithographs reproducing Old Masters, and to the Art Union of London, which offered annual painting prizes and gave all subscribers a print each year—i.e., works of moderate-to-high symbolic functionality, and low-to-moderate scarcity and brand strength. Agnew's starting price in 1879 for oils by living artists was about 50 guineas, ranging up to £2,000 (Agnew's, 1874–1879). S&F described their stock in 1879/1880 as by "well-known English artists ... G. Bassett, R. Marshall, E. Earde, Turner, Wilson, Callow, and others." "Turner, Wilson, Callow", famous artists, conveyed higher scarcity and brand strength but were simply marketing strategy: Turner's oils were fetching at least 100 guineas at auction in 1879/1880, not 50, and were only available on the secondary market, where fraud was prevalent (Matyjaszkiewicz, 2025). Bassett, Marshall and Earde were landscape painters of low-to-moderate rarity and brand strength, and probably glad to have S&F's bulk purchase.

To avoid fraud, collectors had been encouraged since the 1850s to buy work by living artists. S&F assured their customers that "every original work sold by us can be guaranteed" and "all paintings are signed by the artist".[3] These paintings were formulaic, featuring mountains/hills with rivers/lakes, trees, and a figure/dog, elements still popular today, as evidenced in the "Most Wanted" poll conducted by artists Vitaly Komar and Alex Melamid in 14 countries, including the US (Komar & Melamid, 1994–95). Such paintings had mass-market appeal and would have been attractive to non-specialist picture-dealers. They only needed to state to S&F a range and maximum of prices and S&F would choose a crateful.[4] For the traders (S&F's clients), such stock was of high direct functionality and low-to-moderate scarcity and brand strength; for customers, the paintings would have moderate-to-high symbolic functionality. "Higher Class" differentiation was introduced by 1881, when S&F were styling themselves "Picture Dealers & Importers."

"Original Oil Paintings" were accompanied in 1877/1878 by "copies of old and modern masters", and "French oval paintings" of "landscapes, sea views ... female heads ... dead game, fruits, flowers" by "celebrated artists" with whom S&F had arranged to purchase work "at all times for cash," thus offering "prices far below those of the artists themselves".[5] Sourcing is clarified in an 1881/1882 catalogue, where "excellent copies" after "the most eminent artists of the Continental school" (high brand strength) are "by Foreign Artists" and "mostly painted by highly educated ladies and gentlemen".[6] To the landscape, marine, cattle or sporting subjects listed in earlier catalogues are added "Views in Australia or Roman Catholic Subjects, Saints, &c." and "Figure Pictures, comprising Domestic, Historical, and other Scenes," increasing symbolic over direct functionality. S&F's Paris branch would have sourced these copies, like much of S&F's other stock, "from small and large manufacturers in France and Belgium".[7]

The 1881/1882 details are a rare, published reference to sourcing. Copy-painting in museum-galleries was standard practice for artists' training and also an income source, thanks to demand from collectors (and fledgling public galleries) for oil or watercolor copies of works by Old and Modern Masters (high brand strength). Unscrupulous dealers, however, passed off copies as originals (Briefel, 2006). The quantities of miss-sold copies and

[3] S&F (1882), p. 424; S&F (1885), vol. 1, 89.

[4] S&F (1879/1880), iii.

[5] S&F (1877/1878), 90, 93.

[6] S&F (1881/1882a), 178½.

[7] S&F (1882), vol. 1, 464.

intentionally fraudulent works on the nineteenth-century picture-market fueled convictions that there were factories creating fakes, although no documented evidence was presented. S&F's ability to sell crate-loads suggests that production was considerable, even if not in formalized "factories."

5.2 *Silber & Fleming's Print "Multiples" Stock*

Engravings and Etchings

Reproductive engraving production had been growing from the 1830s (Dyson, 1984). It was Gambart's marketing flair (Maas, 1975) that led to increased demand in the 1850s–1860s, with top-quality "proofs" aimed at luxury-goods collectors—as additions or alternatives to oils—and ordinary (lower-end) prints from the same plates for wider clientele. S&F stocked such "First-Class Engravings," detailing about 150 in their 1876 catalogue, over 250 in 1877/1878, and some 1760 titles in 1882 (including sets of up to 100 prints). These were of high symbolic functionality, low-to-moderate scarcity and high brand strength. Over 100 were still listed in 1889, when engravings were less popular than artist-made etchings, which S&F also stocked by 1881. As Dyson noted, "printers and publishers still held gigantic stocks of [engraving] plates" and S&F could supply to order "any subjects not mentioned" unless out of print.

S&F's engravings were sourced from various print-publishers, including the Art Union of Glasgow, Colnaghi & Co., Gambart and his successors Pilgeram & Lefèvre, Henry Graves & Co., Lloyd Brothers, and J. McQueen, although none were named in S&F's catalogues (which also rarely stated producers of other goods except S&F's own patented or trademarked items).

Heading S&F's "First-Class Engravings" were reproductions of Rosa Bonheur's *Horse Fair*, a huge painting and sensation at Gambart's London gallery in 1855. The 4 ft-wide engraving he published was in S&F's 1877/1878 catalogue, with proofs at 5–10 guineas each, the same as official prices declared to the Printsellers' Association (Friend, 1892), founded in 1847 "to prevent the production of proofs beyond an openly declared number".[8] S&F also stocked the "Middle-size" version that Gambart published, and "Small-size" published by his successors,

[8] Gambart was a founding member and also campaigned for copyright laws to prevent illicit print-production that undermined his sales.

Pilgeram and Lefèvre. Prices for the small engraving were 10s 6d to two guineas, medium 2–10 guineas (same as declared prices), with hand-colored versions at 1–4 guineas. S&F's customers thus had all available options of print-quality and price to choose from.

Similarly in the case of William Holman Hunt's famous *Light of the World*, S&F had both "large" and "middle-size" engravings published by Gambart. But they also stocked an undeclared "small-size" costing as little as 1s 6d compared to 12s to eight guineas (declared prices) for Gambart's prints. Without any mention of print-publishers, all S&F's engravings appeared equally valid and Bonheur's top-of-the-range implied high-quality throughout.

Etchings were much quicker to make than engravings and consequently cheaper, though their copper plates wore out and quantities were limited. The most expensive stocked by S&F in 1882 was Charles Waltner's etched reproduction of Gainsborough's *Blue Boy* (characterized by high symbolic functionality and brand strength), priced £2 16s.

Chromolithographs and Oleographs

S&F's chromolithographs and oleographs were similarly ones readily available from British sources and abroad, with no mention of publishers. Chromolithographs include ones published in London by M. & N. Hanhart, J. McQueen, and G. Rowney & Co. Oleographs were mostly imported. Such reproductive prints were the most numerous "Fine art" items S&F stocked: they referred in 1876–1882 to "a detailed catalogue" (untraced) of some 4,000 chromolithograph subjects. Due to their "very low" production price (and consequently high-volume production and low scarcity), chromolithographs had "contributed largely towards increasing a love and taste for the fine arts throughout the whole civilized world," according to S&F, who had therefore given them "special attention".[9] In total, 271 are listed in 1876, 586 in 1877/1878.

Oleograph stock in 1877/1878 comprised 274 titles "From Paintings by Old and Modern Masters." All were available "strained upon canvas, the impression of which is to be seen upon the surface" and "varnished as paintings"—difficult to distinguish from originals once framed—or "on white mounts for framing with a margin." They included Rembrandt's *Night Watch* and Raphael's *Madonna della Sedia*, both

[9] S&F (1876), 216.

sold by London-based publishers Sampson Low & Co. as "sole wholesale agents for England, America, and the Colonies" (Oleographs, 1870). Many listed artists were from Germany, Austria and the Low Countries, where most oleographs were produced. Still bestsellers today were Turner's *Fighting Temeraire*—voted Britain's favorite painting in 2013—and John Constable's *Cornfield*. However, no such "Masters" were chosen to illustrate oleographs in 1880s catalogues, which instead show landscapes, still life, children, and genre scenes.

S&F's largest-size (26 x 50 in) chromolithographs in 1877/1878 were reproductions of Leonardo Da Vinci's *Last Supper* (high symbolic functionality and brand strength) and Italian subjects by Thomas Miles Richardson junior, priced three guineas each, as were chromolithographs after Myles Birket Foster (high symbolic functionality and moderate brand strength), the artist most represented in S&F's catalogues. Three guineas was a high price—as Arundel Society subscribers received five chromolithographs for one guinea in 1877—and implied high quality. Many S&F titles were grouped in pairs (though priced individually), such as *Norham Castle* and *Kirkstall Abbey* after Turner, 7s 6d each. Published by J. McQueen,[10] these are of far poorer quality than S&F's three-guinea chromolithographs after Turner's *Ulysses deriding Polyphemus*—an excellent reproduction published by Rowney[11]—and two Venice subjects,[12] revealing stratification in quality as well as price. Traders could select a range of prices, or focus on higher/lower, according to their client-base. Similar choice was offered with chromolithographs after Thomas Sidney Cooper's cattle paintings, priced £1 11s 6d to 5s and also spanning quality, as described by Westwood (1991). Although S&F boasted that many of their chromolithographs were made using "no less than ... thirty to forty stones ... thereby producing so perfect a facsimile of the original work that even the greatest critic may often be deceived",[13] most of their stock comprised simpler examples of variable quality for as little as 4d each.

Oleographs like Rembrandt's *Night Watch* (high symbolic functionality and brand strength), sourced from Sampson Low, were priced the same as Sampson Low advertised (£3 10s), S&F probably receiving bulk-buy

[10] See British Museum (BM) accession numbers 1893,0612.203 and 202.

[11] See V&A accession number E.5446–1946.

[12] For one of the two Venice subjects see BM 1893,0612.206.

[13] S&F (1876), 216.

discount. S&F in turn offered discount to their customers, who could sell on at the advertised price or more. Oleographs of Turner's *Fighting Temeraire* and Constable's *Cornfield* were each 16s, but unit prices ranged down to 9d for less-famous artists (moderate symbolic functionality and brand strength).

German Prints

S&F called their cheap imported lithographs "German Prints," as the medium had been developed in Germany for mass-printing images at low prices (low scarcity). Silber may have had family contacts there: several Prussian-based Silbers appear in 1860s Paris trade directories. Both black-printed—"plain"—and "in rich colors" were stocked. In 1876 S&F had "1,000 different kinds," the 1882 catalogue describing them as "Landscapes, Sporting and Agricultural Scenes, Historical and Domestic Subjects, Portraits of Crowned Heads, Renowned Generals, Admirals, Poets, Historians, Statesmen, &c.," as well as a "full collection of Religious subjects of every description." Illustrated examples included Landseer's *Dignity and Impudence* (high brand strength) in an unauthorized and copyright-infringing print (low scarcity).

"German Prints" were S&F's cheapest "Fine art" stock alongside photographs. Plain prints, framed-and-glazed, cost as little as 6d each in 1876, and 4¾d in 1882; colored unframed prints as low as 2½d in 1876, 2d in 1882. Like S&F's cheapest photographs, they could be sold on at prices affordable to working-class people. Mayhew (1851), in his mid-century study of London workers, described street-sellers with hand-colored prints from "waste" engravings (low scarcity) priced 1d–2d each.[14] S&F could supply traders with brand-new colored prints of modern subjects at a similar price, which even with mark-up would sell for less than a loaf of bread. This is the lowest end of the art market, very little studied or published, and one where S&F were a major trade supplier.

5.3 Silber & Fleming's "Photographs" Stock

S&F's "Optical Department" in 1876 had "cartes-de-visite" of celebrities and royalty (low scarcity and high brand strength), as well as photo-frames, stereoscopic and lantern slides, while under "Fine art" were over

[14] Mayhew (1851), p. 329.

1,500 photographic views in Great Britain, Europe, the Middle East, India, China and Japan. There were also about 500 hand-colored photographs, some 200 of which were described in 1879 as "from well-known pictures" (moderate-to-high brand strength). Additionally listed in 1877/1878 were 31 reproductions of paintings by photographers Robert Jefferson Bingham, Charles Thurston Thompson and others, most likely sourced from their studios. In 1882, 50 photographic reproductions of paintings from stock of "over 500" were detailed, including works by Millais, Landseer, Delaroche, Raphael and Guido Reni. Many of these would have been sourced from publisher Goupil. There were also "Fine Art Medallions," mostly Old Masters and including Raphael's *Sistine Madonna* angels that are still international favorites (with high symbolic functionality, low scarcity, and high brand strength).

Unit prices for framed photographs in 1876 spanned 31s 6d–5¾d, even 4¾d in 1877/1878, making the cheapest widely affordable. Higher minimum 1880s prices reflect S&F's separation of "Fine art" photographic reproductions from ordinary photography stock. Over 500 photographs reproducing paintings were in 1882 priced 18s per dozen plain (1s 6d each), 48s hand-colored (4s each). Goupil's average price for such photos (plain/uncolored) was five francs each (Gérôme & Goupil, 2000), roughly equivalent to 4s.

6 Silber & Fleming's Unique Selling Propositions

6.1 *A Worldwide Mail-Order Wholesale Outlet*

As wholesalers, S&F supplied "only the wholesale and shipping trade" (S&F, 1879) until sometime between 1886 and 1889 when they extended their custom to "*bona fide* shop-keepers" (S&F, 1889). References in the 1876 catalogue to boots and shoes "for the Foreign and Colonial Markets," hat shapes "for East and West Indies," and features suitable for "hot climates," reflect S&F's client-base across the British Empire. With catalogues describing and illustrating their stock, S&F operated as an international mail-order outlet for wide-ranging merchandise including "Fine art". It was a niche market, without direct competitors among British wholesalers in a growing sector with increased colonial trade and British-staffed administrations, and an expanding, art-hungry middle-class at home and abroad.

According to S&F, their advantages as suppliers were holding large stocks of catalogued merchandise, enabling them to fulfil orders within 24 hours of receipt; having experienced buyers for each department; and being able to "sell as cheaply as, or cheaper than, the manufacturer who supplies customers that buy smaller quantities." Their 1885 catalogue clarified that "our aim has not been to produce every article at the lowest price ... but at such a price that [an] article of the same quality cannot be sold cheaper with a fair profit." Moreover their stock range was suitable for "persons belonging to every grade of society." It spanned high-quality to mass-market imitations, like catalogue-based Argos or Screwfix stores in Britain today but selling to trade customers not the general public.

S&F's cheap "German prints" were the equivalent of their "imitation" jewelry in gilt aluminum and paste (high direct functionality, low scarcity and brand strength). "Artists' proofs" of engravings were like S&F's upmarket gold jewelry (moderate-to-high symbolic functionality for prospective buyers, and moderate scarcity and brand strength). "Ordinary" prints, run off in thousands after limited-edition "proofs," were the equivalent of S&F's cheaper jewelry options in silver (low-to-moderate symbolic functionality, scarcity and brand strength). Traders could select the quality and price point(s) that best catered for the customers they were targeting.

6.2 *Shipping Economies*

S&F offered traders a huge range of merchandise that could be ordered and shipped together, saving on transport costs. A "Carver, Gilder and Picture-frame Maker" like John Sampson of York, for example, selling "Chromolithographs, Oleographs & Autotypes" at his "Fine Art Gallery" alongside various luggage and "Ormolu goods suitable for Wedding and Birthday presents" (York, 1870), could obtain all these, as well as frame-moldings, picture-glass and cord, from S&F. 1880s catalogues grouped "Fine art" with artists' materials, albums, frames and mirrors, as S&F illustrated for Christmas/Birthday gift ideas (S&F, 1881/1882b). "Pictures for Export" were "packed in Cotton Sheets to prevent breakage" and the sale of these sheets provided extra profit.[15]

[15] S&F (1879/1880), 256–257.

6.3 *Pre-Selected Art*

Crates of assorted pictures were S&F's cheapest option and suited traders not particular about exact stock. "Well-assorted" £25 cases of photographs, chromolithographs and oleographs, looking "very effective" in gilt frames, were "specially adapted to auction purposes," according to S&F. By about 1881 they offered 15 themed, ready-crated "Selections" of chromolithographs or oleographs. "German prints" were also preselected, packed in cases of 150. Traders needed only to state "for what market they are intended, and whether for Native or European trade; if European, whether Catholic or Protestant, as the utmost care will be taken to select a class of subjects suited to the market," in which customers would be looking for high symbolic functionality.

6.4 *Ready-Framed in Gilt*

S&F's cheapest "Fine art" was unframed, but ready-framed options were both convenient and inexpensive, providing traders with ready-to-retail stock. Repeated emphasis on gilt or "massive gold" frames—characterized by—reflect their attractiveness to the buying public.

7 Conclusion

S&F's wide-ranging stock provided a one-stop-shop for traders selling low-end art. Instead of having to go to individual print-publishers or suppliers, they could get from S&F any titles still in print. Mixed cases (high direct functionality) were ideal for auctioneers and picture-sellers not particular about artwork choice. Being framed-and-glazed ready for sale also saved S&F's clients the time and trouble of arranging framing themselves. Today, Internet-based wholesalers of art prints and/or fine art offer similar services to traders, including framing, with hundreds of options for subject or medium. They provide stock for high-street shops competing with websites selling direct to the public, who can order prints or oil-on-canvas copies of any painting online, as well as having wide choices of room decoration in stores like IKEA.

Furthermore, catalogues are an important but overlooked resource for art history and study of art markets. The lists of chromolithographs, oleographs and other prints they contain give a unique insight into 1870s–1880s British and international trade in cheap pictures, including 1850s–1860s engravings still stocked and in demand. Most of these were the ordinary prints published in their thousands, quantities of which were not detailed in declarations to the Printsellers' Association. These lists, which contain price information, are worthy of further study, especially in relation to museum/gallery cataloguing of low-end pictures that have hitherto been disregarded, except in the case of Australian museum collections, and are coming to light with digitization. Digitized archive and library holdings may also bring to light pre-1876 S&F catalogues or other sources. Meanwhile the catalogues studied above are a key resource for low-end art-selling that deserve to be more widely known.

References

Agnew, T., & Sons. (1874–1879). *Agnew's picture stock book* (NGA27,1,1,5). National Gallery, London.

Allen, G. (2012). *Inflation: The value of the pound 1750–2011.* House of Commons Library. Retrieved June 2, 2025, from https://commonslibrary.parliament.uk/research-briefings/rp12-31/

Assize Intelligence. Cork. (1871, March 25). *The Freeman's Journal.* n.p.

Bann, S. (2001). *Parallel lines: Printmakers, painters and photographers in nineteenth-century France.* Yale University Press.

Best, G. (1979). *Mid-Victorian Britain 1851–70.* Fontana.

Briefel, A. (2006). *The deceivers: Art forgery and identity in the nineteenth century.* Cornell University Press.

Burnett, J. (1969). *A history of the cost of living.* Penguin Books.

Copyright. (1876, April 25). Painting title 'Look Mamma'. *Records of the Copyright Office, Stationer's Company: The National Archives,* Kew. COPY 1/33/96.

Dyson, A. (1984). *Pictures to print: The nineteenth-century engraving trade.* Farrand Press.

Eliot, G. (1876). *Daniel Deronda.* Penguin Books.

Fletcher, P., & Israel, D. (2007). *London gallery project,* revised September 2012. http://learn.bowdoin.edu/fletcher/london-gallery/

Fletcher, P., & Helmreich, A. (ed.). (2011). *The rise of the modern art market in London, 1850–1939.* Manchester University Press.

Friend, G. W. (1892). *An alphabetical list of engravings declared at the office of the Printsellers' Association, London ... 1847 to the end of 1891.* Printsellers' Association.

Galbally, A., & Inglis, A. (1992). *The first collections: The public library and the National Gallery of Victoria in the 1850s and 1860s.* University of Melbourne.

Gérôme & Goupil. (2000). *Gérôme & Goupil: Art and enterprise*. Réunion des Musées Nationaux.

Inglis, A. (1988). Art at second hand: Prints after European pictures in Victoria before 1870. *Australian Journal of Art, VII*, 50–63.

King, L. S. (1985). *The industrialization of taste: Victorian England and the Art Union of London*. UMI Research Press.

Komar & Melamid. (1994–95) *Komar & Melamid: The most wanted paintings*. https://awp.diaart.org/km/

Limerick Quarter Sessions. (1850, July 3). *The Limerick and Clare Examiner*, 1.

Maas, J. (1975). *Gambart, prince of the Victorian art world*. Barrie & Jenkins.

Macleod, D. S. (1996). *Art and the Victorian middle class: Money and the making of cultural identity*. Cambridge University Press.

Marzio, P. C. (1979). *The democratic art: Chromolithography 1840–1900. Pictures for a nineteenth-century America*. David R. Godine.

Matyjaszkiewicz, K. (2025). Art dealing in "the hands of Abraham's posterity": Jewish art dealers in Victorian London. In S. Davoli & T. Stammers (Eds.), *Jewish dealers and the European art market, c.1860–1940: Negotiating cultural modernity* (37–56). Bloomsbury Visual Arts.

Mayhew, H. (1851). *London Labour and the London Poor* (Vol. 1). Charles Griffin & Co.

Money-Market and City Intelligence. (1886, June 26). *The Times*. 14.

Naturalization Papers. (1856, November 12). *Silber, Albert Marcius, from Denmark: certificate 2351*. The National Archives, Kew. HO 1/77/2351.

Notice. (1876, February 4). *The London Gazette*. 481.

Obituary. (1887, May 26). Mr. Albert Marcius Silber. *The Times 7*

Oleographs. (1870, April 9). Oleographs. After old masters and modern painters. *The Graphic*, 455.

Post Office Directory for Birmingham. (1867). Retrieved February 3, 2025, from https://www.ancestry.co.uk

Post Office London Directory. (1860, 1865, 1870, 1875, 1880, 1885, 1890). Retrieved March 4, 2023, from https://www.ancestry.co.uk

Renié, P. L. (2005). *Une Image sur un mur: Images et decoration intérieure au XIXe siècle*. Musée Goupil.

Rix, B. D. (1983). *Pictures for the parlour: The English Reproductive Print from 1775 to 1900*. Art Gallery of Ontario.

Silber & Fleming Ltd. (1876). *Illustrated catalogue* [1872].

Silber & Fleming Ltd. (1877/1878). *Illustrated catalogue* [1876].

Silber & Fleming Ltd. (1879/1880). *Illustrated catalogue* [1879].

Silber & Fleming Ltd. (1881). *Bound volume containing Silber & Fleming catalogues* [1880–1881].

Silber & Fleming Ltd. (1881/1882a). *Illustrated pattern book of English china ... chimneys, &c.* [188–?].

Silber & Fleming Ltd. (1881/1882b). *A catalogue of Christmas, New Year's, birthday and wedding presents* [186–?].

Silber & Fleming Ltd. (1882). *Illustrated catalogue* [188–?].

Silber & Fleming Ltd. (1885). *Illustrated pattern book of furniture ... paper hangings, etc.*

Silber & Fleming Ltd. (1889/1890). *Illustrated pattern book of sterling silver goods ... guns and pistols* [1889?].

Slater's Directory of Manchester and Salford (1863). 436.

Sociétés commerciales et industrielles. (1861, December 12). *Le Moniteur universel. Journal Official de l'Empire Français. 1738.*

Tedeschi, M. (2005). "Where the picture cannot go, the engravings penetrate": Prints and the Victorian Market. *Art Institute of Chicago Museum Studies, 31*(1), 8–19,89–90.

Verhooght, R. (2007). *Art in reproduction: Nineteenth-century prints after Lawrence Alma-Tadema, Josef Israels and Ary Scheffer*. Amsterdam University Press.

Ward, L. (2020). Quaestio Vexata: Collecting Arundel "chromos" in America and Australasia. *Australian Journal of Victorian Studies, 24*(1), 28–50.

Westwood, K. J. (1991). *Thomas Sidney Cooper: His life and work* (Vol) 1. Master of lithography. Wilson Hunt.

York. (1870, September 3). *The York Herald.* n.p.

Zalesch, S. E. (1996). What the four million bought: Cheap oil paintings of the 1880s. *American Quarterly, 48*(1), 77–109.

Intellectual Property Licensing in Superstar Museums: Transforming Collections Into Creative Products for International Consumer Market

Jiahui Liao

1 Introduction

This chapter examines intellectual property (IP) licensing as an innovative market strategy increasingly adopted by museums worldwide for both commercial and cultural purposes. As a new form of museum-led commercial initiative, this market-oriented approach involves the licensing of museum brands or reproduction rights to external partners, ranging from consumer brands to cultural institutions. This type of brand and licensing partnership is distinct from image licensing, as it often results in jointly produced products (Prokůpek et al., 2023) that combine cultural meanings with practical functionality, and are sold in both consumer markets and museum shops. Through such collaborations, museums adopt a strategic, market-oriented approach to reinterpret their "high art" collections and engage international audiences in "lower-end" markets, spanning a range of sectors including fashion, stationery, homeware, household appliances, and other forms of commercial partnership.

J. Liao (✉)
King's College London, London, UK
e-mail: jiahui.liao@kcl.ac.uk

A.-S. V. Radermecker (ed.), *Low-End Markets for Art and Cultural Goods*, Cultural Economics & the Creative Economy,
https://doi.org/10.1007/978-3-032-27566-0_10

IP licensing and partnerships have evolved from, yet remain distinct from, traditional museum merchandise in at least two key aspects. First, they involve commercial partnerships and licensing agreements concerning intellectual property rights, leveraging the value of a museum's brand and its cultural assets, primarily its collections. Second, in terms of target audience and distribution channels, the focus has shifted from domestic, physical museum shops to international and online markets, opening up new global market opportunities. In this way, it reaches not only museum visitors but also individuals interested in the museum and its collections who may not have the opportunity to visit in person (Total Licensing, 2021). While existing literature has extensively examined museum merchandising and branding, this emerging model centered on commercial partnerships and the production of co-branded products remains largely underexplored. This study also highlights a gap between China-based research on museums' Cultural and Creative Products, or *wenchuang* products rooted in domestic policy and museum practice, and the Anglophone literature on cultural goods and cultural commodities.

While this strategy has gained traction across global markets, including Europe, the United Kingdom, the United States, and East Asia, this study specifically focuses on the Greater China market. This market, as one of the largest markets for IP licensing programs run by international superstar museums, offers substantial market potential, driven by a growing local demand for arts and cultural consumption. However, market specificities and geographic distance necessitate localization strategies and collaboration with local brands and agents. Since the British Museum launched its flagship store on Tmall (Alibaba's B2C e-commerce platform) in 2018 with notable success (Xinhua Finance, 2018), more international museums have followed suit. This study asks: How do international museums develop IP licensing programs and transform their "high art" collections into consumer-market products? And how does this strategy enable museums to engage the Chinese market, enhancing audience accessibility while generating revenue?

To address these questions, this study examines the IP licensing activities of international museums in China between 2018 and 2020, including a period significantly impacted by the COVID-19 pandemic, which disrupted global museum visitation (ICOM, 2021). Methodologically, the study draws on an original dataset of 11 international museums from France, the United Kingdom, the United States, the Netherlands, and Russia, all of which had established IP licensing initiatives in China by the end of 2020. The study aims to develop a fundamental model of museum IP licensing, illustrating an international value chain characterized by cross-cultural collaboration and value co-creation. In addition, it explores how multiple stakeholders, including museums, agents, brands, and market facilitators, collaborate in a market that is not only perceived as "lower end" but also geographically distant.

This study finds that, at its core, such IP licensing activities are characterized by the involvement of superstar museums, and an international, long-tail value chain and value co-creation among multiple stakeholders. This value chain not only seeks to balance commercial profitability with cultural missions but also facilitates the transformation of values from "high art" to more accessible, "low-end" markets across geographic regions. Traditionally, museums and their collections have been viewed as a core segment of the cultural and creative industries (UNESCO & UNDP, 2013), embodying high cultural and symbolic value and serving as a meeting point for fine art, heritage treasures and art professionals. This international value chain extends cultural value from the fine art world into the consumer market, offering more affordable opportunities for cultural consumption to a broader public. In doing so, it blurs the traditional boundary between elite and mass culture, shifting art consumption beyond high-income consumers (Towse, 2006) to a wider audience engaging with more accessible and affordable creative products, or co-branded derivatives of high art.

The next section reviews existing literature on IP licensing strategies in museums, as well as related commercial partnerships and co-branded products as an emerging form of museum merchandising. This is followed by a discussion of the study's methodology, which draws on a dataset of 11 international museums that developed IP licensing programs in China between 2018 and 2020. The findings section introduces a fundamental model of the international value chain, emphasizing the role of partnerships in shaping this process. The chapter concludes by summarizing key insights and outlining directions for future research.

2 Literature Review

Museum IP licensing has typically evolved from earlier forms of museum merchandising and souvenir retail, which have long served as extensions of the museum visit and integral parts of the overall visitor experience (Kent, 2010; McIntyre, 2010). Museum merchandising also plays a key role in museum marketing strategies (Buber & Knassmüller, 2009; Komarac et al., 2019), supporting both commercial and cultural functions (Mottner & Ford, 2005). The broader debate surrounding museum merchandising often centers on (anti)commercialization (Komarac et al., 2019). Within nonprofit museums, revenue-generating activities are generally regarded as a means to support institutional missions, rather than ends in themselves (Marciano & Moureau, 2016). As such, commercial initiatives are expected to remain aligned with a museum's mission, stay relevant to its collections, and not necessarily signal a complete shift toward market-driven operations at the expense of cultural values (Coblence & Sabatier, 2014). Research also suggests that well-managed merchandising can actively advance museum objectives (Prokůpek & Gombault, 2024), by enhancing the visibility of artworks, strengthening institutional reputation, and contributing to public education as a positive externality (Marciano & Moureau, 2016). In the Chinese context, museum merchandising is increasingly seen as a way to vitalize cultural heritage (Li et al., 2022), reflecting local acceptance and a culturally driven perspective.

2.1 *IP Licensing Strategies in Museums*

The form and scope of museum merchandising and museum shop products have evolved, from the retail of self-produced items to co-branded creative products developed through partnerships with commercial brands (Feng & Lin, 2018; Prokůpek et al., 2023). This approach also reflects a new model of the art-commerce relationship, shifting from a once binary opposition to a more complementary dynamic, and from traditional sponsorship to strategic partnership (Lewandowska, 2015).

The motives for museums to pursue licensing programs are generally twofold: generating income and increasing accessibility to collections (Feng & Lin, 2018). On the one hand, the rise of this commercial initiative coincides with the ongoing decline in public funding and cultural subsidies on which museums have traditionally relied (Baumgarth, 2009). As a result, self-generated income has become essential for building more sustainable and resilient financial structures. Many museums have reported a steady increase in earned revenue from sources such as admission fees, exhibition tickets, museum shops, fundraising, memberships, sponsorships, and venue rentals. However, museums are often constrained by policies governing visitor access. For example, public museums in the

UK have been required to offer free admission since 2001 (Finance Act 2001, 2001). Financial strain was further exacerbated by the COVID-19 pandemic, which forced physical closures and led to significant losses in admission income (ICOM, 2021). In response, museums around the world have continued to explore alternative funding sources that can reach new markets and are less dependent on physical presence and geographic location (Prokůpek et al., 2023).

In this way, leveraging intellectual property rights serves as an alternative or complement to cultural subsidies and grant support. Cultural economics research has highlighted "the revenue-earning potential of intellectual property rights" (Throsby, 2008, p. 148) and recognized the rationale for the coexistence and complementary roles of public subsidies and copyright-based revenue models (Towse, 2006). Traditionally, public subsidies have been directed toward "high art," often tied to expectations and evaluations of artistic quality. In contrast, copyright, particularly the economic rights associated with artworks, relates to revenue generation through market sales, driven by consumer demand rather than artistic merit (ibid.). These co-branded products typically draw on Old Master paintings that are in the public domain, which in principle allows their images to be used freely for commercial purposes. While museums hold the physical property rights to these works, they do not necessarily possess the intellectual property rights, including the rights to commercial reproduction (for a more detailed discussion, see Marciano & Moureau, 2016). For similar reasons, copyright infringement typically does not result from the use of public-domain works themselves, but rather from misleading claims of official partnerships or unauthorized licensing associated with the museum (ibid.).

From an art management and marketing perspective, museums' use of intellectual property rights and brand strategies reflects a broader trend toward business-oriented museum management, in which tools and approaches traditionally associated with the commercial sector are increasingly adopted by museums (Ferreiro-Rosende et al., 2023; Prokůpek & Gombault, 2024). IP licensing strategies also align with museums' missions to make their collections more accessible and to fulfill their educational role by reaching the widest possible audience, including both visitors and non-visitors (Total Licensing, 2021; Van Gogh Museum, 2020, p. 20). The high proportion of international visitors—for example, at the Van Gogh Museum, where 85% of visitors in 2019 came from abroad (Bailey, 2020)—highlights the potential for international market exploration. Museums' IP licensing strategy is distinct from related concepts explored in existing studies. Unlike the direct commodification of artworks, as discussed by O'Connor (2007), the creative products involved are not art commodities per se but rather reproductions or newly designed adaptations of original artworks, often incorporating functional elements. Nor are they artist-commissioned works, as the transformation of artworks into creative products does not arise from a direct exchange between artists and the public. Instead, it involves multiple intermediaries, including IP holders, agents, brands, and market feedback, that collectively shape the final product.

2.2 Museum Cultural and Creative Products

The co-branded products resulting from such museum IP licensing programs and brand partnerships (Prokůpek et al., 2023) are commonly referred to in the Chinese context as museum "Cultural and Creative Products," a term translated from *Wenchuang products* (文创产品). Studies on those co-branded products remain limited in much of Western scholarship. The concept of *wenchuang* products in China, especially those resulted from collaborative partnerships with museums, offers a novel perspective that addresses a gap in the Anglophone literature. Developed organically within China, the concept of *wenchuang* products is rooted in the local discourse of Cultural and Creative Industries (CCIs; 文创产业, *wenchuang industry*) and has been widely adopted across the museum sector, cultural policy, and academic research in China (Tu et al., 2019; Zhang & Li, 2024; Zhao et al., 2023).

Wenchuang products are related to, yet distinct from, the concept of "cultural goods." According to the UNESCO Institute for Statistics (2009, pp. 22–23), cultural goods are defined as "consumer goods conveying ideas, symbols and ways of life." *Wenchuang* products similarly function as such goods. However, a distinctive feature of *wenchuang* products lies in their creative inspiration drawn from existing artworks or other forms of creative intellectual property. In this sense, they are more conceptually aligned with art derivatives that involve the reinterpretation and redesign of museum collections, particularly antiques and works of art. This process exemplifies how the "spillover" effect (Throsby, 2008) from core creative industries, namely visual arts and museums, extends into other sectors and the consumer market.

Second, *wenchuang* products are characterized by both their aesthetic value for appreciation and their functional value as everyday consumer goods. In contrast, the consumption of typical cultural goods primarily involves symbolic value, satisfies non-material needs, relies heavily on subjective interpretation and appreciation, and follows a distinctive system of valorization (Chang et al., 2021; UNESCO Institute for Statistics, 2016). *Wenchuang* products are positioned along a spectrum between utility and aesthetic appeal and are designed to combine visual or symbolic richness with practical functionality and occupy a distinct space that bridges the creative industries and consumer markets. More specifically, they fall between what Yin and Phillips (2020) describe as "niche cultural products," such as high art in museums, and "mass traditional products," meaning ordinary consumer goods. Therefore, the traditional definition of cultural goods is insufficient to capture the specific characteristics of *wenchuang* products.

Museum *wenchuang* products may or may not involve IP licensing and partnerships, although they are often developed through such collaborations. In 2019, 72% of museum *wenchuang* products sold on Tmall involved IP partnerships, while only 28% were proprietary products developed by the museums themselves (The Institute of Cultural Economy of Tsinghua University & Tmall, 2019). In either case, museum *wenchuang* products differ from traditional museum souvenirs or merchandise in at least three key aspects.

First, *wenchuang* products place strong emphasis on cultural inheritance and legacy, highlighting the symbolic and cultural meanings embedded in heritage and the authenticity endorsed by museum brands (Li et al., 2022). Design plays a central role in symbolizing and reinterpreting cultural elements drawn from museum collections (Tu et al., 2019).This contrasts with mass-produced reproductions of artworks and objects, such as postcards or T-shirts with printed images, which typically do not qualify for copyright protection on their own, due to minimal creative input. Museum *wenchuang* products typically possess distinct aesthetic and symbolic value and often incorporate new creative elements that extend beyond simple replication. As a result, these products may be eligible for copyright or design protection.

Second, *wenchuang* products are market-oriented, as reflected in both their design and business models. They are developed with reference to consumer purchase intentions (Li & Li, 2022) and are contextualized and localized to meet specific market demands, preferences, and cultural understandings. Finally, internationally licensed creative products are not necessarily distributed through the physical or onsite museum shops of international museums alongside traditional merchandise. Instead, their market presence is primarily global and digital, with transactions taking place through e-commerce platforms or museum-affiliated shops within China. This approach enables engagement with Chinese consumers who may never have visited the licensing museums in person.

Overall, museum *wenchuang* products follow a distinctive business model that reinterprets cultural and symbolic elements from collections into market-driven products. They strategically leverage cultural resources to balance authenticity with commercial viability, while also supporting exhibitions, educational programs, and broader cultural initiatives. This concept demonstrates that non-Western societies possess their own distinctive dynamics and mechanisms for engaging with, shaping, and co-evolving alongside Western-originated initiatives. Rather than serving merely as special-case studies or passive recipients of external frameworks, these contexts can act as "locations where universal theories could be generated" (Tang, 2023, p. 425).

3 Methodology

This study explores how international museums reach out to Chinese audiences and markets through IP licensing partnerships and *wenchuang* products. A dataset was compiled to include international museums identified through systematic search as having publicly declared engagement in such activities in China from the launch of the first case in 2018 through the end of 2020.

The list of museums was compiled through an online search of relevant activities. To identify a broad range of cases, three key touchpoints for the communication and consumption of IP-licensed museum products in China were considered: a social media platform (Sina Weibo), search engines (Google and Baidu), and e-commerce platforms (primarily Tmall and Taobao, Alibaba's B2C and C2C e-commerce platforms). Chinese-language keywords referring to museum-related *wenchuang* products (e.g., *bowuguan wenchuang* [博物馆文创], *bowuguan lianming chanpin* [博物馆联名产品]) were used to search local platforms, to maximise the coverage of relevant cases. The results were concurrently triangulated with English-language keyword searches on Google to cross-check the accuracy of the cases and ensure that they were officially authorized by the museums.

After this, a second-level screening was conducted to ensure the relevance and validity of the identified cases. The following were excluded: (i) products designed using public domain artworks collected by museums, but without any formal IP or brand partnership with the museums; (ii) deceptive collaborations, in which consumer brands claimed partnerships without official endorsement or recognition from the museums; (iii) purely cultural initiatives, where museums used social media solely to communicate with Chinese audiences for cultural or promotional purposes, without any associated commercial or IP licensing activity; and (iv) museum co-branded products developed with international consumer brands but distributed in the Chinese market without a dedicated local partnership (e.g., Louvre x Uniqlo or Casetify), as this study specifically focuses on partnerships with Chinese local brands that reflect localization strategies. In the end, 11 museums were included in the dataset (Table 1), providing a focused and contextually grounded view of this emerging practice.

Based on the compiled list, a dataset of international museums' IP licensing partnerships and activities in China was developed using multiple sources of publicly available secondary data. These sources included official museum websites and annual reports, news releases, product listings on e-commerce platforms, and industry reports. Publicly available materials and statements from museums, IP agents, e-commerce platforms, and

Table 1 List of international museums with IP licensing programs in China (2018–2020)

Country	*Museums*
France (4)	Musée du Louvre *(Louvre)*
	Centre Pompidou
	Musée d'Orsay
	Musée Picasso Paris
United Kingdom (3)	The British Museum
	The National Gallery, London *(National Gallery)*
	Victoria and Albert Museum *(V&A)*
United States (2)	The Metropolitan Museum of Art *(the Met)*
	Museum of Fine Art, Boston *(MFA)*
The Netherlands (1)	Van Gogh Museum, Amsterdam *(VGM)*
Russia (1)	The State Hermitage Museum *(Hermitage)*

Source Author

commercial brand partners were included to facilitate analysis across multiple stakeholder perspectives. The collected data were systematically organized into a dataset under the following categories: museum name, year of establishment, location, collection size, financial structure, governance and organizational model, local agency or representative in China, product licensing cases, other licensing activities, communication and marketing channels, and additional notes. The dataset was then analyzed to identify patterns, shared characteristics, and distinctive features across cases. An analytical synthesis was conducted to examine the licensing and royalty agreements between the parties, as well as the stages of design, production, distribution, marketing, and transaction. Based on this analysis, a conceptual value chain of the IP licensing programs was constructed.

4 Empirical Analysis and Findings

4.1 The Superstar Museum Advantage in International IP Licensing

Based on the dataset, all the museums included in this study qualify as "superstar museums" from a cultural economics perspective, following Frey's (1998) definition. First, these institutions attract large numbers of visitors (both domestic and international) and enjoy significant followings on social media. They are often regarded as "must-visit" destinations for tourists (ibid.). The extensive audience base, along with the economies of scale typical of superstar museums (i.e., high fixed costs and low marginal costs), creates strong potential for generating income through large-scale international commercial activities.

Secondly, all the museums feature some of the world's most renowned artists and artworks. This includes institutions with the largest collections globally (such as the British Museum, the Hermitage, the Met, and the Louvre) as well as those with top-tier niche collections. For instance, Musée Picasso Paris and Van Gogh Museum are both dedicated to individual artists celebrated in art history, while the V&A specializes in a specific domain as the world's largest museum of decorative arts and design. Thirdly, these museums actively engage in, and in some cases lead, commercial initiatives that contribute to the local economy. For example, the British Museum began selling postcards as early as 1911 and opened the world's first museum shop in 1912 and it also acted as the "first mover" in the Chinese market in 2018 (People's Daily Online, 2018). The size and quality of the museums' collection, along with the number of visitors they attract, contribute significantly to their brand value. Compared with smaller institutions, these museums are better positioned to leverage their visitor base, the scale and quality of their collections, economies of scale, and strong brand recognition to expand into international commercial markets.

While market-oriented management is often associated with private museums (Buber & Knassmüller, 2009), all museums discussed here are public institutions that receive at least partial public funding while maintaining a degree of administrative independence and financial autonomy. This reflects a broader trend where lower levels of public funding and larger institutional size tend to correlate with a stronger motivation to innovate in commercial activities (Camarero et al., 2011). The International Council of Museums (2021) also notes that larger museums are often better positioned to experiment with new income-generating strategies. A case in point is the V&A museum, whose self-generated income exceeded 50% of its total revenue in the 2019–20 fiscal year (V&A, 2020). This analysis highlights the complementary relationship between copyright strategies and public funding, demonstrating that the two are not mutually exclusive but can coexist at both policy and operational levels (Towse, 2019). By stepping into the international scenario, these superstar museums embrace a new competitive landscape (Frey & Meier, 2006). Instead of a "monopolistic" environment (Marciano & Moureau, 2016), this market is highly competitive, with museums sharing space with local consumer brands, other *wenchuang* products based on public domain artworks, and other superstar museums in the market. The competition can be particularly direct among museums that hold works by the same artists, leading to overlapping markets. For example, as observed in the dataset, Van Gogh and Monet are among the most frequently licensed IPs, due to their art historical significance, strong market appeal, and the presence of their works across multiple museums in this study.[1]

[1] For example, both the Van Gogh Museum in Amsterdam and the National Gallery in London have released products featuring Van Gogh's *Sunflowers.* Monet's *Water Lilies* appears in the MFA x Pegavision (soft contact lenses) collaboration as well as in the National Gallery x KFC China campaign. Another example is Katsushika Hokusai's 1831 woodblock print *Under the Wave off Kanagawa*, where minor differences across versions (due to the nature of woodblock printing) make commercial reproductions by the British Museum and the MET nearly indistinguishable, except for branding and design choices.

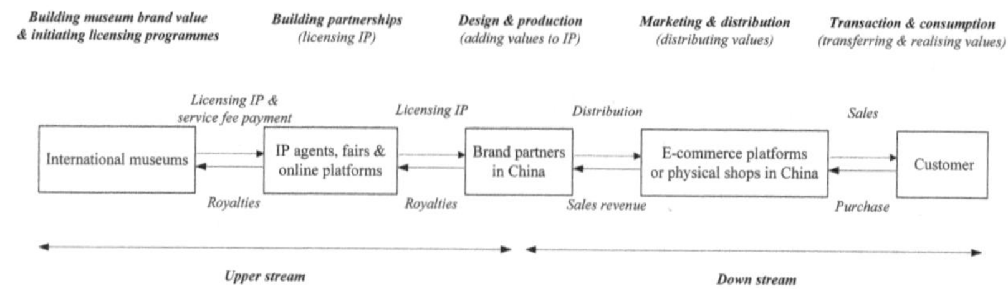

Fig. 1 The international value chain of museum IP licensing activities. *Source* Author

4.2 An International, Long-tail Value Chain

International museums' IP licensing programs in China typically follow an international value chain, illustrating how "high-end" museum collections are transformed into creative products for lower-end market consumption.

Figure 1 presents a fundamental model of this value chain, that begins with museums transforming the cultural value of their collections into IP assets, including museum brands and symbolized art-related IPs. The upstream of the value chain involves partnerships between museums (as licensors) and brand partners (as licensees), typically facilitated by IP agents. The downstream phase, primarily based in China, encompasses product development, distribution, sales transactions, and consumer engagement. Ultimately, the value generated from these activities flows back to the museums, supporting both their cultural missions and long-term financial sustainability. It should be noted that this process is not fully standardized and exhibits variations across the cases.

4.3 The Upstream: The "Museum-Agent-Brand" Partnership

Museums typically play a central role in initiating licensing programs, with some providing official guidelines and support for partners (British Museum, 2025). They leverage their collections as primary sources of cultural value, extending this value through museum branding and symbolized intellectual property. For instance, the British Museum's canonized Gayer-Anderson Cat was reinterpreted as a design element on smart heated scarves produced by Midea, a leading Chinese electrical appliance brand. Through such collaborations, museums mediate the meanings of original artworks, reinterpreting classical, Old Master, or heritage pieces for contemporary consumption. This process is inherently market-oriented and shaped by consumer preferences and market demand. Artwork selection for reproduction is primarily driven by market considerations, with a strong emphasis on the fame and appeal of the IP among Chinese audiences. This corresponds to the art economics analysis that consumers typically do not choose lesser-known works over well-known ones, even when the former are offered at lower prices (Rosen, 1981). Other factors influencing IP selection include the suitability and adaptability of the artwork for the Chinese market—taking into account historical, aesthetic, cognitive, and commercial dimensions—as well as the potential for brand alignment between the museum IP and the consumer brand's identity.

All 11 museums worked with IP agents to carry out licensing activities in China, acting on the museums' behalf when engaging with local brands. Instead of pursuing direct licensing, museums work with IP agents as key intermediaries that bridge international museums and the local market. These agents connect with local brand resources and provide support throughout the licensing process. A notable pattern is the emergence of a clustering effect, whereby certain agents represent multiple museums and form interconnected networks. For instance, Alfilo Brands represents all the UK- and US- based museums listed in this study, while Bomeng Art serves as the China representative for the *Réunion des musées nationaux—Grand Palais* (RMN-GP; renamed GrandPalaisRmn in 2024), covering all the listed French museums, with the exception of a campaign launched by Alibaba specifically for the Louvre in 2020. More broadly, the selection process between museums and IP agents reflects a mutual alignment of strategic interests. International museums generally prioritize agents with strong local brand networks, market expertise, and cultural mediation capabilities. From the other end, IP agents assess museums based on their market potential, often favoring those with popular or niche artworks and well-established brand identities that offer strong commercial appeal.

The collaboration between museums and IP agents typically follows a royalty-based model, which includes a guaranteed royalty (a fixed fee) plus a percentage of sales, generally ranging from 6% to 12%. Alternatively, some partnerships adopt a buyout model, in which the agent pays a one-time fee and independently manages licensing activities on behalf of the museum. This arrangement transfers the commercial risk and uncertainty of predicting market success from the museums to the licensing agents. In addition to IP agents, museum representatives also regularly participate in major licensing fairs in China, such as the Licensing Expo China (LEC) and the China

Licensing Expo (CLE). Furthermore, online platforms like Alibaba's Alifish facilitate licensing collaborations between museums and both local and international brands, further broadening their market opportunities.

Brand partners, as licensees, are also referred to as "corporate partners" (Prokůpek et al., 2023), or "licensing partners" (The Met Store, 2025; Van Gogh Museum, 2025). In this study, the term "brand partners" is used to distinguish them from image licensing agreements. Brand partners often play a crucial role in expanding market reach and managing localized production, leveraging their own marketing channels and distribution networks in coordination with the museum's promotional efforts. Licensing partnerships with museums allow brand partners to capitalize on the aesthetic and symbolic value of artworks and museum brands, which can serve as a "sign of quality" even in non-elitist sectors (Pusa & Uusitalo, 2014, p. 18). For example, Satine Milk, a premium Chinese dairy brand, had faced challenges in communicating its high-end positioning to local consumers. By partnering with the Louvre, Satine leveraged the museum's artistic prestige to elevate the perceived exclusivity of its brand. The collaboration featured bottle caps sculpted with motifs inspired by Louvre artifacts and was accompanied by an extensive social media campaign using the tagline "Every Drop is a Work of Art," reinforcing the association with fine art and luxury. Nevertheless, although local brand partners may enhance their brand positioning and potentially benefit from increased market sales and price premiums through collaborations with museums, they also undertake the risks associated with product development and market performance, in addition to paying royalty fees to the licensors. Despite the advantage of leveraging a museum's brand equity, economic returns are not always guaranteed for brand partners.

For museums, local brand partners can offer benefits beyond financial royalties. Their market presence and established distribution channels can help museums reach broader consumer segments, particularly in regions where direct engagement is limited. As museum IP licensing strategies grow in popularity, museums also face increasing challenges from counterfeit products and self-proclaimed partnerships. These unofficial products, which lack museum approval or endorsement, can potentially harm the museum's image. Some critics also argue that such practices risk over-commercializing the museum's brand identity. However, in the Chinese market, *wenchuang* products are commonly viewed by the public and the museum sector as enhancing the cultural value of commercial goods and contributing to cultural democratization and accessibility. As a result, this approach appears to be generally been welcomed and positively received.

4.4 *The Downstream: From Production to Consumption*

The downstream segment of the value chain begins with design and production, followed by marketing, distribution, and ultimately, the final transaction with consumers. Brand partners typically develop design proposals based on the characteristics of both the product and the museum's IP, while museums provide guidance and final approval. This process often incorporates localization strategies to ensure alignment with market demand and preferences.

Rather than following a standardized model, co-branded products are usually released for a limited period, corresponding to the duration of licensing contracts. Some are launched as special or limited editions and are distributed exclusively within the Chinese market. In this way, they generate a perceived sense of rarity in the consumer market, despite the absence of inherent production constraints and the typically nonexclusive nature of access to purchase. Marketing efforts typically involve multiple stakeholders, including brand partners, e-commerce platforms, and the museums' official social media channels.

Although product categories vary, they primarily include homeware, accessories, stationery, and jewelry. As previously discussed, achieving strong synergy between the museum and brand partner is a central consideration. One notable example of successful collaboration is the partnership between The Beast—a Chinese lifestyle brand (its name referencing Fauvism in Chinese)—and the State Hermitage Museum. Together, they developed a series of Henri Matisse-inspired products in the Fauvist style. The collection included elegantly designed items such as mugs, coffee pots, ashtrays/jewelry trays, silk scarves, and loungewear, blending artistic heritage with contemporary lifestyle aesthetics.

IP licensing and brand partnerships extend beyond consumer products into the food and beverage as well as gaming sectors. One example is Ramen Talk, a Chinese instant noodle brand that collaborated with the National Gallery, London to introduce a series of "food inspired by art." This partnership resulted in a special edition of ramen featuring basil pesto and lotus nuts, as ingredients selected to reflect the colors and objects in Monet's *Water Lilies.* The National Gallery also partnered with KFC China to launch an exclusive, China-only collection of Impressionist-themed ice cream packaging, integrating artworks into everyday consumer experiences.

In the gaming and animation industry, The Met collaborated with Tencent Games to incorporate its artworks and architecture into *Game for Peace*. The partnership included a detailed digital reconstruction of The Met's building and a specially designed gameplay mode, offering players an immersive way to explore its collections. Launched during the COVID-19 pandemic in 2020, the initiative made the museum's artworks accessible to Chinese audiences through digital experiences.

Museum-branded IP products are commonly distributed both in the consumer market and as a distinct category within museum shop offerings. Distribution primarily takes place through the flagship stores of museums and brand partners on Tmall. Tmall also hosts special promotional events, reflecting its ambition to engage more deeply with the cultural sector. Beyond e-commerce, museum-branded products are also available in the physical retail locations of brand partners and in select local museums.

Finally, their sale represents a transfer and exchange of value with consumers, with revenue flowing through shops, brands, and agents before ultimately returning to the museums. Approximately half of these products are priced below 100 Chinese Yuan (around €13 at the 2019 exchange rate), and 85% fall within the 500 Yuan range (around €65) (The Institute of Cultural Economy of Tsinghua University & Tmall, 2019), making them accessible to a broad consumer base beyond the high-value segment of frequent overseas museum visitors. Typical buyers of museum *wenchuang* products in China are female (79.2%) consumers from first- and second-tier cities (66%), and functionality remains the primary driver of consumer purchases, followed by cultural value, design, price, and innovation. (ibid.). Finally, the entire value chain is also supported by a group of auxiliary actors, including international payment providers, big data platforms, and is shaped by copyright laws, regulations, and local cultural policies.

5 Conclusion

This chapter has explored how international museums leverage IP licensing in China, highlighting a global, long-tail value chain and a new form of art-business partnership involving multiple stakeholders. Market-driven and culturally informed, this model enables superstar museums to strategically harness their collections, diversify revenue streams, and engage with audiences in an international consumer market. It not only incorporates localization strategies within China but has also further inspired local

Chinese museums to pursue collaborative development of Cultural and Creative Products, or *wenchuang* products. This trend parallels broader local and international IP collaborations across multiple creative industries, including film, gaming, and online literature. This study contributes to discussions on contemporary museum merchandising and introduces an emerging case within the economics of museums and copyright. It demonstrates how cultural value can be transformed into economic value through IP strategies, generating revenue that, in turn, supports museums' cultural missions and public engagement initiatives.

As international museums enter an increasingly competitive landscape, where they share the market with IP collaborations from other museums and creative sectors, questions arise as to how they can sustain their appeal among local consumers. While all the international institutions involved are superstar museums, the extent to which small and medium-sized museums can adopt this market strategy remains largely unexplored. Furthermore, as more original local cultural IP emerges and domestic consumer brands gain a broader range of collaboration options, the long-term sustainability of this business model becomes increasingly uncertain.

It is therefore worth examining how museums continue to adapt their IP strategies in response to evolving market dynamics while upholding their cultural missions. There is also significant potential for deeper and more diversified collaborations, particularly with local cultural institutions. Examples such as the exhibition partnership between the Centre Pompidou and the West Bund Museum in Shanghai, or the V&A's collaboration with Design Society in Shenzhen to establish its first permanent overseas gallery, highlight promising avenues for co-developing new cultural and creative frameworks.

References

Bailey, M. (2020). Van Gogh Museum to reopen on 1 June, but with only a tenth of its usual visitors. *The Art Newspaper*. https://www.theartnewspaper.com/2020/05/15/van-gogh-museum-to-reopen-on-1-june-but-with-only-a-tenth-of-its-usual-visitors

Baumgarth, C. (2009). Brand orientation of museums: Model and empirical results. *International Journal of Arts Management, 11*(3), 30–45.

British Museum. (2025). *British Museum product licensing*. The British Museum. https://www.britishmuseum.org/commercial/licensing

Buber, R., & Knassmüller, M. (2009). Approaching museum shop marketing from a strategic perspective. *Conference Proceedings of ANZMAC 2009*.

Camarero, C., Garrido, M. J., & Vicente, E. (2011). How cultural organizations' size and funding influence innovation and performance: The case of museums. *Journal of Cultural Economics, 35*(4), 247–266.

Chang, -Y.-Y., Potts, J., & Shih, H.-Y. (2021). The market for meaning: A new entrepreneurial approach to creative industries dynamics. *Journal of Cultural Economics, 45*(3), 491–511.

Coblence, E., & Sabatier, V. (2014). Articulating growth and cultural innovation in art museums: The Louvre's business model revision. *International Studies of Management & Organization, 44*(4), 9–25.

Feng, Q., & Lin, D. (2018). 博物馆 IP 授权与文化衍生品的开发 [Research on the innovative development of the IP derivative cultural products of museum]. *Journal of Archaeology and Museology, 1*, 69–74.

Ferreiro-Rosende, É., Fuentes-Moraleda, L., & Morere-Molinero, N. (2023). Artists brands and museums: Understanding brand identity. *Museum Management and Curatorship, 38*(2), 157–174.

Finance Act 2001, C. 9, s. 98. (2001). https://www.legislation.gov.uk/ukpga/2001/9/section/98

Frey, B. S. (1998). Superstar museums: An economic analysis. *Journal of Cultural Economics, 22*(2), 113–125.

Frey, B. S., & Meier, S. (2006). Chapter 29 The economics of museums. In *Handbook of the economics of art and culture* (Vol. 1, pp. 1017–1047). Elsevier.

ICOM. (2021). *Museums, museum professionals and Covid-19: Third survey*. International Council of Museums. https://icom.museum/wp-content/uploads/2021/07/Museums-and-Covid-19_third-ICOM-report.pdf

Kent, T. (2010). The role of the museum shop in extending the visitor experience. *International Journal of Nonprofit and Voluntary Sector Marketing, 15*(1), 67–77.

Komarac, T., Ozretic-Dosen, D., & Skare, V. (2019). The role of the museum shop: Eliciting the opinions of museum professionals. *International Journal of Arts Management, 21*(3), 28–41.

Lewandowska, K. (2015). From sponsorship to partnership in arts and business relations. *The Journal of Arts Management, Law, and Society, 45*(1), 33–50.

Li, H., Wang, X., & Li, W. (2022). 基于文化元素的故宫博物院文创产品设计研究 [Cultural and creative product design of the Palace Museum based on cultural elements]. *Packaging Engineering, 43*(2), 325–332.

Li, Y., & Li, J. (2022). The influence of design aesthetics on consumers' purchase intention toward cultural and creative products: Evidence from the palace museum in China. *Frontiers in Psychology, 13*, 1–9.

Marciano, A., & Moureau, N. (2016). Museums, property rights, and photographs of works of art. Why reproduction through photograph should be free. *Review of Economic Research on Copyright Issues, 13*, 1–28.

McIntyre, C. (2010). Designing museum and gallery shops as integral, co-creative retail spaces within the overall visitor experience. *Museum Management and Curatorship, 25*(2), 181–198.

Mottner, S., & Ford, J. B. (2005). Measuring nonprofit marketing strategy performance: The case of museum stores. *Journal of Business Research, 58*(6), 829–840.

O'Connor, J. (2007). *The cultural and creative industries: A review of the literature*. Arts Council England.

People's Daily Online. (2018). 大英博物馆借力天猫扩大授权合作范围与周边创新 [The British Museum leverages Tmall to expand the scope of licensing partnerships and Merchandise Innovation]. *People's Daily Online*. http://world.people.com.cn/n1/2018/1213/c1002-30465822.html

Prokůpek, M., & Gombault, A. (2024). Museums and corporate partners: The case of Van Gogh Museum and Shell. *International Journal of Arts Management, 27*(1), 78–87.

Prokůpek, M., Loots, E., & Betzler, D. (2023). Emergency or emerging financing strategies of art museums in the context of a pandemic? *Museum Management and Curatorship, 38*(5), 530–547.

Pusa, S., & Uusitalo, L. (2014). Creating brand identity in art museums: A case study. *International Journal of Arts Management, 17*(1), 18–30.

Rosen, S. (1981). The economics of superstars. *The American Economic Review, 71*(5), 845–858.

Tang, L. (2023). Burning out in emotional capitalism: Appropriation of ganqing and renqing in the Chinese platform economy. *Journal of Sociology, 59*(2).

The Institute of Cultural Economy of Tsinghua University, & Tmall. (2019). *新文创消费趋势报告* [New cultural creative products consuming trend report].

The Met Store. (2025). *Licensing partners*. The Met Store. https://store.metmuseum.org/

Throsby, D. (2008). The concentric circles model of the cultural industries. *Cultural Trends, 17*(3), 147–164.

Total Licensing. (2021, June 2). Interview: The Van Gogh Museum. *Total Licensing*. https://www.totallicensing.com/interview-the-van-gogh-museum-2/

Towse, R. (2006). Copyright and artists: A view from cultural economics. *Journal of Economic Surveys, 20*(4), 567–585.

Towse, R. (2019). *A textbook of cultural economics*. Cambridge University Press.

Tu, J.-C., Liu, L.-X., & Cui, Y. (2019). A study on consumers' preferences for the Palace Museum's cultural and creative products from the perspective of cultural sustainability. *Sustainability, 11*(13).

UNESCO Institute for Statistics (Ed.). (2009). *The 2009 UNESCO framework for cultural statistics.*

UNESCO Institute for Statistics. (2016). *The globalisation of cultural trade: A shift in consumption. International flows of cultural goods and services 2004–2013.* UNESCO Institute for Statistics.

UNESCO, & UNDP. (2013). *Creative economy report, 2013, special edition: Widening local development pathways.* https://unesdoc.unesco.org/ark:/48223/pf0000224698

V&A. (2020). *Victoria and Albert Museum annual report and accounts 2019–2020.*

Van Gogh Museum. (2020). *Van Gogh Museum strategic plan 2021–2024.*

Van Gogh Museum. (2025). *Van Gogh Museum brand licensing.* Van Gogh Museum. https://www.vangoghmuseum.nl/en/about/collaborate/van-gogh-museum-brand-licenses

Xinhua Finance. (2018). 天猫与大英博物馆在伦敦达成深化合作共识 [Tmall and the British Museum reach consensus to deepen cooperation in London]. *中国金融信息网*. http://world.xinhua08.com/a/20181213/1789187.shtml

Yin, E., & Phillips, N. (2020). Understanding value creation in cultural industries: Strategies for creating and managing meaning. *Journal of Humanities and Applied Social Sciences, 2*(3), 165–180.

Zhang, J., & Li, Y. (2024). Copyright protection: A key element in realizing the development potential of digital cultural and creative products in museums. *Museum Management and Curatorship, 39*(4), 497–517.

Zhao, Y., Zeng, J., Zhang, Y., & Yu, J. (2023). Research on the design strategy and application of cultural IP in museums:The example of Henan Provincial Museum. *Highlights in Art and Design, 2*(2), 89–93.

PART IV

Porosity Across Market Segments

Stratification and Price in Art Auctions: How the Presence of Unconsecrated and Lowly Consecrated Painters Impacts the Australian Art Auction Market

Douglas J. Hodgson, Cameron M. Weber, and Bronwyn Coate

1 Introduction

The market for fine art is heterogeneous and stratified (Di Maggio, 1987), with works of varying aesthetic quality by artists of different repute traded such that only a fraction of works by esteemed artists represents the lion's share of sales value in the upper segment of various art markets, including the Australian one (Worthington & Higgs, 2003). Within the secondary market the level of consecration achieved by painters, living or dead, is a key factor associated with auction prices (Cowen, 2000; Beckert & Rössel, 2013; Angelini & Castellani, 2019). While much attention within the literature has traditionally focused upon the high end of the market,

D. J. Hodgson (✉)
UQAM-Université du Québec à Montréal, Montreal, Canada
e-mail: hodgson.douglas@uqam.ca

C. M. Weber
Independent researcher, Brooklyn, USA
e-mail: cameron_weber@hotmail.com

B. Coate
RMIT University, Melbourne, Australia
e-mail: bronwyn.coate@rmit.edu.au

A.-S. V. Radermecker (ed.), *Low-End Markets for Art and Cultural Goods*, Cultural Economics & the Creative Economy,
https://doi.org/10.1007/978-3-032-27566-0_11

we consider the middle and lower range of the auction market for Australian paintings. We concentrate on the role of critical or art historical consecration at the individual artist level as a key determinant not only of price but also of the likelihood that an artist survives in the auction market.

In this chapter we focus on the role of consecration in determining outcomes observed at art auctions. Consecration results from judgments as to art historical status. As Accominotti (2021, p. 9) states: "It enhances the perceived worth of the consecrated, not by confirming that they are individually worthy, but by asserting the existence in a field of a reliable hierarchy of worthiness." As such, consecration is achieved by first being recognized by gatekeepers and tastemakers in the art field, which then serves to transmit a quality signal to the rest of the market and the broader public. Bourdieu (1993b) describes consecration as being determined over time through the judgments made by the various agents in the art field, including artists, critics, dealers, curators, collectors, etc. These various judgments establish a status hierarchy that may be inherently continuous (see Hutter in this volume), but that is often represented through discrete classifications of artists into status categories (a point also made by Accominotti (2021)), which will be the approach we adopt. As outlined in the introduction to this volume, we seek to classify art works by a criterion other than price. We use a somewhat rough criterion of "consecration", defined below, which we see as representing a first approach to what could potentially be a more refined and continuous index in future work.

This study extends recent research (Hodgson et al., 2025) that investigates the presence of Cantillon effects in the Canadian and Australian art markets, focusing on price stratification by consecration status, as monetary policy insiders, such as broker-dealers and banks, bid up prices for highly consecrated art works during periods of expansionary monetary policy.[1] In this chapter, we focus on the segments of the market that are neglected by top collectors. We document the degree of importance (or lack thereof) that the low end (which is comprised of works by unknown artists) holds relative to the highly consecrated segment, and consider possible consequences for prices, sales value, and artist survival, of the failure to achieve top consecration (and collectability) status.

[1] See Weber (2011) for a study of the London art market.

Drawing on research in sociology and economics, we develop conjectures to guide our analysis of a large sample of sales by non-Indigenous Australian artists to examine how artists' consecration impacts prices and returns in this market.[2] Using data on a set of nearly 1,000 artists that yields over 100,000 art auction records observed over a fifty-year period from the early 1970s until recently, we investigate the relative decline after 1990 of both prices and total sales value for lesser consecrated artists, as compared to highly consecrated ones. We also report evidence in the data regarding the relation between consecration and market survival. Our research questions can then be separated into two categories:

(i) Does an artist's consecration status impact prices and total sales value realized at auction for the artist over time?
(ii) Does an artist's consecration status impact the likelihood of the artist's works continuing to be demanded at auction over time?

Hodgson et al. (2025) find that prices for highly consecrated artists in the Canadian and Australian auction markets grow more rapidly after 1990 than for less consecrated ones. Extending on this, the present chapter provides informal statistical evidence suggesting that works by lower consecrated artists are more likely to experience price depreciation to the point that they effectively disappear from the market. To facilitate our analysis, we decompose the Australian market into three segments based on high-, middle-, and low-consecration criteria, informed by art historical sources.

In Sect. 2 we review the literature related to consecration and its possible effects on sales prices and volumes. In Sect. 3 we describe our data set, our partition of the set of artists by consecration category, and the empirical methodology. Section 4 presents and discusses our empirical results, and Sect. 5 concludes.

[2] As the market for Indigenous art has some factors that distinguish it from the market for non-Indigenous art, we focus our analysis here on the market for works by Australian non-Indigenous artists where artists' consecration and reputation is principally bestowed within the national context.

2 Literature Review

For an artist's works to have lasting value on the secondary market, they must attain a high level of consecration. We define consecration as enduring art historical esteem, reflected in an artist's recognition within the established canon of art. While the proportion of professional artists who actually achieve this status is very small, the persistent over-supply of artists suggests that artists either accept these low odds or are overconfident about their talent (Coate & Hoffmann, 2022). With the majority of artists never achieving high consecration, we hypothesize that this will be a key factor explaining why prices for certain artists fall in real (or even nominal) terms over time such that they are no longer traded in the market. This is consistent with Grampp (1989), who describes paintings becoming "worthless" and eventually disappearing from the market as they become almost valueless "rubbish" (Thompson, 1979; Grampp, 1989; Boltanski & Esquerre, 2020).

In this chapter, we focus on the declining presence of artists from auction house salesrooms. Although it may not necessarily be the case that the departure of an artist from the auction market means they have lost all importance or value, we are assuming that a consistent decline in number of sales, accompanied by a decline in price, indicates a decrease in demand among collectors for the artist's work. In particular, if there are many artists for which this is happening, we are assuming that this indicates a general lack of demand for the artists in this group, even if there may be exceptions. There do exist other sales venues (even for what Thompson (1979) calls "rubbish"); these artists' works may be sought out for decorative purposes, due to subject matter, local interest, etc., but there is an assumption that, in general, such artists are losing interest for collectors and that their consecration value (or chances of obtaining it) is diminishing. For example, the auction house the artist appears in may be reduced from the delta to the gamma level or below (second-hand stores and flea markets) signalling a decline in authenticity and prestige as proxied by brand equity (see the Introduction to this volume on the triadic model of value).

At the high end, Rosen (1981) focuses on superstars—a small number of creative producers who dominate the field through their high prices. In addition to studies of the processes by which artists become consecrated superstars (Accominotti, 2021; Bourdieu 1993a, 1996), there is a literature studying the links between consecration and membership in various art movements, styles and historical periods (Hodgson & Hellmanzik, 2019; Hodgson, 2022). The literature on variation of the art historical canon over time finds in general that it does not change much, so that artists who achieve canonical (or highly consecrated) status tend to maintain it, for centuries even.[3] Although changes in taste may affect the status ordering of members of the "pantheon," almost no one loses membership once admitted: "those who are out can get in, but those in cannot get out" (Accominotti, 2021, p. 18). This suggests that highly consecrated artists will not disappear from the market due to lack of demand (although they may due to scarcity as their works land in museums or major corporate collections).

The fate of artists who do not achieve consecration can be hard to analyze, as many artists in the primary, or even secondary, market, wind up failing to achieve major recognition, and tend to disappear from art history, making it difficult to retrospectively track the process of disappearance. Our data set includes such a large number of artists and covers a sufficiently long time period of market activity, that we can track the evolution of the "losers" and observe the process by which artists who fail to achieve consecration disappear from the market as their demand progressively declines.

Notwithstanding the fierce competition, low income and precarity that characterize the visual arts (Throsby & Zednik, 2011), during their lifetime many professional artists may achieve some success in gallery representation and regular sales. Yet, over time, many fail to gain art historical consecration. Additionally, some living artists may see their prices rapidly appreciate only to reach a peak akin to a temporary speculative bubble (Schneider, 2022). Failure of an artist to achieve consecration or even modest renown is more common during their lifetime, often resulting in momentum loss in their market success. This may be observable in the form of downward trends in real prices and sales volumes at auction. Ultimately, as previously described (Grampp, 1989), the market for works by such artists will be completely exhausted as prices fall such that they are not sufficient to cover transaction and time costs and hence cease being traded. Buyers and sellers sensing such declines may turn their attention to the next generation of contenders for consecration.

[3] See, for example, Ginsburgh et al. (2008), Ginsburgh and Weyers (2006, 2008), Graddy (2013), and Milo (1986).

Hodgson et al. (2025) partition the Canadian and Australian markets into segments based on consecration level, and prices and returns are compared for two market segments. For Australia during 1970–2017, artists who are not highly consecrated experience negligible price movement beyond CPI after 1990, suggesting that works by artists not highly consecrated are akin to regular consumption goods, while prices for highly consecrated artists are comparable to financial assets or luxury goods. Hodgson et al. (2025) assign consecration based on textual analysis, categorizing artists as highly consecrated based on inclusion in art history books or display in major art galleries. We extend the analysis with a partition of Australian artists into three categories, as described below. This allows a finer analysis of the effects of consecration on price and returns and a statistical measure of the effect of consecration on market survival. In principle, finer measures of consecration can be imagined, as consecration is an inherently continuous variable. Durkheim (2001, p. 224) observes that things and places are ordered by a consecration hierarchy, with access based on social prestige. In the art market, collectors compete to demarcate their Bourdieusian social status through rivalry to obtain the most highly consecrated works, with an assignment of collectors to market segments based on status and financial means. At the lower end of the market, this competition is—in theory—not present, as no status is connected with the ownership of a work by an unconsecrated artist.

3 Data and Methodology

The data set includes 102,619 observations for secondary auction sales for hundreds of artists of varying historical importance, with which we estimate hedonic time series indexes. The data include only paintings executed in oil or acrylic, on various supports, and any artist for whom at least one painting was sold over the period 1970–2017 is included. We start with 993 artists, being amongst the top 1,000 selling non-Indigenous artists over the period (by sales volume). Our data are sourced from the *Australian Art Sales Digest* (AASD) and due to duplications associated with spelling of the artist's name yields a sample of 993 artists. Of these, 887 have at least one sale.

As mentioned, we partition all artists into three consecration groupings based on presence in selected art history texts. We classify artists as highly consecrated (HC) if they appear in one of three comprehensive surveys of the history of Australian painting (Smith, 1979; Allen, 1997;

Sayers, 2001). To distinguish the remaining artists between medium consecration (MC) and low consecration (LC), we consult the comprehensive and less selective artist encyclopedia of McCulloch (1984), with artists they mention placed in the MC category, and omitted artists considered LC. As shown in the descriptive statistics in Table 1, we have tens of thousands of observations for each category, allowing us to measure the change in price and total sales value (and volume) as a function of consecration status.

As mentioned above, consecration can be thought of as a general (and continuous) consensus on status ranking that a field arrives at through the judgments of many parties. It is unobservable but many observable indices exist, for example art history books or auction prices, which we can think of

Table 1 Summary price statistics by consecration level and decade

Years	*Observations*	*High*	*Low*	*Average*	*Std. Dev.*
Low Consecration					
1971–79	427	18K	50	657	1,254
1980–89	1,488	210K	50	2,084	9,693
1990–99	2,590	340K	45	1,793	8,123
2000–09	3,759	320K	50	2,847	8,607
2010–17	4,581	210K	45	2,689	6,880
Medium Consecration					
1971–79	6,982	51,510	50	906	1,557
1980–89	12,993	700K	50	4,039	12,805
1990–99	17,323	430K	45	4,444	11,546
2000–09	22,195	1.5M	50	8,909	26,208
2010–17	17,981	870K	50	7,794	23,886
High Consecration					
1971–79	1,862	70K	50	3,409	5,001
1980–89	2,295	1.6M	50	22,562	62,728
1990–99	3,799	2.1M	90	31,421	81,136
2000–09	4,702	2.9M	80	73,393	167,268
2010–17	3,434	4.5M	200	95,624	224,681

Source Authors
All prices in Australian dollars
Average and standard deviation rounded to nearest dollar
K = 1,000; *M* = 1 million

as two indicators of the same underlying variable. We use the art historical criterion to define our categories because it provides a clear partition of the sample at the individual-artist level, and represents a separate "observation" on consecration from the one provided by auction prices. The sample could in principle be partitioned in other ways. For example, in an early draft of Hodgson et al. (2025), indexes for this data set were estimated based on the hierarchy of auction houses, with observations partitioned according to high- or low-end salesrooms. The respective estimated hedonic indexes were quite similar to those estimated below, based on a partition of artists. We group observations by artist consecration as it provides a more direct measure of status or quality. Consecration is a property more generally thought of as applying to artists than to works (Bourdieu, 1993b; Accominotti, 2021). In addition, our principal question as to demand decreasing due to consecration status is more appropriately addressed at the level of individual artist than at that of individual work (or auction house).

We estimate the hedonic model in Eq. (1) below three times, once for each grouping of artists into high (HC), medium (MC), and low (LC) consecration. All prices are in nominal terms and are not adjusted for inflation. As we are principally interested in comparison of these indexes with each other, and they would use the same deflator in conversion to real indexes, we do not do the conversion, but in reporting and discussing our results graphically and numerically, we will in several instances provide information on CPI to give an idea of real price changes. The hedonic regression model is written:

$$p_i = \sum_{t=1}^{T} \gamma_t z_{it} + \sum_{j=1}^{J} \alpha_j w_{ij} + u_i, \quad i = 1, \ldots, n, \tag{1}$$

where each observation represents the sale of a painting, p_i is the logarithm of the price of sale i, z_{it} is the value of a period-t dummy variable, equal to 1 if sale i occurred in period t and zero otherwise, with the data being grouped semi-annually. Our estimates of the vector of associated parameters $\{\gamma_t\}$ forms our price index. The regressors $\{w_{ij}\}$ represent the other hedonic characteristics of the painting associated with sale i, including dummies for artist identity and auction house, as wells as artwork dimensions (height, width and surface area). The auction records are taken from a much larger data set that includes works on paper and three-dimensional works, and paintings are often only identified as such, without separate information on medium or support for all works. Work titles are provided, but assignment to genre categories for such a large data set would be a major undertaking. Date of creation is available only for a small number of works. The data set is comprehensive as to auction houses included, with a mix of very high-end houses specializing in consecrated collector-based art (such as Sotheby's, Christies, and Bonhams) and low-end or local ones who offer more highly substitutable works akin to regular consumption goods (Leonard Joel, for example, which includes nearly a third of all observations, and members of the Menzies Art Brands including Deutscher Menzies and Lawson Menzies; see Huda, 2011).

For the estimation of the time period dummies, the data are grouped semi-annually, with all auctions occurring from January 1 to June 30 of a given year grouped together, and likewise for the period July 1 to December 31, and we estimate the index for 1971:1–2017:2, for a time series dimension of $T = 94$. Our parameters of interest in (1) are the price index parameters $\{\gamma_t\}$, with the hundreds of additional parameters being nuisance parameters. The number of these could be reduced to augment efficiency, such as by model-averaging (Galbraith & Hodgson, 2012); we omit the dummy variables for certain categories where a particular member of a category has a small number of observations. In each category, one dummy variable must always be excluded to avoid multicollinearity, so we group together all variables with less than the threshold number of observations in each category into one dummy, which is then omitted. We use 35 observations as the threshold for painters, reducing the number of painter dummies from 886 to 513, and for auction houses, using a threshold of 100 observations, the number is reduced from 46 to 32.

4 Empirical Analysis and Findings

Summary statistics for the three subsamples are reported in Table 1, where for each decade and category we report numbers of observations and descriptive statistics on price. We note that minor works by HC artists can sell for lower prices than the best works by MC and LC artists. We believe this supports our choice to partition by artist rather than individual work, as repeat sales are not readily identifiable in our data set, so that a partition based on other criteria would not allow us to track the relative variation over time of prices for different market segments. The average price is particularly important, not only in that averages correspond strongly with consecration, but also in the implications for the relative increases of financialization and the possible disappearance from the market of artists who fail to achieve consecration. As evidence of this from the 1970s to the 2010s, the percentage (nominal) price increases are 309 for LC, 760 for MC, and 2700 for HC.

We have seen that categorizing observations by auction house yields price indexes that are similar to the ones estimated here. There is no doubt a hierarchy of artists within the offerings of a particular auction house, and an artist who is marginal in one sale might be a "star" in another, depending on the position of the house in the hierarchy of houses. Using a price-based classification criterion, as discussed in the Introduction to this volume, would see lesser works of more consecrated artists being grouped with better works of the less consecrated. We have also seen that status hierarchies can be thought of as continuous, with classifications being arbitrary at the margins, both in terms of houses and individual artists. An interesting question that could be asked with our data is whether there is change over time of artist representation at the house level: do artists whose status is declining tend to "fall" through the hierarchy of auction houses as demand for their works declines? Also, works of certain artists, especially HC ones, can be sold at different points in the auction house hierarchy based on the works' relative importance. For example, the historical consecration level of works by HC artists varies over the life cycle, often peaking for modern artists when they are working in the context of an avant-garde movement associated with their historically most important contributions. Most studies of this phenomenon (for example Galenson, 2000; Galenson & Weinberg, 2000, 2001; Hodgson & Hellmanzik, 2019; Hodgson, 2022) only consider HC artists, there being reason to doubt that such effects would be present in prices of unconsecrated artists.

In Fig. 1, we plot the hedonic log price indices estimated for each segment based on model (1), where each is normalized to equal zero in 1990. If we restrict attention to the period from 1990 to 2017, the results indicate percentage nominal price changes of – 18% for LC, 16% for MC, and 145% for HC. To contextualize these movements, over this period, the Australian Consumer Price Index (CPI) increased by over 90% according to the Australian Bureau of Statistics (see Trading Economics (2025)), so that although HC prices increased substantially even in real terms, the MC and LC market lost significant real value

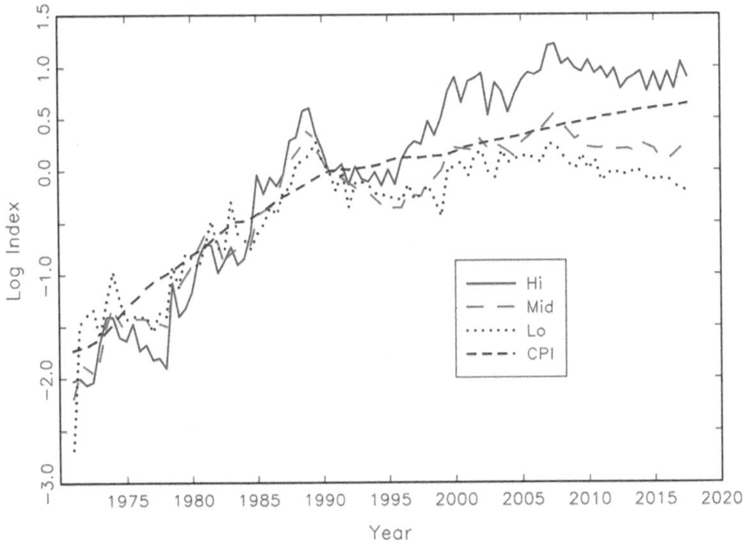

Fig. 1 Log hedonic art index and log CPI. *Source* Authors

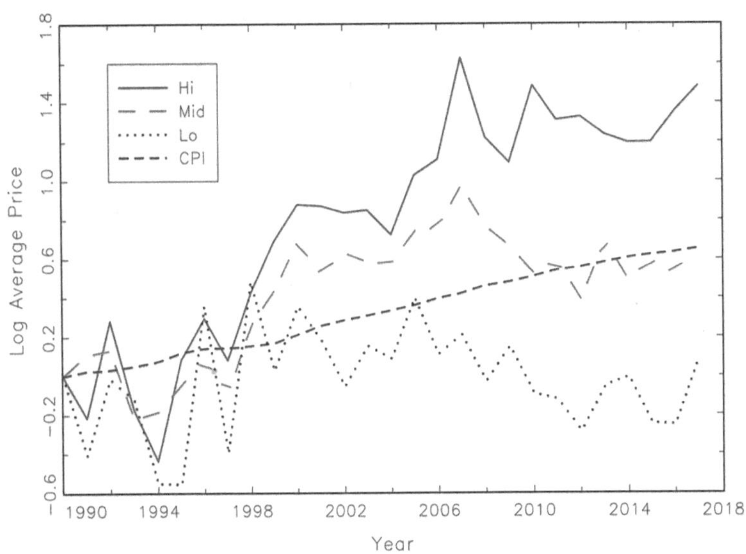

Fig. 2 Log average price (artists who sold pre-1990). *Source* Authors

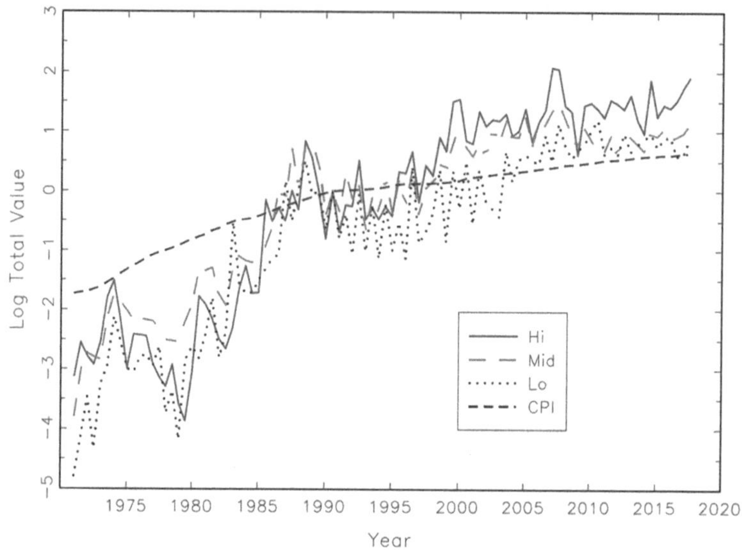

Fig. 3 Log total value of sales and log CPI. *Source* Authors

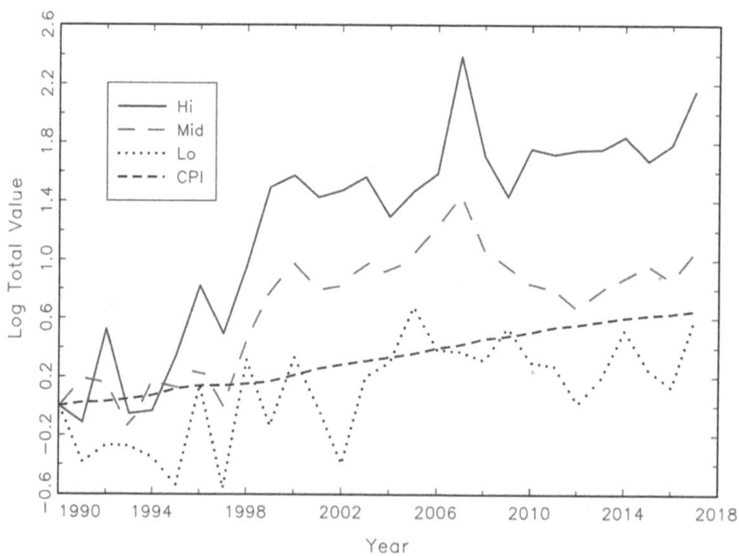

Fig. 4 Log total value of sales (artists who sold pre-1990). *Source* Authors

(for comparison, the CPI is also plotted here, and in Figs 2, 3 and 4.). Log of total sales value, shown in Fig. 3, reveals that increases are much greater for HC than for either MC and LC, with implied respective percentage total value changes of 578%, 211%, and 146%.

The empirical demonstration of declining prices among lesser-consecrated artists reinforces the point made by Radermecker and Moureau that low-end markets function by different logics; for these artists, collectability/investment potential is weak, and prices are more akin to consumer goods. In this respect, the declines in real price for the lower categories suggest the possibility of attrition from the market, so that artists in lower categories, in failing to achieve high consecration, gradually cease to be of interest to collectors, leading to decreasing demand and declining prices and number of sales. This would imply more artist turnover in the lower levels, with failed older artists being replaced by new aspirants who interest collectors until they fail to achieve consecration themselves.

To focus on the possibility of disappearance, we present some sales and price statistics for the post-1990 period, for artists with sales prior to 1990 ("pre-1990 artists"). This enables us to determine whether there are systematic changes, based on consecration level, in prices, sales, and market staying power. Specifically, we evaluate the evidence that MC and LC artists are more likely than HC artists to disappear in later periods, with associated declines in prices and sales volumes. Ideally, we would estimate a fully specified econometric model of market survival, linking decline in demand to hedonic covariates as well as consecration. Such a project is left for future research, but we believe the statistical evidence presented below is highly suggestive.

First, we consider all artists with at least one sale before 1990 and consider those who subsequently disappear from the market. Summary statistics for prices and sales of pre-1990 artists for 1990–2017 are plotted in Figs 2 and 4, which are respectively analogous to Figs 1 and 3 for all artists over the whole period. The larger gap in post-1990 price growth between the upper and lower segments for pre-1990 artists relative to all artists is borne out in the comparison of Figs. 1 with 2 and Figs. 3 with 4. For pre-1990 artists, average price percentage growth for 1990–2017 (Fig. 2) is 341% (HC), 100% (MC), and 10% (LC), and for total value growth (Fig. 4) it is 760% (HC), 188% (MC) and 82% (LC). These larger gaps between HC and

LC for pre-1990 artists as compared to all artists are consistent with our attrition hypothesis, in that pre-1990 artists who fail to achieve consecration see their prices and the total value of sales perform worse than for LC artists as a whole.

Next, we consider the phenomenon of attrition itself in terms of pre-1990 artists who do not have sales after 1990. In Table 2 we report the numbers of pre-1990 artists who continue to have sales after 1990, by decade.

By 2010, none of the HC artists have disappeared from the market, but 32 MC and 6 LC artists have, representing respectively 6.5% and 7.4% of the pre-1990 totals. In a period of 20 years then, 38 non-HC artists, representing about 7% of the total, disappear from the market. Whether this disappearance can be considered as attrition due to declining demand is of course an open question. To provide further insights into this, Fig. 5 plots log average price and log total sales value, for all paintings sold by these 38 artists over the period 1971–2009. Both series, which plot nominal values, peak in 1983, and display no evidence of a trend for a period of nearly 30 years. During 1983–2009, the CPI increased by about 170%, so that the real value of

Table 2 Number of sales by time period, artists present before 1990

	High Cons.	*Mid Cons.*	*Low Cons.*
Artists with at least one sale before 1990			
Number	43	496	81
Artists with at least one sale both before 1990 and during 1990–2017			
Number	43	490	80
Percentage of pre-1990 artists	100	98.7	98.8
Artists with at least one sale both before 1990 and during 2000–2017			
Number	43	483	79
Percentage of pre-1990 artists	100	97.4	97.5
Artists with at least one sale both before 1990 and during 2010–2017			
Number	43	464	75
Percentage of pre-1990 artists	100	93.5	92.6

Source Authors

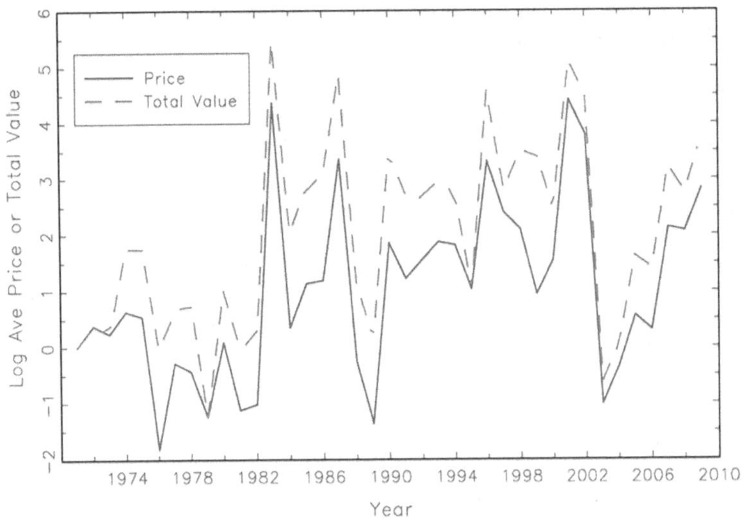

Fig. 5 Artists present before 1990, absent after 2009—log average price and total value. *Source* Authors

prices and sales by this set of artists declined by about 60%, which we take as indicative that demand was declining over this period.

Several of these artists have small number of sales even before 1990, and so it may be possible that their apparent disappearance is due to limited overall supply. To consider the possibility of declining demand more generally, even if not associated with complete disappearance, we consider all artists with at least 30 sales prior to 1990 and consider those who had the greatest percentage decline in number of sales for 2006–2017 as compared to pre-1990. The 25 artists with the largest declines are listed by name in Table 3. It is noteworthy, first, that they are all either MC or LC. Secondly, we compare the average sale price for each artist during 1980–1989 with that for 2010–2017, and find that for 10 artists, the average nominal price declined, and for another 13, the average real price declined. As discussed above, we take a combined decline in sales volumes and prices to indicate a decline in demand and predict that at least some of these artists are on their way out of the auction market.

Table 3 Artists with greatest proportionate decline in sales, pre-1990 to post-2005 (with at least 30 sales pre-1990)

Name	*Number of sales, 1971–1990*	*Number of sales, 2006–2017*	*Average price, 1980–1989*	*Average price, 2010–2017*
Jones, A.E.	50	2	1,102	675*
Stainforth, M.	35	2	3,115	1,700*
Baker, N.H.	31	3	861	1,550*
Tweddle, I.M.H.	34	5	1,118	1,320*
Pownall, G.H.	46	7	965	2,050*
Reynolds, F.G.	64	11	810	624*
Cook, W.D, Sr.	86	15	597	696*
Short, W.H., Jr.	33	6	867	414*
Gritten, H.C.	52	11	8,971	9,195*
Griffin, A.S.	131	28	397	282*
Quinn, J.P.	32	7	2,795	1,353*
Traill, J.C.A.	41	9	5,555	3,445*
Christmas, E.W.	72	16	1,325	877*
Muntz-Adams, J.M.	71	16	1,189	1,455*
Wilkie, L.A.	75	17	922	3,695
Dean, T.	74	17	642	1,417*
Camm, Robert	72	17	1,497	979*
Garrett, T.B.	42	10	2,940	735*
Sher, J.	66	16	1,800	2,809*
Sutherland, J.P.	64	16	255	1,441
Hampel, C.	84	21	918	983*
Lambert, G.W.	75	19	14,242	33,768*
Carse, J.H.	132	34	3,770	4,713*
Woodhouse, F.W., Sr.	69	18	4,625	8,083*
Eyre, G.	37	10	800	1,009*

Source Authors.

1. Ranked by magnitude of proportionate decline in number of paintings sold.
2. Prices rounded to nearest dollar.
3. Names in boldface indicate low consecration (LC). All others are medium consecration (MC).
4. Asterisk indicates decline in real average price with respect to CPI for each period averaged over monthly index values for May and November of all years in the respective time periods, with CPI increase being 165%

5 Conclusion

Our evidence indicates that the auction market for non-Indigenous Australian art is stratified by the consecration status of the artist, and that art historical consecration is a meaningful way to segment the market and to distinguish its low end. Our results indicate that artists can lose value as tastes shift and new artists emerge on the scene. For many artists, their careers and repute may lose steam before significant acclaim is achieved, so that they fail to achieve enduring consecration as an HC artist. The results suggest that the important classification distinction is between being HC (historically important) or not (Accomminotti Accominotti, 2021). Once one has been highly consecrated (inducted into the "Pantheon") one cannot fall out of it. We could say that the MC artists are in a form of purgatory, waiting for induction, but only a very few will achieve it. The fact that we see many MC artists declining (along with LC ones) suggests that unless one gets to HC, one's chances of losing position in the market are always pretty good. This is consistent with the literature on canonicity over time, which finds that HC artists tend to stay HC, that new artists are sometimes added to the canon, but that it is rare to drop out once consecrated.

In Table 3, we see the names of 25 artists for most of whom we can say that demand has decreased over time, quite significantly in some cases. Most of these artists are indeed quite obscure and it is difficult to find information about them online. One artist in this table whose prices have increased over this period is Jane Sutherland, now recognized as being an important contributor to Australian Impressionism. In 2021, she was one of the artists featured in an important exhibition hosted by the National Gallery of Australia. It seems that her status may have increased and that she may have been upgraded to the HC category, and that the decline in sales may be a supply effect, with museums and top collections taking her works off the market as prices are bidden up. In the triadic model of value presented in the introduction to this volume, we find that her scarcity value, in addition to her quality proxy, increased following the 2023 NGA exhibition. Indeed, our paper posits a link between consecration and scarcity, in which the latter is, to some extent, a result of the former: paintings created by formally trained professional artists are not rare, but the consecration process confers rarity on the small contingent of professional artists who achieve high consecration status. This effect is further amplified when works by highly consecrated artists enter museum collections.

Among artists that had fairly high numbers of sales, only to disappear from our sample, we can mention the names of William (Len) Annois, Arnold Jarvis, and Jack Koskie, all of whom have had one sale after 2017. Annois (b.1906) created works around the time of the Great Depression and World War II, Jarvis (b. 1881) is represented by sketches and paintings executed quickly, and Koskie (b. 1914) was an artist most active after returning from WWII and exhibited regularly at the Victorian Art Society. For the other 35 artists who disappear from our data set after 2010, we can find no evidence of subsequent sales.

Salvesen and Cousineau (2005) echo Grampp (1989) in emphasizing that artists who have died without achieving consecration in their lifetime tend to disappear very rapidly from the market unless they have surviving family members (spouses, usually) who actively promote the artists' legacy and reputation as a mechanism used to push for posthumous consecration. Our data set can in principle provide empirical evidence on this issue by tracking the posthumous presence in the market of different artists by consecration level. While beyond the scope of the current chapter, this remains a possibility for future research aiming to investigate how death effects might differ between different cohorts of artists based on the degree of consecration they achieve, and relatedly how death effects might differ between the low end compared to the rest of the market.

Finally, our results show that consecration level, and the associated possibility of loss of demand and market presence, can have significant consequences for the estimation of time series price indexes (as also emphasized by Goetzmann (1996) in the context of repeat sales regressions, even when only using data from higher-end auction houses).Works by HC artists are luxury collectibles or even financial assets, whose consecration acts as an insurance policy that guarantees against major loss of value (Singer, 1988). Works by artists who are not highly consecrated, although having the possibility of moving into the higher level if the artist sees significant increase in esteem by consecrating institutions, often behave more like consumption goods, that can lose value with use and eventually decline into rubbish status. We demonstrate that it can be analytically useful to consider these categories of the overall art market separately.

Acknowledgements We thank two reviewers and the editors for several constructive and helpful suggestions.

References

Accominotti, F. (2021). Consecration as a population-level phenomenon. *American Behavioral Scientist, 65*, 9–24.

Allen, C. (1997). *Art in Australia: From colonization to postmodernism*. Thames and Hudson.

Angelini, F., & Castellani, M. (2019). Cultural and economic value: A critical review. *Journal of Cultural Economics, 43*, 173–188.

Beckert, J., & Rössel, J. (2013). The price of art: Uncertainty and reputation in the art field. *European Societies, 15*, 178–195.

Boltanski, L., & Esquerre, A. (2020). *Enrichment: A critique of commodities*. Polity.

Bourdieu, P. (1993a). *The field of cultural production*. Columbia.

Bourdieu, P. (1993b). *Sociology in question*. Sage.

Bourdieu, P. (1996). *The rules of art*. Stanford.

Coate, B., & Hoffmann, R. (2022). The behavioural economics of culture. *Journal of Cultural Economics, 46*, 3–26.

Cowen, T. (2000). *In praise of commercial culture*. Princeton.

DiMaggio, P. (1987). Classification in art. *American Sociological Review, 52*, 440–455.

Durkheim, E. (2001). *The elementary forms of religious life*. Oxford World's Classics.

Galbraith, J. W., & Hodgson, D. J. (2012). Dimension reduction and model averaging for estimation of artists' age-valuation profiles. *European Economic Review, 56*, 422–435.

Galenson, D. W. (2000). The careers of modern artists. *Journal of Cultural Economics, 24*, 87–112.

Galenson, D. W., & Weinberg, B. A. (2000). Age and quality of work: The case of modern American painters. *Journal of Political Economy, 108*, 761–777.

Galenson, D. W., & Weinberg, B. A. (2001). Creating modern art: The changing careers of painters in France from impressionism to cubism. *American Economic Review, 91*, 1063–1071.

Ginsburgh, V., Mairesse, F., & Weyers, S. (2008). De la narration à la consecration. L'exemple de la peinture flamande de Van Eyck à Rubens. *Histoire & Mesure, 23*, 145–175.

Ginsburgh, V., & Weyers, S. (2006). Persistence and fashion in art Italian Renaissance from Vasari to Berenson and beyond. *Poetics, 34*, 24–44.

Ginsburgh, V., & Weyers, S. (2008). On the contemporaneousness of Roger de Piles' *Balance des Peintres*. In J. Amariglio, S. Cullenberg, & J. Childers (Eds.), *The Aesthetics of Value*. Routledge.

Goetzmann, W. (1996). How costly is the fall from fashion? In V. A. Ginsburgh & P.-M. Menger, *Economics of the Arts Selected Essays*. Elsevier.

Graddy, K. (2013). Taste endures! The rankings of Roger de Piles (1709) and three centuries of art prices. *The Journal of Economic History*, *73*, 765–790.

Grampp, W. D. (1989). *Pricing the priceless: Art, artists, and economics*. Basic Books.

Hodgson, D., Weber, C. M., & Coate, B. (2026). Comparative Cantillon effects in the Canadian and Australian art markets. In press, *Canadian Journal of Economics*.

Hodgson, D. J. (2022). Artistic movement membership and the career profiles of Canadian painters. *Poetics*, *90*, 101595.

Hodgson, D. J., & Hellmanzik, C. (2019). Relationships between artistic movements and careers of modern artists: Evidence from hedonic regressions with auction data. *Journal ofCultural Economics*, *43*, 309–337.

Huda, S. (2011). *Pedigree and Panache: A history of the art auction in Australia*. ANU Press. https://www.jstor.org/stable/j.ctt24hdmd.6

McCulloch, A. (1984). *Encyclopedia of Australian art*. Hutchinson.

Milo, D. (1986). Le phénix cultural: De la resurrection dans l'histoire de l'art L'exemple des peintres français (1650-1750). *Revue Française de Sociologie*, *27*, 481–503.

Rosen, S. (1981). The economics of superstars. *American Economic Review*, *71*, 845–858.

Salvesen, M., & Cousineau, D. (eds.). (2005). *Artists' estates: Reputations in trust*. Rutgers.

Sayers, A. (2001). *Australian art*. Oxford University Press.

Schneider, T. 2022. In finance asset bubbles burst without warning. It turns out the ultra-contemporary art market is even harder to predict. *Artnet*. https://news.artnet.com/market/gray-market-ultra-contemporary-bubble-2124105

Singer, L. P. (1988). Phenomenology and economics of art markets: An art historical perspective. *Journal of Cultural Economics*, *12*, 27–40.

Smith, B. (1979). *Place, taste and tradition: Study of Australian art since 1788* (2nd ed.). OUP Australia and New Zealand.

Thompson, M. (1979). *Rubbish theory*. Oxford.

Throsby, D., & Zednik, A. (2011). Multiple job-holding and artistic careers: Some empirical evidence. *Cultural Trends*, *20*, 9–24.

Trading Economics. (2025). Australian Consumer Price Index (CPI). Available online https://tradingeconomics.com/australia/consumer-price-index-cpi. Accessed February 9, 2025.

Weber, C. M. (2011). *Cantillon effects in the market for art*. Prepared for the Eastern Economic Association meetings, unpublished manuscript. http://cameroneconomics.ipower.com/projects.html

Worthington, A. C., & Higgs, H. (2003). Art as an investment: Short and long-term comovements in major painting markets. *Empirical Economics*, *28*, 649–668.

Illusions of Rarity and Value in Competing Megalodon Tooth Markets

Donna Yates

1 Introduction

On 28 July 2022 a 5 inch, black, fossilized Megalodon shark tooth from South Carolina with no provenance history sold at Sotheby's for $12,600, 530% of its high estimate price of $2,000.[1] On 28 June 2024 (and likely on any other day), a larger 5.5 inch, better preserved and more traditionally desirable Megalodon tooth from Georgia was available at buriedtreasurefossils.com for a "buy it now" price of $1,375.[2] This was one of a total of 351 Megalodon teeth available on that website, several of which were significantly more desirable by traditional standards than the Sotheby's tooth, but none of which were priced at over $10,000. Hundreds of other websites were offering thousands of Megalodon teeth on that day for prices well below the Sotheby's tooth.

Fossils, though natural objects, are a type of cultural property that are traded as a segment of the wider market for art, collectables, and rarities

[1] See https://www.sothebys.com/en/buy/auction/2022/natural-history/megalodon-shark-tooth-south-carolina. Accessed on June 3, 2025.

[2] See https://web.archive.org/web/20241013130305/https://www.buriedtreasurefossils.com/otodus-megalodon-17.html. Accessed on October 13, 2024.

D. Yates (✉)
University of Maastricht, Maastricht, The Netherlands
e-mail: d.yates@maastrichtuniversity.nl

A.-S. V. Radermecker (ed.), *Low-End Markets for Art and Cultural Goods*, Cultural Economics & the Creative Economy,
https://doi.org/10.1007/978-3-032-27566-0_12

(Demeulemeester & Stein, 2022).[3] Megalodon tooth fossils, which can be sourced in locations around the world, are fairly abundant and easily accessible to potential buyers. A long-standing "traditional" trade in Megalodon teeth exists, within which a standardized determination of market value based on size and other features has developed into a common space of understanding among suppliers, dealers, and consumers. These standards are affirmed and reaffirmed through the abundance of Megalodon tooth finds and transactions: Megalodon enthusiasts can easily estimate the market value of a tooth from a photo alone. Indeed, Sotheby's too seemed to know the going rate for a Megalodon tooth as their price estimate for the tooth in question was on the high side of normal for accepted Megalodon tooth value. Despite this, Sotheby's competing bidders, reacting to complicated forces, pushed the price astonishingly high. Why, then, did this tooth sell at auction for more than fossil markets, and indeed more than Sotheby's, would seem to expect?

In this chapter I will use the example of fossilized Megalodon shark teeth to explore the effect of placement within high-end art spaces on the perceived value of lower cost and abundant fossils. Within a conceptual space defined by aspects of commodities theory (Leibenstein, 1950; Brock, 1968; Lynn, 1989, 1991; Mittone & Savadori, 2009) and by considering the "artification" (Naukkarinen, 2012; Shapiro, 2004, 2019; Shapiro & Heinich, 2012) effect of said placement, I will discuss how consumer perception of fossil rarity is amplified by the creation and maintenance of what I have called in previous research a "desirescape" (Yates & Mackenzie, 2021). Potential bidders, responding to this persuasive desirescape and without knowledge of more realistic points of reference for traditional tooth market value, upped the price. The immediate results of this has been a perception of increasing price within traditional Megalodon teeth markets and a sense that access to teeth at a low level is becoming more limited, as well as the appearance of art-like harnessing of perceived value, such as a Megalodon fractional ownership scheme that appears divorced from the traditional construction of tooth availability and

[3] Article 1(a) of the 1970 UNESCO Convention on the Means of Prohibiting and Preventing the Illicit Import, Export and Transfer of Ownership of Cultural Property defines "objects of palaeontological interest" as "cultural property", even before anything recognizable as art or artifact is listed.

value.[4] All told, this view of the Megalodon tooth market shows how low-end objects can become high-end objects through the networked relationships present in high-end marketplaces.

2 Methodology

Gathering data for academic research is an affective, embodied experience. Divorced from the context that it happens within, and forced into the restrictive formulation of feigned neutrality, methodologies sound logical, repeatable, routine, and scientific. The sociological reality of data collection is usually the product of opportunities and choices beyond the researchers' control or heavily influenced by the researchers' perception of the world. The research presented here was conducted by the PI of the *Trafficking Transformations Project* which seeks to unravel aspects of the powerful relationships that develop between humans and desirable objects towards a better understanding of how these objects make people act in seemingly illogical, sometimes irrational, and sometimes illegal ways. A particular focus of this project are paleontological objects, particularly those fossils that interact with humans outside of the "safe" confines of science, such as when the fossils enter the marketplace. The private sale of fossils is socially, ethically, and legally controversial to say the least (Padian, 2000; Larson et al., 2014; Larson & Russell, 2014; Shimada et al., 2014), and at times that controversy spills to the mainstream, forcing the public reckon with their own desires related to fossils, and the discomfort of placing a monetary value on the singular and unique.

The present research stems from a prior focus on unique fossils with high market values. Following research into the placement of *T. rex* fossils in art spaces (Yates & Peacock, 2024) and into the same *T. rex* fossils' destructive and litigious qualities (Yates & Peacock, 2023), I became curious about lower-cost, more abundant fossils. *T. rex* are rare, but many fossils are not. Do the same networks of desire, these object desirescapes (Yates & Mackenzie, 2021), manifest when the fossils in question are not so singularly unique? Is desire diminished when there are simply too many of a type of fossil available?

To explore these initial questions, I decided to focus on Megalodon teeth for an academically reason and a personal reason. The academic

[4] See https://web.archive.org/web/20241104072154/https://www.timeless.investments/en/assets/82dd69a5-e894-4096-9155-7214795e0b77. Accessed on November 4, 2024.

reason is that, based on prior research, Megalodon teeth should be inherently appealing to fossil consumers, as fossil dealers make clear. Multiple dealers agree that generally "carnivores are more sought after than herbivores" on the market (Demeulemeester & Stein, 2022, p. 28). At the time of writing (March 2025) the website for fossil supplier Ck Preparations states that "Our major requests are for teeth and claws. These are the most collectable elements of a dinosaur and therefore are the most expensive due to their supply and demand."[5] Dealer Mike Triebold, quoted by Polsky, has said "There are three important factors in selling dinosaurs: big nasty teeth, big nasty claws, and big nasty horns. That's what gives these creatures sex appeal" (Polsky, 2011, p. 183). While a Megalodon is not a dinosaur but rather a giant shark that swam the seas tens of millions of years after the non-avian dinosaurs went extinct, they were huge, terrifying, and toothy. Their teeth have the same sort of "sex appeal" that provokes dinosaur desire. Having been featured in such blockbuster films as *The Meg* (2018), Megalodon teeth have "brand appeal" as well, as suggested by Radermecker and Moureau.

The personal reason is simply a trick of human geography. My family lives in coastal Georgia in the USA, which is famous for its black Megalodon teeth; the teeth felt 'close to home' to me (which turned out to be literally true). Unlike the *T. rex,* there is something *mine* about Megalodon teeth and as my research is closely tied to emotion, affect, value, and desire (Mackenzie & Yates, 2016, 2017; Yates, 2015, 2022; Yates & Bērziņa, 2023; Yates & Mackenzie, 2021; Yates & Peacock, 2023, 2024; Mackenzie et al., 2024), I invite those feelings in myself into my own research. I wanted Megalodon teeth too.

The data gathering for this chapter occurred in three stages. First, I collected size, collection location, condition, and pricing data from the past 12 years of high-end Megalodon tooth sales at Christie's (2012–2024) and Sotheby's (2020–2024) auction houses. The earliest dates represent the first time that a Megalodon tooth appears in their respective public online sales records, but it is likely that each has offered other Megalodon teeth at earlier dates, and have likely offered teeth since. I also took a "snapshot" of Megalodon teeth (see for the method, Yates, 2014; Brodie et al., 2019; Yates & Peacock, 2025) available for sale on 25 June 2024 from four online Megalodon tooth dealers, again recording tooth size, location where the

[5] See https://web.archive.org/web/20250119003148/https://ckpreparations.com/purchasing-ckp-fossils/. Accessed on January 19, 2025.

tooth was collected, condition, and pricing data where available. All of this data is made publicly available by the sellers and platforms. The data was not collected for quantitative analysis, rather the goal was to gain a broad sense of what Megalodon teeth are available, for what price, and via what platforms, resulting in a qualitative, if numerically supported, understanding of the particulars of these different market strata.

Second, I conducted participatory ethnographic fieldwork on Megalodon tooth diving and collection in Georgia. This was purely opportunistic. Over dinner I asked my brother if he knew anyone who I could buy a Megalodon tooth from. He responded that he "knew a guy," and within 12 hrs I was on a boat heading out into the mouth of the tidal Medway River with two Megalodon tooth divers. Coincidentally, the divers set sail from a dock located where my family lives, and I watched them dive for teeth from a spot that, if on land, would be in walking distance from my family's homes. One diver was a recreational Megalodon tooth hunter, the other had been a professional tooth dealer for a few decades. I spent the morning mostly chatting to the boat captain as we waited for the divers to surface, but also discussing teeth, fossil hunting, and the market with the divers. This diving excursion occurred during the same week of the Apex stegosaurus sale at Sotheby's auction house for a record $44 million (Small & Jacobs, 2024). The Megalodon divers had heard this news, but they did not realize that Megalodon teeth had been offered in the same sale. Showing them the auction results on my phone was an effective icebreaker. The divers gave me a number of Megalodon teeth they found that they considered to be of no market value, and I write this chapter with the teeth on my desk.

Last, I revisited the high-end auction house listings of Megalodon teeth and the sales websites of traditional Megalodon tooth dealers, such as the one who took me out on the water, to consider the social signals and aesthetic differences between the two in relation to price. Throughout this data collection I assumed that the teeth in question were being traded legally and collected no data that would indicate otherwise. This research has been granted ethical approval by Maastricht University's Ethics Review Committee Inner City Faculties.

What emerged from this combined work was a view of the nuanced effects of placement, context, and desire within sales of Megalodon teeth across these unconnected markets. In the correct setting, in this case the high-end auction house, even these demonstrably not-so-rare, arguably-low-value objects can achieve prices that they cannot within the traditional market.

3 Pricing Megalodon Teeth: The Traditional Market

Previously I referred to Megalodon teeth as being not-so-rare and this is true. Megalodons existed for over 22 million years and each had about 250 teeth at any given time (Renz, 2002, p. 81). These sharks constantly shed their teeth throughout their lifetime, growing more to replace those that were lost. Millions of Megalodon teeth dropped to the ocean floor, and some became encased in mud and were eventually fossilized. In places where those mud strata have since come to the (underwater) surface again, such as coastal Georgia, they can be found by anyone with diving equipment, some locational information, and sufficient motivation. A one-hour dive can produce many broken teeth and five or even more whole teeth, depending on location and luck.

While Megalodon teeth are not rare, there are certain qualities of a tooth that are considered more rare and more desirable, and Megalodon teeth are traditionally priced based on the presence or absence of these features. Numerous traditional Megalodon tooth dealers are upfront about how tooth market value is calculated, creating informative guides for assessing the quality and thus value of teeth, all of which agree with each other.[6] According to the guide provided by Dark Water Megs, "arguably the most important factor when it comes to fossilized shark teeth is size" noting that "most people would rather have an item from a [large] shark than a smaller one."[7] Megalodon teeth are normally measured in inches, at their longest diagonal, so "from the tip of the blade to the corner of the root."[8] Teeth that are over 5 inches long are generally considered large, and those over 6 inches

[6] E.g., https://megateeth.com/real-megalodon-teeth-the-collectors-guide/ or https://www.darkwatermegs.com/megalodon-teeth-information/how-much-does-a-megalodon-tooth-cost/how-much-is-a-megalodon-tooth-worth.html or https://www.fossilera.com/pages/megalodon-tooth-buyers-guide. Accessed on June 3, 2025.

[7] See https://www.darkwatermegs.com/megalodon-teeth-information/how-much-does-a-megalodon-tooth-cost/how-much-is-a-megalodon-tooth-worth.html. Accessed on June 3, 2025.

[8] See https://megateeth.com/real-megalodon-teeth-the-collectors-guide/. Accessed on June 3, 2025.

long ("the magical size")[9] are considered very large and thus rare. Teeth over 7 inches long are exceedingly rare, approaching legendary to unbelievable;[10] they are usually not available for sale by anyone. All told, size matters and "the difference in value between a 5.95″ tooth and a 6″ tooth can easily be hundreds of dollars."[11]

Beyond size, the physical condition of a tooth is an important factor in determining its traditional market value. Teeth with broken tips, chipped edges, or cracked or missing roots are worth less than teeth with more intact features, even, at times, if they are smaller. The presence of peeling enamel, too, lowers the value of a tooth, as does the absence of the triangular enamel bourrelet above the root. Roots that have not been, and do not need to be, repaired or restored are significantly more desirable than repaired teeth, and it is considered unethical to not disclose repairs to potential buyers.[12] Features such as the location the tooth came from in the shark's mouth, the location it was collected from, and aesthetic features such as color may also influence price.

So, while each Megalodon tooth is unique, and there is certainly a level of subjectivity to assessment of their value, most dealers price their teeth reliably within a similar range based on the above features with limited variation. As there are numerous Megalodon tooth dealers—each selling a large number of teeth—it can be assumed that traditional dealers who overcharge will be pushed out of the market: there is competition. Yet there is a practical aspect to Megalodon tooth pricing that should be considered: the high production cost. To find these teeth one usually has to scuba dive and that comes with significant costs. Equipment, oxygen tanks, boat upkeep, etc., all mean that the finding a Megalodon tooth is not 'free' or opportunistic; it is expensive and intentional. Dealers sell their teeth to recoup the funds lost on their dives and some do not break even. The act of diving itself is a draw for many dealers, and their fossils sales only partially fund this pastime.

[9] See https://www.fossilera.com/pages/megalodon-tooth-buyers-guide. Accessed on June 3, 2025.

[10] See https://www.fossilera.com/pages/what-is-the-largest-megalodon-tooth-ever-found. Accessed on June 3, 2025.

[11] See https://megateeth.com/real-megalodon-teeth-the-collectors-guide/. Accessed on June 3, 2025.

[12] See https://web.archive.org/web/20250318150048/https://www.fossilera.com/pages/megalodon-tooth-buyers-guide. Accessed on March 18, 2025.

Regarding volume, most traditional Megalodon tooth dealers who trade online offer hundreds of teeth for sale at any given time. At the time of writing, Megateeth.com had over 286 teeth for sale on their website, priced from $35 for one of a random selection of broken 3 inch + teeth to $5,360 (on sale)[13] for a desirable 6.125 in tooth.[14] The site Darkwatermegs.com had over 176 teeth for sale, ranging in price from $17 for a broken tooth that was fashioned into a refrigerator magnet,[15] to $23,000 for an assembled wall display that is made up of 38 megalodon teeth that is offered with the possibility of installation;[16] the most expensive single tooth on the site was a 5.48 in tooth offered for $1,516.[17]

On these sites, the teeth are not presented as singular or rare (Fig. 1). While they may be photographed alone, either on a custom (often rustic) stand of some sort or lying on what seems like a blanket or tarp, they are presented in a web shop format that emphasizes the rows and rows of teeth available to buyers willing to scroll. Buyers can sort by price (low to high, high to low), size, posting date, etc. No shortage of teeth is felt, no competition is present, and it is left to the buyer to purchase within their own price point by putting a pre-priced tooth in their shopping cart. Nearly anyone who wants a Megalodon tooth can have one, with only $17 being the entry price for owning a piece of an ancient beast.

[13] See https://web.archive.org/web/20250514080149/https://megateeth.com/shop/megalodon-shark-teeth/6-1-8-massive-museum-quality-megalodon-shark-tooth/xx068/. Accessed on May 14, 2025.

[14] See https://web.archive.org/web/20241105165647/https://megateeth.com/shop/megalodon-shark-teeth/6-1-8-massive-museum-quality-megalodon-shark-tooth/xx068/. Accessed on November 5, 2025. Note it was listed at the time as Not currently for sale.

[15] See https://www.darkwatermegs.com/megalodon-teeth-for-sale/Megalodon-Magnets-Refrigerator-Etc-p197648270. Accessed on June 3, 2025.

[16] http://www.darkwatermegs.com/megalodon-teeth-for-sale/Large-megalodon-display-wall-p712921036. Accessed on June 3, 2025.

[17] See https://www.darkwatermegs.com/megalodon-teeth-for-sale/5-48-pattern-bladed-megalodon-on-stand-p719074445. Accessed on June 3, 2025.

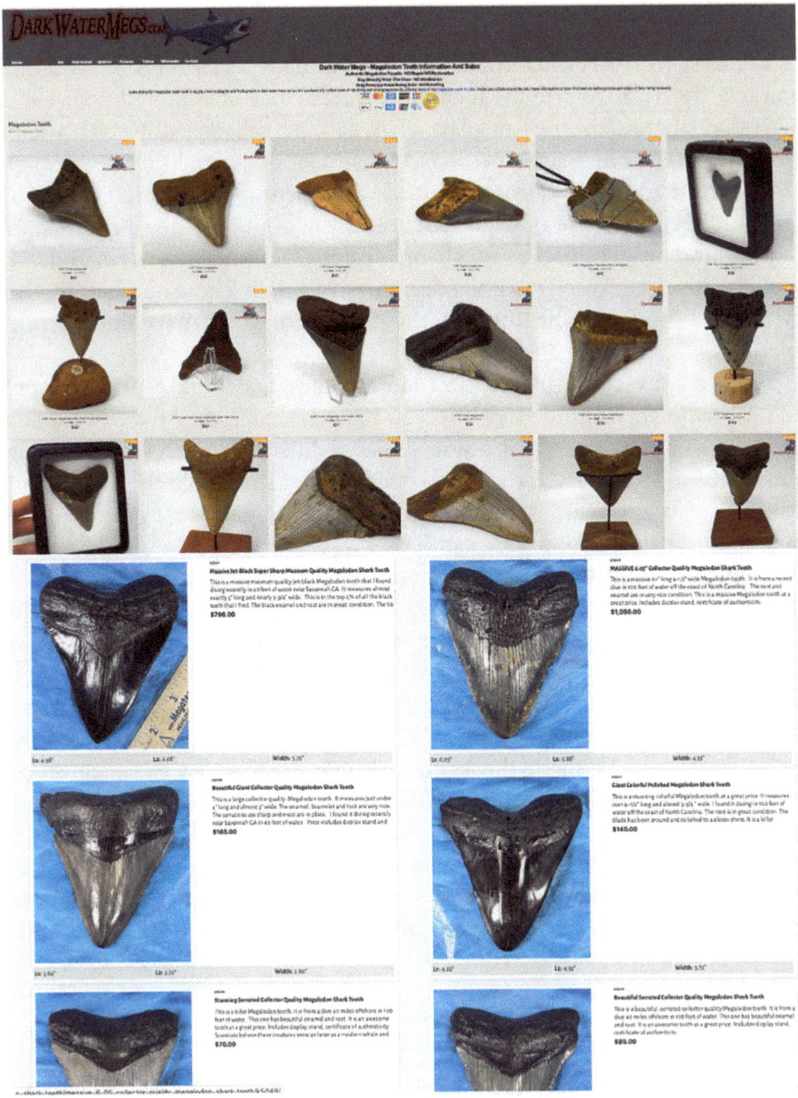

Fig. 1 Screen shots of the websites Darkwatermegs.com and Megateeth.com. *Source* screen shot by Yates, 13 May 2025

4 Placing Megalodon Teeth: The High-end Auction

In contrast to the readily available and abundant teeth on the traditional market, the relatively few Megalodon teeth that are offered for sale at high-end auction houses display what can be called a different pricing structure. Teeth that appear to have no special qualities,[18] at least according to the traditional pricing method described above, normally achieve prices at auction above or even well above the going rate for a comparable (and abundantly available) tooth on dealer platforms. The remainder of this chapter is devoted to considering why this is the case. Before this, however, I provide some notes on the prices achieved in Megalodon tooth auctions.

Limiting myself to the highest end of the auction houses (Sotheby's and Christie's), I found that since 2020, 28 Megalodon teeth were successfully sold at Sotheby's and since 2012, 73 had been successfully sold at Christie's up to 2024. Of these 101 teeth, 47 of them sold for higher than the high price estimate presented in the auction catalogue, even though in most sales the low-price estimate was considerably higher than a traditional Megalodon dealer would charge for the piece. Several of these teeth sold for considerably higher than the high price estimate. For example, lot 231 offered in Sotheby's *Natural History, including Gorgosaurus* sale in July 2022[19] is a nice-looking, dark-colored tooth from South Carolina. While it displays minimal enamel peeling and only a little wear to the edge serrations, it only measures in at 5 inches, so not particularly big. As such, the auction house estimated this tooth at between $1,000 and $2,000: on the high side of the traditional market value of the tooth but not too far off. Yet, after a back-and-forth volley of bidding that I observed while watching the live feed of the auction, the tooth sold for the hammer price of $12,600. This is a startling result that is genuinely difficult to explain, particularly because any bidder could easily buy a 'better' Megalodon tooth for much less money following a basic internet search. This tooth is not alone. To mention a few, a 4.66 in (so,

[18] They have no other unique or desirable qualities other than being present in the auction house. No auction tooth was presented with any history of prior ownership; they had less documentation available; they were listed with imprecise measurements; find-spot information at the state or country level; and they had generic catalogue notes.

[19] See https://web.archive.org/web/20250513122427/https://www.sothebys.com/en/buy/auction/2022/natural-history/megalodon-shark-tooth-south-carolina. Accessed on May 13, 2025.

not "big") tooth from Georgia with no special features sold for $10,160 at Sotheby's in 2023 above an already way too high estimate of $3,000.[20] Also a tooth from South Carolina with visibly peeling enamel was sold for £10,625 at Christie's in 2021 above a high estimate of £3,000.[21] That tooth was purported to be 6 inches, but the perfectly round number makes one wonder if the tooth was measured accurately with callipers.

In high-end auction sales, Megalodon teeth are presented in a noticeably different way than on the websites of traditional dealers (Figs. 2 and 3). Within individual listings, the teeth are inevitably positioned on an unobtrusive and tasteful stand and photographed singularly against a grey or white background. The tooth is nearly always pointed downward, emphasizing its shape and implying the downward movement of a bite while still giving of an impression of artistic display. Recall that on traditional websites the teeth are presented in more "low budget" way, often lying on a table or tarp, with a scale in the photo to prove the tooth's size.

At a whole auction catalogue level, the highest number of Megalodon teeth offered in one sale was six (Sotheby's *History of Science & Technology, Including the World of Richard Feynman, and Natural History*, 13 December 2023; Christie's *Sculpted by Nature: Fossils, Minerals and Meteorites*, 14–20 October 2020), with most sales offering less at one time. In some of the sales that have more teeth, such as the six tooth Christie's sale in 2020, the available Megalodon pieces are not placed next to each other in the auction lot order, instead they are lots 26, 53, 116, 126, 132, and 134 respectively. Recall that traditional Megalodon sales websites are characterized by hundreds of teeth lined up together and presented as for sale (Fig. 1). The much lower volume of teeth available at high-end auctions and the clear attempt to not have too many teeth in a row give an impression of Megalodon tooth rarity and thus value that the traditional dealers do not.

[20] See https://web.archive.org/web/20250514080831/https://www.sothebys.com/en/buy/auction/2023/natural-history/megalodon-shark-tooth-georgia-4. Accessed on May 14, 2025.

[21] See https://web.archive.org/web/20250514081314/https://onlineonly.christies.com/s/sculpted-nature-fossils-minerals-meteorites/large-megalodon-tooth-15/117691. Accessed on May 14, 2025.

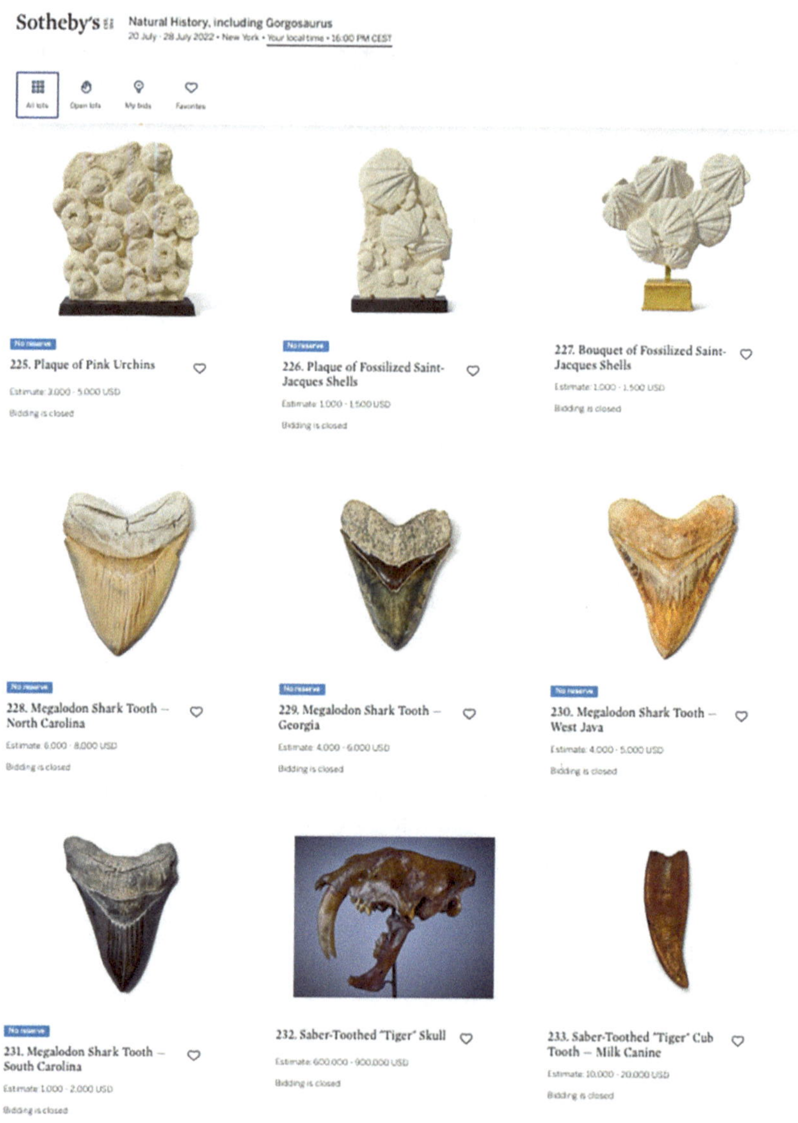

Fig. 2 Megalodon teeth offered for sale at Sotheby's *Natural history, including gorgosaurus* sale in New York in July 2022. *Source* Screen shot by Yates, 14 May 2025

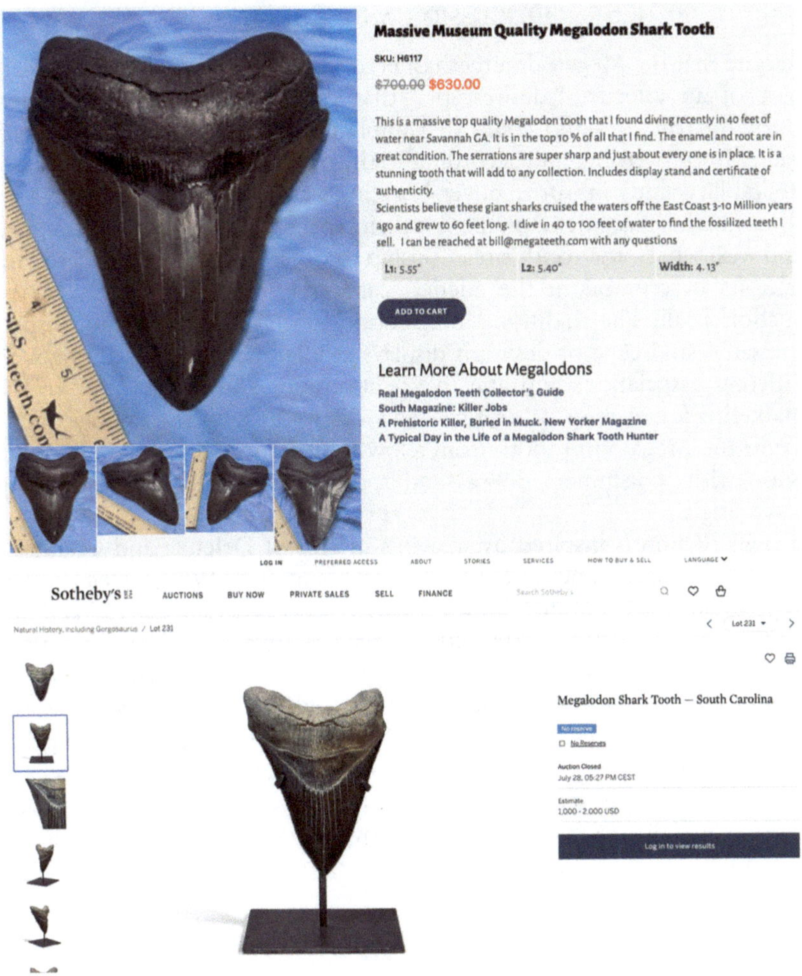

Fig. 3 Above, a Megalodon tooth offered for sale on megateeth.com for a discounted price of $630; below, a Megalodon tooth offered for sale at Sotheby's on 28 July 2022 that ultimately sold for $12,600. *Source* screenshots taken by Yates on 13 May 2025

5 Discussion and Conclusion

I argue that the Megalodon teeth offered for sale at the auction houses are part of an affective "desirescape" that provokes desire in consumers through structures and codes that imply uniqueness and high monetary value. In this setting, and according to the triadic model, scarcity increases desirability and, in turn, buyers' willingness to pay. This is achieved through the placement of the tooth in space (how it is photographed and with what), the tooth's relationship to other objects being offered for sale, its description in the auction catalogue, and its presence in the auction at all. The traditional Megalodon tooth market does not display the same landscape of desire; it displays a different desire landscape with different associations and affective relationships and shows none of the marketing of scarcity or rarity.[22] This desirescape of associations transforms the Megalodon tooth from a low value commodity to a high value one, with consumer desire and purchasing behavior responding accordingly.

This section is inspired by weaving strands of Deleuze and Guattari's assemblage/agencement (Deleuze & Guattari, 1987; Deleuze & Lapoujade, 2006), into Actor Network Theory (Callon, 1984; Law, 1992; Latour, 1999, 2005, 2009), past singularity (Kopytoff, 1986; Karpik, 2010), through to a desirescape "where a spatial array of myriad agentic objects cultivates desire among people to collect, own, possess, and show off" (Yates & Mackenzie, 2021, p. 119). Acknowledging that those bodies of theory have directly informed what follows, I now focus in on three concepts: commodities theory, artification, and desirescapes. I will briefly discuss each in turn and how they connect to our seemingly over-valued auction Megalodon teeth.

5.1 *Commodities Theory: Scarcity, Snobs, Uniqueness, and Desire*

Within greater commodity theory (Brock, 1968), the *scarcity effect* (or scarcity bias) (Mittone & Savadori, 2009) states that perceived scarcity makes consumers see a commodity as more desirable. This is further associated with *uniqueness theory* which postulates that "consumers may

[22] The differences in the desirescapes likely mirror the differences in the profiles of auction vs. traditional tooth market buyers. As humans are important components of a desirescape, what they desire is manifest within each.

desire scarce goods as a way to differentiate themselves from others" (Mittone & Savadori, 2009, p. 454). This, in turn, is tied to Leibenstein's *snob effect* (Leibenstein, 1950, p. 189) which "represents the desire of people to be exclusive; to be different," and postulates that in some circumstances, demand for a consumer good decreases when others are perceived to be consuming that commodity." To synthesize this briefly, these theories and effects map a situation where a scarce and unique commodity appears (more) desirable to certain consumers.

An interesting outcome of Lynn's research on the scarcity effect is the connection between scarcity, desirability, and knowledge of a commodity's price. Lynn found that "scarcity increased the desirability of art prints only when subjects had been primed to think about the expensiveness of art prints in general" and that "scarcity enhanced the desirability of wine only when subjects did not know how much the wine cost" (Lynn, 1989, p. 257). To rephrase slightly, Lynn's subjects found wine and art prints desirable when they assumed the commodities were expensive and were told (or assumed) that the commodities were scarce. This is supported by Verhallen (1982, p. 321) who found that "the effect of scarcity is hypothesized to be strongest when no other information about the good is available." Lynn (1991, pp. 53–54) found that "scarcity tactics will be more effective when targeted at consumers who possess greater than average need for uniqueness" and further postulated that the desirability of uniqueness would be strongest for commodities that are "valued for their symbolic and self-defining properties" rather than their utility.

Those who wish to profit from these consumer's desires, then, might choose marketing techniques that emphasize a commodity's scarcity, that cause consumers to assume the commodity is expensive, but also do not provide much information about the commodity's cost. Bringing this back to Megalodon teeth, to make the teeth more desirable to the sort of uniqueness seeking consumers who buy at high-end auctions, the teeth need to be made to seem scarcer than they are with limited background information provided to challenge that message of scarcity. This can be achieved through the identification of that commodity with something that consumers already feel to be scarce, unique, and valuable, without offering any additional information about the true market value or rarity. In this, and in many cases, this means creating a scenario where the object is identified with and as art. Art has long been seen sociologically as a stand in for the possessor's appreciation for the rare and unique,[23] and to make something into art, to *artify* it, brings with it the resulting implications of value.

5.2 *Artification*

Put succinctly, *artification* has been defined as "situations and processes in which something that is not regarded as art in the traditional sense of the word is changed into something art, [. . .] to processes where art becomes mixed with something else that adopts some features of art" (Naukkarinen, 2012, p. 1). It can be seen "to be an all-encompassing process of change, both practical and symbolic" (Shapiro & Heinich, 2012). Shapiro (2019) generally considers artification to be a series of microprocesses, many of which (such as displacement, renaming, reshuffling rankings, institutional change, differentiation of function, normative and legal consolidation, and aesthetic formalization), I believe, are clearly present within the auction market presentation of Megalodon teeth, as they were in our previous work on *T. rex* artification (Yates & Peacock, 2024). The goal here is not to thoroughly document these microprocesses, but their tangible manifestations are important. Perhaps the easiest way to present the artification of Megalodon teeth is through a visual comparison.

At the top, Fig. 3 shows a typical presentation of a Megalodon tooth for sale on a traditional market website; at the bottom is the typical presentation of a Megalodon tooth in a high-end auction, having undergone artification. In the traditional presentation, the tooth is laying on a blue cloth or tarp, next to a ruler for scale. In various other photographs, the tooth is flipped and turned, with the impression that it has been handled and thus is something you can and should touch. It lacks a stand or other mode of display, and thus does not imply anything about how the buyer should interact with the piece. It is listed with a price which has noticeably been reduced, with the new price in red, indicating that this is a good deal.

In contrast, the auction presentation frames the tooth as an artwork. The tooth is first shown singularly, alone on a white background, evoking the "white cube gallery" style of art spaces which has become inseparably identified with the display and sale of modern art. In most pictures, the tooth interacts only with a minimal

[23] See Bourdieu's concept of cultural capital where art serves as his primary example (Bourdieu, 1986).

stand, the stand itself indicating to the viewer that this is a display object, and thus an art object. In various photos, the tooth has been turned on its stand, but one imagines that a hand only touched the stand, not the tooth: the tooth being presented as perhaps too special to touch. Like in all auction catalogues, the price is presented as an estimated range, but the implication is that tooth might sell for more (it did); there is neither a commitment on the part of the auction house as to the monetary value of the tooth in the form of a set price, nor is there further information for the buyer as to why the estimate was set to that presented. This is in contrast to the traditionally presented tooth which is sold both with links at the bottom of the listing that serve to educate buyers (e.g., "Real Megalodon Teeth Collector's Guide" leads to a page that explains exactly how value and price of Megalodon teeth are assessed), and an invitation for buyers to compare prices with hundreds of other Megalodon teeth listed on the site.

In the introduction to this volume, Radermecker and Moureau offer a model of the art market built upon three axes: functionality, scarcity, and brand strength, positing that the placement of objects along these axes shape both pricing strategies and value. It follows that those who seek to increase the monetary value of an item would need to modify the positioning of that item on one or more of those axes. Megalodon teeth are minimally functional: they are objects of curiosity or decoration and that is unlikely to change. They already have a high degree of brand strength both from the cultural cache of fossils generally, the "sex appeal" of teeth, and from being featured in recent popular films. What they do not truly have is scarcity. The presentation of Megalodon teeth within the signalling frameworks of the auction serves to increase their placement on the scarcity axis in the minds of buyers, thereby increasing their monetary value.

All told the auction Megalodon tooth is made to feel more like art, thus feel more valuable, and feel more expensive. In contrast to the traditional site, the auction site simultaneously presents the Megalodon tooth as (rare, unique, valuable) art while withholding all information about true scarcity and market value. The traditional site provides an abundance of information about true rarity and pricing in the tooth market in both written and visual format. Sotheby's was able to sell their Megalodon tooth for 20 times what the traditionally presented tooth is being offered for.

5.3 *Megalodon Tooth Desirescapes: Objects Working Together Towards Scarcity Signals*

Within this admittedly complicated space filed with transforming and translating assemblages and networks of human and non-human actors,[24] I and a colleague (Yates & Mackenzie, 2021, p. 119) proposed the idea of an art world desirescape, "where a spatial array of myriad agentic objects cultivates desire among people to collect, own, possess, and show off artworks." We expanded upon this concept specifically for fossils in later papers (Yates & Peacock, 2023, 2024). Our desirescapes display elements of a Deleuzian idea of *territorial assemblages* (Nail, 2017) in that within desirescapes the heterogeneous objects, people, and associations that form them display strong territorial coding, admitting and excluding based on clearly delineated codes: a nineteenth-century sculpture from Gabon is admitted into a "Contemporary Art" evening by way of sculptures by Picasso and Brancusi (Yates & Mackenzie, 2021, pp. 124–125); a 66-million-year-old *T. rex* is admitted into a "twentieth/twenty-first Century Art Evening" via an artification process that placed the fossil between paintings by living artists Pat Steir and Jonathan Gardner (Yates & Peacock, 2024).

The desire generated by these networks of objects finds its perceived relief in consumption. The artworks (or in this case Megalodon teeth that have been artified) are for sale, and the evocative territorial assemblages of art and culture that provoke desire are intimately tied to perceived value, availability, and scarcity. The formation of a desirescape, as a powerful assemblage or network of objects, people, and ideas, can greatly increase the experience of an object's value. The cultivation of value enhancing desirescapes, then, can be financially lucrative to the people involved. The desirescape can be initially curated by human actors in ways that allow the non-human actors to act on particular targets.

When it comes to art, and artified Megalodon teeth, it seems that maximisation of market value is achieved when a desirescape is able to enhance the perceived rarity of an object while masking the inherently transactory quality of offering the rare thing for sale. When the networks and associations leading up to and including sale and purchase are masked

[24] Back to Deleuze and Guattari, and particularly Latour, etc. By non-human actors I mean entities that are not people that cause other entities to act. They have some form of agency, but they do not have to be conceived of as having intentionality.

by associations that are coded towards something else, the consumer is left only with the sense of rarity that they feel coming from the object and the sense of value that the object, and its desirescape, engenders. This can be seen, for example, in the art commerce space of the major art fairs, where art dealers create atmospheric experiences for their art to sit within (resembling museums, temples, even tombs) that are usually unencumbered by commercial signifiers such as price tags (Yates, 2021; Yates & Mackenzie, 2021; Yates & Bērziņa, 2023).

This is what has happened to the artified auction Megalodon teeth. The bidders, who ultimately paid much more than the traditional market would argue they should for the limited number of Megalodon teeth offered at Christie's or Sotheby's, were responding to the affective desirescape emanating from the scarcity signals presented by the auction catalogue. To move back to the auction tooth in Fig. 3, the interaction between the tooth itself, the stand, the white cube space, the (lack of) information, the (lack of) a set price, the weight of the printed catalogue page, the (artified) presentation of the other items offered for sale and, very importantly, the implied presence of all the high-priced and valuable art that has been sold in the same auction location in the past, created an affective desirescape that disturbed consumer reason. For this to happen, an assemblage was created or transformed, a network of human and nonhuman actors was modified or translated, and a desirescape formed. This assemblage, this network, this active desirescape of human/object relationships serves to make the commodity seem rare and scarce, seem unique, and thus seem valuable and desirable. Consumers paid more for something that was not rare because it felt rare, and that feeling emanated not only from the object of desire itself, but from the networked context of that object of desire.

5.4 *Byproducts and Market Changes*

What does this mean for Megalodon teeth markets? I admit that my research was not designed to directly consider the wider implications and effects of the movement of low-value Megalodon teeth to high-value spaces, but rather to document its occurrence and consider some of the possible mechanisms that transform these fossils. Yet in conducting this research, I have encountered what appear to be some interesting byproducts of the artification of these teeth and the desire that these processes inspire.

Take for example a 6-inch Megalodon tooth with peeling enamel and what may be restorations, presented on Timeless, a platform that allows users to fractionally invest in collectables.[25] First appearing on the website on 13 July 2023, the platform claims the tooth has a market value of €7,500 at the time of writing. In an "About the Megalodon Tooth" section, the platform states "Megalodon teeth specifically often exceed initial auction house estimates, with prices ranging above the $10,000 mark for a single tooth." When I showed this listing to a traditional Megalodon tooth dealer he identified it as being from South Carolina and gave it what he portrayed as a charitable valuation of about $700, less than a tenth of what Timeless claims the piece is worth. This is not fraud, Timeless is correct about the auction results, and yet something feels unsettling about this listing. The artified Megalodon tooth has now become an investment, following art's example, but this value can only be maintained within the narrow confines of this particular desirescape. When the tooth, or the investor, moves anywhere else, the tooth becomes low-end again.

Then again, maybe not. There is some indication that the traditional Megalodon tooth market is experiencing changes. On an webpage that was produced after 2021 and updated in 2024, the diver and dealer behind DarkWaterMegs.com sought to explain "Why the Price of Megalodon Teeth is Increasing."[26] The author portrays a situation where more people are becoming aware of Megalodon Teeth (more demand), fossil find locations are becoming restricted or exhausted (less supply), and requisite dive equipment is more expensive (higher production cost). The diver I observed in Georgia also cited an increase in tooth demand (and an increase in what he charges), however he attributed that to people gaining new interests during the Covid pandemic. All told, Megalodon teeth may be becoming exactly what the auction houses are portraying them as—scarce—and their prices are responding accordingly.

[25] See https://www.timeless.investments/en/assets/82dd69a5-e894-4096-9155-7214795e0b77. Accessed on June 3, 2025.

[26] See https://web.archive.org/web/2/https://darkwatermegs.com/megalodon-teeth-information/why-are-megalodon-teeth-getting-more-expensive/megalodon-tooth-prices-are-increasing.html. Accessed on June 3, 2025.

5.5 *Final Thoughts*

Still, most Megalodon teeth are not scarce or particularly valuable. The survey of the traditional Megalodon market spaces discussed here, as well as the pile of free Megalodon teeth I currently have sitting on my office desk, are clear proof of this. While extremely large Megalodon teeth are very rare and valuable, they are truly unavailable to the market at any cost and are not a part of this discussion. Although Megalodon teeth are not rare, the general consuming public is not aware of this. People do not normally encounter Megalodon teeth and their perceptions of them are, thus, developed from cultural experiences that assume fossil rarity even when that is not reality. Megalodon teeth are startling survivors of a startlingly ancient past: they are fossils and we are taught that fossils are rare things that belong in museums. Like dinosaur bones, they feel exclusive, impossible, and expensive.

At this point, Megalodon teeth appear to be objects that the commodity theorists discussed above would see as ripe for the scarcity effect. They are valued for their symbolic properties and have no utility. They are assumed to be expensive. No other information is available about them. The only issue, then, is that they are not actually scarce. But that is where the affective qualities of these objects and their desirescapes take over.

Funding The funding for this research was provided by the European Research Council (ERC) under the European Union's Horizon 2020 research and innovation programme (grant agreement n° 804851).

References

Bourdieu, P. (1986). The forms of capital. In J. Richardson (Ed.), *Handbook of theory and research for the sociology of education* (pp. 241–258). Greenwood.

Brock, T. C. (1968). Implications of commodity theory for value changel. In A. G. Greenwald, T. C. Brock, & T. M. Ostrom (Eds.), *Psychological foundations of attitudes* (pp. 243–275). Academic Press. https://doi.org/10.1016/B978-1-4832-3071-9.50016-7

Brodie, N., Yates, D., Slot, B., Batura, O., & van Wanrooij, N., & op't Hoog, G. (2019). *Illicit trade in cultural goods in Europe Characteristics, criminal justice responses and an analysis of the applicability of technologies in the combat against the trade*. European Commission. https://op.europa.eu/en/publication-detail/-/publication/d79a105a-a6aa-11e9-9d01-01aa75ed71a1

Callon, M. (1984). Some elements of a sociology of translation: Domestication of the scallops and the fishermen of St. Brieuc Bay. *The Sociological Review, 32* (1_suppl), 196–233. https://doi.org/10.1111/j.1467-954X.1984.tb00113.x

Deleuze, G., & Guattari, F. (1987). *A thousand plateaus: Capitalism and Schizophrenia*. University of Minnesota Press.

Deleuze, G., & Lapoujade, D. (2006). *Two regimes of madness: Texts and interviews 1975–1995*. MIT Press

Demeulemeester, T., & Stein, K. (2022). *Dinosaurs are collectible: Digging for dinosaurs: The art, the science*. Lannoo Publisher.

Karpik, L. (2010). *Valuing the unique: The economics of singularities*. Princeton University Press.

Kopytoff, I. (1986). The cultural biography of things: Commoditization as process. In A. Appadurai (Ed.), *The social life of things: Commodities in cultural perspective* (pp. 64–91). Cambridge University Press.

Larson, N. L., Stein, W., Triebold, M., & Winters, G. (2014). What commercial fossil dealers contribute to the science of paleontology. *AAPS Journal*. https://www.aaps-journal.org/Fossil-Dealer-Contributions.html

Larson, P. L., & Russell, D. (2014). The benefits of commercial fossil sales to twenty-first century paleontology. *Palaeontologica Electonica, 17*(1).

Latour, B. (1999). On Recalling ANT. In J. Law & J. Hassard (Eds.), *Actor network theory and after* (pp. 15–25). The Sociological Review.

Latour, B. (Ed.). (2005). *Reassembling the social: An introduction to actor-network -theory*. Oxford University Press.

Latour, B. (2009). Where are the missing masses? The sociology of a few mundane artifacts. In F. Candlin & R. Guins (Eds.), *The object reader* (pp. 229–254). Routledge.

Law, J. (1992). Notes on the theory of the actor-network: Ordering, strategy, and heterogeneity. *Systems Practice, 5*(4), 379–393. https://doi.org/10.1007/BF01059830

Leibenstein, H. (1950). Bandwagon, Snob, and Veblen effects in the theory of consumers' demand. *The Quarterly Journal of Economics, 64*(2), 183–207. https://doi.org/10.2307/1882692

Lynn, M. (1989). Scarcity effects on desirability: Mediated by assumed expensiveness? *Journal of Economic Psychology, 10*(2), 257–274. https://doi.org/10.1016/0167-4870(89)90023-8

Lynn, M. (1991). Scarcity effects on value: A quantitative review of the commodity theory literature. *Psychology & Marketing, 8*(1), 43–57. https://doi.org/10.1002/mar.4220080105

Mackenzie, S., & Yates, D. (2016). Collectors on illicit collecting: Higher loyalties and other techniques of neutralization in the unlawful collecting of rare and precious orchids and antiquities. *Theoretical Criminology, 20*(3), 340–357.

Mackenzie, S., & Yates, D. (2017). What is Grey about the "Grey Market" in Antiquities. In M. Dewey & J. Beckert (Eds.), *The architecture of illegal markets: Towards an economic sociology of illegality in the economy* (pp. 70–86). Oxford University Press.

Mackenzie, S., Yates, D., Hübschle, A., & Bērziņa, D. (2024). Irregularly regulated collecting markets: Antiquities, fossils, and wildlife. *Crime, Law and Social Change*, *82*(5), 1111–1130. https://doi.org/10.1007/s10611-024-10171-9

Mittone, L., & Savadori, L. (2009). The scarcity bias. *Applied Psychology*, *58*(3), 453–468. https://doi.org/10.1111/j.1464-0597.2009.00401.x

Moureau, N., & Radermecker, A.-S. V. (2006). Recontextualizing and modeling the low-end market for art and cultural goods. In N. Moureau & A.-S. V. Radermecker (Eds.), *Low-end markets for art and cultural goods*. Palgrave Macmillan.

Nail, T. (2017). What is an assemblage? *SubStance*, *46*(1), 21–37.

Naukkarinen, O. (2012). Variations on artification. *Contemporary Aesthetics*, *4*. https://digitalcommons.risd.edu/liberalarts_contempaesthetics/vol0/iss4/2

Padian, K. (2000). Feathers, fakes, and fossil dealers: How the commercial sale of fossils erodes science and education. *Palaeontologica Electonica*, *3*(4), 1–8.

Polsky, R. (2011). *Boneheads: My search for T. rex* (1st ed.). Council Oak Books.

Renz, M. (2002). *Megalodon: Hunting the hunter* (3 ed., 2 print). PaleoPress.

Shapiro, R. (2004). The aesthetics of institutionalization: Breakdancing in France. *Journal of Arts Management Law and Society*, *33*, 316–335. https://doi.org/10.3200/JAML.33.4.316-335

Shapiro, R. (2019). Artification as process. *Cultural Sociology*, *13*(3), 265–275. https://doi.org/10.1177/1749975519854955

Shapiro, R., & Heinich, N. (2012). When is Artification? *Contemporary Aesthetics (Journal Archive)*, *4*. https://digitalcommons.risd.edu/liberalarts_contempaesthetics/vol0/iss4/9

Shimada, K., Currie, P. J., Scott, E., & Sumida, S. J. (2014). The greatest challenge to twenty-first century paleontology: When commercialization of fossils threatens the science. *Palaeopntologia Electronica*, *17*(1).

Small, Z., & Jacobs, J. (2024, July 17). T. Rex Dethroned? A Stegosaurus Fossil sells for a record $44.6 Million. *The New York Times*. https://www.nytimes.com/2024/07/17/arts/design/stegosaurus-auction-44-million.html

Verhallen, T. M. M. (1982). Scarcity and consumer choice behavior. *Journal of Economic Psychology*, *2*(4), 299–322. https://doi.org/10.1016/0167-4870(82)90034-4

Yates, D. (2014). Church theft, insecurity, and community justice: The reality of source-end regulation of the market for Illicit Bolivian cultural objects. *European Journal on Criminal Policy Research*, *20*, 445–457.

Yates, D. (2015). 'Value and doubt': The persuasive power of "authenticity" in the antiquities market. *PARSE*, *2*, 71–84.

Yates, D. (2021). Crime and its objects: Human/object relationships and the market for illicit latin american antiquities. *Mélanges de La Casa de Velázquez, 51–2*, 307–312. https://doi.org/10.4000/mcv.15543

Yates, D. (2022). Creative compliance, neutralization techniques, and palaeontological ethics. *The Geological Curator, 11*(7), 428–435. https://doi.org/10.55468/GC1458

Yates, D., & Bērziņa, D. (2023). Affective atmosphere in an Art fair Jewel Heist. *European Journal on Criminal Policy and Research*. https://doi.org/10.1007/s10610-023-09549-7

Yates, D., & Mackenzie, S. (2021). Crime, material and meaning in art world desirescapes: How matter matters for art crime. In N. Oosterman & D. Yates (Eds.), *Crime and art: Sociological and criminological perspectives of crime in the art world* (pp. 119–133). Springer.

Yates, D., & Peacock, E. (2023). *T. rex* is Fierce, *T. rex* is Charismatic, *T. rex* is Litigious: Disruptive Objects in affective desirescapes. *International Journal of Cultural Property, 30*(4), 396–418. https://doi.org/10.1017/S0940739124000055

Yates, D., & Peacock, E. (2024). The artification of fossils in commercial art spaces: Dinosaurs in a desirescape. *Journal of Material Culture, 29*(3), 287–310. https://doi.org/10.1177/13591835241248291

Yates, D., & Peacock, E. (2025). Exploring aspects of the online trade in antiquities through snapshot analysis. In A. M. Dominicé, S. Vigneron, & J. Ulph (Eds.), *Elgar research handbook on art, culture, and heritage*. Elgar.

Sector Insights: The Valuable Low End of the Auction Art Market

Jean Minguet

1 Introduction

In the art market, prices are generally expected to reflect the historical importance of each piece, in combination with its notoriety and rarity, while also accounting for various formal and material attributes—including size, technique, and the condition of the work. Academic research has further established that external factors, such as the venue of sale or the provenance of the work, exert a significant influence on market outcomes. In addition, artistic tastes naturally evolve over time: artists who are in vogue may see their prices temporarily rise, whereas those falling out of fashion are gradually overlooked. As a result, the art market undergoes price fluctuations for reasons that are often independent of the inherent qualities of the works themselves. The low end of the market is no exception to this phenomenon. In fact, at auction, the least expensive lots offer the greatest potential for financial appreciation.

It is arguably a common aspiration among collectors to acquire a long-forgotten piece, or conversely, a newly created work that has yet to be appreciated at its full value—and to see it reclassified as a masterpiece. Within its immense diversity, the low end of the art market undoubtedly contains works that may gain substantial value over time, whether due to

J. Minguet (✉)
Artprice, Paris, France
e-mail: jminguet@artprice.com

A.-S. V. Radermecker (ed.), *Low-End Markets for Art and Cultural Goods*, Cultural Economics & the Creative Economy,
https://doi.org/10.1007/978-3-032-27566-0_13

shifting tastes, reattribution, or relocation to a more receptive geographic context. Conversely, this segment also absorbs works that were once highly priced but have since lost appeal among collectors. These contrasting trajectories are nonetheless conflated in the lower strata of the art market, which comprises an intimidating volume of works across a wide spectrum of quality.

According to the Cambridge Dictionary, the term *low-end* refers to the cheapest products available within a given market. This superlative is, by nature, relative: in the context of art, even the least qualitative items may still command significant prices. Any definition of the low end should in any case be based exclusively on price thresholds and must not carry implicit artistic judgments.

A detailed analysis of the auction market's price structure helps clarify what might constitute its lower segment. Works sold for under $10,000—often grouped in this way in market reports—account for only a small share of total market value. Nonetheless, they play a key role in terms of market dynamism and structural resilience, sustaining engagement from collectors and professionals alike, even during periods of economic uncertainty. By demonstrating greater resistance to macroeconomic shocks, the low end of the auction market has acquired strategic importance in the eyes of auctioneers. In response to increasing demand for smaller and more accessible transactions, auction houses have multiplied sales specifically dedicated to lower-priced works—beginning with the popular "Prints and Multiples" sessions—and have expanded their digital platforms accordingly.

Despite its growing role, the low end has received limited attention in academic literature. To date, the lowest-priced lots have not been the subject of dedicated studies and are typically included only marginally in broader research on the market as a whole. One key obstacle is the sheer volume and heterogeneity of this segment, which complicates both data collection and analysis. Furthermore, low-priced lots often lack essential information, including title, date of creation, provenance, and even dimensions if the works have not been removed from their frames for inspection. In many cases, catalogue reproductions are missing, which makes comparative analysis and provenance tracing especially difficult. The combination of overwhelming quantity and imprecise documentation likely explains why the low end of the art market remains understudied and poorly understood in both academic and professional circles.

2 Literature Review

While numerous monographic publications are dedicated to prints by artists such as Edvard Munch, Pablo Picasso, and Pierre Soulages—works that are generally far less valuable than their paintings but nonetheless retain clear artistic significance—macroscopic studies focused on the low end of the art market remain virtually non-existent. This gap can be attributed, first and foremost, to the difficulty of analyzing the most heterogeneous segment of a market whose boundaries are already inherently ambiguous.

Given that a comprehensive representation of the art market is considered utopian, scholars have become accustomed to conducting research based on samples of auction sales, as these data are publicly accessible. However, access to such information varies across auction houses and tends to be more readily available for prestigious firms, notably Christie's and Sotheby's, thereby disproportionately highlighting the high-end segment of the market. Even within this limited scope, researchers often narrow their focus to an even more restrictive and homogeneous subset. For instance, in one of the earliest papers addressing art as an alternative investment, Anderson (1974) examined the financial performance of art by analyzing paintings—still the dominant medium on the market.

The construction of price indices has become a prominent tool for assessing the financial characteristics of art as an investment, not only in terms of expected returns but also regarding volatility and correlation with other asset classes. By breaking down indices according to medium or time period, researchers can also compare various market segments. One of the most widely known indices, developed by Mei and Moses (2002) and later acquired by Sotheby's in 2016, is based on a database of repeat sales of thousands of artworks. As the authors explain, their dataset comprises "paintings sold at the main salesrooms of Sotheby's and Christie's (and their predecessor firms) from 1950 to 2000. If a painting had listed in its provenance a prior public sale, at any auction house anywhere, we went back to that auction catalog and recorded the sale price (p. 1657)." Since their focus lies on painting—the dominant medium—and on sales occurring in major auction venues with traceable provenance, it is likely that lower-priced works are underrepresented.

The academic preference for the high-end segment is further evident in recurring investigations into whether the most expensive artworks financially outperform the rest of the market, a hypothesis often referred to as the "masterpiece effect." The mixed empirical results associated with this hypothesis can largely be explained by differences in methodology—particularly the distinction between hedonic and repeat-sales models—as well as variation in sample composition and in the definition of a masterpiece. While studies by Pesando (1993), Mei and Moses (2002), and Ashenfelter and Graddy (2003) conclude that the highest-priced artworks underperform the broader market, Renneboog and Spaenjers (2013), adopting a different methodological approach, arrive at the opposite conclusion. They argue that much existing research is flawed because masterpieces are identified endogenously, based on their prices. In their study, they test for a "masterpiece effect" using a non-price measure of quality. Specifically, they replicate their hedonic regression analysis for all sales by artists who had already been included in the textbook *Gardner's Art Through the Ages* prior to the beginning of their study period.

To maintain consistency with a price-based definition of the low-end segment of a market, the present study opts for a straightforward segmentation relying exclusively on transaction price—eschewing more sophisticated approaches such as that of Renneboog and Spaenjers (2013), which implicitly incorporate an element of artistic judgment. Even this simplified approach necessitates methodological decisions, particularly regarding which price to use at auction: the starting bid, low and high estimates, reserve price, price with or without fees, taxes and royalties. The hammer price represents the final accepted bid, from which the auction house typically deducts the seller's commission. In addition, a buyer's premium is applied and disclosed publicly and is usually included in the final price announced by the auctioneer.

Auction estimates play an indirect but notable role in this analysis, as they influence the quality of catalogue information: the higher the estimated value, the more documentation is typically provided. As a matter of practice, all information disclosed in a catalog serves the goal of optimizing the sale. Accordingly, gallery names and even those of previous collectors may be included in the provenance section. Similarly, references to relevant literature and exhibitions are more often featured for highly valued works. In this context, the systematic omission of art fairs—even major ones such as Art Basel—from auction catalogues raises questions about why auction houses believe that such details cannot stimulate demand, as discussed in Minguet (2017). Overall, the content of auction catalogues is highly variable, becoming increasingly detailed as estimates rise.

The considerable challenge of obtaining reliable information on low-estimated works—which are also most likely to fetch the lowest prices—partially explains why databases such as Artnet exclude them. As noted in its *Intelligence Report: The Year Ahead 2025*, "[Artnet's] databases include only items with low estimates of at least $500." The heterogeneity of low-estimated lots and the unequal nature of the available information are key reasons why both academic studies and market reports tend to exclude the low end of the market—beyond merely omitting lots estimated below $500. Reports published by Artnet, Art Basel & UBS, and Artprice generally treat this market segment with minimal attention, typically aggregating all sales below $10,000 into a single category. This practice reflects both habitual reporting conventions and a widespread assumption that the low end is less likely to yield meaningful insights into market trends.

3 Methodology

Auction sales represent one of several channels through which artworks are exchanged. While they entail relatively high operating costs, they offer a consistent and relatively transparent view of the art market. According to the 2025 *Art Basel and UBS Global Art Market Report*, public auction sales totaled $19.0 billion in 2024, accounting for approximately 33% of the global art market's total value of $57.5 billion. Moreover, auction results are publicly disclosed and legally certified, making them particularly valuable for academic inquiry. The present research is based on Artprice's Fine Art database, one of the most comprehensive repositories available for auction-based art market data. Covering the period from 2000 to 2024, the database includes 15.8 million public auction results without applying any exclusion criteria based on price or estimate. It encompasses eleven categories: Painting (41%), Drawing (26%), Print-Multiple (19%), Sculpture (7%), Photography (4%), Object (2%), Ceramic (0.5%), Tapestry (0.2%), Miniature (0.2%), Audiovisual (0.02%), and the more recent category of NFTs (0.01%).

Each work in the database must be attributed to a clearly identified artist, typically including both name and date of birth, although pseudonyms—such as the Master of Frankfurt or Banksy—are accepted. Alternative attributions follow the terminology outlined by Sotheby's in its *Guide for Buyers. Glossary & Important Notices*, which includes distinctions such as:

- By [artist]: "In our opinion, a work by the artist."
- Attributed to [artist]: "In our opinion, probably a work created during the artist's lifetime, with substantial grounds to believe it is by the artist's hand, but with less certainty than the previous category."
- Studio of [artist]: "In our opinion, a work by an unknown hand in the artist's studio, possibly executed under the artist's direction."
- Additional designations include Circle of, Follower of, Style of, After, among others.

From a pricing perspective, this study adopts the most consistent metric available: the sum of the hammer price and the buyer's premium. This figure, now standard across most auction houses, closely approximates the total amount paid by the buyer. For the sake of international comparability, all values are converted to U.S. dollars using the exchange rate applicable on the day of sale.

The analysis of Artprice's database is structured around two primary objectives. Section 4 investigates the global auction market's price structure in order to establish a clear, objective threshold for identifying its lower segment. Section 5 offers case studies of artworks that have transitioned into or out of this segment over time, enabling a closer examination of the external factors that impact pricing. Together, these sections aim to illustrate the structural relevance of the low end of the market and to shed light on the dynamics that can alter both perception and valuation of individual artworks.

In its approach, Sect. 4 deliberately avoids speculative analyses of financial performance in favor of a more foundational economic framework. This decision mitigates several of the key limitations that plague financial studies of the low end, such as the absence of previous sales in the provenance section necessary for repeat sales index construction, or the incomplete or imprecise descriptive attributes required by hedonic pricing models. It also circumvents the challenge of accounting for hidden costs—especially substantial seller fees—and the complexity of operating within an open market. Indeed, works can exit circulation by entering museum collections or being forgotten in private attics, while simultaneously, the market continuously absorbs newly created artworks and even new categories. This phenomenon is not exclusive to the lower segment: the advent of NFTs, for instance, was marked by Beeple's *Everydays: The First 5,000 Days* selling for $69.3 million at auction in 2021. However, the lower end has particularly witnessed the influx of mass-produced editions—sometimes unnumbered or unsigned—marketed by galleries, museums, or online platforms. These releases tend to dilute the market by obscuring original works among a flood of editions.

Section 5 likewise refrains from attempting to quantify the average investment potential of low-priced lots. Instead, it seeks to reveal the mechanisms through which select artworks emerge from the low end—either gradually or through sudden revaluation. While the low end of the market is often perceived as a black hole where artworks lose both visibility and informational integrity, it is precisely this opacity that merits scrutiny. By examining extreme cases of price transformation, the study shows how the value of certain works can sometimes be revealed.

4 Structural Importance of the Lowest Price Ranges

Given that a painting by Willem de Kooning is reported to have sold privately for $300 million, while works by lesser-known or discredited artists may be acquired for a nominal sum at flea markets, one may ask: what does the price distribution actually look like in the art market?

Auctioned lots represent approximately one-third of the market's total value, as previously noted, and they are subject to professional vetting. Despite this partial scope, auction sales nonetheless offer one of the most reliable and publicly accessible portraits of the market's structure. By design, the presence of a reserve price introduces asymmetry into price dynamics: while bids cannot fall significantly below the estimates, nothing prevents a work from reaching unexpectedly high final prices. Furthermore, auction houses typically avoid transactions at the very lowest price levels, as these are unlikely to cover fixed costs related to marketing, storage, logistics, and cataloguing. Consequently, the price structure of the auction market is expected to exhibit a positively skewed distribution—more akin to a diamond than a pyramid.

Based on data from Artprice, which encompasses fine art auction sales from 1,060 auction houses worldwide, without applying upper or lower price thresholds, the shape of the distribution can be clearly observed. In 2024, sales under $10 (including the buyer's premium) represented only 0.6% of all recorded transactions. However, sales below $100 already accounted for 13% of the total volume. The prominence of slightly upper prices is even more notable: in 2024, 48% of auctioned works were sold within the $100–$1,000 range, although these generated just

1.5% of the total revenue for the fine art auction market. More broadly, sales below $10,000 accounted for 91% of all transactions, contributing 9.5% of total turnover.

This study defines the low end of the art auction market using a $10,000 threshold, for two principal reasons. First, sales in this bracket exert a non-negligible impact in terms of value, representing nearly 10% of total market proceeds, compared to only 1.6% for sales below $1,000. Second, the $10,000 figure serves as a practical and symbolic benchmark: it is commonly used in art market reports and online platforms, and is more operationally useful than the precise but variable statistic that 90% of all 2024 transactions were concluded at prices below $9,450—a figure that would, in any case, require annual adjustment (Table 1).

The 8.6 million transactions recorded by Artprice between 2000 and 2024 for fine art works sold under $10,000 represent the foundational base of the auction art market. In contrast, the upper segment of the market constitutes a long tail that contributes disproportionately to volatility in annual revenue figures. While total auction turnover tends to fluctuate significantly from year to year due to the success or absence of a small number of exceptionally expensive masterpieces, the total volume of sales has followed a steady upward trajectory, largely driven by activity in the lowest price ranges. This contrast is particularly evident between

Table 1 Distribution of fine art sold lots at auction in 2024 (n = 811,300)

x% of lots sold under	
100%	$121,160,000
99%	$142,815
98%	$66,704
96%	$30,480
94%	$18,638
92%	$12,600
90%	$9,450
80%	$3,506
70%	$1,750
60%	$1,003
50%	$629
40%	$413
30%	$270
20%	$160
10%	$80

Source Artprice

2022 and 2023. During this period, global auction turnover declined by 9% (equivalent to a $1.32 billion drop), a decrease that may be attributed to the sole extraordinary result achieved by the Paul G. Allen collection. Auctioned by Christie's New York in November 2022, this landmark sale generated $1.5 billion in a single evening, including six lots that exceeded $100 million each. The magnitude of this event was not matched in the following autumn season, leading to a natural contraction in total revenue. In parallel, however, the number of auction results under $10,000 rose by 6% between 2022 and 2023. This segment alone generated a 5% increase in revenue year-over-year.

A comparison between the evolution of lots sold by price range and the turnover they generated reveals that transactions under $10,000 have demonstrated greater consistency than the rest of the market over the past twenty-five years (Fig. 1). Although the low end was not immune to downturns following the 2008 subprime mortgage crisis or the onset of the COVID-19 pandemic, this segment recovered more rapidly in both cases than did higher price tiers.

In 2020, amid an unprecedented global health crisis, online sales enabled auction houses to resume operations even before public health restrictions were lifted. The swift deployment of online platforms facilitated the continuity of market activity. As a result, the number of dematerialized sales more than tripled within a single year, rising from 670 online sessions in 2019 to 2,080 in 2020.

To this day, online sales remain better suited to lower-priced works. In 2024, lots sold for under $10,000 accounted for 13.5% of sales (748 lots) in Sotheby's live auctions, while they comprised as much as 49% (2,878 lots) of the firm's online sales (Fig. 2). This disparity underscores the strategic role of online platforms in supporting accessibility, liquidity, and volume at the lower end of the auction art market.

A key factor driving the recent expansion of the low-end segment of the art market is the increasingly frequent inclusion—particularly in online sales—of large-edition works such as prints, 3D multiples, jewelry, and design objects. Although editions have long been popular among modern artists—most notably with Pablo Picasso's prolific ceramic and print series—post-war and contemporary artists have further contributed to this trend by introducing new types of editions that auction houses have gradually integrated into their catalogues.

As a result, the number of editioned works appearing at auction has risen significantly. In 2024 alone, Artprice recorded 1,169 editions sold at

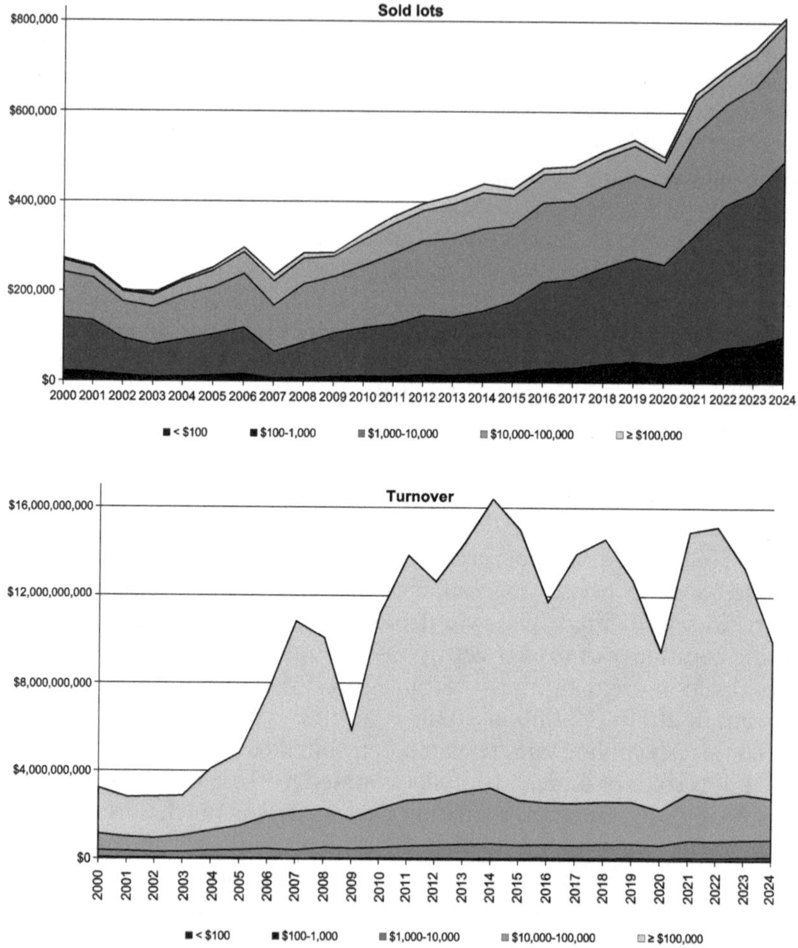

Fig. 1 Yearly number of fine art lots sold and revenue by price Range at auction. *Source* Artprice

auction for Takashi Murakami, followed by Banksy with 881 and Damien Hirst with 709. This proliferation illustrates how editioned works have played a central role in shaping the dynamics of the lower-priced segment, particularly within the context of digital platforms and expanding collector bases.

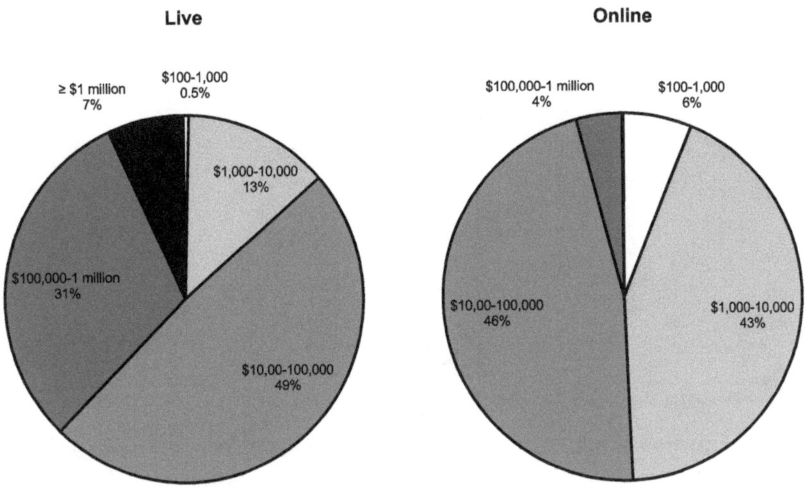

Fig. 2 Sotheby's fine art lots sold in 2024: Live vs. online sales breakdown by price range

5 Escaping or Falling Into the Bottom End

The price volatility observed within individual editions of the same artwork highlights the relative inefficiency of the art market, where the "law of one price" seldom applies. This deviation is largely attributable to the significant influence of external factors on sale outcomes.

A particularly illustrative example can be found in Jeff Koons' *Balloon Dog (Plate)* series, which comprises five color variants—red (2005), blue (2002), yellow (2015), magenta (2015), and orange (2015)—each issued in 2,300 copies, plus 50 artist's proofs. Although a time lag is generally required for newly released editions to enter the secondary market, trading activity has clearly accelerated over the past fifteen years, accompanied by pronounced price fluctuations (Fig. 3).

Among the many sales recorded for this series, one especially striking example is that of a red edition numbered 331/2,300. Estimated between $8,000 and $12,000 by Christie's, it was ultimately sold for $52,500 on 14 November 2013. This exceptional result occurred just two days after the record-breaking $5.4 million sale of *Balloon Dog (Red)*—a monumental, three-meter-high sculpture by Koons and the only red version among five unique colors. It is highly likely that the impact of this headline-

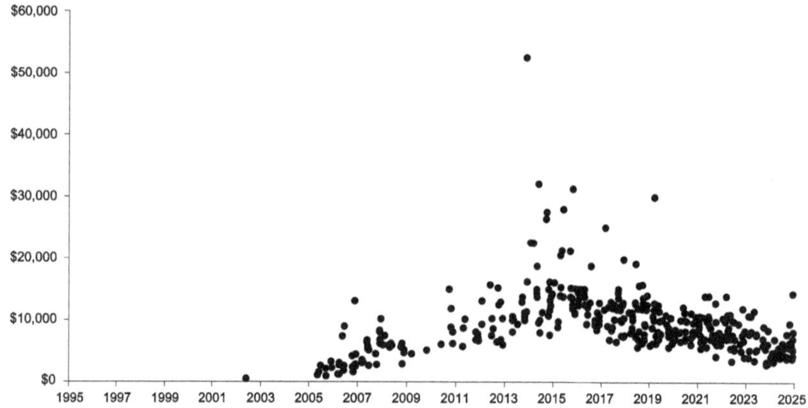

Fig. 3 Auction results recorded for Jeff Koons's *Balloon Dog (Plate)* Series. *Source* Artprice

grabbing event contributed to a significant bidding surge for the plate edition, well above its average market value of $10,600 recorded over the ten months preceding the sale.

While the day of the sale and the venue are key drivers of short-term price volatility, more enduring changes in an artwork's market value—those that can propel it sustainably into or out of the low-end segment—typically result from more substantive shifts. These transformations are generally rooted in new interpretations of a work, either due to evolving market tastes or the emergence of new information that significantly alters its desirability. Although such changes used to take time to be absorbed by the market, the current ecosystem is capable of reacting more swiftly to major developments in an artist's career, such as the receipt of a prestigious award, representation by a leading gallery, or a solo exhibition at a major museum.

The following cases trace individual lots through successive auction sales, exploring the mechanisms that appear to have most significantly altered their market value. The pace and degree of these shifts vary widely, and their origins range from spontaneous market intuition to deliberate intervention. A substantial increase in price can indeed result from the informed foresight of a collector, but also from the strategic efforts of an expert capable of identifying an undervalued work.

Investing in contemporary art involves inherent risk but may, as a result, yield extraordinary returns over the long term. The evolution in value of *Pumpkin* (1989), a small acrylic on canvas by Japanese artist Yayoi Kusama, exemplifies this potential. Initially acquired for $1,380 at Sotheby's Arcade in New York on 24 June 1998 (estimated between $1,000 and $1,500), the work was resold at Christie's New York on 13 May 2022 for $529,200. Over the 24 years between these transactions, Kusama's global reputation expanded significantly, bolstered by representation from Gagosian and later David Zwirner, alongside major institutional exhibitions at the Tate Modern, the Whitney Museum, and the Centre Pompidou.

Conversely, the low end absorbs works that once commanded high prices but have since fallen out of favor. Although the intrinsic quality of such works remains unchanged, collector demand may collapse. This downward trajectory is illustrated by abstract painter Ned Vena, whose *Untitled* (2012)—a large ink and acrylic on canvas—was acquired for $125,000 at Phillips New York on 12 November 2013, but sold for only $3,720 at Sotheby's Paris on 22 September 2022.

Incomplete or ambiguous information can introduce a degree of uncertainty that informed actors may exploit. When a work is reattributed to a more prominent artist (works by old masters usually do not bear a signature, so attribution to an artist must be made by experts based on stylistic and technical characteristics. This attribution can therefore always potentially change) or successfully presented to a more relevant audience, acquisitions at the low end can yield fantastic returns. In such cases, the expertise and institutional credibility of the new auction house often play a critical role in securing market acceptance of revised attributions.

One notable example is the *Portrait of Caterina Cornaro*, presented as a "Studio of Titian" painting in Christie's London online sale on 9 July 2021, where it achieved $69,300. Just a year earlier though, the same painting had been acquired for $6,300 at Gardiner Houlgate Auctions in Corsham, near Bath. At that time, the work had been catalogued as "After Titian," under the more descriptive title *Portrait of a Lady Said to Be Catherine Cornaro, the Last Monarch of Cyprus, Painted as Saint Catherine of Alexandria*—emphasizing the subject rather than the ambiguous attribution. Christie's likely contributed to a more refined scholarly positioning by conducting further research, and its institutional reputation helped reassure buyers by supporting the revised attribution to Titian's studio.

Official certificates of authenticity issued by an artist's studio or estate can also radically shift market perception—particularly in cases where the work's attribution is in doubt and forgery is a known concern. Consider *Radar Rat* (2002), an aerosol work on cardboard listed as "Attributed to Banksy" and sold for $2,500 by Millea Brothers Auctions on 26 March 2020 (New Jersey). A year later, on 13 May 2021, the same piece achieved $352,800 at Sotheby's New York. By then, it was accompanied by an official "Pest Control Certificate" from Banksy's authentication body and had been displayed in Sotheby's prestigious York Avenue building.

In other instances, avoiding the major hubs of the art market may paradoxically increase a work's appeal. This effect was demonstrated by the resale of *Bach Cantata*, a double-sided drawing by Austrian artist Oskar Kokoschka. Initially acquired for $2,375 at Christie's New York on 6 February 2013, the drawing was resold two years later, on 12 May 2015, at im Kinsky in Vienna for $114,400. Research conducted by im Kinsky to reconstruct the work's provenance elevated its significance and visibility, whereas it had received minimal attention in the earlier Christie's catalogue.

This study does not aim to provide an exhaustive list of factors that influence price variation, nor of the complex interactions among them. In several cases described above, location shifts were intertwined with scholarly advances. Each variable that contributes to an artwork's valuation can, in theory, be adjusted—either corrected or enhanced—in ways that affect market demand. In that sense, hedonic regression models, which quantify and weigh such variables, may help identify the factors with the greatest transformative potential. Ultimately, however, it is the intuitive eye of a seasoned collector or the analytical expertise of a connoisseur that determines which works, hidden within the vast heterogeneity of the low end, have yet to reveal their full market value.

6 Conclusion

The least expensive works of art are not only perceived as less attractive but are also those for which it is most difficult to gather clean and complete information. They bring together a multitude of qualities, are exchanged in every corner the world and can be described by imprecise or incomplete information. For reasons of convenience and methodological consistency, academic research has too often focused on paintings successfully sold at the most prestigious auction houses and scholars have shown a greater propensity to test the so-called "masterpiece effect" than to engage critically with the low end of the art market.

The first contribution of this article lies in its use of Artprice's fine art database, which compiles auction results for eleven categories of works without filtering based on price or estimated value. The initial investigation conducted here aims to examine the price structure of the global fine art auction market—both in terms of transaction volume and sales revenue—in order to establish a more robust and meaningful delineation of the low end. A price-segmented approach reveals a positively skewed distribution: in our dataset, sales under $100 are relatively rare, as auction houses generally avoid transactions too low to cover operational costs. However, slightly higher price ranges play a more significant role in shaping the auction market. In 2024, lots sold for less than $10,000 accounted for 91% of all fine art auction transactions and 9.5% of total revenue. This lower segment has shown sustained growth since the beginning of the twenty-first century, particularly with the rise of editions, whose circulation was further accelerated by the expansion of online sales during the COVID-19 pandemic.

Alternative definitions of the low end of the art market are possible, notably by lowering the price threshold to $1,000. This segment represents more than half of all transactions and undoubtedly conceals high-quality works. However, its weight in terms of total turnover remains marginal. This study therefore adheres to the conventional demarcation, grouping all transactions under $10,000. Crucially however, the findings of this study challenge the marginal status often assigned to this low-end segment. First, because of its structural significance within the market. Second, because it serves as a primary point of entry for new collectors, new artworks, and evolving buying behaviors. And third, because it constitutes one of the most dynamic and compelling parts of the art market—capable of generating both surprising discoveries and substantial capital gains.

An analysis of several concrete resale cases in which artworks experienced substantial price variation revealed two principal categories of value transformation. The first involves superficial changes linked to the influence of sale context and venue, which typically generate short-term volatility. The second involves deeper and more enduring revaluations, often driven by external factors such as changes in attribution or provenance.

Together, the two parts of this study lead to a common conclusion: the low end of the art market is both understudied and undervalued in academic literature and professional reporting. It deserves renewed analytical attention and a more prominent place in the empirical and theoretical discourse surrounding the economics of art.

References

Anderson, R. C. (1974). Paintings as investment. *Economic Inquiry, 12*(1), 13–26.

Ashenfelter, O., & Graddy, K. (2003). Auctions and the price of art. *Journal of Economic Literature, 41*(3), 763–786.

Mei, J., & Moses, M. (2002). Art as an investment and the underperformance of masterpieces (NYU Finance Working Paper No. 01-012).

Minguet, J. (2017). *The brief impact of art fairs on prices.* Scalpenti Editore.

Pesando, J. E. (1993). Art as an investment: The market for modern prints. *The American Economic Review, 83*(5), 1075–1089.

Renneboog, L., & Spaenjers, C. (2013). Buying beauty: On prices and returns in the art market. *Management Science, 59*(1), 36–53. https://doi.org/10.1287/mnsc.1120.1580

PART V

Mechanisms of Trust and Value Creation

A Study of the Low End of the Auction Market for Australian Indigenous Art

Tim R. L. Fry and Bronwyn Coate

1 Introduction

In this chapter we focus on understanding the low end of the secondary auction market for fine art using a large dataset comprised of Australian Indigenous art sold at auction between 1991 and 2020. In responding to the challenge of defining the low end of the market and recognizing the inadequacy of relying on realized prices alone as addressed in the introduction by Radermecker and Moureau, our novel approach draws attention to the role played by pre-sale estimates. We show how the presence of these estimates strategically influences buyers' perceptions about the value of various artworks offered for sale and examines how auction houses set pre-sale estimates differently for the low-end compared to the rest of the market. Our contribution is twofold. First, we outline an approach that uses pre-sale estimates to assist in identifying the low end as a frequently neglected segment of the market. Second, we show how the strategic behavior of auction houses differs within the various

T. R. L. Fry (✉)
Nottingham Trent University, Nottingham, UK
e-mail: tim.fry@ntu.ac.uk

B. Coate
RMIT University, Melbourne, Australia
e-mail: bronwyn.coate@rmit.edu.au

A.-S. V. Radermecker (ed.), *Low-End Markets for Art and Cultural Goods*, Cultural Economics & the Creative Economy,
https://doi.org/10.1007/978-3-032-27566-0_14

segments of the market and compare the low end relative to the middle and high-end segments of the market.

Pre-sale estimates which are presented in catalogues prior to auction, represent a publicly advertised price range based on expert appraisal and are designed to convey an indicative range which a given work offered for sale may be expected to fetch. Previous research on pre-sale estimates in relation to fine art has examined various questions related to issues such as whether they are unbiased predictors of price (Bauwens & Ginsburgh, 2000; Farrell & Fry, 2017) and their usefulness in identifying reserve prices that can assist with explaining non-sales (Czujack & Martins, 2004; McAndrew & Thompson, 2007). In this chapter we add to the ways that pre-sale information can be used to address questions concerning the workings of art auction markets. Insights gained from segmenting the Indigenous art market suggest that, at an aggregate level, the market might be better conceptualized as comprising several smaller but related markets that behave in distinct ways. Viewing the Indigenous art market in this way has the advantage of bringing greater insight to appreciate and better account for the heterogeneity that exists between works traded which also comes to characterize the way art markets themselves operate.

While most research concerning auction markets for art has traditionally focused on the high-end of the market where works by famous artists that typically sell for high prices, there is emerging research that takes a more encompassing view of art markets (by including a wider breath of works produced by a wider representation of artists), that lends support to segmenting art markets. For instance, using quantile regression models (Farrell & Fry, 2017) and finite mixture models (Fry, 2020), it has been shown using large representative samples that the auction market for Australian Indigenous art has clear price segmentation. Building on these contributions we show how pre-sale estimates can be used to effectively segment the auction market for Australian Indigenous art. An advantage pre-sale estimates offer over using hammer price when segmenting the market, is that works that fail to sell do not become excluded from the analysis and are able to be better recognized as constituting a special case of supply with implications for behavior within the market.

For our study of the low end, we use the case of the auction market for Australian Indigenous art which is sometimes also referred to as Australian

Aboriginal art.[1] This unique art market possesses some distinguishing features that make it ideally suited to our investigation of the low end. As a specific category of art, Indigenous art attracts widespread interest that tends to be more global in its reach compared to non-Indigenous Australian art which is principally produced, consumed and traded within the domestic Australian market. As a highly collectable commodity that possess both aesthetic qualities to drive utility as well as the potential to act as an investment, the market for Indigenous art rapidly expanded and had reached a state of maturity by the time data for our study picks up in the early 1990s. To provide further context about the history and development of the Indigenous art market, it is of interest to consider that despite being one of the longest continuous traditions of art in the world, dating back at least fifty millennia, the art of Indigenous Australia remained relatively unknown until the second half of the twentieth century (Caruana, 2003). As wider interest in Indigenous art by non-Indigenous people gained increasing momentum during the 1950s and 1960s and Indigenous cultural products shifted from being viewed as ethnographic curiosities to art, the market for Indigenous art gradually developed creating new opportunities for Indigenous artists as works produced left the communities where they were created and found their way into exhibitions and galleries in major cities across Australia and overseas.[2]

[1] Today the wide range of Australian Indigenous art traded and represented in major collections covers several distinctive styles featuring a variety of media and mediums as well as motifs and stylistic elements. Within the Indigenous art market there are three prominent styles of work, although it is important to note that while these styles have been popularized and found favor within the broader market for Indigenous art, by no means do they represent the entirety of what constitutes Indigenous art. The first dominant style is the Hermannsburg School typified by watercolor works on paper, often depicting Central Australian as exemplified in the paintings by Albert Namatjira. The second dominant style is found in the distinctive dot paintings that are synonymous with arguably the most influential movement in Aboriginal art, the Western Desert movement that first formed around the government settlement of Papunya in the Northern Territory. The third dominant style is associated with traditional art from the region of Arnhem Land in the north-eastern corner of the Northern Territory, that is typically produced on bark using a limited color palette derived from natural ochres, where the artist employs the use of 'rarrk' or cross-hatching to produce X-ray like representations of subjects that often depict animals and human figures in which bone structures and internal organs are clearly visible.

[2] While Australian Indigenous art began to appear in galleries, and was traded in the auction market as far back as the 1940s and 1950s (Morphy, 2001; Sloggett, 2014), the market—and in particular the secondary market grew substantially during the 1980s (Farrell & Fry, 2017; Fry, 2020).

While the imperatives to produce Indigenous art for traditional purposes continued (and continues), the expanded environment and art market in which Indigenous art circulates has been heralded as bringing Indigenous culture to the world.[3]

The chapter is structured as follows. In the next section we outline our approach to defining the low end and segmenting the auction market. We draw upon insights from literature that also informs conjectures we put forth about auction house practices and why we expect these to differ across different segments of the market when it comes to setting pre-sale estimates. In Sect. 3 we describe our data which comprises a large sample of Australian Indigenous art presented for auction over a 29-year period and present our methodology. Our extensive data set for the Indigenous art market enables us to effectively segment the market and draw comparison between high, middle and low segments which we present as part of our results in Sect. 4. Additionally, we analyze differences between auction houses across the three market segments and focus upon the strategic behavior observable with regards to the setting of pre-sale estimate. In Sect. 5 we discuss implications from the research focusing on how information conveyed in pre-sale estimates differs across segments of the art market—indicative of auction houses' strategic behavior. We suggest further avenues for research and conclude.

2 Defining the Low End of the Auction Market for Art

Defining the low-end of the art market in a robust and non-arbitrary manner is a major issue. In the case of the Australian Indigenous art market, empirical studies conducted to date have largely relied on samples reflecting sales by a limited number of blue-chip artists (e.g., Taylor & Coleman, 2011). Issues of data availability mean that it may be tempting to crudely define the top end of the market by concentrating on sales by reputed artists; however, such an approach risks muddying the waters to bias perceptions about not only the high end but also the low end of the market. For instance, as we find using an extensive dataset based on sales by over 2,000 Indigenous artists, blue-chip artists invariably have works

[3] The growing market and interest in Indigenous art has also attracted some controversy at different points in time centered around the authenticity of works, including the black art scandals in the late 1990s and more recently the white hands black art scandal in the early 2020s (see Coslor & Fry, 2024).

traded outside the high end when segmentation is based on either realized price or pre-sale estimates. As such selecting a narrow sample based on convenience should invite caution when it comes to drawing generalizations about the broader market and its high and low ends.

Leifer and White (2004) show that, for markets with differentiated products in which expert evaluations (pre-sale price estimates) may differ, it is appropriate to segment. Given then the heterogenous characteristics of art, segmenting the market to reflect its constituent parts makes sense. Yet less apparent is the question, also posed in the introduction to this volume, of how precisely to segment. What criteria is best applied to segment a given market in a meaningful, transparent and consistent way? Simply segmenting a large market, such as a national art market or part of it such as the Australian Indigenous art market, based on realized prices is problematic insofar that works that may have depreciated in value to the point of being worthless or which fail to sell will be excluded in the absence of any notable price. Excluding works that fail to sell ignores an important aspect of how art markets function and effectively understates in volume terms, the full extent of the segment in question.

Our approach involves using pre-sale estimates rather than prices per se, to classify expert opinion and market perceptions about the worth of disparate artworks of different quality, from different time periods and by artists of varying degrees of repute. Pre-sale estimates are routinely provided by the auction houses—indeed 97.24% of the works offered in our data which comprises over 47,000 observations of Australian Indigenous art works put up for auction have a pre-sale estimate. In looking closely at the data, we find that beyond sharing a similar level of pre-sales estimate, there is little that unites works in the low end in terms of their work level attributes. For Australian Aboriginal art at least, the market does not delineate high, mid and low ends based on features such as the style of art, iconography and motifs that are used and whether an artist is linked to a particular school or movement. However, authenticity is a quality that appears to matter for the high end.[4] For the low end, a feature that is noteworthy concerns the high prevalence of sales by artists with a single or very few sales compared to the high end. This features

[4] Indicative of the importance attached to authenticating works since the market exploded throughout the 1990s and into the early 2000s, the Indigenous Art Code introduced in 2009, brought in protocols designed to protect First Nations Cultural and Intellectual Property.

makes information about the low end of the art market more dispersed meaning supporting the view put forward by Radermecker and Moureau that information failures may be more acute in the low end of the market. This is further indicative of the heterogenous nature of the art market and, in particular, the low end. As such we assert that despite the heterogeneity of works traded, sharing a similar level of pre-sale estimate provides a convenient and meaningful way to classify and segment the market and for our purposes to distinguish the low-end.

We conjecture that a defining characteristic for works in the low-end of the market where the likelihood of future marketability is negligible, is that pre-sale estimates will be predictably set higher compared to other market segments. Given evidence that is overwhelming based on studies focused on the high end that find pre-sale estimates are biased predictors of price that are typically set low, with some sales data even attesting that reserve prices are below the low estimate (McAndrew & Thompson, 2003), we expect to find differences in the degree of bias in setting pre-sales estimates across the three segments of the market we define. Our hypothesis is that deflating pre-sale estimates to the extent witnessed in other higher market segments would function as a warning to prospective buyers that works offered are of low quality and hence risk decreasing demand further to drive prices even lower. As such a more profitable strategy for auction houses dealing with low end art is to provide a more transparent signal, reflecting a more honest pre-sale estimate compared to the pre-sale estimates in the high and middle segments. As such we expect that pre-sale estimates in the low-end of the market are typically less biased and closer to actual prices unlike the top-end of the market where they tend to be consistently understated to attract buyer interest and stimulate bidding (Farrell & Fry, 2017; Fry, 2020).

If, in fact, pre-sale estimates do differ in their degree of bias across different market segments, this indicates that they perform a different signaling task across the distinct segments of the market, meaning that the use of pre-sale estimates to define segments, including the bottom-end is not merely an arbitrary exercise but also has salience if we are interested in understanding the behavior of the market (and its segments) and the ways in which auction houses operate. The future valuation of works is particularly pointed at the low end of the market. This is because at the low end of the market, the quality of a work is not simply uncertain but also highly risky (D'Souza & Prentice, 2002). For works in the low end, the likelihood of having enduring value over time is less than the middle and top end of the market as works once valued may depreciate and become "worthless" as the fate of the overwhelming majority of art is destined to be (Grampp, 1989). Hence pre-sales estimates may attempt to mask or camouflage this trajectory towards worthlessness by erring towards being less deflated and closer to reality compared to other market segments in order to attract interest. As such rather than having a lower estimate to attract interest as occurs in other market segments, the estimates provided for works offered in the low end may be set closer to what experts expect a work will fetch in a strategic move designed by the auction house to increase the likelihood of a sale occurring. In this way, pre-sale estimates that are "too low," like in other market segments, might inadvertently signal to warn potential buyers that the work is in fact "rubbish" (Thompson, 1979) that results in a prospective buyer dismissing a work on this basis.

3 Data and Methodology

The data we use comprises Australian Indigenous art works traded at auction over the period 1991 to 2020 sourced from *Australian Art Sales Digest* (AASD) (Furphy, 2021) and is comprised of 47,005 art works offered for sale created by over 2,000 artists. Most of the works traded are classified as paintings; however, the market also includes works executed on bark as well as some decorative objects including pottery and totems. Importantly our dataset includes works that fail to sell. The inclusion of buy-ins compliments understanding about the workings of the art auction market including strategic behavior on the part of auction houses as we can compare not only prices realized but clearance rates. Of the works offered at auction, 29,469 (62.7%) are sold with the total realized (hammer) value of these sales over the period equating to 210.3 million Australian dollars.

Using data that encompasses the Indigenous art market, we address our research questions which are stated as follows:

(i) How well do pre-sales estimates perform in segmenting the market and do the resulting segments show evidence of being sufficiently distinct to justify segmentation in the first place?
(ii) Do auction houses engage in strategic behavior in setting pre-sale estimates across different segments of the Indigenous art auction market, and if so what is the nature of this behavior?

To address these questions, we first segment the market based on the mid-point of the high and low estimates that together form the pre-sale estimate. We then divide the sample into quartiles defining the low end as the bottom quartile of mid-point pre-sale estimates, while the middle market comprises the sales occurring in the second and third quartiles while finally the top end of the market represents works with the highest mid-point pre-sales estimates.

These data, categorized in this manner to define three segments—low end, middle and top end, are then analyzed using a Heckman selectivity model (Heckman, 1976, 1979). This approach enables us to investigate the effect that pre-sale estimates have on the resultant hammer prices observed at auction as well as the rates of sale across lots within each of the three different segments we identify. We are also interested in examining whether the types of artists represented within the various segments differ in any discernible way. While characteristics associated with the artist are an important determinant of price (Anderson, 1974; Ashenfelter & Graddy, 2003), within the market for Indigenous art we observe a high degree of price variability across many individual artists' oeuvres. For instance, prolific artists such as Clifford Possum Tjapaltjarri who has the highest valued work in the dataset—*Warlugulong* created in 1977 and sold in July 2007 for a hammer price of $2 million Australian dollars by Sotheby's in Melbourne—also has works that appear in the middle and lower ends of the market. This characteristic of the market whereby variability exists not only between different artists but also within a given artists body of works that are traded, supports our approach of looking to pre-sale estimates rather than characteristics associated with the artist alone in identifying the low end that may constitute works by well-known and lesser-known artists. We categorize the artists within our dataset as well unknown and lesser known based on whether a given artist's name appears and is referenced in the Oxford Art Online database (Rodenbeck & Olivier, 2021). Applying this criterion across our sample of artists, we find that 28 (0.8%) are well-known and account for 3.2% of all works offered and 3.4% of all works sold.

In our testing that follows and results presented in the next section that aims to understand how the low-end of the market is different (or not) from the rest of the Australian Indigenous art market, our analysis draws attention to the following: (i) comparing pre-sale estimates and the effect these have on the lots offered and lots unsold and (ii) comparing practices across different auction houses in terms of setting pre-sale estimates across different segments of the market.

4 Empirical Analysis and Findings

Table 1 presents summary statistics for the three segments of the market—low end, middle and top end—that we identify from our data set which comprises just over 47,000 observations for Indigenous art works offered for sale between 1991 and 2020. Across each of the three segments the clearance rate is highest in the low end with 72.6% of works selling. This may be due to works offered for sale in this segment having either negligible or no reserves in place. It is of interest to compare the average mid-point of the pre-sale estimate across each segment relative to the average realized price. In doing so, we find that the gap between average pre-sale estimates and average prices widens as we shift from the low end towards the high end of the market. For the low end of the market, pre-sale estimates are on average 6% below average hammer prices with this increasing to 9.7% below and 12% below respectively for the middle and high ends of the market. As expected, the low end of the market accounts for just under 2% of the total value of sales despite contributing around

Table 1 Descriptive statistics by segment

	Low End	*Middle*	*Top End*
Number of works offered	12,126	21,527	13,352
Number of works sold	8,8	12,437	8,152
Clearance rate (%)	72.6	57.8	61.1
Average pre-sale estimate	\$500	\$2,925	\$24,170
Average hammer price	\$470	\$2,640	\$21,260
Percentage of total market value	1.9	15.7	82.4
Percentage of works with unknown artist	3.5	2.2	1.6
Number of artists with works offered	2,326	2,298	1,005
Number of artists with works sold	1,919	1,736	789
Artist clearance rate	82.5	75.5	78.5
Number of famous artists with works offered	27	27	28
Percentage of works offered by famous artists	3.1	10.0	29.1
Number of auction houses	50	53	56
Number of locations	11	13	14
Number of countries	3	5	5

Source Authors

a quarter of the total volume of works offered. Expectedly, we observe that from defining our market segments based on pre-sale estimates, the presence of unknown artists is most apparent in the low end particularly compared to the high end. It is also worth noting that, while usually in the high end we would expect there to be possibly no unknown artists, the character of Indigenous art, particularly for traditional works executed on media like bark that have ethnographic and historic value, may be by artists whose identity is unknown. Another point to note when comparing across segments concerns the number of artists and the clearance rates observed at the artist level. Interestingly, while the low end has the highest presence of artists, it also has the highest artist clearance rate, although this may be driven by the fact that artists in the low end of the market typically have—on average—a smaller number of works offered for sale over the period of our analysis.

In terms of the presence of sales venues across different market segments, as Table 1 shows, the numbers of auction houses are similar across segments. However, while this suggests that auction houses that trade in Indigenous art tend to do so across all segments within the entire market, Table 2 reveals that many auction houses dominate in a particular segment of the market, even if they trade across all the three segments we identify. For instance, in the case of Sotheby's, an auction house that in Australia conducted specialist auctions dedicated to fine Aboriginal Art, around half of its total sales are concentrated in the top end with only a small share of works falling into the low end. At the other end of the spectrum, the volume of works put up for auction at lower tier auction houses, such as Leonard Joel, are concentrated in the low end of the market.

In Table 3, we present results that apply a Heckman selectivity model (Heckman, 1976, 1979) to our data, scaling our hammer and presale estimate values to AU$10,000 across each of the three segments to test the effect that pre-sale estimates have on hammer prices as well as a probit model to predict the likelihood that a given lot sells at auction. The Heckman model also allows us to test whether the clearance (Sale (Y/N)) equation and the hammer value equation are independent. Interestingly, we see that the two are independent for the low end but not for the middle or top end of the market.

From the modelling, it is observed—as expected—that across all market segments, the inclusion of pre-sale estimates in the models is highly significant. In the lower end of the market, however, pre-sale estimates tend to be closest to realized hammer prices: specifically, as the midpoint

Table 2 Number of works offered by auction house

	Low End	*Middle*	*Top End*	*Total*
Sotheby's	458	3,275	3,405	7,138
Leonard Joel	2,084	2,505	767	5,356
Lawson ~ Menzies	688	2,154	1,215	4,057
Lawsons	1,793	2,658	499	495
Deutscher and Hackett	61	1,256	1,527	2,844
Mossgreen Auctions	442	1,604	904	295
Bonham's	209	904	668	1,781
Davidson Auctions	1,127	377	65	1,569
Elder Fine Art	797	819	262	1,878
Theodore Bruce Auctions	1,037	747	196	198
Shapiro Auctioneers	354	926	403	1,683
Bonham's & Goodman	396	525	330	1,251
Christie's	88	432	427	947
Deutscher ~ Menzies	85	542	366	993
GFL Fine Art	169	301	155	625
Cooee Art Marketplace	1	144	440	585
McKenzies Auctioneers	392	184	19	595
Philips Auctions Australia	282	315	99	696
Other auction houses	1,663	1,859	1,605	5,127
Total	12,126	21,527	13,352	47,005

Source Authors

of the pre-sale estimate increases by 0.9%, hammer prices in this segment rise on average by 1%. The finding that pre-sale estimates are closest to hammer prices at the low end may reflect the fact that this segment is characterized by greater information asymmetry than the others.

The results of the probit model estimating whether a work sold reveal further distinctions across the market's three segments. Across all segments, we find highly significant results between the pre-sales estimate and whether a work sells, although interestingly this effect varies considerably across the segments. In the high-end segment, there is a small positive effect on the likelihood a work sells as the mid-point of the pre-sale estimate increases which stands in contrast to the middle and low ends where increasing mid-point estimates reduce the likelihood of a sale occurring. In comparing the size of the coefficient, this is most profound in the low end. Furthermore, in modelling the quadratic function for the mid-point of pre-sale estimates, we find that, in the low end and middle segments, the relationship between pre-sale estimates and the likelihood of

Table 3 Heckman Selectivity Model Estimation Results

Hammer Value	*Low End*			*Middle*			*Top end*		
	Cofficient	*s.e.*		*Cofficient*	*s.e.*		*Cofficient*	*s.e.*	
pre-sale estimate	0.9022	0.0265	***	0.8932	0.0138	***	0.8499	0.0301	***
Auction House: Reference Others									
Sotheby's	0.0260	0.0067	***	0.0453	0.0076	***	0.8354	0.1110	***
Leonard Joel	0.0040	0.0011	***	−0.0126	0.0070	*	−0.1345	0.1196	
Lawson ~ Menzies	0.0036	0.0022		−0.0513	0.0075	***	0.1754	0.1261	
Lawsons	−0.0010	0.0010		−0.0150	0.0068	**	−0.3807	0.1484	**
Deutscher and Hackett	0.0207	0.0098	**	0.0166	0.0079	**	0.6577	0.1081	***
Mossgreen Auctions	0.0156	0.0029	***	0.0314	0.0102	***	0.0664	0.1138	
Bonham's	0.0147	0.0039	***	0.0304	0.0094	***	0.7544	0.1371	***
Davidson Auctions	0.0018	0.0011	*	−0.0122	0.0086		0.2382	0.2491	
Elder Fine Art	0.0031	0.0016	*	−0.0279	0.0082	***	0.2100	0.1403	
Theodore Bruce Auctions	0.0018	0.0014		−0.0367	0.0076	***	−0.9862	0.2014	***
Shapiro Auctioneers	0.0167	0.0038	***	0.0300	0.0105	***	−0.3170	0.1450	***
Bonham's & Goodman	0.0009	0.0023		−0.0040	0.0136		−0.5259	0.1818	***
Christie's	0.0452	0.0077	***	0.0329	0.0118	***	0.0346	0.1522	
Deutscher ~ Menzies	0.0051	0.0037		0.0023	0.0097		0.4962	0.1488	***
GFL Fine Art	−0.0009	0.0020		−0.0116	0.0075		0.5473	0.1860	***
Cooee Art Marketplace	0.0387	0.0012	***	−0.0061	0.0132		0.6428	0.1271	***
McKenzies Auctioneers	0.0027	0.0019		−0.0084	0.0081		0.4931	0.3581	
Philips Auctions Australia	0.0008	0.0015		−0.0170	0.0139		−0.3893	0.2315	*
Entry in Oxford Art Online (Y/N)	0.0113	0.0061		0.0358	0.0065	***	0.3508	0.0640	***
Constant	0.0002	0.0012		0.0068	0.0072		−1.4552	0.1543	***

(continued)

Table 3 (continued)

Hammer Value	*Low End*			*Middle*			*Top end*		
	Cofficient	*s.e.*		*Cofficient*	*s.e.*		*Cofficient*	*s.e.*	
Sold (Y/N)									
pre-sale estimate	−18.6416	1.2016	***	−1.8656	0.1444	***	0.0792	0.0131	***
pre-sale estimate^2	69.7059	7.1314	***	1.2758	0.1547	***	0.0003	0.0003	
Auction House: Reference Others									
Sotheby's	0.5416	0.0753	***	0.4859	0.0373	***	0.2326	0.0485	***
Leonard Joel	0.3355	0.0453	***	−0.0078	0.0390		−0.1406	0.0582	**
Lawson ~ Menzies	0.5948	0.0661	***	0.4623	0.0407	***	0.1806	0.0712	**
Lawsons	−0.1856	0.0449	***	−0.3223	0.0399	***	−0.2519	0.0728	***
Deutscher and Hackett	1.0419	0.2043	***	0.8065	0.0485	***	0.2054	0.0499	***
Mossgreen Auctions	0.2459	0.0726	***	0.2388	0.0434	***	−0.0948	0.0570	*
Bonham's	1.1412	0.1378	***	0.8538	0.0559	***	0.2219	0.0607	***
Davidson Auctions	0.3058	0.0550	***	0.2826	0.0730	***	0.0479	0.1253	
Elder Fine Art	0.1826	0.0586	***	0.1900	0.0529	***	0.0019	0.0686	
Theodore Bruce Auctions	0.1989	0.0540	***	−0.2912	0.0553	***	−0.5536	0.0958	***
Shapiro Auctioneers	−0.0406	0.0770		0.1997	0.0506	***	−0.2912	0.0706	***
Bonham's & Goodman	0.4576	0.0772	***	−0.0628	0.0631		−0.3673	0.0877	***
Christie's	0.8188	0.1666	***	0.4347	0.0688	***	−0.1285	0.0694	*
Deutscher ~ Menzies	0.5653	0.1642	***	0.6189	0.0651	***	0.1203	0.0713	*
GFL Fine Art	0.8222	0.1315	***	0.7914	0.0885	***	0.1664	0.0914	*
Cooee Art Marketplace	5.3715	0.1831	***	0.9668	0.1250	***	0.2560	0.0570	***
McKenzies Auctioneers	0.4646	0.0802	***	0.1095	0.0981		0.1075	0.1803	

(continued)

Table 3 (continued)

Hammer Value	*Low End*			*Middle*			*Top end*		
	Cofficient	*s.e.*		*Cofficient*	*s.e.*		*Cofficient*	*s.e.*	
Philips Auctions Australia	−0.2517	0.0845	***	−0.1542	0.0785	**	−0.2272	0.1137	**
Entry in Oxford Art Online (Y/N)	0.1640	0.0764	**	0.1833	0.0304	***	0.1301	0.0255	***
Constant	1.1165	0.0494	***	0.3460	0.0395	***	−0.3150	0.0677	***
Log Pseudo-likelihood	−8945.714			−9293.116			−19,971.780		
Wald Test of Independence	0.430			12.490			156.940		
p-value	0.5142			0.0004			0.0000		

Source Authors

a sale occurring is non-linear while in the high end of the market results do not support this. For the low end, as the pre-sale estimate increases, the effect this has on reducing the likelihood of a non-sale increases at a decreasing rate.

The measure we use to reflect artist renown, namely whether an artist is recorded in Oxford Art online, is significant for the low end although it is also highly significant for both the middle and high ends of the market. The marginal effects from the Heckman model (that incorporate both the clearance and value components) show that, overall, hammer value increases by 24.0% for the low-end, by 16.5% for the top-end and by 12.3% for the middle of the market. In terms of auction houses, we saw in Table 2 that there was specialization within sectors by the houses, with Sotheby's focused on the top-end and Lawsons in the low-end. The Heckman model estimates show that works offered in Sotheby's have both increased probability of sale and higher hammer values in all segments and, conversely, works offered in Lawsons have both decreased probability of sale and lower hammer values in all segments. This suggests that there may also be a reputation effect for the auction houses. Indeed, well established auction houses may seek a reputation for accuracy. Future work might investigate differences between such auction houses by focusing upon the larger auction houses operating across all segments but with focus on particular segments.

5 Conclusion

Using an extensive dataset that covers Australian Indigenous art sold at auction over almost 30 years, we have presented evidence to show how pre-sale estimates can be used to effectively segment the market and identify the low end; and furthermore, we have revealed evidence about the strategic behavior by auction houses in setting pre-sale estimates across different segments of the market. As such, this study of the auction market for Australian Indigenous art provides new insights into the strategic role of pre-sale estimates and their effective use in segmenting the market. By highlighting the differences in auction house behavior and the unique characteristics at the low end of the market, the research expands our understanding of how art markets function beyond just high-value transactions.

One of the key implications is that pre-sale estimates play a crucial role in shaping buyer perceptions, especially in markets where the quality and future marketability of art works are uncertain. Within the low end of the market, we find that auction houses set higher price estimates compared to the middle and top ends. To explain this behavior, we conjecture that by setting higher pre-sale estimates on low valued works, auction houses can minimise the risk of devaluing art works further and maintain buyer interest, suggesting a deliberate strategy to mask potential quality issues at the low end of the market. This conjecture is consistent with the view offered by Radermecker and Moureau that recognizes auction houses as key market influencers whose behaviors, including in setting estimates, ultimately affects buyer perceptions and segment composition. Ideally future research would pick up on the conjecture offered to test whether the reasoning suggested for different practices in setting pre-sale estimates is supported by those at the coalface involved in setting the estimates. Most likely the type of evidence needed to understand auction houses strategic behavior and decision making with regards to pre-sale estimates would come from a variety of sources including qualitative data obtained from hearing from experts involved in setting estimates.

Beyond deepening understanding of auction houses strategic behavior, the findings open other avenues for future research. One area worth exploring is how differing pre-sale strategies impact long-term market trends and how these play out at the individual artist level, particularly for Indigenous artists whose reputations are not settled and whose work may fluctuate significantly in value over time. Relatedly, future research to examine artist attrition rates as the composition of works traded changes over time, and some artists effectively cease to be traded, would add to understanding how artwork that were once considered valuable become "worthless" or "rubbish" (Grampp, 1989; Thompson, 1979). Another promising direction would be to investigate the role of digital platforms, such as Invaluable, and to examine how they might influence pre-sale estimates in the art auction market.

As we have shown, segmenting the market is relevant for several reasons. Firstly, excessive aggregation in large datasets that treat the art market as a single entity is problematic. In practice, broadly defined markets, such as the Australian Indigenous art market, are more accurately able to be understood as comprising multiple smaller markets that are distinct and behave differently. Secondly, market segmentation can help shed light on previously overlooked parts of the market such as the low end. Like much research using auction market data, including other studies about the Australian Indigenous art, the focus has been on the top end (e.g., Farrell et al., 2018, 2021). While attention given to the top end is often justified by the concentration of such markets where works by a few artists account for a large proportion of the total market value, they neglect to shed light on the market that exists for the majority of works traded that fetch little compared to the top end of the market. Thus, little is known about how the low end of the auction market may work in practice.

By segmenting the market using pre-sale estimates rather than realized prices, our research provides insights into overlooked market dynamics and the behavior of auction houses. This segmentation offers a nuanced understanding of the distinct roles pre-sale estimates play across market segments, particularly in managing perceptions of art with uncertain futures.

References

Anderson, R. C. (1974). Paintings as an investment. *Economic Inquiry, 12*(1), 13–26.

Ashenfelter, O., & Graddy, K. (2003). Auctions and the price of art. *Journal of Economic Literature, 41*(3), 763–786.

Bauwens, L., & Ginsburgh, V. (2000). Art experts and auctions: Are pre-sale estimates unbiased and fully informative? *Recherches Économiques de Louvain/ Louvain Economic Review, 66*(2), 131–144.

Caruana, W. (2003). *Aboriginal art* (New ed.). Thames & Hudson.

Coslor, E., & Fry, T. R. L. (2024). Misattribution stigma and contagion: How did the art auction market react to Australian "Black art scandals"? *Journal of Cultural Economics*. https://doi.org/10.1007/s10824-024-09526-w

Czujack, C., & Martins, M. F. O. (2004). Do art specialists form unbiased pre-sale estimates? An application for Picasso paintings. *Applied Economics Letters, 11*(4), 245–249.

D'Souza, C., & Prentice, D. (2002). Auctioneer strategy and pricing: Evidence from an art auction. *Marketing Intelligence & Planning, 20*(7), 417–427.

Farrell, L., Fry, J. M., & Fry, T. R. L. (2018). Determinants of sales and price at auction for three Australian Indigenous artists: To pool or not to pool? *Journal of Cultural Economics, 42*(3), 507–520.

Farrell, L., Fry, J. M., & Fry, T. R. L. (2021). Gender differences in hammer prices for Australian Indigenous art. *Journal of Cultural Economics, 45*, 1–12.

Farrell, L., & Fry, T. R. L. (2017). Pre-sale information and hammer prices for Australian Indigenous artists. *Scottish Journal of Political Economy, 64*(2), 483–500.

Fry, T. R. L. (2020). Heterogeneity in auction price distributions for Australian Indigenous artists. *The Economic Record*, *96*, 177–186.

Furphy, J. (2021). *Australian Art Sales Digest*. http://www.aasd.com.au

Grampp, W. D. (1989). *Pricing the priceless: Art, artists, and economics*. Basic Books.

Heckman, J. J. (1976). The common structure of statistical models of truncation, sample selection and limited dependent variables and a simple estimator for such models. *Annals of Economic and Social Measurement*, *5*(4), 475–492.

Heckman, J. J. (1979). Sample selection bias as a specification error. *Econometrica*, *47*(1), 153–161.

Leifer, E. M., & White, H. C. (2004). A structural approach to markets. In F. Dobbin (Ed.), *The new economic sociology: A reader* (85–108). Princeton University Press.

McAndrew, C., & Thompson, R. (2003). Pre-sale estimates, risk analysis, and the investment quality of fine art. In V. A. Ginsburgh & D. Throsby (Eds.), *Handbook of the economics of art and culture* (Vol. 1, pp. 571–603). Elsevier.

McAndrew, C., & Thompson, R. (2007). The collateral value of fine art. *Journal of Banking & Finance*, *31*(3), 589–607.

Morphy, H. (2001). Seeing Aboriginal art in the gallery. *Humanities Research*, *8*(1), 37–50.

Rodenbeck, J., & Olivier, V. C. (Eds.). (2021). *Oxford Art Online*. Oxford University Press. https://www.oxfordartonline.com/

Sloggett, R. (2014). Has Aboriginal art a future? Leonhard Adam's essay and the development of the Australian Aboriginal art market. *International Journal of Cultural Studies*, *18*(2), 167–183.

Taylor, D., & Coleman, L. (2011). Price determinants of Aboriginal art, and its role as an alternative asset class. *Journal of Banking & Finance*, *35*(6), 1519–1529.

Thompson, M. (1979). *Rubbish theory: The creation and destruction of value*. Oxford University Press.

From Canvas to Confidence: How Trust Shapes Barcelona's Low-End Art Market

Isabel Causadias

1 Introduction

Trust is a fundamental structural mechanism in art markets, particularly in the primary sector and its lower segments. While its role has been widely acknowledged, academic research has predominantly focused on the secondary market, where provenance tracking and institutional validation facilitate price formation (Moulin, 1987; Radermecker, 2022). In contrast, trust in the primary market—especially within its lower tiers—remains underexplored, despite being a core element that structures transactions, sustains professional networks, and enables market participation in the absence of formalized institutions.

In this study, trust is explicitly defined as a relational expectation within interpersonal networks that reduces economic uncertainty, facilitating transactions despite limited institutional guarantees. Unlike trust in upper art-market segments, primarily grounded in formal certifications and provenance records, trust in Barcelona's low-end primary art market operates predominantly through informal reputation mechanisms, direct interpersonal relationships, and repeated reciprocal exchanges.

This study examines how trust operates in the low-end primary art market of Barcelona, a segment characterized by high information

I. Causadias (✉)
University of Barcelona, Barcelona, Spain
e-mail: icausadias@ub.edu

A.-S. V. Radermecker (ed.), *Low-End Markets for Art and Cultural Goods*, Cultural Economics & the Creative Economy,
https://doi.org/10.1007/978-3-032-27566-0_15

asymmetry, limited institutional support, and economic instability. It adopts an approach rooted in economic sociology, which conceptualizes markets as embedded social networks where economic exchanges are shaped by interpersonal relationships, reputation systems, and symbolic capital (Granovetter, 1985; Bourdieu, 1993; Velthuis, 2005). Specifically, trust is analyzed both as a market signal that mitigates uncertainty and as a form of social capital that provides access to economic and symbolic resources (Casson & Della Giusta, 2006; de Bliek 2015).

Despite the assumption that low-end market players—such as galleries, dealers, and artists—are inherently "less branded" than their high-end counterparts, empirical evidence suggests that trust mechanisms within this segment vary significantly. Some low-end galleries establish enduring reputations, attract a stable clientele, and develop artist representation strategies that resemble those in higher-end markets. This challenges the idea that trust functions solely as a substitute for institutional validation and invites further inquiry into the vertical segmentation of the art market.

Barcelona provides a compelling case study for investigating these dynamics. Although considered Spain's second-largest art market, its gallery sector remains underexplored from an economic and sociological perspective (Ulldemolins, 2012). Institutional reports by the Catalan Department of Culture offer only a partial overview, often excluding low-end galleries that do not participate in official associations. This statistical invisibility reinforces the perception that the low-end market is marginal, despite its significant role in Barcelona's art economy. To address these gaps, this study explores three key research questions:

i) How do low-end galleries construct and maintain trust among artists, buyers, and professional networks?
ii) What valuation and reputation mechanisms replace institutional validation in this market segment?
iii) How do trust dynamics in the lower tiers of the primary art market differ from those in the high-end art market?

To answer these questions, the research follows a qualitative methodology based on semi-structured interviews with gallery owners and art professionals, direct observation of exhibition spaces and art fairs, and documentary analysis of market reports and promotional materials. By integrating these methods, the study aims to uncover the processes through which trust is built, maintained, and operationalized in a market with weak institutional frameworks.

This research contributes to broader discussions on market stratification in art market studies, challenging the assumption that low-end galleries are inherently precarious or lack brand identity. Instead, it highlights how some galleries—despite operating with fewer financial resources—leverage reputation, social capital, and trust-based networks to secure long-term sustainability.

2 Literature Review

Trust has long been recognized as a fundamental mechanism in market functioning, particularly in sectors characterized by information asymmetry and structural uncertainty, as noted by Akerlof (1978), Rousseau et al. (1998) and Fehr (2009). The art market exemplifies such an environment, where trust plays a crucial role in structuring commercial and institutional relationships. The absence of objective reference points for determining the value of an artwork, combined with the intangible nature of prestige and reputation, requires market participants to rely on social networks and institutional frameworks to legitimize artists, establish pricing mechanisms, and ensure transactional continuity. These dynamics are particularly salient in cultural and art markets, where valuation relies less on functional attributes and more on symbolic and reputational processes.

Following Casson and Della Giusta (2006), trust within economic contexts functions as an essential coordination mechanism, particularly vital in markets with high information asymmetry and structural uncertainty. In cultural markets, as emphasized by Benhamou (2011a, 2011b), trust compensates for the inherent instability and subjective valuation of cultural goods. This dynamic is particularly pronounced in cultural markets, where valuation remains inherently subjective and unstable, reinforcing the role of trust as a regulatory mechanism (Benhamou, 2011a, 2011b). As Möllering (2006, 2012) and Bianchi (2015) have highlighted, trust is not merely a risk-reduction strategy but a structural component that underpins market interactions.

Within the field of cultural economics, scholars have extensively examined the role of trust in price formation and reputation building in the art market. Li et al. (2024) argue that the willingness to trust an artist or an artwork is shaped by factors such as the artist's career trajectory, exhibition history, and coverage in specialized literature. This aligns with

Van der Ploeg's (2002) assertion that trust functions as a valuation mechanism in markets where objective economic benchmarks are scarce. Similarly, Gambetta (1988) and Adler (2001) define trust as a coordinating force that operates alongside price mechanisms and institutional authority, reinforcing its structural importance in market organization.

A key distinction emerging from the literature is the differentiation between interpersonal trust and institutional trust. Coleman (1990a, 1990b) identifies three principal mechanisms through which trust is established: direct interpersonal interactions, reputation within a network, and institutional influences on market behavior. This distinction is particularly relevant in understanding how trust functions across different segments of the art market. In the upper segment, trust tends to be institutionalized through certifications, auction results, and formal validation procedures. In the lower segment, however, what functions as trust often emerges from informal coordination mechanisms—such as repeated interpersonal exchanges, local reputation, and social proximity (Choi and Storr, 2020)—that help actors reduce uncertainty and make decisions under conditions of incomplete information.[1] While these may not constitute 'trust' in its strictest calculative sense, they act as substitutes for institutional guarantees in low-information contexts, enabling cooperative behavior through embedded social norms and expectations.

Beyond its role in economic transactions, trust has been examined from a broader perspective regarding its function in market organization. Fukuyama (1995; 2001) argues that trust is a fundamental element of social cohesion and a key driver of efficient economic exchanges. This principle is particularly relevant in the art market, where the sustainability of transactions depends on the strength of relationships between artists, gallerists, and collectors. Lin (1999) and Bourdieu (1980) further emphasize that trust facilitates information flow and reinforces positions within market networks. In this sense, trust does not equate to social or cultural capital but interacts with them: social capital refers to the resources embedded in networks of relationships (Coleman, 1988; Putnam, 1994),

[1] The notion of trust in low-end markets may not always meet the criteria of instrumental or calculative trust (Williamson, 1993; Coleman, 1990a, 1990b), where actors assess the risk-reward ratio of cooperation. Rather, it aligns more closely with relational and social-embedded forms of trust, where expectations of trustworthiness are based on reputation, mutual identification, and shared norms (Putnam et al., 1993; Sztompka, 1999; Nooteboom, 2002). These mechanisms often serve to reduce transaction costs and uncertainty in the absence of formal enforcement, acting less as hard trust and more as informal proxies for decision-making under bounded rationality and incomplete information.

while cultural capital denotes specialized knowledge, symbolic recognition, and embodied artistic competencies. Trust serves as a relational mechanism that mediates access to both, helping define participation thresholds and cooperation levels within specific segments of the art market.[2]

Recent studies have also underscored the relationship between trust and vulnerability in economic decision-making. Hamm et al. (2024) argue that trust is not merely a risk-mitigation strategy but is also shaped by the perceived vulnerability of market participants. This is particularly relevant in the lower end of the art market, where galleries operate with limited financial safeguards and rely heavily on personal relationships to maintain business stability.

From an economic perspective, trust acts as a coordination mechanism that reduces uncertainty and facilitates transactions in markets characterized by information asymmetries and the absence of objective valuation standards (Van der Ploeg, 2002, Fehr, 2009). From a sociological standpoint, trust operates within social networks but should not be conflated with social capital itself. Rather, it constitutes one of the relational norms that enables social capital to function (Coleman, 1990a, 1990b; Fukuyama, 1995). Trust allows networks to support cooperative behavior and to distribute symbolic and economic resources, yet it is not the structure of the network per se. These complementary perspectives help explain how trust operates across different segments of the art market, from highly formalized institutions to informal, relationship-driven spaces within the lower tier. The present study builds on this literature to explore how trust operates in the lower tiers of Barcelona's primary art market, where institutional validation is limited and informal networks are expected to shape both artistic visibility and transactional credibility.

[2] Fukuyama (1995) conceptualizes trust as "the expectation that arises within a community of regular, honest, and cooperative behavior" based on shared norms. In his framework, trust constitutes a precondition for generating social capital, which he defines as the "capability that arises from the prevalence of trust in a society." Trust facilitates cooperation and reduces transaction costs, but should not be conflated with social capital itself. Social capital refers to the structure and quality of social networks, while trust is one of the norms that makes those networks function. Bourdieu, on the other hand, situates cultural capital within a system of symbolic goods, where trust among actors often depends on shared dispositions and recognition codes. In the context of informal or low-end art markets, trust enables access to relational resources (social capital) and supports symbolic legitimation (via cultural capital), but remains conceptually distinct from both.

3 Data and Methodology

This study adopts a qualitative methodology informed by field-based traditions in cultural economics and the sociology of art markets (Moulin, 1987, 1992; Benhamou et al., 2002; Velthuis, 2005), as well as by recent analyses of non-central markets (Halle & Tiso, 2008; Kim, 2007; Macedo Rubião, 2018; Patin, 2016; Radermecker, 2022.). Methodologically, it draws on the premise that market dynamics are mediated by the interpretative frameworks through which actors navigate their environment (Komarova & Velthuis, 2018, p. 61). The empirical strategy combines a field-validated mapping of the local gallery landscape with interviews, observations, and documentary materials, seeking robustness through triangulation rather than statistical representativeness (Bewley, 2002). In this context, trust is conceptualized not as a psychological attitude but as a situated coordination mechanism embedded in symbolic hierarchies, role-dependent dependencies, and informal reciprocities.

To identify and classify low-end galleries, a multi-stage mapping process combines institutional data, ethnographic fieldwork, and digital verification. While existing sources—such as the *Estadística d'Arts Visuals 2022* published by the *Departament de Cultura de la Generalitat de Catalunya*, the *Gremi de Galeries d'Art de Catalunya (GAC)*, and the selective *Associació Art Barcelona*, which currently comprises 33 member galleries—offered a partial overview of the gallery landscape, they exclude unaffiliated and hybrid spaces with consistent activity that fell outside official registries. According to official figures from 2022 (Catalunya. Departament de Cultura, 2022), a total of 121 galleries were active across Catalonia, with 69% located in the Barcelonese area. Of these, 32% were affiliated with the GAC, 31% with Art Barcelona, and 26% with the *Consorcio de Galerías de Arte Contemporáneo*, while 37% reported no professional association. These institutional limitations were addressed through direct observation in key art districts of Barcelona, complemented by a snowball sampling strategy,[3] whereby gallery owners and staff identified other venues with similar pricing models, artistic profiles, or client bases. Additional galleries were located via systematic online searches,

[3] Also known as purposive sampling. Purposive sampling was selected as the sampling method. According to Matthews and Ross (2010), it is often used for research where the focus is on in-depth insights and qualitative results, with participants being selected based on predefined characteristics.

which enabled the detection of clusters in digital directories, exhibition calendars, and promotional platforms. This process resulted in an original, field-validated census of 148 active galleries in Barcelona—slightly above the official figures—of which approximately 18–20% (27–30 galleries) were classified as operating in the lower segment. This estimate combines direct verification of galleries included in the interview sample with indirect identification of additional spaces through field-based extrapolation, peer-referencing, and digital clustering techniques. These spaces typically featured limited representation contracts (if any), high exhibition turnover (between 11 and 24 shows per year), and frequent price visibility through gallery websites, even if not all platforms function as transactional marketplaces. Although comprehensive digital sales data are not available, official reports from 2019 suggest that nearly 50% of Barcelona-based galleries maintain online sales platforms, with even higher prevalence among unaffiliated galleries.

Primary data were collected through 26 semi-structured interviews with gallery owners, upper-segment professionals, artists, critics, and institutional agents, including one of the most active auction houses in the city, which regularly includes works by emerging artists in its "twenty-first-century painting" category,[4] given the central role that such institutions play in the consolidation of art markets (Baia Curioni, 2012; Vermeylen, 2015; Komarova & Velthuis, 2018). Interviewees were selected purposively to capture variation in organizational models, mediation practices, and degrees of institutional embeddedness, with the census-based mapping used to ensure coverage across distinct profiles, and were recruited through a combination of direct contact during field visits, outreach based on the census, and referrals. Interviews ranged from 50 to 90 minutes and explored internal operations, pricing and discount routines, client relationships, artist selection, and legitimacy-building strategies. Interviews were recorded when consent was granted; otherwise, detailed notes were taken. In parallel, ethnographic observation at exhibitions and local fairs

[4] Although auction houses are generally associated with the secondary market, one of the interviewees represented a prominent Barcelona-based auction platform that has consistently promoted emerging artists and incorporated works of recent production into its "twenty-first-century painting" category. This platform collaborates with art competitions and offers sales opportunities to young creators, positioning itself as a hybrid actor at the intersection of the primary and secondary market. Its inclusion in the sample is justified by literature emphasizing the role of auction houses in activating and legitimating local art market structures.

documented rhetorical framings and informal practices not always articulated during interviews. Documentary sources included gallery websites, price lists when available, promotional materials, institutional reports, and official statistical outputs. All participants were informed of the research purpose and were offered anonymity in reporting.

Analytical procedures followed an iterative logic based on constant comparison across interviews, observations, and documents. Rather than addressing "trust" as a topic per se, the study elicited situational accounts of collaboration, negotiation, and discretion, interpreted through the lens of symbolic positioning (Bourdieu, 1993) and informal normative structures (Becker, 1982; Granovetter, 1985). Coding focused on recurring sequences in which actors managed uncertainty (for example, first-time sales, price justification, informal discounts, delayed payments, and selection decisions) and on the conditions under which interpersonal credibility substituted for institutional safeguards. Trust was treated as an analytical category when it produced observable coordination effects: stabilizing relations with artists, enabling repeat purchases, sustaining referrals, or mitigating reputational fragility in situations of price dispersion. The resulting interpretations were cross-checked against field observations and publicly available documentary traces to strengthen internal consistency. These analytical criteria informed both the interpretation of coordination mechanisms and the comparative construction of the gallery typology reported in Sect. 4.

Four different types of galleries were inductively identified by comparing cases along four analytical dimensions: (i) revenue model (commissions, volume strategies, artist-borne costs, or mixed arrangements); (ii) curatorial and selection logic (coherent projects, eclectic mixes, decorative "chromos," or seasonal hybridization); (iii) the degree of formalization (contracts, exclusivity, and documentation); and (iv) client-relationship routines (price visibility, negotiation practices, and repeat-buyer strategies). The resulting typology distinguishes: (i) commercially oriented venues focused on sales, high turnover, and non-exclusive representation; (ii) promotional spaces supporting emerging artists and career-building with minimal resources; (iii) para-commercial points of sale,[5] offering highly accessible

[5] This category echoes Moulin's (1992) concept of "points de vente" or "chromos" galleries: retail spaces that offer highly accessible, often decorative artworks targeting non-specialized buyers, including tourists. These venues typically operate outside professional networks, and their selection is driven more by salability than curatorial coherence.

works; and (iv) retail-oriented venues operating on the basis of artist-borne exhibition costs and/or gallery space rental—akin to the *galeries locatrices* described by Patin (2016)—and often driven by current art-oriented selection logics. While these categories are not mutually exclusive, they reveal stable patterns of role specialization and institutional positioning. This typology also resonates, albeit partially, with earlier classifications in art market literature: the "chromos" (drawing on Francine Couture's earlier work), "classified works," and "contemporary" markets distinguished by Moulin (1992). Yet the Barcelona context required further refinement to capture the fluidity, informality, and symbolic ambiguity of its lower segment.

4 Empirical Analysis and Findings

4.1 Market Position and Segmentation

This section applies the previously defined conceptual framework of trust as a relational coordination mechanism substituting for institutional guarantees, specifically examining operational practices in Barcelona's lower-tier galleries. In this context, trust refers to the interpersonal credibility attributed to the gallery's artistic choices, pricing transparency, and consistency in client relations. It mitigates buyers' and artists' uncertainty in the absence of contractual protection or symbolic endorsement and serves as a stabilizing force amid reputational fragility and price dispersion. In the terms of the triadic model proposed by Radermecker and Moureau, the segment addressed here is largely characterized by works with predominantly symbolic functionality, limited scarcity at the level of individual emerging artists, and weak brand legitimacy. Trust therefore operates as the relational infrastructure through which galleries and artists compensate for limited third-party validation and gradually consolidate reputation.

Despite Barcelona's historical prominence, the city's primary art market exhibits characteristics typical of provincial cultural economies: notably limited international visibility, strong reliance on local networks, and uneven institutional support (Debroux, 2017). Spatial proximity and social embeddedness crucially shape artistic production and commercial mediation (Velthuis, 2011; Zorloni, 2013). International benchmarks typically define the lower-tier market as comprising artworks priced below $50,000 (McAndrew, 2023). However, Barcelona's lower-tier galleries rarely exhibit works above €9,000, with most priced between

€1,000 and €6,000. In contrast, galleries associated with the upper tiers exhibit a wide price dispersion, with works ranging from €10,000 to over €80,000. However, publicly visible prices tend to remain considerably lower than these peaks, particularly in local gallery spaces. Interviewees explained that top-tier pieces are generally withheld from display or sold through art fairs, where price confidentiality and client profiling are standard practices. Higher-priced works exceeding €50,000 appear primarily at international fairs, reflecting local demand limitations and strategic symbolic positioning (Rea, 2025).

Empirical findings from Barcelona's galleries show substantial operational variation, countering Moulin's (1992) general characterization of low-end galleries as primarily "chromos" or commercial decorative art venues. Based on qualitative assessments, four typologies were identified:

i) Coherent artistic projects with local artists, occasionally including recognized Catalan artists (approximately 7%).
ii) Eclectic emerging artist galleries without defined curatorial lines, mixing original and commercially accessible art (around 39%).
iii) Galleries exclusively showcasing decorative "chromos," illustrations, and reproductions (around 7%).
iv) Hybrid galleries adapting inventory based on seasonal demand (remaining galleries).

Table 1 synthesizes key operational traits observed across Barcelona's lower-tier galleries, including curatorial practices, institutional affiliation, pricing strategies, and audience orientation. While price levels signal segmentation, they alone cannot explain how galleries position themselves. Trust-based mechanisms—substituting for formal validation—emerge as crucial for navigating symbolic hierarchies and reputational uncertainty. These gallery types also reflect differentiated trust configurations: hybrid models tend to rely on recurring informal collaborations, while promotional galleries depend more on artist referrals and relational credibility in the absence of institutional support.

These galleries frequently cluster along high-traffic commercial streets, driven by urban regeneration policies and cultural tourism (Kim, 2007; Debroux, 2017). Such locations foster transactional strategies like eclectic displays and public-facing pricing. Nevertheless, clustering does not imply operational homogeneity, highlighting diverse responses to local economic pressures and demand (Velthuis, 2005, Rius Ulldemolins, 2012).

Table 1 Dimension and Characteristics of Barcelona's Lower-tier Galleries

Dimension	*Characteristics*
Institutional Affiliation	Not affiliated with major professional associations (e.g., ARTBarcelona; *Gremi de Galeries d'Art de Catalunya*); in some cases, affiliated only with the Gremi (GAC).
Exhibition Rhythm and Format	Over 10 exhibitions per year; frequent use of large collective shows (20 + artists).
Display Techniques	Use of wire-hung systems (tracks and fishing lines); minimal wall intervention.
Curatorial Standards	Dense, visually crowded displays; limited thematic or conceptual coherence.
Price Transparency	Prices visibly displayed alongside works and/or online.
E-commerce Orientation	Integration of online sales platforms or visible purchasing/ reservation options.
Artist Filtering	No systematic vetting; open-door policy toward artist submissions.
Client Relationship Model	Limited client cultivation; oriented toward occasional or tourist buyers.
Artistic Offer	Mixed typologies: decorative, contemporary, and experimental art may coexist.
Target Audience	General public and untrained buyers; emphasis on visual appeal and affordability.
Artist Profiles	Many artists with fragmented careers, secondary professions, or low institutional visibility.
Sales Model	Works often include small formats, multiple editions, or chromos.
Representation Model	No formal artist representation or contracts.
Storage and Investment Capacity	Limited storage; no investment in production or artist development.
Organizational structure	Gallery owners are also practicing artists whose works are permanently or recurrently exhibited alongside guest artists.
Location Strategy	Situated in commercial streets; oriented toward walk-in traffic.
Fair Participation	Minimal or no participation in local or international art fairs.
Business Model Hybridization	Gallery often functions as a framing shop, design store, or illustration outlet.
Programming Flexibility	Occasional deviation from usual art style to accommodate social ties or convenience.
Opening Practices	No formal openings or solo shows; exceptions are occasional.
Artist Charges	Artists often pay to exhibit or to access international opportunities.
Commission Rates	Commission rates may exceed 50% of sale price.
Staffing Structure	Small teams (1–2 people); limited division of roles.
Pricing Range	Wide dispersion: from €60–€300 for prints/chromos to €2000–€10,000 for unique works.

Source Author

4.2 Operational Practices and Typologies

Low-end galleries in Barcelona exhibit operational models shaped by limited institutional support, scarce financial resources, and a high degree of organizational informality. Interview data indicate the prevalence of two dominant profiles: commercial galleries that prioritize rapid turnover with minimal artist commitment, and promotional galleries that support emerging artists through visibility rather than sales. These are complemented by retail-oriented spaces focused on graphic or decorative works, and rental or vanity galleries where costs are shifted to artists.

Price transparency is widespread across these venues and constitutes a key mechanism for reducing entry barriers. Field observations reveal that works are commonly exhibited with visible price tags and technical descriptions. While this contrasts sharply with the opacity of high-end galleries, it does not eliminate uncertainty for potential buyers or exhibitors. Instead, it signals an alternative model of trust—one based on accessibility and clarity rather than exclusivity or symbolic value.

Exhibitions tend to be frequent and densely populated, with collective shows often featuring twenty or more artists. Staff is typically limited to one or two individuals who handle curatorial, commercial, and administrative tasks simultaneously. Interviews and direct observation underscore the extensive reliance on informal labor arrangements. Approximately two-thirds of the galleries studied reported regularly drawing on personal and professional networks to assemble exhibitions, manage logistics, or cover absences. These practices, grounded in long-standing relationships and reciprocal exchanges, exemplify what we term relational delegation—a non-contractual form of task allocation rooted in interpersonal trust. As one gallerist put it: "When we do a collective show, it's always a bit chaotic—but we know who to call. It's like family. Everyone helps, no questions asked."

4.3 Trust Mechanisms in Artist Selection and Representation

Artist selection in Barcelona's low-end segment rarely follows standardized or formalized procedures. Instead, decisions are mediated through social proximity, shared aesthetic sensibilities, and informal endorsements. According to interview data, 27 out of 29 galleries do not operate with exclusive representation contracts. Rather, they invite artists through peer recommendation, prior collaboration, or even spontaneous proposals. "If someone is introduced by an artist we trust, we'll give them a wall," one gallery owner explained. In this sense, trust acts not only as a filter for entry but as a resource-saving mechanism. Some galleries incentivize trusted artists to recommend others, offering reduced commissions or discounts on exhibition fees in exchange. For rental-based models, where a consistent flow of participants is needed, such referral strategies become particularly salient.

However, this informality also entails reputational risks. One gallerist shared: "We used to find artists via Instagram, but it made us look desperate. Now we rely on word of mouth and our circle." In this ecosystem, trust functions as a social infrastructure for risk management. It substitutes for missing validation channels such as fair participation or institutional endorsements, helping galleries avoid problematic partnerships.

The absence of formal evaluation does not imply randomness. Artists are often assessed through a combination of intuitive judgment, informal conversation, and shared background. As another gallerist described: "We don't ask for CVs or portfolios. We look at the work, we talk to the person. If we click, that's enough."

4.4 *Buyer Relations and Transactional Trust*

In the context of Barcelona's low-end art galleries, buyer relationships are constructed on immediacy, openness, and interpersonal cues rather than on investment value or institutional signaling. The clientele consists predominantly of casual visitors, tourists, and first-time buyers unfamiliar with the codes of the contemporary art world. Unlike high-end venues, which rely on exclusivity and symbolic barriers, these galleries seek to generate accessibility through conversational engagement and emotional connection. One gallerist recounted: "People need to know what they're looking at. If they have to ask the price, they might not ask at all. We want it to feel easy." Many galleries allow clients to reserve works without deposit or even take them home "on trial." This form of transactional informality is grounded in mutual trust and repeated experience: "Nine out of ten times, they come back and pay," a gallery assistant noted.

Trust is also cultivated through storytelling. Gallerists frequently describe artists' backgrounds, working processes, and personal anecdotes to build relational proximity and embed artworks in meaningful narratives. This helps mitigate the absence of institutional validation or collector experience on the buyer's part. Over time, occasional buyers can become repeat clients, especially in tourist areas, where trust and familiarity evolve into informal patronage. Thus, transactional trust operates not as an exception but as a central feature of how economic and affective exchanges unfold in this market segment (Zelizer, 2005).

4.5 *Trust as Market Infrastructure*

In the absence of formal contracts, stable funding, or institutional endorsement, trust functions as a foundational infrastructure for Barcelona's low-end galleries. It sustains production, mediates access, and ensures continuity through embedded social practices. Gallerists repeatedly emphasized that without trust-based cooperation—among artists, assistants, and informal collaborators—their operations would be unsustainable. One gallery owner explained: "Trust is the glue holding everything together—without it, we wouldn't survive." This is not merely rhetorical. Several galleries coordinated entire exhibitions without written agreements, relying instead on verbal commitments and shared professional values. Yet this dependency on trust also introduces vulnerabilities. As noted by one interviewee: "We've all had conflicts. Not everything goes smoothly, but we try not to talk about it. We solve it quietly."

While galleries in the upper segment refer to "follow-up processes" and "market-building efforts" before representing an artist, those in the lower segment operate in real time, under uncertain conditions. Trust replaces vetting, contracts, and institutional gatekeeping with ongoing relational labor. In this sense, trust in low-end art markets is neither residual nor secondary—it is the mechanism that makes the market possible.

5 Discussion

The empirical findings of this study challenge residualist understandings of trust in low-end art markets. Rather than functioning as a secondary social lubricant or an ad hoc response to resource scarcity, trust emerges as a primary coordination mechanism that sustains operational continuity, transactional reliability, and symbolic legibility in the absence of formalized structures. In the context of Barcelona's lower-tier primary market, trust is not merely compensatory but constitutive: it underpins the relational architecture through which galleries, artists, and clients navigate structural fragility, build credibility, and reproduce market practices. This section articulates four interrelated dimensions through which the role of trust acquires systemic relevance: market coordination, symbolic positioning, infrastructural substitution, and relational labor.

5.1 *Trust as a Market Coordination Mechanism*

The data refine theoretical contributions in cultural economics (Throsby, 2001; Velthuis, 2005) by showing that trust is not only relevant in high-end segments—where it filters investment risk or stabilizes symbolic value through institutional validation—but also actively organizes market functionality in under-institutionalized contexts. Practices such as verbal agreements, open-door artist policies, chain-referral recruitment, and non-remunerated labor exchanges do not simply reflect resource constraints; they constitute a decentralized system of market coordination. These trust-based arrangements replace formal protocols and enable key functions—artist selection, exhibition production, buyer engagement—to unfold without bureaucratic mediation. As Radermecker (2022) suggests in her work on legitimacy-building in peripheral art markets, informal mechanisms are often not provisional but adaptive logics of operation in structurally constrained environments. The present study builds on this insight by demonstrating how trust structures, rather than supplements, market organization in the low-end segment.

5.2 *Differentiated Trust Configurations and Symbolic Stratification*

Trust in this context is neither uniform nor ideologically neutral. It is differentiated by gallery typology, symbolic ambition, and audience orientation. Commercial, promotional, retail, and hybrid spaces activate distinct configurations of trust: interpersonal trust based on familiarity and proximity; delegated trust through peer recommendations; and symbolic trust grounded in curatorial discourse or mimetic references to higher-tier aesthetics. These configurations are not only responses to internal capacity but also instruments for navigating symbolic hierarchies. Even in precarious market niches, distinctions persist—not only in pricing and visibility but in the semiotics of legitimacy. Trust, then, operates as both a currency of inclusion and a mode of differentiation, echoing Bourdieu's (1993) insight that symbolic capital is unequally distributed even within dominated fractions of the field. Galleries leverage trust not simply to reduce uncertainty, but to position themselves within a stratified symbolic economy.

5.3 *Trust as Infrastructure for Valuation and Participation*

In environments marked by low curatorial density and weak institutional filtering, trust substitutes for formal mechanisms of valuation. It functions as a pragmatic infrastructure that reduces interpretive ambiguity for buyers and lowers access barriers for artists. For clients unfamiliar with art world codes, trust is enacted through transparent pricing, narrative engagement, and interpersonal fluency—strategies that signal sincerity and credibility without recourse to connoisseurship. For artists, exhibition opportunities are less contingent on institutional reputation than on social embeddedness and relational momentum. As Radermecker (2022) observes in her analysis of lowbrow art markets, informal validation circuits are not peripheral but integral to how value is constructed and circulated. The present findings extend this argument, showing that in Barcelona's low-end market, trust performs dual valuation work: it legitimates artistic participation and facilitates buyer decision-making in the absence of authoritative cues.

5.4 *Relational Labor and the Organizational Logic of Low-end Galleries*

The study also contributes to a finer-grained understanding of the organizational rationality of low-end galleries. Here, relational labor—mobilizing personal networks for installation, delegating tasks to collaborators based on affective trust, or managing reputational risks through informal vetting—replaces institutional infrastructures. This labor is not merely operational; it is symbolic and strategic. It sustains programming frequency, preserves gallery identity, and buffers reputational shocks. Trust becomes a form of organizational capital, enabling resilience without formalization. Crucially, this model is not an imperfect version of high-end galleries but a structurally distinct one, governed by its own norms, constraints, and strategies. As with other informal economies, the low-end art market operates through logics of improvisation, reciprocity, and adaptive coordination. Its legitimacy, while fragile, is not fictive—it is negotiated and reproduced through embedded relational work.

In sum, this research encourages a rethinking of trust not as an exception to governance, but as a constitutive element of cultural markets operating under institutional scarcity. It contributes to emerging scholarship (Radermecker, 2022; Habelsberger & Bhansing 2021) that treats informal and peripheral segments as structured, agentive, and analytically productive. By reframing trust as both an economic and symbolic technology—through which actors generate continuity, reduce ambiguity, and construct shared meaning—this study opens new directions for understanding how underrecognized sectors of the art market maintain viability and shape cultural value. Further comparative research could examine how these mechanisms function across different cities or market segments, advancing a more pluralistic and grounded understanding of market infrastructures in the cultural economy.

6 Conclusions

This study has demonstrated that low-end galleries, far from being peripheral or merely decorative components of the art market, perform a critical and under-recognized function in sustaining its structural and symbolic integrity. By analyzing the role of trust as an infrastructural mechanism, the research reframes the lower tiers of the primary market not as informal replicas of elite segments but as structurally distinct arenas governed by their own logics of coordination, valuation, and credibility.

The empirical evidence presented confirms that these galleries actively generate access to artistic careers, promote visibility for emerging and lesser-known artists, and cultivate aesthetic literacy among audiences often excluded from institutionalized cultural spaces. Their function is not merely economic but civic and pedagogical: they democratize the act of looking, collecting, and engaging with art. As Moulin (1967) already observed, small galleries operating at the margins of dominant circuits play a decisive role in the formation of taste, the identification of new talent, and the renewal of local art ecologies. In Barcelona, their proximity to artistic production and their embeddedness in relational networks allow them to respond to local conditions with agility, experimentation, and symbolic inclusiveness.

The heterogeneity of the gallery landscape—ranging from high-end blue-chip spaces to mid-size commercial venues and small, often precarious galleries—does not weaken the market; it enhances its adaptability and reach. Each segment contributes to the diversification of audiences, the pluralization of aesthetic values, and the circulation of artworks across different economic and symbolic regimes. Low-end galleries, in particular, act as interfaces between cultural production and local publics, mediating not only transactions but also meanings, affiliations, and forms of participation. In doing so, they maintain the connective tissue of the art ecosystem, absorbing risks, activating latent demand, and offering an entry point for both artists and buyers.

Reconceptualizing trust as an organizational and symbolic infrastructure within this context enables a richer understanding of how art markets function beyond institutional centers. It also foregrounds the importance of informal mechanisms—reciprocity, delegated judgment, affective labor—as durable logics of governance in cultural economies. This perspective invites future research to examine how these mechanisms operate across different territories, levels of formality, and cultural policy frameworks. Ultimately, acknowledging the structural relevance of low-end galleries requires us to rethink not only the geography of art markets but also their epistemology. Peripheral does not mean insignificant. As this study shows, it is often in these fragile, adaptive, and socially embedded spaces that the foundational work of cultural markets is performed.

References

Adler, P. S. (2001). Market, hierarchy, and trust: The knowledge economy and the future of capitalism. *Organization Science, 12*(2), 215–234.

Akerlof, G. A. (1978). The market for "lemons": Quality uncertainty and the market mechanism. In *Uncertainty in economics* (pp. 235–251). Academic Press.

Baia Curioni, S. (2012). A fairy tale: The art system, globalization, and the fair movement. In M. Lind & O. Velthuis (Eds.), *Contemporary art and its commercial markets: A report on current conditions and future scenarios* (pp. 115–151). Sternberg Press.

Becker, H. S. (1982). *Art worlds.* University of California Press.

Benhamou, F. (2011a). *L'économie de la culture* (2nd ed.). La Découverte.

Benhamou, F. (2011b). Artists' labour markets. In R. Towse (Ed.), *A Handbook of Cultural Economics* (2nd ed., Ch. 7). Edward Elgar Publishing.

Benhamou, F., Moureau, N., & Sagot-Duvauroux, D. (2002). Opening the black box of the white cube: A survey of French contemporary art galleries at the turn of the millenium. *Poetics, 30*(4), 263–280.

Bewley, T. (2002). Interviews as a valid empirical tool in economics. *Journal of Socio-Economics, 31*, 343–353.

Bianchi, M. (2015). Willingness to believe and betrayal aversion: The special role of trust in art exchanges. *Journal of Cultural Economics, 39*, 133–151.

Bourdieu, P. (1980). Le capital social. *Actes de la Recherche en Sciences Sociales, 31*, 2–3.

Bourdieu, P. (1993). *The field of cultural production.* Columbia University Press.

Casson, M., & Della Giusta, M. (2006). The economics of trust. In *Handbook of Trust Research*. Edward Elgar Publishing.
Catalunya. Departament de Cultura. (2022). *Estadística d'arts visuals 2022: galeries d'art* [online]. Barcelona: Generalitat de Catalunya. Departament de Cultura. http://hdl.handle.net/20.500.12368/32468
Choi, G. S., & Storr, V. H. (2020). Market interactions, trust and reciprocity. *PLOS ONE, 15*(5), e0232704.
Coleman, J. S. (1988). Social capital in the creation of human capital. *American Journal of Sociology, 94*(Supplement), S95–S120.
Coleman, J. S. (1990a). Commentary: Social institutions and social theory. *American Sociological Review, 55*(3), 333–339.
Coleman, J. S. (1990b). *Foundations of social theory*. Harvard University Press.
Corominas-Bosch, M. (2004). Bargaining in a network of buyers and sellers. *Journal of Economic Theory, 115*(1), 35–77.
de Bliek, R. (2015). Empirical studies on the economic impact of trust (No. EPS-2015-324-ORG).
Debroux, T. (2017). The visible part: Of art galleries, artistic activity and urban dynamics: Presentation and first results of a research project. *Articulo: Journal of Urban Research, 15*. https://doi.org/10.4000/articulo.3409
Fehr, E. (2009). On the economics and biology of trust. *Behavioral & Experimental Economics*.
Fukuyama, F. (1995). *Trust: The social virtues and the creation of prosperity*. The Free Press.
Fukuyama, F. (2001). Social capital, civil society and development. *Third World Quarterly, 22*(1), 7–20.
Gambetta, D. (1988). Can we trust trust? In D. Gambetta Ed., *Trust: Making and breaking cooperative relations* (pp. 213–237). Blackwell.
Granovetter, M. (1985). Economic action and social structure: The problem of embeddedness. *American Journal of Sociology, 91*(3), 481–510.
Habelsberger, B. E. M., & Bhansing, P. V. (2021). Art galleries in transformation: Is COVID-19 driving digitisation? *Arts, 10*(3), 48.
Halle, D., & Tiso, E. (2008). The sociology of the new art gallery scene in Chelsea, Manhattan. In J. Amariglio, J. W. Childers, & S. E. Cullenberg (Eds.), *Sublime economy: On the intersection of art and economics* (pp. 220–249). Routledge. https://doi.org/10.4324/9780203890578
Hamm, J. A., Möllering, G., & Darcy, K. (2024). Integrating focal vulnerability into trust research. *Journal of Trust Research, 14*(2), 237–255.
Kim, H. H. (2007). The creative economy and urban art clusters: Locational characteristics of art galleries in Seoul. *Journal of the Korean Geographical Society, 42*(2), 258–279.
Komarova, N., & Velthuis, O. (2018). Local contexts as activation mechanisms of market development: Contemporary art in emerging markets. *Consumption*

Markets & Culture, *21*(1), 1–21. https://doi.org/10.1080/10253866.2017.1284065
Lin, N. (1999). Social networks and status attainment. *Annual Review of Sociology*, *25*(1), 467–487.
Li, X., Ma, X., & Renneboog, L. (2024). In art we trust. *Management Science*, *70*(1), 98–127. https://doi.org/10.1287/mnsc.2022.4633
Macedo Rubião, R. (2018). A short but deep dive into the economics of arts: Art entrepreneurs in a peripheral market. *Artivate: A Journal of Entrepreneurship in the Arts*, *7*(2), 3–26.
Matthews, B., & Ross, L. (2010). *Research methods: A practical guide for the social sciences*. Pearson Longman.
McAndrew, C. (2023). *The Art Market 2023: A Report by Art Basel & UBS*. Art Basel and UBS.
Möllering, G. (2006). *Trust: Reason, routine, reflexivity*. Emerald Group Publishing.
Möllering, G. (2012). Trusting in art: Calling for empirical trust research in highly creative contexts. *Journal of Trust Research*, *2*(2), 203–210.
Moulin, R. (1967). Le marché de la peinture en France. Les Éditions de Minuit.
Moulin, R. (1987). *The French art market: A sociological view*. (No Title). https://cir.nii.ac.jp/crid/1971712334742997538
Moulin, R. (1992). *L'artiste, l'institution et le marché*. Flammarion.
Nooteboom, B. (2002). *Trust: Forms, foundations, functions, failures and figures*. Edward Elgar.
Patin, C. (2016). La fabrique de l'art au Japon: Portrait sociologique d'un marché de l'art. CNRS Éditions.
Putnam, R. D. (1994). Social capital and public affairs. *Bulletin of the American Academy of Arts and Sciences*, 5–19.
Putnam, R. D., Leonardi, R., & Nanetti, R. Y. (1993). *Making democracy work: Civic traditions in modern Italy*. Princeton University Press.
Radermecker, A.-S. (2022). Selling lowbrow art and cultural goods in times of pandemic: The case of a provincial art market. *International Journal of Cultural Property*, *29*(3), 283–310. https://doi.org/10.1017/S0940739122000340
Rea, N. (2025, June 13). The art market has lost its grip on pricing. Now what? *Artnet News*. https://news.artnet.com/market/the-art-market-has-lost-its-grip-on-price-2653663
Rius Ulldemolins, J. (2012). Gallery districts of Barcelona: The strategic play of art dealers. *The Journal of Arts Management, Law, and Society*, *42*(2), 48–62. https://doi.org/10.1080/10632921.2012.678929
Rousseau, D. M., Sitkin, S. B., Burt, R. S., & Camerer, C. (1998). Not so different after all: A cross-discipline view of trust. *Academy of Management Review*, *23*(3), 393–404.
Sztompka, P. (1999). *Trust: A sociological theory*. Cambridge University Press.
Throsby, D. (2001). *Economics and culture*. Cambridge University Press.

Van der Ploeg, R. (2002). In art we trust. *De Economist, 150*(4), 333–362.
Velthuis, O. (2005). *Talking prices: Symbolic meaning of prices on the market for contemporary art*. Princeton University Press.
Velthuis, O. (2011). Art markets. In R. Towse (Ed.), *A handbook of cultural economics* (2nd ed., pp. 33–42). Edward Elgar.
Vermeylen, F. (2015). The India Art Fair and the market for visual arts in the Global South. In O. Velthuis & S. Baia Curioni (Eds.), *Cosmopolitan canvases: The globalization of markets for contemporary art* (pp. 31–54). Oxford University Press.
Williamson, O. E. (1993). Calculativeness, trust, and economic organization. *Journal of Law and Economics, 36*(1), 453–486.
Zelizer, V. A. (2005). *The purchase of intimacy*. Princeton University Press.
Zorloni, A. (2013). *The economics of contemporary art: Markets, strategies and stardom*. Springer.

Trash or Treasure? Interviews with a Dealer from the Chinese Folk Antiques Market

Yuqing Song

1 Introduction

> In this world, first comes Bo Le, and then comes the thousand-mile steed. Thousand-mile steeds are not uncommon, but not so with Bo Le. So even if such a horse exists, it will often die in obscurity, never being recognized for its true worth.
>
> —Han Yu (768–824), *On Horses*[1]

"Sleepers" are artworks that are undervalued because one or more characteristics go unrecognized (Marrone & Beltrametti, 2020). Once awaken, i.e., identified with the right attribution, the market value of the object often increases considerably. Although the artwork itself does not change, in many cases, cleaning and restoration are essential in the discovery of a sleeper (Bandle, 2016). Sleeper cases are subject to disputes because of the economic and legal ramifications. The handful of studies on sleepers often focus on public auctions because of the accessibility of their sales

[1] *Ma Shuo* Han Yu.

Y. Song (✉)
Université libre de Bruxelles, Brussels, Belgium
e-mail: yuqing.song@ulb.be

A.-S. V. Radermecker (ed.), *Low-End Markets for Art and Cultural Goods*, Cultural Economics & the Creative Economy,
https://doi.org/10.1007/978-3-032-27566-0_16

records, their privileged position in the art market, and the high-profile sales of sleeper cases.

In this interview-style chapter, I focus on the Chinese *mincang* market (Folk Antiques Market) and argue that the phenomenon of sleepers is far more widespread than is typically recognized and emerges from the low-end art market. I identify the factors that contribute to the realization of such hidden value, highlighting jargons specific to the Chinese antiques trade and concepts central to the art market, including trust, discretion, expertise, and reputation. These elements closely mirror the triadic framework (functionality-scarcity-brand) introduced in this volume. Functionality refers to whether an item has direct practical or symbolic use; in the Chinese context, this includes ritual value or aesthetic appeal, often captured by the term *you maixiang* (having buyer appeal). Scarcity is closely tied to the practice of *jianlou* (picking up bargains), which motivates many dealers to remain in the trade and actively seek undervalued object. Brand, in this market, is less institutional and more narrative-driven—constructed through reputation, storytelling, and dealer authority. These dimensions interact to shape how value is perceived and negotiated. In addition to object-level attributes, I also identify contextual factors that significantly influence valuation, such as regional price differences (*diqu cha*), next buyer differences (*xiajia cha*), and the dealer's expertise (*yanli*). This chapter sheds light on the inner workings of the lower end of the art market, offering insights not only into the supply but also into the demand side and the roles of other key market players.

More specifically, I adopt in-depth interviews as the main methodology (Seidman, 1998). This approach allows to capture rich, nuanced, and contextually informed insights that might not emerge from multiple general respondents. In addition, the fact that the interviewee is a close relative of the researcher grants access to insider knowledge, allowing me to obtain rare first-hand insider information that would otherwise be difficult to acquire (Goldman & Swayze, 2012). The interviewee is a Chinese antique dealer with over 30 years of experience running his business (for privacy concerns, hereafter I use *Quan* when refering to the antique dealer) in a second-tier city in Northeast China. Quan mainly deals in Chinese antique coins, but also sells other antiques such as porcelain, paintings, silverware (see Appendix for Figs. 1, 2, 3 and 4). In total, I conducted two interviews—one was online (18 August 2024), the other was in his antique shop (6 January 2025)—each covering a length of over 3 hours. Our conversations were originally in Chinese, covering a wide range of topics within the antiques business.[2]

2 *Jianlou* and Sleepers

Bandle (2016) argues that, potentially, each sleeper can be discovered once it is traded on the market. However, the less valuable an art object appears to be initially, the less effort an auction house expends on it for scrutiny and authentication, and the less likely it will be reattributed. A misattributed artwork is at material risk because it may receive low recognition on the market. It is more likely to remain hidden and is less likely to be exhibited, auctioned, or to be conserved. Jauregui (1996, p. 195) comments that "probably many great masterpieces have disappeared, been destroyed or forgotten, because they were not recognized in time for their full worth."

Similar to the notion of sleepers, *jianlou*[3] is a Chinese term referring to purchasing a valuable item at a low price. Originated from the antiques market, the term is now widely used in everyday conversations to refer to any situation where someone gets something valuable for less than its worth, especially in contexts such as antiques markets, second-hand shops, and online shopping platforms. Contrary to *jianlou*, *dayan*[4] refers to mistakenly assessing an item's value, authenticity, or quality. In broader everyday use, it describes any situation where someone makes a poor judgment or error, particularly when someone is deceived or misled into making a wrong choice or decision. Closely related to *dayan* is *chiyao*[5] and *jiaoxuefei*,[6] where the former means suffering a loss and the latter paying a price for gaining experience. Speaking of the low-end antiques market in China, Hua (2005) argues that it is the existence of large numbers of fakes that makes the antiques market a fascinating place for collectors to continue to *jianlou*, *chiyao*, or *jiaoxuefei*.

[2] The interviews were very much conversational, expanding spontaneously across subjects. The excerpts shown have been selected and reconstructed to improve the flow and readability.

[3] Literally means picking up what is left out. *Lou* also refers to a bargain.

[4] Literally means hitting the eyes.

[5] Literally means taking medicine, used especially in markets like the stock market or in gambling.

[6] Literally means paying tuition.

YS: Tell me about your experiences with *jianlou*/sleepers?

Quan: Well, it all started when I was reading books as a kid. I spent a lot of time at a book stall at the flea market, then one day, I found a book on old coins. In it, there were some coins marked with prices that I had seen before, I thought to myself, "These could even sell for money?" I bought the book and started my journey with antiques. Back then, there were a lot of people selling second-hand stuff at the flea market. It was easy to *jianlou* (pick up bargains). Most people didn't have much education, maybe just at the elementary school level. When I went there, I was considered having a higher level of education. Since I could recognize the traditional characters, especially the ones used in books and coins, when I held the items, I could instantly recognize the characters and spot the real thing. It's really about having a good instinct. At the market, for example, someone might offer you something for 500 yuan, but it could be worth 4000 yuan. Back then, my salary was 180 yuan. But with just one good deal, I could make a lot more. Of course, I got interested! The more I learned, the more I realized how profitable it could be.

Eventually, I travelled to other places to see what the market was like, especially in smaller towns or villages. There, people would trade without much knowledge about the value of objects. I could buy things for as little as five yuan and sell them in Beijing for 500. Back then, people in small towns didn't have easy access to information as it is now when basically anyone can check prices online, so there were significant price differences.

For me, business is always about adapting. If something can sell at 500, I buy it at 400 and make 100 in profit. If prices drop to 5, I buy it for 4 and still earn 1. That's just how it works. Either way, there's always a way to earn. But when the market is down, there are fewer buyers, so business slows down. Right now, people don't have much money to spend. In the past, we could sell in bulk. Now, it's mostly one piece at a time. The domestic economy is in a rough spot; in fact, this might be one of the worst times among recent years. You see, there's a lot going on globally: economic pressures, foreign sanctions, trade restrictions. Everything is declining, and prices for all kinds of goods are dropping. There's not much we, as small business owners can do, unfortunately. We just wait.

Some would think that, when the prices are low during these downturns, it is the perfect time to take advantage of it and stock up antiques, hoping to sell later when the market recovers. But it's actually not quite the right approach. You should follow rising trends, not falling ones. Because when prices are falling, they usually keep falling. Let's say something was worth 500, and it drops to 300. If you buy it, thinking it's a bargain, it might drop even further to 100. And when the market is at its lowest, people don't rush in to buy. Prices don't start rising just because they're cheap—buyers stay cautious. People tend to buy when prices are rising, not when they're low. So only serious collectors keep buying no matter what, they don't care about market trends. They buy consistently, whether prices are high or low, just because they love antiques. But there aren't many people like that. Most people follow the hype. When something is trending, everyone rushes to buy, afraid of missing out. That's when prices skyrocket. So real investment is about timing. You make money when the market is hot, not when it's cold.

YS: Nowadays, can everything be considered a sleeper?

Quan: Sleepers can be quite common. For instance, some regions will always have different prices due to demand, collector preferences, and the overall economic situation. Beijing is more likely to have higher prices because there are more wealthy collectors. Some Tibetan items are sold cheaply here, while Tibetan products from Tibet itself are sold at high prices.

There can be a lot of factors influencing the value of antiques, including the item itself and how it's sold. We call this *you maixiang* (having appeal). If something has appeal, it is good-looking and easily sells well. People will like it when they see it. They'll know it has value and will want to buy it. Something might be rare, and if you overestimate it, not everyone with money will buy it. But if something has appeal, however, then people may be willing to pay a high price for it. The price can vary depending on whether the item has been restored or whether it's a genuine piece or a reproduction. Even with modern tools, such as scanning an item and checking the price online, there will still be these differences, especially when it comes to things like quality and authenticity. You can still make good profits by understanding those differences.

Importantly, *xiajia cha* (next buyer differences) is another factor. Say, my buyer is an average person, and they buy my items as part of their ordinary middle-class collection. But their buyer might be a big boss, and they can sell the items for much higher prices. In Buddhist statues, people who believe in Buddhism might value them as part of their faith; thus, they would rather spend a high price to acquire them, which is very different for a non-Buddhist. In a way, the final value of a sleeper doesn't depend solely on the item itself. It depends on how the value is realized. Sometimes, items at auctions may fetch high prices but not always. The item itself, regional differences, buyer differences are just a few of the factors that determine its value.

I remember there was once the case of an ivory Guanyin statue in Jilin City, it must be at least 20 years ago. Someone bought it for a few hundred yuan, but people thought it was fake and returned it. After being promoted, it was sold again at a few thousand to an antique dealer from Tianjin. Then this person sold it in Shenyang at tens of thousands of yuan. Then eventually, the buyer took it to an auction where it was sold for 600,000 yuan. Does this count as a case of sleeper? It's a gradual process, and what's important is recognizing its value. For that, you will need adequate expertise of course.

Another time, I went to a market to buy coins and saw a porcelain bottle. It had a hexagonal shape and twelve floral motifs, which were common in late Qing pieces. But something about it didn't match Guangxu or Tongzhi styles, many people hesitated to buy it for fear that it was a Republic-era or modern reproduction. I could tell it was old but couldn't pinpoint the era. I bought it for 3000 yuan. Later, a porcelain expert from Dalian came, bought it from me for 4000 yuan, and told me, "This isn't late Qing—it's Xianfeng-era porcelain," that expert explained, "Xianfeng-era porcelain is rare because it was a time of war, so fewer pieces survived. That's why people don't recognize it easily." So you see, that person had a sharper eye and greater level of expertise than I did, so he was able to exploit the lack of knowledge in others, and that's how people at different levels of expertise work with each other. On the high end, experts sell to wealthy collectors who are willing to pay top prices. Major collectors and auction houses compete for rare pieces, that's where items get sold for tens of thousands or even millions.

So basically, it is a process of constant value creation, and each layer adds value. A piece might sell for 10,000 at one level but 100,000 at another. Some people feel they lose money by selling too early, but that's not how it works. Every level has its own buyers. A wealthy collector won't trust a random street vendor; they trust top-tier experts. In a local antiques market, for example, a gold-speckled incense burner might sell for a few thousand yuan. But if it's from a famous collector's estate, it could sell for over 100,000 yuan at auction. It's about the name. Even if a piece isn't that special, if it was owned by a famous collector, it becomes valuable. Sometimes, if a major collector's name shows up, people might buy out the entire collection at an auction. They'll keep raising their cards for every item, regardless of the price. You see, this is why we call this business *guwan* (old things to play with), they don't care about the money.

YS: Would you regret it if you later learned that a sleeper slipped from your own hands? That you later discovered their true values?

Quan: No, in fact, I feel happy for those who buy from me and make a profit from it. Long-term success in business comes from making sure your customers profit, too. You know, a lot of people insist on listing at the highest possible price and they get upset if they don't sell at a high price or even at the standard market price. Yet, this is a distorted mindset to have. To be happy when your buyer purchases from you and losts money? If you're always obsessed with selling at the highest price, you'll be tormented by greed and constantly anxious. You'll eventually come to understand that, in this business, it's more about relationships. When you're familiar with the trade, it becomes more of a game, something enjoyable. You make money without a fuss. I don't always care about whether I get a high or low price. Sometimes, people buy at a high price; sometimes, they get a deal. If I buy at a high price, I sell higher; if I buy low, I sell lower. It all balances out. Real dealers don't focus on just one sale—they think about the bigger picture. That's why in this business, you need a steady flow of clients and suppliers. It's about trust. Buyers aren't always hunting for the cheapest deal, either—they care about authenticity and relationships. When I acquire a new item, I am in the habit of asking my familiar collectors first before listing it online. Over time, these relationships grow like friendships. It's mutual—like friends helping each other out. If they need something, they come and take it without hesitation. Some had delayed payments, but later, they'll send gifts during holidays. Over time, most of them become long-term friends with me, and we stay in touch for decades.

When you build trust this way, your clients stay with you. You can confidently buy new goods, knowing they will sell, and more people come to you because they trust that they won't lose money when they buy from you. The suppliers, too, trust you. Those people who source gather old objects from rural areas, they just take whatever they can get—old coins, liquor bottles, antique utensils—whatever people have to sell. When they bring a variety of goods, you buy them all. That way, they know that every trip to me will be worth it. If you only focus on one type, say rare coins, suppliers won't bother with you. They'll sell everything elsewhere, including the coins. Ultimately, it's about convenience for both buyers and suppliers. If I buy everything they bring, they save time and effort. Once this system is in place, the actual amount of profit per deal becomes secondary.

Don't trap yourself. If you're not making enough money, think of other ways to improve your business. But don't always focus on squeezing the highest price from every sale. You should also work on acquiring more goods and developing sources. If you know people who collect at the grassroots level, let them bring things to you first. These are the areas where you should put in effort. Nobody can be an expert in everything. Even experienced collectors make rough estimates. If you specialize in coins but see a porcelain piece, you make an educated guess about its value. Sometimes you buy high, sometimes you buy low—it's all part of the game. It's all about rough estimation, and no one can be 100% certain. If you buy high and then find another buyer, you might say, "I bought this for too much." But sometimes that buyer might still take it at a high price. You often run into these situations, you know? That's why real, serious deals are rare—unless you're buying fakes. As long as you're buying genuine pieces, losses are uncommon. Some things just need time.

A real businessman should aim for maximum profit, right? But in this trade, people do business while also enjoying the process. It's not like manufacturing cars, where you just push products to old customers and aggressively market them. It doesn't work that way. So sometimes, you might sell something at a loss—it happens. That's just how it is. As long as you're making money, then it's fine—there's no need to stress over it. For example, if you're selling something at a certain price here, it might worth a different price in Shenyang, and another price in Beijing, and yet another in the U.S. But can we directly take the item to the U.S. to sell? No, prices go up one step after another. It is not realistic to say that you only sell in the U.S.; you can only sell within your market. There's no need to overthink it.

YS: Why do you say that it is not a good idea to talk about *jianlou* openly?

Quan: Who would talk about such things? Picking up others' bargains and selling for a high price, you know? Writing about your own experience is no good. For business owners, it is a taboo. Imaging that you said you bought something from someone for one yuan and sold it for 50,000 yuan. After doing this for a long time, people will notice. Eventually, they'll figure it out. If you keep talking about picking up bargains, no one will want to sell you things, since it raises suspicion and gets attention. Yes, it shows that you have good *yanli* (expertise), which is fine, but some people just can't accept it. If you picked up a bargain, they can't get over it.

Actually, there are too many examples like this among us, we can't even count them. In the market, we don't boast about picking up bargains or talk about these things openly, we talk about other people's things, you know? When you're in the circle and talk about *jianlou* all the time, people will notice you, and the next time they sell you something, they'll be extra cautious. For these things, when people in the same circle get together say at a dinner table, they talk among themselves, you know? But they don't talk to outsiders. If you run into someone in the trade, you can chat with them casually. If you're too pushy, however, they won't want to talk to you anymore. It is a circle hard to get into: you just need to introduce yourself, make people see you, and gradually take off from there. Some famous antiques dealers such as Ma Weidu may openly talk about it in public, but not us.

3 *YANLI* AND GUT FEELINGS

Yanli[7] is the ability to discern the authenticity, quality, or value of an item. *Yanli* is distinct from *vision* in the literal sense, it reflects the comprehensive knowledge, experience, and more broadly, the feeling of an expert. In the world of folk antique collecting, the development and experience of *yanli* is often not through formal educational channels, but from years of practical experience in purchasing and collecting (Wu, 2017). Similar to connoisseurship, which is the "sensitivity of visual perception, historical training, technical awareness, and empirical experience needed by the expert to attribute the object" (Spencer, 2004, p. 29). The visual aspect of connoisseurship is often referred to as judgment by an informed eye (Johnson, 2015). Gut feelings of experts, as subjective as they might appear to be, are crucial to determining the value of an artwork. It can be difficult for an expert to explain his gut feelings to a lay person, especially when they are based on connoisseurship knowledge (Paintin, 2015).

YS: Is there such thing as gut feelings in the connoisseurship of antiques? Something that the expert may not necessarily be able to explain?

Quan: Antique identification is never vague, in fact, the specific conditions are very concrete and subtle. Whether a porcelain is from the early or

[7] Literally means eye power.

late Kangxi period (1662–1722), they all have specific characteristics. For instance, thin-walled porcelain is from the early period or middle period. For some details, outsiders may have a difficult time getting the point. Some people just need one sentence to see it, while others can't tell the difference with all the explanations. Experienced collectors have seen many things. Do you know that they don't even need to see real objects sometimes? When I look at the *baojiang* (old patina), I can tell exactly how it's aged. Although this is a general statement, specific situations can be explained. The way the old patina was applied and its layers differ from artificial patina. Although in theory there may be 100 criteria for identification, when we identify items in the market, once we look at certain areas, we can judge the authenticity. Sometimes experts don't even look at something; they just feel it and immediately know it's a high-level piece. The shape and curve behind the kiln are different. Every dynasty made it differently, the craftsmanship was different, and the habits and aesthetics also varied.

There are those people who we call *guobao bang* (the national treasure gang). They only know the theories from books but when it comes to practice, they are at complete loss. They follow the books and call everything national treasures, but it's all fake. You ask them, and they say it's correct, all according to the book, step by step, but it's still wrong. These people with mechanical thinking will argue that our connoisseurship is mysterious, but that is the real distinction between insiders and outsiders. Some experts and scholars know these terms better than them, even in a state of absolute certainty. They think the 10 criteria are written by experts, but they have no idea that some criteria are for reference, others are only supplementary.

YS: How do you develop *yanli*/expertise?

Quan: You need to learn and practice. Follow the books and then have actual objects to experiment within the collectors' circle—that's the fastest way to improve. You'll immediately understand what the books are telling you. You see, every year, even for me, not everything I buy is genuine. Sometimes I buy fakes, but that's part of the learning process. Fakes are constantly being improved every year; therefore, your skills need constant development as well. Whatever comes out, you have to know it. If you don't, you'll buy it and learn from it. You can't guarantee with your eyes that everything you see is genuine. Nobody can. Every year you should set aside 20% of your funds for learning, the other 80% be for profit. Sometimes, if you feel unsure about something, you just have to be cautious. If you're uncertain, buy it within your range and use it to learn. That's the way it works. Nobody is going to teach you; you learn from your own mistakes. The market is your school.

Books give you the framework, but when you bring that knowledge to the market, people can deceive you easily because they make the fakes using those very principles. You see, the real difference is in the experience and the skill to recognize things. That's why practice is key. It's not like someone just comes to me and says, "Hey, can you teach me how to spot these things?" That's not how it works. You can't just tell someone one thing and expect them to understand right away. Sometimes you can tell them, for example, how to spot a certain thing. But it just works differently between using the naked eye and the magnifying glass, which is perplexing to a lot of people. Sometimes, it's about *wuxing* (talent), whether you have it or not. Real understanding is something that really takes time and experience.

It's all about having *yanli* (a good eye). For some people, you can't teach them anything, no matter how hard you try, while others just get it immediately. We've all encountered that in the market. It's not just about eyesight; it's about the ability to discern. Good eyesight doesn't guarantee the ability to distinguish between real and fake. What's needed is a comprehensive understanding, built through knowledge and experience. You start to feel when something's off. For instance, the texture of the old patina, or the surface of the item, is something you feel and understand with time. It's not just abstract; it's very concrete and specific. It's not scientific, it's more intuitive. The feeling comes from years of practice. A machine won't give you that feeling, which is why experienced people rely on their judgment.

The more you handle antiques, the more you'll know when something doesn't fit. Books won't always be able to explain the exact difference, but the hands-on experience in the market will teach you. Once you've been in the field long enough, you can point to the exact reasons behind why something is fake. Some books are written by experts, but if you don't understand the subject, you won't get anything out of it. The real experts explain things in very specific terms. When people read these books, the ones who don't understand the subject will see the information as vague, while someone with knowledge will see the details and know exactly what's being described. Only through handling real items and comparing them to the information in the books will you truly understand what's being said. Some people can write books even if they don't understand the subject, but experts can tell right away if someone's book is legitimate or if it's just a collection of random information.

Again, in the antiques industry, isn't it all about people? It's about *yanli* (expertise) and reputation. Indeed, some people with a high reputation may not necessarily have good judgment. But if someone is really skilled, they can make money easily in this industry, and they don't need to deceive people to make profits. When you can appraise items accurately, people will come to you. Gaining reputation is about getting better and better at recognizing the real thing; it is a contest between you and others within the industry. How does someone stand out from the others? Let's say I have a certain level of expertise. Suppose you bring me a piece of porcelain, and I take a look—I can tell if it's old and roughly determine its period. With deeper knowledge, I can tell if it's from the Republic of China, the late Qing Dynasty, or even earlier. Someone with a higher level than me can pinpoint whether it's from Guangxu (1875–1908), Jiaqing (1796–1820), or Qianlong (1736–1796) directly. An expert beyond that doesn't even need to look; just by touching the porcelain, they can tell whether it's from early, mid, or late Qianlong, or if it's a Qianlong-era imitation of a Ming piece. That's how skill levels are distinguished. If I'm just giving a general assessment, experts can give judgments on little details. For example, the clay material, the glaze texture, the shape of the foot ring, how different dynasties crafted their porcelain, how they painted blue-and-white ceramics, and how they made monochrome glazes. If you can't explain these details, people will know your level isn't high enough.

Another important part of the learning process is through the exchange with others. For example, if I sell something to a collector who specializes in a certain type, and he comes back and shares his knowledge with me about it, that's also a way to learn. Also, we have trade fairs all over the country, which is a great venue for exchange. As long as you want to go, you will be like a horse which does not stop its hooves[8] all year round. At these trade fairs, we usually occupy an entire hotel, where food and accommodation are taken care of and each dealer gets a room. In the day, the organizers set up conferences, small auctions, and networking events. In the evening, we have this thing called *chuangjiaohui* (bed exchange meetings), where people informally lay their items out on beds

[8] Chinese figurative idiom.

and go from room to room. If you want to buy something, you just go in, check it out for yourself, and make deals on the spot. Nowadays, collectors can buy anything online and, with seven-day return guarantees, it's much easier. But you know, antiques are best assessed in person, that's why trade fairs are still so important. Face-to-face sales are faster, whereas people tend to hesitate in online sales due to poor photo conditions and you can't see flaws or repairs clearly. Also, if you can't sell something locally, you can try a different market where your items are rarer and in higher demand. At the fairs, everything is concentrated—if you're into gold coins, all the gold coin dealers are there. You can browse freely. Everyone gathers and learns from each other. Over time, you get to know people. Plus, you can learn about counterfeits. Seeing how fake items evolve helps you avoid getting scammed in the future. You learn so much in big markets. Locally, you only see the same stuff, but at large fairs, you see everything. Learning about antiques is all about gaining experiences.

YS: Do you always offer an authenticity guarantee?

Quan: I mostly guarantee it, because if you have regular customers, you can't afford not to. You can't keep selling counterfeit goods, right? If someone buys antiques from you, and you don't guarantee authenticity, you say you're following industry regulations, they won't come back next time. Who would come back to you after you have sold counterfeit goods to you? Yes, there might be some cases where I misjudged, one uses their naked eyes to see after all. When that happens, we should refund the money, right? There are also cases where some people think say it's counterfeit, but I believe it's genuine. After the item is returned, I sell it again. But now the object has appreciated in value, I initially sold it for 3,000 and now I can sell it for 6,000.

It's also about your own morality. You need to conduct yourself; you can't keep earning money by fooling others, right? If you keep pulling this stunt, people won't let you. If it's fake, it's fake. Everyone discusses where the fake is with evidence. People in the industry discuss it among themselves, and everyone understands. It's not like the street vendors, where everything is counterfeit. If you're a serious collector, you go inside the store. Whoever has good business, you buy from them. If it's counterfeit, they're responsible. If you buy from a street vendor, you just have to accept it. Because they might be gone tomorrow, you won't be able to find them again.

Antique authentication has its own difficulties. Our country now has some judicial appraisal institutions, but these institutions require 100%

certainty in their appraisals before they can convict someone. If you're only 99% certain, you can't convict them. Yes, we have the law, but there are things the law can't control. Because sometimes, it's purely a matter of opinion. The police can't verify it, so you have to go to court. Go to court, they can't decide for you either, they have to rely on verification. You say it's fake, I say it's real, and I also say that what I sold you is yours not from here, so it's all very chaotic. Who am I threatening to give you a refund? Nowadays, in the antique business, isn't it all about people? It's all about expertise and reputation.

4 Discussion and Conclusion

How are sleepers awakened? Through interviews with an experienced antique dealer from the Chinese folk antiques market, I argue that sleepers can be brought to light through a combination of factors: having appeal (*maixiang*), dealer expertise (*yanli*), market dynamics such as regional price differences (*diqu cha*), next buyer differences (*xiajia cha*), and variations in market levels. While every sleeper has the potential to be awakened, that is, to realize its true value, my conversations with an industry insider reveal that value realization depends on more than just price considerations.

The antiques market, like other markets, is subject to economic downturns, fluctuations in disposable income, and global pressures. The value of sleepers is realized through layers of transactions, with each step adding value. Long-term success in the antiques trade, however, lies not in maximizing profit from every transaction, but in building trust and ensuring mutual benefit for buyers and sellers and other market participants. Further, I highlight the importance of discretion and reputation within the trade. Publicly discussing *jianlou* (picking up bargains) may damage trust and deter sellers from offering items in the future.

Expertise in the antiques trade is developed through hands-on experience, learning from mistakes, and continuous exchanges with other insiders. As the dealer emphasizes, true expertise comes from getting into the business, physically engaging with objects, rather than solely studying them in books. This perspective aligns with the literature on *situated learning*, which holds that much of knowledge is specific to the situation in which it is learned, and that abstract instruction alone is of little use; but needs to be done in complex, social environments (Greeno et al., 1992; Anderson et al., 1996). While books can offer a general overview of the principles of the trade, they are limited in conveying the nuanced, context-dependent knowledge required to develop a good eye (*yanli*) and in imparting the interpersonal skills essential for navigating the variety of people involved in the antiques trade.

Although limited to a single case study of an antique dealer operating in the Chinese context, several of our findings resonate with insights presented in *How Not to Be an Antiques Dealer* by the British antique dealer Pritchard (2023), suggesting that certain rules of thumb may be broadly applicable of the antiques business in a larger scale, across different cultural settings. For instance, both dealers emphasize the importance of gut feeling, or having a good eye (*yanli*) as central to developing an expertise. Pritchard (2023) maintains that it all comes down to taste, "the 'eye' cannot be taught" (p. 10), even in the low-end market. Similarly, both stress that experience, rather than theoretical knowledge alone, is the best teacher. As Pritchard notes, "The only way to get experience is to buy things and to make mistakes" (p. 34), echoing the Chinese saying *jiaoxuefei* (literally, to pay tuition). In addition, trust, reputation and discretion emerge as cornerstones in long-term success for both dealers. The concept of sleepers—undervalued objects with hidden value—resonates across both contexts. In Chinese, the term *jianlou* (literally "picking up what is left out") captures this idea, while Pritchard describes scoring big bargains at auctions as "trawlers," lots that fail to sell but carry potential value. He also cautions against bragging about getting a bargain, advising that advising that "there's nothing more off-putting than playing the 'Big I am'" (p. 114), reinforcing a shared ethos that discretion enhances reputation in the trade.

Yet, there are also meaningful differences in how each dealer approaches the business. In the Chinese *mincang* (Folk Antiques Market), also referred to as the *guwan* (literally, old toys) market, the dealer Quan emphasizes a playful, relaxed attitude, rather than one that is businessman-like. He argues that, once familiar with the trade, it becomes something enjoyable—a game, rather than purely a business. As such, Quan downplays the importance of profit, arguing that one should not fuss over making money. In contrast, Pritchard (2023) underscores that "it's the antiques business. It's not the antiques game show" (p. 32), advocating for a more serious mindset governed by established rules. This divergence is particularly apparent in how the two dealers handle returns. While Quan supports accepting returns and providing refunds as a way to build trust—even in a market where no guarantees is a common principle—Pritchard adheres strictly to the trade norms, asserting that "a trade sale is a trade sale" (p. 46), and emphasizing the importance of "standing on" a deal (p. 45). Both dealers recognize the business relies heavily on trust, but their interpretations of how to cultivate it differ: Quan shows that trust is built by providing guarantees and prioritizing personal relationships and flexibility, while Pritchard highlights consistency with industry codes as the right way. These observations may point toward fundamental principles that govern the antiques trade across different cultural contexts, suggesting a promising direction for further exploration.

To conclude, this chapter reflects several aspects of the antiques market, such as discretion, trust, and reputation, which are also essential features of the higher-end auction market (Ashenfelter & Graddy, 2003). Similar to British antique dealer Pritchard (2023), the Chinese dealer Quan acknowledges the central role of auction houses, noting that auction sales often serve as industry benchmarks and tend to produce exceptionally high prices. However, Quan also critiques that auction houses do not always reflect the true market value. He observes that good deals can still be found in auction settings as local market prices sometimes surpass those achieved at auction. As he explains, "It works like this: when collectors from different regions have money to spare, they're very generous when they purchase. For example, if something is worth 800 in the market, I can buy it at an auction and immediately sell it to my buyer for 1,000."

In contrast to the impersonal, businesslike sales environment of auction houses, what emerges from our conversations with the dealer as key to the realization of hidden value in sleepers is a good understanding of the demand, maintaining a strategic relationship with stakeholders, in particular buyers and other key players operating closely to one's own trade. These insights align with the triadic framework—functionality, scarcity, and brand—introduced in this volume. Functionality is often reinterpreted through symbolic or aesthetic appeal, such as ritual use or decorative value (*you maixiang*). Scarcity is contextual and dynamic, shaped by local availability and the dealer's ability to recognize overlooked objects (*jianlou*). Brand is not institutional but constructed through narrative, reputation, and dealer expertise—what Quan calls *yanli*, the cultivated eye.

Sleepers are not simply discovered; they are actively molded through layered transactions, storytelling, and understanding of the market. The triadic framework helps clarify how these dimensions interact in practice, offering a grounded lens for understanding price formation and buyer behavior in the low-end art market. While the case study is situated in the Chinese context, parallels with the British trade suggest that these mechanisms may resonate across cultural settings, pointing toward broader principles in the global antiques business.

Glossary of Jargons

baojiang 包浆
chiyao 吃药
chuangjiaohui 床交会
dayan 打眼
diqu cha 地区差
guobao bang 国宝帮
guwan 古玩
Han Yu 韩愈
jianlou 捡漏
jiaoxuefei 交学费
Ma Shuo 马说
mabutingti 马不停蹄
maixiang 卖相
mincang 民藏
wuxing 悟性
xiajia cha 下家差
yanli 眼力

Appendix: Chinese Antiques at Quan's Shop

See Figs. 1, 2, 3 and 4.

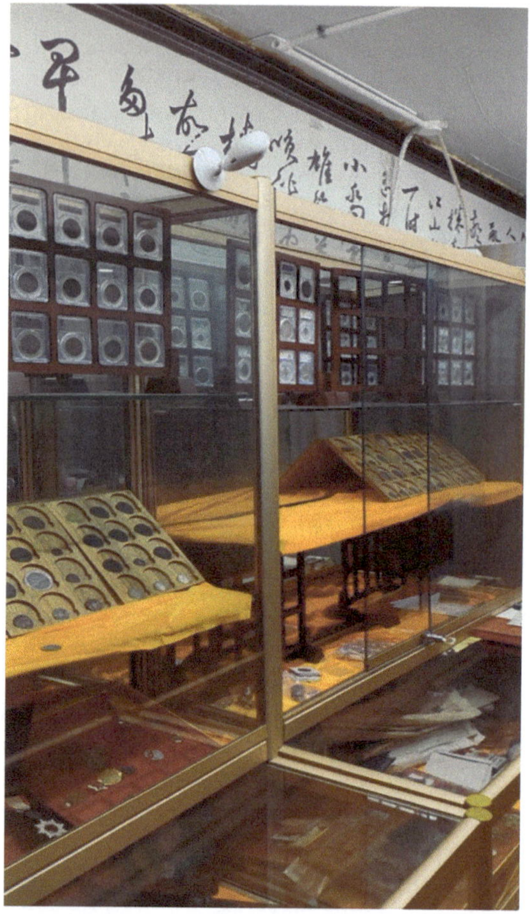

Fig. 1 Antique coins. *Source* Author

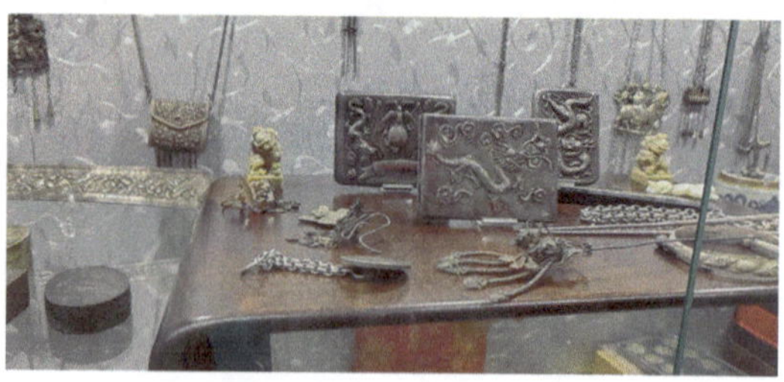

Fig. 2 Silverwares and Jadestones. *Source* Author

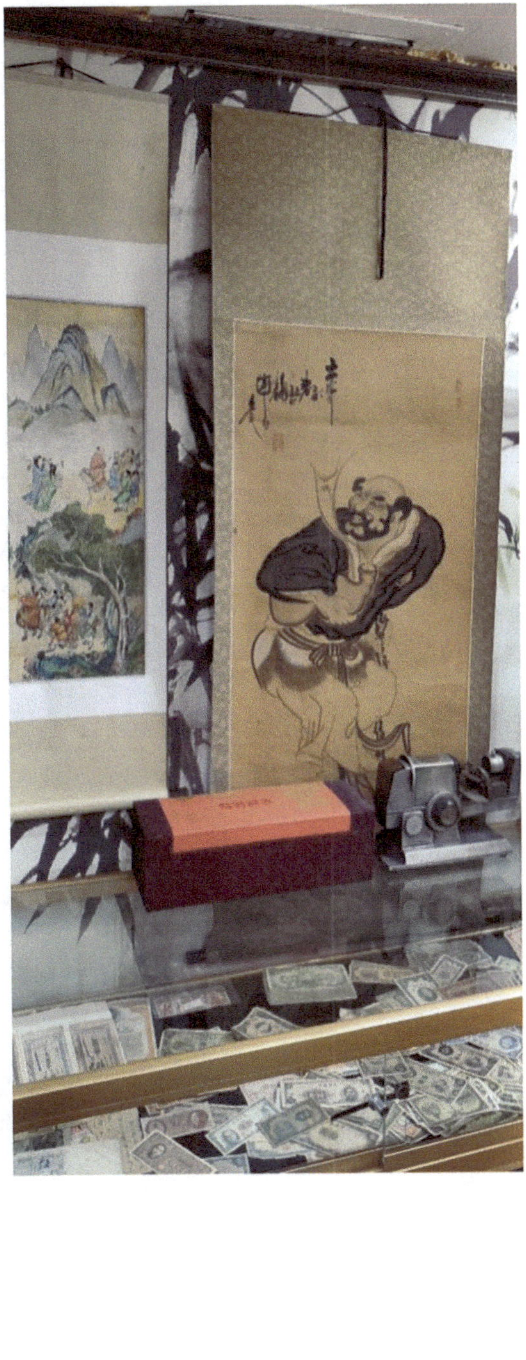

Fig. 3 Paintings. *Source* Author

Fig. 4 Porcelain and ornaments. *Source* Author

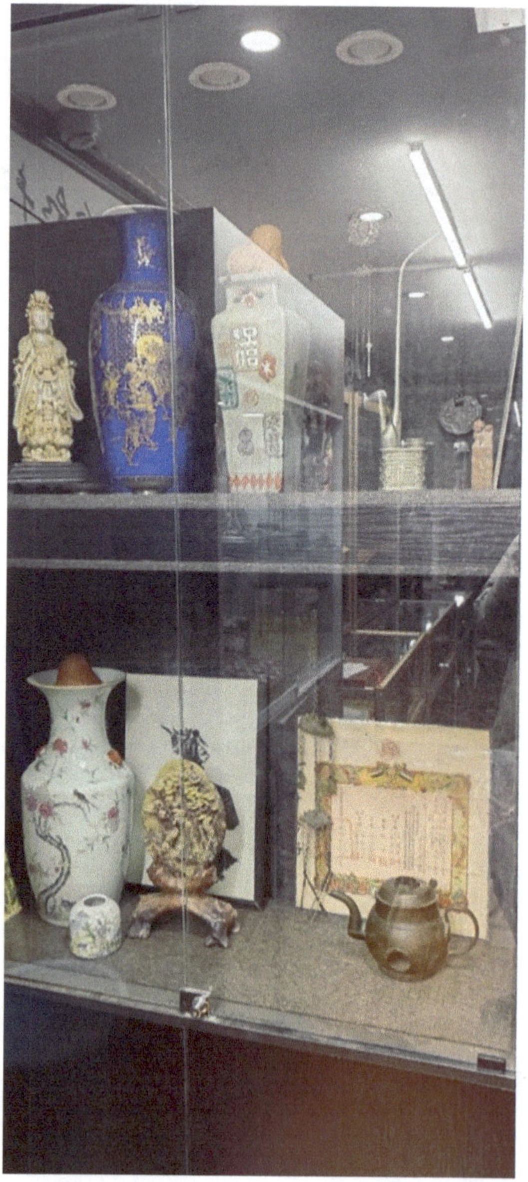

References

Anderson, J. R., Reder, L. M., & Simon, H. A. (1996). Situated learning and education. *Educational Researcher, 25*(4), 5–11. https://doi.org/10.2307/1176775

Ashenfelter, O., & Graddy, K. (2003). Auctions and the price of art. *Journal of Economic Literature*, 31.

Bandle, A. L. (2016). *The sale of misattributed artworks and antiques at auction*. Edward Elgar Publishing.

Goldman, E. F., & Swayze, S. (2012). In-depth interviewing with healthcare corporate elites: Strategies for entry and engagement. *International Journal of Qualitative Methods, 11*(3), 230–243. https://doi.org/10.1177/160940691201100304

Greeno, J. G., Smith, D. R., & Moore, J. L. (1992). Transfer of situated learning. In D. Detterman & R. J. Sternberg (Eds.), *Transfer on trial: Intelligence, cognition, and instruction* (pp. 99–167). Ablex.

Hua, B. (2005). Zhongguo Diduan Guwan Shichang Tanlue. *Nanjing Yishu Xueyuan Xuebao, 4*, 158–160.

Jauregui, R. (1996). Rembrandt portraits: Economic negligence in art attribution. *UCLA Law Review, 44*, 1947.

Johnson, H. (2015). Is it authentic—Who may say—A fresh look at connoisseurship and its role in art attribution. *Journal of Art Crime, 14*, 47–54.

Marrone, J., & Beltrametti, S. (2020). "Sleeper" antiquities: Misattributions in sales of ancient art. *International Journal of Cultural Property, 27*(1), 3–52.

Paintin, I. (2015). The art of connoisseurship through judicial eyes: The law of negligence and fine art attribution. *Art Antiquity and Law, 20*(2), 101–124.

Pritchard, D. (2023). *How not to be an antiques dealer: Everything I've learnt, that nobody told me*. Ebury Spotlight.

Seidman, I. (1998). *Interviewing as qualitative research: A guide for researchers in education and the social sciences* (2nd ed.). Teachers College Press.

Spencer, R. D. (2004). Introduction. In R. D. Spencer (Ed.), *The expert versus the object: Judging fakes and false attributions in the visual arts* (pp. 143–187). Oxford University Press.

Wu, H. (2017). Yanli de Faze—Dangdai Minjian Guwan Quanwei Diwei de Hefahua Yanjiu. *Huazhong Shifan Daxue Xuebao, 56*(02), 29–40.

Sector Insights: Stay Local, Sell Global: Regional Auctioneers, Platforms and Questions of Locality in the Digital Age

Julia Marie Wendl

1 Introduction

Auction houses, like most storefront-businesses, have traditionally benefited from local core client-communities, but have also been subject to an increasing shift towards online representation and sales over the past three decades (Boll, 2021; Brown, 2024). This chapter addresses the transformative power of digitization and platformization on locality and practice of regional auctioneers for art and antiques.[1] While digitization has previously been analyzed for top-tier auction houses and the primary art market (Boll, 2021; McAndrew, 2023, 2024), little has been written about its effects on the lower secondary market, despite the larger number of auction houses operating in it.

The term "regional auctioneer" is typically descriptive of geographical location, though it is also used colloquially to refer to smaller auction houses dealing in the lower to mid-market segments from a singular location. Their size, auction rhythms, schedules and client bases differ

[1] For this chapter, which discusses market dynamics rather than examinations of singular works, the terms "art" and "artwork" will refer to both fine art and applied art, including antiques.

J. M. Wendl (✉)
Kunst-Auktionshaus WENDL, Rudolstadt, Germany
e-mail: j.wendl@auktionshauswendl.de

A.-S. V. Radermecker (ed.), *Low-End Markets for Art and Cultural Goods*, Cultural Economics & the Creative Economy,
https://doi.org/10.1007/978-3-032-27566-0_17

significantly from top-tier players such as Christie's and Sotheby's (Radermecker, 2022). While their existence used to rely strongly on local bidders and traditional practices, smaller auction houses were arguably quicker to embrace digital solutions, and today almost all regional auctioneers host their sales on one or more auction-aggregator platforms (Radermecker, 2022; McAndrew, 2023). The latter accumulates catalogues from numerous auction houses, providing bidding opportunities on vast numbers of artworks through searches based on general categories, key words and price ranges across multiple auctions, regions, and sale dates (Boll, 2024). Consequently, auctioneers adapted their sale practices and client interactions to those new digital platforms and bidding pools.

Being an auctioneer and director of the studied auction house, I analyze this process with an autoethnographic perspective. Data access and inside knowledge of both auctioneer and client-experiences, combined with a reflective but interpretive research philosophy, contribute to the interpretation of the case study, namely Kunst-Auktionshaus WENDL. Founded in 1991 in Rudolstadt, within the former GDR-state of Thuringia, Kunst-Auktionshaus WENDL grew parallelly to the spread of digital solutions in the global economy, changing from a traditional model to a hybrid one with the incorporation of a website and online catalogues (2001), platform-integration (2002) and live-bidding (2010, as only the second German house to host live-sales on Lot-tissimo). Today, it offers between 10,000 and 12,000 lots of art and antiques in three yearly four-day auctions with 99.99% under the value of $50,000, catering to both national and international clients (WENDL, 2025). Most artworks on offer can therefore be placed within the lower art market segment, both by definition of a traditional market segmentation by price and the triadic model by Radermecker and Moureau in the introduction to this volume.

This case study grants insights into the complex challenges and opportunities faced by auctioneers of lower value art and antiques in today's globalized digital economy. Various digital tools influence regional auctioneers either directly or indirectly. However, for the scope of this chapter, the focus rests on auction-aggregator platforms and their live-bidding formats that broadcast from salerooms to online spaces, as they affect most directly the *modus operandi* of regional auction houses. Attention is given especially to the change in bidder location distribution, bidding formats, and social aspects of auction dynamics. While the case study is based on observations in the German market, many findings translate to other countries due to the international reach of said platforms.

2 Literature Review

Although general literature can be found on the traditional role of auctioneers, studies specifically concerned with regional auctioneers and their needs are scarce. A noteworthy contribution is Radermecker's (2022) exploration of provincial actors in the lowbrow art market, which also explored the locality and adaptiveness of smaller auctioneers during the Covid-Pandemic. The article identified main differences in the high-end and low-end art market, naming the adaptiveness of the latter's players and their early embrace of online channels as key factors for favorable market conditions during the pandemic. Amongst other points, Radermecker investigated local loyalties by returning collectors as well as online purchases by the newer client pool of Generation Y in a provincial market setting, drawing relevant conclusions for today's hybrid (lower) art market. Generally, the fundamentals explored by Smith (1989), Velthuis (2005), Thompson (2008) and various others, are contextualizing auction structures across market segments, especially Boll's (2021, 2024) analysis of recent art market crisis and their propelling effects on digital solutions (Kalbermatten & Rausch, 2021). While recent scholarship frequently addresses the digitization of the modern-day art auction market, most of it concentrates on early attempts of online-only auctions by the top-tier players and their final establishment during the COVID-pandemic (Boll, 2021; Kalbermatten & Rausch, 2021; Häußler, 2023; Brown, 2021, 2024; McAndrew, 2024). These studies are valuable points of comparison when investigating differences in experience for auctioneers in the lower art market compared to the top tier and for the contextualization of wider economical and societal developments.

Online-only-formats (as used by eBay), although offered by many platforms, are often covered in digital auction literature but are not explored here. Their key difference is the absence of a human auctioneer who asks for bids, decides over bidsteps and assigns them to competing bidders before closing the sale by calling the highest bid (thrice) and bringing down the hammer. In many legislations, such as Germany (where auctioneering requires a license), timed or online-only auctions are therefore strictly not considered auctions due to the lack of the auctioneer's mediation, which offers the latter type certain differences in legal status to regular purchases (such as the exception of the standard 14-day return period in the EU; see Boll, 2021, p. 84).

Samdanis (2024) analyzes various aspects of platformization, including the benefits of accessibility, democratization of the segment and strategic partnerships with digital platforms. While many of his points relate to the use of platforms by brick-and-mortar businesses, auction-aggregator platforms were not part of his investigation. This chapter attempts to bridge the gap in literature on how digitization transformed traditional auctions in the lower-value art market and how their online-translation affects the (once considered essential) factor of locality.

3 Data and Methodology

I use a mixed methodological approach with an interpretive research philosophy. At its core is the case study of Kunst-Auktionshaus WENDL in Rudolstadt, Germany—a traditional, family-lead auction house for fine art and antiques operating mainly in the lower-market segment. Due to its foundation in 1991 in newly reunited Germany, it is a prime example of a regional auction house having established itself in a local market gap and having grown parallelly to the spread of digital solutions in the global economy. As the daughter of the founders and current owner, I am conscious of potential personal bias. Consequently, personal observations and autoethnographic perspectives are cross-checked with the quantitative analysis of auction and bidder data between 1991 and 2024. This allows for unique insights into the geographical distribution of clients and use of digital and non-digital bidding methods over the course of 110 auctions. Combining the perspective of practicing auctioneer with data generally inaccessible to the public allows for a unique opportunity to investigate how general art market trends fit into the rarely analyzed reality of those operating at the lower end of the market. To highlight specific shifts in auction culture, selected autoethnographic datapoints are provided.

Further triangulation is achieved by comparison with relevant literature on art market dynamics and observations of the wider auctioneer community, exclusively focusing on traditional, auctioneer-led, rising sales (or English Auction) with their digital translation to online live-auctions, such as offered on platforms like Lot-tissimo, The Saleroom and Invaluable (Boll, 2021). They require active auctioneers and sale operators that manage the digital presentation of asking prices and acceptance of bids from online bidders clicking respective buttons on the live-auction interface.

To measure the impact of live-bidding and auction aggregator platforms, the proportion of local, regional, national, and international (DACH and worldwide) clients from a 33-year period is analyzed, as well as analogue and digital bidding formats active (and measurable) during this time. The data is extracted from two sets of back-office software as well as the three main auction aggregator platforms used by WENDL during this period. Personal data has been anonymized and archival datasets processed for maximum comparability. Slight changes in the collection parameters of the data as well as a 4-year data gap (due to faulty historic backups from the DOS-Software) could not be prevented, but are considered, which shows the importance of digital data conservation for art markets studies. National and global economic developments have not been contextualized as their relevance seems minor to the drawn conclusions.

To determine client locality, this case study uses the following geographical definitions:

Local: Within a 50 km radius of Rudolstadt, where the auction house is located.
Regional: Districts bordering the Saalfeld-Rudolstadt district, identified by postcode.
National: Within Germany.
DACH: Germany, Austria, and Switzerland, grouped by their common language.
World: All other countries.

4 Empirical Analysis and Findings

4.1 Auctioneer Locality

Physical, local accessibility used to be key for auction houses, as they lead to spontaneous interactions and sales, longstanding client-relationships and the ability to build and reinforce a reputation through constant interactions and exposure (Velthuis, 2005). Although some regional auctioneers also have adjacent shops and dealerships, the rarity and event character of an auction traditionally extends their geographical reach to a wider area (Brown, 2024). Auctions are events one makes the effort to travel to, thus benefiting local cultural tourism and economic stimulation. They are often scheduled taking local festivities and holidays into account, which highlights their interwoven contribution to the local cultural economy.

The sourcing and selling of artworks contribute to current local market trends and collecting dynamics, influencing regional perception of art (market) histories and networks (Velthuis, 2005). At times, like for WENDL, there was no other auctioneer of comparable size and portfolio in geographic vicinity, granting them a certain monopoly and unrivaled possibility to set up and grow (local) auction standards and communities pre-digitization (Radermecker, 2022). Following the triadic model, an auction monopoly could add to the perceived scarcity factor of the sold artworks solely by their limited supply channels. Today, most local auctions are available online, making them accessible outside of their geographic area and around the clock. This leads to more competition both amongst auctioneers when attracting consigners and bidders, and between bidders from various (international) locations (see below) (Radermecker, 2025).

Even with no physical local competitor, auctioneers and their fee structures, lots, pricing, expertise, and services are under more competitive pressure post-digitization. When hosting their catalogues on international auction-aggregator platforms, they compete globally against a previously unparallelled number of comparable auctions for the attention of potential bidders. However, the international exposure also helps to balance drops in regional bidding performance. I have observed less lower value lots being passed amongst the large offer in our sales. What the local market could not absorb, online-bidders did. Following the triadic model, although the actual number of similar artworks does not change, the perception of scarcity does, as greater exposure is given to those works. In effect, the perceived scarcity factor increases because a larger pool of bidders competes for a single lot, but it simultaneously decreases because a larger pool of comparable artworks becomes sourceable and accessible.

For bidders, online catalogues contribute to market democratization as they decrease the relevance of geographic proximity and increase time-flexibility by providing access to bidding channels outside of auction house opening times (Brown, 2021). Anyone from anywhere might bid during the weekend or late at night. Autoethnographic data confirms strong bidding activity on the WENDL-website on days following the auction when premises are closed. Even before the staff has finished physically moving unsold lots to the aftersales, many of them have parallelly sold online—both to local and more remote bidders.

4.2 Cultural Community

Traditionally, geographical factors of a local auction community influence social factors, habits, and customs, thus shaping the value-creating process and practices applied by bidders and auctioneers (Smith, 1989). Indeed, regional auctioneers fulfill various further cultural roles adjacent to their core business to various, individually varying degrees. Frequently, auctioneers are supporters and sponsors of their local art scenes, participating in exhibition openings, theatre premieres and other socio-cultural events. Their presence grants consecration and social capital (Bourdieu, 1996). Through their support and networking, auctioneers impact local culture beyond simple donations or artworks they sell. Regional auctioneers and auction house specialists like me frequently serve as jury members, specialist contacts and boards members to local, regional, and even national cultural institutions and competitions. I even experienced my auction house serving to promote my region's cultural assets during visits by (international) delegations. Some auctioneers, including myself, engage in teaching or research and provide professional internship opportunities. Hence, an auctioneer's social connections can serve the (local) cultural community and vice versa. Auctioneers act as access-providers to information, knowledge, networks and artworks, record-keepers of art historical and ownership data, and exposure-creators for little-known (local) artists not commonly found in public attention or the canon of art history (Smith, 1989). They contribute to the preservation and promotion of local heritage and their community's cultural economy, often fostering access through partnerships with local museums, exhibitions, cultural events and more (Velthuis, 2005; Brown, 2024). To illustrate, WENDL hosted the preview to the estate sale of the deceased German artist and set designer Gerd Kraus in a temporarily empty museum space of the local castle museum Schloss Heidecksburg. The subsequent sale established publicly accessible price references and a market for Kraus' artworks (mainly framed collages and paintings), which still sell mainly through WENDL when resurfacing. During the preview and sale, both the museum and the auction house benefitted from common audiences and cross-advertising. To set this example within Radermecker and Moureau's triadic model: while the direct functionality and quality of those works were low to moderate, the scarcity was higher. It was the first time a larger body of the deceased artist‘s work had entered the market and the estate sold exclusively through WENDL. These factors established a stable pricepoint mainly between 100 and 400 EUR per artwork, which reduced slightly over the next few years when a smaller number of collages and paintings continued to be auctioned.

Community engagement, although aided by digital means and often advertised online, has arguably not been affected as strongly by digitization as other aspects of an auctioneer's work. However, the time-investment necessary for online presences and constant development and integration of technological advances as well as digital communication and administration have affected the time and resources left for the immediate local community to some extent. In 2024, WENDL made the decision to discontinue their printed catalogue, which by then was mostly used by local and national clients with lower average spending. While disappointing for local audiences that reported using it as a coffee-table book and for their preview-weekend visit, the arguments of environmental considerations while saving on increasing printing costs, which were re-invested in online-advertising and company-wide pay rises, overweighed. Due to the limitation to a single image per lot, no searchability and only one language (German), most active bidders who received the print catalogue had already been using the online version parallelly. For today's auctioneers, online-access to new client pools (as provided by platforms) poses the question if constant local engagement and visibility is still necessary to generate interest in sales—or if it is mainly a question of image and philanthropy—as (inter)national online-buyers could potentially absorb the loss of local bidders in the digitized auction economy.

4.3 Social—Local—Saleroom

Art auctions are inherently social events. As opposed to the high-end art market, where entry barriers are (perceived) high and cultural codes are plentiful, regional auction houses offer a more informal atmosphere (Smith, 1989; Velthuis, 2005). Some may offer entry level talks and tours during previews and a selection of lots with affordable pricing (with prices starting at €20 at WENDL). Couples attend to furnish their homes, and porcelain may be bought for display but also as dinner sets for family meals. Regional auctioneers thus provide a valuable entry point for new collectors into the art market and facilitate a practical appreciation of living with art and ordinary antiques. Within the triadic model, Radermecker and Moureau addressed this factor as the direct practical functionality that is high in the entry level art market—and a sustainable option complementing the current *Zeitgeist* (Radermecker, 2022).

Traditionally, print catalogues, (art-)newspaper announcements and sales previews inform local audiences about upcoming auctions (Boll, 2021). Especially in the lower-value market segment, auction catalogues could only feature a limited number of images and information due to high printing costs (Adelaar, 2000). Hence, personal inspection of lots and direct interaction with specialists and auctioneers were essential to taking informed bidding decisions (Boll, 2014, 2024). Today, the online catalogue of WENDL hosts up to 10 additional images showing signatures/marks, frames, and details indicative of the work's quality or condition (e.g., restored areas). While this is preferable to the limitations of print catalogues, even digital, two-dimensional photographs (or 360-degree-views) cannot replace the feeling clients develop from handling three-dimensional art-works, ideally complimented by a conversation with auction house staff that have investigated the object for a period of time. Simultaneously, many collectors are highly specialized in their niche area of interest, leading to a mutual exchange of knowledge and industry contacts amongst collectors but also between potential buyers and auction house experts, as I have often benefitted from myself. Evidently, social interactions at auction events enhance the community experience of art collecting and the social role of auctioneers expands past price-building mechanisms (Bourdieu, 1996; Graddy & Ashenfelter, 2002; Karpik, 2010).

Regional auctioneers have tried to digitize social experiences during the pandemic, for example a broadcast of the 100th WENDL-auction in 2020, celebratorily interspersed with theatrical performances by actors from the local theatre and a befriended singer, even though clients were only "present" online. While digitization has brought a wealth of online advertising options that can convey expertise digitally, such as chat groups and forums for collectors and even 360-degree-tours through auction previews (the latter especially during Covid-lockdowns but on continuous offer at WENDL), the social component of a preview experience hardly translates online, especially for those attending "to see and to be seen" (Boll, 2021; Brown, 2024). Personal observations reveal selected preview-attendees with more interest in peer-interaction than in bidding. While having little relevance to the economic success of the auction, they actively contribute to the social atmosphere of the event.

4.4 *Client Locality*

WENDL's auction previews in the small town of Rudolstadt attract a variety of guests, most of them repeat-clients. When specific clients enter, the staff already knows who else will attend during this day. There are friendships or collegial bonds formed during those visits; collectors and even families scattered in different parts of the country coming together, finding its location in the center of Germany and the event of mutual interest a convenient meeting point. The rarity factor of these thrice-yearly events adds to the motivation of making an invested effort for both: the artworks and the community experience of talking to likeminded collectors, specialists and auctioneers. Interestingly, while room audiences during sales have never returned to pre-digitization or even pre-pandemic levels, the number of preview visitors has recovered. The more relaxed, familiar atmosphere, supported by free biscuits, coffee and specialist talks, still carries a social attraction to be experienced offline.

4.5 *Consigner Locality*

The auctioneers' social role is tangible in their relationships with vendors and buyers and can essentially be stripped down to the notion of trust and opportunity (Beckert & Rossel, 2013). Experienced dealers and collectors enjoy cordial relationships with auctioneers due to years of fruitful collaboration. I witnessed multiple times how collectors have explicitly entrusted my auction house with the dissolution of their collection in their will—a large part of it having been previously acquired at the very same saleroom operated by my parents. Equally, first-time consigners approach auctioneers for guidance, often relying on their expertise and trusting them as an independent third-party agent, striving alongside them for the highest possible hammer price and the transfer of treasured possessions to a worthy new owner. The emotional component of auction buying and selling should not be underestimated. The connection between perception of value and the sale of art at specific auction houses was investigated by Thompson (2008) looking at the top-tier market segment. On a much smaller scale, the symbolic transfer of value from the selling auction house to the artwork can still be observed for regional auctioneers and their consigners, especially when an emotional relationship to the work and/or auction house exists.

Digitization has a limited effect on consigner localities. Digital solutions benefit different stages in the consignment process, like initial contact and pre-evaluation, but do not eradicate the need to move physical artworks to the auction location. Thus, the low investment costs of using local salerooms for lower-priced art, even if no trust-relationship has previously been established, can be preferable. Figure 1 demonstrates the clear dominance of individual local, regional and national consigners for the years 2020 to 2024 of the digitized art market, especially when comparing it to buyers in Fig. 2. Long-standing trust relationships and auction profiling, however, can motivate non-local consignments despite geographical constraints.

Consignments from local and regional vendors, even in the period displayed post-digitization, are stable, averaging 40% altogether (Fig. 1), and therefore are essential for business-survival, as strong consignments

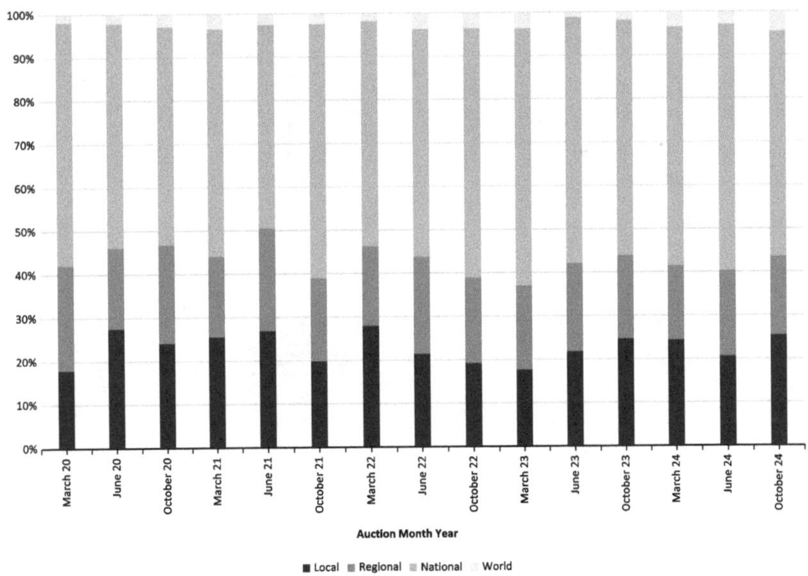

Fig. 1 Consigner location distribution (in percentage), 2020–2024. *Source* Author

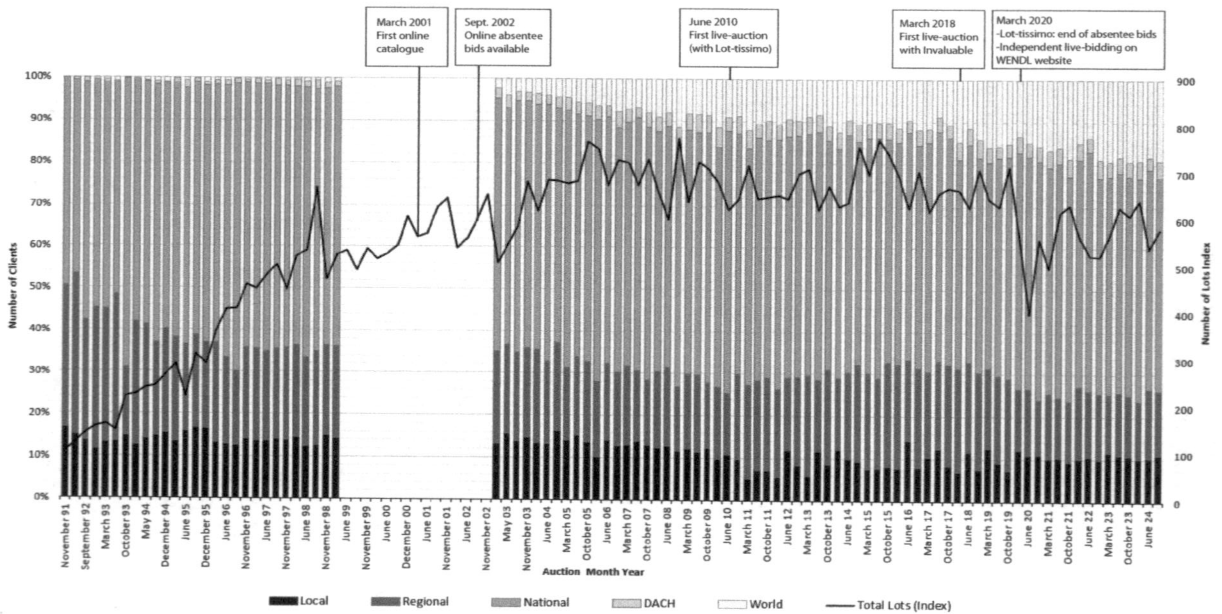

Fig. 2 Buyer location distribution (percentage) in relation to number of lots (index), 1991–2024 (Winning bidders = buyers. Data gap due to faulty backups from early 1999 to late 2002). *Source* Author

are the starting point of any auction, attracting bidders from various locations. Platformization, however, influences even local vendors indirectly by questions of reliability and trust in the purchasing online-bidders. Autoethnographic data suggests that many vendors are still skeptical of sales to platform bidders, especially those bidding from abroad. They are worried about non-payment and the added difficulty as well as associated costs of prosecuting buyers through various legislative spheres. As mediators of trust, auctioneers rely on semiautomated vetting systems provided by aggregator-platforms to aid the sale-registration process. They include successful bidder statistics and feedback from other auctioneers, essentially being the digital version of former personal requests for auctioneer-to-auctioneer client references.

4.6 *Buyer Locality and Bidding Formats*

Buyer localities were significantly affected by digitization and platformization, which is clearly observable over the history of WENDL. Figure 2 is based on historical auction and invoice data and shows the development of WENDL's buyer localities in percentage per auction. The years 1991 to September 2002 show non-digital development starting at their first-ever sale. It is noteworthy that while the number of clients and lots quickly increased, there was relatively little change to the percentage of the local bidder core. The regional reach reduced more significantly by ca. 10% in the first five years, before reaching a plateau. Instead, there was a rising percentage of national clients. During this first decade of offline operations, the small number of international buyers were either overseas tourists or mainly from the German-speaking DACH region, where advertising and word of mouth could easily reach and logistical barriers (such as language, transport costs, and varying national auction legislation and practices) were lower. The auction house was dependent on their local, regional and national audiences, with a solid, increasing room audience and absentee bidders (Fig. 3), both growing in correlation with the quantity and quality of lots on offer (Fig. 2).

From 2001, WENDL hosted digital catalogues and advertising on their website, using the Lot-tissimo white label-solution and platform catalogue from November 2002. An increasing number of digital commission bids from national and international bidders were received soon after (Figs. 2 and 3). By June 2010, when WENDL held their first live-auction (hybrid model) through Lot-tissimo, international client rates expanded from 2%

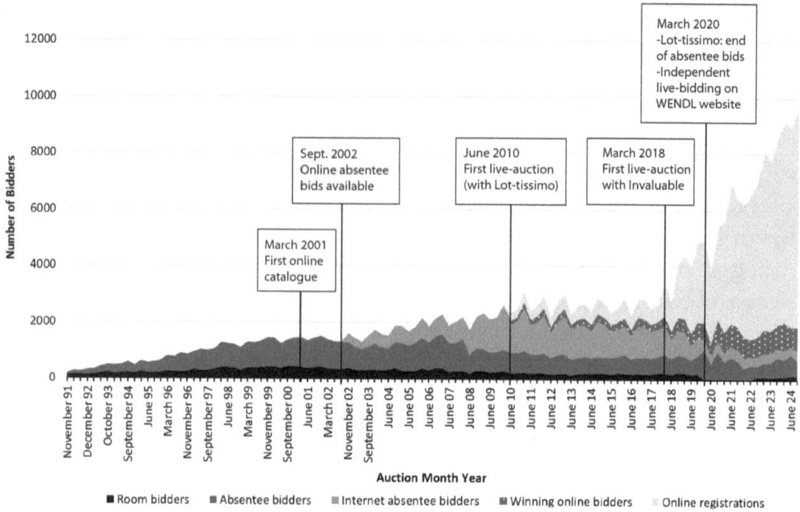

Fig. 3 Bidders by bidding method, 1991–2024 (Absentee bidders include telephone bidders). *Source* Author

pre-digitization in 1999 (last reliable figure before data gap) to 12% (Fig. 2). Further growth of non-German buyer-percentage continued much slower but got lifted when joining the internationally-oriented aggregator-platform Invaluable in March 2018, doubling to 24% by October 2024.

Changes in bidder-locality can be further contextualized by a shift in bidding practices. As seen in Fig. 3, at the beginning both direct bidding in the saleroom and absentee bidding grew steadily, reaching their highest point in the early 2000s. The effects of internet absentee bidding took several years to surpass analogue absentee bids, but from 2008 the offline versions decreased significantly, suggesting a migration of bidders to online formats, especially once live-bidding was introduced. The convenience of bidding from home and over long distances while staying in full control was a winning argument over traditional formats, even considering additional live-charges of 3–5% on the hammer price (depending on platform and year). Consequently, the number of registrations and winning live-bidders grew steadily, while room attendance and offline bidders continued to decline. The exponential growth of live-bidding-registrations since 2018, however, is largely due to the automated sale-registration systems of

Invaluable and not representative of bidder participation. Inflated registration-rates, I must report, pose a significant administrative challenge to auctioneers, who may host on several platforms and have limited resources to vet ever larger amounts of potential bidders. The total amount of active live-bidders could not be retrieved historically but the increase in winning live-bidders over the past 14 years is indicative.

In 2020, the COVID-Crisis forced bidders and auctioneers around the globe to operate online, as physical access to salerooms was restricted or, as with WENDL, completely impossible until October 2022. Effectively, Invaluable reported a 70-percent-increase in partnering auction houses between April and May 2020 compared to the previous year, with a 132% gain in turnover and 52% more buyers (Kutscher, 2020). Those numbers substantiate Radermecker's (2022) identification of the investigated provincial market participant's particular adaptiveness to alternative (online) sale strategies. She observed a synergetic advantage with younger, digitally-versed client groups and attributed a positive effect in stability of sales to auctioneers that had previously migrated to online channels–both effects can be seen in the above-mentioned overall statistics and those of this case study.

The significant drop in lot numbers for WENDL's June 2020 auction was due to unclear local policies regarding personal interactions during consignments, which the WENDL-team used as an opportunity for re-consigning older inventory into a smaller summer sale, thus freeing time for internal restructuring processes during the adaptation of their new software and web-systems. The following sales featured significantly more lots but still less than pre-Covid. This was not primarily due to a lack of consignment requests but also a conscious reduction of workload. An investigation of consignment-to-profit ratio would be necessary for weighing of both factors. Nonetheless, while live-auctions had been successfully run and steadily improved by the auction house for eight years when the first lockdown was imposed, more traditional competitors reported serious hardships, some even decided to close their business instead of rushed adaptation to online sales.

Auctioneers on Lot-tissimo were further subject to adaptation when the platform discontinued their online absentee bids (directly forwarded to the auctioneer at no additional cost to them or the client) in favor of auto-bids ("secret" absentee bids activated in the live-bidding software and thus unknown to the auctioneer and subject to live-fees). WENDL had re-introduced their independent web-catalogue with online absentee-bid-option at the same time, continuously offering the service to their bidders, hoping to keep their loyalty. Nonetheless, the effect of these platform changes and the pandemic's move towards more active online participation is visible within the shift of numbers from internet absentee bids to live-bidding (Figs. 3 and 4). Getting used to bid online even for local sales, international bidders easily transitioned to bid on more remote auctions as well. The "one search catches all"-model of aggregator platforms and their prominent advertising tools for auctioneers helped catch the attention of visiting bidders. Once they are invested, the bidding process is the same regardless of the artwork's location, and post-sale logistics are more likely to become an afterthought.

Although the local and regional bidder core stayed stable in the last five years, gravitation towards live-bidding is noticeable even within those groups. During each auction, I observe their hybrid bidding activity: many local clients bidding during several days within a multi-day auction split their time between online-bidding and personal attendance according to convenience. Eventually, many still enjoy the thrill of visiting the saleroom, the social interaction with the auctioneer and staff, and the comfort of paying and collecting their lots in person. The auction room at WENDL (and reportedly at most regional salerooms), however, is filled

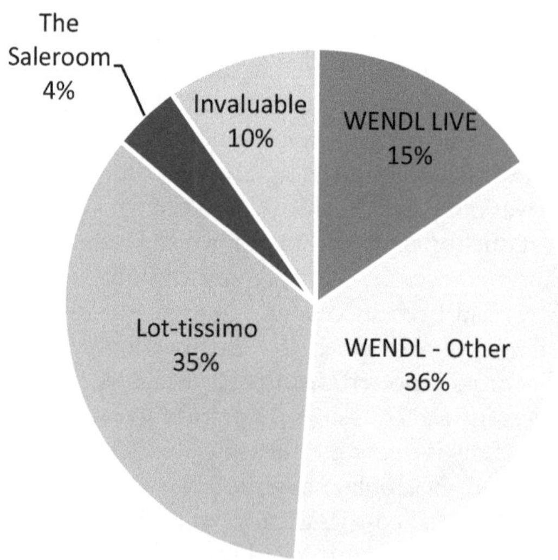

Fig. 4 Average share of winning bidders at WENDL by auction platform (in percentage), 2021–2024. *Source* Author

less densely than in pre-live-bidding times 15 years ago. Currently, an average of 64% of bidders win their lots online, with 49% coming from external platforms. (Fig. 4). This shows the weight of these platforms in auction operation and bidding practices for regional auction houses, even for those few with their own live bidding systems like WENDL.

Meanwhile, auctioneers are faced with the "amazon-mentality" of online-buyers that expect lots to be packed, shipped, and delivered immediately, at preferably no cost. In times of increased labor and material costs, those demands are impossible to meet and post-sale logistics increasingly consume the time of auction house staff, taking workforce and attention away from their core roles of art experts and sale-facilitators (Boll, 2021). It is not surprising that shipping companies like Mail Boxes Etc. in the UK (with the-saleroom.com) and ThePackengers in France (with Drouot.com) have formed platform-partnerships, providing those services for clients and auctioneers as an alternative to in-house shipping. Interestingly, what digitization economized in personal interaction on location, it seems to add in the need for intermediaries instead. Online-bidders have essentially outsourced their physical presence to the auction house or third parties as service providers.

The parallel success of digital bidding formats and expanded platform presence (Figs. 3 and 4) compared to the growth in international bidders (Fig. 2) suggests a strong correlation, further supported by the analysis of platform-bidder localities in Fig. 5.

4.7 *Platform Locality*

Auction-aggregator platforms possess their own locality or native focus within their bidder base. This geographical focus is, amongst other factors, a main consideration for auction houses deciding on their platform co-operations. For Germany, the predominant platform is Lot-tissimo, with its monopoly in the DACH region.[2] The Saleroom (owned by the

[2] The platform was founded and is still registered in Germany and is available in two languages: German and English. As of 07.06.2025, from 325 currently listed auction houses, 181 are from Germany (55.65%), 13 from Austria and 8 from Switzerland, accounting for a 62.15% DACH share. The 44 houses from the UK are mainly cross-platform postings via the-saleroom.com, although Italy (19), the Netherlands (15) and Belgium (11) are also stronger target markets. Similar numbers found on invaluable.com seem less reliable as several of the listed houses have not uploaded an auction in 12 months or more.

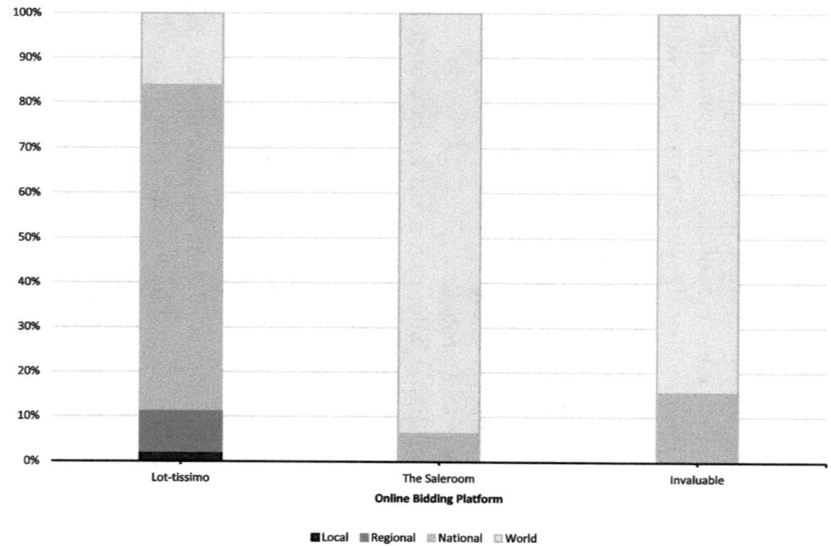

Fig. 5 Average share of winning bidders by locality per auction-aggregator platform (in percentage), 2021–2024. *Source* Author

London-based ATG Group which also acquired Lot-tissimo in 2018) caters mainly to the UK and other English-speaking markets, including the Commonwealth (ATG, 2025), Drouot.com to France and French-speaking audiences, while Invaluable is especially strong on the American and Asian markets (McAndrew, 2023, lists more platform data). WENDL initially joined Lot-tissimo, extending their audience in German speaking countries. By later joining The Saleroom and Invaluable, WENDL grew their international reach. The comparison of winning bidder localities between platforms supports this strategy, with local and regional bidders exclusively found on Lot-tissimo (10%), while the-saleroom and Invaluable show over 90% and 80% international reach respectively (Fig. 5).

By paying careful attention to the compatibility of their auction profile (language, lot types, international logistic capacity), auctioneers can use platforms to tap into their native bidder pools, specifically targeting certain national markets. Arguably, platforms are joining regional auction houses in their role as mediators between local and broader art markets, preserving regional culture while facilitating trade (Velthuis, 2005). The case study shows that even a regional auction house, situated far from any major art-market hub, can establish an international reach (Fig. 6). In a way, platforms can provide regional auctioneers with a similar effect to the "source locally, sell globally"-strategy of top-tier auction houses, arguably acting as a digital, globally accessible satellite office (Boll, 2021). In the lower-value market, however, international exposure is humbler, and quieter compared to world-record-breaking auctions. Low-value artworks reach homes across boarders instead of international headlines.

4.8 Auctioneer Interaction in Hybrid Salerooms

While the convenience of bidding online from home has certainly reduced physical bidder attendance, so far, it has not left regional salerooms entirely empty. Among those attending WENDL-sales in person are clients from all locations—even international, with an obvious majority of local origin. Auctioneers, however, are facing the challenge of upholding traditional auction customs and bidding methods while also catering to online audiences and formats. This does not only lead to various administrative challenges, but also to the need for flexibility and creativity when negotiating the social complexities of hybrid sale audiences.

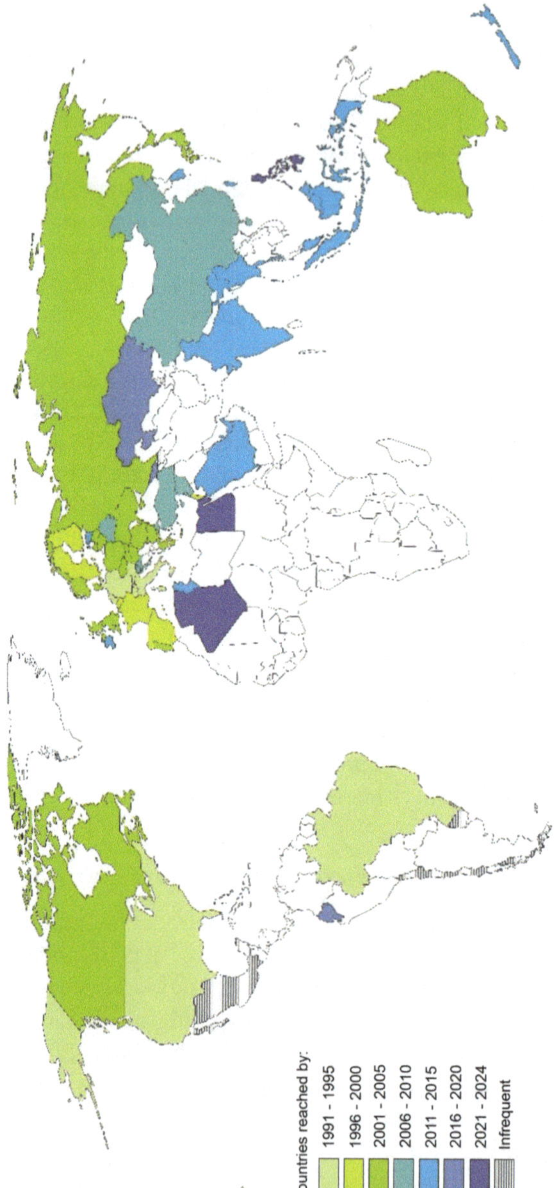

Fig. 6 Global reach of Auktionshaus WENDL by 5-year indication of first sale to country. *Source* Author

The local, social, and cultural roles all meet in the auction room and in the performative power of the auctioneer. Being occasionally a highly theatrical experience, even subtle nuances in auction practices can have a strong effect (Boll, 2024; Kathryn Brown, 2024; Smith, 1989). Regional auctioneers with successful live-auctions have adapted their social role to a digital audience (Kalbermatten & Rausch, 2021). They now serve as virtual hosts, maintaining a sense of immediacy and trust in an impersonal online environment. Trust is formed by fairness and transparency and being able to follow the price-building process in the saleroom is a key argument for bidders choosing auctions over other forms of art sales transactions (Boll, 2024). While auctioneers are ideally skilled in controllably performing the sale, digital bidding formats can be hard to control.

Live-auction broadcasts use software that features lot information, starting prices, and asking bids with the possibility for registered bidders to actively participate by clicking on the current bid step. All bids and the auctioneer's response to them must be translated by an operator into the software, thus enabling a clear yes-or–no-decision for live-bidders on the other side of the screen. The auctioneer sees incoming bids either by a show of hand from the operator, or by looking at the provided auctioneer screen. The latter has improved over time, and depending on the platform, can give additional information such as the country codes of bidder location, the total amount of online bidders currently attending, the hovering of undecided bidders over the bid button, and (more recently) the arrival at the second-last and final steps of an auto-bid. It does not, however, substitute social signals an auctioneer would get from looking in the face of a bidder in the saleroom. Subtle nuances in facial expressions or the quick word with a partner cannot be observed, nor can individual requests be made.

The live-bidder, on the other hand, can see and hear the auctioneer through audio—and video-broadcasts. Initially, some auctioneers were reluctant to broadcast any audio or video. Sometimes, this was due purely to consideration of additional costs and wanting to become more comfortable with the integration of live-bidding systems into their auctioneering without the pressure of an extended audience. Others worried about the added transparency and public assessment of their auctioneering tactics, not least by the competition. Providing video-broadcasting correctly, however, increases the user experience considerably and leads to stronger engagement of bidders as they create a more immersive and personal experience of interacting with the auctioneer, ultimately benefiting hammer prices (Boll, 2021). In the early days, many auctioneers set up the camera out of their visual field and treated it as a mere recording device to the effect that live-bidders reported feeling left out and confused whether their bids were even received. In contrast, WENDL set it up close to the auctioneer, who addressed online bidders by looking and talking into the camera, asking directly if they wished to increase their bid. This proved so successful that bidders started calling after the auction apologizing for their untidy living rooms, as they could not fathom that they themselves were not actually seen by the auctioneer. WENDL livestreams were soon used as training examples for successful auction broadcasts by Lot-tissimo operators.

Anecdotal evidence from WENDL's first live-auction during the infancy of this format confirms the social importance of auctioneering skills. Being unused to this new technology, bidders in the auction room got the impression that they were constantly outbid by invisible online bidders that only the auctioneer could see. When the auctioneer announced that a live-bid had actually been received last-second, thus continuing the bidding after a floor bidder had already thought himself the winner, some started to suspect exploitation. While there was familiarity with auctioneers assigning bid steps to commission bids at the rostrum, the immediacy of the live-bidders' reaction to their own bids, not even anticipated by the auctioneer on many occasions, was new. Immediate reactions within the room audience quickly spread an atmosphere of disbelieve and mistrust. Being aware of the bidders' discontent, Anke Wendl had her staff install a room-facing screen during a break, that mirrored the auctioneer monitor. Soon, the room audience did not only nod their agreement at incoming bids, but they even informed the auctioneer on occasion when they feared live-bids were overlooked. The atmosphere changed back to one of trust and well-meaning curiosity, as bidders tried to decipher country codes, exclaiming in awe when an international bid arrived. While this makes for an entertaining anecdote, it demonstrates the fragile social balance of auctioneer-bidder-relationships with the element of trust at its very core.

Quite often when auctioneering, I even switch languages according to the country codes displayed to prompt international bidders. Nonetheless, the necessity to simplify the bidding process into "to-click-or-not-to-click" decisions for online participants results in auctioneers either sacrificing some of their more flexible tactics of auctioneering or to accept a certain inequality of participation between room and online audiences. For example, live-bidding operators can rarely adjust asking prices below the starting price as pre-set in platform-hosted online catalogues. Therefore, the in German regional sales once common practice of asking for an offer below the starting price (conditional to the vendor's approval), if made to room audiences, would seem unfair to online participants who only have the option to click on the original starting price if wanting to bid. Some, including WENDL, therefore completely abandoned the practice during their hybrid sales. However, it is still common for room or phone bidders to ask for a reduction of the next bid step once high values are reached. Online, live-bidders cannot enter an alternative sum, and it is upon the auctioneer to offer an alternative step, then made available through the live-operator, with the bidder's choices still being restricted to pure acceptance or refusal. Digital democratization and flexibility stopps at those finer practical nuances.

4.9 Outlook

Digital bidding formats in the lower art market, most frequently provided by auction-aggregator platforms, are well established and will continue to have a democratizing and homogenizing effect on bidding and auctioneering practices. As a country with long-standing auction legislation, Germany has recently updated the *Versteigererverordnung*, establishing auctioneer-led virtual and hybrid live-sales as fully-fledged auctions, also eradicating the necessity of so-far mandatory physical sale previews.[3]

Nonetheless, the needs of auctioneers and clients in the lower-value art market, whether online or offline, are frequently overlooked by policy makers. In 2023, the EU released consumer protection laws for online purchases with strict quality guidelines.[4] Although antiques are generally exempted, they are vaguely defined by use of a previous directive as

[3] See Versteigererverordnung, https://www.gesetze-im-internet.de/verstv_2003/BJNR0e54710003.html.

[4] See REGULATION (EU) 2023/988, http://data.europa.eu/eli/reg/2023/988/oj.

"Goods, other than works of art or collectors' items, which are more than 100 years old".[5] In reality, many sought-after auction lots, for example functional ordinary antiques and design objects such as Art Deco lamps, mid-century tables, and vintage jewelry, have not yet reached a century in age, neither can they fulfill the demands of the legislation (e.g., providing the manufacturer's postal and electronic addresses). Resultingly, their online sellers, including auction houses, are left to operate in a dangerous grey area. I strongly suggest closer collaboration with practitioners from all segments of the market when deriving such legislation to ensure practicability as the art market has undoubtedly become part of the e-commerce universe. A proposed solution could be general exemptions for online auctions by acknowledged auctioneers for art and antiques (at least in countries like Germany where they are licensed and registered, offering a minimum of quality-control). Additionally, cross-border sales encouraged by online solutions pose significant logistical challenges, such as varying import and export restrictions depending on national legislation. Ideally, international regulations and declaration processes would be unified. Finally, attention should be given to the power of monopoly-holding platforms. By restricting their offered bidding formats too intensely, aggregator-platforms potentially force auctioneers to discard regional or national differences in auction practices, as many houses are quite dependent on the platforms' infrastructures. A loss in regional differences in both artworks and auction practices would be a loss in cultural diversity of local art markets.

Various further routes of enquiry remain open after this limited scope. Though difficult to gain access to, larger datasets from other auction houses would benefit further investigations, such as comparisons of client localities between live-online and online-only auctions. Additionally, imbalances of geographical artwork circulation could be analyzed, considering this case study suggests a stronger local and regional origin of consigners as opposed to buyers. Albeit, within those preliminary results, underlying variables such as a potential discrepancy in consigner location (registered address) and lot origin (potentially varying address in case of inheritance, etc.) were not considered.

[5] See Annex IX to Council Directive 2006/112/EC, https://eur-lex.europa.eu/eli/reg/2023/988/oj#ntr13-L_2023135EN.01000101-E0013.

5 Conclusion

This chapter showed that regional auctioneers have transitioned from local intermediaries to international market participants through the integration of digital platforms, balancing their core local, regional and national audiences and traditional community roles with new demands of an interconnected marketplace. The introduction of live-bidding and auction-aggregator platforms has affected established auction practices and brought various challenges and opportunities to regional auctioneers—including an interdependence with this new digital "intermediary of intermediaries." A careful selection of aggregator-platform partnerships allows expansion to desired (inter-)national bidder groups, thus diversifying audiences and decreasing dependency on the stability of local markets. This could affect the perception of the scarcity factor of entry-level artworks established by Radermecker and Moureau in the triadic model, as (inter-)national online exposure may balance geographically varying levels of supply. Online bidders have embraced live-bidding for its convenience and independence of physical location, although their influence to shape the auction process is more limited than with room attendance. While this case study suggests that, currently, the fear that local bidders would not be able to succeed against global online competition can be refuted, a co-relation between the use of platform-live-bidding and international reach is found. Ultimately, locality factors remain a relevant consideration for the sale of physical artworks and their collecting communities. The successful bridging of the physical auction room with the digital sphere during hybrid live-auctions requires careful negotiation by an auctioneer, making their social role in the saleroom more challenging but not less relevant today.

Acknowledgements I am grateful to my colleague Graciela Gamboa Moyano for her help with data mining and processing and to the peer-reviewer and scientific committee for their informative feedback on the first draft of this chapter.

References

Adelaar, T. (2000). Electronic commerce and the implications for market structure: The example of the art and antiques trade. *Journal of Computer-mediated Communication*, *5*, JCMC531.

ATG. (2025). https://www.auctiontechnologygroup.com/about-us/our-history/

Beckert, J., & Rossel, J. (2013). The price of art. Uncertainty and reputation in the art field. *European Societies, 15*, 178–195.

Boll, D. (2014). Distributions system und Ereignis: Die Auktion auf dem internationalen Kunstmarkt In A. Hausmann, *Handbuch Kunstmarkt* (pp. 177–198). transcript Verlag. https://doi.org/10.14361/transcript.9783839422977.17

Boll, D. (2021). *Was ist diesmal anders? Wirtschaftskrisen und die neuen Kunstmärkte: 1990, 2001, 2009, 2020.* Hatje Cantz.

Boll, D. (2024). *Die Kunst und ihr Markt.* Hantje Cantz.

Bourdieu, P. (1996). *The rules of art: Genesis and structure of theliterary field.* Chicago University Press.

Brown, K. (2021, July 11). Germany's auction market has remained strong through the pandemic. Now, it's poised to make even bigger gains. *Artnet.* https://news.artnet.com/market/germany-has-it-all-why-german-auctions-are-making-major-gains-1987567

Brown, K. (2024). *Art auctions: Spectacle and value in the twenty-first century.* Lund Humphries Publishers, Limited.

Graddy, K., & Ashenfelter, O. (2002). *Auctions and the price of art.* University of Oxford. https://ora.ox.ac.uk/objects/uuid:af5f7921-b77f-4e46-ac62-f4009a525885/files/sst74cr031

Häußler, H. (2023). *Die Schöpfer des Kunstmarkts: Von den Anfängen in der Antike bis zur Digitalisierung in der Gegenwart.* transcript Verlag. https://doi.org/10.14361/9783839464526

Karpik, L. (2010). *Valuing the unique: The economics of singularities.* Princeton University Press.

Kalbermatten, S., & Rausch, C. (2021). Bidding better online in Belgium: The value of auction house expertise during the COVID-19 pandemic. *Arts, 10*(4), 75. https://doi.org/10.3390/arts10040075

Kutscher, B. (2020). Enorme Nachfrage bei Verkäufen im Netz. *Handelsblatt.* https://www.handelsblatt.com/arts_und_style/kunstmarkt/zeitgenoessische-kunst-enorme-nachfrage-bei-verkaeufen-im-netz/25988056.html

McAndrew, C. (2023). *The art Basel and UBS art market report 2023.* Art Basel and UBS. 2023. https://www.ubs.com/global/en/our-firm/art/art-market-insights/download-report-2023.html?campID=NL-ANY-GLOBAL-ENG-ANY-ANY-ANY

McAndrew, C. (2024). *The art Basel and UBS art market report 2024.* By Arts Economics. 2024. https://www.ubs.com/global/en/our-firm/art/art-market-insights.html#artmarketreport2024

Radermecker, A.-S. (2022). Selling lowbrow art and cultural goods in times of pandemic: The case of a provincial art market. *International Journal of Cultural Property, 29*(3), 283–310. https://doi.org/10.1017/S0940739122000340

Radermecker, A. S. V. (2025). The legal and reputational implications of the platformization of the market for 'ordinary'antiques: The case of Drouot. com. In *Law and finance in international art markets* (pp. 69–84). Routledge.
Samdanis, M. (2024). Platformisation and transparency in the global art marketI. et al., *Global art markets* (219–231). Routledge. https://doi.org/10.4324/9781003400868
Smith, C. W. (1989). *Auctions: The social construction of value.* University of California Press.
Thompson, D. (2008). *The $12 million stuffed shark: The curious economics of contemporary art.* Palgrave-MacMillan.
Velthuis, O. (2005). *Talking prices: Symbolic meanings of prices on the market for contemporary art.* Princeton University Press. https://doi.org/10.1515/9781400849406
WENDL. (2025). https://www.auktionshauswendl.de/tcms/en/about-us/our-house/the-history

PART VI

Beyond Traditional Art Values

Consumer Behavior in the Low-End Art Market: A Comparative Analysis Among Consumers of Fine Antiques, "Ordinary" Antiques, and Collectibles

Federica Aramu

1 Introduction

Within the art market, consumption is mostly associated with collecting practices, which have been extensively studied in academic literature (Chen, 2009; Lazzaro et al., 2015; Kossenjans & Buttle, 2016; Rojas & Lista, 2022), with a specific focus on the high-end segment. While the motivations in collecting fine art are well-documented in the history of collecting (Zolfagharian & Cortes, 2011; Lee et al., 2021; Spaid & Matthes, 2021), less attention has been dedicated to the low-end art market.

This chapter examines consumer behavior in the low-end segment of the art market by drawing on the Theory of Consumption Values, developed by Sheth et al. (1991). The theory proposes five consumption values that influence consumer choice behavior. A comparative approach is employed to examine to what extent consumption values and motivations differ among buyers of the following object categories belonging to the low-end art market: fine antiques (below the $50,000 threshold),

F. Aramu (✉)
Université libre de Bruxelles, Brussels, Belgium
e-mail: federica.aramu@ulb.be

A.-S. V. Radermecker (ed.), *Low-End Markets for Art and Cultural Goods*, Cultural Economics & the Creative Economy,
https://doi.org/10.1007/978-3-032-27566-0_18

"ordinary" antiques and collectibles. While academic literature proposes definitions of antiques, it often overlooks distinctions among the already mentioned object categories.

Fine antiques are typically characterized by exceptional craftsmanship with very curated details and high-quality materials (e.g., Mahogany in furniture making, precious metals for dinnerware or lighting). They are usually appreciated not only for their high aesthetic value and superior craftmanship, but also for their historical significance, eventually reflecting historical events or being associated with prominent figures of the past (e.g., members of royalty, aristocracy). Agedness is a necessary condition of being an antique, with the style reflecting the past and showing material signs of aging (Rosenstein, 2009). However, conventional classification of antiques stipulates a minimum age of 100 years (e.g., Palmer & Forsyth, 2006; Rosenstein, 2009). Ordinary antiques, despite being later reproductions of fine antiques, also have historical significance. They show lower quality in the materials and techniques adopted (e.g., a twentieth-century Louis XV furniture reproduction). They might be handmade or the result of semi-industrial production and mostly serve a utilitarian purpose. Additionally, they are not usually associated with historical personalities or events but rather reflect social trends or the habits of the users (e.g., the middle and working classes). If fine antiques are distinguished by uniqueness or are part of limited editions or even commissioned work, ordinary antiques are often the result of serial production. Antiques can even signal social status. While historically associated with the upper class, antiques collecting has diffused to the lower-middle and working classes, acquiring distinct symbolic meanings across social strata (Belk et al., 1988). This distinction is mirrored in the market itself, where dealers specialize in either high-end antiques characterized by rarity and craftsmanship, or later, mass-produced pieces that cater to broader consumption patterns (Nelsen, 1970).

If both fine and ordinary antiques can reasonably be classified under the category of decorative arts, collectibles form a separate category. Collectibles—such as coins, memorabilia, militaria, toys, stamps—are considered having between 15 and 99 years old (Zolfagharian & Cortes, 2011) and are cultural goods valued for their set completion and sometimes rarity. They are usually produced in series or handmade and some of them even target the collectibles market. According to Carey (2008, p. 339), collectibles exist in sets, and the act of collecting is often "the active pursuit of completing the set." Ordinary goods can also become collectibles when they are considered instruments to enhance or evoke some memories or past experiences (Carey, 2008). Their value lies in their potential to be collected as part of a series.

In this study, the three object categories—although they may reflect different consumption behaviors and appeal to distinct buyers—are considered part of the low-end segment of the art market, as, in terms of price, all three categories usually fall within the market's low-end segment, defined as below \$50,000 (McAndrew, 2024). However, a conceptual challenge appears as fine antiques, which are sold at higher prices than ordinary antiques and collectibles (due to scarcity and higher quality of craftmanship, materials, and historical significance), are expected to belong to the high-end segment of the market. Although the intrinsic qualities of fine antiques align more closely with high-end market goods, fine antiques are usually sold below \$50,000, despite some exceptions. Ordinary antiques, by contrast, are more accessible in terms of price value, due to their lower quality, serial production and the utilitarian purposes they offer. This distinction is also evident in the marketplaces through which these objects circulate. If fine antiques are often sold in prestigious auction houses and highbrow antiques stores, ordinary antiques are typically traded in local auction houses, flea markets, antiques or second-hand shops. This dissonance concerning fine antiques shows that other approaches are needed to capture the specificities of the art market, beyond classification based on prices.

Three magazines—each one providing interviews with consumers of either fine antiques, ordinary antiques or collectibles—were selected, as differences among these object categories and the related types of consumption are expected. The British magazine *Apollo* features fine art and antiques, and the French periodicals *Antiquités-Brocante* and *Collectionneur & Chineur* are respectively dedicated to ordinary antiques and collectibles. Each of them contains interviews with their respective consumers. A content analysis with a comparative approach has been conducted on 120 interviews (40 per magazine) to identify and compare consumption patterns.

The findings reveal a complex and layered art market where perceived values and motivations shape consumer choices alongside the intrinsic qualities of the objects themselves. Consumers of fine and ordinary antiques acquire similar objects with different price points and levels of quality (e.g., furniture, glassware, porcelain), driven by distinct values and motivations. Consumers of collectibles share the marketplace with ordinary antique consumers, but they align more with fine antique consumers in values and motivations. Consumers of ordinary antiques challenge traditional collecting motivations, prioritizing utilitarian purposes, and contributing to sustainable consumption. Since the high-end market for fine art is well-documented in terms of collecting literature, this research offers new insights into consumer values and motivations within the low-end segment of the art market. This chapter is divided as follows: a literature review on collecting motivations and consumer behavior in the art market, followed by a theoretical framework based on the Theory of Consumption Values; data collection and methodology; the empirical part with findings; and a final section that interprets the results and concludes the chapter.

2 Literature Review

2.1 *Consumer Behavior in the Art Market: Collecting Motivations and Beyond*

Academic research on consumer behavior in the art market has predominantly focused on collecting, often overlooking other forms of consumption, such as occasional or utilitarian purchasing of art and cultural goods. Existing literature has examined collecting practices (Chen, 2009; Lazzaro et al., 2015; Kossenjans & Buttle, 2016; Rojas & Lista, 2022) with an emphasis on fine art and the high-end segment of the art market. Scholars have also explored the history of collecting (Zolfagharian & Cortes, 2011; Spaid, 2018; Lee et al., 2021; Spaid & Matthes, 2021) and how to define collector profiles (Dillon, 2019). Literature on art collecting has traditionally focused on various motivations, including psychological factors (Belk et al., 1988; Muensterberger, 1994; Pearce, 1995; McIntosh & Schmeichel, 2004), socio-cultural influences (Bourdieu, 1984; Belk, 1995; McIntosh & Schmeichel, 2004; Johnson Jorgensen et al., 2023), and economic considerations (Coslor et al., 2020; Velthuis, 2005; Mandel, 2009; Frey & Eichenberger, 1995).

Psychological motivations play a crucial role in art collecting. Collecting is often a goal-oriented process that generates satisfaction in both acquiring items and maintaining collections (McIntosh & Schmeichel, 2004), but it can also be a means of self-enhancement, allowing individuals to reinforce their identity (Belk et al., 1988; Muensterberger, 1994). Some collectors experience nostalgia, acquiring objects that evoke memories of their past, especially of their childhood (Muensterberger, 1994). However, collecting can sometimes take on problematic dimensions, becoming compulsive or even addictive (Belk et al., 1988; Formanek, 2012), although this behavior is usually socially acceptable, unlike other more stigmatized addictions (Belk, 1995). Beyond individual motivations, collecting is also a social activity, fostering relationships and a sense of belonging. This activity can allow individuals to establish and maintain relationships with peers through shared interests (Bourdieu, 1984; Veblen, 1899). Lee et al. (2021) introduce the concept of "social membership" to explain how collecting enables individuals to connect with others and become part of a community, with dynamics including both cooperation and competition. Additionally, some collectors view their activity as a way to preserve cultural history, rescuing objects from obsolescence (Belk, 1995; Grable & Watkins, 2016). Legacy reflects another significant factor, as some collectors aim to pass their collections to future generations (Lee et al., 2021; Spaid, 2018). Pearce (1995) also highlights the educational aspect of collecting, noting how acquiring and categorizing items can contribute to knowledge acquisition. Economic reasons are another crucial motivation, with many collectors viewing their activity as a financial investment. Velthuis (2005) and Mandel (2009), for instance, discuss the investment potential of collecting, especially in art markets, where items may be appreciated over time. While much of the research on collecting has focused on the non-monetary aspects of behavior, Lee et al. (2021) point out that economic considerations are relevant, even if they are not always the primary motivation for all collectors. Importantly, economic motivations often operate in conjunction with psychological and social motivations.

Despite the extensive literature on art collecting, research on broader consumption behaviors within the art market—particularly in its lower-end segment—remains limited. While collecting constitutes a form of consumption, it is not the sole way individuals engage with cultural goods. Bulk purchasing and one-time acquisitions also constitute important yet understudied modes of consumption. Belk (1995) articulates a comprehensive definition of collecting as the passionate and selective acquisition of items removed from ordinary use and viewed as part of a larger, non-identical set. Dillon (2019) critiques the rigid distinction between the use and non-use of objects in collections, noting that collectors of art, books, or musical recordings may engage with their items in both utilitarian and nonutilitarian ways. For example, art collectors may display their pieces decoratively, and book collectors may not read every book they own but still view them as potential resources. Similarly, Stebbins (1992) differentiates between "systematic" collectors, who follow a structured approach to building comprehensive collections and "casual" collectors, who acquire goods more opportunistically. In exploring consumer behavior within the art market, it is important to extend the focus beyond fine art collecting to include the lower-end segment, which might feature similar or contrasting consumption practices and motivations, if compared to the high-end segment. The focus on fine art collecting calls for a critical re-evaluation, as it neglects key aspects of consumption in the art market, limiting the understanding of how consumers engage with this market.

2.2 *The Theory of Consumption Values*

Since the low-end market includes more utilitarian and affordable types of objects, this study adopts a broader perspective, beyond traditional collecting practices, to investigate which values motivate consumer choices in the art market, by employing the Theory of Consumption Values (hereinafter TCV) (Sheth et al., 1991), a theoretical framework rooted in marketing and consumer behavior research. The TCV provides a multidisciplinary approach to understanding consumer choice by identifying five key perceived values that influence purchasing decisions: functional, social, emotional, epistemic, and conditional. While these values are conceptually independent, their influence varies according to the consumer's context. Some values align with key motivations in collecting literature, whereas others offer new insights into consumer behavior. The values encompassed within the theory are the following:

(i) Functional value refers to the perceived utility derived from an alternative's ability to fulfil functional, utilitarian, or physical performance needs (Sheth et al., 1991). In the art market, cultural goods can be acquired for their functional and practical use. Consumers may evaluate art market goods based on their condition, functionality, affordability, and durability.

(ii) Social value refers to the perceived utility acquired from an alternative's association with demographic, socio-economic and cultural groups (Sheth et al., 1991). In the art market, purchases may signal social distinction or belong to a community of collectors and enthusiasts, reinforcing social bonds through shared interests.
(iii) Emotional value refers to the perceived utility acquired from an alternative's association with the capacity to arouse feelings or emotions (Sheth et al., 1991). The act of acquiring cultural goods can be an emotionally engaging experience, fostering sentimental attachments.
(iv) Epistemic value refers to the perceived utility acquired from the alternative's capacity to arouse curiosity or provide a desire for knowledge or novelty (Sheth et al., 1991). The process of acquiring cultural goods can offer opportunities for learning and exploration.
(v) Conditional value depends on situational factors influencing consumer choice (for instance, some products only have seasonal value or are associated with events happening only once) (Sheth et al., 1991). Acquisition of cultural goods can also be influenced by demographic shifts, economic conditions, lifestyle changes and personal circumstances.

Already applied to understanding consumer choices across a wide range of products and services (Sheth et al., 1991; Lin & Huang, 2012; Koay et al., 2022), the Theory of Consumption Values (TCV) provides a useful framework for exploring value-based consumption within the art market. Despite existing research on collecting practices, there remains limited understanding of broader consumption behavior across different segments of this market. The framework, extended in this study to the analysis of art market consumption, is motivated by the intention to shed light on the low-end segment of the art market, which also encompasses utilitarian and affordable goods (e.g., ordinary antiques). This approach enables a comprehensive analysis of the values—and related motivations—that shape consumption within this segment, bridging the gap between collecting motivations and the broader spectrum of consumer behavior.

3 Data and Methodology

This research analyzes three magazines that feature interviews with consumers and collectors of fine antiques, ordinary antiques and collectibles. The relevance of the proposed magazines was assured by the adoption of the following selection criteria: first, the presence of interviews with consumers and collectors related to these categories; second, the publication frequency of the interviews to ensure a consistent dataset; third, publication of articles related to one of the object categories (e.g., publishing information about auction results, collecting trends, detailed description of the objects, art market analysis); fourth, broad circulation of the magazine among readers interested in one of the object categories. Based on such criteria, the following magazines were selected: *Apollo* for fine antiques, *Antiquités-Brocante* for ordinary antiques and *Collectionneur&Chineur* for collectibles.

Apollo is an international monthly magazine in publication since 1925. With 30,000 readers across 25 countries—54% is represented by female and 46% by male readership—[1]it covers topics related to fine and decorative arts, including art history, contemporary art, exhibitions, auctions, and art market trends. It is well-known for its insightful analysis and reports on the art market, including auction results, emerging trends, and profiles of collectors and dealers. The magazine is also known for its scholarly approach, with articles written by leading art historians, curators, and critics. More broadly, it offers a global perspective on the art world, covering art from various cultures and regions. Since similar magazines do not publish such detailed interviews with collectors recurrently (e.g., *Frieze*, *ArtReview*), the selection of *Apollo* was motivated by the interviews with collectors of fine antiques, accessible via its digital archive. Additionally, in other magazines, the interviews were more market-oriented (ARTnews), or the role of collectors was captured more in the art ecosystem (e.g., *The Art Newspaper*).

Antiquités-Brocante and *Collectionneur&Chineur* are both in French and belong to the same media company. They share structural similarities, including recurrent interviews with consumers and collectors of items displayed in the respective magazines. What differentiates these two magazines from *Apollo* is that they provide a section for readers to buy, sell, or

[1] This information was included in the 2024 media kit shared by the magazine editor during an email exchange with the author.

trade items. *Antiquités-Brocante* is a French monthly magazine since 1997, dedicated to the world of low-end antiques. It has around 28,000 monthly readers, 45% of whom are female and 55% male, with an average age of 64.[2] It serves as a comprehensive guide to collecting, buying, and selling ordinary antiques (e.g., furniture, ceramics, glassware, clocks), but also art, jewelry and vintage items, with a focus on French and European items. It contains specific insights into the antiques market, including trends, price guides, and auction results, but also practical advice for collectors and enthusiasts, including tips on identifying authentic items, restoration, and care of antiques. The event agenda is another service of the magazine, with listings and reviews of antiques fairs, flea markets, and other events where readers can buy and sell antiques. Articles often incorporate historical context for various types of antiques, helping readers understand the provenance and significance of their collections. It also features interviews with collectors, dealers, and experts in the field of antiques and *brocantes*, and touches on how antiques and vintage items can be incorporated into modern décor and lifestyle. Although other magazines specialized in antiques can be found (e.g., *Home & Antiques*, *Antiques Trade Gazette*), only *Antiquités-Brocante* specializes in low-end cultural goods.

Collectionneur and Chineur is a French bi-weekly magazine in publication since 2006, with 13,000 readers, 75% male and 25% female, and an average age of 55.[3] This magazine covers a wide range of collectibles, including toys, books, postcards, stamps and various other items of interest to collectors. It provides in-depth coverage of the collecting world, publishing valuable information and resources for both seasoned collectors and beginners. It publishes updates on the antiques and collectibles market, including trends, auction results, and price guides. The magazine also displays practical advice on collecting and maintaining collections. Sometimes, it publishes themed issues focused on specific types of collectibles or particular periods, conveying specialized content for niche interests. Like *Antiquités-Brocante*, it includes comprehensive listings of upcoming events such as antiques fairs, flea markets, and auctions, but also articles that delve into the historical and cultural significance of

[2] Ibid.

[3] Ibid.

various collectibles, providing readers with a deeper understanding of the items they are interested in. Similar magazines usually focus on specific types of collectibles such as toys (*Collectors Gazette*) or any type of goods available on the art market (*Collezionare*).

These magazines show some differences among themselves, but they represent a specific segment of the art market and target a specific readership each. They show different formats and languages and yield multiple insights, most likely aligned with the magazines' purpose and narrative. After the identification of the relevant magazines, data collection encompassed the selection of 120 interviews (40 per magazine) to examine consumer behavior related to fine antiques, ordinary antiques, and collectibles. The digitized interviews were analyzed through a qualitative content analysis adopting a comparative approach, supported by NVivo software. Content analysis, widely used in media communication research (Krippendorff, 2004; Bryman, 2012), enabled the systematic categorization and interpretation of consumer values. Despite the two languages encountered in the data set (English and French), the analysis was conducted in English and encompassed two main phases: first, I employed a deductive approach, with the operationalization of the Theory of Consumption Values to identify consumer values and compare them among the three categories second, I coded the interviews into NVivo to identify consumer values and motivations behind consumer choice (see in Appendix 1, Table 3, the operationalized definitions of the codes). Furthermore, additional values and motivations that emerged inductively during the coding process were included in the analysis. All the observations detected in the analysis—including both dominant and less frequent patterns—are reported in the section dedicated to the findings.

This study relies on existing magazine content rather than firsthand interviews; therefore, findings may reflect editorial choices and not fully capture consumer diversity. Social desirability bias can affect interviewees' responses that align with the publication's tone or readership expectations. Also, confirmation bias is a potential issue, as the interviews might reflect existing audience preferences instead of objective representation. Additionally, the longitudinal perspective, with articles from 2023 and earlier, does not track interviews across fixed intervals throughout the three magazines. Despite these limitations, the research delivers a valuable analysis of consumer motivations within the art market, laying a foundation for further studies. Future research could feature a more thorough understanding of the dynamics characterizing the low-end market, but also exploring consumption values, motivations and trends directly involving consumers of these three categories.

4 Empirical Analysis and Findings

Drawing on the Theory of Consumption Values (Sheth et al., 1991), the analysis focused on interviews published between 2007 and 2023 in *Apollo* (APO), between 2012 and 2023 in *Antiquités-Brocante* (AB), and between 2022 and 2023 in *Collectionneur & Chineur* (CC). A total of 293 instances reflecting the values of the TCV and additional values were identified. As reported in Table 1, all consumption values proposed by the TCV were observed in the interviews. Emotional value was the most recurrent among the consumers (30.4%), followed by Social (16.8%), Epistemic (10.2%), Functional (6.5%) and Conditional value (6.2%).

Table 1 Overview of values across consumers of fine antiques, ordinary antiques and collectibles. *Source* AB, APO, CC and author

Values		*Fine antiques*	*Ordinary antiques*	*Collectibles*	*TOT*
The TCV	Emotional	8.9% (*n* = 26)	5.8% (*n* = 17)	15.7% (*n* = 46)	30.4% (*n* = 89)
	Social	8.9% (n = 26)	1.4% (n = 4)	6.5% (*n* = 19)	16.8% (*n* = 49)
	Epistemic	7.5% (*n* = 22)	1.0% (*n* = 3)	1.7% (*n* = 5)	10.2% (*n* = 30)
	Functional	–	6.5% (n = 19)	–	6.5% (n = 19)
	Conditional	–	3.8% (*n* = 11)	2.4% (*n* = 7)	6.2% (*n* = 18)
Other values	Aesthetic	8.2% (*n* = 24)	0.7% (n = 2)	0.7% (n = 2)	9.6% (*n* = 28)
	Economic	1.4% (n = 4)	0.7% (n = 2)	–	2.1% (*n* = 6)
	Experiential	–	9.1% (*n* = 27)	–	9.1% (n = 27)
	Environmental	–	9.1% (n = 27)	–	9.1% (n = 27)
TOT		34.9% (*n* = 102)	38.1% (*n* = 112)	27.0% (*n* = 79)	100.0% (*n* = 293)

Beyond the values included in the framework, additional dimensions emerged, namely Aesthetic (9.6%), Experiential (9.1%), Environmental (9.1%) and Economic value (2.1%). Overall, consumers of ordinary antiques presented instances of all the values (38.1%) while both consumers of fine antiques (34.9%) and collectibles (27.0%) did not display Environmental, Experiential and Functional value. Furthermore, consumers of ordinary antiques shared the Conditional value with collectors of collectibles and the Economic value with collectors of fine antiques.

4.1 *The TCV Within the Low-End of the Art Market*

Building on the overview of the values discussed above, this subsection explores the values and the motivations underlying the purchase of fine antiques, ordinary antiques, and collectibles as expressed by the interviewed consumers. While the analysis was guided by the Theory of Consumption Values (TCV), the specific consumer motivations were identified inductively during the coding process, emerging directly from the empirical material rather than being predefined by an existing theoretical framework. These motivations were subsequently associated with the values outlined in the TCV framework, as well as with additional values identified during the analysis. The relationship between values and motivations across the three object categories is summarized in Table 2.

Emotional, Social and Epistemic values were the most recurrent ones and appeared across the three categories.[4] Emotional value was primarily reflected in the following motivations to purchase the object categories that the consumers expressed: "nostalgia" (15.4%) and "attachment" to cultural goods (15%). Concerning "attachment," the highest number of motivations were detected among the interviewed collectors of collectibles (8.9%), who personalized and formed deep bonds with items, such as toys evoking adolescence and cinematic fantasies.[5] Examples were also detected among collectors of fine antiques (5.1%), who developed emotional bonds with their objects, often valuing them beyond their monetary worth, such as a collector showing an intense attachment to his Sèvres porcelain collection:

[4] The referencing system to indicate the magazines is the following: Name of the magazine (APO for *Apollo*; AB for *Antiquités-Brocante*; CC for *Collectionneur&Chineur*); Number of the issue; Year of the issue publication; Month of the issue publication; Day of the issue publication (only in *Collectionneur&Chineur*, as it is a bi-weekly magazine).

[5] CC, 390, 2023, 06, 01.

Table 2 Overview of values and motivations (numbers and percentages) among consumers of fine antiques, ordinary antiques and collectibles. *Source* AB, APO, CC and author

Values	*Motivations*	*Fine antiques*	*Ordinary antiques*	*Collectibles*	*TOT*
Emotional	Attachment	5.1% (n=15)	1.0% (n=3)	8.9% (n=26)	15.0% (n=44)
	Nostalgia	3.8% (n=11)	4.8% (n=14)	6.8% (n=20)	15.4% (n=45)
Social	Social membership	4.8% (n=14)	1.4% (n=4)	6.5% (n=19)	12.6% (n=37)
	Legacy	4.1% (n=12)	–	–	4.1% (n=12)
Epistemic	Educational motivations	7.5% (n=22)	1.0% (n=3)	1.7% (n=5)	10.2% (n=30)
Functional	Utilitarian purpose	–	6.5% (n=19)	–	6.5% (n=19)
Conditional	Gifting	–	3.8% (n=11)	2,4% (n=7)	6.1% (n=18)
Aesthetic	Aesthetic appreciation	8.2% (n=24)	0.7% (n=2)	0.7% (n=2)	9.6% (n=28)
Economic	Investment value	0.7% (n=2)	0.7% (n=2)	–	1.4% (n=4)
	Market influence	0.7% (n=2)	–	–	0.7% (n=2)
Experiential	Experiential value	–	9.1% (n=27)	–	9.1% (n=27)
Environmental	Lifecyle extension	–	6.1% (n=18)	–	6.1% (n=18)
	Waste avoidance	–	3.0% (n=9)	–	3.1% (n=9)
TOT		34.9% (n=102)	38.1% (n=112)	27.0% (n=79)	100.0% (n=293)

"I know the works so well that I would walk into any room and tell in a heartbeat if something were moved or missing".[6] Meanwhile, a very limited number of instances were found for ordinary antiques (1.0%), with consumers stressing the emotional value of their possessions over monetary

[6] APO, 668, 2018, 10.

worth.[7] This shows that attachment was not an important motivation for buyers of ordinary antiques. The other significant motivation is "nostalgia," which was particularly salient for collectors of collectibles (6.8%), who usually referred to childhood memories.[8] For consumers of ordinary antiques, nostalgia (4.8%) was associated with objects recalling their childhood[9] or the work of their relatives.[10] Nostalgia was also identified among collectors of fine antiques (3.8%), who often replicate their family's collecting habits or see collecting as a way to honor their family's memory.[11] All the consumer categories shared the same values with similar trends and motivations behind the consumption of these goods.

Social value, although manifested across the three categories, revealed different nuances depending on the object type. Consumer choices were mostly motivated by "social membership" (12.6%) and "legacy" (4.1%). "Social membership" played a crucial role in fostering connections and engagement within communities, although it materialized in different ways across the three categories. It was mostly observed among collectors of collectibles (6.5%), some of whom assumed leadership roles, such as becoming presidents of their respective associations of coins and Champagne plates.[12] Other collectors built social connections through collector associations,[13] but also had their dedicated websites or join platforms like Instagram[14] to share their collections. Similarly, but with a very low percentage (1.4%), consumers of ordinary antiques usually shared their passion on Instagram, selling pieces and exchanging decoration ideas or showcasing how they restored or repurposed items. With 4.8% of instances, collectors of fine antiques often emphasized the role of dealers or friends in the creation of their collections.[15] For some collectors, the desire to leave a "legacy" shaped their approach to collecting. This motivation was evident only with collectors of fine antiques (4.1%) who

[7] AB, 183, 2014, 01.

[8] CC, 394, 2023, 08, 03; CC, 396, 2023, 09, 07.

[9] AB, 195, 2015, 01.

[10] AB, 276, 2021, 10; AB, 298, 2023, 08.

[11] APO, 705, 2022, 02.

[12] CC, 392, 2023, 07, 06; CC, 389, 2023, 05, 18.

[13] CC, 389, 2023, 05, 18; CC, 392, 2023, 07, 06.

[14] CC, 391, 2023, 06, 15; CC, 392, 2023, 07, 06; CC, 403, 2023, 12, 21.

[15] APO, 559, 2008, 11; APO, 607, 2013, 03; APO, 669, 2018, 11; APO, 680, 2019, 11.

donated portions of their collections to renowned museums, emphasizing the public value of their objects.[16] Different consumer motivations were attached to social value, showing how collectors of collectibles and fine antiques were engaged in communities of collectors, although legacy was present only among collectors of fine antiques. Social motivations appeared marginal among consumers of ordinary antiques.

Epistemic value was exemplified by "educational motivations" (10.2%), representing an important dimension of the low-end segment of the art market, particularly among consumers who engaged with antiques to explore history, craftsmanship, and cultural significance. This motivation was most prominent among fine antiques collectors (7.5%), who remarked how their initial appreciation has deepened into passion through study.[17] Inspiration frequently stemmed from museum visits and the purchasing process itself,[18] but also from reading specific books on the topic.[19] This motivation appeared less central in the other two categories. With a very low percentage of instances (1.7%), collectors of collectibles acquired specialized books or catalogues,[20] and studied the provenance[21] and history[22] of these objects. Although very marginal, consumers of ordinary antiques accounted for only 1.0% of examples, such as a chef who loved uncovering the history behind objects,[23] while another one conducted research to trace the provenance of her items.[24] Educational motivations were most strongly associated with fine antiques, showing the importance of provenance in their consumption.

The least frequently observed values were Functional (6.5%) and Conditional (6.1%). The first was exclusive to consumers of ordinary antiques, who acquired these goods for "utilitarian purposes." For instance, one interviewee, a guest house owner, reported purchasing tables for guest rooms—stressing that they were needed to furnish her

[16] APO, 549, 2007, 12; APO, 691, 2020, 11; APO, 687, 2020, 06.

[17] APO, 569, 2009, 10.

[18] APO, 607, 2013, 03.

[19] APO, 670, 2018, 12.

[20] CC, 389, 2023, 05, 18.

[21] CC, 392, 2023, 07, 06.

[22] CC, 400, 2023, 11, 16.

[23] AB, 195, 2015, 01.

[24] AB, 296, 2023, 06.

place.[25] Similarly, other consumers acquired furniture from flea markets or auction houses to be used in their houses.[26] Another described using the plates, glassware and silver cutlery on the table purchased at antique fairs and flea markets.[27] The second value, mostly linked to examples of "gifting" and inheritance, appeared only among consumers of collectibles (2.4%) and ordinary antiques (3.8%). Collectors of collectibles stated that their passion began after receiving the first piece as a gift, usually from their partner[28] or parents.[29] Similar trends appeared among consumers of ordinary antiques, where both gifting and inheritance frequently overlapped. For example, a decorative arts collector recalled when she obtained her first pieces of furniture gifted by an aunt,[30] while another inherited an Art Deco furniture that continued to shape interiors and collections.[31] This practice did not emerge in interviews with collectors of fine antiques, although it may also have existed within this group.

Although the TCV values were observed across the three consumer categories, they manifested differently within the low-end art market. It is nevertheless important to acknowledge that these categories may overlap and that exceptions in consumer behavior can occur in practice. Overall, consumers of fine antiques and collectibles reflect distinct motivations, whereas consumers of ordinary antiques are primarily driven by practical considerations, as indicated by the functional value identified exclusively within this category.

5 Additional Values

5.1 Aesthetic and Economic Values

Four additional values characterizing the low-end market and not included in the TCV were detected. To start with, Aesthetic value was represented by the perceived utility acquired from the visual appreciation of

[25] AB, 194, 2014, 12.

[26] AB, 234, 2018, 04; AB, 250, 2019, 08; AB, 300, 2023, 10.

[27] AB, 271, 2021, 05.

[28] CC, 395, 2023, 08, 17; CC 400 2023 11 02.

[29] CC, 395, 2023, 08, 17.

[30] AB, 177, 2013, 07.

[31] AB, 252, 2019, 10; AB, 238, 2018, 08; AB, 267, 2021, 10.

a cultural good. "Aesthetic appreciation" was most prominent among collectors of fine antiques (8.2%), who prioritized craftsmanship and artistic significance over functionality or monetary value.[32] Some collectors selected pieces with historical significance and, more importantly, those they find beautiful.[33] Although this motivation has been widely identified in art collecting literature (e.g., Pearce, 1995), it was less prevalent among collectors of collectibles (0.7%) and consumers of ordinary antiques (0.7%), where it was mostly related to decorative appreciation.[34]

Economic value was the least recurrent among all the values, with examples of "investment value" and "market influence" appearing only among consumers of fine and ordinary antiques. Some collectors viewed their acquisitions as assets, considering the investment potential of their acquisitions (1.4%). Considering the instances of collectors of fine antiques (0.7%), a decorative arts collector considered his collection an asset while also emphasizing that he was motivated primarily by his appreciation of the objects.[35] With examples among consumers of ordinary antiques (0.7%), the investment value acquired another meaning, referring instead to the high quality-price ratio of the acquired ordinary antiques, particularly when compared to new items.[36] In the case of "market influence" (0.7%), collectors based their choices on market trends. Examples were found only among collectors of fine antiques: one of them was not only fascinated by antiques furniture but also by the unconventional business practices observed within the antiques market: "I began to notice some strange business practices—strange from standard economics perspective—in the world of antiques [. . .]."[37] The other collector listed the core ingredients of a collection, the role of market opportunities, together with passion, spending power and knowledge.[38] The literature on economic motivations to purchase art market goods is quite extensive (e.g., Velthuis, 2005; Mandel, 2009; Renneboog & Spaenjers, 2013), with some examples focusing on antiques as investment (Nelsen, 1970; Graeser, 1993), while

[32] APO, 549, 2007, 12; APO, 569, 2009, 10.

[33] APO, 559, 2008, 11.

[34] CC, 389, 2023, 05, 18; AB, 195, 2015, 01.

[35] APO, 559, 2008, 11.

[36] AB, 276 2021 10; AB, 292, 2023, 02.

[37] APO, 638, 2016, 01.

[38] APO, 716, 2023, 02.

here only marginal results appeared, probably due to the narrative of the magazines which did not focus on this aspect of purchasing.

5.2 *Experiential and Environmental Values*

Experiential (9.1%) and Environmental (9.1%) values were the most recurrent among consumers of ordinary antiques and did not appear among consumers of the other categories. Experiential value was reflected by the enjoyment derived from the process of acquiring items ("consumer experience"). Consumers described the experiential aspects of acquiring ordinary antiques rather than stressing the pleasure of collecting per se, with some of them visiting flea markets or garage sales for the pleasure of going and eventually hunting.[39] For either retired or younger couples, hunting for treasures together at flea markets became a shared ritual.[40] Surprisingly, a young couple refused to purchase goods online because they found it less interesting, expressing their pleasure in looking for an object at flea markets or garage sales.[41] Although the low-end art market has an online presence through various sales platforms, it is possible that, for some consumers, the in-person buying experience was more valuable (e.g., direct interaction with dealers, physical inspection of the objects).

Environmental value referred to the utility derived from purchasing items that contribute positively to the environment (Kim et al., 2021). According to previous studies, consumers with strong environmental consciousness are more likely to engage in responsible consumption behaviors, such as purchasing second-hand goods to extend product life cycles (Gonçalves et al., 2016). In line with this literature, 3.1% of instances reflected "waste avoidance," as consumers acquired ordinary antiques to prevent them from becoming waste. Examples included collectors rescuing discarded antiques,[42] with some embracing the mindset of "it can be useful" and "you shouldn't waste it."[43] Similarly, one collector emphasized that antiques yield a better quality-to-price ratio compared to new products.[44] Consumers

[39] AB, 206, 2020, 06; AB, 229, 2017, 11.

[40] AB, 252, 2019, 10; AB, 178, 2013, 08; AB, 262, 2020, 08.

[41] AB, 271, 2021, 05.

[42] AB, 177, 2013, 07.

[43] AB, 288, 2022, 12.

[44] AB, 292, 2023, 02.

valued antiques for their quality, durability, and affordability compared to mass-produced items,[45] seeing them as a more ethical and sustainable choice. Additionally, in some cases, the consumption of ordinary antiques reflected a responsible lifestyle, especially after buying old houses to be restored.[46] "Lifecycle extension" of goods was also a central argument (6.1%), where consumers repurposed dismantled furniture or adapt ordinary antiques to fit their homes.[47] Furthermore, some transform old furniture into new creations,[48] such as a chest of drawers belonging to the former owner transformed into a bathroom cabinet.[49] Creativity was an important component in these practices, as seen in the work of a retired architect described by the magazine as "an inspiring artist" who showcased objects he had repurposed into original works of art.[50] If ordinary antiques have the potential to be modified due to their functional value, fine antiques tend to be preserved in their original state.

Overall, the values not included in the TCV framework highlighted significant differences among consumer groups in the low-end art market. While Aesthetic value was a common thread across all groups, Environmental and Experiential values were particularly prominent among consumers of ordinary antiques, reflecting their focus on sustainability and the process of acquiring items. Additionally, Economic value, with very few instances, was most noticeable among collectors of fine antiques. These findings suggest the heterogeneity of this market segment, influenced by a set of values and motivations.

5.3 *Other Aspects of the Low-End Segment*

Beyond the perceived values and motivations detected in this study, additional insights from the magazines highlighted important factors, such as demographics, acquisition contexts and pricing. A demographic comparison revealed some patterns in gender distribution. Male collectors accounted a significant percentage in both fine antiques (25%)

[45] AB, 276 2021, 10.

[46] AB, 284, 2022, 06; AB, 292, 2023, 02.

[47] AB, 287, 2022, 09; AB, 177, 2013, 07; AB, 296, 2023, 06.

[48] AB, 246, 2019, 04; AB, 262, 2020, 08.

[49] AB, 267, 2021, 01.

[50] AB, 264, 2020, 10.

and collectibles (25%), while collecting as a couple appeared more common among ordinary antique buyers (16%). Females constituted 10% and 8% of consumers of ordinary antiques and collectibles respectively, and only 1% for fine antiques. This shows that, in the context of the magazines, there was a predominance of males dealing with collecting activities. Regarding acquisition context, again, *Antiquités-Brocante* and *Collectionneur&Chineur* suggest that—unlike fine antiques—both ordinary antiques and collectibles were typically sourced from similar marketplaces, with flea markets being the most common, followed by online platforms, garage sales, and second-hand shops. The very few examples found in *Apollo* showed auction houses and antiques shops as marketplaces.

In addition to differences in sourcing practices, pricing patterns also diverge across categories. In *Collectionneur&Chineur,* collectible prices were usually displayed in the interviews and were very low—sometimes even under one euro, especially for objects in series like postcards. While high-priced collectibles exist, this magazine focused on more affordable options. It is important to specify that collectibles with very high prices appear in the market, but this is not the focus of this magazine. For ordinary and fine antiques, prices were usually not disclosed in the magazines. In *Apollo*, likely due to social desirability bias, collectors' status and achievements within their collections frequently appeared. Additionally, object prices may also reflect different socio-economic categories, suggesting that the consumption of fine antiques is also influenced by economic capital. Despite differences in object price and marketplace, collectors of both collectibles and fine antiques shared common values driving their acquisition often reflecting established collecting practices. The vertical segmentation of the art market—primarily structured around price tiers (McAndrew, 2024)—provides an insufficient analytical framework for explaining the dynamics of the low-end segment. For example, fine antiques, although conventionally associated with the high-end market, frequently fall within the lower price range (below $50,000) (McAndrew, 2024). This discrepancy shows the limitations of the price-based segmentation as a manipulated parameter typically used in art market studies. A more robust approach must instead account for the specific characteristics of distinct object categories, including both their intrinsic and extrinsic values. This necessity is also underscored in the first chapter of this book, which provides a triadic model for a more comprehensive understanding of price formation and consumer behavior, according to three core attributes: functionality, scarcity and brand strength. The present chapter lends empirical support to this framework by demonstrating that the low-end segment encompasses objects characterized by both direct (e.g., ordinary antiques) and more symbolic functionality (e.g., fine antiques and collectibles).

To conclude, this comparative analysis demonstrates that the Theory of Consumption Values, unlike art collecting theories, introduces a novel perspective on consumer choice within the art market. To capture the entirety of the consumer choices, additional values that emerged inductively during the coding process were included in the analysis. The results portray the art market as a rich and multifaceted environment, where a multitude of values and motivations appear in the consumption of the three object categories. Emotional value was the most prevalent, driven by attachment and nostalgia, while Social and Epistemic values reflected social membership and educational motivations respectively. Aesthetic value was significant for fine antique collectors, whereas Experiential and Functional values were unique to ordinary antiques. Environmental considerations played a key role in ordinary antiques, emphasizing sustainability and reuse, as practices with potential applicability in the low-end art market. Overall, consumer choices appear closely tied to the intrinsic characteristics of objects and to the relationships individuals establish with them. Although the magazine-based material may not fully mirror real-world practices, it nonetheless reveals meaningful distinctions among object categories and their respective consumers.

6 Conclusions

Within the low-end art market, fine antiques, ordinary antiques and collectibles reflect distinct values, consumption patterns and object characteristics. If the consumption of fine antiques and collectibles largely aligns with established collecting motivations, the consumption of ordinary antiques challenges traditional collecting definitions. Belk's definition of collecting as "materialist luxury consumption" seems applicable primarily to fine antiques, where acquisition reflects luxury and aesthetic appreciation (1995). According to Belk, collecting entails acquiring goods removed from ordinary use and viewed as part of a set. Although some collectibles covered in *Collectionneur & Chineur* consist of everyday items rather than luxury goods, they are indeed removed from their practical function. Some of them might also hold functional value (e.g., ceramics, glassware), further complicating distinctions. Carey (2008) notes that ordinary goods can become collectibles when tied to personal experiences, challenging McIntosh and Schmeichel's (2004) definition of collectors as individual uninterested in an object's practical utility. This suggests a need to reconsider the boundaries between collecting and general consumption.

Ordinary antiques, despite often being reproductions of fine antiques and being priced similarly to collectibles, display distinct patterns of consumer behavior. This divergence raises critical questions about the nature of collecting and highlights differences in consumption practices within the low-end segment. Interviewed consumers of ordinary antiques appeared to derive greater enjoyment from the acquisition process—primarily at flea markets—rather than from the possession of objects themselves. This suggests a shift from aesthetic or symbolic engagement with cultural goods to the contextual and practical dimensions they entail. Another critical aspect of ordinary antiques consumption lies in its intersection with second-hand markets. While all three categories belong to the secondary market, as most likely are pre-owned items, ordinary antiques are more frequently acquired for utilitarian purposes. This reinforces their already recognized position within second-hand consumption practices, and their contribution to sustainable consumption (Aramu & Radermecker, 2025). These findings highlight the diversity of practices within the secondary market, where sustainability considerations, lifestyle choices, and practical needs provide new insights into consumption dynamics within the art market more broadly.

This chapter contributes to art market research by demonstrating how distinct values drive the consumption of cultural goods, revealing implications that extend beyond traditional market segmentation based on price (McAndrew, 2024). Within the low-end segment, fine antiques and collectibles share similar acquisition motivations, yet they differ in pricing and acquisition settings. In contrast, ordinary antiques stand apart for their strong functional value (i.e., direct utility other than just decorative). Though fine antiques and collectibles may include functional items (e.g., furniture, kitchenware), they are typically acquired for reasons beyond practicality. Although ordinary antiques and collectibles are often found in the same marketplaces (e.g., flea markets, thrift stores) and can have similar price points, the values influencing consumer choices vary due to the objects' intrinsic characteristics. Furthermore, ordinary antiques constitute a unique avenue within the art market, revealing consumer motivations that align more closely with second-hand consumption rather than with the more conventional collecting practices observed in the other two categories. More broadly, this study expands the understanding of cultural consumption in the low-end art market and highlights how the engagement with ordinary antiques extends beyond traditional art collecting.

Acknowledgements The author is grateful to the participants of the TIAMSA conference (online and in Melbourne, July 2024) and the LEAM workshop (online, December 2024) for their feedback. The author thanks Prof. Anne-Sophie Radermecker and the anonymous reviewers for their extremely valuable feedback.

Funding The funding for this research was provided by the European Research Council (ERC) under the European Union's Horizon 2020 research and innovation programme (MOOVA—Making Old Objects Valuable Again. The Economic, Cultural Challenges and Sustainability Opportunities of Ordinary Antiques in the twenty-first Century, #101075828).

Appendix Section: Appendix 1.

Table 3 Operationalization of values and motivations

Functional value	*The acquisition of goods fulfils functional, utilitarian, or physical performance needs*
Utilitarian purpose	Consumers acquire objects with the purpose to primarily use them
Social value	The acquisition of goods may signal social distinction or belonging to a community of collectors and enthusiasts
Social membership	The engagement with communities or individuals where consumers can share their interests and find a sense of belonging among like-minded enthusiasts
Legacy	Collectors are motivated by the desire to leave behind a tangible legacy through their collections, with assets that can be passed on to future generations as part of their personal or family history
Emotional value	The acquisition of goods may arouse feelings or emotions
Attachment	The emotional connection developed with objects or collections
Nostalgia	Consumers acquire objects that evoke memories of their past
Epistemic value	The acquisition of a good is connected to a desire for knowledge or novelty
Educational motivation	Collectors engage in research and study, often before and during the collecting process, to gain deeper insights into the items they collect
Conditional value	The consumption of a good is related to a specific situation or circumstance
Gifting	Consumers receive or inherit pieces that become part of their collection
Aesthetic value	The acquisition is determined by the aesthetic appreciation for a good
Aesthetic appreciation	The acquisition of a good for its beauty, artistic value or visual appeal
Experiential value	The acquisition of a good may signal an attachment to the context where it is sourced
Consumer experience	The engagement with the context wherein objects are sold (e.g. flea market) is seen as an experience
Environmental value	The acquisition of goods is related to the willingness to produce positive outcomes for the environment
Lifecycle extension	Consumers modify objects to make them last longer
Waste avoidance	Consumers acquire pre-used and pre-owned goods to prevent them from becoming waste and as a valid alternative to new items
Economic value	The acquisition of goods is related to financial considerations
Investment value	Consumers acquire items considering potential financial returns
Market influence	Collectors are influenced by market trends, acquiring items that are currently popular or anticipated to increase in demand

References

Aramu, F., & Radermecker, A. S. (2025). Preserving the past for a sustainable future: Circular practices in the consumption of ordinary antiques. In E. Salvador & I. Pappalepore (Eds.), *Responsible consumption and production in the cultural & creative industries. Actions, policies, and strategies for a sustainable future*. Routledge. Forthcoming.

Belk, R. W. (1995). Collecting as luxury consumption: Effects on individuals and households. *Journal of Economic Psychology, 16*(3), 477–490. https://doi.org/10.1016/0167-4870(95)98956-X

Belk, R. W., Sherry Jr, J. F., & Wallendorf, M. (1988). A naturalistic inquiry into buyer and seller behavior at a swap meet. *Journal of Consumer Research, 14*(4), 449–470.

Bourdieu, P. (1984). The market of symbolic goods. *Poetics, 14*(1–2), 13–44. https://doi.org/10.1016/0304-422X(85)90003-8

Bryman, A. (2012). *Social research methods*. Oxford University Press.

Carey, C. (2008). Modeling collecting behavior: The role of set completion. *Journal of Economic Psychology, 29*(3), 336–347. https://doi.org/10.1016/j.joep.2007.08.002

Chen, Y. (2009). Possession and access: Consumer desires and value perceptions regarding contemporary art collection and exhibit visits. *Journal of Consumer Research, 35*(6), 925–940.

Coslor, E., Crawford, B., & Leyshon, A. (2020). Collectors, investors and speculators: Gatekeeper use of audience categories in the art market. *Organization Studies, 41*(7), 945–967. https://doi.org/10.1177/0170840619883371

Dillon, A. (2019). Collecting as routine human behavior: Personal identity and control in the material and digital world. *Information & Culture, 54*(3), 255–280.

Formanek, R. (2012). Why they collect: Collectors reveal their motivations. *Interpreting Objects and Collections*, 327–335.

Frey, B. S., & Eichenberger, R. (1995). On the return of art investment return analyses. *Journal of Cultural Economics, 19*, 207–220.

Gonçalves, H. M., Lourenço, T. F., & Silva, G. M. (2016). Green buying behavior and the theory of consumption values: A fuzzy-set approach. *Journal of Business Research, 69*(4), 1484–1491.

Grable, J. E., & Watkins, K. (2016). Quantifying the value of collecting: Implications for financial advisers. *Journal of Family and Economic Issues, 37*, 639–648.

Graeser, P. (1993). Rate of return to investment in American antique furniture. *Southern Economic Journal*, 817–821.

Johnson Jorgensen, J., Sorensen, K., & Spilinek, M. (2023). Motivations to collect: How consumers are socialized to build product collections. *Social Sciences, 12*(12), 671. https://doi.org/10.3390/socsci12120671

Kim, I., Jung, H. J., & Lee, Y. (2021). Consumers' value and risk perceptions of circular fashion: Comparison between secondhand, upcycled, and recycled clothing. *Sustainability, 13*(3), 1208.

Koay, K. Y., Cheah, C. W., & Lom, H. S. (2022). An integrated model of consumers' intention to buy second-hand clothing. *International Journal of Retail & Distribution Management, 50*(11), 1358–1377.

Krippendorff, K. (2004). *Content analysis: An introduction to its methodology*. Sage Publications Inc.

Kossenjans, J., & Buttle, F. (2016). Why I collect contemporary art: Collector motivations as value articulations. *Journal of Customer Behavior, 15*(2), 193–212.

Lazzaro, E., Moureau, N., & Vidal, M. (2015). *What drives the VIPs of the art world? Collectors in the light of textual analysis.*

Lee, C., Brennan, S., & Wyllie, J. (2021). Consumer collecting behavior: A systematic review and future research agenda. *International Journal of Consumer Studies, 46*(5), 2020–2040. https://doi.org/10.1111/ijcs.12770

Lin, P. C., & Huang, Y. H. (2012). The influence factors on choice behavior regarding green products based on the theory of consumption values. *Journal of Cleaner Production, 22*(1), 11–18.

Mandel, B. R. (2009). Art as an investment and conspicuous consumption good. *American Economic Review, 99*(4), 1653–1663. https://doi.org/10.1257/aer.99.4.1653

McAndrew, C. (2024). *The art Basel and UBS art market report 2024.* Art Economics. https://theartmarket.artbasel.com/

McIntosh, W. D., & Schmeichel, B. (2004). Collectors and collecting: A social psychological perspective. *Leisure Sciences, 26*(1), 85–97. https://doi.org/10.1080/01490400490272639

Muensterberger, W. (1994). *Collecting: An unruly passion: Psychological perspectives.* Princeton University Press.

Nelsen, H. M. (1970). The democratization of the Antique: Meanings of antiques and dealers' perceptions of customers. *The Sociological Review, 18*(3), 407–419.

Palmer, C. E., & Forsyth, C. J. (2006). Antiques, auctions, and action: Interpreting and creating economic value. *The Journal of Popular Culture, 39* (2), 234–259.

Pearce, S. M. (1995). *Interpreting objects and collections.* Psychology Press.

Renneboog, L., & Spaenjers, C. (2013). Buying beauty: On prices and returns in the art market. *Management Science, 59*(1), 36–53.

Rojas, F., & Lista, P. (2022). A sociological theory of contemporary art collectors. *The Journal of Arts Management, Law, and Society, 52*(2), 88–100.

Rosenstein, L. (2009). *Antiques: The history of an idea.* Cornell University Press. https://doi.org/10.7591/9780801463822

Sheth, J. N., Newman, B. I., & Gross, B. L. (1991). Why we buy what we buy: A theory of consumption values. *Journal of Business Research, 22*(2), 159–170.

Spaid, B. I. (2018). Exploring consumer collecting behavior: A conceptual model and research agenda. *Journal of Consumer Marketing, 35*(6), 653–662.
Spaid, B., & Matthes, J. (2021). Consumer collecting identity and behaviors: Underlying motivations and impact on life satisfaction. *Journal of Consumer Marketing, 38*(5), 552–564. https://doi.org/10.1108/JCM-09-2019-3413
Stebbins, R. A. (1992). *Amateurs, professionals, and serious leisure.* McGill-Queen's Press-MQUP.
Veblen, T. (1899). *The theory of the leisure class.*
Velthuis, O. (2005). An interpretive approach to meanings of prices. *The Review of Austrian Economics, 17*(4), 371–386.
Zolfagharian, M. A., & Cortes, A. (2011). Motives for purchasing artwork, collectibles and antiques. *Journal of Business and Economics Research.*

Collecting the Past: Motivations and Meanings in the Low-End Antiquities Trade

Emily Peacock

1 Introduction

> 'You know what they say, one man's junk is another man's treasure.' (Collector A)

Collecting remnants of the past is a global enterprise, shaped by diverse motivations and spanning legal, ethical, and cultural boundaries. It has been claimed that one in three Americans identify as collectors (Belk et al., 1988, p. 548). The motivations behind collecting have long attracted scholarly interest, from early behavioral theories (Pavlov & Gantt, 1928) to more recent work on meaning-making and identity (Dillon, 2019). Yet scholarly attention has traditionally focused on elite collecting, and dominant narratives still rely on "anachronistic conceits about enlightened patrons, narratives of heritage and donors, and unexamined assumptions about the psychology of accumulation" (Fyfe, 2006, p. 42). This neither represents the collecting practices at the low end of the art market generally, nor of low end antiquities collecting, the focus of this chapter, specifically. As Belk observed, "we cannot hope to understand consumer

E. Peacock (✉)
University of Maastricht, Maastricht, The Netherlands
e-mail: emily.peacock@alumni.york.ac.uk

A.-S. V. Radermecker (ed.), *Low-End Markets for Art and Cultural Goods*, Cultural Economics & the Creative Economy,
https://doi.org/10.1007/978-3-032-27566-0_19

behavior without first gaining some understanding of the meanings that consumers attach to possessions" (Belk, 1988 p. 139).

For the purpose of this chapter, archaeological material for sale shall be referred to as "antiquities," because once archaeological material enters the art market as consumer goods, it is often so defined. The ethics of private ownership of archaeological material remain hotly contested, especially around antiquities sold without due diligence and good provenance information (Chippindale & Gill, 2000; Hicks, 2020; Brodie et al., 2021; Yates & Graham, 2023). As the low-end trade makes up a large percentage of this "gray market," and material is often sold without provenance, much of the extensive literature on the illicit antiquities trade is pertinent (Renfrew, 2006; Proulx, 2011; Felch & Frammolino, 2011; Campbell, 2013; Yates & Peacock, 2023; Yates & Brodie, 2023). However, this chapter does not specifically focus on the legality of the material for sale, taking a broader view of the low end trade.

While the online trade in antiquities has attracted regulatory and journalistic attention, the motivations and behaviors of low-end buyers remain underexplored. This is partly because such purchases are informal, decentralized, and often dismissed as trivial or hobbyist. However, two key developments are encouraging closer scrutiny. First, researchers now have improved access to online forums and user-generated content, making it easier to observe how these communities operate in real time. Second, this shift aligns with broader disciplinary trends in archaeology, heritage studies, and criminology that increasingly focus on everyday practices, marginal markets, and informal modes of expertise.

As Radermecker and Moureau establish in the introduction to this volume, the art market is well known to be polarized, and this is clear in the antiquities segment of the market. While high-value objects dominate headlines, they represent a smaller volume of transactions compared to the low-end, where inexpensive goods change hands in large numbers (Bērziņa, 2021). According to the 2025 Art Basel & UBS Art Market Report, overall sales in the global art market declined by 12% in 2024 to an estimated $57.5 billion, with the main drag on growth coming from stagnation at the high end (McAndrew, 2025). Meanwhile, the low-end antiquities trade has been "thriving" since researchers first began investigating it online (Brodie, 2014, p. 435). This segment represents the long tail of the market: high in volume, globally dispersed, and increasingly accessible to individuals with lower budgets. Applying the triadic model presented in the introduction to this volume, and considering the low end antiquities trade through the interaction of functionality, scarcity, and brand strength, proves interesting. Under these market conditions of lower pricing, uneven documentation, and limited institutional oversight, these dimensions do not disappear; they are reworked. Considering prices, "low end antiquities" are typically defined as items under £5,000, with most selling for under £100, and, here, refer to archaeological objects dating before 1700. While this chapter adopts a price threshold for analytical clarity, following Radermecker and Moureau, it moves beyond price as the primary differentiator. Instead, the low-end antiquities trade is examined through the interaction of functionality, scarcity, and brand strength. These dimensions structure value even where prices remain low.

The term "antiquities" is used loosely across platforms but includes everything from prehistoric tools to early modern relics, often of European or Near Eastern origin. Examples include Roman nails, arrowheads, corroded rings, and pottery shards. The kinds of objects unlikely to appear on the covers of auction catalogues or museum vitrines. This market thrives on platforms like eBay, specialist dealer sites, and enthusiast forums (Altaweel & Hadjitofi, 2020). The central research question explored here is: ***Why do individuals collect such low-end antiquities, and what forms of meaning and value do they assign to these objects?*** To investigate this, I conducted non-participant observation across five open-access online forums over the course of one month in early 2024. These forums function both as peer knowledge hubs and as performative spaces where collectors express their values, anxieties, and passions. The aim is to understand how authenticity, authority, and affect are negotiated within these informal heritage economies. In doing so, this chapter challenges Joseph Alsop's assertion that collectors have no inner relationship with the objects they acquire. Instead, it demonstrates that even broken or corroded antiquities can carry deep symbolic significance.

2 Theoretical Framework

This chapter approaches low-end antiquities collecting as a socially embedded, meaning-making practice shaped by informal economies, symbolic value, and digital participation. Understanding these dynamics requires an interdisciplinary conceptual framework that draws from material culture sociology, heritage studies, psychological theory, and learning theory. At its core, collecting is not merely an act of acquisition but a cultural and symbolic practice through which individuals construct identity and assert value. Fyfe (2006) considers collecting within sociological traditions that link material accumulation to taste hierarchies and the production of cultural legitimacy. While his focus is on institutional collecting, the same symbolic logic applies to low-end collectors, who, in this case outside of the museum, engage in similar acts of distinction and value-making.

Macdonald (2022) extends this by framing heritage not as something institutions bestow but as something that is co-created through participation and emotional engagement. Collectors in informal spaces like online forums enact their own "heritage work" by identifying, contextualizing, and narrating the meaning of objects, often in dialogue with others. This emotional and symbolic labor is not purely cultural; it is also existential. Drawing from terror management theory, originally posited by Pearce (1992), and extended by Solomon et al. (1991), this chapter considers how collecting may function as a way of managing mortality salience. Material engagement offers a means of symbolic immortality, especially when collectors articulate a sense of connection to history or legacy through objects. As later sections demonstrate, many collectors describe their practices as responses to trauma, life transition, or personal loss, reaffirming identity and continuity through tangible links to the past.

Equally important is the informal and digital nature of these collecting communities. Rather than relying on institutional expertise, knowledge and authority emerge from within communities themselves (Radermecker, 2025). Lave and Wenger's (1991) concept of legitimate peripheral participation provides a useful model here. Their theory of situated learning shows how expertise is developed through social practice, with newcomers learning from more experienced participants via meaningful engagement. Online collector forums exemplify this structure: novices begin by asking identification questions and gradually move toward offering their own insights, gaining symbolic capital through interaction and peer recognition. In this way, the forums function as "communities of practice" where learning, identity, and authority are co-constructed. This chapter approaches low-end collecting as part of a broader informal economy, both symbolically and structurally. Bourdieu's (1984) concept of distinction underpins the analysis of how taste and legitimacy are performed differently across cultural hierarchies. While elite collecting operates within established circuits of capital and prestige, low-end collecting relies on narrative construction, emotional resonance, and peer validation. Rather than viewing this informality as a deficit, this chapter argues that it enables forms of value creation not available through institutional channels.

The dynamics observed in online collector forums reflect what Oosterman, Mackenzie and Yates (2021) conceptualize as *symbolic security bubbles*. While their study focuses primarily on the elite end of the trade, similar structures are evident at the low-end of the market. Within these symbolic bubbles, trust and reputation substitute for due diligence, and market participants rely on closed, informal networks to manage risk and define legitimacy. As in the high-end market, these bubbles simultaneously provide a sense of protection while potentially shielding problematic or illicit practices from external scrutiny. In the low-end forums I studied, community norms, affective bonds, and shared knowledge claims work to create parallel forms of informal governance.

This framework informs the three empirical themes that follow: (i) informal knowledge economies; (ii) ritual and symbolic practices; (iii) authenticity and authority. Together, they illustrate how low-end collectors produce cultural meaning not in spite of informality, but precisely through it.

3 Data and Methodology

This study is based on qualitative online ethnography, specifically non-participant observation of posts on five public forums dedicated to antiquities collecting. These forums were selected via keyword searches such as "antiquities collecting," "collecting ancient treasure," and "archaeology collecting," using an English-language search engine. The posts were collected over a one-month period (March 2024), and only publicly accessible content was included. A total of approximately 1,000 user posts were sampled. Posts were analyzed using inductive thematic coding in NVivo, with anonymized usernames replaced by pseudonyms to preserve confidentiality. Themes were developed iteratively, and coded for repeated patterns of language, sentiment, and narrative emphasis. Following best practices in digital ethnography, the forums are treated both as sites of discourse production and community formation.

Key selection criteria for inclusion focused on posts explicitly discussing motivations for collecting, the perceived value of objects, community interactions, and debates around authenticity. Low-end antiquities were defined as items sold for less than £5,000 and identified by both their listed value and material characteristics (e.g., size, wear, absence of provenance, utilitarian forms). It is of note that numerology and coin collection function as a unique sub-hobby within antiquities collecting, and due to time constraints, the forums dedicated to coins were excluded from the study, despite containing material which could be considered pertinent. This methodology allows for the exploration of "thick data" (Wang, 2016; Bērziņa, 2024, p. 140), capturing how meanings and motivations are discursively constructed by collectors themselves. While such forums do not represent the entirety of the low-end collecting population, they provide valuable insight into the global informal knowledge economies and symbolic worlds that structure this subcultural practice.

4 Empirical Analysis and Findings

4.1 Informal Knowledge Economies

The forums function as open learning environments, where mentorship, peer validation, and the sharing of knowledge form the core of community interaction. Exchanges between members frequently emphasize camaraderie and enthusiasm. One poster responds to a shared acquisition with "Holy moly, that's a relic and a half," (Collector B) while another states: "Beautiful Egyptian artifacts. I love this thread—makes me feel like Indiana Jones" (Collector C). These interactions are often reciprocated with compliments, such as "You've posted a lot of amazing artifacts yourself in this thread! I am extremely impressed" (Collector D). This collective spirit reflects the centrality of peer influence in collecting culture (Cockrill, 2012) and reveals how community affirmation contributes to the construction of value.

Unlike many online spaces, the dominant tone in these forums is notably respectful, encouraging, and positive. They feel friendly. Community and shared enthusiasm are foundational, yet there are two subjects that disrupt this overall ambiance: selling collections, and accusations of fakes or forgeries. Selling is treated as a transgressive act, rarely discussed and often framed as a last resort. Despite some forums being attached to customer-to-customer sales platforms, the forum posters themselves tend to express a distinct disinterest in monetizing collections. Posts about selling are typically met with sympathy or subtle rebuke, and never with practical guidance. For example, one user wrote: "My cat needed a specialized soft tissue surgery (ear canal removed), so I sold a small handful of broken chains and rings. It covered the surgery with $150 to spare" (Collector E). Another replied, "If I had to sell my collection to live, I would starve" (Collector F). These interactions suggest that to sell is to break the social contract of collecting. It introduces commodification into what is otherwise framed as a morally and emotionally meaningful practice.

The second topic that generates discord is the exposure of members who attempt to pass off or sell forgeries. In one post, a collector warns: "[Name] has sold fakes in the past. He is not a respected seller on most antiquities collectors forums where I am a member" (Collector G). These moments of conflict underscore the extent to which authenticity is not just desirable but essential to the social and symbolic structure of the community. While selling for necessity is tolerated with reluctance, misrepresenting authenticity is treated as a violation of the group's ethical framework.

Forum participants frequently turn to others for help identifying objects, a process that plays out through threads with titles such as "Can somebody tell me what this is?" (Collector H). These questions are usually met with patience, and even when the answer is disappointing, responses remain courteous; "If it's [sp] correct, these are stones. They're not made by humans but by wind and water. They're so-called pseudo-artifacts, because they look like some kind of tool" (Collector I). Expertise is thus sourced not from dealers or professionals, but from within the community itself. This dynamic marks a notable shift from the traditional offline antiquities market, which tends to rely on institutional or commercial authentication. Online forums, by contrast, democratize the collecting process by allowing authority to emerge from within.

This structure exemplifies what Lave and Wenger (1991) term a "community of practice," where learning occurs through "legitimate peripheral participation." New collectors begin on the margins by asking questions, requesting identifications, and over time, through repeated interaction, observation, and participation, become core contributors. Their status is not granted externally, but earned through meaningful practice within the group. The forums thus serve not only as information-sharing spaces but as sites of identity formation and social learning. These low-end objects, though no longer serving their original purpose, are now situated in what Kopytoff (1986) describes as the afterlife stage of their commodity biography. As antiquities, they become heritage items and are valued not for their utility but for their perceived connection to the past, with no distinction for their previous uses. This transformation is enacted through identification: when a collector determines the origin or historical use of an object, it is endowed with significance. In this sense, collectors are engaged in a self-sustaining cycle where knowledge confers heritage status, and heritage status in turn increases perceived value. Commercial worth may remain negligible outside of these communities, but internally, objects become symbolically invaluable.

Forum language reflects this dynamic. Posts such as "Thank you to … community elders … who have contributed a wealth of knowledge to these topics" (Poster J) highlight the role of hierarchy and mentorship. These "elders" function as what Lave and Wenger describe as "old-timers" (ibid) within a community of practice: they guide newcomers not through formal instruction, but through lived engagement with shared problems and routines. The act of identification itself is a ritual of inclusion, a signal that the poster is becoming a fuller participant in the community's practice. This process mirrors Appadurai's (1986, p. 13) assertion that consumption is "eminently social, relational, and active." The transformation of ambiguous finds into meaningful artifacts happens not in isolation but through public, social discourse. The very act of posting an image of a new acquisition and receiving responses embeds the object in a web of shared values and negotiated interpretations. Lave and Wenger's situated learning theory further emphasizes that such learning is most powerful when embedded in authentic tasks. Forums provide precisely this context: asking for authentication, debating forgeries, or recounting the object's imagined past are not abstract exercises but affective, high-stakes practices that matter to the participants. These interactions are not only about knowledge; they are about community membership, legitimacy, and symbolic authority. Jarvenpa's (2003) concept of "collective witnessing" in antiques auctions is also useful here. He describes auctions as rituals where commodities are transformed into valuables through public performance. A similar phenomenon occurs in online antiquities forums, where the identification and interpretation of objects become a public act. Knowledge is not simply exchanged; it is performed. In this context, collectors participate in socially constructed ceremonies where senior members validate the heritage value of newly acquired items by providing historical context or stylistic insight.

Online collector forums, therefore, represent informal knowledge economies where heritage is constructed through peer expertise and affective labor. Authority is distributed horizontally rather than hierarchically, yet patterns of seniority and recognition persist. Within these digital spaces, low-value artifacts are made valuable not through provenance or price, but through a communal process of storytelling, identification, and ritualized engagement. These spaces are not merely information hubs, instead they are symbolic arenas where the cultural status of objects is collaboratively produced and sustained through practices that echo those described in Lave and Wenger's (1991) model of communities of practice.

These observations underscore the heterogeneity of the low-end antiquities market. Far from representing a uniform category of "minor" objects or marginal actors, this segment encompasses diverse motivations, identities, and value logics. As the introduction to this volume suggests, the entry market should not be treated as homogeneous; rather, its internal differentiation becomes particularly visible when examined through everyday practices.

4.2 *Ritual and Symbolic Practices*

Collectors in the low-end antiquities market frequently frame their engagement in emotional, existential, and identity-affirming terms. For many, collecting is not simply a hobby but a deeply personal and symbolic practice. One forum user, for example, wrote: "After some close calls and being injured in Iraq in 04 my eyes opened to what really matters in life" (Collector J). Another commented, "If I had to sell my collection to live I would starve" (Collector K). These expressions suggest that collecting is invested with meaning far beyond the economic value of the objects. It is instead positioned as a stabilizing practice in the face of life's precarity and trauma. Such narratives align with terror management theory (Solomon et al., 1991), which posits that individuals engage in culturally meaningful activities to cope with the awareness of their mortality. Though collecting, individuals construct a form of symbolic immortality, with antiquities functioning as enduring legacies. The survival of ancient objects into the present grants them a timelessness that collectors may identify with, transforming ownership into a means of asserting permanence, identity, and control.

In many cases, collectors describe turning to antiquities in mid-life, often after careers in military service, law enforcement, or other high-risk professions. Similarly to Hardy's findings (Hardy, 2021), low-end collectors often include professionals, veterans, and members of the business and political elite. Many forum members explicitly self-identify with such roles, often introducing themselves in threads dedicated to collector backgrounds. For instance, one poster states, "I've been in law enforcement for 15 + years and I'm a veteran of the Iraq War 2004." This demographic trend suggests that collecting may serve as a response to experiences of trauma, career transition, or existential reassessment, particularly for those who have long held historical interests but only recently acquired the means, time, or emotional impetus to collect. These identity performances are not merely private reflections but are negotiated within the collective norms of online collector communities. Forum discussions reveal a moral economy that distinguishes "authentic" collectors from opportunistic outsiders. Acts such as selling one's collection or questioning the authenticity of a peer-reviewed item can be read as violations of group norms, reinforcing Bourdieu's (1984) concept of symbolic distinction. Taste and knowledge become mechanisms of insider status, while community cohesion is maintained through shared rituals of validation, display, and protection of the group's epistemic boundaries.

Moreover, the act of collecting often becomes a form of personal mythology, where individuals use antiquities to narrate continuity with the past. Whether through imagined kinship with Roman soldiers or medieval craftsmen, collectors inscribe themselves into a larger historical arc. This symbolic self-positioning mirrors broader cultural dynamics. As Macdonald (2020) notes, the late twentieth century saw collecting become a response to anxieties about cultural loss and social fragmentation. Martin, building on Debord's *Society of the Spectacle*, argues that popular collecting serves as a "masquerade" (quoted in Macdonald, 2002) for individuals increasingly alienated from stable social identities. In this light, collecting material heritage, however modest in monetary terms, can be interpreted as an act of emotional repair and identity anchoring amid uncertainty. Further, despite the low financial value of the objects, the act of collecting is heavily symbolic. Spooner (1986) observes in the context of Oriental rug buyers that commodities help individuals establish points of personal order and identity in an amorphous society. Likewise, Kersel (2023), studying tourists in Israel, shows that antiquities function as ideological souvenirs. They are tangible links to a past shaped by religious, ethnic, and national narratives. These insights are echoed in the low-end antiquities forums, where the appeal of an object often lies in its symbolic and affective resonance rather than its market value.

In terms of the triadic model, these objects exhibit low direct functionality yet high symbolic functionality. They no longer serve their original practical purposes, but operate instead as markers of taste, continuity, and personal narrative. Importantly, despite the low-end segment lacking the cultural prestige and institutional validation enjoyed by high-end collectors, who participate in the elite art market (Macdonald, 2020), it is this very marginality that can amplify the symbolic function of collecting. While elite collecting is associated with social distinction and aesthetic connoisseurship, low-end collecting often becomes a personal, even redemptive practice—imbued with emotion, memory, and identity work. In these contexts, collecting becomes a negotiation of mortality, memory, community, and personal history. It is within this symbolic economy that material heritage takes on deeply felt significance in everyday digital life.

4.3 *Authenticity and Authority*

> "It's the thrill of seeking out the answers ... I may be turning to you guys for some guidance and learning how to follow through on my quest" (Collector L).

Within the low-end antiquities market, authenticity occupies a paradoxical position: it is both a central concern and a source of productive uncertainty. Rather than discouraging participation, ambiguity over whether an object is "genuine" often intensifies its affective and symbolic appeal. Where documentary certainty is limited, experiential engagement and relational forms of authenticity tend to carry greater weight, suggesting that the three dimensions of the triadic model operate in a compensatory rather than strictly hierarchical manner. Scarcity, meanwhile, derives less from original rarity than from survival. In this respect, the antiquities trade exemplifies how scarcity in the low-end market is often historically produced rather than economically engineered. Unlike limited editions in contemporary art, rarity here is the unintended consequence of endurance across time. Even artefacts that were once mass-produced acquire singularity through endurance, their material persistence conferring a form of distributed uniqueness. Finally, what might elsewhere appear as brand strength manifests here primarily as authenticity itself. In the absence of recognised makers, institutional validation, or established signatures, authenticity becomes the primary quality signal. It functions as a substitute for brand in stabilizing trust and legitimizing exchange.

The thrill of the "hunt," the process of communal verification, and the imaginative engagement with the object's past all work to sustain collectors' interest. As one poster puts it: "The excitement of the hunt, not knowing what you'll find, keeps me going, even the junk. I love it" (Collector M). This emotional and cognitive investment resembles what

Csikszentmihalyi (1990) describes as "flow": a state in which engagement is sustained because the task feels challenging but attainable. Authenticating antiquities occupies precisely this liminal space for collectors: a challenge that requires skill, community input, and persistence, but one that remains within the realm of achievable knowledge. Drawing on the work of Celsi et al. (1993) and Arnould and Price (2000), parallels can be seen between antiquities collecting and the language of risky sports. Both activities are described using terms like "thrill," "challenge" and "personal discovery," suggesting that the appeal of collecting lies not only in the object itself but in the affective intensity of the process.

This framing also aligns with existential and affect theory, particularly in terms of risk, uncertainty, and the drive toward meaning-making. Beck (1992) and Browning (2016) argue that individuals in high-modern societies experience elevated levels of ontological insecurity, leading to greater investment in identity work and stabilizing routines. For low-end collectors, the pursuit of authenticity may function as one such stabilizing structure, providing a sense of mastery and continuity in a precarious cultural and economic landscape.

Further compounding this dynamic is the analogy to gambling behavior. Belk et al. (1988) describe collecting as a form of compulsive consumption, frequently labelled an "obsession" or "addiction" by collectors and their families. This is echoed in forum discourse: "Why do I want to buy nearly every single one of them? I know quite well two things at this point: A) I don't need any more stuff. B) I don't need any more stuff. … Does anyone else suffer from this?" (Collector N). The low-end market, particularly online platforms like eBay, mirrors the structure of online gambling environments, as accessible, fast-paced, and based on small, low-risk transactions with uncertain outcomes. Tabri et al. (2022) argue that gambling is not just about material reward but the psychological anticipation of resolution, a logic that closely parallels the emotional arc of acquiring and authenticating antiquities. Within this economy of risk and reward, authenticity emerges as a symbolic prize. It is less about verifiable historical truth and more about affirming one's expertise and belonging within a collecting community. One collector writes with remarkable technical authority, "I'm afraid your third one (bull's head on discus) almost certainly belongs to the Bulgarian Volute Series and has all the characteristics … of the First Batch, made from about 2004 to 2011" (Collector M). This kind of encyclopedic identification reinforces the collector's status within the group while simultaneously confirming that authenticity is constructed through shared knowledge practices, not institutional provenance.

This social construction of knowledge reflects Etienne Wenger's theory of communities of practice, in which knowledge is generated through collective participation, negotiation, and peer validation. On low-end antiquities forums, authenticity is not verified by laboratories or museums, but by fellow enthusiasts drawing on personal expertise, intuition, and accumulated experience. The authentication process becomes performative and iterative. It is less about fixed truth and more about communal alignment and mutual recognition. This contrasts sharply with the high-end antiquities trade, where authenticity is policed through expert certification, provenance documentation, and legal infrastructures. There, authenticity is often used to secure economic value and cultural legitimacy (Appadurai, 1986; Kopytoff, 1986). In low-end collecting, by contrast, authenticity may be flexible, even negotiable. One collector jokes after learning they had bought a fake: "Thank you very much. I appreciate you're informing me of this. I guess it's something that happens to most of us in this hobby at one time or another. Maybe in 2000 years it will be valuable!" (Collector O).

While authenticity is a key concern among forum participants, explicit attention to due diligence, such as verifying provenance or assessing legal status, is largely absent. Unlike the high-end market, where provenance research has become increasingly essential for dealers and institutions, low-end collectors appear to accept the absence of documentation as a normative feature of the trade. This is not necessarily a deliberate effort to save information costs but rather reflects a cultural expectation within these communities that provenance is typically unavailable and, therefore, not required. Where documentary certainty is limited, experiential engagement and relational authenticity tend to carry greater weight, suggesting that the three dimensions of the triadic model operate in a compensatory rather than hierarchical manner.

Walter Benjamin (1973) famously argued that an object's "aura," its unique presence in time and space, underpins its authenticity. Though Benjamin saw mechanical reproduction as the death of aura, many low-end collectors effectively reconstitute aura through narrative. As Spooner (1986, p. 199) suggests, people often "reconstruct context" around ambiguous objects, using their imagination and social networks to imbue them with meaning. This is not merely wishful thinking, it reflects what Thompson (2016, p. 172) calls the use of heritage to "support self-conception," allowing individuals to manipulate or integrate the past into their own identity narratives. In this sense, authenticity is less a static property and more a relational, affective, and performative process. The satisfaction is not merely in the possession of the antiquities, then, but in the process itself, as the object becomes aligned with the collector's self-concept, blurring the lines between "me" and "mine" (Belk et al., 1988). Therefore, in reaffirming the authenticity of another collector's acquisitions, they are reaffirming the very self of other collectors and simultaneously affirming that person's identity and their own role within the moral economy of the group. The repeated use of phrases like "great find" or "textbook example" works not only to classify the object, but to recognize the collector's status and legitimacy.

This narrative construction operates within a broader tension: the structural scarcity of authentic antiquities. Most countries now prohibit the sale of unprovenanced archaeological material, and the 1970 UNESCO Convention serves as a key marker for legal acceptability. Given the finite nature of licit supply, the demand for "authentic" antiquities must either be met by illicit looting or by increasingly sophisticated forgeries. Indeed, the latter may have become an entrenched feature of the market. Thompson (2016, p. 77) posits we may soon witness a "counterfeit feedback loop," where new forgeries are modelled on older fakes, further complicating the authenticity landscape. Major media coverage often focuses on forgery scandals at the top of the market, such as the Getty Kouros or the case of New York dealer Sadigh, who sold thousands of forgeries over decades before his conviction in 2021 (Moynihan, 2021). Yet for low-end collectors acquiring antiquities on platforms such eBay, where a majority of listings make unverifiable claims about authenticity (Brodie, 2017), and the platform itself avoids liability, presenting its role as akin to that of a classifieds page rather than a vetting institution, the acquisition of "authenticity" (Fay, 2011) can, perhaps, be seen as more symbolic than financial.

Ultimately, for low-end collectors, authenticity functions as both aspiration and affect. It represents a form of symbolic capital that is accumulated through knowledge, performance, and participation. Even in the face of forgery, collectors persist, not simply because of denial or naivety, but because the object's narrative and communal resonance matter as much, if not more, than its archaeological veracity. Returning to the forum poster, Collector O, who concluded: "Maybe in 2000 years it will be valuable," this ironic deferral underscores a core point: the value of authenticity in low-end collecting lies not in fixed truth, but in the affective labor and collective imagination that brings it into being.

5 Conclusion: The Stories We Tell Ourselves

> "Objects are important to the study of human history because they provide a concrete basis for ideas, and can validate them ... preserved objects also validate memories; and the actuality of the object, as opposed to a reproduction or surrogate, draws people in and gives them a literal way of touching the past."
> —*UNESCO, 1994*

In Hegel's *Philosophy of History*, he states, "History combines in our language the objective as well as the subjective ... It means both *res gestae* (the things that happened) and *historia rerum gestarum* (the narration of things that happened)." The historical value created and attached by antiquities collectors is an example of *historia rerum gestarum*—the stories told around history—which infuse it with "Memory with a capital M," full of nostalgia and emotional resonance. It is for this reason that authenticity emerges as the essential value: the transformative element that turns 'junk' into heritage material. In this light, low-end antiquities collectors are not merely hobbyists. They are symbolic actors engaging in meaning-making, boundary maintenance, and informal heritage economies. Much to the frustration of those combating the illicit antiquities trade, most of the low-end material discussed has little to no provenance information. This absence precludes the types of emotionally driven cultural biographies (Kopytoff, 1986) that many second-hand marketplaces rely on. However, rather than weakening emotional attachment, this lack of documentation often opens a space for collectors to invent their own histories. The only essential component required is the belief that the object is genuinely from antiquity, that is, authenticity. Although this market is not overtly illicit, its informality and reliance on peer validation may enable gray-market dynamics. Forums can serve as double-edged tools: they help mitigate forgery risks through community expertise (Radermecker, 2025), yet may also normalize the circulation of unprovenanced objects, unintentionally creating a hospitable environment for the sale of illicit antiquities.

Given how strongly the desire for connection to the past is reflected in collector discourse, and how this intersects with broader debates about the ethics of private ownership, there may be alternative ways to harness this impulse. Museums are often hesitant to allow public handling of collections, yet events such as touch tours for the visually impaired have proven to be extremely popular (Saeed, 2024). As we have seen, it is not only iconic or high-value objects that satisfy this need for tactile engagement with history. If museums and heritage sites offered more opportunities to handle lower-end, less financially valuable artifacts, they might meet this deep-seated desire while also providing a meaningful alternative to the expanding low-end antiquities trade.

Collectors' motivations also diverge significantly from those of the high-end art market. While elite buyers may pursue investment, social prestige, and institutional recognition, low-end collectors are more often driven by emotional resonance, personal meaning, and historical curiosity. Yet both forms of collecting remain embedded in broader narratives of cultural value and symbolic distinction. In each case, the object is not just a thing but a signifier of identity, knowledge, taste, or belonging. The low-end antiquities market, despite lacking financial prestige, is rich in meaning for its participants. Further, far from representing a diluted version of higher end markets, this segment reveals the flexibility of the triadic model under conditions of informality and low price. Functionality remains central, though it is symbolic and experiential rather than practical. Scarcity becomes a matter of survival through deep time, which is directly related to the endurance of certain kinds of material within the archaeological record. Brand strength/ quality is translated into relational authenticity. Indeed, collectors find value not only in the objects themselves but in the stories they construct around them, the connections they imagine with the past, and the camaraderie of fellow collectors. This chapter has demonstrated that collecting at this level is not a passive act of ownership, but an active process of meaning-making, identity formation, and community building. Ultimately, the motivations for collecting antiquities, particularly at the low end, extend well beyond financial or aesthetic considerations, revealing the deeply personal and symbolic significance of these seemingly mundane relics of the past.

Read alongside other segments examined in this volume, the low-end antiquities trade demonstrates the flexibility of the triadic model under conditions of informality and limited institutional oversight. Functionality becomes symbolic and existential, scarcity is grounded in survival rather than exclusivity, and brand strength is translated into relational authenticity. Rather than occupying the bottom of a hierarchical system, this segment reveals alternative configurations of value within the broader art market ecology.

References

Altaweel, M., & Hadjitofi, T. G. (2020). The sale of heritage on eBay: Market trends and cultural value. *Big Data & Society*, *7*(2). https://doi.org/10.1177/2053951720968865

Appadurai, A. (1986). *The social life of things: Commodities in cultural perspective*. Cambridge University Press.

Arnould, E. J., & Price, L. L. (2000). Authenticating acts and authoritative performances: Questing for self and community. In S. Ratneshwar & D. G. Mick (Eds.), *Inside consumption: Consumer motives, goals, and desires* (pp. 140–163). Routledge.

Beck, U. (1992). *Risk society: Towards a new modernity*, (M. Ritter, Trans.). Sage Publications

Belk, R. (1988). Possessions and the extended self. *Journal of Consumer Research*, *15*(2), 139–168.

Belk, R., Wallendorf, M., Sherry, J., Holbrook, M., & Roberts, S. (1988). Collectors and collecting. *Advances in Consumer Research*, *15*, 548–553.

Benjamin, W. (1973) The work of art in the age of mechanical reproduction. In (H. Arendt & H. Zohn, Trans.). (pp. 217–252). Schocken Books.

Bērziņa, D. (2021). More than just money. In N. Oosterman & D. Yates (Eds.), *Crime and art* (Vol. 1). Springer. https://doi.org/10.1007/978-3-030-84856-9_14

Bērziņa, D. (2024). Between crime and commemoration: Human–object relationships in the treasure hunting for World War II objects. *Critical Criminology*, *32*, 139–153. https://doi.org/10.1007/s10612-023-09738-0

Bourdieu, P. (1984). *Distinction: A social critique of the judgement of taste*. Routledge & Kegan Paul.

Brodie, N. (2014). The antiquities market: It's all in a price. *Heritage & Society*, *7*(1), 32–46. https://doi.org/10.1179/2159032X14Z.00000000017

Brodie, N. (2017). *How to control the internet market in antiquities? The need for regulation and monitoring*. Antiquities Coalition.

Brodie, N., Kersel, M. M., Mackenzie, S., Sabrine, I., Smith, E., & Yates, D. (2021). Why there is still an illicit trade in cultural objects and what we can do about it. *Journal of Field Archaeology*, *47*(2), 117–130. https://doi.org/10.1080/00934690.2021.1996979

Browning, C. S. (2016). Ethics and ontological security. In J. Nyman & A. Burke (Eds.), *Ethical security studies: A new research agenda* (xx–xx). Routledge.

Celsi, R. L., Rose, R. L., & Leigh, T. W. (1993). An exploration of high-risk leisure consumption through skydiving. *Journal of Consumer Research, 20*(1), 1–23. https://doi.org/10.1086/209330

Campbell, P. B. (2013). The illicit antiquities trade as a transnational criminal network: Characterizing and anticipating trafficking of cultural heritage. *International Journal of Cultural Property, 20*(2), 113–153. https://doi.org/10.1017/S0940739113000015

Chippindale, C., & Gill, D. W. (2000). Material consequences of contemporary classical collecting. *American Journal of Archaeology, 104*(3), 463–511.

Cockrill, A. (2012). Does an iPod make you happy? An exploration of the effects of iPod ownership on life satisfaction. *Journal of Consumer Behavior, 11*(5). https://doi.org/10.1002/cb.1385

Csikszentmihalyi, M. (1990). *Flow: The psychology of optimal experience*. Harper & Row.

Dillon, A. (2019). Collecting as routine human behavior: Personal identity and control in the material and digital world. *Information & Culture, 54*(3), 255–280. https://www.jstor.org/stable/26855128

Fay, E. (2011). Virtual artifacts: EBay, antiquities, and authenticity. *Journal of Contemporary Criminal Justice, 27*(4), 449–464. https://doi.org/10.1177/1043986211418887

Felch, J., & Frammolino, R. (2011). *Chasing Aphrodite: The hunt for looted antiquities at the world's richest museum*. Houghton Mifflin Harcourt.

Fyfe, G. (2006). Social aspects/sociological perspectives. In S. J. Macdonald (Ed.), *A companion to museum studies* (pp. 33–49). Blackwell.

Hardy, S. (2021). It is not against the law, if no one can see you: Online social organisation of artefact-hunting in former Yugoslavia. *Journal of Computer Applications in Archaeology*, 169–187. https://doi.org/10.5334/jcaa.76

Hicks, D. (2020). *The Brutish Museums: The Benin Bronzes, colonial violence and cultural restitution*. Pluto Press.

Jarvenpa, R. (2003). Collective witnessing: Performance, drama, and circulation of valuables in the rural auction and antiques trade. *Journal of Contemporary Ethnography, 32*(5), 555–591. https://doi.org/10.1177/0891241603255676

Kersel, M. M. (2023). Innocents abroad? The consumption of antiquities from the Holy Land. *Journal of Ancient Judaism, 14*(2), 263–290. https://doi.org/10.30965/21967954-bja10042

Kopytoff, I. (1986). The cultural biography of things: Commoditization as process. In A. Appadurai (Ed.), *The social life of things: Commodities in cultural perspective* (pp. 64–91). Cambridge University Press.

Lave, J., & Wenger, E. (1991). *Situated learning: Legitimate peripheral participation*. Cambridge University Press.

McAndrew, C. (2025). *The Art Basel and UBS global art market report 2025* (Annual report). Arts Economics. https://theartmarket.artbasel.com/

Macdonald, B. (2022). Pausing, reflection, and action: Decolonizing museum practices. *Journal of Museum Education*, *47*(1), 8–17. https://doi.org/10.1080/10598650.2021.1986668

Macdonald, S. (2020). On 'old things': The fetishization of past everyday life. In N. Thomas & K. Hill (Eds.), *British subjects: An anthropology of Britain* (pp. 89–106). Routledge. https://doi.org/10.4324/9781003084822-10

Moynihan, C. (2021, October 13). Antiquities dealer admits mass-producing fakes he sold for years. *The New York Times*. https://www.nytimes.com/2021/10/13/arts/design/fake-antiquities-mehrdad-sadigh.html

Oosterman, N., Mackenzie, S., & Yates, D. (2021). Regulating the wild west: Symbolic security bubbles and white collar crime in the art market. *Journal of White Collar and Corporate Crime*, 1–9.

Pavlov, I. P., & Gantt, W. H.Trans. (1928). *Lectures on conditioned reflexes: Twenty-five years of objective study of the higher nervous activity (behavior) of animals*. Liverwright Publishing Corporation

Pearce, S. M. (1992). *Museums, objects and collections: A cultural study*. Smithsonian Institution Press.

Proulx, B. B. (2011). Organized criminal involvement in the illicit antiquities trade. *Trends in Organized Crime*, *14*, 1–29. https://doi.org/10.1007/s12117-010-9115-8

Radermecker, A. S. V. (2025). Connoisseurship from below exploring "informal" expertise in art on social media. *Journal of Cultural Economics*, 1–38.

Renfrew, C. (2006). *Loot, legitimacy and ownership*. Duckworth.

Saeed, K. (2024, August 1). What are touch tours? Royal National Institute of Blind People. https://www.rnib.org.uk/news/what-are-touch-tours/

Solomon, S., Greenberg, J., & Pyszczynski, T. (1991). A terror management theory of social behavior: The psychological functions of self-esteem and cultural worldviews In M. P. Zanna (Ed.), *Advances in experimental social psychology* (Vol. 24, pp. 93–159). Academic Press.

Spooner, B. (1986). Weavers and dealers: The authenticity of an oriental carpet. In A. Appadurai (Ed.), *The social life of things: Commodities in cultural perspective* (pp. 195–235). Cambridge University Press.

Tabri, N., Xuereb, S., Cringle, N., & Clark, L. (2022). Associations between financial gambling motives, gambling frequency and level of problem gambling: A meta-analytic review. *Addiction*, *117*(3), 559–569. https://doi.org/10.1111/add.15642

Thompson, E. L. (2016). *Possession: The curious history of private collectors from antiquity to the present*. Yale University Press.

Wang, T. (2016, May 13). Why big data needs thick data. *Ethnography Matters*. http://ethnographymatters.net/blog/2016/05/13/why-big-data-needs-thick-data/

Yates, D., & Brodie, N. (2023). The illicit trade in antiquities is not the world's third-largest illicit trade: A critical evaluation of a factoid. *Antiquity, 394*, 991–1003.

Yates, D., & Graham, S. (2023). Reputation laundering and museum collections: Patterns, priorities, provenance, and hidden crime. *International Journal of Heritage Studies, 2*, 145–164.

Yates, D., & Peacock, E. (2023). T. rex is fierce, T. rex is charismatic, T. rex is litigious: Disruptive objects in affective desirescapes. *International Journal of Cultural Property, 30*(4), 396–418. https://doi.org/10.1017/S0940739124000055

From Physical to Virtual: The Shifting Landscape of a Collectors' Community of Advertising and Packaging Paraphernalia in Northwestern Europe

Sanne Rossel

1 Introduction

Digitalization has transformed the way collectors of packaging and advertising material in Northwestern Europe trade and curate their collections. Once, collectors were reliant on printed works, personal networks and physical markets, the latter consisting of in-person venues such as flea markets, antiques fairs, and collector conventions. Nowadays, they also navigate online platforms, where social dynamics and curatorial practices are reshaped by increased information exchange and evolving digital etiquette—the informal norms and social expectations governing behavior in online collecting communities (Radermecker, 2025). This significantly impacts the information asymmetry that can be observed in markets that value seller expertise, such as the collectibles market (Gertsberg, 2019, p. 53).

This study explores the question: *How has digitalization changed the social dynamics of trade and the curatorial practices of Northwestern European collectors of packaging and advertising material?* This research aids in our understanding of the structure and functioning of contemporary collecting communities in Northwestern Europe. It highlights how

S. Rossel (✉)
Independent researcher, Ghent, Belgium

A.-S. V. Radermecker (ed.), *Low-End Markets for Art and Cultural Goods*, Cultural Economics & the Creative Economy,
https://doi.org/10.1007/978-3-032-27566-0_20

digitalization reshapes social aspects of collecting, such as etiquette and knowledge exchange, within a small community. It also shows how digitalization alters the spatial dynamics of collecting, revealing both continuity and change.

The research has a clear scope and delineation. Geographically, the focus is on Northwestern Europe, where the collecting network in question is primarily located. Private collecting has a particularly long tradition in this region, forming the basis upon which the first Western museums were built (Bennett, 1995, pp. 1–10). The research took place over a space of five months and is qualitatively informative in nature. Its focus lies on one collector network in particular. Since such networks are generally understudied in anthropology, it is difficult to determine how far the results apply to other groups or regions. However, comparable studies report similar findings regarding social dynamics in collecting, suggesting broader relevance.

2 Literature Review

This literature review draws from different fields such as anthropology, cultural economics, heritage studies, information science and psychology and predominantly focuses on studies regarding digitalization and collecting, as well as social analyses of collector networks. This category of research has received little academic attention, but the few studies that have been conducted are particularly informative. Two dominant and recurring themes within this literature are the relation between collectors and the wider population and the role of information exchange within collecting.

The limited body of literature on collector communities primarily addresses themes related to the social inclusion of collectors. Key comparable studies include Ellis and Haywood (2012)'s research on vintage radio collectors in the UK, Case (2009)'s work on American coin collectors, and Lee and Trace (2009)'s study of international rubber duck collectors. Within this scholarship, social inclusion is often examined through concepts such as "insider-outsider relationships," "spaces of knowing and unknowingness," and "interactions with the lay public versus the collegial public" (see Lee & Trace, 2009; Desjardins, 2012; Ellis & Haywood, 2012; Bainbridge, 2014; Shuker, 2017). This focus is unsurprising given the longstanding European tradition of depicting the archetypal "Collector" as eccentric, possessing unusual social or personal traits

(Pearce, 2013, p. 226). A notable finding across these studies is that, despite the common assumption that collecting is an antisocial and solitary pursuit, most collectors consider social interaction with like-minded peers to be both valuable and enjoyable. Such exchanges not only provide opportunities for knowledge sharing but also foster a sense of belonging within specialized collecting networks.

A recurring theme in previous research on the digitalization of collecting is the central role of information in both collecting practices and the collectibles market. Studies in this area examine the creation of distinct collector types based on the kinds of information they seek, as well as the mechanisms of knowledge exchange within collecting communities (Lee & Trace, 2009; Lai & Chen, 2014). Case offers a particularly insightful analysis, observing that the development of "expertise and knowledge [...] enhances [collectors'] standing and self-image in relation to other collectors" (2009, p. 749). Similarly, Ellis and Haywood (2012) and Radermecker (2025) explore how digital market spaces contribute to the democratization of knowledge about collectibles, reshaping traditional hierarchies of expertise. This emphasis on information naturally connects to broader economic theories of information asymmetry, which describe situations in which one party in a potential transaction possesses more knowledge about the good being exchanged than the other (Löfgren et al., 2002; Gertsberg, 2019). One well-known consequence of such asymmetry is "adverse selection," whereby buyers, uncertain about an item's quality, are unwilling to pay premium prices. This reluctance can drive sellers of high-quality goods out of the market, ultimately reducing overall market quality (ibid). Given that collecting is fundamentally an information-driven activity, and that the collectibles market places a high premium on accurate and specialized knowledge, information emerges not only as a key determinant of market transactions but also as a significant factor shaping social hierarchies and dynamics within collector networks (Lee & Trace, 2009, p. 626; Gertsberg, 2019, p. 53).

2.1 *The Collectors and Collectibles*

The interviewed collectors primarily focus on packaging dating from 1880 to 1940, typically in the form of tin, wooden, or paper boxes. These containers, characterized by direct functionality, were originally used to store foodstuffs and household products such as coffee, tea, cocoa, tobacco goods, various types of sweets, and gramophone needles. For some collectors, the appeal lies not only in the objects themselves but also in the identity of the designer or the company that produced them. As a result, most collections extend beyond packaging to include related commercial artifacts, such as advertising signs and other promotional paraphernalia. Many of these objects fall into the category of *ephemera*—items originally intended to be discarded after use, but which have survived due to the historical, cultural, or aesthetic value attributed to them over time (Fig. 1). The objects can be described as "everyday collectibles" and are characterized by their low direct functionality. As shown in Fig. 1, these once predominantly utilitarian objects are now displayed in collectors' homes for symbolic purposes, in line with subsegment 2 of Radermecker and Moureau's triadic model.

These collectibles can be considered cultural goods, as they embody both economic and cultural value (Angelini & Castellani, 2018, p. 13). They circulate through antique shops, flea markets, and, increasingly, digital platforms. The packaging itself reflects the aesthetic preferences,

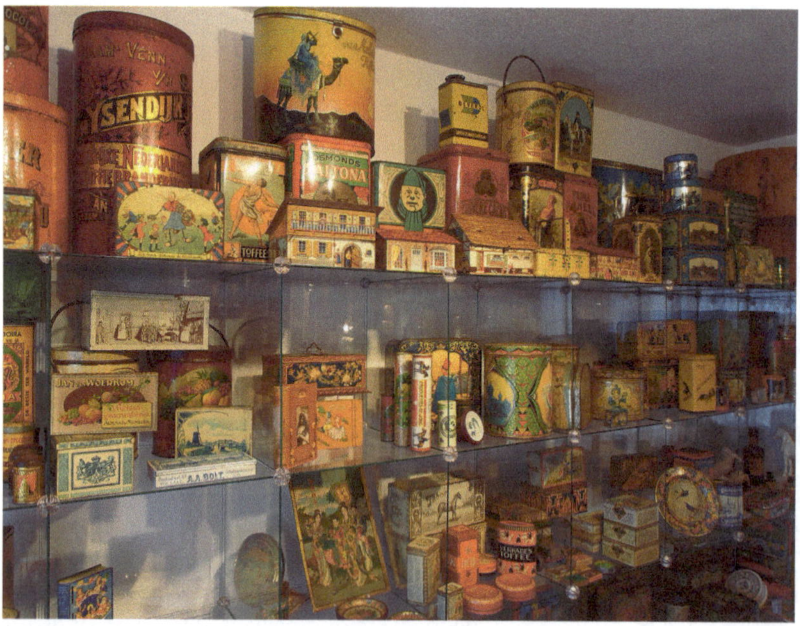

Fig. 1 Tin display in the house of a collector, similar to those in participants' homes. 2013. *Source* Alf van Beem—Wikicommons

commercial design practices, technological capabilities, and social norms of its time, qualities that often form the basis of their appeal to collectors. The examples discussed here typically sell for anywhere between a few euros and a few hundred euros, with rare exceptions reaching into the low thousands. Several participants suggested that their relatively modest financial value stems from their mass-produced origins, in contrast to the perceived uniqueness of individually created artworks. At the same time, many feel that the cultural significance of these objects is substantially underestimated by the broader public. In response, they often see themselves as advocates and guardians of this heritage—a stance frequently observed among collectors of ephemera (Belk, 2012, p. 2; Iskin & Salsbury, 2019, p. 122). This discrepancy, in which high cultural and economic value is recognized within the collector community but overlooked outside it, echoes Bourdieu's observation that the value of playing cards depends entirely on the game being played (Bourdieu & Wacquant, 1992, p. 98).

The term *community* in this context draws from its broader social-science usage, referring to a group bound by shared values and interests rather than physical proximity (Hess, 1987, p. 36; Wilson & Peterson, 2002, p. 455). As Marcus (1995) notes, communities can flourish despite spatial dispersion, and in the case of these collectors, physical and virtual interactions are equally vital. This aligns with Wilson and Peterson's (2002) argument that digital spaces should be studied with the same anthropological tools as physical ones, since both reflect and operate within broader socio-political realities (pp. 455; 462). Estimating the size of this community is challenging due to limited academic research, but evidence drawn from collector testimonies, book sales, and online group memberships suggests that several thousand individuals across Northwestern Europe share an interest in these objects, with only a few dozen deeply engaged (Rossel, 2024, p. 21).

Within this network, three overlapping profiles of central actors emerge. The first is the collector, who acquires items primarily for personal enjoyment and may occasionally sell surplus pieces, but without profit-making as a primary goal. The second is the collector-dealer, whose engagement with the market is more deliberate and sustained, investing considerable time in tracking market trends, cultivating relationships with buyers, and negotiating favorable deals. The third is the dealer-collector, typically a professional antiques or art dealer with a substantial private collection, who trades across a wide range of objects but collects in a narrow, specialized niche. These identities are not fixed; they blur and shift over time, as Case (2009, p. 731) observed in his study of coin collectors, with individuals often moving between roles depending on circumstances and opportunities.

3 Data and Methodology

There is an element of auto-ethnography in this research that warrants acknowledgment. My father is an avid tin collector, and through his passion, I have acquired first-hand experience with the processes of collecting, valuing, and curating such objects. This peripheral yet informed positionality provided me with a unique vantage point: it facilitated access to what is, in many respects, a private world. I was welcomed into the homes of participants and, by extension, into aspects of their financial and social lives, with minimal gatekeeping.

Participants were recruited through a combination of convenience sampling and exponential discriminative snowball sampling (Leavy, 2022, p. 149). I began with collectors to whom I had direct access, and subsequent participants were identified through recommendations and their relevance to the study. Inclusion criteria were straightforward: participants had to be collectors of packaging and related commercial materials. In cases where participants were also dealers, their trade needed to include these categories. Snowball sampling proved particularly suitable given the community's dispersed geography, niche focus, and potential reluctance to discuss sensitive social and financial matters with unfamiliar researchers.

The final sample consisted of seven participants from the Netherlands, Germany, and Switzerland, aged between 50 and 80 years old. Six were male and one was female. Data collection relied primarily on in-person, in-depth, semi-structured interviews. This format was chosen for its capacity to capture participants' unique perspectives on the phenomenon under study and to explore complex social research questions (Adams, 2015, p. 49; Adeoye-Olatunde and Olenik, 2021, pp. 3–5). The interviews followed a predetermined set of open-ended questions, organized thematically (Leavy, 2022, pp. 139–140). The themes included: motivations and routines surrounding collecting; buying and selling practices; community dynamics and collector networks; personal relationships with objects; methods of value assessment; issues of trust and authenticity; approaches to curation and display; documentation and cataloguing practices; and strategies for knowledge acquisition. Each of these themes was also examined in light of the impact of digitalization, drawing on the foundational literature on collecting (see Elsner & Cardinal, 1994; Pearce, 2013; Bennett, 1995).

Interview transcripts were analyzed through manual, cyclical coding to identify key themes and recurring patterns across responses (Basit, 2003; Saldaña, 2013; Hacking et al., 2023). This method enabled the organization of diverse perspectives into a coherent thematic structure, rather than forcing them into a singular, linear narrative.

4 Empirical Analysis and Findings

4.1 Collecting Before the Internet

To understand in which ways digitalization has affected the manner in which these collectors engage with their hobby and each other, a reconstruction of how they collected before the digitalization of collecting practices is necessary. This reconstruction is based on the characterizations that collectors gave of their activities in the conducted interviews.

Knowledge Gathering and Exchange Before Digitalization

Before the advent of digitalization, acquiring information about an object's value, function, history, and scarcity required considerable effort from collectors. Much like their initial entry into the collecting world, knowledge acquisition often occurred serendipitously. Many collectors described learning through firsthand experience—visiting markets with a curious eye, observing transactions, and spending time with more seasoned peers. One participant recalled offering ten guilders for a tin in his youth, only to be sharply corrected by the seller, who informed him it was worth at least ten times that amount—a lesson he never forgot. Another recounted a more dramatic episode from his early twenties: attempting to haggle down a five-guilder price by offering half, only for the vendor to stomp on the box and hand it to him in its crushed state, remarking, "Now you can have it for two and a half guilders." Such vivid encounters, combined with the routine observation of market goods and discussions with fellow collectors, helped shape an intuitive understanding of an object's market value, grounded in factors such as scarcity, quality, and demand. For many, the collector community itself served as a crucial source of learning. Several participants explained that they had partnered with peers or informally assumed the role of mentee under the guidance of a more experienced collector. Knowledge exchange most often took place through visits to markets and private collections, where objects could be examined and discussed in depth. Printed resources—such as auction catalogues, themed books, and collectors' magazines—also played a role, though most interviewees considered them secondary to social learning. Not only could such materials be expensive, but their information was not always up to date, and their scope was not necessarily relevant to a collector's specific niche. In contrast, interpersonal exchange provided nuanced, context-specific knowledge and fostered relationships that were as valuable as the information itself.

Curatorial Practices Before Digitalization

Likewise, before the advent of the Internet, curatorial practices among the interviewed collectors varied considerably, both in terms of acquisition strategies and methods of cataloguing. Some—particularly those who relied on dealing for part of their income—invested significant effort in documentation, meticulously handwriting files, maintaining detailed logs, and even taking Polaroid photographs of individual objects. Most, however, did not keep thorough records of their collections until more time-efficient tools became widely accessible through the Internet. This tendency toward looser documentation mirrored another pre-digital pattern: relatively unrestricted collecting parameters. Many participants explained that they acquired objects opportunistically, based on what they happened to encounter. If an object outside their established focus caught their interest, they often expanded their collecting scope rather than rejecting it. This approach was partly shaped by the scarcity of comprehensive information that could provide an overview of all available collectibles, reducing the perceived need for strict boundaries. In other words, less information meant less pressure to work systematically. It is also worth noting that many participants began collecting during this same pre-digital period, when they were still relatively inexperienced. A lack of specialization may thus have reflected not only limited access to information but also the natural progression of a collecting career. As Belk (2012, p. 2) observes, the tendency to narrow one's focus and specialize often emerges only as collectors become more deeply engaged in their pursuits.

Social Dynamics of Trade Before Digitalization

The importance of social interactions in the collecting experience cannot be overstated. Every participant emphasized that relationships with other collectors were central to their enjoyment of the hobby. While many joked about fitting the popular stereotype of the eccentric enthusiast, they also described their collector networks as spaces where such eccentricities were validated and transformed into a shared passion. As Belk et al. (2012, p. 2) note, recognition from peers legitimizes what might otherwise be viewed as abnormal acquisitiveness, offering both a sense of purpose and a feeling of belonging. Goodwill, mutual enthusiasm, and the willingness to share knowledge were described as essential to both the social and commercial dynamics of collecting within this network, reinforcing the importance of sustaining the community over time.

This ethos often extended to welcoming newcomers. Interviewees recounted offering discounted prices to encourage new collectors, or overlooking minor breaches of etiquette from enthusiastic beginners. Similar practices have been observed in other collecting cultures (Case, 2009, p. 746; Lee & Trace, 2009, p. 633). While such gestures could be viewed as a form of long-term relationship-building with potential customers, they were also framed as investments in the survival and vitality of the collector community as a whole. Participants frequently described the social hierarchy of the network through the metaphor of a "monkey rock," where status and influence were determined by a combination of collection quality, business acumen, and specialist knowledge. Before the rise of the Internet, dealer-collectors and well-connected collectors with extensive expertise and financial resources acted as central hubs. They typically enjoyed first access to desirable pieces, not because they possessed hidden information about a specific object's attributes—most transactions occurred in person, allowing both parties to assess physical qualities equally—but because they had superior knowledge of the market as a whole. These individuals had a more complete picture of the volume, relative quality, and financial value of available goods, enabling them to trade more competitively and, most likely, to command a larger share of the market (Gertsberg, 2019, p. 10). It is unsurprising, then, that many of these "big players" also served as key social connectors, sharing information and creating opportunities that allowed others in their network to enhance their collections.

However, social capital was as important as financial capital. While some dealer-collectors could, in theory, operate with a ruthless, profit-maximizing approach, doing so risked long-term exclusion from the community's informal channels of exchange. Many participants cited a well-known collector whose unsociable business practices had earned him a reputation for self-interest. Though not formally excluded, he was seldom invited to private gatherings or offered attractive buying opportunities, despite owning highly valued cultural goods. This underscores a central theme: in a community where reputation was paramount, trustworthiness, fair dealing, and reciprocity were essential to maintaining privileged access to desirable pieces. Importantly, several interviewees who did not occupy central positions in the hierarchy stressed that this did not prevent them from building meaningful social connections. Shared passion for the objects often transcended status differences, allowing even peripheral members to experience the camaraderie and knowledge-sharing that form the lifeblood of the collecting community.

4.2 *The Arrival of the Internet*

All participants reported that the advent of the Internet fundamentally transformed how they pursue and experience their collecting activities. While there is no comprehensive quantitative data on the number of physical antiques markets held annually in Northwestern Europe, it is clear that online platforms such as eBay and Marktplaats have had a profound impact on the geographical and structural dynamics of the antiques trade (Combs, 2005, p. 1). This shift was echoed by the participants, who observed that the nature of physical markets has changed significantly with the rise of digital marketplaces.

Before digitalization, major physical markets were landmark events in the collecting calendar. Collectors and dealers would spend months preparing, stockpiling goods, and ensuring they had sufficient financial resources to maximize their chances of striking large deals. The anticipation surrounding these events created a charged atmosphere; as one dealer recalled, he could "always count on potential buyers having money burning a hole in their pocket from excitement." Today, this dynamic has shifted. The constant, year-round availability of online offers means that by the time a physical event occurs, potential buyers may have already exhausted their budgets and dealers may have sold much of their best stock. High-value deals are often negotiated and secured online before the event, leaving the physical market to function primarily as a social gathering and a venue for finalizing pre-arranged transactions.

The Internet has also become embedded in the daily routines of the interviewed collectors. Most reported checking online marketplaces for new acquisitions at least once a day, if not more frequently. A 2010 report by the Central Bureau of Statistics noted that in that year alone, over 3,330,000 advertisements were posted in the "Art and Antiques" section of Marktplaats, with an average selling price of €79 (Kuipers et al., 2010, p. 8). Since then, collectors report an even greater shift of their business activities online. The centrality of digital markets in the collecting community has inevitably reshaped traditional practices, challenging long-established routines and fostering new forms of interaction, etiquette, and community norms (Ellis & Haywood, 2012, p. 45).

A Change in Knowledge Gathering and Exchange

Perhaps the most significant change brought about by digitalization is the unprecedented availability and accessibility of information. One dealer-collector reflected that, in the past, his knowledge had been his "super-power" as a dealer—a hard-earned advantage that set him apart from competitors. He recalled the considerable effort once required to acquire this knowledge and continued:

> "The way we gathered information was like the early hunter-gatherers running through the fields and getting some food. With the digital world, you sit in front of your computer and you're getting drowned by information. So, there's a big, big change in the game, both for a dealer and for a collector. The availability of information and buying opportunities ... it's a really big change."

These days, if you were to find an old tin in your grandmother's attic, you could simply photograph it, upload the image to Google Images, and be met with page upon page of listings from platforms such as Marktplaats and eBay, showing similar tins along with their prices and sale dates. This instant accessibility has effectively democratized knowledge, reshaping both the social dynamics between dealers and collectors and influencing how collectors curate their collections and pursue knowledge exchange within their networks. However, the most financially valuable objects are rarely sold through public online marketplaces. Instead, sellers typically rely on their personal networks to connect with buyers known to be willing to pay premium prices—a pattern also observed in comparable collecting communities (Ellis & Haywood, 2012, p. 56). This demonstrates that while increased access to market information has leveled the playing field to some extent, networking remains a crucial component of the trade, and significant segments of the collectibles market remain invisible online. Although some traditional information-sharing practices continue to play a role in the studied collector network, digital systems now dominate. Books on the subject are still published, but instead of relying on conventional brick-and-mortar publishers, collectors increasingly self-finance limited-run publications, which are often enthusiastically supported within the community. Even so, such print materials are far less common than digital alternatives. Websites, online databases, and social media platforms now form the primary infrastructure for information exchange, having almost entirely replaced the once-essential collectors' magazines.

(Online) Curatorial Practices

Digitalization has significantly influenced curatorial practices, affecting both acquisition parameters and methods of display and registration. The increased transparency of the market has reshaped how collectors curate their holdings. With easier access to information about the full range of objects available within their broader area of interest, immersion in digital markets has pushed collectors toward greater specialization, encouraging them to identify a niche within their collecting domain. The sheer volume of available material makes such focus almost inevitable (Ellis & Haywood, 2012, p. 52). One collector explained that once you truly understand the scope of objects that could fall within your collection's parameters, you begin to feel the need to narrow those boundaries. The pursuit of completion within a defined niche is, after all, a prominent motivation for many collectors (Pearce, 2012, p. 157). He also noted that shifting price dynamics shape acquisition strategies. For instance, one subcollection he owned proved to be more valuable in the United States than in the Netherlands when sold online, and the profits from these sales became a funding source for developing other areas of his collection. While specialization has long been a natural tendency in collecting, it is noteworthy that digitalization appears to accelerate this process (Belk, 2012, p. 2).

In terms of registration and display, the shift has been equally pronounced. Whereas collectors once relied on polaroids and handwritten notes, many now maintain Google Drives, specialized databases, or social media pages dedicated to their collections. These serve as both private and public digital archives, most of them image-based, enabling collectors to document and showcase their holdings. Interestingly, most participants expressed a long-standing desire to create a shared, community-sourced archive. When I asked one collector why he wanted to make his objects visible online, he replied:

> "I am not interested in meeting new people online [. . .] I want to challenge the youth to engage with the history of advertising, and over the past years I think I have managed that. I notice that I speak to a lot of young graphic designers, historians and architects when I go to antiques markets, and they are interested!"

He is one of several collectors who have taken website-building courses and learned to use various digital tools in order to fully capitalize on the opportunities the Internet offers for showcasing their collections.

Changing Social Hierarchies

The abundance of readily available online information has significantly altered the social dynamics between dealer-collectors and their customers. Two dealer-collectors noted that while their expertise remains valuable, it no longer holds the same weight it did 20 years ago. Consequently, they now rely on alternative strategies to encourage customer loyalty, such as deliberately fostering personal relationships. One collector-dealer observed that, in the past, dealers naturally came to know their customers through informal interactions at physical meetups—connections that are far less organic in an online environment.

> "Now, it is suddenly possible that you have been dealing for years with a customer that lives in the USA or Singapore, but you have never seen them before. [. . .] I try to speak about more than just the tin, also talk about life. Eventually I even visited these people's home because it is good for the business relationship, but also because I just like visiting, [. . .] seeing them and their collection face to face".

The same interviewee explained that roughly 80% of his clients are repeat customers, while the remaining 20% are first-time buyers who may eventually become regulars. Even when an initial interaction feels distant, he makes a point of identifying the customer's collecting interests so he can proactively offer relevant items in the future. In this way, he deliberately cultivates relationships by maintaining personal correspondence online and offering to leverage his own network on the customer's behalf.

Another collector-dealer shared that he has been in ongoing correspondence with a man in Denmark whom he first met through an online market platform. The two regularly exchange photos of their latest tin acquisitions—not only for the social enjoyment, but also to provide each other with business advice. Because their networks differ significantly, this exchange does not threaten their respective markets. While the digital availability of information may have reduced the degree of information asymmetry that once characterized collectibles markets (Gertsberg, 2019, p. 53), the evolving market infrastructure has also shifted the nature of the information exchanged between buyers and sellers.

4.3 *Issues of Authenticity*

As most collectors now conduct business online rather than in person, sellers often hold more detailed knowledge about an individual object than potential buyers do. Before the rise of the Internet, most transactions took place with buyer and seller in the same physical space, where it was customary for the buyer to handle, open, and thoroughly inspect the object. In contrast, online listings typically provide only basic details—such as the brand, approximate age, a brief description of the object's type and condition—alongside a set of photographs. For the interviewees, high-quality images from multiple angles were considered the most essential form of information. Additional details may be shared during personal exchanges, often for social rather than strictly commercial reasons, but such disclosures are not standard practice. Without the opportunity to physically examine an object, buyers must rely heavily on what the seller chooses to show. This opens the door for selective presentation: opportune lighting and strategic camera angles can conceal blemishes, while alterations such as makeshift restorations or unsuitable replacements for missing parts can be downplayed—or entirely hidden—from view.

Digital Etiquette

It is likely due to the combined need to cultivate loyal trading relationships and manage heightened quality uncertainty that a relatively clear online etiquette has developed within this community. Adhering to this etiquette can significantly influence both a buyer's ability to secure high-quality pieces for their collection and a seller's capacity to obtain the best possible price for their cultural goods.

Participants identified several behaviors that constitute "breaking etiquette" on market websites. These include reneging on agreements, publicly outbidding acquaintances to drive up prices, ignoring bids, and misrepresenting one's intentions—for example, claiming an object is for a personal collection when it is in fact intended for resale, in order to appeal to the seller's sensibilities. Another common breach involves using photographs that deliberately conceal flaws or damage to an object.

Compliance with etiquette, particularly on the dealer's side, can also be understood through the lens of "signaling": actions taken by a seller to convey legitimacy, as well as the value and quality of the object offered (Löfgren et al., 2002, p. 199). In this context, signaling may include investing in professional-quality photographs, guaranteeing secure delivery through tracked shipping and protective packaging, or maintaining high customer ratings on market platforms. Such strategies are designed to reassure prospective buyers that their risk is minimal, thereby encouraging them to bid more confidently and competitively without fear of opportunistic exploitation.

Anonymous or Not?

Another notable effect of digitalization on the social sphere of collecting is the community's evolving relationship with the concept of anonymity. Most participants described the anonymity of online trading and information exchange as one of the less appealing aspects of conducting collecting activities in digital spaces. As a result, they tended to interact online primarily with people they already knew personally, or with those connected to them indirectly through real-life acquaintances. When encountering new potential contacts, participants often made a conscious effort to establish a personal relationship—particularly when they anticipated future opportunities for trade or information exchange. In practice, this meant that there was surprisingly little genuine anonymity in the network's online interactions.

This tendency toward transparency stands in contrast to the art market, which is widely recognized for its opacity, discretion, and reliance on anonymity (Oosterman et al., 2022, p. 7). Several collectors explained that anonymity was not a major concern in their own community, citing the relatively modest financial stakes, the limited interest from outsiders, and the inherently low level of privacy in such a close-knit network where business moves are often widely known. Nevertheless, anonymity still functions as a strategic tool—most notably in the withholding of provenance information in selling contexts. In a market as small as this, former owners often belong to the same narrow pool of potential future buyers. If a buyer's intention is to resell an item for profit, knowledge of its previous owner can limit resale opportunities and therefore reduce the price they are willing to pay.

Within this research context, expectations for digital etiquette largely mirror those for socially acceptable behavior offline. Participants reported that breaches of etiquette were rare, and that they seldom encountered problematic behavior from other users online. This dynamic may be explained through the lens of the "online disinhibition effect," a phenomenon described by Lapidot-Lefler and Barak (2015, p. 1) as "the lowering of psychological restraints, which often serve to regulate behavior in the online social environment." They argue that a sense of anonymity can foster disregard for accepted social norms in digital interactions. In this community, however, anonymity is deliberately reduced through the cultivation of personal relationships—both with strangers and with known acquaintances—within the same cyberspace. This relational approach appears to encourage members to maintain the same standards of social etiquette online as they would in person. This finding contrasts with Ellis and Haywood (2012)'s earlier study of vintage radio collectors, which found that many older participants resisted online engagement altogether, deeming it too impersonal and preferring "the traditional way" (p. 46).

4.4 *Changing Geographies*

A major change brought about by digitalization is the ability to buy and sell from virtually anywhere—whether at home, in the office, or even while on holiday. Despite the surge in online trading and communication, participants reported that they still attend physical markets regularly. These events are valued not only as opportunities to browse for new acquisitions but also as enjoyable social outings—occasions to reconnect with fellow collectors, view each other's latest finds, and finalize previously discussed trade agreements. However, the nature of these markets has evolved. The Internet now enables collectors to source objects from much farther afield, but it has also reduced the incentive to travel long distances for physical markets. Many participants explained that they can no longer justify the expense of traveling to what is now largely a social event, when in the past such trips also yielded substantial financial gains.

The shift to online spaces has also changed curatorial practices. Physical space is no longer the sole arena for displaying a collection: many participants now complement their home displays with dedicated websites or social media profiles showcasing their holdings. This allows them to share their collections more widely and maintain a network without leaving their home. Yet, despite the convenience and expanded reach of online engagement, many of the core social aspects of collecting have remained intact. The sense of community—and the enjoyment derived from it—continues to be regarded as a vital component of the collecting experience.

5 Conclusion

As shown in the analysis of previous research in this field, the interview results largely align with earlier findings—particularly regarding the importance of the social dimension of collecting and the central role of information in shaping trading dynamics between actors in the network. Nonetheless, this study reveals several noteworthy points that merit further discussion.

In contrast to many examples in the literature, the collectors in this study were not only willing to improve their digital literacy but also succeeded in creating an online social community that, to them, does not feel anonymous (Ellis & Haywood, 2012, p. 46). They actively embrace the opportunities the Internet offers for information exchange and collection display. This raises an intriguing question: to what extent might this increasingly public digital presence influence the cultural, social, and financial value of their objects, both within and beyond the collecting field?

The interviews also re-emphasize the centrality of the social sphere in the collecting experience. Information asymmetry remains an important factor in the relationships between collectors, but its focus has shifted over time. Before digitalization, it largely concerned knowledge about an object's position in the market; after digitalization, it is more often tied to assessing the object's quality, as also observed by Radermecker (2025). This raises further questions: has this shift led to adverse selection? The most valuable collectibles in this network are rarely sold online and are instead offered privately to a small circle of prospective buyers via the seller's personal network. Is this practice driven by concerns over quality uncertainty, by a level of market opacity that this research has only partially uncovered, or simply by the fact that these are niche cultural goods with few serious buyers in a tightly knit community? Another promising avenue for inquiry is whether the methods used by dealer-collectors to build customer loyalty could be understood as forms of "signaling" designed to counter the new types of information asymmetry introduced by digitalization.

More broadly, the aim of this research was to shed light on how digitalization has reshaped the social dynamics of trade and the curatorial practices of Northwestern European collectors of packaging and advertising materials. This question was addressed through semi-structured interviews with seven collectors. The findings indicate that the Internet has fundamentally changed the value of market knowledge: increased transparency has democratized access to information, reducing the relative advantage of specialized insider knowledge. In response, dealers have shifted their focus to fostering loyal customer relationships, as their informational edge is no longer as decisive as it was before the digital era.

The abundance of available information online has also pushed collectors to specialize within their interests; faced with an overwhelming array of objects, many have tightened their acquisition parameters in the pursuit of completion. Furthermore, physical markets have lost their former role as fixed milestones in the trading calendar. Rather than being events for which buyers save up and dealers prepare months in advance, markets now function primarily as social gatherings and occasions to finalize deals already arranged online. Yet despite these structural changes, many aspects of the social sphere remain remarkably resilient. Newcomers are still welcomed, reputation continues to be paramount, and social interactions remain essential to the enjoyment of collecting.

Future research could build on these findings in several ways—for example, by exploring the role of digital anonymity on online trading platforms, assessing how digitalization affects the perceived cultural value of collectibles outside the collecting community, and examining in greater depth the trust-building strategies dealer-collectors employ to signal credibility and reliability to potential buyers.

References

Adams, W. C. (2015). Conducting semi-structured interviews. *Handbook of Practical Program Evaluation*, 492–505.

Adeoye-Olatunde, O. A., & Olenik, N. L. (2021). Research and scholarly methods: Semi-structured interviews. *Journal of the American College of Clinical Pharmacy, 4*(10), 1358–1367.

Angelini, F., & Castellani, M. (2018). *Cultural and economic value: A (p)review*. University of Bologna. https://doi.org/10.13140/RG.2.2.34355.32803/1

Bainbridge, J. (2014). "Gotta catch 'em all!" Pokémon, cultural practice and object networks. *The IAFOR Journal of Asian Studies, 1*(1), 1–15.

Basit, T. (2003). Manual or electronic? The role of coding in qualitative data analysis. *Educational Research, 45*(2), 143–154.

Belk, R. W. (2012). Collectors and collecting. In *Interpreting objects and collections* (pp. 317–326). Routledge.

Bennett, T. (1995). *The birth of the museum: History, theory, politics*. Routledge.

Bourdieu, P., & Wacquant, L. (1992). *An invitation to reflexive sociology*. University of Chicago Press.

Case, D. O. (2009). Serial collecting as leisure, and coin collecting in particular. *Library Trends, 57*(4), 729–752.

Combs, H. J. (2005). The Internet's impact on the antiques trade. *Material Culture*, 26–41.

Desjardins, M. (2012). Ephemeral culture/eBay culture: Film collectibles and fan investments. In *Everyday eBay* (pp. 31–43). Routledge.

Ellis, R. M., & Haywood, A. (2012). Virtual_radiophile (163*): EBay and the changing collecting practices of the UK vintage radio community. In *Everyday eBay* (pp. 45–61). Routledge.

Elsner, J., & Cardinal, R. (Eds.). (1994). *Cultures of collecting*. Reaktion Books.

Gertsberg, M. (2019). *Asymmetries in art markets* (Doctoral thesis, Maastricht University). ProefschriftMaken Maastricht. https://doi.org/10.26481/dis.20190906mg

Hacking, C., Verbeek, H., Hamers, J. P., & Aarts, S. (2023). Comparing text mining and manual coding methods: Analysing interview data on quality of care in long-term care for older adults. *PLOS ONE, 18*(11), e0292578.

Hess, R. E. (1987). Anthropology, the meaning of community, and prevention. In *Prevention* (pp. 45–74). Routledge. https://doi.org/10.4324/9781315791609-7

Iskin, R. E., & Salsbury, B. (Eds.). (2019). *Collecting prints, posters, and ephemera: Perspectives in a global world*. Bloomsbury Publishing USA.

Kuipers, A., Mocking, R., & Schürmann, R. (2010). *Programma Impact ICT Onderzoeksrapport nr. 1: Marktplaats en statistiek*. Centraal Bureau Voor Statistiek.

Lai, H. M., & Chen, T. T. (2014). Knowledge sharing in interest online communities: A comparison of posters and lurkers. *Computers in Human Behavior, 35*, 295–306.

Lapidot-Lefler, N., & Barak, A. (2015). The benign online disinhibition effect: Could situational factors induce self-disclosure and prosocial behaviors? *Cyberpsychology: Journal of Psychosocial Research on Cyberspace, 9*(2).

Leavy, P. (2022). *Research design: Quantitative, qualitative, mixed methods, arts-based, and community-based participatory research approaches.* Guilford Publications.

Lee, C. P., & Trace, C. B. (2009). The role of information in a community of hobbyist collectors. *Journal of the American Society for Information Science and Technology, 60*(3), 621–637.

Löfgren, K. G., Persson, T., & Weibull, J. W. (2002). Markets with asymmetric information: The contributions of George Akerlof, Michael Spence and Joseph Stiglitz. *The Scandinavian Journal of Economics*, 195–211.

Marcus, G. E. (1995). Ethnography in/of the world system: The emergence of multi-sited ethnography. *Annual Review of Anthropology, 24*(1), 95–117.

Oosterman, N., Mackenzie, S., & Yates, D. (2022). Regulating the wild west: Symbolic security bubbles and white collar crime in the art market. *Journal of White Collar and Corporate Crime, 3*(1), 7–15.

Pearce, S. (2012). *Interpreting objects and collections.* Routledge.

Pearce, S. (2013). *On collecting: An investigation into collecting in the European tradition.* Routledge.

Radermecker, A. S. V. (2025). Connoisseurship from below exploring "informal" expertise in art on social media. *Journal of Cultural Economics*, 1–38.

Rossel, S. (2024). *The transformation of private collecting* (Master's thesis). Leiden University, Faculty of Archaeology. https://hdl.handle.net/1887/4011243

Saldaña, J. (2013). *The coding manual for qualitative researchers.* Sage Publications.

Shuker, R. (2017). *Wax trash and vinyl treasures: Record collecting as a social practice.* Routledge.

Wilson, S. M., & Peterson, L. C. (2002). The anthropology of online communities. *Annual Review of Anthropology, 31*(1), 449–467.

Outsiders or Forgotten? Independent Artists Creating Alternative Career Paths in the Low-end Market

Matilde Ferrero

1 Introduction

From the supply-side perspective of the art market, is it appropriate to describe non-profit artist-run spaces as part of the low-end art market? This question is relevant as the art market grows more polarized. As argued in the introductory chapter, the high-end segment combines strong scarcity, symbolic functionality, and brand legitimacy, which tend to translate into high prices and institutional visibility (Zorloni & Ardizzone, 2016; Isales 2015). While "low-end" may suggest lesser commercial value, it also raises questions about legitimacy, innovation, and autonomy. Recent scholarship has foregrounded the polarized structure of the contemporary art market: a small, hyper-visible high-end segment (art fairs, auction houses, elite galleries) coexists alongside a more diffuse ecosystem of emerging, independent producers. The triadic model proposed in the introduction to this book offers a comprehensive framework for examining market segmentation through the attributes of traded goods and identifies, within sub-segment 4, the distinguishing characteristics of artist-run artworks. Nevertheless, this chapter argues for a necessary reorientation of analysis from objects to practices. By investigating the organizational structures and career strategies of artists affiliated

M. Ferrero (✉)
Université libre de Bruxelles, Brussels, Belgium
e-mail: matilde.ferrero@ulb.be

A.-S. V. Radermecker (ed.), *Low-End Markets for Art and Cultural Goods*, Cultural Economics & the Creative Economy,
https://doi.org/10.1007/978-3-032-27566-0_21

with Bastione, it demonstrates that value emerges both from the formal or material properties of artworks and from collaborative ways of creating art whose output is not necessarily physical. In doing so, the chapter expands the scope of the model beyond object-centered segmentation to encompass practice-based modalities of value production that function within, alongside and at times beyond the entry-level art market. At the same time, the transposition of the low-end art market concept to non-profit, artist-run environments remains insufficiently theorized. Accordingly, this chapter critically assesses whether applying the "low-end" category to independent artists operating in artist-run spaces provides analytical insights, or whether it instead imposes an overly market-centric interpretive framework.

The chapter is structured as follows. Section 1 reviews key literature on the art market and independent spaces. Section 2 outlines the research methodology. Section 3 presents the case study and findings, while Sect. 4 concludes.

2 Literature Review: Artists' Careers in the Contemporary Art Market

In high-end market analyses, success is measured by auction prices, critical acclaim, and institutional validation (Zorloni & Ardizzone, 2016; Beckert & Rössel, 2013). By contrast, research on artist-run spaces highlights their role as incubators of experimentation, collective agency, and urban commons (Blessi et al., 2011; Grodach, 2011; Lenna and Trimarchi 2019). Given the confusion surrounding the definition of these spaces, which are defined in many ways (e.g. independent, alternative, commons, grassroots), this chapter does not seek to add to this confusion by suggesting a new definition—that of "low-end"—but rather to ascertain the extent to which the term aligns with, supports, complements or excludes the concept of the independent art scene.

2.1 The Dynamics of the High-End Art Market: How Artists Create Their Own Path

Artists, who are the creative force behind the contemporary art market, create works that reflect their unique perspectives and have a substantial impact on the categories of works available in the market from an economic perspective. The definition of an artwork is often contested. Santagata (1998) argues that an artwork functions as both an object and an image, a symbol and a commercial commodity. This duality highlights how the physical manifestation of contemporary visual art connects intrinsically to its broader expression in both space and time. This is evident in art forms such as photography, video, canvas, and performance art, which requires a specifically designated time and place to reach its full artistic potential. As such, the concept of an artistic good is often defined by originality, craftsmanship, and a sense of "uselessness," pointing to its unique artistic identity.

Artistic production begins with the artist, who dedicates significant time to creation, but success is largely determined by critics, curators, and collectors who shape market visibility and pricing (Fillis, 2013; Fletcher, 2008; Frey & Pommerehne, 1989; Thompson, 2008). Entry into national and international markets remains highly competitive, with barriers to visibility disproportionately favoring a select few (Zorloni & Ardizzone, 2016). Unlike traditional patronage models, where recognition stemmed from personal networks, today's market is shaped by globalized competition, yet only a small number of artists attain sustained recognition (Sacco, 2004).

The arts labor market differs significantly from other sectors, characterized by a younger, highly educated workforce facing high self-employment rates, income instability, and underemployment (Menger, 1999, 2001; Abbing, 2003). Increased precarity, fueled by globalization and the shift toward project-based work, exacerbates these challenges (Morgan & Nelligan, 2018). Despite growing interest in arts education, economic rewards remain limited, creating a paradox where creativity does not guarantee financial stability (Abbing, 2003; Ball, 2003).

To face these conditions, artists increasingly adopt multidisciplinary, entrepreneurial, and mobile career strategies (Hall, 2004; Throsby & Zednik, 2011). The acceleration of digitalization, particularly post-pandemic, has reshaped the way artists approach their work, decentralizing creative processes and fostering new forms of artistic expression. While these changes offer new opportunities for visibility and flexibility, they also raise concerns about market saturation, creative control, and the precarization of employment (Farchy & Denis, 2020; Hearn, 2020). Therefore, artists in the digital era face the challenge of balancing artistic expression with commercial success, and many adopt strategies like portfolio-to-platform models to secure financial stability while pursuing creative projects (Clague, 2023). This entrepreneurial shift underscores the growing need for artists to develop business acumen, and more broadly, to engage in collaborative efforts to sustain their careers (Puletti et al., 2024; Bosma et al., 2024). The intersection of art and commerce creates new challenges, and it continues to evolve as artists experiment with new forms of mutual support and self-determination in their professional lives.

2.2 *Independent Artist-Run Spaces as an Alternative of the High-End Art Market?*

Independent artist-run spaces have long operated on the margins of the art market, overshadowed by dominant players such as galleries and foundations due to limited resources and visibility (Sharon, 1979; Blessi et al., 2011; Arthurs, 2012). Despite this, they play a crucial role in contemporary art by fostering artistic experimentation beyond the constraints of market-driven pressures (Komarova, 2018; Działek, 2021). Historically, these spaces emerged in the 1960s as a response to the commercialization of art, aligning with broader social movements and challenging institutional structures (Lippard, 1965).

Today, artist-run spaces serve as creative spaces, providing platforms for emerging artists while navigating economic precarity. Operating with limited funding, they often rely on public or independent sources (Lange & Bürkner, 2013; Gritzas & Kavoulakos, 2016; Bertacchini et al., 2022). Their focus on avant-garde practices places them in the "low-end" market, where works may struggle to gain commercial traction or critical recognition (Bourriaud, 2002). While high-end artists gain international visibility, these spaces primarily engage with local communities, fostering cultural specificity but limiting global reach (Blessi et al., 2011; Zebracki & Smulders, 2012). As a matter of fact, these spaces have been analyzed beyond the market and through the lens of urban commons, collectively managed resources that resist privatization and market-driven exclusions (Harvey, 2012). Grassroots artistic practices transform underutilized spaces into cultural hubs, countering neoliberal dominance in the arts (Malatjie, 2013; Wright, 2024). Through the reimagination of urban culture, these practices reinforce commons-based cultural production while challenging commodification (Borchi, 2018; Lenna and Trimarchi 2019; Zilberstein, 2019; Morea & Sabatini, 2023).

Nevertheless, financial sustainability remains a key challenge. Many artist-run spaces face organizational vulnerabilities, such as short-term funding and a lack of managerial expertise (Blessi et al., 2011; Hoffmann et al., 2022). However, they also serve as incubators for artists, helping them face both creative and entrepreneurial demands (Rota & Salone, 2014; Salone et al., 2017).

3 Methodology

Based on these premises, the chapter addresses the following question: *To what extent the concept of the low-end art market can be meaningfully applied to independent artists operating in artist-run spaces?* This research employs an in-depth case study of Bastione, an independent art space in Turin's grassroots ecosystem (Bertacchini et al., 2022). Initially emerging informally in a neglected historic building, Bastione fostered artistic experimentation outside institutional frameworks. After its eviction, it re-established itself as a non-profit in a new location, continuing its activities despite limited institutional support. The case study approach allows for an exploration of the social dynamics shaping the space and its resilience within the broader cultural landscape (Simons, 2014). A mixed-methods strategy was used, integrating deductive and inductive approaches (Fig. 1). The selection of Bastione as a case study is grounded in its transformation from an informal occupation into a formally constituted association, as well as its integration within Turin's wider art ecosystem. This trajectory renders it a particularly strategic site for analyzing how the dimensions articulated in the triadic model intersect with artistic practices and career-oriented strategies within the entry-level segment of the art market. Although the findings are not intended to be broadly generalizable across all artist-run initiatives, the case affords substantive analytical insight into a specific configuration of autonomous artistic production operating within a hierarchically structured market environment.

The deductive phase guided interview design, grounding it in existing theoretical frameworks, while the inductive phase allowed themes to emerge organically from the data (Newman, 2000). Data collection combined semi-structured interviews and participant observation. Interviews with 10 artists (60–90 minutes each, totaling 14 hours) explored artistic practices, governance, and sustainability (Mannan & Afni, 2020). A six-month observation period (January–June 2024) included weekly meetings, project development, and guest artist residencies, providing deeper insights into Bastione's operations and collaborative strategies (Musante, 2015).

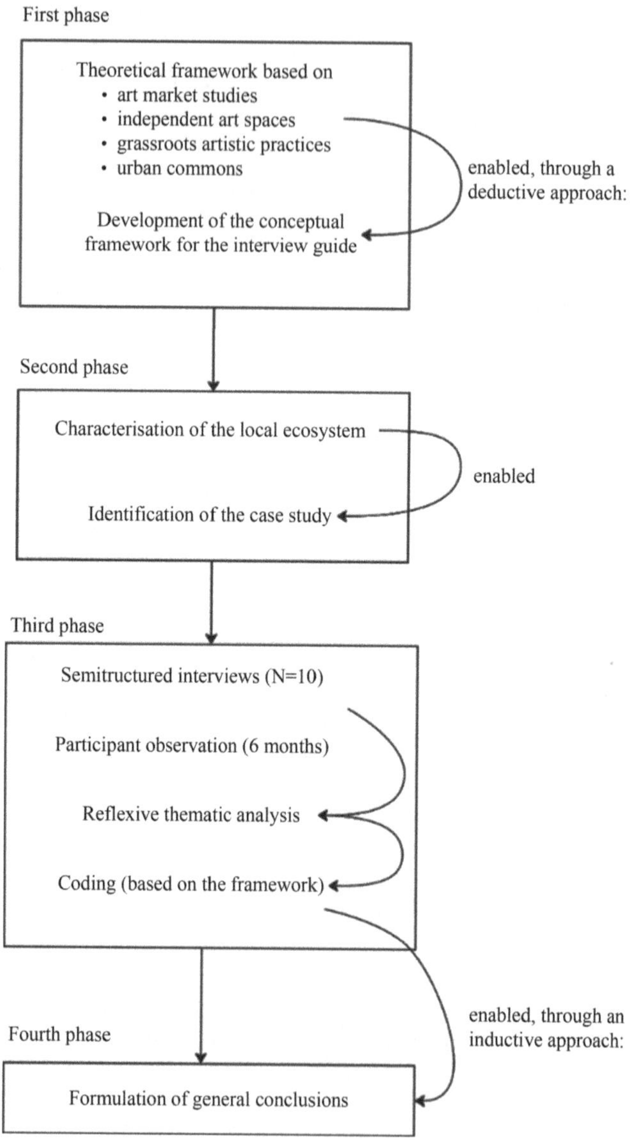

Fig. 1 The Four Phases of the Research Design. *Source* Elaborated from Ferrero (2025)

Data analysis used reflexive thematic analysis within *Atlas.ti*, systematically coding interview transcripts and observation notes to identify recurring themes (Clarke & Braun, 2021). This approach gave the opportunity to deepen Bastione's artistic and organizational model, positioning it as a case study in development and adaptability of independent art spaces.

4 Empirical Analysis and Findings

4.1 Context

Once a major industrial center, Turin has undergone a transformation in recent decades, moving from a manufacturing-based economy to one centered on culture, creativity and innovation. The collapse of its industrial base in the late twentieth century, particularly with the Fiat crisis and wider deindustrialization, led to widespread unemployment, urban decay and the need for new economic strategies (Vanolo, 2015). In response, the city embraced a post-industrial model of regeneration that prioritized cultural production, creative industries and technological innovation. This transition was further accelerated by major events such as the 2006 Winter Olympics, which attracted significant public and private investment in infrastructure, tourism, and the arts (Della Sala, 2023).

Some scholars argue that Italy's major HEAM centers are Milan and Rome, with Turin historically more peripheral (Zorloni, 2013). However, a recent wave of established galleries and art fairs suggests a more complex picture. Although smaller in scale compared to Milan, established galleries such as Franco Noero (founded in 1991) regularly showcase works by internationally recognized artists, contributing to the city's visibility on the global art stage (Frieze, 2025). Meanwhile, galleries like Sonia Rosso (opened in 2005) emphasizes emerging Italian and international practices, with artworks priced between €10,000 and €50,000, positioning it within the "low-end" market, though occasionally engaging in middle- and high-end sales. This layered market structure is further exemplified by Artissima, Turin's leading contemporary art fair, which presents both prestigious international galleries accounting for the HEAM, and more experimental sections where artworks typically sell for €5,000–€10,000. Such pricing strategies blur the lines between low-end and middle-end markets. On the other hand, institutions like the Castello di Rivoli reinforce the city's integration into the high-end art market through consistent programming of internationally significant exhibitions

Independent art spaces in Turin have historically emerged as a response to the high-end art market, providing a platform for emerging artists and experimental practices that struggle to gain access to established institutions (Bertacchini et al., 2022). Despite their role in fostering artistic innovation and community engagement, independent art spaces face significant challenges related to financial sustainability, legal recognition, and institutional constraints. Unlike the structured high-end markets of France and Germany, where national policies have helped to integrate contemporary artists into the global market, Italy's fragmented cultural ecosystem offers limited career opportunities for young artists (Zorloni, 2013; Bertacchini and Borrione 2021). As a result, independent spaces have become important sites of artistic production, but they remain vulnerable to changing urban policies and redevelopment pressures.

To understand Bastione's practice, it is essential to consider the broader institutional context that shapes Turin's cultural ecosystem. Beyond its grassroots activities, the association is influenced by macro- and *meso*-level dynamics, including government policies, funding bodies and cultural institutions. Decentralization reforms since the 1970s have given local authorities greater control over cultural initiatives, supporting urban regeneration and heritage conservation efforts. At the *meso* level, foundations such as Fondazione CRT and Compagnia di San Paolo, as well as social innovation incubators such as SocialFare, play a key role in funding and promoting cultural projects. Meanwhile, Turin's independent art scene continues to be driven by grassroots initiatives that reclaim urban spaces for artistic and social purposes, often operating outside formal institutional frameworks. Figure 2 provides a picture of the presence of cultural organizations belonging to the high and low-end market in Turin.

Bastione emerged from the independent cultural landscape, originally rooted in the Cavallerizza Occupata movement, which challenged traditional notions of public space and cultural production.[1]

[1] The *Cavallerizza Occupata* (Occupied Cavallerizza) movement was the name under which the occupation initiative emerged in 2014 at the Cavallerizza Reale complex. The main objective of the movement was to oppose plans for privatization and real estate speculation in the complex, promoting instead a model of participatory and inclusive management based on free access to culture and shared spaces. This movement, which emerged in response to the perceived under-utilization of public spaces, sought to reclaim these spaces for cultural and artistic production, challenging conventional norms of public space use and ownership in urban contexts (Dellarossa, 2020).

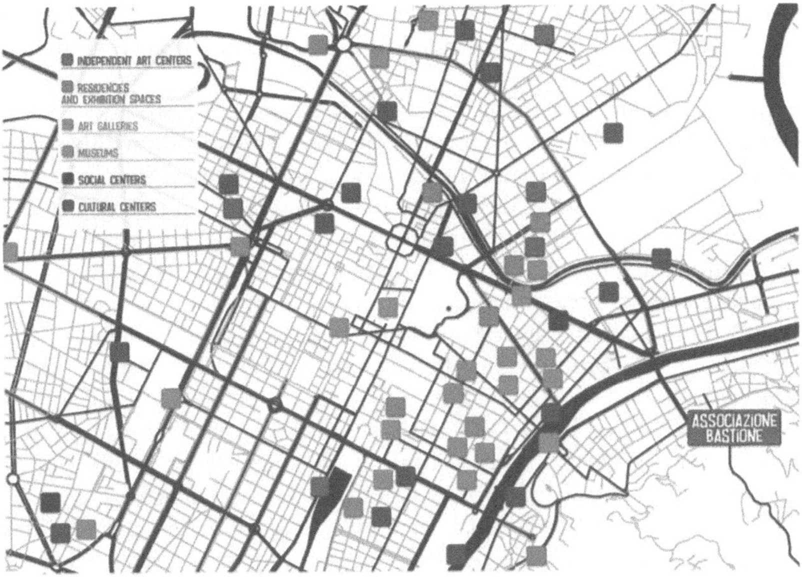

Fig. 2 Map of Turin's Cultural Ecosystem. *Source* Author's own elaboration based on secondary data

4.2 *Case-study*

The group of artists now known as Bastione originated in Turin in 2017, when 15 young artists began the occupation of the Bastione San Maurizio, one of the buildings of Cavallerizza Reale. Their aim was to work together to activate the potential of the space through collaborative artistic practices, though an architectural and creative restauration. After about a month of experimenting within the site, the group formalized their efforts in a project called "Apotema" (2017)—their first public exhibition at the bastion (Dellarossa, 2020). The name, derived from geometry, refers to the radius of an inscribed circle and symbolizes the relationships and movements within the space, the way the artists liked to visually describe their ongoing activities in the space at the time. This project marked the official start of the architectural and creative interventions in the building, and the bastion became a house of sculptures, where the architectural features and individual works merged into an evolving installation. Each artist left a trace, creating a layered history of interventions within the space. For example, Emanuele Marullo's "Nord-Est" featured a bamboo dome originally intended for the adjacent gardens but assembled indoors.

By the end of the first year (2017), the expected restoration of the Bastione San Maurizio by the local government had not begun, giving the artists the freedom to expand their presence and activities. This led to the launch of "AFFITTASI"[2] in January 2019, a project that invited external artists and groups to engage with the bastion and its artists, transforming the location into an artistic hub. The initiative facilitated performances and installations from a wider artistic community, extending the reach of the group's influence. In general, multidisciplinarity was the fil rouge that linked these and other events: between 2017 and 2019, similar artistic projects have been hosted and co-organized, such as "K_Night" by the "Mrzb" collective and "DISCARNATE: the flesh failures" by the American artist Qualiatik, as well as documentaries and sound performances such as "Gang of ducks x Cripta 747." According to the artists, "music, performance and visual art have allowed different personalities, both hosted and belonging to the main group of artists, to express themselves during this period."

However, this period of experimentation came to an end on 19 November 2019 with the start of the eviction process led by local authorities. This marked a significant turning point for the artists in the group, but also for all the artists and people who used the spaces in Cavallerizza as an artistic hub. From that moment on, the artists of the bastion began to reflect on important questions about their role in caring for abandoned urban spaces and their relationship with the creation of communities.

The Need for a Space to Create

The first informal years of the group of artists, spent in the bastion at Cavallerizza (2017–2019), illustrate a tension that is central to this chapter: to what extent can the term "low-end," which is market-based, be meaningfully applied to the independent art scene, which tends to identify itself as separate from the market (Sharon, 1979; Blessi et al., 2011; Komarova, 2018)? Rather than positioning themselves in opposition to the art market, the artists' main concern at that time was finding a space to

[2] The Italian word means "to rent." In fact, it was a project based on the contradictory idea of renting space in the occupied building for free.

create, experiment, and build relationships. Their experience points to how "independence" was, above all, a strategic and material response to the absence of institutional infrastructure—not an ideological rejection of the market.

Their accounts often returned to the lack of accessible workspaces at the academy and the invisibility they felt within more formal circuits. "Sometimes we invited the artists who taught at the Academy," one of them recalled, "but very few of them came to see our practice and our work at the bastion." Another put it more plainly: "The Academy itself didn't have spaces for us to meet, create, and think. So we had to find our own space." The occupation of the bastion was not framed as resistance, but as necessity: "The Bastione San Maurizio was like a blank canvas where we could make things happen without waiting for permission." These statements reveal a form of independence that is not grounded in ideology but in the need to support artistic creation outside the limitations of both market and institutional environments.

This understanding contrasts with how independent spaces are often framed in the literature—as initiatives operating outside market boundaries, defined by their own rules, ideologies, and organizational forms (Sharon, 1979; Blessi et al., 2011). In Bastione's case, such boundaries were far more porous. The artists were not focused on avoiding the market, but on building a supportive context to sustain both individual projects (often tied to their thesis work) and collective experimentation. Their practice was collaborative, multidisciplinary, and improvisational, involving not just visual artists, but musicians and performers as well. The bastion offered a platform to test out ideas and co-create with others in an open-ended way.

Notably, the term "independent" was never used by the artists themselves in interviews or conversations. Yet their practice aligns with what is often described in scholarship on artist-run initiatives: temporary, adaptive, shaped by resource scarcity, and focused on shared cultural production (Arthurs, 2012; Borchi, 2018). Their relationship to the market was complex and variable. For some, the bastion was a safe space to experiment, while for others, it became part of a parallel path alongside occasional exhibitions and gallery contacts. In this sense, the early years of Bastione do not fit neatly into a "low-end" market frame—understood as a transactional space for undervalued goods—nor are they entirely "independent" in the oppositional sense. What emerges instead is a flexible and strategic use of autonomy, shaped by practical needs and the desire for artistic self-determination. In this context, applying the term "low-end" to their practice risks oversimplifying what was, in fact, a complex relationship with institutional structures and market expectations.

4.3 *The Emergence of New Networks and Careers*

The previous section explains how the creation of the informal group at the bastion was not that ideological, but rather a practical need for creative experimentation in a shared space. Although the artists never framed their activity as explicitly "against" the market, they were fully aware of the structural barriers that prevented them from entering it. The galleries felt inaccessible, and the academic system did not offer viable alternatives: "There were no opportunities to work together at the academy or in the galleries," one artist said. "We needed a space where we could just try things out together, without formalities." And, "it wasn't so much a decision to reject the system ideologically, but rather to find a place where we could work and experiment without having to wait for someone to give us a chance." The development of the group at the Bastione San Maurizio is another example of how the creation of such spaces is a response to specific practical needs to create their own ecosystem. This section explores the reasons why these spaces have emerged as practical solutions: the need for informal networking, and the desire to build careers independent of the conventional art market through their own network and relationships.

For young artists, the early stages of their careers are characterized by a strong need to experiment, collaborate, and connect with fellow artists and, at the same time, high barriers set by gatekeepers. In fact, the rigid structures of the traditional art market and its associated institutions often limit opportunities for young emerging artists (Sacco 2004). Galleries, museums, and established networks are often inaccessible to those without the right connections or sufficient market recognition (Thompson, 2008). As one artist argued, "We felt cut off from the mainstream galleries because we were young and had no network. It felt like a closed club." As a result, artists face significant barriers when trying to enter the art world through these traditional channels. The early members of the group, many of whom were recent art school graduates, were frustrated by the lack of accessible, shared spaces for co-creation and artistic dialogue. For some, the bastion offered a space where they could develop a body of work that would later be shown elsewhere, in group exhibitions or small galleries. Others continued to work in parallel, combining their independent practice with moments of more market-oriented engagement. In both cases, the bastion thus became a self-constructed ecosystem that combined informal support networks with modes of presentation and collaboration that were not available elsewhere and enhanced mobility. These networks were essential in building visibility, relationships, and potential career trajectories.

A major factor behind the creation of the space at the bastion was the desire to build careers that did not depend on the market conventional careers, which always lead artists to the mechanism of building visibility (Sacco 2004). In their plans, the creation of a space for creation and relationships could allow them to pursue parallel careers—one that could potentially interact with the market and another that existed outside. For those who already wanted to engage with the market and exhibit in galleries as a parallel career to the independent art space, the space offered a way to maintain a sense of autonomy and creative freedom. They could continue to experiment and develop their artistic voices independently, without being beholden to the demands of the market. "The bastion gave us a space to continue working on projects that the galleries might not be interested in, but that were important to us as artists," explained one of them. For others, the decision to bypass the market altogether was already a conscious one. These artists refuse the commodification of their work and the constraints imposed by galleries, collectors, and museums. Instead, they focus on building autonomous careers, supported by alternative forms of support such as collaborations, residencies, and teaching. As one artist described: "For me, it's not about selling art. It's about creating something meaningful and connecting with people through that process." For them, the existence of spaces such as the bastion was crucial, providing an environment in which they could work without the pressure of market expectations.

However, there is more to it than that. As they experienced the creation of artworks and the organization of exhibitions and performances with hosted artists, they began to realize that their way of working was no longer limited to the creation of art. They could build their artistic practice and careers around the organization of such art projects, which relied much more on hospitality and co-creation than on individual creation or creation as a collective of artists. Over the next few years (especially at Villa Rey), this possibility of a new career in their practice became visible to most of them, while others continued to focus on making art between their safe space and the market. In this sense, their words and practices may reflect a wider shift in which artists are taking control of their careers and artistic practices. Rather than waiting for market validation, they are creating their own platforms where they define their careers. This autonomy could allow for greater flexibility and freedom, enabling artists to pursue projects that may not be commercially viable but remain artistically significant. As one artist said: "The collaborations we have built at the bastion are some of the most important relationships of my career. They're not about money, they're about shared ideas and support."

Read through the lens of the triadic model, Bastione's practices reveal a configuration typical of the entry-level segment, characterized by symbolic functionality but limited scarcity and weak institutional brand recognition. However, the case also shows that brand strength and legitimacy may be constructed relationally, through networks and collaborative infrastructures rather than through established market institutions. This suggests that segmentation at the entry level cannot be understood solely through the attributes of traded goods, but must also account for the organizational and career practices that shape value production.

5 Conclusions

In contrast to the high-end art market, which operates through international galleries, auction houses, and institutional legitimation, the low-end art market offers alternative artistic and organizational forms that foreground community participation, interdisciplinary collaboration, and experimentation. Co-creation is an integral part of these practices: Bastione's programs, for example, rely on artists, musicians, and performers working together to generate participatory projects that are far from traditional modes of display or sale. Because many of these collaborative works are site-specific or process-driven, they can be functionally unsellable in conventional terms, underscoring a core difference between the low-end and the high-end of the art market.

The need for spaces to create shows that artists of Bastione did not turn away from the art market for ideological reasons, as might have been the case with the emergence of the first independent spaces in the 60s (Sharon, 1979), but sought pragmatic strategies to overcome the obstacles they encountered in traditional institutions (i.e., the Art Academy). Their case suggests that independence does not means rebellion to the conventional structures of the high-end art market but stems from the necessity for spaces that allow for artistic experimentation and alternative ways of working, leaving room for the creation of a low-end market.

For some, the bastion offered a space where they could develop a body of work that would later be shown elsewhere, in group exhibitions or small galleries. Others continued to work in parallel, combining their independent practice with moments of more market-oriented engagement. In both cases, Bastione was not conceived as a marginal or anti-market space, but as an enabling context. "The bastion gave us a space to continue working on projects that the galleries might not be interested in," one artist explained, "but that were important to us as artists." At the same time, some artists described their involvement as a conscious decision to remain outside the market logic altogether. For these individuals, the bastion allowed them to build alternative careers, grounded in collaboration, teaching, residencies, and co-curation. As one said: "For me, it's not about selling art. It's about creating something meaningful and connecting with people through that process."

This coexistence of different orientations—towards, alongside, or outside the market—demonstrates that Bastione functioned as more than just a creative space. It became a site of career experimentation. In the years that followed, especially during the Villa Rey period, some members began to focus on producing and organizing events and residencies, understanding this work as part of their artistic trajectory. Others moved between exhibition projects and self-organized initiatives, balancing autonomy with occasional institutional support.

These developments reflect a broader shift: rather than waiting for external validation or visibility, artists are increasingly building their own platforms. The collaborations and informal infrastructures developed at Bastione became central to how many artists framed their careers through a redefinition of what artistic work can be. "The collaborations we have built at the bastion are some of the most important relationships of my career," one artist noted. "They're not about money; they're about shared ideas and support."

As such, Bastione cannot be reduced to a "low-end" position within the art market. It served as a hybrid arena—at once a self-organized creative space, a point of entry into broader networks, and, for some, a pathway toward institutional or market visibility. If the concept of the low-end art market is to be meaningfully applied here, it must be reframed to account for these roles: the focus here is on autonomy, recognition and the construction of alternative infrastructures, rather than on sales or economic value. In this sense, Bastione's approach aligns with the triadic segmentation of the art market, while also extending it. This is demonstrated by showing that value in the entry-level segment can be generated through practice-based and relational infrastructures, as well as the characteristics of artworks as traded goods.

References

Abbing, H. (2003). *Support for artists. A handbook of cultural economics* (pp. 55). Edward Elgar Publishing.

Arthurs, K. E. (2012). *Creative cities, creative spaces, and urban policy: The impacts of regulations on artist-run centres and independent arts spaces in Vancouver, British Columbia* (Doctoral dissertation, University of British Columbia).

Ball, L. (2003). *Future directions for employability research in the creative industries. ADM (The higher education academy subject centre for arts, design and media)*. The Higher Education Academy.

Beckert, J., & Rössel, J. (2013). The price of art: Uncertainty and reputation in the art field. *European Societies, 15*(2), 178–195.

Bertacchini, E. E., & Borrione, P. (2021). Arte al futuro. Indagine su percorsi di formazione, carriere artistiche e spazi emergenti in Italia. CSS-Ebla.

Bertacchini, E. E., Pazzola, G., & Puletti, F. (2022). Urban alternative cultural production in Turin: An ecological community approach. *European Urban and Regional Studies, 29*(3), 350–368.

Blessi, G. T., Sacco, P. L., & Pilati, T. (2011). Independent artist-run centres: An empirical analysis of the Montreal non-profit visual arts field. *Cultural Trends, 20*(2), 141–166.

Borchi, A. (2018). Culture as commons: Theoretical challenges and empirical evidence from occupied cultural spaces in Italy. *Cultural Trends, 27*(1), 33–45.

Bosma, B., Loots, E., Stroet, P., & van Witteloostuijn, A. (2024). Passionately or reluctantly independent? Artistic and non-artistic self-employment compared. *Journal of Cultural Economics*, 1–31. https://doi.org/10.1007/s10824-024-09525-x

Bourriaud, N. (2002). *Relational Aesthetics.* Les presses du réel.

Clague, M. (2023). From portfolio to platform career. *Artivate, 12*, 1–22.

Clarke, V., & Braun, V. (2021). Thematic analysis: a practical guide.

Della Sala, V. (2023). The legacy of the Turin 2006 Olympic Games through a long-term development perspective: Reflection and opinion about the physical and social change in the post-Olympic period. *Cambio: Rivista Sulle Trasformazioni Sociali, 25*(1), 229–247.

Dellarossa, G. (2020). Una corteccia linfatica. *Osservatorio Futura*. Retrieved October 4, 2024, from https://archivio.osservatoriofutura.it/una-corteccia-linfatica/

Działek, J. (2021, July). A spatial history of independent art spaces in Krakow from the 1970s to 2019. *Arts, 10*(3), 45. MDPI.

Farchy, J., & Denis, J. (2020). Artificial intelligence and cultural creation. In T. Brille, A. Mignosa, & R. Towse (Eds.), *Teaching cultural economics* (pp. 198–203). Edward Elgar Publishing. https://www.elgaronline.com/abstract/edcoll/9781788970730/9781788970730.00037.xml.

Ferrero, M. (2025). *Artists beyond the market. The case of independent art spaces and their role in contemporary society*. PhD dissertation.

Fillis, I. (2013). The artist as marketer and entrepreneur. In I. Fillis, B. Lee, & A. Broadbridge (Eds.), The Routledge companion to arts marketing (2nd ed.). Routledge.

Fletcher, R. (2008). The Artist-entrepreneur in the New Creative Economy. *Organizational Aesthetics, 2*(3).

Frey, B. S., & Pommerehne, W. W. (1989). *Muses and Markets: Explorations in the Economics of the Arts.*

Frieze. (2025). *Turin*. Retrieved from https://www.frieze.com/tags/turin

Gritzas, G., & Kavoulakos, K. I. (2016). Diverse economies and alternative spaces: An overview of approaches and practices. *European Urban and Regional Studies, 23*(4), 917–934. https://doi.org/10.1177/0969776415573778

Grodach, C. (2011). Art spaces in community and economic development: Connections to neighborhoods, artists, and the cultural economy. *Journal of Planning Education and Research, 31*(1), 74–85.

Hall, D. T. (2004). The protean career: A quarter-century journey. *Journal of Vocational Behavior, 65*(1), 1–13. https://doi.org/10.1016/j.jvb.2003.10.006

Harvey, D. (2012). *Rebel cities: From the right to the city to the urban revolution.* Verso books.

Hearn, G. (2020). The future of creative work: Creativity and digital disruption. In G. Hearn (Ed.), *The Future of Creative Work* (pp. 1–12). Edward Elgar Publishing. https://www.elgaronline.com/edcollchap/edcoll/9781839101090/9781839101090.00007.xml.

Hoffmann, R., Coate, B., Chuah, S.-H., & Arenius, P. (2022). What makes an artrepreneur?: An exploratory study of artrepreneurial passion, personality and artistry. In J. Woronkowicz (Ed.), *Arts, entrepreneurship, and innovation* (pp. 39–58). Springer Nature Switzerland. https://link.springer.com/10.1007978-3-031-18195-5_3

Isales, A. M. (2015). *An analysis on the correlation between commercial success and institutional success for contemporary artists* (Master's thesis, Sotheby's Institute of Art-New York).

Komarova, N. (2018). Between the market and noncommercial art institutions: Early career strategies of contemporary artists in emerging art scenes. *Poetics*, *71*, 33–42.

Lange, B., & Bürkner, H.-J. (2013). Value creation in scene-based music production: The case of electronic club music in Germany. *Economic Geography*, *89*(2), 149–169. https://doi.org/10.1111/ecge.12002

Lenna, V., & Trimarchi, M. (2019). For a culture of urban commons. Practices and policies. In *Art, economics and the city* (pp. 205–242).

Lippard, L. (1965). Biting the hand: Artists and museums in New York since 1969. *Alternative Art, New York*, *1985*, 79–120.

Malatjie, P. (2013). Alternative/experimental art spaces in Johannesburg. *Third Text*, *27*(3), 367–377.

Mannan, S., & Afni, M. (2020). Best practices of Semi-structured interview method. *Chittagong Port authority*, 1–12.

Menger, P.-M. (1999). Artistic labor markets and careers. *Annual Review of Sociology*, *25*(1), 541–574. https://doi.org/10.1146/annurev.soc.25.1.541

Menger, P.-M. (2001). Artists as workers: Theoretical and methodological challenges. *Poetics*, *28*(4), 241–254. https://doi.org/10.1016/S0304-422X(01)80002-4

Morea, V., & Sabatini, F. (2023). The joint contribution of grassroots artistic practices to the alternative and vital city. The case of Bologna and Venice (Italy). *Cities*, *135*, 104234.

Morgan, G., & Nelligan, P. (2018). *The creativity hoax: Precarious work in the Gig economy*. Anthem Press.

Musante, K. (2015). Participant observation. *Handbook of methods in cultural anthropology*, 251–292.

Newman, I. (2000). *A Conceptualization of Mixed Methods: A Need for Inductive/Deductive Approach to Conducting Research.*

Puletti, F., Bertacchini, E. E., Borrione, P., & Arenella, O. (2024). "A place for my art": Independent artist-run spaces as incubators of artistic careers in Italy. *Cultural Trends*, 1–18.

Rota, F. S., & Salone, C. (2014). Place-making processes in unconventional cultural practices. The case of turin's contemporary art festival paratissima. *Cities*, *40*, 90–98. https://doi.org/10.1016/j.cities.2014.03.008

Sacco, P. L. (2004). La giovane arte italiana nel contesto internazionale: opportunità, vincoli e incentivi. *De Luca M. et al.*

Salone, C., Bonini Baraldi, S., & Pazzola, G. (2017). Cultural production in peripheral urban spaces: Lessons from barriera, turin (Italy). *European Planning Studies*, *25*(12), 2117–2137. https://doi.org/10.1080/09654313.2017.1327033

Santagata, W. (1998). *Simbolo e merce: I mercati dei giovani artisti e le istitutzioni dell'arte contemporanea*. Il Mulino.

Sharon, B. (1979). Artist-run galleries—A contemporary institutional change in the visual arts. *Qualitative Sociology*, *2*(1), 3–28.
Simons, H. (2014). Case study research: In-depth understanding in context. *The Oxford handbook of qualitative research*, 455–470.
Thompson, D. (2008). The $12 million staffed shark.
Throsby, D., & Zednik, A. (2011). Multiple job-holding and artistic careers: Some empirical evidence. *Cultural Trends*, *20*(1), 9–24. https://doi.org/10.1080/09548963.2011.540809
Vanolo, A. (2015). The Fordist city and the creative city: Evolution and resilience in Turin, Italy. *City, Culture and Society*, *6*(3), 69–74.
Wright, J. D. (2024, April). The Power of Convening: Towards an Understanding of Artist-Led Collective Practice as a Convener of Place. *Arts*, *13*(2), 67. MDPI.
Zebracki, M., & Smulders, L. (2012). Artists-Accompanied Urban Regeneration: Insights and Lessons from Utrecht and Rotterdam. *Tijdschrift voor Economische En Sociale Geografie*, *103*(5), 615–623.
Zilberstein, S. (2019). Space making as artistic practice: The relationship between grassroots art organizations and the political economy of urban development. *City & Community*, *18*(4), 1142–1161.
Zorloni, A. (2013). *The economics of contemporary art* (Vol. 60). Springer.
Zorloni, A., & Ardizzone, A. (2016). The winner-take-all contemporary art market. *Creative Industries Journal*, *9*(1), 1–14.

PART VII

Unveiling the Heritage Dimension of Low-End Art and Cultural Goods

Guardians of Lesser-Known Artists: The Role of Public and Private Actors in Cultural Preservation

Annick Schramme and Laura D'hoore

1 Introduction

The preservation of cultural heritage is a fundamental component of public museums mission, namely maintaining the cultural identity and history of societies. While high-value "masterpieces" are often prioritized for protection through legal frameworks, such as the Flemish *Topstukken* Decree (Belgium), a gap exists in safeguarding lesser-known local artists. By "lesser-known artists," we refer to a broad category that spans both living and deceased creators, ranging from contemporary artists currently active in local circuits, to recently deceased artists whose legacies are at risk of erasure, to historical artists whose contributions have been marginalized over time. Consider, for instance, the renewed recognition of premodern female painters such as Artemisia Gentileschi (1593–1654) who, despite some acclaim during her lifetime, was long overlooked in canonical narratives. Similar dynamics are evident in the nineteenth and twentieth centuries: artists like Vincent van Gogh or Berthe Morisot only achieved widespread recognition posthumously, while figures such as Hilma af Klint, Claude Cahun, and Alice Neel were integrated into the canon decades after their deaths. Lesser-known artists can thus be understood

A. Schramme (✉) · L. D'hoore
University of Antwerp, Antwerp, Belgium
e-mail: annick.schramme@uantwerpen.be
e-mail: laura.dhoore@uantwerpen.be

A.-S. V. Radermecker (ed.), *Low-End Markets for Art and Cultural Goods*, Cultural Economics & the Creative Economy,
https://doi.org/10.1007/978-3-032-27566-0_22

as those whose work, despite artistic or cultural relevance, has not been canonized, institutionalized, or integrated into the mainstream market or museum circuits. These artists, though not (yet) recognized as top-tier, hold substantial cultural and historical value, contributing to the richness and diversity of a region's artistic heritage. This article takes a public-institutional perspective and focuses specifically on the validation of lesser-known artists through public-private collaboration (PPC). It asks how private and public actors can work together to address the systemic under-recognition of culturally relevant artists who remain outside dominant circuits of value and visibility. Rather than addressing "preservation" in the narrow sense of conservation, this article uses the term to refer to a broader process of recognition, acquisition, and integration into institutional narratives. This shift in focus allows for an exploration of strategic complementarities between public institutions and private actors in enabling long-term cultural inclusion.

A key conceptual departure in this article lies in the focus on lesser-known artists, rather than on lesser-known artworks produced by already recognized names. This distinction is critical: the former involves structural invisibility, the latter situational underexposure. Lesser-known artists often operate outside established market mechanisms, academic narratives, and curatorial frameworks. They may be regionally known, niche, ephemeral, or deliberately resistant to institutional norms. Their relative obscurity is not necessarily a reflection of artistic value or relevance but often a result of systemic omissions in canon formation, collecting practices, and cultural policy. The category of "lesser-known" is thus not objective but socially produced. This observation invites further clarification of what is meant by "preservation" in the context of this article. The term is often used interchangeably with "safeguarding," "conservation," or even "promotion," yet these concepts carry distinct operational meanings.

As Heinich (2009) argues in *La fabrique du patrimoine: De la cathédrale à la petite cuillère*, patrimonialization is not merely about safeguarding objects, but involves a layered and socially mediated process, including recognition, categorization, valorization, and public dissemination. In this article, the term "preservation" is used in an expansive sense that reflects this processual view: not only the physical conservation or archiving of artworks, but also the institutional and discursive mechanisms through which lesser-known artists are studied, promoted, and integrated into broader cultural narratives. Clarifying these dimensions is essential to understand the roles that different actors, public and private, can or should play in ensuring the visibility and continuity of lesser-known artists.

To that end, the article adopts an ecosystemic approach that places emphasis on the public-private interface as a site of cultural negotiation. This approach starts from the premise that the art world consists of a multitude of interconnected public and private actors, including public museums, private collectors, commercial galleries, auction houses, art fairs, artist-run initiatives, philanthropic foundations, cultural policy-makers, academic researchers, and civic organizations. These actors operate with different logics, resources, and timeframes, yet are interdependent in shaping what counts as culturally valuable and institutionally visible. The ecosystem metaphor emphasizes these mutual dependencies, feedback loops, and the importance of building sustainable cultural environments. While recognizing this broader complexity, the article focuses specifically on two key actors within this ecosystem: the private collector and the public museum. By examining their respective roles, constraints, and potential complementarities in the validation of lesser-known artists, the article seeks to identify strategic entry points for more inclusive forms of cultural preservation. In doing so, it also addresses questions of governance, legitimacy, and curatorial authority, namely, who has the power to recognize, acquire, and narrate cultural value within evolving institutional frameworks. The ecosystem lens foregrounds the roles of intermediaries, informal networks, and local knowledge, which are often overlooked in top-down cultural strategies.

Why is this relevant? A prioritization of high-value artworks seems to shape the public art scene in Flanders. The Flemish *Topstukken* Decree (Belgium), for example, is designed to protect works deemed of exceptional importance ("rare and indispensable") to Flemish cultural heritage . However, this approach often overlooks lesser-known art pieces that may not fit the traditional definitions of "masterpieces" but are still nonetheless significant. Besides the Masterpieces approach, there is the more interesting regulation of key pieces or *sleutelwerkenregeling* focused on the protection of key works of art. This more pragmatic and effective approach was introduced in 2004 in Flanders after the near sale of James Ensor's *Christus aan het volk getoond*. It highlights a critical moment in this discourse. The sale's prevention underscored the importance of safeguarding key works that, while perhaps not universally acclaimed, play a vital role in the context of a specific collection or cultural narrative. This regulation allows the Flemish government to acquire works based on their significance to both the overall Collection of the Flemish Government and/or their critical role within recognized institutions such as museums, heritage libraries, and cultural archives (Resonant, s.d.).

Despite these protections, there remains a notable absence of a comprehensive strategy that incorporates the preservation of works of lesser-known artists. This gap necessitates a closer examination of the roles and interactions between private and public actors involved in cultural preservation. This research aims to address this gap by exploring the dynamics between these actors, their motivations, strategies, and the outcomes of their efforts, with a particular focus on how they contribute to preserving artworks that do not receive the same level of attention or resources as recognized masterpieces. The research employs a qualitative approach, including case studies of private foundations, which actively acquire and preserve artworks from artists outside the mainstream museum circuit. Additionally, the study examines the role of public actors such as public museums in facilitating the preservation and accessibility of these works through collaborations with local governments and private collectors.

2 Literature Review

2.1 *The Value of Art and Artists*

Art, as a culture-based asset, is notoriously difficult to value in standardized or objective terms, especially in the case of lesser-known works and artists whose reputational capital has not yet been consolidated within dominant institutional circuits. As stated by Latour (2005), the social is not a stable domain but a network of heterogeneous associations constantly in the process of being assembled. In this view, value emerges not from intrinsic qualities but through the dynamic interplay of actors, both human and non-human, within specific networks. Plante et al. (2021) build further on that by demonstrating how art valuation is a performative and socially constructed practice that relies on modes of categorization and valuation work, including interpreting, credentialing, and projecting. These modes are unevenly distributed across artwork categories, such as decorative, emerging, trending, and blue-chip, with lesser-known works often relegated to the periphery due to their limited cultural recognition. The authors demonstrate that valuation is not only hierarchical but also circular, where recognition enables valuation, and valuation further reinforces recognition, thereby posing a significant barrier to the appreciation and institutional acquisition of obscure or marginalized art forms (Plante et al. 2021). This challenge is compounded by what Cleeremans et al. (2016) demonstrate through experimental methods: simply revealing the name of a well-known artist significantly increases the perceived aesthetic value of a work, even when the artwork itself remains unchanged. Their findings reveal the strength of name recognition in shaping aesthetic judgments, irrespective of intrinsic artistic qualities. Although reputation and name recognition enhance valuation, as Cleeremans et al. (2016) show, Kaube and Rahman (2024) nuance this effect by demonstrating that even highly recognized names can evoke negative aesthetic judgments when biographical information is morally compromising. Their neurocognitive study found that artworks by artists associated with negative biographical traits (e.g. domestic abuse or involvement in financial fraud), regardless of their fame, were rated less favorably and induced stronger emotional arousal. Conversely, positive biographical cues, including charity work or overcoming personal adversity, led to more favorable aesthetic evaluations. The neutral profiles, containing non-emotionally charged information, generally resulted in moderate aesthetic evaluations, which differed significantly from both the positive and negative conditions. This suggests that reputational capital is not a monolithic asset: while name recognition facilitates attention and baseline valuation, the *quality* of that reputation, its ethical framing, modulates the affective and evaluative response. Therefore, the presence of fame does not guarantee positive valuation; it amplifies both the rewards of admiration and the costs of moral disapproval. This insight complements Plante et al. (2021), who describe valuation as a circular process embedded in broader social narratives and power structures. Fame may open the door to recognition, but the framing of that recognition, positive or negative, ultimately conditions the cultural legitimacy and preservation potential of the work. The act of preservation becomes an exercise in narrative construction as much as technical safeguarding. Van Mensch (2019) links these insights to the concept of "musealization," where the transformation of objects into heritage depends on value attribution that is contingent and relational. Institutional missions shape which objects are deemed worthy of preservation, underscoring that lesser-known artworks are often excluded not due to lack of value, but because they do not fit within existing interpretive logics. These studies suggest that extrinsic social context, including name recognition, biographical knowledge and "musealization," plays a crucial role in aesthetic evaluation, making lesser-known artworks particularly vulnerable to reputational narratives, whether absent or misaligned with dominant cultural norms.

2.2 The Expanding Role of Private Actors in the Public Cultural Scene

Over the past two decades, private actors have emerged as powerful players in the preservation and promotion of art, including lesser-known works. The rise of private museums represents a major institutional transformation in this regard. Kolbe (2024) explores how private museums, often founded by elite collectors, serve dual purposes: enhancing public access to their art collection while also operating as instruments of elite self-legitimation. Through discursive strategies that position these museums as flexible, innovative, and socially responsible alternatives to public institutions, founders attempt to distinguish themselves not only from the broader category of wealth elites but also from state actors. Importantly, these private museums sometimes claim to champion neglected artists, incorporating their works into the collection for example as a way to differentiate themselves from more traditional institutions. Yet in Kolbe's study, it is noted that they simultaneously construct intra-group status hierarchies via notions of the autonomous and ethical collector-founder versus other ostentatious private collectors and unethical wealth elites more widely (Kolbe 2024).[1] Quemin (2020) add further weight to this critique by highlighting how the global circulation of works, exhibitions, and artists is increasingly mediated through market mechanisms that favor visibility and financial speculation over curatorial rigor. This tension is echoed by Brown (2019), who warns that the increasing influence of private collectors in public display practices, through board appointments, artwork loans, and even national representation at international exhibitions, threatens to influence the interpretation of the mission of public museums. As a result, lesser-known or locally significant works are frequently bypassed in favor of more marketable options, an outcome that undermines public museums cultural missions.

[1] The study of Kolbe is based on interviews with founders, directors, and curators of Germany-based private museums.

However, these perspectives overlook a parallel circuit of smaller, less mediatic private initiatives, often driven by personal commitment to specific artists working outside academic training, public institutions or market circuits. As David Maclagan (2009) explains in *Outsider Art: From the Margins to the Marketplace*, outsider art often starts completely outside of official institutions but gradually becomes more accepted and visible in the mainstream art world. This process raises important questions: when does something stop being "outside"? And who decides what counts as "real" art? Smaller private initiatives that support "outsider" or "marginal" artists show that not all private actors reinforce existing power structures. On the contrary, some create alternative spaces where lesser-known artists can be collected, exhibited/presented, and valued, often in ways that large public or commercial institutions overlook.

Despite the above critiques, the public-private divide is not inherently antagonistic. Several studies suggest that under the right conditions, public-private partnerships (PPPs) can contribute positively to the preservation of cultural heritage, including lesser-known works. Dubini et al. (2012) examine Italian case studies in which private actors were entrusted with conservation and promotion activities traditionally handled by public authorities. They find that successful outcomes hinge on clearly defined roles, shared commitments, and the effective integration of competencies. Their research points to the potential of hybrid models in addressing resource constraints and institutional inertia that often plague public museums, particularly with regard to maintaining and exhibiting non-mainstream art. Reynaers (2013) extends this analysis by evaluating PPPs through the lens of public values. Her findings challenge the binary view that privatization necessarily undermines public interest. Instead, the impact of PPPs on public values is context-dependent, shaped by governance structures, transparency, and accountability mechanisms. In the field of cultural heritage, this means that private involvement can either dilute or amplify public commitments to diversity, inclusivity, and long-term stewardship, depending on how these collaborations are designed and managed.

As a consequence, the label "lesser-known" should not be treated as an absolute condition but as a relative, context-dependent position within layered cultural ecosystems. As Velthuis (2005) and Zorloni (2013) illustrate in their analyses of the contemporary art market, recognition and value are constructed through actor-driven processes, where galleries, collectors, and institutions play pivotal roles in legitimizing artists and their work. This also holds in smaller, local contexts: while often overlooked, these micro-ecosystems replicate similar mechanisms of inclusion and exclusion. Spiridon and Sandu (2015) build on this broader perspective, advocating for participatory conservation models that actively engage local communities in the preservation process. By mobilizing cultural volunteers and fostering interdisciplinary collaboration, they argue that conservation can become more democratic and inclusive. This model is especially relevant for preserving lesser-known artists, which often hold localized or subcultural significance that may not be immediately apparent or appreciated by traditional institutional gatekeepers.

Borin (2017) advances this argument by analyzing PPPs in four European countries. Her empirical findings show that PPPs that evolve into multi-stakeholder partnerships (MSPs) tend to foster more inclusive and adaptive governance. By integrating public institutions, private entities, and community actors, MSPs create "territorial cultural ecosystems" that embed lesser-known heritage within local identity and development strategies. The evolving definition of museums themselves reflects the broader shifts in cultural policy and institutional ethos. In 2022, the International Council of Museums (ICOM) adopted a new definition emphasizing inclusivity, accessibility, community participation, and ethical operation (ICOM 2022). This definition aligns with the principles advanced in the literature on participatory and integrated conservation and provides an institutional framework for evaluating the legitimacy and effectiveness of both public and private actors in heritage management.

In sum, existing literature has shed light on how value is constructed within the art ecosystem and how public and private actors co-produce legitimacy. However, there remains a research gap concerning the preservation of lesser-known artists, particularly in relation to coordination between public and private actors across institutional levels. This study seeks to extend these debates by exploring how coordination unfolds within art ecosystems, particularly in the preservation of artists operating outside canonical circuits. Specifically, we ask: *How do public and private actors currently coordinate in preserving lesser-known artists? What mechanisms enable or hinder the long-term safeguarding of such practices in institutional settings?*

3 Methodology

This study adopts a qualitative research design, appropriate for exploring complex, context-dependent phenomena such as the roles of public and private actors in the preservation of lesser-known artists. Qualitative methods are particularly suited for capturing stakeholder perceptions, institutional dynamics, and the socio-political nuances of cultural governance. Mitchell et al. (1997) proposed a classification of stakeholders based on their power, the legitimacy of each stakeholder's relationship with the organization, and the urgency of each stakeholder's claim on the organization. This study adopts an ecosystemic approach (Holden, 2015), not only conceptually but also methodologically. The ecosystem metaphor, as introduced earlier, provides a lens through which to understand the interdependence of public and private actors, intermediary institutions, and regulatory frameworks. It also legitimates the use of a multi-method research design that draws from diverse sources, interviews, case studies, policy analysis, across multiple national contexts. Rather than seeking linear causality, this approach embraces complexity, heterogeneity, and relationality as defining features of the art preservation landscape. In terms of analysis, the empirical material was examined through thematic coding, guided by key ecosystemic dimensions such as actor interdependence, governance structures, resource distribution, and modes of valuation. By identifying recurring patterns and relational dynamics across interviews and case studies, the research reconstructs how preservation efforts emerge, succeed, or break down within particular institutional constellations. Comparative insights from different countries further help to situate these dynamics within distinct policy environments.

The core empirical basis for this article stems from two consecutive studies commissioned by the Flemish government. In the first study (D'hoore & Schramme, 2022), conducted between 2021 and 2022, we interviewed 45 stakeholders involved in collaborations between private collectors and public museums across Flanders, France, and the Netherlands. Participants included museum directors, cultural policymakers, private collectors, foundation representatives, and intermediary organizations. These interviews explored perceived benefits, risks, and practical challenges in hybrid cultural partnerships. The study included in-depth explorations of notable cases, such as the integration of the Matthys-Colle Collection into the public domain through a long-term loan and partial acquisition by the S.M.A.K. and the Flemish Government

(Belgium), Museum Voorlinden (The Netherlands), Musée Groesbeeck de Croix (Belgium). These cases highlighted both the mutual value of public-private exchange and the fragility of such arrangements, underscoring the need for sustained dialogue between collaboration partners and policymakers, as well as long-term trust frameworks.

In 2025, we conducted a follow-up study on the feasibility of establishing a private foundation for acquiring masterpieces in Flanders, which entailed an additional 25 expert interviews with stakeholders in legal, financial, ethical, and cultural heritage domains (D'hoore and Schramme, 2025). This study deepened the exploration of governance tensions by combining interview data with case study analyses of international models, including the Vereniging Rembrandt (Netherlands) and the Art Fund (UK). The findings highlighted both the potential and limits of private foundations in strengthening public collections. To deepen our understanding in light of ongoing debates around lesser-known artists, we conducted additional expert interviews with different profiles: cultural heritage professionals, curators, and policy advisors. These interviews provided insights into current institutional strategies, valuation practices, and the shifting roles of private actors in cultural ecosystems.

In parallel, we conducted a documentary review of key policy texts, legal frameworks, and institutional strategies at regional, national, and international levels (including documents from UNESCO, ICOM, and national cultural heritage bodies). This allowed us to situate empirical findings within broader cultural policy developments and to identify common trends and divergences in heritage governance.

This ecosystemic and comparative approach enables a more systematic interpretation of the findings, highlighting both structural patterns and context-specific divergences in how lesser-known artists are recognized and preserved.

4 Empirical Analysis and Findings

4.1 *The Fragility of Visibility for Lesser-Known Artists: A Multi-Stakeholders Perspective*

From our literature review, we can conclude that the visibility and recognition of an artist is contingent on a complex interplay of factors, networks, institutional recognition, media circulation, gallery representation, and historical timing. Some artists remain outside the canon due to lack of access to institutional support, marginalization based on gender, ethnicity or geography, or simply because their work does not align with prevailing aesthetic or political narratives. This understanding challenges romantic notions of the *undiscovered genius* and instead foregrounds the relational and systemic conditions under which recognition occurs. So, Canon formation is not an organic outcome, but a cumulative process of selection, repetition, and legitimation involving academia, media, market actors, and public institutions.

Our interviewees reaffirmed that recognition is a layered process, often based on *a public private interaction* one could say. Museums function as validators, once an artist enters a museum collection, their symbolic value increases. But prior to that point, selection often relies on the art critics, the gallery system, auction houses and private collectors. This reveals the limitations of the notion of "neutral" curatorship and highlights the influence of market logic and existing social capital.

Drawing from our empirical data, "lesser-known" artists emerge as a diverse and unstable category. They include living artists who never entered formal market circuits, recently deceased artists whose estate is at risk, and historically marginalized artists whose practices were sidelined due to factors such as gender, medium, or geography. In other cases, families of deceased artists struggle to preserve or valorize an oeuvre due to the lack of interest or institutional outreach. What is at stake, then, is not only the material preservation of artworks, but the safeguarding of cultural memory, alternative narratives, and the possibility of later re-interpretation.

It also challenges cultural policy to rethink its assumptions: should value be confirmed by existing hierarchies, or cultivated through proactive and reparative strategies? The question of recognition is further complicated by scale. An artist may be considered "lesser known" from an international perspective, while enjoying substantial local resonance. Conversely, globally circulating artists may have limited local relevance. This duality invites a rethinking of what constitutes "success" in cultural, institutional and market terms. It also prompts critical reflection on how institutional frameworks (e.g., museums, funding bodies) and gatekeepers (e.g., curators, critics, collectors) navigate these layered geographies of recognition.

"Lesser-known" artists thus do not constitute an objectively stable category but rather reflect structural imbalances in processes of cultural recognition. Visibility and recognition are not simply a product of artistic merit, but the result of strategic positioning within institutional and market-driven logics. Public museums act as custodians of collective memory, whereas galleries, auction houses and dealers selectively valorize a narrow spectrum of works based on their market potential. This asymmetry creates a system in which countless valuable oeuvres fall outside dominant acquisition and exhibition circuits. Moreover, certain artists consciously resist commodification, either by working outside of market-compatible formats (e.g. performance, installation, visual poetry) or by intentionally avoiding commercial representation. In these cases, public institutions have a strategic responsibility to identify, research, and preserve such practices, precisely because the private market cannot or will not sustain/acquire them. Failing to do so risks the silent disappearance of entire cultural trajectories.

4.2 *Evaluating the Key Works Regulation in Flemish Cultural Policy*

In the Flemish context , cultural policy has historically placed a strong emphasis on safeguarding artistic heritage through legal frameworks and institutional support. However, despite growing discursive attention to diversity, inclusion, and participation, the infrastructures for recognizing and supporting lesser-known regional artists remain limited and fragmented. Cultural policy in Flanders tends to prioritize established criteria of quality, often based on artistic excellence, international recognition, and institutional prestige.

The *Topstukkenfonds*, developed under the 2003 *Topstukken Decree*, is geared primarily toward the acquisition and protection of exceptional works of national or international significance, often tied to established canons of art history (and the criteria "rare and indispensable"). By contrast, the Key Works Regulation (*sleutelwerkenregeling*) was introduced in 2004 to create space for the recognition and safeguarding of contextually important works that may not meet the "masterpiece" threshold but hold cultural, social, or historical relevance within specific communities or disciplines or can be interesting from a museum's collection management perspective. In theory, this dual structure acknowledges the need for a more inclusive and layered approach to heritage preservation. In practice, however, significant limitations persist. As previously noted by Schramme and D'hoore (2022), the Key Works Regulation suffers from low visibility, ambiguous scope, and a lack of dedicated funding or legal status. Its relationship to the broader acquisition framework of the

Topstukkenfonds remains unclear. According to expert interviews, the criteria for designating "key works" are insufficiently defined, and no standard exists to assess cultural relevance outside dominant valuation paradigms. As one respondent noted, "while the Key Works Regulation theoretically creates space for recognizing non-canonical value, the lack of clear procedures and criteria means that the regulation opens a door, but no one knows what's behind it." This conceptual vagueness hampers implementation. Moreover, the mechanisms used to define or justify the value of "key works" often revert to existing standards, academic legitimacy, formal aesthetics, or indirect market value, thus risking a reproduction of the exclusions the regulation was intended to counteract. The framework continues to privilege practices already recognized by dominant cultural systems, while lesser-known, marginal, or interdisciplinary practices remain invisible.

4.3 *Brief Comparison of Policy Models in France, the Netherlands and the UK*

France's cultural policy operates under a strongly centralized framework, in which the Ministère de la Culture plays a direct and directive role in both acquisition policy and heritage protection. Legal instruments such as the *Code du Patrimoine*, the *Trésor National* classification, and the *Loi LCAP* (2016) formalize the state's responsibility to safeguard nationally significant cultural goods (French Ministry of Culture, 2021). Tax incentives like the *loi Aillagon* (2003) have enhanced private philanthropic engagement, yet always under tight state oversight (Compendium of Cultural Policy and Trends, 2023b). The rigidity of the French system was long illustrated by the role of the *Commission Scientifique Nationale des Collections* (CSNC), which exercised strict control over deaccessioning from public collections. However, in 2020, the CSNC was dissolved because of its complexity and low throughput and was replaced by a streamlined administrative procedure that maintains scientific oversight while aiming to simplify the process (Droit, patrimoine & culture, 2022). While the French model ensures long-term security and institutional legitimacy for works that have been canonized, it is less accommodating to lesser-known or emerging artists. The criteria for recognition are often steeped in national symbolic value, and the administrative weight of state mediation can slow down the acquisition or exposure of non-canonical works. In contrast to this centralized model, France also maintains a decentralized support mechanism through the FRACs (*Fonds Régionaux d'Art Contemporain*). Established in the early 1980s, the FRACs play a pivotal role in collecting, exhibiting, and promoting contemporary art at the regional level. They actively support emerging and lesser-known artists by acquiring their works and organizing public exhibitions across non-metropolitan territories. The FRACs operate semi-independently but receive structural funding from both regional authorities and the state, making them a hybrid model within the French cultural system. Their activities often fill the gap left by national institutions, offering visibility and preservation for practices that may not meet the symbolic thresholds of central collections. As such, the FRACs contribute significantly to a more pluralistic and territorially grounded cultural ecosystem (Compendium of Cultural Policy and Trends, 2023b; French Ministry of Culture, 2021, (s.d.). Furthermore, the near-impossibility of deaccessioning and the emphasis on patrimonial permanence create little flexibility for experimenting with newer or underrepresented voices. As a result, lesser-known artists risk being excluded from visibility due to the high thresholds of recognition and the formalized, top-down nature of state validation.

The Dutch cultural policy model delegates acquisition decisions and heritage support to autonomous institutions, for example through the *Mondriaan Fonds* (Fonds, n.d.) and philanthropic organizations like the *Vereniging Rembrandt* (Vereniging Rembrandt, n.d.). In addition, the Dutch preservation landscape is shaped by the *Rijksdienst voor het Cultureel Erfgoed* (RCE), which operates under the Ministry of Education, Culture and Science. The RCE plays a crucial coordinating and advisory role in implementing the *Erfgoedwet* (2016, Rijksoverheid, 2016a) which supports broad definitions of heritage value, including historical, artistic, and social significance, and supports museums, municipalities, and private owners in matters related to cultural heritage management, including conservation standards, registration of protected cultural property, and long-term care. While the RCE does not directly fund acquisitions, it provides the legal and technical backbone for cultural property governance in the Netherlands and facilitates alignment between national heritage priorities and decentralized institutional practices (Rijksoverheid, 2016b). Policy continues to be shaped by the previously discussed *Erfgoedwet*. Furthermore, the *Geefwet* offers tax benefits to donors, and the cultural sector is encouraged to seek co-financing and partnership models (Commissie Collectie Nederland, 2022; Compendium of Cultural Policy and Trends, 2023a). The Dutch system is relatively open to the inclusion of lesser-known artists, as the grant-based model allows for more nuanced justifications rooted in context, innovation, or historical relevance. Institutions can apply for funding for acquisitions of works by emerging or regionally significant artists, and private co-financing (e.g. via *Vereniging Rembrandt*) can help bridge the funding gap. However, access to funding depends on curatorial initiative and the ability to articulate cultural value within the frameworks required by the fonds. This can disadvantage practices that lack immediate institutional advocates or research infrastructures. Still, compared to France, the Netherlands offers more flexibility and access points for lesser-known artists to enter public collections, provided institutions are proactive and strategically supported.

The UK's model focuses less on direct state control and more on incentivizing private giving through tax schemes. Instruments such as the Acceptance in Lieu Scheme and Cultural Gifts Scheme allow art to enter public collections through in-kind tax arrangements (Arts Council England, 2025a, 2025b). The Arts Council England and the National Lottery Heritage Fund offer grants, but much of the momentum for acquisitions comes from private initiative and negotiation (Compendium of Cultural Policy and Trends, 2023c). Donors often retain influence over where works are placed or how they are interpreted. The British system supports a broad range of acquisitions but relies heavily on donor interest and the perceived symbolic or financial value of the artwork. Works by lesser-known artists are less likely to be part of estates with sufficient value for tax negotiation, and donors often prefer gifting already-validated works to maximize recognition and legacy. Additionally, expert panels and institutional gatekeepers may default to traditional hierarchies in deciding which donations are accepted. Thus, while the system allows for flexibility, it tends to reward prestige and visibility, making it less structurally supportive of underrecognized artists unless there is a strong curatorial or donor advocate. The lack of centralized acquisition strategy may also lead to uneven collection development, with lesser-known practices falling between the cracks.

4.4 Roles and Dynamics of Public and Private Actors

The preservation efforts of both private and public actors are crucial in maintaining a diverse cultural heritage /collection. Public museums are essential in this regard, as they serve not only as repositories for well-known masterpieces but also as guardians of lesser-known works of local/regional artists and cultural artifacts that might otherwise fade into obscurity. The focus on preserving a wide range of cultural expressions has gained more attention in recent years. This approach aligns with recent international guidelines, such as the 2015 UNESCO Recommendation and the updated ICOM definition of a museum from 2022, both of which highlight the importance of museums and collections in promoting cultural diversity and emphasize their social role in fostering a more inclusive and participatory approach to museology (ICOM 2022; UNESCO, 2024). Public museums continue to wield significant symbolic power in canon formation. During our interviews it was pointed out that inclusion in a museum collection still functions as a major validation mechanism—affecting both symbolic and financial value. However, institutional practices remain uneven. Some museums, like the Stedelijk Museum Amsterdam or Van Abbemuseum Eindhoven, have begun proactively addressing historical exclusions, through targeted acquisition policies or reinterpretation of existing collections.

However, a distinction must be made between national and local museums in terms of scope, resources, and curatorial focus. While national institutions often prioritize artists with international or canonical significance, local organizations tend to concentrate on regionally rooted practices and emerging or underrepresented voices. This includes, but is not limited to, local artists. It is important to note, however, that "lesser-known artists" and "local artists" do not always overlap: while some local artists may be well recognized within specific circuits, others may be regionally unknown yet internationally relevant, or historically significant yet institutionally overlooked. From a macro-level (national) perspective, this distribution of roles may allow for a more complete representation of cultural diversity across the institutional spectrum. Yet from a micro-level view, the segmentation may also result in fragmented visibility, where some local practices remain marginalized due to limited institutional outreach or capacity. Fostering strong coordination and knowledge-sharing between local and national institutions is of major importance in sustaining cultural diversity. Furthermore, in evaluating the recognition and canonization of lesser-known artists, it is crucial to distinguish between artists who are well-known within a national context and those who have gained international acclaim. Visibility on a local or national scale does not automatically translate into international recognition, and vice versa.

In the ecosystem, public museums and regional heritage institutions are often caught in a bind: they are expected to be inclusive and innovative but operate within policy frameworks that offer little flexibility or funding for exploratory acquisitions or experimental partnerships. This institutional misalignment poses a major obstacle for the long-term preservation of cultural diversity, especially when it comes to supporting regional artists who remain structurally under-recognized. This situation is compounded by the fact that validation tends to happen post-factum: once a work is purchased, exhibited, or canonized, its cultural value is reinforced. But the processes that lead up to that recognition, the research, interpretation, and justification, are often under-resourced. As a result, policy continues to reward outcomes rather than enable discovery, reinforcing a circular logic where only already-visible practices gain institutional support. While budgetary constraints are frequently cited as a barrier to expanding museum collections, this argument is less compelling when it comes to acquiring works by lesser-known artists. These works are often more affordable than high-end art, offering institutions an opportunity to diversify their holdings without incurring substantial financial risk. Rather than being a limitation, the lower market value of these works could be seen as an advantage, especially for institutions committed to cultural inclusion. Importantly, acquisition policy encompasses more than the initial purchase cost; it also entails long-term financial planning for the preservation, conservation, and sustainable care of the acquired works. Another challenge, however, lies in audience engagement. Exhibiting lesser-known artists may not immediately resonate with mainstream audiences, particularly if the work lacks name recognition or familiar aesthetic cues. Yet this gap in appeal is not insurmountable; it is often shaped by curatorial framing, institutional branding, and the quality of public engagement strategies. When contextualized through compelling narratives, thematic relevance, or community linkages, lesser-known art can attract meaningful interest and broaden institutional relevance. A telling example occurred during the COVID-19 pandemic, when the Flemish Government implemented an acquisition program aimed explicitly at supporting local and under-recognized artists. With a budget of nearly €4 million, the initiative led to the purchase of 281 artworks by 180 artists, many of whom were emerging or had limited institutional exposure. These works were added to the Collection of the Flemish Community and distributed across six public museums of contemporary art, including S.M.A.K., M Leuven, and the FOMU in Antwerp. A committee composed of both independent curators and experts from these six museums ensured a high-quality selection (Departement Cultuur, Jeugd en Media 2021; S.M.A.K, 2021, 2022). Some of these acquisitions have since resulted in solo exhibitions and increased visibility, illustrating how strategic, publicly funded acquisitions can act as a catalyst for long-term recognition. This model demonstrates that inclusion is not only possible within constrained budgets, but also potentially transformative, provided that acquisition policy is coupled with curatorial commitment and sustainable care. However, as public institutions increasingly embrace the role of tastemakers and talent incubators, the line between public museums and other actors in the ecosystem such as galleries begins to blur, raising new questions about institutional identity and responsibility.

A key insight from our research is that the critical phase prior to formal recognition, including research, contextual valuation, and engagement with communities of relevance, is often structurally unsupported. Without proactive investment in curatorial and academic inquiry, many works of potential significance remain unrecognized and unpreserved. A relevant Flemish case is that of M HKA, which recently acquired works by Hugo Roeland, a lesser-known Belgian artist active in the 1960s-90s. His practice, marked by experimental uses of ephemeral materials and an anti-institutional stance, had long remained outside mainstream museum circuits. He was someone who quite deliberately chose to operate outside the market. The acquisition resulted from a targeted trajectory by the museum's collection team, who recognized the work's historical significance within both Belgian conceptualism and countercultural movements. Roeland's inclusion in the permanent collection was not a response to market or public demand, but the outcome of curatorially driven discovery supported by internal institutional reflection and external close relationships to relevant private actors in the ecosystem. This example demonstrates how investment in research and curatorial initiative can bring overlooked *œuvres* of regional artists into public visibility. Furthermore, institutions such as the Van Abbemuseum in Eindhoven also offer a notable example. Through participatory collection reviews and collaborations with local communities, the museum re-evaluates its holdings not just in terms of artistic significance, but in relation to contemporary social debates such as decoloniality, accessibility, and local relevance. Another important factor is the vulnerability of an artist's legacy after their death, especially when no clear preservation plan exists. In such cases, families may feel compelled to sell the work on the market for financial reasons, which risks dispersing or even losing cohesive bodies of work. Investing in relationships with artists and their families during their lifetime is therefore not only a curatorial concern, but also a preventative strategy that can secure long-term preservation.

Private actors, on the other hand, including foundations, collectors and philanthropists, often step in to preserve artworks, for other reasons such as familial legacy, regional identity, or the desire to support new upcoming and often yet underappreciated artists—that may otherwise be neglected by public institutions. Their activities extend beyond mere acquisition. Private foundations are often involved in restoration and conservation, ensuring that artworks remain in good condition for future generations (Dubini et al., 2012). Foundations like the *PASfoundation* in Flanders for example play a significant role in acquiring and preserving artworks outside the mainstream museum circuit. This foundation in particular focuses on oeuvre collections from living Belgian artists (Schramme and D'hoore 2022). By preserving and making artworks available outside the commercial circuit, the *PASfoundation* aims to build bridges between people, companies, communities, and generations. The foundation focuses on collecting works that offer a representative cross-section of the oeuvre of living Belgian modern and contemporary artists. These works are acquired by the *PASfoundation* and subsequently donated to the King Baudouin Foundation. In doing so, the collection is not only safeguarded for future generations, but also actively used to make art visible and accessible in unique and unexpected locations (PASfoundation, 2025). However, their long-term structural integration into the broader museum ecosystem remains underexplored. Increasingly, these private entities are also opening their own private museums, creating new platforms for the display and appreciation of art that might not fit into the traditional scope of public collections. Their flexible acquisition policies, swift decision-making capabilities, and commitment to cultural stewardship position them uniquely to fill gaps left by public entities. As highlighted in interviews, such private actors are not always driven by financial or symbolic return, but often by a strong personal or local commitment to specific artists or cultural narratives. Private collectors or foundations can, and sometimes do, act with a public mission. The challenge lies in aligning intentions, ensuring legal clarity, and fostering shared frameworks of value. However, our study also reveals that this agility can come with challenges. Some museum professionals expressed concerns about the asymmetry of influence when private actors enter into partnerships with public institutions. The risk lies in blurred boundaries between public interest and private agenda, especially when collections are shared, co-managed, or exhibited together. While this can lead to innovative and generous cultural contributions, it also introduces symbolic competition between forms of legitimacy, curatorial versus philanthropic, institutional versus entrepreneurial. A more sustainable public-private model would require clear governance agreements, mutual respect for institutional roles, and shared commitment to the visibility and consequently recognition of underrepresented artistic practices.

5 Discussion in Relation to the Triadic Model

The triadic model proposed in this volume offers an analytical framework for situating different types of cultural goods within the low-end art market, based on the interaction between functionality, scarcity, and brand strength. From this perspective, much of the empirical material discussed in this chapter corresponds to artworks characterized by moderate to high symbolic functionality, weak or emerging brand strength, and low to moderate scarcity, which aligns with the fourth sub-segment of the model. This includes regionally recognized or historically marginalized artists whose works circulate in limited institutional and market circuits and whose symbolic value is primarily stabilized through local museums, collectors, and intermediaries rather than through international reputational hierarchies. In this configuration, market prices remain relatively accessible not because of a lack of cultural value, but because brand legitimacy has not yet been consolidated within dominant systems of recognition.

However, our findings also reveal cases where artworks display high levels of rarity but remain associated with weak or absent brand strength. This applies, for instance, to unique artistic estates, archival collections, or singular practices by artists who operated outside established market and institutional frameworks. In such cases, rarity does not translate into higher market valuation or symbolic legitimacy, precisely because the reputational and institutional mechanisms that transform rarity into value are lacking. This suggests that rarity alone is insufficient as an economic driver in the low-end segment and that its effect is strongly mediated by institutional recognition and processes of musealization.

Finally, our empirical findings underline that the interaction between functionality, scarcity, and brand strength should not be understood as an abstract structural relation between object attributes, but as a relational process actively produced by a constellation of actors within the art ecosystem. Museums, curators, collectors, foundations, policymakers, and intermediaries do not merely respond to pre-existing levels of scarcity or brand legitimacy; they actively construct, interpret, and negotiate these dimensions through practices of selection, research, acquisition, exhibition, and narrative framing. In this sense, the triadic model seems within our article best interpreted as an actor-mediated framework, in which the three dimensions acquire empirical relevance through institutional work and social interaction. Our study thus confirms the explanatory power of the model while extending it by showing that the relative positioning of artworks within the triadic space is not a purely market-driven outcome, but the result of strategic and relational processes of valuation , in which public and private actors function as key mediators between latent cultural value and realized symbolic and economic recognition.

6 Conclusions

The findings of this research suggest that there is a need for a more nuanced approach to cultural preservation—one that recognizes the value of lesser-known artists and actively integrates them into broader heritage/museum strategies (Heinich, 2009; Van Mensch, 2019). This includes developing frameworks for collaboration that optimize resources and expertise, while balancing the interests, capacities, and motivations of both private and public sectors. Such frameworks could help address the challenges associated with preserving art at the "lower ends" of the market and ensure a more inclusive and representative approach to cultural heritage preservation (Dubini et al., 2012; Reynaers, 2013).

Moreover, this article argues that recognition is not binary (known/unknown), but multiscalar, context- and actor-dependent, building further on the perspectives of Velthuis (2005), Zorloni (2013), Spiridon and Sandu (2015), and Borin (2017). One of the key insights emerging from this research is the inherently relative nature of the term "lesser-known." An artist might be unknown to national museums or international audiences, yet enjoy substantial recognition in a local context (Plante et al. 2021). In such cases, smaller-scale institutions, including regional museums, local galleries, and cultural centers—often enact the same public mission as larger museums, albeit at a different scale. Through collaborations with collectors, critics, or community actors, these institutions contribute to mechanisms of local value co-creation (Spiridon & Sandu, 2015). As a result, some artists gain a place within local art histories, even while remaining absent from the dominant narratives of canonical Art History. However, local ecosystems are not immune to hierarchy. In some cases, a handful of actors can dominate the recognition process, forming what could be called a "local monopoly" on legitimacy. At the same time, other artists may fall outside both circuits, national and local, and remain effectively invisible. Recognizing these layered dynamics of recognition allows for a more situated and plural understanding of what it means to be "lesser-known."

Several structural and practical challenges persist in preserving artworks that lack mainstream market or institutional validation. One of the most pressing among these is the lack of coordination, both within the public sector and between public and private actors. Focusing first on public institutions: from a macro-level perspective, cultural diversity may appear to be reasonably distributed across the institutional landscape. However, at the micro level, a distinct segmentation emerges: national museums tend to prioritize artists with broader (inter)national visibility, while local museums are more attuned to regional or emerging figures. This division of labor largely reflects structural differences in governance and funding, but it also risks reinforcing institutional silos, where visibility, legitimacy, and recognition remain unevenly allocated. To address this fragmentation, it is essential to foster active dialogue and collaboration between institutions operating at different scales. Such collaboration could include joint curatorial platforms, shared acquisition strategies, co-organized exhibitions, or long-term knowledge exchange initiatives. In this regard, expanding existing mechanisms, such as the *sleutelwerkenregeling*, could also prove beneficial, offering additional support for the preservation of culturally significant yet often overlooked works. These mechanisms not only enhance mutual visibility but also enable a more integrated and inclusive preservation infrastructure, one that values both local specificity and broader cultural narratives.

Beyond the public sector, the absence of coordination mechanisms between private and public actors further complicates preservation efforts. Without structured collaboration, initiatives risk becoming fragmented, culturally significant works may go underrecognized, and efforts may be duplicated rather than complementary. Moreover, the complexity of balancing public and private interests becomes particularly evident in acquisition policy and long-term stewardship. Public institutions, as museums, frequently face budgetary constraints and fixed procedures that limit their capacity to act swiftly or expansively. Private actors, by contrast, tend to operate with greater agility and autonomy. Their involvement is often driven by a combination of personal interest, emotional attachment, financial gain and occasionally philanthropic motives. Private collectors, galleries and foundations play a growing role in maintaining, exhibiting, and sometimes revalorizing overlooked works. Their preservation efforts may stem from emotional/personal motivations, such as familial legacy, regional identity, or the desire to support new upcoming and often yet underappreciated artists, yet such efforts are not immune to issues of self-legitimation and conflicting values.

The motivations behind preservation efforts on both sides are therefore diverse and multifaceted, reflecting different time horizons, operational logics, and notions of public value. The success of hybrid heritage/museum strategies depends not only on legal or financial instruments, but also on the ability to negotiate and identify shared values. Finding this common ground, between curatorial independence and patron involvement, between historical responsibility and contemporary relevance, is essential for building sustainable and trust-based collaborations. Equally vital, yet persistently overlooked in current frameworks, is the pre-acquisition phase, the main focus of this article. This early stage, comprising research, contextual valuation, artist and community engagement, collection management and institutional reflection, is where the visibility and legitimacy of lesser-known works often begins. Yet it remains structurally under-resourced and undervalued. Without dedicated funding and time for exploratory curatorial work, many culturally significant artists may never be identified, let alone preserved. Public acquisition tools tend to reward finalized transactions, purchases, donations, catalogued objects, while overlooking the invisible labor that precedes them. In practice, this early-phase work often depends on proactive museum directors who have developed personal networks over time. However, such initiatives are grounded in personal trust rather than institutional trust. While the former can be effective in the short term, it is the latter that is crucial for continuity and long-term impact (King & Schramme, 2023). When a director leaves, their network and momentum often leave with them, underscoring the need to embed trust structurally within institutions. Strengthening this phase means recognizing discovery itself as a critical act of preservation, one that requires time, trust, and shared values between the public institutions and private stakeholders involved. In doing so, policy can move beyond reactive validation and begin actively shaping a more inclusive, reflexive, and future-oriented cultural memory.

References

Arts Council England. (2025a). *Cultural Gifts Scheme.* Retrieved from https://www.artscouncil.org.uk/supporting-arts-museums-and-libraries/supporting-collections-and-cultural-property/cultural-gifts-scheme

Arts Council England. (2025b). *Acceptance in Lieu Scheme.* Retrieved from https://www.artscouncil.org.uk/supporting-arts-museums-and-libraries/supporting-collections-and-cultural-property/acceptance-lieu

Borin, E. (2017). *Public-private partnership in the cultural sector. A comparative analysis of European models.* Peter Lang Verlag.

Brown, K. (2019). Private Influence, Public Goods and the Future of Art History. *Journal of Art Market Studies, 3*(1), 1–17. https://doi.org/10.23690/jams.v3i1.86

Cleeremans, Axel et al. (2016). What's in a name? The effect of an artist's name on aesthetic judgments. *Empirical Studies of the Arts, 34*(1), 126–139.

Commissie Collectie Nederland. (2022). *Brochure cultuurgoederen.* Retrieved from: https://www.inspectie-oe.nl/publicaties/brochure/2016/11/16/brochure-invoer-en-uitvoer-van-cultuurgoederen

Compendium of Cultural Policy and Trends. (2023a). *Cultural policy in the Netherlands.* Retrieved from https://www.culturalpolicies.net/database/search-by-country/country-profile/category/?id=28&g1=1

Compendium of Cultural Policy and Trends. (2023b). *Cultural policy in France.* Retrieved from: https://www.culturalpolicies.net/database/search-by-country/country-profile/category/?id=13&g1=3

Compendium of Cultural Policy and Trends. (2023c). *Cultural policy in the UK.* Retrieved from https://www.culturalpolicies.net/database/search-by-country/country-profile/category/?id=42&g1=3

Cultuur, D., & En Media, J. (2021). *Aankoop hedendaagse kunst.* Vlaamse overheid. Retrieved from https://www.vlaanderen.be/cjm/nl/cultuur/kunsten/andere-diensten-kunsten/aankoop-hedendaagse-kunst

D'hoore, L., & Schramme, A. (2022). *Samenwerking tussen privé verzamelaars en (semi)publieke cultureel-erfgoedinstellingen in Vlaanderen.* Departement Cultuur, Jeugd en Media, Vlaamse Overheid.

D'hoore, L & Schramme, S. (2025). *Haalbaarheidsstudie van een stichting met als doel het verwerven van Topstukken ter ondersteuning van de collectie van Vlaamse Erfgoedinstellingen.* Departement Cultuur, Jeugd en Media.

Droit, Patrimoine & Culture (1 février 2022). Suppression de la Commission scientifique nationale des collections: un aperçu de la nouvelle procédure administrative de déclassement. *Droit, patrimoine et culture*. Consulté le 28 mars 2025 à l'adresse. https://doi.org/10.58079/nwaz

Dubini, P., Leone, L., & Forti, L. (2012). Role Distribution in Public-Private Partnerships: The Case of Heritage Management in Italy. *International Studies of Management and Organization*, *42*(2), 57–75. https://doi.org/10.2753/IMO0020-8825420204

Fonds, M. (n.d.). *Subsidies voor aankopen*. Retrieved from https://www.mondriaanfonds.nl

French Ministry of Culture. (2021). *Code du patrimoine*. Retrieved from https://www.legifrance.gouv.fr/loda/id/LEGITEXT000006074236/2021-08-26

French Ministry of Culture. (s.d.). *Les Fonds régionaux d'art contemporain*. Retrieved from https://www.culture.gouv.fr/thematiques/arts-plastiques/les-arts-plastiques-en-france/les-fonds-regionaux-d-art-contemporain

Heinich, N. (2009). *La fabrique du patrimoine* (1-). Éditions de la Maison des sciences de l'homme, Ministère de la culture. https://doi.org/10.4000/books.editionsmsh.2642

Holden, J. (2015). *The ecology of culture*. Arts and Humanities Research Council.

International Council of Museums (ICOM). (2022). *Extraordinary General Assembly: Final report and new museum definition proposal*.

Kaube, H., & Abdel Rahman, R. (2024). Art perception is affected by negative knowledge about famous and unknown artists. *Scientific Reports*, *14*, 8143. https://doi.org/10.1038/s41598-024-58697-1

King, I. W., & Schramme, A. (2023). Institutional trust and cultural governance. In: *Cultural Governance. Current and Future European Perspectives*. Edited By Bailey, C., Theodoulou Charalambous, E., Drien, G. Cultural Governance: Current and Future European Perspectives (1st ed.), 17p. Routledge. https://doi.org/10.4324/9781003380535-6

Kristina Kolbe. (2024, July). The art of (self)legitimization: How private museums help their founders claim legitimacy as elite actors, *Socio-Economic Review*, *22* (3), 1119–1140, https://doi.org/10.1093/ser/mwad051

Latour, B. (2005). *Reassembling the Social: An Introduction to Actor-Network-Theory*. Oxford University Press.

Maclagan, D. (2009). *Outsider art: From the margins to the marketplace*. Reaktion Books.

Mitchell, R. K., Agle, B. R., & Wood, D. J. (1997). Toward a Theory of Stakeholder Identification and Salience: Defining the Principle of Who and What Really Counts. *The Academy of Management Review*, *22*(4), 853–886. https://doi.org/10.2307/259247

PASfoundation. (2025). *Missie & visie*. Geraadpleegd op 8 april 2025 via: https://www.pasfoundation.be/missie-visie

Plante, M., Free, C., & Andon, P. (2021). Making artworks valuable: Categorisation and modes of valuation work. *Accounting, Organizations and Society*, *91*, 101155. https://doi.org/10.1016/j.aos.2020.101155

Quemin, A. (2020). The market and museums: The increasing power of collectors and private galleries in the contemporary art world. *Journal of Visual Art Practice*, *19*(3), 211–224.

Resonant – Centrum Muzikaal Erfgoed (s.d.) *Collectie Vlaamse Gemeenschap.* Geraadpleegd op 31 augustus 2024 via: https://www.muzikaalerfgoed.be/voor-erfgoedliefhebbers/over-muzikaal-erfgoed/53-muzikale-erfgoedtopstukken/128-collectie-vlaamse-gemeenschap

Reynaers, A.-M. (2013). Public Values in Public-Private Partnerships. *Public Administration Review*, *73*(1), 41–50.

Rijksoverheid (2016a). *Erfgoedwet.* Retrieved from https://www.rijksoverheid.nl/onderwerpen/cultureel-erfgoed/erfgoedwet

Rijksoverheid (2016b). Erfgoedwet. Retrieved from https://www.cultureelerfgoed.nl/onderwerpen/erfgoedwet#:~:text=In%20de%20Erfgoedwet%20is%20vastgelegd,mogelijk%20bij%20het%20erfgoedveld%20zelf.

S.M.A.K. (2021). *Vlaamse overheid koopt kunstwerken voor Collectie Vlaamse Gemeenschap.* Retrieved from https://smak.be/nl/nieuws/vlaamse-overheid-koopt-kunstwerken-voor-collectie-vlaamse-gemeenschap

S.M.A.K. (2022). *Motel Corona – Exhibition Catalogue.* Retrieved from https://smak.be/volumes/exhibitions/Motel-Corona/MotelCorona_digitaal_N.pdf

Spiridon, P., & Sandu, I. (2015). Conservation of cultural heritage: From participation to collaboration. *ENCATC Journal of Cultural Management and Policy*, *5*(1), 43–52.

UNESCO. (2024). Bridging Cultures: Moving Towards New Perspectives in Museums. Concept note, UNESCO, 24 May 2024. Retrieved from UNESCO Headquarters, Paris.

Van Mensch, P. (2019). Private collecting as public challenge: Visions for the future. *Arthistoricum*, *402*, 85–100.

Velthuis, O. (2005). *Talking Prices: Symbolic Meanings of Prices on the Market for Contemporary Art.* Princeton University Press.

Vereniging Rembrandt. (n.d.). *Over ons.* Retrieved from https://www.verenigingrembrandt.nl

Zorloni, A. (2013). *The Economics of Contemporary Art: Markets, Strategies and Stardom.* Springer.

Sector Insights: The Low-end in the *Mobilier National*'s Collections: From Splat Back Chairs to Bouillotte Lamps

Vincent Lamouraux and Camille Mestdagh

1 Introduction

The history of the *Mobilier national*, originally the *Garde-Meuble de la Couronne* (Crown Furniture Repository), dates back to the reign of Henry IV, who, in 1604, created the first administration dedicated to the management of royal furniture, headed by an *intendant des meubles de la Couronne* (Castellucio, 2004). At the time, there was no specific jurisdiction governing furniture collections, which were considered by contemporaries to be ephemeral—subject to wear and tear and to changes in taste. The royal collections of gold and silverware and silver furniture were, therefore, treated as monetary reserves and were melted down on several occasions. It was under Louis XIV that "the furniture of the Crown," considered rare and precious, became "inalienable" (Gaillard, 2012).[1] However, this principle remained subjective, depending on symbolic and monetary value (jewelry, arms and armor, tapestries), excluding works intended for practical use, such as furniture and fabrics, which could be sold if they were considered

[1] Letters patent of December 1663, registered in the Parliament and the Chamber of Accounts on January 4, 1664. See Castellucio (2004, p. 46).

V. Lamouraux · C. Mestdagh (✉)
Mobilier National, Paris, France
e-mail: vincent.lamouraux@culture.gouv.fr
e-mail: camille.mestdagh@culture.gouv.fr

A.-S. V. Radermecker (ed.), *Low-End Markets for Art and Cultural Goods*, Cultural Economics & the Creative Economy,
https://doi.org/10.1007/978-3-032-27566-0_23

out of fashion. Old pieces could then be sold to fund new commissions from the royal manufacturers, allies of the *Garde-Meuble*. The melting down of precious metals, the destruction of fabrics to recover gold and silver threads, and the auctioning of furniture considered obsolete continued until the mid-eighteenth century. The Age of Enlightenment was more conservative, accompanied by a growing awareness of the heritage value of objects. In the new building on *Place Louis XV* (now *Place de la Concorde*), where the *Garde-Meuble* moved in 1774, rooms were specially designed to display the most illustrious pieces in the collection to the public. However, during the Revolution, a large part of the royal furniture—consisting of pieces considered "duplicates" or in poor condition—was not reserved for the future Louvre Museum and was largely dispersed at auction,[2] and the melting down did not resume until the end of the *Directoire*. The *Garde-Meuble de la Couronne* was liquidated before it became the *Garde-Meuble impérial* (Tisseau des Escotais, 2020), and later the *Mobilier national*, responsible for the furniture collections of the French Republic. During the Third Republic, a *musée du Garde-Meuble* (Furniture Repository Museum) was created. It displayed historical collections of furniture and decorative objects from the Ancien Régime and the Empire, before the first major transfer of collections of royal origin to the Louvre Museum in 1901, followed by others that made it possible to refurnish the palace-museums associated with the memory of the Monarchy and the Empires. Today, the *Mobilier national* does not have a museum,[3] but it is responsible for a collection of decorative arts comprising 100,000 cultural items, including tapestries (dating from the sixteenth century onwards), carpets, furniture, textiles and gilt bronzes (clocks, chandeliers, wall-lights, etc.), mainly from the Empire period to the present day. Among its missions, in direct continuity with the *Garde-Meuble*, the institution is responsible for providing the décor and furnishings for the residences assigned to representatives of the major bodies of the State, as well as ensuring the maintenance, inventory, and promotion of the furniture and objects in its collections. However, as the collections are very extensive, valorizing them can sometimes be complex. On the one hand, the furnishing purpose of the collection is subject to changes in taste, and certain pieces of furniture or objects may no longer be valued for their stylistic qualities, or their use may be

[2] Among the furnishings of Versailles, Marly, Saint-Cloud, and Bellevue, around 40,000 lots were put up for sale between 1793 and 1795.

[3] It benefits from the Galerie des Gobelins as a temporary exhibition venue.

questioned due to new habits. On the other hand, the *Mobilier national* makes its historical collections available to French museums, but many objects do not fall within the scope of museum loans, as institutions often seek exceptional pieces or those associated with specific interiors or historical narratives. For example, the last major loan to the Louvre Museum was the furniture from the throne room of Louis XVIII at the Tuileries Palace,[4] and there are many other deposits at national palace-museums that seek to reunite works originally belonging to their interiors. Less expensive works of art constitute an integral part of the art market, but they can also be found in collections held by public institutions. The collection at the Mobilier national illustrates well the wide array of objects and materials that make up the segment known as the decorative arts, associated with decoration, interiors, and furnishing, which, as highlighted in the book introduction, embody a hybrid of artistic, functional, and historical value. While some objects display a degree of scarcity, quality, and recognized cultural significance, such as signatures or provenance, others cannot be evaluated through conventional frameworks and may be considered "low-end" when their practical use has become obsolete. In that case, they fall outside the three core attributes of the triadic model discussed in this volume: functionality, scarcity, and brand strength/quality. If we look at the surplus of these "low-end" objects—often part of series, containing little or no precious materials—what might their future be?

2 The Large Series of Chairs from the First Empire in Heritage: Reviving a Tradition

In the current collections of the *Mobilier national*, the number of pieces of furniture preserved from the *Ancien Régime* is small due to the dissolution of the *Garde-meuble* and the revolutionary sales. However, since the reconstitution of the *Garde-Meuble* during the Consulate, there has been uninterrupted continuity to the present day. All the furniture commissioned by Bonaparte and later Napoleon to refurnish empty palaces is still held in the *Mobilier national* collections.[5] It should be remembered that, starting with just two palaces—the Tuileries and Saint-Cloud—under the

[4] This room opened at the Louvre Museum in 2024.

[5] With the exception of furniture destroyed in fires, those pieces that were lost—which may still reappear in private collections—or sold legally and sparingly by the administration during the Restoration and for two centuries thereafter.

Consulate, Napoleon eventually appropriated up to 47 palaces across Europe by the end of the Empire, all of which passed through the administration of the *Garde-Meuble*. As a result, the First Empire collections now contain around 1,700 pieces of cabinetry and 6,400 seats. Chairs are, in essence, prone to being delivered in series. However, while a set of living room chairs often consists of four to ten pieces, dining rooms may contain one, two, or even three dozen, and some larger reception rooms more than a hundred. The question of how to preserve these large series thus becomes a specific challenge.

The case of the so called *chaise à grille* (a type of splat back chair with vertical bars)[6] is the most emblematic. This typology of chairs appeared under Louis XVI,[7] flourished under the Consulate (chairs in the dining room at Saint-Cloud in 1802, by Jacob Frères) and became widespread under the Empire, thanks to Jacob Desmalter (1770–1841). It is impossible to know how many examples were made at the time, but of the approximately 720 chairs of this type in the *Mobilier national* collections, around 520 were produced during the First Empire. Much work remains to be done on the provenance of these items, which appear to have been the archetypal dining chair under Napoleon. Although a standard form was established at the beginning of the Empire, many variations exist (Fig. 1).[8]

How should we manage more than 520 items, similar in general form but different in detail, whose heritage value is questionable? While their value is significant because of their provenance—all were commissioned by the Imperial Furniture Repository to furnish imperial palaces, whose marks they still bear—it is diminished by the large number originally produced and still extant. A museum institution would likely have sampled each type, preserving around twenty examples suitable for an exhibition gallery.

[6] The *chaise à grille* is a type of openwork chair with a back composed of four or five vertical bars. The term has been in use by the *Garde-meuble*, where it frequently appears in nineteenth-century records alongside other recurring types, such as lyre chairs, or lattice chairs.

[7] Chairs of the Princesse de Lamballe, by Jean-Baptiste Claude Séné (1743–1803).

[8] This design features a back with a "grille": a central five-bar splat motif, set between a base and a solid crowning and flanked by two opened sides, with Etruscan-style rear legs and baluster-style front legs. A formal study of the *Mobilier national* collections has identified ten types of "grille" backrest, which differ mainly in the shape of the base and the top of the splat, as well as the presence or absence of a hand grip, which, when present, can be oval, almond-shaped or semi-circular. Some of these ten models are further subdivided according to subtle ornamental details, such as the presence of scrolls at the end of the crowning, and five types of legs result in numerous possible combinations.

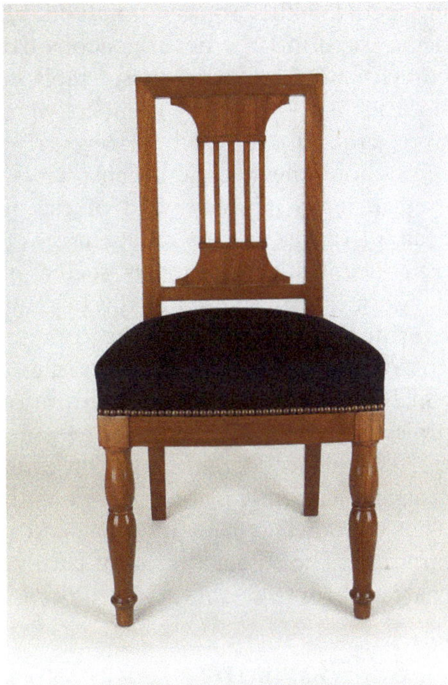

Fig. 1 *Chaise à Grille*. Société Jacob-Desmalter (1803–1813) *Mobilier national* (GMT-7702-002. *Photographer* Vincent Lamouraux)

However, if we consider their value as furniture, their worth also derives from their quantity. Although identical chairs still occasionally appear at auction, fetching around a hundred euros each, the interest of the *Mobilier national* collection also lies in the reconstruction of coherent sets.

However, the original sets were quickly dispersed in the nineteenth century.[9] This dispersion resulted in incoherent groupings when the items were returned to the *Garde-Meuble*. When the 1894 inventory was drawn up, all the splat-back chairs—which were then very numerous—were

[9] A recent study of the chairs delivered for the dining room of the Palace of Saint-Cloud—the only homogeneous group to have been the subject of exhaustive historical research—shows that, of the 35 chairs delivered in 1802 and dispersed from 1830 onward, only small sets of four or six, or even pairs, remained in use during the Second Empire and can be traced, by the end of the nineteenth century, across an impressive number of different palaces and institutions (Saint-Cloud, the Tuileries, the Palais-Royal, the Hôtel des Pyramides, Rambouillet, and the Ministry of Finance).

grouped together to save time and, above all, mixed with other types, being listed in large heterogeneous batches unified only by their textile covers.[10] This grouping considerably complicated their use as furniture, since identical inventory numbers were assigned to different chairs that were difficult to match. However, this remained standard practice throughout the twentieth century, as the cane chair continued to be used in many ministries and official apartments, both as an occasional chair in offices and in dining rooms or large meeting rooms. Unlike other openwork chair models, such as lyre-back chairs, its sleek geometric design meant that, even at the beginning of the twenty-first century, it remained compatible with the contemporary furniture introduced into government offices. The difficulty of meeting demand with uniform series, which threatened the continued use of these items, led to a collecting project in 2022 that formally regrouped them. Several new lots were created independently of their original inventory numbers. Seventy-five chairs are currently being restored so that they can be put back into use, while the others remain in storage and are likely to be matched with other furniture. The reconstitution of clearly identified, coherent sets has thus enabled them to retain their furnishing function.

3 Bouillotte Lamps and Louis XVI-Style Chairs: On the Road to De-Accession?

The problem of preserving series also arises with objects and lighting. The bouillotte lamp is particularly well represented in the *Mobilier national*'s lighting collection, which includes more than 400 examples. Of these, only 13 date back from the First Empire—the period when the production of this lamp, known as a *bouillotte* first developed. Of the remainder, more than 200 are standard models manufactured between the 1960s and 1990s. These quantities attest to the enduring popularity of this type of lamp during the twentieth century. Initially designed to be placed on a table to light *bouillotte* games, it consists of a candelabrum with two, three, or four lights, set on a curved-shaped base originally intended to hold the game chips. It was also one of the first lamps to feature an adjustable-height lampshade, allowing the brightness to be regulated. The most famous example—exceptional in its execution—is undoubtedly the six-branched

[10] See GMT 1347, GMT 1356 et GMT 2363 for groups of more than 100 pieces.

lamp in vermeil (including the lampshade), designed by the silversmith Martin-Guillaume Biennais (1764–1843) for the service of Emperor Napoleon. Delivered in 1809, the set included six lamps placed in the *grand cabinet de l'Empereur* at the Tuileries Palace.[11] The model of this lamp is unique and hybrid, featuring a tripod base rather than a curved one (Fig. 2). It was probably designed by Charles Percier (1764–1838). Part of the ornamentation was modified during the Restoration to replace the imperial symbols, as evidenced by the eight examples preserved today, five of which are in the *Mobilier national.*[12]

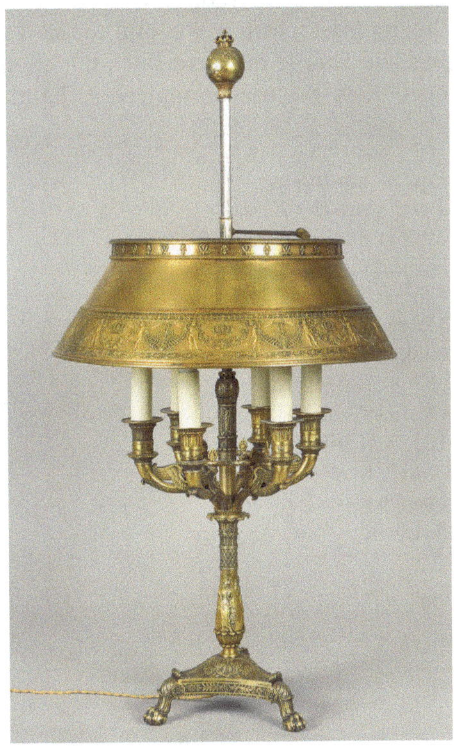

Fig. 2 *Bouillote Lamp. Mobilier national* (GML-8990-001. *Photographer* Isabelle Bideau)

[11] Further commissions will bring the total number to 12.

[12] GML 1319/1 à 5.

These lamps are considered masterpieces, with one on display at the Louvre Museum and two others at the Château de Fontainebleau. One of these lamps was placed on Charles de Gaulle's presidential desk at the Élysée Palace, which was photographed many times, and three others followed in the 1970s. Although the days of playing the *bouillotte* game were long gone, these lamps became very fashionable as desk lamps in the 1960s and 1970s. The demand was such that the *Mobilier national* acquired more than 200 *bouillotte* lamps from the lighting manufacturer Delisle between 1960 and 1990 to furnish various ministries, sometimes in sets of 15, 20, or even 30 (Fig. 3). However, today more than half of these lamps have been returned to storage. Their lampshades project light downwards, which was useful for card games and writing, but they have become almost obsolete since the adoption of computer screens, which encourage the use of anglepoise lighting. Nowadays, a few Empire-era

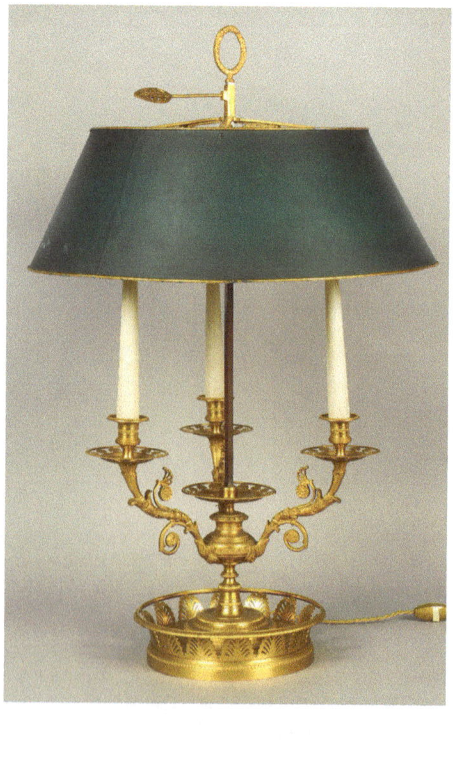

Fig. 3 *Bouillote Lamp* from the "Grand cabinet de l'Empereur" at the Tuileries palace. Charles Percier (1764–1838), Martin-Guillaume Biennais (1764–1843), Jean-Charles Cahier (1772 1857) *Mobilier national* (GML-1319-001. *Photographer* Isabelle Bideau)

examples can be placed in historical reconstructions of imperial palaces, but what about the modern examples, which certainly reflect the official aesthetic choices of an era but have no historical or significant monetary value today (with prices ranging from €200 to €300 on eBay)?

The same problem arises even more acutely in the case of the numerous pieces of furniture in the neo-Louis XV and, above all, neo-Louis XVI styles, which were produced in France from the July Monarchy onwards and which, as with the *bouillotte lamps*, the *Mobilier national* continued to purchase until the end of the twentieth century! The *Mobilier national* has more than 2,000 Louis XVI-style chairs in its collection, the style being understood as retrospective, made during the nineteenth and twentieth centuries. Most of these chairs are of average quality, and a third was made in the twentieth century, offering little hope in terms of their formal inventiveness or historical interest (Fig. 4).

The Louis XVI style remained in vogue in French government offices throughout the twentieth century. Despite the introduction of contemporary furniture at the Élysée Palace under Georges Pompidou (only in the private apartment) and later under François Mitterrand (in a few selected rooms in the central building), it was not until 2017, when Emmanuel and Brigitte Macron arrived, that all the antique furniture still present—furnishing in particular the seven salons on the ground floor of the central building—was returned to the *Mobilier national*. As the Élysée's taste easily imposed itself on the ministries, several of them began to change their furniture during the same period. Until recently, therefore, the Louis XVI style reigned supreme, prompting the *Mobilier national*—which, as we have seen, possessed few original Ancien Régime pieces—to enrich its holdings with furniture in this style. Acquisitions took the form of payments by administrations for worn sets, which were then restored in workshops, reupholstered, and returned to service, as well as purchases of new furniture from regular suppliers who, in the 1980s, were still providing series of more than twenty seats each.[13] The inclusion of these items in the inventory gave them a level of protection that became cumbersome when fashion changed. Within a few years, a sudden shift led

[13] In the 1930s and 1940s, the *Mobilier national* purchased sets of Louis XVI-style chairs for the living rooms, offices, and meeting rooms of Charles Dugast, Pierre-Laurent Roustan, Baptistin Spade, and Edmond Vérot; after the war, it continued to do so with pieces by Béchard, Dumesnil and Pequignot, Ramette in the 1970s, and Guillemin in the 1980s.

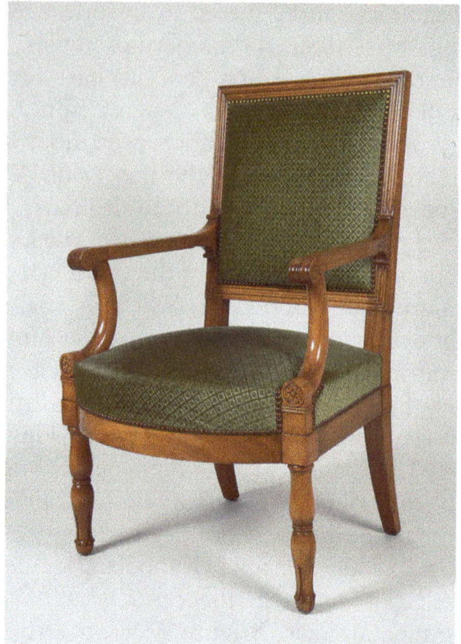

Fig. 4 Empire Style Armchair. Société Dumesnil, 1967. *Mobilier national* (GMT-22688-004. *Photographer* Isabelle Bideau)

to most of these chairs being returned to storage and replaced by contemporary chairs that showcase the creativity of the current French design scene. What should be done with these hundreds of chairs now? What value should be assigned to them? Their heritage value is virtually nil, except insofar as these sets bear witness to an official taste that remained largely unchanged in this respect for more than a century. Their value as furniture remains theoretically significant, since these sets are largely complete. However, changing tastes have led to a drop in demand. Furthermore, as they are mostly in poor condition and have not been restored since, these sets would not be reusable unless disproportionate restoration costs were incurred. A few remain in storage or in offices far from the heart of power—only a few dozen pieces out of the 2,000 counted.

For both bouillotte lamps and modern Louis XVI-style chairs, the question of deaccessioning arises: they are no longer relevant to the *Mobilier national*'s furnishing mission, many similar examples are already preserved, and they are of little current interest to the public from an art-historical perspective.[14] However, while the decision seems rational for objects that have undergone significant alterations and whose restoration costs far exceed their market value, for pieces in fair condition the assessment of their significance remains highly subjective, depending on how the object is received—a perception that varies over time as it continues to bear witness to craftsmanship and official taste destined to become part of history.

4 Refurnishing Local House-Museums: Widening Our Conception of Heritage

As part of making the collections available to French museums, the *Mobilier national* furnishes regional house-museums, *maisons des illustres*, and historic residences open to the public. Until then, the furniture removed from the furnishing mission was mainly from former royal castles—later imperial and then national—which, after being stripped of their furnishings during the Revolution, gradually regained a palatial appearance, if not a palatial life, by opening to the public as museums. During the twentieth century, precious pieces of furniture were thus returned to Versailles, Malmaison, Fontainebleau, and Compiègne, to resume their former places of use. The turn of the 2010s saw a different desire to open historic residences, sometimes national[15] but also belonging to local authorities, and to offer a more or less faithful restoration of their former interiors, using equivalent pieces from the *Mobilier national* collections that had been relegated to storage due to changing tastes. Certain pieces of furniture and objects are thus contributing to the reconstruction of the furnishings of an era. This could present a new opportunity for bouillotte lamps and Louis-style furniture, as they remained in fashion throughout the nineteenth century and most of the twentieth century. This is also the case for Louis-Philippe and Second Empire furniture. The *Mobilier national* has nearly 3,000 chairs made during the July Monarchy or the

[14] Decree of 26 November 2024 on the removal from the inventory and de-accession of items belonging to the *Mobilier national* collections: "General reason for declassification: common or everyday furniture and seats from the twentieth century, lacking significant historical interest, present in large numbers in the collections and in poor condition. Light fixtures from the late nineteenth and twentieth centuries, without significant historical interest, of average quality or in poor condition."

[15] Managed by the *Centre des Monuments Nationaux*.

Second Empire. They vary in quality, with a few gems among them. However, most are of good quality, going beyond the retrospective style without standing out in the visual landscape of the time. From Louis-Philippe, we have rather heavy armchairs with bowed legs and wide volute armrests, as well as numerous openwork chairs with various motifs. From Napoleon III, we have inherited armchairs whose decorative richness combines Louis XIV and Louis XVI ornamentation; others in a "Louis XV style" with curves less balanced than those of older models; as well as new forms, such as light chairs with lyre or crook backs, and comfortable seats, which became markers of the taste of the era. The fortunes of these pieces of furniture varied, but overall declined throughout the twentieth century. The turn of the twentieth and twenty-first centuries dealt a fatal blow to furniture from this period, whose lines were considered too sinuous or too ornamental. It was largely to save these pieces that the *Mobilier national*—a unique public institution about which the Heritage Code remains laconic, leaving it free to develop its own rules—developed this new mission of refurnishing in 2012.

Through the dozen or so house-museum refurnishing projects carried out over the past ten years, or still in progress, the nineteenth century—especially its second half—has been restored to prominence. The collections are too limited in *Ancien Régime* furniture to support coherent refurnishing schemes of this kind, while twentieth-century creations remain too much in demand for everyday use to be withdrawn from what remains the institution's primary mission. At the Château de Chaumont-sur-Loire, since 2014, it is the last owner, Marie Say, Princesse de Broglie—expropriated by the State in 1938—who has been honored through a predominantly neo-Louis XIII ensemble, complemented by smoking chairs and occasional chairs. At Azay-le-Rideau, the refurbishment inaugurated in 2017 likewise chose, for the ground floor, to evoke the period of the Biencourts, the last private owners of the château before it was acquired by the State in 1905: a diverse ensemble of neo-Gothic chairs, gondola armchairs, and comfortable chaise longues, complemented by bookcases with metal marquetry.

At the Caillebotte house in Yerres, since 2018, the setting known to the painter in the 1860s and 1870s has been revived through a faithful reconstruction of the atmosphere of the period: Charles X-style cross-back chairs in the dining room, a Louis-Philippe-style drawing-room suite, and a billiard room furnished with comfortable Second Empire chairs with openwork backs. This work continued at the Château de Duras and the Villa Arnaga in Cambo-les-Bains, giving a second life to furniture that, in some cases, had lain forgotten in the *Mobilier national*'s storage since the beginning of the twentieth century.

5 In Conclusion: Innovative Initiatives ...

To avoid the destruction or deaccessioning of obsolete, unusable objects in poor condition, the Aliénés programme (2020–2024) made these pieces available to designers and artists for reuse in new creations. The programme enabled creators to showcase their work and present exhibitions at the Galerie des Gobelins featuring contemporary works based on older items.[16] More than 150 works, including both lighting and furniture, have since entered the *Mobilier national* collections. A small number have been selected for use as furnishings, while the others now form a collection considered to be of cultural interest and intended for public display, notably at the Château de Biron.[17]

The obsolescence and devaluation of objects is inevitably an issue faced by an institution whose main mission is furnishing, which is subject to changing tastes and to the evolution of functionality, If there is a consensus on these objects, with limited brand and minimal scarcity—considered of lesser quality due to their modern manufacturing, and/or less meaningful as they were made as part of large series—they still serve as witnesses to an official taste and to a system of commissions deployed by the *Garde-meuble* at a certain time. They bear cultural significance regardless of their low perceived value and to support this vision, finding solutions to give these objects a second life is a mission in itself.

References

Castellucio, S. (2004). *Le Garde-Meuble de la Couronne et ses intendants du XVIe au XVIIIe siècle*. Éditions du Comité Des Travaux Historiques Et Scientifiques.

Gaillard, R. (2012). Les commissaires-priseurs et les ventes révolutionnaires du mobilier royal. *Bibliothèque de L'école Des Chartes, 170*(1), 183–207.

Tisseau Des Escotais, A. (2020). *Le Garde-Meuble sous la Révolution et l'Empire*. Éditions du Comité des travaux historiques et scientifiques.

[16] *Les Aliénés du Mobilier national* (June 2022), *Les Aliénés du Mobilier national, le retour* (October 2023-January 2024).

[17] Opening planned for 2026.

Sector Insights: Coins as Cultural Goods: Promoting Conservation Over State Control

Peter K. Tompa

1 Introduction

Coins are among the most common historical artifacts. The large numbers still extant require both collectors and a healthy numismatic trade to ensure their proper preservation, study, and display. Collecting also promotes scholarship, cultural understanding, and people to people contacts. Efforts to suppress collecting in favor of source country ownership and/or control are detrimental to the preservation, study, and appreciation of historical coins. There are far too many coins extant for them all to be properly cared for and displayed by museums or cultural bureaucracies. Regulating metal detectors is far less drastic and a far more effective measure to protect archaeological context than limiting trade or restricting collector access.

In support of this analysis, this essay first discusses supply-side and demand-side factors as background. Section 2 reviews supply-side factors. It explains that coins are amongst the most common artifacts due to the great numbers of multiple examples of the same type produced and hoarded over the centuries. Section 3 discusses demand-side factors. It explains how the large number of historic coins available at low prices has

P. K. Tompa (✉)
International Association of Professional Numismatists (IAPN), Washington, D.C., USA
e-mail: pkt@pktcounsel.com

A.-S. V. Radermecker (ed.), *Low-End Markets for Art and Cultural Goods*, Cultural Economics & the Creative Economy,
https://doi.org/10.1007/978-3-032-27566-0_24

stimulated collecting but discouraged the retention of provenance information. Section 4 then discusses different regulatory schemes and why this large number of coins is accompanied with little, if any, collecting history, making compliance difficult, if not impossible. Section 5 critiques the justifications often given for regulating collectors' coins. Section 6 promotes regulating metal detectors as a less drastic, more effective alternative to the problem of looting. This essay then argues that such regulation is best combined with recording programs akin to those found in the United Kingdom's Portable Antiquity Scheme (PAS) and Treasure Act. These programs work in conjunction to preserve context and encourage coins with recorded provenances. Finally, Sect. 7 concludes that such programs foster numismatic study and preservation with additional benefits of promoting cultural understanding and museum donations.

2 Supply-Side Factors

The immense number of coins that have been produced over millennia and their wide dispersion first as currency and then as collectibles makes it difficult to link individual coin types to particular modern nation states. In an era before modern banking systems, staggering numbers of coins were produced and then hoarded, leaving immense numbers that have survived today.[1]

Over 25 years ago,1.5 million ancient Greek coins were estimated to be held in public and private collections (De Callataÿ 1998, p. 45). More recent figures focusing on Roman coins are even more eye catching. As of May 27, 2025, the Coin Hoards of the Roman Empire Database listed 15,805-coin hoards containing over six million coins found from 1707 AD to the present.[2] Mintage figures and survival rates of one of the world's first international trade coins, the Athenian Tetradrachm, illustrate this point further (Fig. 1).

These silver coins, which feature the city's patron goddess, Athena, on the obverse, and her familiar, an owl, on the reverse, were minted over a 500- year period from approximately 561–42 BC. They are found in great numbers in the Middle East, with imitative issues struck in what is today

[1] Silver Die Studies Database. ENS de Lyon. https://silver.kbr.be/Die_Studies_Database. Accessed on May 27, 2025.

[2] Coin Hoards of the Roman Empire database, https://chre.ashmus.ox.ac.uk/. Accessed on May 27, 2025.

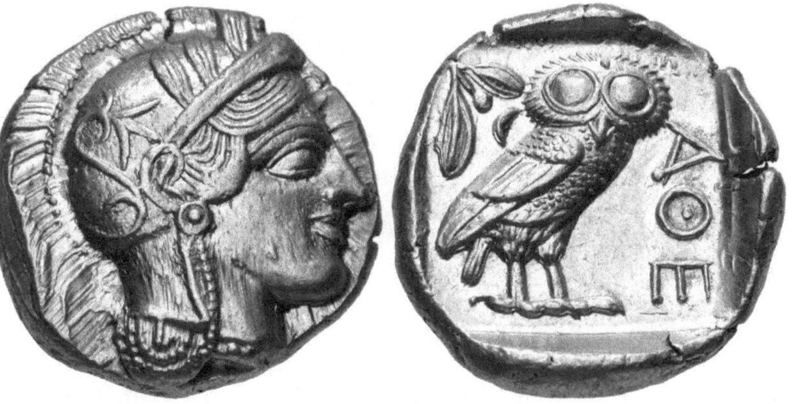

Fig. 1 Ancient Greece, Athens. Circa 454–404 BC. Silver Tetradrachm, Image courtesy of Classical Numismatic Group, LLC, Copyright © CNG 2025

modern Egypt, Israel, Iraq, and Afghanistan also attesting to their popularity as trade coins.

Based on contemporary sources as well as modeling such factors as the numbers of coins that may be struck by individual dies, one recent study concluded that over 14 million Athenian Tetradrachms were made in a 34-year period from 561 to 527 BC (Sverdrup & Schyyter, n.d., p. 6). After reviewing the numbers of such coins on the market and other factors, that study also concluded that there were approximately 40,000 such coins extant above ground in 2010 (idem, p. 18).

Coins from Eastern cultures are even more numerous. In 1992, one of the greatest ancient coin deposits of all times was discovered in Afghanistan (Bopearachchi, 1999–2000). The hoard consisted of three to four tons of gold, silver, and bronze coins or about 500,000 Greek, Graeco-Bactrian, Indo-Greek, Indo-Scythian, Indo-Parthian, and Kushan coins. In 2011, 10 tons of cash coins were found in the burial chamber of a Chinese official who died circa 92–59 BC (Giedroyc, 2019). The widespread use of metal detectors since the 1960s has drastically increased the number of historic coins available on the market, in private collections, and in the custody of museums and other repositories. The British Museum's Portable Antiquities Scheme (PAS) website provides some indication of this drastic increase in supply. That database, which had its first record uploaded in 1998, as of May 27, 2025, listed 1,812,071 objects (mostly Celtic, Roman, and Medieval coins) found in

Britain and Wales alone within 1,172,704 records.[3] Given these immense numbers, values are often quite modest, as low as $10-$20 for late Roman bronze coins. Truly valuable coins are a distinct minority, even at auction.

Comparative esthetic appeal, scarcity, condition, and precious metal content are what drives value. Generally speaking, archaic and classical Greek silver coins, first- second century Roman Imperial gold coins, and early modern silver and gold coins in exceptional condition exhibit "brand strength" that translates into high prices. In response to an inquiry from US regulators, one large auction house reported that 90% of its lots of ancient coins sold for under $1,000 hammer with a median lot price of $240.[4] Another reported in the past year that 18,030 items sold for less than $1,000, 4079 sold from $1001–$10,000, 499 sold from $10,001–$100,000, 17 sold from $100,001–$500,000, 1 sold from $500,000–$1,000,000, and 0 sold for over $1,000,000.[5]

3 Demand-Side Factors

Rome's first Emperor, Augustus, is one of history's first recorded coin collectors (Vico, 2019). During the Middle Ages, old coins instead were typically treated as bullion or as decorative items. One scholar has inventoried 47 instances where ancient coins were incorporated into reliquaries that were venerated in medieval churches and monasteries in Europe (Travani, 2022). Many of these coins only survived the melting pot as imagined relics of Christ's passion (Idem). For example, the Hunt Museum in Limerick, Ireland, exhibits a repurposed silver Decadrachm of ancient Syracuse, a large silver coin from the 5th c. BC, depicting a quadriga with its charioteer crowned by Nike on the obverse and a beautiful nymph surrounded by dolphins on the reverse.[6] Sometime in

[3] Portable Antiquities Scheme database. https://finds.org.uk/database. Accessed on May 27, 2025.

[4] International Association of Professional Numismatists & Professional Numismatists Guild. (October 21, 2021). Comments to FinCEN's advanced notice of proposed rulemaking: Anti-money laundering regulations for dealers in antiquities at 10. https://www.regulations.gov/comment/FINCEN-2021-0006-0017.

[5] Idem, pp. 10–11.

[6] Hunt Museum. (n.d.). Decadrachm of Syracuse / One of the thirty pieces of silver. https://www.huntmuseum.com/stories/silver-anniversary-silverware-at-the-hunt-museum/dekadrachm-of-syracuse-one-of-the-thirty-pieces-of-silver/.

the thirteenth or fourteenth c. AD, the coin was mounted in a gold frame with the inscription, *Quit premium sanguines est* ("Because it is the price of blood"), a reference to the 30 pieces of silver paid out to Judas for his betrayal of Christ (Travani, 2022, pp. 190–191). It may seem strange to us today that that anyone would associate a large silver coin from ancient Greek Sicily with Judas' betrayal, but perhaps the jeweler who created the frame was engaged in a flight of fancy or sought to say something more profound about the wages of sin.

With the coming of the Renaissance, ancient and then medieval coins started to be collected systematically and exchanged as gifts amongst humanist elites (Cunnally, 1999). After first being considered the "hobby of kings," coin collecting became democratized between the late nineteenth and mid-twentieth centuries as incomes grew both in Europe and the Americas. In the past fifty years, collecting coins has also become newly popular in Eastern Europe, Russia, the Middle East, and Asia with increasing wealth in those societies. At first, collectors in these rising economies focused on local issues, but increasingly more sophisticated collectors have started purchasing high grade ancient and modern coins of other cultures.

The creation of numismatic organizations in such countries helps demonstrate this growth. For example, the China Numismatic Society, founded in 1982, currently has 77 institutional members, involving 62,000 individual members.[7] Historically, lower value coins were traded among collectors or purchased at antiques markets while more valuable coins were sold in specialized stores, at coin shows, or at auctions. More recently, coins have also been traded over the Internet, with dealers, and auction houses either creating their own websites or listing on sales platforms featuring the offerings of multiple vendors. For example, on May 27, 2025, a search for "Roman coins" on the V coins platform generated a list of 11,057 items for sale.[8]

[7] China Numismatic Society, China Numismatic Museum, http://www.cnm.com.cn/qbbwgyw/143050/index.html. Accessed 27 May 2025.

[8] Vcoins, https://www.vcoins.com/en/Search.aspx?search=true&searchQuery=roman+coins&searchQueryExclude=&searchCategory=0&searchCategoryLevel=2&searchCategoryAncient=True&searchCategoryUs=True&searchCategoryWorld=True&searchCategoryMints=True&searchBetween=0&searchBetweenAnd=0&searchDate=&searchUseThesaurus=True&searchDisplayCurrency=&searchDisplay=1&searchIdStore=0&searchQueryAnyWords=&searchExactPhrase=&searchTitleAndDescription=True&searchDateType=0&searchMaxRecords=100&SearchOnSale=False&Unassigned=False. Accessed on May 27, 2025.

Such Internet sales have also made it much easier to reach collectors well outside one's own geographic area. For example, one recent Swiss auction reportedly attracted 1,694 different bidders from 73 different countries (Coins Weekly, 2021). The Internet also serves as a useful tool to transmit provenance information. As of May 27, 2025, Coin Archives Pro had captured 2,563,383 sales records from 6,472 Internet-based auctions.[9] While some of these entries reflect multiple sales of the same coin, this platform captures precise price and provenance information, at least for coins valuable enough to be auctioned off since the Internet became widely used in 1990s. Another promising initiative, pioneered by Swiss-based Ex-Numis,[10] involves the use of facial recognition technology to recover old provenances by comparing coins to images uploaded onto a computer database from printed auction catalogues and lists dating back to the nineteenth century (Tompa, 2020).

Despite these advances, the vast majority of coins still fail to retain much provenance information beyond the most recent purchase. Sales invoices and other documentary information get lost or discarded over time. Most coins have never been illustrated in printed price lists and auction catalogues. It was too expensive to photograph all but the most valuable coins before digital cameras came into widespread use in the 1990s. Indeed, before that time, provenance information was not typically retained at all except for rarer ancient Greek coins from famous collections. Even today, information about the most recent sale may be hard to ascertain because dealers typically do not want buyers to learn the extent of their price markup.

4 Regulatory Schemes

Until recently, there have been few regulations on purchasing coins, particularly in wealthy countries in Northern Europe and North America. In "source countries" where coins are regularly found the

[9] Coin Archives Pro, https://pro.coinarchives.com/a/. Accessed on May 27, 2025 (behind paywall).

[10] Ex Numis, https://www.ex-numis.com/page/the-idea.html. Accessed on May 27, 2025.

situation has been much more complicated. Often, there has been a disconnect between laws on the books and the reality on the ground. In many such countries that appear to have strict cultural patrimony laws, there are still vibrant local coin markets. These range from quite open and legal markets in Italy and China to "grey markets" in places like Bulgaria, Jordan, and Ukraine.

Both Italy and China have robust legal markets for historical coins. The *Numismatici Italiani Professionisti* association, founded in 1993, includes over 70 firms, many of which have operated for decades.[11] In China, five large auction houses, all of which have links to the Communist Party, control the market in more expensive coins.[12] In addition, two American auctioneers, Heritage and Stack's Bowers, and one from the United Kingdom, Spink, conduct regular sales of ancient and modern coinage in Hong Kong. Coins are also available for sale in China online, at local stores, at numismatic conventions, and in traditional markets, most notably the Liulichang in Beijing.[13]

Collecting coins is also tolerated in countries like Bulgaria, Jordan, and Ukraine despite questions about its legality raised by confusing or contradictory local laws. In Bulgaria, coins are traded legally at numismatic exchanges that take place several times a year in multiple locations.[14] In Jordan, there is an annual numismatic bourse in Amman and old coins are sold to tourists at Petra.[15] Finally, in Ukraine, the "Violity" website lists numerous cultural goods, including coins, for sale. As of May 27, 2025, the website listed 238,379 numismatic items for purchase.[16]

[11] *LA NIP—Italian Numismatists Professionals, About Us,* https://numismaticinip.it/chi-siamo. Accessed on May 27, 2025.

[12] Chen, S., & Cheng, Z. (2017, August 10). Coin and China—A comprehensive Chinese coin market research report. California State University. https://scholarworks.calstate.edu/concern/theses/1r66j164h?locale=it.

[13] Idem.

[14] Center for the Study of Democracy. (2007). The antiquities trade—dealers, traffickers, and connoisseurs. In *Organized Crime in Bulgaria: Markets and Trends* (p. 181). https://www.academia.edu/2,891,301/Organized_crime_in_Bulgaria_markets_and_trends.

[15] Jordan's Official Calendar of Events. Undated. The 5th Amman International Numismatic & Philatelic Exhibition, Jordan's Official Calendar of Events, https://calendar.jo/events/6612/the-5th-amman-international-numismatic-and-philatelic-exhibition. Accessed on May 27, 2025.

[16] Violity. Numismatics, https://violity.com/en/auction/174-numizmatika. Accessed on May 27, 2025.

Supply side regulatory schemes focus on registration, exports, and metal detectors. While there are few outright bans on collecting in source countries, nations like Bulgaria, Greece, and Türkiye require collectors and their coins to be registered. Given the low value of most coins and the Byzantine rules collectors often face, it should not be surprising that compliance lags, with some wealthy collectors going so far as to store their coins abroad at homes in more collector friendly countries.

In Bulgaria, collectors are hesitant to pay exorbitant fees associated with registering their collections and fear registration will just act as an invitation for one's coins to be stolen by the authorities.[17] In Greece, coins found locally are treated as State property.[18] While collectors may still legally "hold" coins purchased from foreign auctions or price lists as long as that the lot is photographed, packages containing such coins must be opened and recorded in the presence of a government official.[19] In Türkiye, the ability to collect legally depends on personal relationships with local museum officials. Historic coins imported from abroad or found within Türkiye itself may be legally held, but any collection must be registered with a local museum (Giedroyc, 2024).[20]

The 1970 United Nations Educational, Scientific, and Cultural Organization Convention on the Means of Prohibiting and Preventing the Illicit Import, Export, and Transfer of Ownership of Cultural Property (UNESCO Convention, 1970) assumes that coins and other common artifacts will be exportable with a permit,[21] but Middle Eastern countries such as Jordan do not issue such permits even where coins are offered to tourists.[22] Other countries allow coins to be exported with or without

[17] Center for Study of Democracy (2007, p. 193).

[18] Tompa, P. K. (Jones, 2016, April 20). Letter to Prof. Patty Gerstenblith, Chair of the Cultural Property Advisory Committee. https://www.regulations.gov/document/DOS-2020-0036-0024.

[19] Idem, pp. 9–10.

[20] Tompa, P. K. (Tompa, 2020, January 6). Letter to Jeremy Sabloff, Chair of the Cultural Property Advisory Committee, p. 11. https://www.regulations.gov/comment/DOS-2019-0043-0036.

[21] See 1970 UNESCO Convention, Art. 6 (a) (State parties undertake "[t]o introduce an appropriate certificate in which the exporting State would specify that the export of the cultural property in question is authorized.").

[22] Tompa, P. K. (2019, March 20). Letter to Jeremy Sabloff, Chair of the Cultural Property Advisory Committee, p. 11. https://www.regulations.gov/comment/DOS-2024-0015-0004.

a permit depending on rarity, value, and whether the coin is the direct product of an archaeological dig. Such export rules range from relatively permissive ones in countries like the UK[23] to more stringent regulations like those found in Italy.[24] Where export permits are required for even low value coins, associated costs and delays can function as a disincentive to compliance.

Increasing regulation also has prompted numismatic trade associations to update ethics rules for their members. For example, members of the International Association of Professional Numismatists (IAPN) promise "[t]o guarantee that good title accompanies all items sold, and never knowingly to deal in any item stolen from a public or private collection or reasonably suspected to be the direct product of an illicit excavation, and to conduct business in accordance with the laws of the countries in which they do business".[25] More focused measures relate to metal detectors (Fig. 2).

Here, there are only two rational methods of regulating metal-detector use: outright bans, such as those in Ireland, or recording statutes, such as those in force in England and Wales, which also give local museums a right of first refusal over finds (Tompa, 2012). A third approach, such as that used in Ukraine, which allows metal detectors to be sold but not used in sensitive areas, is naive at best (Boguki & Myzgin, 2021).

The 1970 UNESCO Convention contemplates that State Parties will institute demand side import controls to meet their treaty obligations. Most countries that have acceded to the UNESCO Convention will

[23] Coins over 50 years old and under £65,000 pounds in value that are not archaeological items found in the United Kingdom can be exported without a license. Arts Council England. (n.d.). Export licensing. https://www.artscouncil.org.uk/supporting-arts-museums-and-libraries/export-licensing#t-in-page-nav-1.

[24] Italian law previously allowed export of coins over 70 years old that are not archaeological items found in Italy that are over € 13,500 in value with a license. Legance Avvocati Associati. (2020, June). Global art and heritage law series: Italy & the EU. *Committee for Cultural Policy*, 42. https://culturalpropertynews.org/cultural-property-law/. All ancient coins of Italy were assumed to be archaeological items under this rule. Recently, however, the Italian Parliament increased this monetary threshold to € 50,000 and Italian legal experts believe that this threshold may also apply to "ancient coins in trade," i.e., those coins on the market not known to be the products of archaeological digs. Legge 17 marzo 2026, n.40. https://www.gazzettaufficiale.it/eli/id/2026/03/30/26G00055/sg.

[25] International Association of Professional Numismatists. Undated. Code of Ethics, https://www.iapn-coins.org/code-of-ethics. Accessed on 27 May 2025.

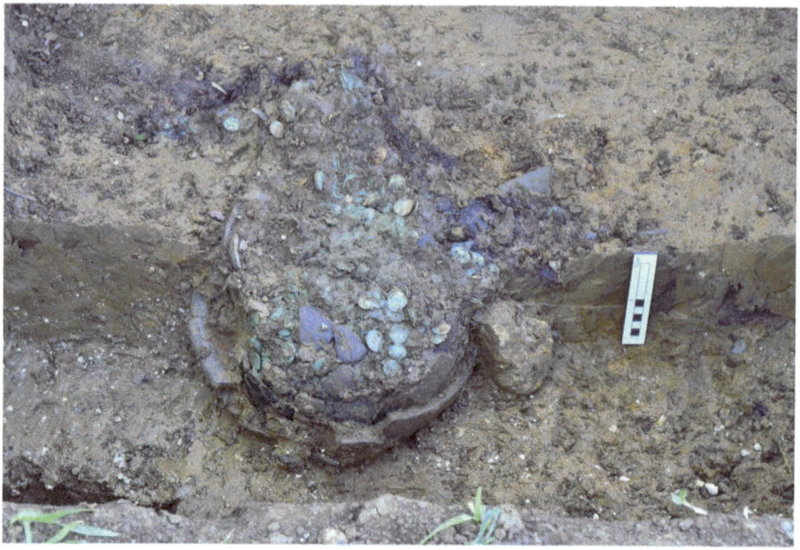

Fig. 2 So-called "Muddy Hoard" of 9,274 Roman coins found in 2018 near Huntingdon, Cambridgeshire, England, and reported to the Portable Antiquities Scheme. *Source* Courtesy of Portable Antiquities Scheme and British Museum, CC License

enforce all the export controls of other signatories. However, the US only acceded to the Convention with reservations designed to protect its "independent judgment" in such matters (Senate Report 97–564, 1982, p. 6). As a result, the Cultural Property Implementation Act (CPIA) was passed into law to effectuate this "independent judgment" by placing what on their face appear to be significant procedural and substantive constraints on executive authority (19 U.S.C. § 2601 *et seq.*). In particular, the CPIA requires a series of specific findings before the President or his designee may enter into a Memorandum of Understanding (MOU) with another UNESCO State Party that authorizes focused, prospective import restrictions meant to protect archaeological sites, and clearly delineated artifacts of cultural significance (idem §§ 2602, 2603, 2604). To assist in reaching this "independent judgment," Congress also required the executive branch to vet MOUs through a Cultural Property Advisory Committee (CPAC) which includes representatives of museums and the public and experts in the fields of archaeology, anthropology, ethnology as well as the international trade in archaeological, ethnological, or other cultural property (idem § 2605).

For the first 25 years that the CPIA was in operation there were no restrictions on coins. This should not be surprising. It is difficult to link coins—which by their very nature are instruments of monetary exchange —to one modern nation state. Indeed, when the CPIA was being considered, Mark Feldman, one of the State Department's top lawyers, represented to Congressional legislators that "it would be hard to imagine a case" where coins would be restricted (Cultural Property Treaty Legislation, 1979, p. 8).

In 2007, however, the State Department first imposed import restrictions on Cypriot coins under controversial circumstances. According to CPAC's chairman, the State Department improperly suggested that the decision was consistent with his Committee's recommendations in official reports made to Congress and the public.[26] Subsequently, another CPAC member representing the interests of the trade resigned his Presidential commission after new import restrictions were placed on ancient coins from Italy.[27] In doing so, he protested that this decision, as well as others imposing import restrictions on coins for Iraq, China, and Cyprus, were also made without CPAC's knowledge or consent.[28]

After that, what Mark Feldman represented to Congress as "hard to imagine" instead became commonplace. As of May 2025, the US Government has imposed overlapping import restrictions on numerous types of ancient, medieval, and early modern coins made as recently as 1774 on behalf of 20 additional countries[29] with new restrictions being imposed each year.[30] To the further consternation of collectors, despite

[26] Declaration of Jay I. Kislak ¶ 9, p. 3, (April 20, 2009); *Ancient Coin Collectors Guild v. U.S. Department of State,* Civ. Act 07–72,074 (RSL) (DDC). https://www.regulations.gov/comment/DOS-2025-0003-0014.

[27] Korver, R. B. (2011, February 18). Resignation letter to President Barack Obama. https://www.regulations.gov/comment/DOS-2025-0003-0014.

[28] Idem, p. 3.

[29] Ancient Coin Collectors Guild (2025, May 22). U.S. Import Restrictions on Ancient Coins (current as of May 22, 2025). https://accguild.org/news/13,502,343.

[30] Cultural Heritage Center, Bureau of Educational and Cultural Affairs, U.S. Department of State (Undated). Current Agreements and Import Restrictions, https://eca.state.gov/cultural-heritage-center/cultural-property/current-agreements-and-import-restrictions. Accessed on 27 May 2025.

statutory language limiting restrictions to coins "first discovered within, and subject to export control by" these countries (19 U.S.C. § 2601 (2)) restrictions have been placed on a wide variety of coins that circulated both regionally and even internationally, including popular ancient, medieval, and early modern trade coins.[31]

Moreover, the mere appearance of a coin type on a "designated list" is sufficient to trigger the government's authority to detain, seize, and repatriate similar coins to their supposed countries of origin.[32] Such restrictions impose the *probatio diabolica* or devil's proof on coin collectors. The problem for coin collectors is that most historical coins simply do not carry with them the detailed provenance information necessary for legal imports under the CPIA's current "safe harbor" provisions. Based on the broad discretion provided to border control officers, US Customs can demand references to an auction record predating any restrictions when the vast majority of collectors' coins are not valuable enough to be sold at auction. While enforcement may be inconsistent, widely publicized repatriations of "undocumented" coins that are then assumed to be "stolen" are meant to have a chilling effect on the market (Tompa, 2023).

Other UNESCO State parties will also repatriate coins to their countries of origin, but typically this only happens where there is a reasonable suspicion such coins were smuggled. Recently, however, the European Union (EU) promulgated import controls (Regulation EU, 2019/880) on a wide variety of cultural goods including coins. These regulations went into effect on 28 June 2025 after the rollout of a web-based system to enable the authorities to track imports. There is a consensus in the trade that these rules, which apply to all cultural goods created or first discovered outside the EU, will be highly problematical (Valentin, 2023; Pryor, 2024).

The regulations generally require that all cultural goods created or discovered outside the EU have been exported legally from their country

[31] See Ancient Coin Collectors Guild (2025) (listing restrictions on trade coins such Greek Tetradrachms, Roman Imperial coins, Byzantine coins, Venetian coins, and eighteenth century talers).

[32] *United States v. Ancient Coin Collectors Guild,* 899 F.3d 295 (4th Cir. 2018) (holding that government must only establish that a coin is a "listed type" before it can be detained, seized, and forfeited for repatriation).

of origin.[33] Such cultural goods, including coins, are then placed in "high risk" or "low risk" categories. Under these rules, coins over 250 years old traced to archaeological sites are treated as "high risk" items under Category B and can only be imported with a license issued in advance by an EU member state. In contrast, all other coins originating outside the EU that are over 200 years old that are valued over €18,000 are considered "low risk" under Category C and may gain entry with an "importer's statement." Even if a coin does not require an import license or an importer's statement, that does not necessarily mean they can be traded freely. All imports remain subject to possible investigation for violations of customs laws, including whether the coins were legally exported from their countries of origin.

Moreover, the distinction between "high risk" and "low risk" categories is not as significant as it may seem because the documentation required for both an "importer's statement" or an "import license" will be equally difficult, if not impossible, to obtain (Valentin and Dorking, 2025). As we know where most coin types were minted, a derogation for objects where the country of creation and/or discovery are unknown will likely be unavailable. Accordingly, the importer will typically be required to produce information proving either legal export from the country where the coin was created or discovered or demonstrating that the restricted coin was both removed from the country where it was created or discovered before 24 April 1972 and was subsequently exported lawfully from the last country where it has been for at least five years.

Unfortunately, such documentation will simply be impossible to produce in most instances for coins and other artifacts that require either an import license or an importer's statement. Moreover, the dramatic increases in value for high grade rare coins in high grades since 1972 will only exacerbate these problems for coins falling under "Category C." Thus, while coins under age and date thresholds, those created or discovered in countries like the US without export controls, or coins created or discovered within the EU will continue to gain entry, many, if not most coins, that fall within these regulations will not.

[33] For a detailed explanation of these complicated rules, see European Commission. (n.d.). Questions & answers on the EU legislation on the introduction and the import of cultural goods (Regulation (EU) 2019/880) (2nd ed.). https://taxation-customs.ec.europa.eu/customs-4/prohibitions-and-restrictions/cultural-goods_en.

5 Justifications for Increasing Regulation

Justifications for these increasing regulations in the US and EU have shifted over time. Initially, proponents argued that they were necessary to protect archaeological context. More recently, such justifications have been expanded to include headline grabbing claims that collecting coins and other cultural goods support terrorism and money laundering. Finally, decision-makers have made repatriating artifacts, including common artifacts like coins, a priority because repatriation is perceived as a "soft power" diplomatic tool.[34]

Such justifications may be critiqued on several grounds. First, justifying regulating coins to protect archaeological context depends on the claim that they are important tools for dating purposes. However, hoard evidence establishes that ancient coins circulated for as long as hundreds of years, and in any case, only the few coins found in undisturbed "secure contexts" have any use for dating archaeological stratum.[35]

Second, a claim that such restrictions will act to limit demand in the collector market and therefore help preserve archaeological context ignores legal or grey markets in historical coins in most countries, meaning that there is already a large enough internal demand for coins to encourage looting. Indeed, a number of the countries with current or pending US import restrictions, including Bulgaria,[36] China,[37] India,[38] Italy,[39]

[34] Tompa, P. K. (2025. May 6, 2025). Letter to Alexandra Jones, Chair of the Cultural Property Advisory Committee, pp. 2–3 (reporting statement of high-ranking State Department official about how MOUs are a positive way to collaborate with unfriendly governments). https://www.regulations.gov/comment/DOS-2025-0003-0014.

[35] Tompa, P. K. (2025. January 10). Letter to Alexandra Jones, Chair of the Cultural Property Advisory Committee, p. 15. https://www.regulations.gov/comment/DOS-2025-0003-0018.

[36] Center for the Study of Democracy. (2007, p. 181) (discussing legal numismatic exchanges).

[37] Chen, S., & Cheng, Z. (2017, August 10).

[38] Tompa, P. K. (2024, January 19). Letter to Alexandra Jones, Chair of the Cultural Property Advisory Committee, pp. 7–8. https://www.regulations.gov/comment/DOS-2023-0040-0028.

[39] Tompa, P. K. (2025, January 10, p. 9, n.10).

Jordan,[40] Lebanon,[41] Pakistan,[42] Türkiye,[43] Ukraine,[44] and Vietnam,[45] have significant "white" or "grey" markets internally. That, of course, raises the obvious question whether the point of this exercise is really to protect archaeological context or simply to promote governmental controls, particularly where such countries make it difficult, if not impossible as a practical matter, to export coins legally.[46]

Third, justifying regulations as necessary to promote the protection of coins as cultural heritage ignores the fact that museums already possess large collections, often formed through donations from collectors (De Callataÿ, 1998; Vico, 2019). Indeed, efforts to preserve, publish, and display coins in source country museums often remain substandard, despite a recent increase in digitization efforts.[47]

[40] Tompa, P. K. (2019, March 20, p. 5–6).

[41] Tompa, P. K. (2024, September 12). Letter to Alexandra Jones, Chair of the Cultural Property Advisory Committee, p. 10. https://www.regulations.gov/comment/DOS-2024-0028-0021.

[42] Tompa, P. K. (2022. April 14). Letter to Stefan Passantino, Chair of the Cultural Property Advisory Committee, pp. 3–4. https://www.regulations.gov/comment/DOS-2022-0008-0010.

[43] Tompa, P. K. (Tompa, 2020, January 6, pp. 10–13).

[44] Tompa, P. K. (2024, May 14). Letter to Alexandra Jones, Chair of the Cultural Property Advisory Committee, p. 6. https://www.regulations.gov/comment/DOS-2024-0015-0012.

[45] Committee for Cultural Policy and Global Heritage Alliance. (n.d.). Testimony on the proposed Memorandum of Understanding (MOU) and the imposition of import restrictions between the United States and the Socialist Republic of Vietnam, pp. 3–5. https://www.regulations.gov/comment/DOS-2025-0003-0011.

[46] It appears that India, Jordan, Lebanon, Pakistan, and Türkiye do not issue export permits, even for common artifacts like coins. Moreover, even where local law provides for their issuance, bureaucratic intransigence and delays can make the process unworkable. Tompa, P. K. (2025. January 10, pp. 26–28) (discussing increasing difficulties in securing Italian export permits).

[47] Center for the Study of Democracy. (2007, p. 193) (discussing poor recording practices); Tompa, P. K. (2016, April 20). Letter to Prof. Patty Gerstenblith, Chair of the Cultural Property Advisory Committee, pp. 12–14 (describing situation in Greek museums). https://www.regulations.gov/document/DOS-2020-0036-0024; International Association of Professional Numismatists. (2020, June 26). Report on Roman Republican and Roman Imperial coins (pp. 17–29). https://www.regulations.gov/comment/DOS-2020-0022-0143.

Fourth, knowledgeable commentators have questioned sensationalist reports that historical coins and other artifacts are a major source of terrorist and criminal financing (Felch, 2014; Jones, 2016; Brennan & FitzGibbon, 2017; FitzGibbon, 2017; Press, 2017; FitzGibbon, 2019; FitzGibbon, 2020). A more sober analysis from the RAND Corporation instead suggests that coins and other artifacts are at best a limited funding source for terrorists.[48]

Finally, it is debatable that repatriating common artifacts like coins will have any long-term benefit to foreign relations, particularly when compared to repatriation of far more significant objects. Moreover, if a coin purchased legitimately abroad was seized based on nothing more than its "type," any such seizure can only harm people to people contacts between domestic purchasers and foreign sellers.

6 What Best Promotes Preservation, Study, and Display?

The regulation of metal detectors is the best way to protect archaeological context because it is difficult, if not impossible, to find small metallic objects like coins without such devices. There are two rational ways to regulate metal detectors, an outright ban or the creation of a system that encourages reporting but leaves most coins with the finder. Permitting the sale of metal detectors while presuming they will be kept away from sensitive areas is, at best, unrealistic.

Of the two rational approaches, PAS and Treasure Act programs akin to those already operating in England and Wales for the past 30 years offer the best alternative (Fig. 3). These programs work in conjunction to encourage finds to be reported and recorded, and to discourage state institutions from retaining more material than they have the resources to manage. The PAS lists these finds on a public database[49] and provides State museums with a right of first refusal over coins and other artifacts that are reported. Funds to purchase coins come from a variety of sources, including donations and grants. The criteria for exercising a right of first

[48] Sargent, M., Marrone, J. V., Evans, A. T., Bilyana, L., Nemeth, E., & Dalzell, S. (2020, May 12). Tracking and disrupting the illicit antiquities trade with open-source data. *RAND Corporation*, p. 87. https://www.rand.org/pubs/research_reports/RR2706.html.

[49] Portable Antiquities Scheme database, https://finds.org.uk/database. Accessed on May 27, 2025.

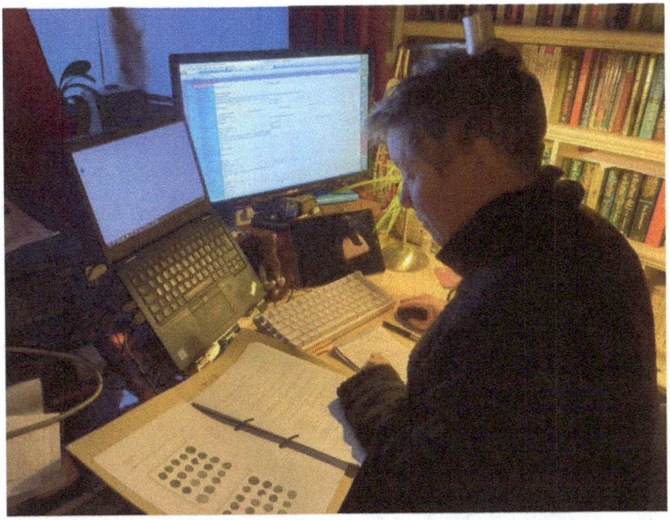

Fig. 3 Studying a hoard at the Oxfordshire Museum. *Source* courtesy of Angie Bolton and Cultural Property News, © 2025 Cultural Property News

refusal include whether the coins "have a good story to tell," have "research potential" as well as "condition" or "displayability" factors.[50] Coins not purchased at fair market value are returned to the finder and may end up in the collector market. The added bonus for collectors is that they can learn something about the findspot of their coins from the PAS database.

Critics may be quick to point out the challenges that institutions may face raising funds to purchase coins at fair market value or that some looting still persists, but it remains undisputed that these programs have greatly enriched archaeology in England and Wales. Since the Treasure Act was introduced in 1996, 15–20 times more finds have been reported than before this legislation was introduced (FitzGibbon, 2024). Some 1.7 million objects have been recorded in less than three decades in a publicly accessible database. The database has also stimulated educational research with data being used for almost 900 research projects (idem). Finally, reports about find spots can apprise archaeologists of sites that would not otherwise have been discovered. As a result of these programs, we

[50] Bolton, A. (n.d.). Oxfordshire Museum Service: Treasure PowerPoint. *Ancient Coin Collectors Guild*. https://accguild.org/news/13,367,474.

know far more about ancient and medieval economic activity in Britain and Wales than we do in most other countries.

7 Conclusions

Byzantine import and export rules aimed at controlling collectors and their coins hurt the legitimate trade due to their unrealistic documentation requirements. Focusing on recording metal detector finds with programs akin to the PAS and Treasure Act offers a less drastic and more focused alternative than draconian rules aimed at collecting. The vast numbers of coins available means that there are plenty to go around, and, indeed, cultural bureaucracies and museums cannot possibly conserve, study, and display all of them. If anything, private collectors and a healthy numismatic trade are instrumental in preserving large numbers of coins and promoting cultural understanding and people to people contacts. Finally, private collections ultimately can enrich museum collections through donations of important coins. Indeed, most of the world's greatest institutional numismatic collections have only been built through such generous donations (De Callataÿ, 1998; Vico, 2019). Promoting conservation, not state control, should be the primary goal.

References

Bogucki, M., & Myzgin, K. (2021). The law and practice regarding coin finds: Poland and Ukraine. *Compte Rendu*, *68*17, 21–24, International Numismatic Council

Bopearachchi, O. (1999). Coin production and circulation in Central Asia and North-West India (before and after Alexander's conquest). *Indologica Taurinensia*, *25*, 15–121. https://www.academia.edu/15798938/

Brennan, K., & FitzGibbon, K. (2017, December 1). Bearing false witness: The media, ISIS and antiquities. *Cultural Property News*. https://culturalpropertynews.org/bearing-false-witness-the-media-isis-and-antiquities/

Center for the Study of Democracy. (2007). The antiquities trade-dealers, traffickers, and connoisseurs. In *Organized crime in Bulgaria: Markets and trends*. https://www.academia.edu/2891301/Organized_crime_in_Bulgaria_markets_and_trends

Chen, S., & Cheng, Z. (2017, August 10). Coin and China-A comprehensive Chinese coin market research report. California State University. https://scholarworks.calstate.edu/concern/theses/1r66j164h?locale=it

Convention on Cultural Property Implementation Act, 19 U.S.C. § 2601 et seq.

Coins Weekly. (2021). Bidding fights over special collections at Leu sale. https://coinsweekly.com/special-collections-contested-at-leu-sale/

Cultural Property Treaty Legislation: Hearing on H.R. 3403 before the Subcommittee on Trade of the Committee on Ways and Means, 96th Cong. 8 (1979).

Cunnally, J. (1999). *Images of the illustrious*. Princeton University Press.

De Callataÿ, F. (1998). Estimating the number of Greek coins: A note on the probable evolution of the stock. *Minerva*, *9*(6), 44–45.

European Union. (2019). *Regulation (EU) 2019/880 on the introduction and the import of cultural goods*.

Felch, J. (2014, November 18). Danti's inference: The known unknowns of ISIS and antiquities looting. *Chasing Aphrodite*. https://chasingaphrodite.com/2014/11/18/dantis-inference-the-known-unknowns-of-isis-and-antiquities-looting/

FitzGibbon, K. (2017, August 24). Facts on terrorism and the art trade: Important study by Dutch National Police contradicts media hoax. *Cultural Property News*. https://culturalpropertynews.org/facts-about-the-art-trade-terrorism-and-the-size-of-the-illicit-market/

FitzGibbon, K. (2019, July 14). Was ILLICID report 'buried' for failing to show illegal trade? *Cultural Property News*. https://culturalpropertynews.org/was-illicid-report-buried-for-failing-to-show-illegal-trade/

FitzGibbon, K. (2020, July 30). RAND Corp report demolishes assumptions on antiquities and terror. *Cultural Property News*. https://culturalpropertynews.org/rand-corp-report-demolishes-assumptions-on-antiquities-and-terror/

FitzGibbon, K. (2024, June 24). A closer look at the Portable Antiquities Scheme. *Cultural Property News*. https://culturalpropertynews.org/a-closer-look-at-the-portable-antiquities-scheme/

Giedroyc, R. (2019, December 19). Details of Chinese coin hoard published. *Numismatic News*. https://www.numismaticnews.net/world-coins/details-of-chinese-coin-hoard-published

Giedroyc, R. (2024, April 30). France returns ancient coins to Turkey. *Numismatic News*. https://www.numismaticnews.net/world-coins/france-returns-ancient-coins-to-turkey

Jones, C. (2016, January 12). How much money is ISIS making from antiquities looting? *Gates of Nineveh*. https://gatesofnineveh.wordpress.com/2016/01/12/how-much-money-is-isis-making-from-antiquities-looting/

Press, M. (2017, December 7). How antiquities have been weaponized in the struggle to preserve culture. *Hyperallergic*. https://hyperallergic.com/415471/how-antiquities-have-been-weaponized-in-the-struggle-to-preserve-culture/

Pryor, R. (2024, March 18). Art trade figures voice major concerns over new EU import licensing regulations. *The Art Newspaper*. https://www.theartnewspa

per.com/2024/03/18/members-of-art-trade-voice-major-concerns-over-new-eu-import-licensing-regulations

Sargent, M., Marrone, J. V., Evans, A. T., Bilyana, L., Nemeth, E., & Dalzell, S. (2020, May 12). Tracking and disrupting the illicit antiquities trade with open-source data. *RAND Corporation* at 87. https://www.rand.org/pubs/research_reports/RR2706.html

Senate Report No. 97-564 (1982).

Sverdrup, H. U., & Schlyter, P. (n.d.). Modeling the survival of Athenian owl tetradrachms struck in the period from 561–42 BC from then to the present. *System Dynamics Society*, https://proceedings.systemdynamics.org/2012/proceed/papers/P1192.pdf.

Tompa, P. K. (2012, March 12). The future of recording the past in England, Wales, Scotland, Ireland and the United States. *Cultural Property Observer Blog*. https://culturalpropertyobserver.blogspot.com/2012/03/future-of-recording-past-in-england.html

Tompa, P. K. (2020, June 2). Rediscovering old provenances for ancient coins. *Cultural Property News*. https://culturalpropertynews.org/rediscovering-old-provenances-for-ancient-coins/

Tompa, P. K. (2023, July 6). Customs repatriation to Greece raises questions for collectors. *Coins Weekly*. https://new.coinsweekly.com/news-en/customs-repatriation-to-greece-raises-questions/

Travani, L. (2022). The thirty pieces of silver. In *Images of the illustrious* (pp. 176–217). Routledge.

United Nations Educational, Scientific and Cultural Organization. (1970). *Convention on the Means of Prohibiting and Preventing the Illicit Import, Export and Transfer of Ownership of Cultural Property*, No. 11806, 823 U.N. T.S. 231 (November 14, 1970).

United States v. Ancient Coin Collectors Guild, 899 F.2d 295 (4th Cir. 2018).

Valentin, P. (2023, September 25). New rules to restrict the importation of cultural goods into the EU. *LinkedIn*. https://www.linkedin.com/pulse/new-rules-restrict-importation-cultural-property-eu-pierre-valentin/

Valentin, P., & Dorking, Y. (2025, February 24). Art collectors beware – Changes to importing cultural property into the EU in 2025. *Fieldfisher Insights*. https://www.fieldfisher.com/en/insights/art-collectors-beware-changes-to-importing-cultural-property-in-the-eu-in-2025

Vico, A. (2019). From the market of archaeological antiquities to the creation of archaeological museums. *Boletín de la Asociación Española de Amigos de la Arqueología, 49–50*, 11–36.

Concluding Remarks

Anne-Sophie V. Radermecker

This volume set out to address a striking asymmetry in art market research. Whereas the upper tiers of the market have long attracted academic attention, its lower segments have remained comparatively neglected, often relegated to the margins of both art history and cultural economics. One of the book's central contributions has been to redress this imbalance by documenting, in a more systematic and interdisciplinary manner, the diversity, complexity, and significance of these understudied market spaces. Far from constituting a residual or secondary domain, the low end emerges throughout the volume as a crucial site for observing how value is produced, negotiated, stabilized, and contested in contexts where conventional hierarchies of legitimacy, price, and quality prove insufficient.

In line with the objectives articulated in the introduction, the volume first sought to provide a conceptual foundation for approaching the low-end market beyond price alone. The contributions assembled here collectively demonstrate that low-end cultural markets cannot be reduced to a simple condition of affordability or weak monetary value. Rather, they are structured by shifting combinations of functionality, scarcity, and brand strength—as developed in our triadic model—upon which trust

A.-S. V. Radermecker (✉)
Université libre de Bruxelles, Brussels, Belgium
e-mail: anne-sophie.radermecker@ulb.be

A.-S. V. Radermecker (ed.), *Low-End Markets for Art and Cultural Goods*, Cultural Economics & the Creative Economy,
https://doi.org/10.1007/978-3-032-27566-0_25

and reputation mechanisms, as well as symbolic attachment and social mediation accrue and confer value. The chapters gathered in the first part of the volume are especially important in this respect, as they revisit established art market theories and show that more nuanced analytical tools are required to account for the forms of exchange, uncertainty, and valuation that characterize these segments. Whether examined through sequences of markets, bazaar-type economies, or the investment logics attached to "everyday luxury goods," the low end appears not as a fixed category but as a relational and dynamic space in which the attributes of artistic and cultural goods—as well as the knowledge and practices that surround them—are continuously reassessed and acquire distinct forms of value depending on demand-side actors, their resources, and their purchasing intentions.

A second major contribution of the volume lies in the breadth and heterogeneity of the empirical terrain it covers. The chapters move across flea markets, decorative arts, cemetery ornamentation, print subscriptions, oleographs, wholesale art trade, museum-derived consumer products, auction markets, folk antiques, collectibles, advertising ephemera, and utilitarian heritage goods. This diversity is not merely cumulative. It demonstrates that the low end cannot be apprehended as a homogeneous market tier, since the goods circulating within it occupy unstable positions at the intersection of art, craft, luxury, consumer goods, and junk. Some retain strong practical functions; others derive their value primarily from symbolic, nostalgic, local, or historical significance. Some are embedded in relatively formalized channels of expertise and distribution; others circulate in settings marked by opacity, informality, and fragmented knowledge. All these contributions show that the low end is best understood not as a single market category, but as a set of porous, shifting, and internally differentiated segments.

Another important achievement of the volume is its identification of several key mechanisms that organize behavior across different market segments. A number of chapters highlight the role of information asymmetries, bargaining, social relationships, trust, endorsement, locality, and intermediation in shaping the circulation and valuation of goods. Others show how boundaries between market segments remain permeable, and how the low end may capitalize on high-end legitimacy, institutional recognition, or reputational spillovers. In that respect, the volume does more than describe a neglected market segment; it also proposes a broader analytical framework through which coherent logics can be identified across markets that may initially appear fragmented or incommensurable. The low end is thus revealed as a space in which general market mechanisms become especially visible, precisely because uncertainty, heterogeneity, and weak formalization are often more pronounced there than in more consecrated sectors.

Finally, the volume has also fulfilled its ambition to foster a genuinely interdisciplinary dialogue. Economists, art historians, anthropologists, archaeologists, criminologists, heritage scholars, among others, as well as practitioners, illuminate distinct yet complementary dimensions of this broad marketplace. This plurality of approaches allows the low end to be examined simultaneously as a market structure, a social space, a cultural ecosystem, and a field of material practices. In doing so, the book expands the study of value systems beyond conventional metrics of price and quality, demonstrating why such measures are often inadequate when applied to goods whose significance depends on context, use, mediation, circulation, and recognition. The dialogue established across disciplines reveals the low end as a particularly fertile observatory for understanding how art and cultural goods acquire meaning outside the narrow frame of consecrated art.

The chapters gathered in this volume also point to a broader research agenda that remains largely open. Although this volume has identified mechanisms that either resemble those operating at the upper end of the art market, display dynamics specific to its lower segments, or exert varying degrees of influence within them, the convergences and divergences between the two ends of the spectrum still warrant further investigation. Future scholarship should continue to examine more systematically whether theories commonly applied to the high-end art market retain their explanatory power in lower segments or whether the latter require distinct conceptual frameworks. Is there, for instance, a "superstar effect" among low-end artists, makers, or objects, albeit operating at different scales of recognition? Can a "masterpiece effect" be identified in the valuation of lower-priced goods, especially when symbolic singularity compensates for weak market legitimacy? Does the "law of one price" apply in informal, bazaar-type, or digitally fragmented markets where information asymmetries remain pervasive? Are expert estimates biased differently in the low end, and are authenticity, attribution, and forgery as economically consequential there as they are in more consecrated segments? More generally, the low end calls for an inquiry into its own endogenous logics rather than the simple downward application of models developed for elite markets. This includes the study of the mechanisms through which goods, artists, or brands move from one segment to another, thereby empirically testing Thompson's theory: what stylistic, historical, reputational, institutional, or contextual criteria govern such mobility, and how do they reshape perceived scarcity and legitimacy over time? Exploring these issues would deepen and refine our understanding of market stratification, in combination with critical reflection from more legal- and policy-oriented approaches.

In this regard, two final reflexive points emerging from this volume, both linked to terminology, deserve emphasis. In the introduction, we highlighted the weight of polarized terms in the collective imaginary, irrespective of their initial economic relevance, and the ways antonyms (such as "high" and "low") affect how goods are apprehended. If this book has shown anything, it is that shifts in perception and understanding require not only documentation and analysis, but also critical attention to language itself. Terms do not merely describe markets; they also classify them, shape expectations, and influence the status of the goods and actors they designate. Whereas the notion of the low end was prevalent in most contributions, some authors deliberately used the term "entry-level" segment to describe this specific marketplace as a way of better capturing its role as a space of access, initiation, and possible upward mobility, rather than as a merely residual tier of low value. For this reason, we suggest that future scholarship and professional discourse move, where analytically appropriate, from the terminology of the "low-end markets" to that of the "entry-level markets." This is not an attempt to replace one label with a more marketable euphemism. Rather, it is an effort to adopt a vocabulary that better captures the structural role and social meaning of this segment. While, in theory, the low-end market refers to the lower tier of a market hierarchy, usually defined in relation to lower prices, weaker quality, and limited recognition, the entry market emphasizes accessibility. It denotes the segment through which new buyers, collectors, users, or goods enter the market and begin to participate in its value systems. Similarly, "low-end" tends to evoke inferiority, disposability, or weak legitimacy, whereas "entry-level," by contrast, foregrounds access, initiation, and possible progression. For consumers and collectors, this difference matters. To be positioned as a "low-end buyer" may imply stigma, while to be situated in an "entry market" suggests inclusion in a trajectory of acquisition, learning, and cultural participation. Conceptually, the notion of the entry market is also more dynamic. It allows us to think of this segment not as a fixed bottom layer, but as a threshold, a zone of circulation in which goods, actors, and forms of value may move upward, stabilize, or disappear. In that sense, rescaling the familiar power-law image of the market would also change our perspective. What is usually and visually represented as a long tail (on the right) beneath the high end (on the left) may instead be understood as the ***broad, necessary, and resilient base*** (on the left) on which the upper tiers depend (on the right).

This terminological shift also invites a complementary concept that the present volume has only begun to suggest: that of the "exit market." If the notion of entry markets refers to the zone through which cultural goods and consumers enter systems of recognition, exchange, and accumulation, that of exit markets refers to the point at which such goods leave cultural and creative circuits, temporarily or definitively, to become junk, waste, scrap, or undifferentiated secondhand products. Here, Kopytoff and Thompson's theories, among others, remain particularly useful. Goods may move from durable to transient, and from transient to rubbish, depending on changing demand, classificatory frames, and valuation mechanisms. From this perspective, the entry market is not only an entry point into culture; it is also a site where reversals of status occur. It is where neglected or devalued cultural objects may be requalified and reenter circulation, but also where once-valued cultural goods may slip toward obsolescence. Future research, at the intersection of cultural economics, anthropology, sociology and marketing, should therefore pay closer attention to the relation between entry and exit markets, asking under what social, economic, and institutional conditions goods cross these thresholds. What kinds of intermediaries, narratives, or devices prevent cultural goods from becoming waste? Which objects are allowed to reenter the market, and which are not? How do heritage, nostalgia, brand strength, scarcity, or functional reuse intervene in these processes? Such questions point to a broader analytical horizon, one in which the study of low-end—or, more precisely, entry—markets is inseparable from the study of dispossession, revaluation, and the unstable boundaries between culture, commodity, and trash.

A second and final reflexive point concerns a segment that this volume has deliberately not addressed in a systematic way, but which its chapters implicitly bring back into view: the "middle-end market." In both professional discourse and academic commentary, one often encounters the recurring claim that there is, in fact, no real "middle market" in the arts. This assertion is revealing. It suggests that while the two ends of the spectrum—the highly consecrated upper end and the more accessible entry end—can be more readily identified, the middle remains elusive, difficult to delimit, and conceptually unstable. It occupies a gray zone at the intersection of high and low, one that resists the neat dichotomies through which value is often mapped. From an economic perspective, the middle market may be understood as the segment situated between mass accessibility and elite exclusivity, i.e., a zone in which prices, symbolic recognition, and market visibility are substantial but not dominant, and where goods and actors have neither the inclusiveness of entry markets nor the strong consecration effects of the high end. Unsurprisingly, this segment remains underdefined. Even the conventional visualizations used in art market studies—power-law graphs, long-tail models, or highly aggregated art market reports—tend to obscure rather than clarify its contours. The middle often disappears between the spectacular concentration of value at the top and the broad base of low-price circulation below. This is particularly evident in market reporting, where categories such as "mid-market" may encompass extremely wide and analytically unmanageable ranges of value, from $50,000 to $1,000,000, thereby masking rather than identifying a coherent segment.

The difficulty of conceptualizing the middle market may also reflect a broader structural challenge. In many cultural and creative industries, occupying the middle tends to be more precarious than operating at either end. Mid-sized firms are often the most vulnerable to competitive pressures, mergers, and absorption by larger competitors, while also lacking the cost advantages or broad reach of low-cost models. Comparable dynamics can be observed across sectors. In the music industry, independent intermediaries are increasingly acquired by major groups (e.g., [PIAS] by Universal in 2024). In the auction sector, mid-sized houses have been consolidated into larger international structures (Cornette de Saint Cyr acquired by Bonhams in 2022). In fashion and retail, the erosion of mid-range brands contrasts sharply with the resilience of both luxury and discount segments. These patterns suggest that the middle end may be not only elusive from a theoretical perspective, but also economically fragile. Applied to the art market, this raises a number of hypotheses that future research should explore. Is the middle market difficult to identify because it is structurally unstable, constantly pulled upward by aspirations to consecration and downward by competitive pressure from more accessible segments? Does its relative invisibility stem from the fact that it lacks a clear symbolic identity, unlike the prestige of the high end or the accessibility of the entry market? Or does the middle market function less as a stable segment than as a transitional space through which artists, goods, intermediaries, and buyers circulate? The contributions in this volume suggest that much of the most important movement in cultural markets may occur precisely in these in-between zones. If so, then the often-repeated claim that "there is no middle market" may need to be taken seriously—not as a factual statement, but as an indication that the middle has yet to be theorized with the same precision as the two extremes of the market for art and cultural goods.

Index

A.-S. V. Radermecker (ed.), *Low-End Markets for Art and Cultural Goods*, Cultural Economics & the Creative Economy,
https://doi.org/10.1007/978-3-032-27566-0

C

D

E

FSC
www.fsc.org
MIX
Papier | Fördert gute Waldnutzung
FSC® C083411

Kolibri 360 GmbH
Ferdinand-Jühlke-Straße 7
99095 Erfurt, Deutschland
produktsicherheit@kolibri360.de